The Private Papers
OF
Senator Vandenberg

Copyright by Harris & Ewing

"Courteously receiving testimony." Senator Vandenberg at a Senate Hearing. During many such sessions, he learned the mind of the people on controversial measures.

The Private Papers
OF
Senator Vandenberg

EDITED BY
ARTHUR H. VANDENBERG, JR.
WITH THE COLLABORATION OF
JOE ALEX MORRIS

1 9 5 2

ILLUSTRATED

HOUGHTON MIFFLIN COMPANY · BOSTON
The Riverside Press Cambridge

COPYRIGHT, 1952, BY ARTHUR H. VANDENBERG, JR.
ALL RIGHTS RESERVED INCLUDING THE RIGHT TO REPRODUCE
THIS BOOK OR PARTS THEREOF IN ANY FORM
L. C. CARD NO. 52–5248

The Riverside Press
CAMBRIDGE · MASSACHUSETTS
PRINTED IN THE U.S.A.

Acknowledgments

A VERY special word of recognition and appreciation is due to those who have worked with me in the editing of this book. Their collaboration has made the book possible.

Joe Alex Morris, who has been foreign editor of the New York *Herald Tribune* and the United Press, managing editor of *Collier's*, and is a contributor to the *Saturday Evening Post*, has spent full time with me in organizing the material and has discharged the chief responsibility for shaping the material into a book.

John L. Steele, of the United Press, now on leave as a Nieman Fellow at Harvard University, has collaborated on the section dealing with the years 1946 through 1949 — a period in which he was a Senate correspondent for the United Press specializing in foreign affairs and in almost daily contact with my father's Washington activities.

Francis O. Wilcox, Chief of Staff of the Senate Foreign Relations Committee, has been the source of original material gained from his intimate association with my father in Committee work. Though he was not responsible for the actual selection of material from the Vandenberg papers which has been included, he has served as a check on the accuracy of facts in the entire manuscript.

In addition, a number of friends and men in public life have given generously of their time to help fill in details and interpret events discussed in the book. Their contributions have added greatly to the substance of the book and will be easily and individually recognized.

I hope it will be considered proper if I hereby express my deepest gratitude to all of those who have thus helped me to honor the memory of my father.

A. H. V., Jr.

January 10, 1952

Contents

Introduction	xi
1. "That Day Ended Isolationism"	1
2. "We Must Not Fumble the Peace"	21
3. "Hunting for the Middle Ground"	37
4. Skirmish with the State Department	66
5. "The MacArthur Adventure"	75
6. Committee of Eight	90
7. "At the Water's Edge"	108
8. A Speech Heard Round the World	126
9. Yalta: "This Will Raise Hell"	146
10. San Francisco Conference: "Town Meeting of the World"	172
11. San Francisco Conference: Showdown with Russia	199
12. Atomic Bomb: "Is the Wit of Man Competent?"	220

13. London: "What Is Russia Up To Now?"   237

14. Atomic Control: Military vs. Civilian   252

15. Paris: "Firmness and Patience" with Russia   262

16. Paris: The Ice Begins To Break   289

17. "More Than a Personal Victory"   304

18. Wearing Three Hats   318

19. "Calculated Risk"   337

20. The Marshall Plan   373

21. The Vandenberg Resolution: "Within the Charter But Outside the Veto"   399

22. On Not Running for President   421

23. The 1948 Campaign   446

24. Cracks in Nonpartisan Policy   461

25. The North Atlantic Treaty   474

26. Implementing the Pact   502

27. China: "The Conundrum of the Ages"   519

28. "And This Too Shall Pass"   546

    Notes   581

    Index   591

List of Illustrations

FRONTISPIECE
FACING TITLE PAGE

Senator Vandenberg at a Senate hearing

GROUP I
FOLLOWING PAGE 232

1. Greeting voters at a 1940 rally
2. Senator Taft, Wendell Willkie, and Senator Vandenberg
3. In his favorite chair at home
4. At the Mackinac Conference
5. The Senator and Governor Dewey
6. Signing the United Nations Charter
7. The Charter in the Senate. Cartoon by C. K. Berryman
8. Setting out for Paris with Senator Connally and Secretary Byrnes

LIST OF ILLUSTRATIONS

GROUP II
FOLLOWING PAGE 424

9. Voting with Mrs. Vandenberg and their son, Arthur Vandenberg, Jr.

10. Senators Vandenberg and Taft as the 80th Congress convenes

11–14. Doodles

15. Mr. Bernard Baruch with Senators Vandenberg and McMahon

16. Off for the Inter-American Conference

17. During the Petropolis Conference

18. "The Sphinx." Cartoon by Berryman, in the Washington *Evening Star*

19. Governor Stassen confers with the Senator at the Republican Convention of 1948

20. Senator and Mrs. Vandenberg

Introduction

UNDER the terms of the will of my father, Arthur Hendrick Vandenberg, I was bequeathed his papers, scrapbooks, diaries, documents, and other items of a like nature relating to his official position in public life. Whether any of this material was to be published was left to my discretion, but with the admonition that "great care be used in making any portions of these records available for publication."

Frankly, I don't know whether he would have wanted me to publish this book.

My association with him was unusual because I worked with him in his office in the United States Senate for fourteen of the twenty-three years of his public career. I was in the midst of each of his four campaigns for election to the Senate, beginning with the plush Republican days of 1928 when his nomination in Michigan was tantamount to election; through 1934 when he was the only Republican Senator from the populous states of the Middle West to survive a New Deal sweep; through 1940 when he rode the tail of the Isolationist kite to a respectable win; to 1946 when he won a thumping victory without making a political speech or an appearance in the State in behalf of his campaign.

I attended him at three of the four Republican National Conventions between 1936 and 1948, when he declined a draft for the vice-presidential nomination in 1936, was an unsuccessful nonactive, *isolationist* candidate for the presidential nomination in 1940, and refused to yield to a formidable demand that he become an *internationalist* candidate for President in 1948. Also, I was able to spend many hours of relaxation with him when he was testing his ideas and shaping his judgments for a political campaign or an important speech in the Senate.

Thus, my father was willing to trust me with the decision as to whether this material should be published now. By suggestion in his will, his official papers would otherwise have been sealed and deposited in the William L. Clements Library at the University of Michigan, not to be opened until ten years after his death. Although obviously he intended to use the records himself as a basis for the memoirs he hoped to write some day, he cannot be held responsible for the present publication of anything in this book. The decision to publish the book was made by me after his death without any prior consultation with him or any prior effort on his part to edit the records with publication in mind.

I recognize the time-honored prejudice against the quick publication of the personal papers of a public figure, especially when so much of the material in the papers centers about personalities still active in public life. But the trend in recent times seems to have veered sharply in the direction of the contemporary publication of political papers. If misstatements are made or false impressions are created, they can thus be corrected by those who know the facts at firsthand. I concluded that the publication of this book was not only justified by current, general practice but that there was a certain degree of compulsion confronting me to consolidate the record of my father's career and to redefine his viewpoints now for the sake of clarity in the 1952 presidential campaign.

The book is not in any sense a standard type of historical biography. It is more in the nature of a narrative account of the decade — from Pearl Harbor until my father's death in 1951 — in which the mass mind of America reluctantly forsook its isolationist traditions and accepted the challenge to world leadership. Looking back upon this decade of evolution, it seems to me that my father can fairly be described as a symbol of the average American mind which, prior to Pearl Harbor, honestly and conscientiously believed that it was possible for the United States to confine its responsibility to our own hemispheric shores, but which gradually faced up to the hard realities of a changing world and became converted to the concept of collective security among free nations everywhere on earth.

That is what this book is about — ten years of dramatic change in the thinking of America to cope with changing world conditions. It was a period in which bipartisanship in foreign affairs — or nonpartisanship, as my father preferred to call it — was born and nurtured and finally adapted as a governmental mechanism through which a Democratic Executive Branch and a Republican opposition in Congress united to speak with a single foreign-policy voice at the water's edge.

In his last public speech on September 15, 1949, at a dinner given by the Overseas Writers in honor of a group of visiting journalists from Western Europe, my father pridefully summed up the results of bipartisanship at that time:

> It seems to me that our basic pattern is clear. The Senate of the United States ratified the United Nations Charter by a vote of 89 to 2. It ratified the Inter-American Rio Treaty by a vote of 72 to 1. It approved the initial Marshall Plan by a vote of 69 to 17. It adapted the Senate Resolution 239 [the so-called Vandenberg Resolution] fifteen months ago, demanding more effective strength for all these faiths, by a vote of 64 to 4. It ratified the North Atlantic Pact by a vote of 82 to 13. Last Monday the Joint Senate Committee on Foreign Relations and Armed Services reported an arms bill to implement the North Atlantic Pact by a vote of 22 to 3.
>
> There is powerful consistency in these attitudes . . . They asserted — and I believe they still assert — our general and very deep conviction that the free world must work together for its common interest in collective peace and that no other character of peace can be dependable in this foreshortened world. I believe they asserted — and still assert — our relentless purpose to stop another war before it starts, and to avoid appeasements which, as I have said before, are but surrender on the installment plan.
>
> I believe they asserted — and still assert — our disposition to render every rational, economic aid within our prudent power, not as a matter of charity but as a matter of intelli-

gent self-interest, to help build a sound as well as a peaceful society in which the hopes of men may thrive.

My father used words as carefully as a master craftsman uses his tools. It gave him great satisfaction to be able to write prose that seemed to sing and to condense the essence of a subject into a single catch phrase or a pungent sentence.

His papers were in the form of scrapbooks, diaries, and letters. In the course of his twenty-three years in Washington, he kept a yearly scrapbook in which he entered chronologically all of his Senate speeches and many hundreds of newspaper and magazine articles relating to matters in which he had a special interest.

His diaries were written irregularly. Sometimes he would let weeks pass without making an entry. Then he would write at one sitting a complete account of some lengthy series of events in which he had participated. On other occasions he would make brief entries to accompany newspaper clippings that he pasted in his scrapbooks. Again he would take notes or write out dialogue during an important conference, and later transcribe an almost stenographic account of what had happened. And on some occasions, such as the San Francisco conference to draw up the United Nations Charter, he wrote several hundred words almost every day recording the details of the controversies in which he was involved and setting down his own reactions to the results.

His letters, as many recipients know, were often little essays in themselves. He wrote a tremendous number of them — many were long explanations of current problems. Not infrequently they were replies to inquiries from persons of whom he had never heard before and would never hear again. Often they were written to people who were not even his own constituents. These letters illustrated his eagerness for everyone to understand the important questions before Congress, but they also afforded him an opportunity to think out problems, to try out phrases and slogans that he would use later in Senate debate.

As far as possible these records are presented intact in this book. Some minor changes have been made where he obviously typed the wrong word; but if there was any doubt about the word he intended to use, the word substituted by the editors has been enclosed in brackets with a question mark. He also continued an editorial-writing habit of scattering superfluous quotation marks, underlinings, capital letters, and asterisks with wild abandon through letters and diary entries. In the editing of the papers some of these have been modified for the sake of readability, but in general the character and personality of the original record have been preserved. He could split an infinitive at twenty paces with consummate ease, and seldom missed an opportunity to do so. These have not been altered because he believed that they were essential to his style. He was, to put it charitably, a careless speller, especially of names; and such errors have been corrected. It also should be mentioned that he sometimes omitted dates from his diaries and letters and that some of the missing dates have been supplied by the editors whenever the time of writing could be accurately determined.

The contribution of the collaborators who worked with me in editing the papers is acknowledged on a separate page in the book in order to give it the emphasis that I feel it deserves. But I mention them collectively at this point to record the agreement among us that the story in these pages should be told in my father's words as completely as possible. This is *his* account of what happened in the evolution of the foreign policy of the United States — and how it happened, and in many cases, how it almost didn't happen between the years of 1941 and 1951. Editorial comment has been interpolated only for the purposes of clarification and continuity. Opinions of what my father *may* have meant or how he *may* have felt in any given situation have been restrained unless I have been perfectly sure that I knew the thoughts behind his words.

As a result I believe we have made the closest possible approach to the creation of an historical narrative told in the intimate words of a man who himself was not on earth to write it. I feel that many Americans who followed and supported the broad outlines of the development of bipartisan foreign policy will find in this book a chance to go behind the Congressional scenes to see what actually happened *to themselves* in the evolution of their own thinking during this important period. . . .

Since this book is not intended to be a biographical type of work, many important events in my father's life will not be found. And thinking back over the years, it is difficult for me to pick out the little things and the big things that show in a few paragraphs what kind of a man he was. There are too many episodes to recall; too many memories from which to choose. But there was one particular entry in his diaries of the earlier days which told a great deal about him. In 1936 when the Republican National Convention was in session in Cleveland and Governor Alf Landon of Kansas had won the presidential nomination, John D. M. Hamilton, who was Landon's campaign manager, called on my father and asked him to accept second place on the ticket. (Landon himself, incidentally, did not extend the invitation. He later wrote that he had wanted a running mate from the rebellious faction of the Democratic party.) In reply to Hamilton's proposal, my father gave a number of sound political reasons for refusing, and then as a kind of afterthought he added in his diary: "I think I should die of inaction in the VICE presidency."

The remark that he might "die of inaction" under the restrictions placed on the Vice-President contained no disrespect for that office, but it was revealing in respect to his own psychology. He always had an irrepressible urge to get things done; he instinctively avoided a philosophical attitude toward affairs of state unless the philosophy could be translated into direct action. In using capital letters to type the word VICE in reference to the presidency, he was giving emphasis to the fact that he strongly disliked a position that would require him to restrict his activities to the policies laid down by someone else — even if that someone else was the President of the United States.

This love of independent action dated from his early boyhood. When he was nine years old the family income vanished in the panic of 1893 that ruined my grandfather's once-prosperous business as a harness maker. My father began facing realities then — this time the fact that the family needed money in order to eat. He promptly got a job hauling freight in a pushcart and soon had a couple of other boys working for him. He continued to work at various jobs until he was graduated from high school. His formal education was later concluded with one year at the University of Michigan in a pre-law course, when he found that his health would not permit him to pursue a college career and earn a living at the same time. After working as a cub reporter on the city hall beat of the Grand Rapids *Herald*, he was plucked out of the city room at the age of twenty-two by his friend and patron, William Alden Smith, and made editor of the almost bankrupt newspaper. This position he held until he was appointed to the Senate.

He had plenty of opportunity for action as editor of the *Herald*. He solicited ads. He wrote news stories. In a pinch he set type. He used a megaphone to announce election results and world series scores in a booming voice to crowds gathered in front of the newspaper office. He wrote the most pungent and sometimes the most flamboyant editorials published in the state of Michigan. He made speeches whenever anyone asked him. He built the newspaper into a valuable property and he made a name for himself in state political affairs.

In his spare time he set out to become a man of letters, and with his typical direct approach, he simply sat down at the typewriter and actually turned out more than one hundred short stories — which nobody chose to publish. At another time he attempted writing lyrics to popular songs — of which two were published but which few people chose to buy. His total royalties from the songs were six dollars and fifty cents. He wrote three scholarly and ponderous books that extolled the virtues of Alexander Hamilton as the "Greatest American," and generally proclaimed his faith in the nationalist point of view.

In 1928 he was appointed by Governor Fred Green to serve out the unexpired term of Senator Woodbridge N. Ferris, who died in office.

In view of what happened later, it is interesting to recall that in the beginning of his Senate career my father did not conform to the general rules which sharply limit the activities of freshmen senators. For one thing, he had only six months to serve before the next election, and he fully intended to be re-elected. With this in mind, and with his penchant for direct action, he introduced a bill to provide for the reapportionment of representation in Congress by which Michigan gained four seats in the House of Representatives on the basis of increased population. Other states represented by influential senators stood to lose ground by reapportionment, and there was powerful Senate opposition to the bill. But my father fought it through with youthful zest that reassured his election victory in Michigan even if it did nothing for his popularity rating in the Senate.

The reapportionment battle may have added to his natural aggressiveness at the time. He was a leader of the "Young Turks" who rebelled against the Republican Old Guard leadership during the Hoover Administration and were denounced by Senator George Moses of New Hampshire as "the sons of wild jackasses." He was self-confident. He was probably a little cocky. He spoke in a powerful voice, and early in his career was inclined toward purple prose and clichés. Some newspaper reporters described him as a disciple of the "boom-boom" technique in oratory.

But he got things done — things like the act for federal bank deposit insurance. And, when he squeaked through the New Deal landslide and won re-election in 1934 while a number of well-known Republicans were being eliminated from the Senate, his position in the Party hierarchy was assured. In the next few years he became a spearhead of opposition to President Roosevelt and the New Deal, and later a leading spokesman for isolationism in America. As an effective opponent of the New Deal he became a familiar national figure.

But these years were essentially preparation for the task that he was to face during the war and in the postwar period when, although belonging to the anti-Administration party, he achieved a unique position in the history of the United States Senate as an influential figure in the development of American foreign policy.

There has always been some speculation as to the reasons for my father's abandonment of the isolationist attitude that marked his Senate career before the war. The fundamental reasons — the gradual shifting of ground to face the realities of a changing world — are explained in this book. But it is also worthy of note that there was a personal influence exerted by his nephew, Hoyt S. Vandenberg, who later became Chief of Staff of the United States Air Force.

My cousin, Hoyt, came to live with us in Grand Rapids in

1918 and was appointed to the United States Military Academy from Michigan. After he was graduated from West Point he kept in touch with us. On cross-country flights to Washington from his various Air Force locations, he often spent several hours with my father, talking over problems of the Air Force and arguing that the airplane would be a dominant factor in any future wars. Later he was assigned to the War College and then to other duty in Washington, and there were opportunities for many more long sessions about what air power meant to the future of the United States and the world. I can recall many conversations in which the then junior officer in the Air Force argued heatedly against my father's belief that the oceans were "moats" protecting America from foreign wars. Pearl Harbor ended the argument.

If I tried to single out any one thing to show how my father was conditioned to the change that he made during the war, I would choose his devoted relationship with Hoyt. I would also like to emphasize that both of them were extremely careful never to permit this personal relationship to become involved with their official positions. They both scrupulously avoided any act or gesture that anyone could remotely interpret as an attempt to capitalize on the fact that a rising young officer in the Air Force had an uncle in an influential position on Capitol Hill.

In addition to this personal factor, it is obvious that chance played a part in my father's emergence as a molder of the nation's foreign policy — the circumstances that brought him to the right place at the right time. But the important factors were his tremendous drive, his need for action, his stubborn defense of broad principles, and his championship of what became known as bipartisanship in the foreign relations of the United States. It was his dedication to bipartisanship that dominated the last years of his life and brought into sharp focus a generally unrecognized spiritual side of his nature.

His favorite Biblical character was Saint Paul, the dynamic convert to Christianity, the author of Epistles to the Corinthians, and the great missionary of the New Church. My father enthusiastically hoped to write a life of Saint Paul. Perhaps one of the reasons — although he never expressed it to me — was that he found in the story of Saint Paul an inspiration that sustained him in the trying days of his own conversion from isolationism to a belief in collective safeguards for the maintenance of peace.

Before setting out to organize the papers for use in this book, I conferred with a few of my father's closest friends. They stressed the spiritual quality that marked his work for peace during the last years of his public life. They seemed to come to mutual agreement — although they expressed it in different terms — that the key to my father's character lay midway between his tremendous urge for action and his later dedication to the ideal of keeping politics out of peace.

Somewhere in this book I had hoped to have a completely objective analysis of my father's contribution to the history of his times. But it seemed to me it would violate the character of the book if the editors had attempted to write it themselves. So I submitted the following question to Mr. Walter Lippmann, noted journalist and authority on world affairs: "What will history show to have been the contribution of Senator Vandenberg in the evolution of the United States from a basically isolationist country in 1940 to our present-day position of world leadership?"

Lippmann was troubled by the phrasing of the question because understandably he did not wish to seem to set himself up as anticipating the judgment of history. But he was good enough, without having read the manuscript of the book, to write me the following personal letter for use in this introduction:

> If I were asked that question by an historian who had lived abroad and had never known your father personally, but wanted, nevertheless, to write a book about him, I would urge him to give great importance, indeed primary importance, to the influence of a conspicuous personal example.
>
> We do not any of us like to change our minds, particularly in public. And when we have taken a public stand we tend to be stuck in it. Once an issue has been fought over a long time, most of us are too proud and too timid to be moved out of our entrenchments by reason and evidence alone. Nothing

then is likely to change quickly, and in time before it is too late; the minds of a whole people accept a collision with the brutal facts and being run over by them — as in Pearl Harbor.

But when a sudden and tremendous change of outlook has become imperative in a crisis, it makes all the difference in the world to most of us to see a man whom we have known and trusted, and who has thought and has felt as we did, going through the experience of changing his mind, doing it with style and dash, and in a mood to shame the devils of his own weakness. I would argue at the bar of history, if ever I got the chance, that his spiritual experience, which great masses of our people entered into vicariously, was the creative element which made his other political powers so enormously effective.

In all men who lead multitudes of human beings there is a bit of magic. When it is working, then their other powers — such as the ability to see through an argument to the crucial issue, and to know at all times not only what they themselves are thinking but what others are feeling, and the gift of judging what is and what is not feasible, and what has priority, and the gift of eloquence — all these become incandescent with an effective energy that in themselves they would not possess.

I think that our friend, the imaginary historian, would find that it was well worth his while if he worked this vein.

Thus Mr. Lippmann has said what I myself could not say. In stressing my father's spiritual experience, he has sounded a note which serves to prepare the reader for the story that is about to be told. I wish only to add the final paragraph from my father's speech to the Overseas Writers' Club, which was quoted on an earlier page. In the opinion of some who heard him that night, he knew that this might be his last public statement.

After expressing pride in the record that the United States "had written in the annals of human history," he told the foreign correspondents:

We are joined together in a crusade for enduring peace. We

grip friendly hands across the sea. We have no enemies unless aggressors nominate themselves as such. Our common cause is human rights, fundamental liberties and a free world of free men. So long as we preserve and strengthen and expand that fraternity, we labor in the vineyard of the Lord and I dare to believe He will bless our dedications.

A. H. V., Jr.

January 12, 1952

The Private Papers
OF
Senator Vandenberg

I

"That Day Ended Isolationism"

SENATOR Arthur Hendrick Vandenberg wrote his diary on his own portable typewriter throughout his senatorial career, and he often took advantage of lazy Sunday afternoons to do the writing and to paste clippings in his scrapbook. One such Sunday was December 7, 1941, when the smell of cigar smoke and mucilage hung heavily over the Senator's bedroom desk as he brought up to date the record of his long battle against what he regarded as President Roosevelt's steps toward participation in the war against the Axis Powers.

Vandenberg was a symbol and a leader of isolationism — or, as he preferred to say, "insulationism" — in the United States up to four o'clock that Sunday afternoon. His determination to keep out of foreign wars was in harmony with the dominant feeling of the people of America at that time. But at four o'clock the telephone on his desk rang and he was informed that the Japanese had attacked Pearl Harbor. "In my own mind," he wrote later, "my convictions regarding international cooperation and collective security for peace took firm form on the afternoon of the Pearl Harbor attack. That day ended isolationism for any realist."

Perhaps that was correct; perhaps it was hindsight that enabled him later to recognize the turning point in his career. The record shows that on Pearl Harbor Day Vandenberg's reaction merely reflected what was happening all over America, where people who had been divided over the development of Rooseveltian foreign policy were suddenly and tightly united by a grim determination to win the war. "It is too late," he said in a public statement, "to argue why we face this challenge. . . . The answer so far as I am concerned is victorious war with every resource at our command." It was understandable that the Senator lost no time in issuing such a statement in order to prevent any misconception of the answer of isolationists to the Japanese attack. Vandenberg was not just an ordinary isolationist. He had been an internationally recognized spokesman for isolationism. He had almost made a career of it, particularly in the period leading up to Pearl Harbor and, in 1940, he had been the leading isolationist choice for the Republican presidential nomination.

Looking back on the record, there may be some question whether the Senator had wholeheartedly wanted to be President. "I think I can honestly say that I have never been bitten by the 'presidential bug,'" he wrote in a diary entry of November 27, 1938. "I abhor the thought of running for President — much more, the thought of actually being elected." But he was a logical isolationist candidate as a result of his prominent role in the Nye Munitions Investigating Committee and in framing the Neutrality Law of 1937, which included an arms embargo clause designed to keep the United States out of foreign wars by making illegal the sale or shipment of munitions to belligerents. Later, in 1939, his opposition to Mr. Roosevelt's program of assisting the Allied nations in the European war reached a climax when he vainly fought to prevent repeal of the arms embargo provision. In his diary at that time, he wrote:

September 15, 1939

The Battle Over the Arms Embargo: The story of 1917–18 is already repeating itself. Pressure and propaganda are at work to drive us into the new World War. . . . The same emotions which demand the repeal of the embargo will subsequently demand still more effective aid for Britain, France and Poland. . . . It is a tribute to the American *heart* but not to the American *head*. Oh yes, all these good people abhor the thought of our entry into the war; they are all opposed to that. President Roosevelt has given them their cue, however, in his use of the treacherous idea that we can help these countries by methods "short of war." My quarrel is with this notion that America can be half in and half out of this war ... which — if we are really in earnest about this business of "helping the democracies" — is utterly cowardly as a public policy for a great country like ours. I hate Hitlerism and Nazism and Communism as completely as any person living. But I decline to embrace the opportunist idea ... that we can stop these things in Europe without entering the conflict.

October 27, 1939

The Arms Embargo Battle: This dramatic contest closed tonight in the Senate. We were beaten 63 to 30. But we won a great moral victory. . . . It is going to be much more difficult for F.D.R. to lead the country into war. We have forced him and his Senate group to become vehement in their peace devotions — and we have aroused the country to a peace vigilance which is powerful. . . . Everybody is for "peace." This lip service may last quite a time. But we have definitely taken sides with England and France. There is no longer any camouflage about it. Repealist Senators speak frankly about it. In the name of "democracy" we have taken the first step, once more, into Europe's "power politics." . . . What "suckers" our emotions make of us!

Throughout this period prior to Pearl Harbor, Vandenberg grimly held to his conviction that America should take every precaution to keep out of the European war. But at the same time he was not blind to changing conditions. For instance, he promptly accepted repeal of the arms embargo as the will of the Congress and thereafter acknowledged the new situation. He wrote:

February 2, 1940

It is probably impossible that there should be such a thing as old fashioned isolation in this present foreshortened world when one can cross the Atlantic Ocean in 36 hours. We still want all the isolation we can get — despite the triumphs of modern science — and we still can look upon the two great oceans as the God-given guarantee of our international detachment (if we still have sense enough to maintain an unentangled foreign policy). But probably the best we can hope for from now on is "insulation" rather than isolation. I should say that an "insulationist" is one who wants to preserve all of the isolation which modern circumstances will permit.

In the period leading up to the National Conventions of 1940 — and to the fall of France — the Senator seemed to be frustrated by his inability to keep up with the behind-the-scenes maneuvers of the White House to assist the Allied cause. The President had the advantage of conducting much of our foreign relations in secret with the British and French. Vandenberg, without intimate knowledge of what was going on, seldom had a chance to oppose what he believed was a trend toward participation in the war until after the Administration's actions became publicly known — and usually that was too late. He had always been a man who loved action, who enjoyed a fight, but now he seemed to feel that he was being held impotently on the sidelines. This may have had some influence on his attitude toward the Vandenberg boom for the Republican presidential nomination despite the fact that he "abhorred" the thought of life in the White House. A group of Michigan Republicans, under the leadership of Howard C. Lawrence, a political associate and long-time friend, had organized a movement to promote his candidacy. Vandenberg didn't actively campaign for the nomination but he indirectly encouraged the sponsors of his candidacy and he made it clear that he would accept.

His attitude toward the President may also have been a consideration. By the spring of 1940, it was almost certain that Mr. Roosevelt would seek a third term. Vandenberg was opposed to that break with tradition, but he also must have felt an intense rivalry with the President, and he had relished his frequent past attacks on some of Mr. Roosevelt's pet New Deal ideas such as the Passamaquoddy tide-harnessing and Florida Ship Canal projects. That this antagonism was mutual was suggested by a note in the Vandenberg diaries as early as 1939.

June 8, 1939

At the White House reception tonight for visiting British royalty when I went down the line, the President introduced me to the King in an amazingly ungracious way. With a grim growl (and not a bit of facetiousness) — he didn't even give the King my name. He simply said: "Here's a chap who thinks he is going to succeed me in the White House; but he isn't." Whereupon two of the Roosevelt boys (Elliot and Jimmy) standing just behind, laughed loud and long. Senator White of Maine, who followed me in the line, heard the whole thing. He was shocked. I was greatly amused. At the same time, I was surprised because the President usually is very generous to me in his greetings. Perhaps he was trying to be funny. If so, he might at least have smiled.

Relations between the President and the Senator apparently were no better when the major parties chose their nominees for the 1940 campaign at their conventions in Philadelphia. Governor Thomas E. Dewey of New York, Vandenberg, and Senator Robert A. Taft appeared to be the popular choices as the conventions opened, but there also was a late-starter named Wendell Willkie. It is a commentary on the speed with which Willkie came to the front as well as on Vandenberg's frequent misspelling that the Senator wrote the newcomer's name with one "l" throughout his diary entry on the convention sessions.

[Undated]

Inside Stuff — Real History. Willkie came to Washington the Tuesday preceding the convention and asked me to have breakfast with him — which I did at the Carlton. He said that all he needed to put him over was the support of some outstanding, recognized Republican leader like me. I thanked him and told him that I thought the final show-down would come between the two of us (in which I was wrong). We parted good friends — but nothing doing. . . .

Before the balloting ever started, Dewey had a chance to control the convention if he had been willing to take a sporting chance. On June 25th, about 10:30 A.M., Senator Bridges came to my headquarters in the Adelphia and said he had a direct message for me from Dewey. "He wants you to take the vice presidency with him . . . ; he says this will sew up the whole thing on the first ballot."

This was my reply: "Tell Dewey that I think the vice presidency is very important and that if I were not a Senator I would take it, but I think — as I did in 1936 — that my place on the Senate floor is more important than on the Senate rostrum. Also tell him that if he will take the vice presidency with me . . . I shall be a pre-pledged one-termer [and] he will be in direct line for the White House in 1944. Also tell him that if this is too much for him to swallow all at once, I'll make him a sporting proposition. I'll meet him at eleven o'clock and flip a coin to see which end of the ticket we each take."

That was the end of the negotiations. I never heard from Dewey again until the convention approached the final voting on Thursday night. But it was too late. He missed the boat when he clung to his own first place ambitions. Between us we could have controlled the convention if it had been done in the first instance.

Joe Pew, in charge of Pennsylvania's 72 votes, could have nominated Taft on the fourth ballot if he had swung to him at that time. He waited too long. When he finally got around to doing business on the 6th ballot, Michigan had declared for Willkie and the die was cast.

Governor Carr of Colorado had agreed to make a seconding speech for me. . . . He . . . switched to Willkie and he wound up with a seconding speech for Willkie. Sam Pryor, National Committeeman from Connecticut, was originally in my corner and had planned on having Governor Baldwin of Connecticut make a seconding speech for me. On the showdown, Connecticut went over solidly to Willkie and Baldwin seconded his nomination.

It was interesting, in connection with the 1940 convention, that Vandenberg later wrote in his diary a complete denial of an item that appeared in the political column "Washington Merry-Go-Round" concerning an alleged telephoned offer by Vandenberg to swing the Michigan delegation to Taft at a critical moment.

[*Undated*]

> There is not one word of truth [in the story]. At no time during the . . . convention did I telephone the Taft headquarters or have any contacts, directly or indirectly, with Senator Taft or any of his representatives. At no time did I promise Taft or any of his people that I would deliver anything to them. Nor did I promise anything to anyone else — with the single exception that when Dewey . . . phoned me on the night of the balloting and begged me to join in getting adjournment ahead of the final balloting, I said I would have my floor managers talk with his about it (and they reported back that it was "no go" because the Taft managers insisted they could win by battling straight through without a further recess). That was the real Taft "tragedy." . . . The only time I had any communication with Taft at all was when he phoned my apartment after the nomination had been made, the next morning, and told . . . me that he was distressed to find himself interviewed that morning in the Philadelphia newspapers as expressing some critical wonderment as to why my Michigan delegates finally went to Willkie. He denied having said anything of the sort — and said his checkup on the ultimate disposition of these Michigan votes had convinced him early in the game that whenever I released them they would go to Willkie and not to him.

As for Vandenberg's diary comment on the outcome, it was terse and to the point: "The Willkie blitzkrieg hit me just as it hit everybody else."

Following the re-election of Mr. Roosevelt for a third term Vandenberg led the last, all-out isolationist fight against the Administration's program for lend-lease aid to the Allied Powers. It began with the President's message to the new Congress, in which he proposed lend-lease assistance.

January 7, 1941

President Roosevelt delivered his "total aid to England" war speech. I subsequently described it as a powerful statement in behalf of *"Peace Through War By Proxy."* The President received less applause than usual, even from his own partisans, when he entered and left the chamber and in the course of his address. The Republicans applauded very little — except courteously at the beginning and the end. But for the *first* appearance of the *Third Term President* whose third-term election the Joint Session had just previously certified, his reception was a flop.

Of course, in such circumstances, there has to be a "goat." So the First Lady, Mrs. Eleanor Roosevelt, laid it all to the Republicans and published a bitter statement criticizing the Republicans for their rank partisanship in not giving the President of the United States a *big hand* when he made his "war-by-proxy" speech.

But she reserved her chief anathema for me. At her subsequent press conference (for women correspondents) at the White House, she picked me out (alone) for personal condemnation for the statement that I issued following the speech — my "War-By-Proxy" statement. She said it was terrible; and that no statesmen had a right to "play with words when the world is on fire." Those who heard her said she showed more raw anger than ever before.

I had no thought of even being critical when I used the phrase — "Peace Through War by Proxy." I was simply trying to condense the President's policy into the fewest possible number of words; and I think I did it accurately and without prejudice. After Eleanor's attack, I asked a dozen Democratic Senators whether my phrase was improper from any aspect. The unanimous verdict was that I had been exactly accurate in describing the President's policy — and that *that very fact* was probably my chief crime because the Roosevelts did not relish facing the reality of what they are trying to do. At any rate, the limitations on "free speech" are getting constantly more apparent — and I suppose it won't be long now before *lèse majesté* is an *American* crime.

The fight on the lend-lease bill was vital both to the Administration and the isolationists. It was perhaps a last chance for the United States to turn back from the policy of aiding the Allies by all measures short of war. Defeat of the measure might have profoundly affected the course of the European conflict. Vandenberg made the case for keeping out, for stopping short of war while there still was time. He delivered a carefully prepared and impassioned speech to the Senate to support his position. But it wasn't a winning case. Slouched in his Senate seat, his long legs comfortably crossed, his chin sunk against his collarbone, his bright eyes darting restlessly from senator to senator as the roll was called, he knew that he had reached the end of a trail.

For months — for years — he had been carefully creating for America a kind of Portrait of an Isolationist; a portrait in which he sought to symbolize the obvious desire of the people to avoid war. The lessons of a century and a half of protected democracy, the yearnings of a hundred and fifty million Americans had been assembled in the picture. The outlines had been adjusted skillfully to the changing times — to what he had begun to call a "foreshortened" world. The final details had been painted with passion and with a firm hand. Nothing had been omitted that might catch the eye or stir the emotions. And at 7:10 P.M. on the night of March 8, 1941, the Portrait was put up for sale — and rejected. After the final Senate vote of 60 to 31, the Senator reviewed the fight in his diary.

Saturday, March 8, 1941, 7:10 P.M.

If America "cracks up" you can put your finger on this precise moment as the time when the crime was committed. It was at this moment that the Senate passed the so-called Loan-Lease Bill. It was passed because it wore the popular label of an aid-to-England bill and because the Roosevelt Administration left no stone unturned to drive its votes in the Senate into a goose-step — backed by a nation-wide emotion and a nation-wide propaganda of amazing proportions.

Nothing of the sort was necessary to give maximum material aid to Britain, *short of war*. The Taft substitute (for which I voted) provided direct and immediate "aid to Britain" without any of the "trimmings" which needlessly make President Roosevelt the Ace Power Politician of The World, and which turn The White House into G.H.Q. for all the wars of all the world. Nothing of the sort was necessary in order to demonstrate that the Senate is a unit against Hitler. *Eighty-nine* out of ninety-five Senators voted for the substitute or for the Bill — and thus voted for "aid to Britain" — and the other six (Bone, Chavez, La Follette, Nye, Langer and Walsh) all openly declared on the Senate floor that they wanted Britain to win.

But when H.R. 1776 passed the Senate, and thus negotiated its final hurdle, we did vastly more than to "aid Britain." I doubt if *all* those who supported it realized its implications. I hope I am wholly wrong when I say I fear they will live to regret their votes beyond anything else they ever did. I had the feeling, as the result of the ballot was announced, that I was witnessing the suicide of the Republic.

This is what I believe is the result. We have torn up 150 years of traditional American foreign policy. We have tossed Washington's Farewell Address into the discard. We have thrown ourselves squarely into the power politics and the power wars of Europe, Asia and Africa. We have taken the first step upon a course from which we can never hereafter retreat. We have said to Britain: "*We will see you through to victory*" — and it would be unbelievably dishonorable for us to stop short of full participation in the war if that be necessary to a British victory. We have said to Britain and all of her Allies, present and prospective: "You can charge your war bills to us from now on — we are your arsenal and your treasury." We have said to Hitler and Mussolini and Japan: "We are at undeclared war with you, and we will never sheath the sword until you have suffered a *conclusive military defeat.*" And we have said to the President that which not even embattled England has said to Churchill: "*You* pick our allies; *you* pick our enemies; *you* reward the former and punish the latter as *you* see fit; *you* can use our resources to suit *yourself* in thus roaming the world in martial stride; *you* lend, lease or give away what you please (with only casual limitations) out of our own defense facilities or out of the reservoir of our resources; *you* are *monarch of all you survey*. The proponents of this Bill say this is the way to *peace*. I pray to God that they are right. I pray to God that I am wholly in the wrong. Heaven has always protected us from our mistakes before; perhaps Heaven will do so again. But I believe we have *promised* not only Britain but every other nation (including Russia) that joins Britain in this battle that *we* will see them through. I fear this means that we must actively engage in the war ourselves. I am *sure* it means *billions upon billions* added to the American public debt — to a point which cannot be borne without ultimate depreciation and devaluation of the dollar to the vanishing point of value. . . . I do not believe we are rich enough to underwrite all the wars of all the world. I fear it means the ultimate end of our own democracy. Only "totalitarians" can do what will be expected of us.

[Such forebodings as Vandenberg noted in this diary entry on a night when his emotions were deeply stirred did not, however, halt the "evolution" into which he had been forced by a rapidly changing world. He immediately accepted the Congressional action as the future basis of American foreign policy and put himself in the position of trying to make it work.]

If we stand *any* show, it will be from pursuing this new, revolutionary foreign policy to the last limit with swiftest speed. I shall vote hereafter accordingly — but *only* because the Senate, on this historic night, has committed America to these illimitable obligations. . . . Our fate is *now* inseverably linked with that of Europe, Asia and Africa. We have deliberately chosen to "sit in" on the most gigantic speculation since Time began.

This attitude he elaborated on March 19 when he wrote to a Michigan friend: "I fought it from start to finish. I think it was wrong. . . . I think it will *not* stop short of war. But it is now the law of the land. It is now our fixed foreign policy whether we like it or not. We have no alternative except to go along unless and until H.R. 1776 is used by the President in a fashion which is not short of war."

The letter suggested that, despite the deep convictions that had guided him for twenty years, despite his stubbornness and despite the political bridges he had burned behind himself, a change was taking place in Vandenberg's philosophical outlook. It wasn't any sudden or dramatic change. It was so subtle that you could hardly put your finger on it or find a direct reference to it in the Senator's writings or speeches. It is certain that in his own mind it was not immediately a change at all — merely an adjustment to meet the demands of a changing world. If conditions changed for the worse through no fault of his own, Vandenberg was not a man to keep on defending an outpost when the enemy had overrun him and was attacking the fort. He intended to be where the fighting was going on. But something else had happened, too. By the spring of 1941 he felt that only a miracle could keep America out of the war, and he was now becoming convinced that unity at home was essential in the face of the world crisis. Therein lay the seeds of what was to become the nebulous idea of a bipartisan or nonpartisan foreign policy.

In the following months the Administration continued its pressure for measures short of war to aid the Allies. German and Italian ships in American ports were seized, and the Senate defeated a Vandenberg amendment to the bill authorizing seizure which would have prevented their transfer to Great Britain. The United States steamship *Robin Moor* was sunk by a German submarine, and on June 20 Mr. Roosevelt told Congress that the sinking was "outrageous and indefensible" and the "act of an international outlaw."

In a personal letter at this time, Vandenberg wrote:

[*Undated*]

> The President's message on the sinking of the Robin Moor was a typical statement of equivocal propaganda from the standpoint of naked truth. The important thing to establish is what precise rights the Robin Moor had, in international law, at the particular spot where she was torpedoed, and especially whether her cargo was contraband. Of course,

nothing is said about these matters. . . . I have been reliably informed that 1,173 items in the ship's cargo (about 70 percent of the cargo) was on not only the German contraband list but also on the British contraband list and also on our American contraband list in the last war. If that is anywhere near the truth, it puts a totally different light on the episode (although it would not excuse the utterly unexplainable fact that the sub-commander did not take off the passengers and crew before the sinking). But the country and Congress are entitled to *all* the facts — and don't get them.

Vandenberg wrote to Secretary of State Hull on June 20 asking whether the *Robin Moor* carried contraband war material. He got no reply to this letter but, after he had written again, the State Department replied that the *Robin Moor*'s manifest was ninety-five pages long and said, in effect, that they weren't sure whether it included war materials.

Lord Beaverbrook came to Washington early in September and his talk with Vandenberg was recorded in the Senator's diary.

[*Undated*]

Beaverbrook (And National Unity). Lord Beaverbrook came to Washington the first week in September, 1941, in his capacity as Chief Procurement Officer for Great Britain. He is an old, personal friend of mine and was very nice to me upon the occasion of my visit to England ten years ago. He phoned that he wanted to see me. . . . I went to the British Embassy and spent a very candid and interesting hour with him. He looks better than I have ever seen him before and seems to be thriving upon his difficult task which he is administering with supreme skill and effectiveness.

Beaverbrook immediately launched into a discussion of American *disunity* and its dangers. It seemed to be the chief burden of his soul. "Hitler never scared us more," said he, "than your House of Representatives did when it voted 203 to 202 for the extension of the draft act, and missed a repudiation of the Roosevelt leadership by the thin margin of only one vote in 405."

I took that as an example to show how *needless* this situation is. The Administration itself is responsible for most of its own hazards. I told him this story of the draft extension Act.

General Marshall, Chief of Staff, speaking of course for the President, told us in June that *four* things were necessary to avoid dire consequences to America. (1) The Draft Act must be amended to allow an unlimited Army in size. (2) It must be amended to permit keeping draftees indefinitely. (3) It must be amended to permit the use of this Draft Army *anywhere* in the world. (4) These things must be done by August first. That was the dead-line. What happened?

First the Administration discovered that it could not possibly get Congressional consent to an unlimited sphere of service because that meant a second American Expeditionary Force abroad. So this "indispensability" was quietly dropped. Second the Administration found it could not possibly get an unlimited total Army personnel. So this "indispensability" was dropped. Third, the debate ran on past the dead-line of August first. Nothing untoward happened. We heard nothing more of it.

That left just one of the critical "indispensables" remaining — namely unlimited tenure of service for draftees. Opposition in the Senate (where the Bill was first considered) stiffened against *this* demand — the last of the "indispensables." The Administration capitulated by proposing an outside limit of a total of thirty months of service. This, we were told, was the last thin line of national safety. The opposition offered eighteen months (the so-called Taft substitute). It was hooted down as impossible. The Senate voted thirty months — in a vote ratio of two to three. The House voted, as above indicated, thirty months by a single vote. There could not have been a heavier blow to the Administration. It was close to a repudiation. *Two weeks later the Administration voluntarily announced that it would ask only for a maximum of eighteen months extension in draft service, and that it would release at the end of fourteen months of service. On that basis, it could have had practically unanimous Congressional support and national unity.* But it preferred to first force a Congressional surrender to the executive program.

Nothing could better illustrate why "national unity" is so difficult. The failure to give *real* and serious consideration to its "opposition" is the Administration's most serious flaw. It *pretends* this unpartisan attitude by the device of inviting certain external Republicans into its counsels — but they are always Republicans who are *known in advance* to be "yes men" to the President's policies. A country, living under *representative, Constitutional government* cannot be united in any such totalitarian fashion.

When I told Beaverbrook this story, he said: "Do you tell the President these things?" I replied: "I have not been invited into the executive office in eight years." I do not care to record Beaverbrook's responsive comment. But it would burn a hole in this paper.

In these months, after the Nazis had suddenly turned and invaded Russia, the idea of putting all thought of politics aside and trying to find some solution to the world crisis was very much in Vandenberg's mind, and he seemed to feel keenly the President's failure to seek the active help or co-operation of the Republican minority. In November of 1941 he wrote: "It is dangerous to attempt to lump all of us (who oppose intervention in the war) into one standard isolationist bracket. . . . If I had to choose between being an isolationist or an internationalist I should unhesitatingly proclaim myself to be the former. But the path of wisdom and prudence lies somewhere between." That was, basically, Vandenberg's attitude when the Japanese struck at Pearl Harbor and united political figures of every hue in Washington behind the President's prosecution of the war to total victory.

At the White House, according to notes jotted down by Harry Hopkins late on December 7, the atmosphere seemed to include almost a tinge of relief that at last the decision had been forced by the Japanese in an entirely unexpected way. Hopkins remarked that the scene was "not too tense . . . because I think that all of us believed that in the last analysis the enemy was Hitler and that he could never be defeated without force of arms; that sooner or later we were bound to be in the war and that Japan had given us an opportunity."

At the other end of Pennsylvania Avenue, Vandenberg's thoughts in the next few days were running along a different line. On the day after Pearl Harbor he put down in detail his reactions:

December 8, 1941

Congress declared war on Japan today — with but one dissenting vote. The Senate was unanimous. There was no other recourse — in answer to what was probably the most treacherous attack in all history.

The news of the attack on Hawaii came into Washington around 4 o'clock yesterday afternoon. I immediately issued [a press] statement. I then phoned Steve Early, White House Secretary, and asked him to tell the President that, despite all differences on other things, I would support him without reservation in his answer to Japan. Marvin McIntyre, another White House Secretary, shortly phoned me the President's thanks.

Today at 12:30 the President addressed a joint session of Congress — asking a formal declaration of a state of war. With a speed and unanimity that show how a *democracy* can function in crisis, the Resolution was through both Houses within one hour.

I made the only speech that was made in the Senate before the vote was taken there. I felt it was absolutely necessary to establish the reason why our non-interventionists were ready to "go along" — making it plain that we were not deserting our beliefs, but that we were postponing all further argument over policy until the battle forced upon us by Japan is *won*. I felt it was necessary, too, in order to better swing the vast anti-war party in the country into unity with this unavoidable decision. The Administration leaders, with typical short-sightedness, had *not* wanted it done. They wanted no speeches at all — and even tried to cut me off.

[This was almost an understatement. Senator Tom Connally of Texas, Chairman of the Foreign Relations Committee, resisted on the floor when Vandenberg arose to speak and gave in only gruffly with the remark that "of course, the Senator has a right to speak if he insists."]

But I insisted — and I was greatly pleased, when I had finished my brief statement, to have Senator Glass cross over, shake my hand, and thank me for my statement. In the course of the afternoon, 21 other Senators phoned similar messages to my office; and Majority Leader Barkley himself later said that, upon reflection, he was very glad that I had done exactly as I did.

We were no longer "free agents" after the infamous Japanese attack and Japan's Declaration of War on America. There was nothing left to do but to answer in kind. But I continue to believe that a wiser foreign policy could have been followed — although now no one will ever be able to prove it.

We have little or no information regarding the peace-negotiations which have been going on for ten days as a result of the visit of the Mikado's special emissary. It has all been secret — secret even from the Senate Foreign Relations Committee. Perhaps this was necessary. But I hope that some day the whole record will be laid bare. I should like to know what the *price* of peace in the Far East would have been. I have the feeling that it would have been necessary for us to yield but relatively little — and nothing in the nature of "appeasement" — in order to have pacified the Far Eastern situation; and certainly any such pacification, virtually taking Japan out of the Axis, would have been the deadliest blow we could have struck at Hitler. For example, Japan has been in Manchukuo for 15 years — despite our refusal to recognize her title under the "Stimson Doctrine" (which, by the way, Britain rejected). To recognize Japan's title in Manchukuo, speaking loosely, would be simply to acknowledge an accomplished fact which will *remain* an accomplished fact whether we like it or not. I may frankly add that I think China is big enough so that additional territorial concessions, or trade zones, might have been arranged to the advantage of China herself in return for a guaranteed peace. This is pure speculation — except as the general notion is sustained by many conversations I have had with responsible Japs visiting America. Without condoning for an instant the *way* in which Japan precipitated hostilities, I still think we may have *driven* her *needlessly* into hostilities through our dogmatic diplomatic attitudes.

I fear this means a virtual end to our "lend-lease" aid to Britain et al. because *we are not adequately* prepared ourselves — as I have been saying for months. I fear we shall pay dearly for this lack of preparedness on our own account. I am *certain* it was worth infinitely much to Britain et al. to have us continue to remain out of the actual shooting war — and I doubt whether these values were appropriately assessed in determining what it was cold-bloodedly worth to *all* of us to take Japan virtually out of the Axis and to substantially pacify the Far East — thus permitting concentrated attention to Hitler.

But we have asked for this — and other — wars. Now we are in it. Nothing matters except *victory*. The "arguments" must be postponed.

December 11, 1941

War with Germany! War with Italy! Two declarations today! Unanimous! The news of German and Italian declarations against us reached us by radio this morning after the morning papers were out. The Committee on Foreign Relations met at 11:30 and passed upon the text of our Resolutions. The preamble proposed by the State Department describing the German action as a culmination of its longtime plan against us was rejected by the Committee in favor of a more factual statement which avoided the moot question of why we face this challenge. The Resolution was reported at 12:30. It was passed in ten minutes. A democracy *can* function when it has to.

The body of the Resolution was identical with that against Japan, and followed the precise language used in the Declaration of 1917 against Germany. It accepted "the state of war that has been *thrust* upon the United States."

That is the moot question which, as I said in the Senate on Monday, will have to be settled by the historians in some cooler, calmer moment. There is no use debating it now. So far as the *immediate* issue is concerned, these wars certainly *have* been "thrust" upon us. There is nothing to do but to repel the "thrust" — forever. I shall co-operate without reservation to that end. The argument is "on ice" for the duration so far as I am concerned.

But when historic appraisals finally are made, I want my own view-point preserved against that day of judgment.

Perhaps it was ultimately inevitable that we should be involved — no one can successfully deny that thesis. But I contend that this inevitability was *certain* in the light of the foreign policies which we pursued. We "asked for it" and "we got it." The interventionist says today — as the President virtually did in his address to the nation — "See! This proves we were right and that this war was *sure* to involve us." The non-interventionist says (and I say) — "See! We have insisted from the beginning that this course would lead to war and it has done exactly that."

Perhaps, in a sense, we are *both* right. But I do not see, on the face of the record, how it can be denied that *we* certainly have been right.

I remember saying, in my speech two years ago against the repeal of the arms embargo (the first step away from neutrality): *"You cannot be the arsenal for one belligerent without becoming a target for the other."* Well — aren't we?

We repealed the arms embargo frankly to help Britain. We established "cash and carry" frankly to help Britain. When British cash failed, we invented "lease-lend" to help Britain. We traded 50 destroyers, partially for the benefit of getting air bases for ourselves, but chiefly to help Britain. By this time, the President and his spokesmen (including the particularly bellicose Secretary of the Navy Knox) had abandoned all pretense to the contrary. They were loudly calling for the defeat of Germany — by proxy. We repealed practically all that was left of the Neutrality Act and voted to arm our ships and send them into combat zones and into belligerent ports to help Britain. By "we" I mean the Administration majority of interventionists. They said it was all done "to promote peace" — God save the mark. They promised peace in the 1940 campaign. They were "keeping the war from our shores," we were always told. I do not question the sincerity of these interventionists. But I *do* question their *candor*. Certainly I question their logic — then and now. It may have been the *right* course to "help Britain." God knows I have wanted Britain to win and win conclusively. That is not the present point. The point is that we did *everything* we could — by proxy — to help defeat Germany, and said so. We finally ordered the American Navy on Atlantic patrol under orders to shoot down *any* German craft on sight; and Roosevelt and Churchill sealed what they called "The Atlantic Charter" for Germany's doom. I do not here question the *justification* of these policies — they may have been right and necessary. But I say that when, at long last, Germany turned upon us and declared war against her most aggressive enemy on earth, it is no contribution to "historical accuracy" (to put it mildly) for us to pretend to say that this war has been *"thrust upon us."*

It may not be politically expedient for the interventionists to tell the truth at the moment — because they would thus have too many anti-war promises to swallow. But if this war is worth fighting, it is worth accepting for what it is — namely, a belligerent cause which we openly embraced long ago and in which we long since *nominated ourselves* as active participants. The "thrusting" started two years ago when we repealed the Arms Embargo.

2

"We Must Not Fumble the Peace"

THE WAR was not yet a week old when Vandenberg received a telephone call from the British Embassy asking him to come for a talk with Lord Halifax. Their conversation turned out to be interesting but, in itself, of only passing significance. The important thing was that the Ambassador, representing a foreign government, told the Senator more about the war situation in the course of an hour than he had been able to learn from the State Department in a long time. Vandenberg was surprised, gratified and more than ever convinced that there were powerful reasons why his own government should deal more frankly with the leaders of Congress in the prosecution of the war.

December 13, 1941

At the request of Lord Halifax, British Ambassador, I called on him this morning at the Embassy. The primary reason was a personal message which he wished to relay to me from Lord Beaverbrook.

I was received in one of the south rooms on the second floor looking out upon the famous Garden. As I glanced through the window out upon the cold, empty, silent, rain-swept lawn, I could not help but contrast it with memories of the gay, colorful, flashing Garden Parties of happy men and women from all quarters of the globe who have annually gathered here on the King's birthday. It seemed like a picture of what has happened to the world.

Beaverbrook was again urging me to visit England as his guest to see the British war effort at first hand. Halifax joined in the pressure. I declined. There might have been some utility in it prior to our entry into the war when many mutual misunderstandings needed to be cleared away. But our entry into the war has done all the necessary clearing. Furthermore, I doubt the propriety of such a visit except at the suggestion of my own government.

But I had a most interesting hour with Halifax and in our discussion of the Far Eastern situation, I learned more from *him* about *our own* Far Eastern policies than I have learned from our own secretive governmental circles. He agreed with me that it would have been worth a "reasonable price" — short of "appeasement" — to have pacified the Far East by agreement and thus to have taken Japan out of the Axis, and we pretty much agreed on what a "reasonable price" would have been. But he said he was certain that no "reasonable" agreement would have been possible; that he thought Secretary Hull had labored to the last feasible limit for at least an interim accord; but that anything within the realm of possibility would have been a staggering blow to Chiang Kai-shek and the Chinese "democracy." I could not help but think, as I left, that it is unfortunate our own Congress and our own People are not given *more* official information. Sound popular conclusions cannot be based on ignorance....

Halifax read to me an amazingly interesting, confidential memorandum from a British diplomat who had been interviewing Dr. Beneš, President of the exiled Czech-Slovak government and a man exceptionally well informed. Dr. Beneš expressed the belief that the German offensive against Russia was forced on Hitler by his younger militarists against the advice of his older generals and advisers; that this has caused an internal schism in the Nazi Party which is calculated shortly to cause serious trouble; that such men as Goering and Goebbels have now been set pretty much aside, and that only Himmler (of Gestapo fame) is still close; that Hitler's sources of man-power have now been used up and that the re-organization of his Divisions into smaller units proves his shortening resources; that, in the event of any serious set-backs Hitler will probably be liquidated by his own "older generals" who will attribute it to a "British bomb" and then take over. Halifax said: "This may be wishful thinking; but Beneš usually knows what he is talking about." But he agreed with me that the new Jap war-actions are likely to bolster German morale and postpone the end of the total war.

I bluntly asked Halifax if he trusted Russia. He did not answer for a moment. Then he said slowly — "Yes, I think I do." More silence — and then he repeated it more firmly. As proof he quoted a conversation with Litvinoff, the new Russian Ambassador, when he arrived here. He said to Litvinoff: "I see the Germans say they are stopping the war on the Eastern front till Spring." And Litvinoff vigorously replied: "It takes two to stop a war, and we shall never stop."

Halifax had much to say — as did Beaverbrook in my interview with him when he was here — about the great need for *national unity* in the United States. He apologized for making any comments on our internal affairs; but he said he hoped every effort will be made to perpetuate the *unity* which America spontaneously disclosed in answer to "Pearl Harbor." Halifax frankly conceded that American defense necessities are likely to substantially slow down "lend-lease" aid for Britain; but he added — "From now on we must consider everything as a common problem."

This meeting with Halifax made a strong impression on the Senator. The Ambassador, obviously interested in Vandenberg's good will, had spoken very frankly and had made him feel that he was being given access to significant information that was of great importance in helping him to form his own opinions. That was, he noted, a great deal more than he had learned from his own government. He chafed at his own lack of knowledge and inability to act. He believed the Administration's secretiveness raised an important question in the conduct of the United States' war effort, and two days later he did something about it. The following letter was written to President Roosevelt:

December 15, 1941
Dear Mr. President,
   . . . I am seeking your reactions in advance so that I may initiate no needless controversy if there be persuasive reasons why the subject should not be opened.
   I am constantly impressed by the fact, on the one hand, that the direction of this war must be essentially an executive function; and by the fact, on the other hand, that legislative responsibilities still persist which are not calculated to be ignored even though they are necessarily subordinated in the first instance. Therefore, I am wondering whether it would not be highly useful to both the Executive and the Legislature if a more intimate connecting link should be created between us for the duration.
   [He then went on to point out that he was not suggesting legislative interference with conduct of the war and that he realized much critical information could not be communicated to all members of Congress.] But in many . . . situations . . . there may be understandable Congressional demands for information . . . and many situations will develop where the Executive would be happy to partially share this responsibility with Congress — to the extent of full, free, frank consultation — if it could be done in a dependable partnership.
   It is in this spirit — and . . . in full understanding that this war cannot be conducted by a town meeting — that I invite your comment upon the creation of a Joint Congressional Committee on War Cooperation to be composed of six Senators and six Representatives with the proviso that not more than four of each group of six should come from the same political party. . . . It seems to me that Congress might well be more content to curb whatever suspicions or irritations may arise if it were to know that its own selected representatives are in full and first hand contact with all essential facts. . . . On the other hand, it seems to me that the Executive might find not only comfort but great aid in such a group. . . .

   This proposal was of considerable significance — although nothing came of it except a good deal of discussion — because it showed how Vandenberg's feeling of frustration was pushing him toward some kind of a bipartisan approach to problems of foreign policy; some kind of formula for collaboration between the Administration and the Opposition without requiring the Opposition to agree with everything that the President did. It was important, too, that Mr. Roosevelt recognized both the sincerity of the suggestion and the opportunity it offered him to make a conciliatory gesture to the Senator. It is doubtful that he wanted such a committee, but his reply was friendly and open-minded — and a little flattering.

"Of course," he wrote on December 27, "I am in hearty accord with the apparent objective. If the Congress believes greater cooperation can be had by the appointment of such a Committee, I will be only too happy to consult with and seek the advice of the members of the Committee." He then pointed out certain difficulties in the way of creating such a liaison but added: "If Congress thinks the proposal wise, I will be delighted to accept its judgment. . . . I appreciate the good faith in which you submit your inquiry and your offer to serve in any assignment. . . . Each of us in this crisis must labor where we are best fitted to serve. In the Senate you have an opportunity granted few men to be of real service in promoting unity in the Congress and in the country. Even without your offer, I would know that I could rely upon you."

This exchange was as sincere as the President and the Senator had ever been in their correspondence. More than once Mr. Roosevelt had brushed off the Senator's suggestions or offers of willingness to be of service in some domestic problem. Vandenberg had on more than one occasion stung the President with his well-documented political attacks. Their active dislike for one another was inevitably an additional barrier to the still nebulous idea of foreign policy collaboration.

Progress was made, however, in the following weeks, as Vandenberg noted in his diary:

January 7, 1942

Senator Connally, Chairman, initiated an excellent new practice today in the Senate Foreign Relations Committee. He arranged for a representative from the State Department to meet with us confidentially once a week and give us the "inside dope." Assistant Secretary Breckinridge Long came in today to serve this function.

Among many other illuminating things, he told us about the efforts of ex-King Carol of Rumania to get into the U.S. It touches the lighter side of this crisis. It came the same day that Carol (with his red-headed friend, Lupescu) was announcing himself as the head of a new anti-Axis movement in behalf of "Free Rumania" — with the purpose of getting out of Mexico and into the U.S. to "campaign" for his new devotion.

Long told us that Carol had been trying to get into the U.S. ever since his abdication. He went first to Spain and tried — and was refused. He fled to Portugal and tried — and was refused. At that point Cuba agreed to take him — and we agreed that he could go via Bermuda. He got to Bermuda and the only available boat to Cuba took him as far as the Virgin Islands. There he got on a cruise ship (the "America") bound for Havana. But no sooner did this ship put out to sea than it was notified that it had been requisitioned by the U.S. Government and should make immediately for New York. Thus Carol would have found himself bound for the U.S. in spite of all our official refusals to let him in. The State Department moved into action. It definitely did *not* want Carol and his notorious consort in the U.S. But it was not until a direct appeal to the President was made that the ship was ordered to continue its original course to Cuba. And *so* Carol landed in Havana instead of New York. From there he finally went to Mexico. It remains to be seen whether he can *now* get into the U.S.A.

These tentative maneuverings toward some kind of liaison between the State Department and Congress didn't add up to much except perhaps to achieve a change in the atmosphere — probably not enough to be noticeable. Vandenberg wrote:

January 12, 1942
This war is the most desperate responsibility which America ever faced . . . and it will take the country's best to win it.

Certainly the country's best is not mobilized at the present time in positions of control. The worst of it is that there is still a substantial New Deal sector in high places which will constantly think of the war in terms of new opportunities for further New Deal experiments. . . . Obviously the country should be given the confidence which would flow from a White House demonstration that the country's best (regardless of politics) is to be assigned to this frightful responsibility. . . . But nothing will ever come of it until the President himself recognizes the present jeopardy. . . . We are now living under government by executive decree. . . . The president . . . is the one who must get . . . new vision before it is too late.

The Senator's dissatisfaction with Mr. Roosevelt's attitude was further intensified by two speeches Winston Churchill delivered in the House of Commons in January and February. Both of them underlined the Vandenberg contention that the Congress and the American people were not getting enough information about the war. He recorded the speeches in his diary as follows:

January 27, 1942
Churchill spoke to the British Commons today. *And we learned something of very great importance over here in the U.S.A.* In discussing events leading up to the war in the Far Pacific he said:

What was the likelihood of the Far Eastern theatre being thrown into war by Japanese attacks? I will explain how delicately we walked and how painful it was at times — how very careful I was that every time *we should not be exposed single-handed to this onslaught.*
On the other hand, the probability since the Atlantic Conference, at which *I discussed these matters with President Roosevelt, that the United States, even if not herself attacked, would come into the war in the Far East* and thus make the final victory assured, seemed to allay some of these anxieties, and that expectation has not been falsified by the events.

In other words, Churchill said that when he met Roosevelt the first time — and wrote "The Atlantic Charter" — he talked with the President about the fact that Britain must not *fight alone* in the Far East, and got some sort of an assurance, evidently satisfactory to him, that the U.S. would go to war with Japan *regardless of whether* Japan attacked us or not. In still other words, *we were slated for this war by the President before Pearl Harbor*. Pearl Harbor merely precipitated what was "in the cards." To whatever extent this is true, it indicates how both Congress and the Country were in total ignorance of the American war-commitments made by the President and never disclosed.

I saw the full text of the Churchill speech *only* in The New York Times. . . . Senator Danaher of Connecticut put this material in the Congressional Record for January 28. *Not a paper mentioned it.* Does this mean that censorship is now at work to complete the task of keeping the people in ignorance regarding what has happened to them?

And if the implications of Churchill's statement are valid, is there not *very high responsibility* for not *ordering* Hawaii to be on "total alert" ahead of "Pearl Harbor"?

February 16, 1942

Churchill spoke to the British Commons again today. *And again we learned some of the things which heretofore we have only suspected.* With bad news from Singapore and the successful German running of the Dover Straits by German battleships, Mr. Churchill faced a difficult subject. But he found one reason, dominating all others, why, in spite of disasters, Britain should cheer up:

When I survey and compute the power of the United States and its vast resources, and feel that *now* they are in with us, in with the British Commonwealth of nations all together, however long it lasts, till death or victory, I cannot believe there is any other fact in the whole world which can compare with *that*. *That is what I have dreamed of, aimed at and worked for, and now it has come to pass.*

In other words, the major objective of British Diplomacy all through these recent years (when all our British co-operation was *supposed* to be for the purpose of *keeping us out of the war*) has been to *get us into the war*. I don't blame 'em. But if any non-interventionist, prior to last December 6th, had accused Churchill of "working to get us into the war" he would have been condemned by the interventionists as a pro-Nazi. "Just give us the tools and we will finish the job" was what Churchill was saying *then*. And so the American people were told that if we *would* "furnish the tools," they *would* "finish the job." But all the while, the *real* "job" was to *get us into the war*.

Too late to argue about it. Being in, we must *stay* in to the point of total victory. But I hope the historians will one day straighten out the record. The non-interventionists "weren't so dumb," as they say on the street.

These Churchillian revelations, however, did not affect the Senator's determination to press for greater liaison between the Administration and Congress, although he acquired doubts as to the wisdom of his proposal that Congress set up a Joint Committee on War Cooperation. "I am frank to say," he wrote on February 20, "that I am not entirely clear that it [Congress] should do so. I think the members of any such committee would occupy an exceedingly difficult role . . . because of the obvious limitations within which they would operate.

"Nevertheless . . . I think Congress and the country must be brought very much closer to the realities of this war. I think there must be a broader sharing of vital responsibility. I think there must be closer 'team work' in Washington."

During the winter and spring of 1942 Willkie had again become a highly controversial figure. After going on a mission for Mr. Roosevelt to bomb-wrecked London, the titular leader of the Republican party had stepped far out ahead of many of his colleagues with positive views on the internationalist role which the United States should play after the war — views that developed into his One World theory, much to the chagrin of some Republicans. Vandenberg had not enjoyed the Willkie "blitzkrieg" at the 1940 Republican convention, but he had developed a considerable respect and admiration for the man's aggressiveness, his willingness to fight all the way and his ability to catch the popular imagination and hold the loyalty of a large following. Their relations were friendly and relaxed. They had worked together during the 1940 campaign. In the spring of 1942, however, the Senator did not approve Willkie's use of the Republican National Committee meeting in April as a sounding board to further the swing toward internationalism.

April 21, 1942

The Republican National Committee "resolved" today not only to fight the war to unqualified victory, but also that the nation has an obligation "to assist in the bringing about of understanding, comity and co-operation among the nations of the world in order that our liberty may be preserved and that the blighting and destructive processes of war may not again be forced upon us and upon the free and peace loving peoples of the world." And this was nationally hailed as the death of so-called "Isolationism." It was advertised as a great victory for Willkie, the internationalist. As a matter of fact it is all sheer bunk. It is mere shadow-boxing with platitudes. *I* agree with this general statement. *I* do not see how *anybody* could disagree with it. *I* think that Senator Taft made a great mistake in going to this Chicago meeting and opposing this declaration and in thus *giving* Willkie the pretense of a "victory." The statement is one of sheer generalities. *Everything* depends upon the ultimate "bill of particulars" — and no one can foresee the future — until *after* the war itself is won — sufficiently to deal in specifications at all. *Of course* we shall have to "co-operate" in the peace. I have no doubt that we shall "co-operate" much more than we did after World War Number One. But how? In a "World Union"? In a new "League of Nations"? Not even Willkie would dare be specific. The so-called former "Isolationist" will simply insist upon consulting the best welfare of "America First" when the time comes to chart this "co-operation" — and *that* sort of "isolationism" will be found very much alive (despite all these Willkie funeral orations) *when the time comes* to deal with the post-war world. The Chicago meeting was just a "show" in which the best "actor" stole the lime-light and got the most applause.

As a matter of *fact*, the National Committee has no control whatever over "party policies" and its "resolution" is sheer dictum. "Policies" will be determined by *elected* Republican Senators and Congressmen until the Convention of 1944 when they will be settled by a National Convention called for that purpose and authorized to act.

The fact that Soviet Russia was in the Allied line-up against the Axis was a matter of no little concern to Vandenberg almost from the beginning of our participation in the war. He had always been a sturdy foe of communism. He repeatedly recalled in letters and speeches that he was one of two senators who voted against recognition of the Soviet Union, and he had on several occasions before the war protested that the Russians were brazenly violating the Roosevelt-Litvinov agreement upon which United States recognition of Moscow was based. This was an agreement by which Russia promised to abandon all relationships with internal revolution inside the United States or with any agencies engaged in "any act overt or covert liable in any way whatsoever to injure the tranquility, prosperity, order or security of the whole or any part of the United States." He urged that relations with Russia be broken off in 1939 and, later, he wrote in his diary that Russia "has brutally, relentlessly and without the shadow of justification moved in on Finland and bombed and fired her Capital." In 1942, when postwar problems were first attracting attention in Washington, the Senator struck a prophetic note in observing in his diary that Stalin seemed to be demanding a price from the United States and Britain in return for Russia's efforts against the Axis.

June 4, 1942

By unanimous Senate vote we declared war today on Bulgaria, Rumania and Hungary. It took just 25 minutes for the three roll calls. The Foreign Relations Committe met in the morning to canvass the situation. The first question asked was *why* we had waited until *now* to declare war on these three countries — since they all declared war on us within a week after Pearl Harbor. The superficial answer was that *their* original declarations were considered by us to be little more than a formality under Hitler's orders and they weren't worth paying any attention to. But since they are now very definitely *in the war* on the Russian front, we must "keep the record straight."

The *real* reason for the President's recommendation, however, is that Molotoff (Russian Foreign Minister) is secretly in Washington (the censors have not allowed even a suggestion of this fact to get into print). *He* has undoubtedly demanded these declarations of war on our part. It is perfectly logical and appropriate that we should make them. But it is significant that we do it *in response to Russian demand*. The "argument" seems to be that "we are all in a common war against a common enemy" and we should *say so*. But when some member of the Committee suggested that "it's a poor rule which doesn't work both ways" and that, by the same token, Russia should either declare war on Japan or should at least let us have Russian air bases to bomb Nippon, there was no answer.

I was particularly interested in the fact that Russia seems, in this instance, to be perhaps *starting* a series of demands upon Britain and upon us as the price of her continued belligerence (which is so totally indispensable to our war effort). I inquired if it was true that Russia had *also* asked of Britain (and perhaps of us) a present agreement that she shall have Latvia, Lithuania and Estonia *after* the war is won. The request certainly was made of Britain. Chairman Connally said, confidentially, that all he could say was that any such demand regarding these three little countries would *not* be granted. Probably so — right now. Certainly it would reduce the famous "four freedoms" to a "scrap of paper." But I wonder if Russia isn't in position to *force* almost *any* "price" upon us during the balance of 1942 if she really *wants* to do so! How could either Britain or we refuse? Russia is doing a magnificent job. She is the key to the present and prospective success of the United Nations. Moscow has always been a shrewd trader — for Moscow. Will there be any "four freedoms" left by the time this show is over? Will there be a paraphrase of the "secret treaties" in World War Number One by which the Allies divided up the spoils in advance of victory and without any knowledge?

These are just some of my speculations today — as we take the first step (however logical and justified) in response to Russian demands. It will be horribly interesting to check the final results, one day, against June 4, 1942.

Close collaboration between the Senate and the Administration was pretty well stalled on dead center in these months and for the remainder of 1942. Vandenberg grew increasingly restless and more than ever convinced that some closer form of liaison was essential in Washington. In the winter of 1943 he wrote numerous letters on the subject. To Major George Fielding Eliot he complained on February 10 about the

> complete and total lack of authentic liaison between the White House and Congress in respect to war responsibilities. . . . Perhaps we can muddle through. . . . I can give . . . two examples, one positive and one negative. The State Department's recent White Paper proves that Congress . . . knew little or nothing of the international realities . . . in policies and events for six critical months preceding Pearl Harbor. It is not strange that one cannot see in a dark room. . . .
> On the other hand, when General Marshall called a group of representative Senators and Congressmen to the War Department when General Eisenhower landed in North Africa and frankly explained to them the necessities of the Darlan relationship [Eisenhower's cease-fire deal with Admiral Jean François Darlan, which was denounced in many quarters because of Darlan's past co-operation with Hitler] he "turned on the light" and . . . in a completely confidential way it served . . . to relieve Eisenhower of what otherwise might have been a most embarrassing Congressional barrage. [Vandenberg drove home this point on the Senate floor by defending Eisenhower's deal with Darlan and in doing so indirectly attacked Willkie, who had been one of the most outspoken critics of the arrangement.]

The Administration — and Mr. Churchill's cabinet in London, too — was under very bitter attack for the Darlan deal, but if anyone regarded it as significant that Vandenberg helped in relieving the pressure, it was not recorded by the Senator. It is interesting, however, to note that in the following months his idea of closer teamwork in Washington — without in any way tying the hands of the opposition — began to bear some fruit. On March 12, for example, the Senate appointed a Special Committee on Post-War Economic Policy and Planning, with Senator Walter George of Georgia, as Chairman and Vandenberg as one of four minority members. "I think," Vandenberg wrote in his diary, "this may be the most important committee in the history of the Senate." The Committee had no connection with foreign policy, being designated to prepare for postwar reconversion legislation, but he noted later that it did a good job and it also served to illustrate the benefits of such bipartisan collaboration.

Most important in this period, however, was the sudden but vast interest in postwar objectives, particularly some kind of international agreement that would provide a safeguard against future wars. The United States' refusal to join in the League of Nations after World War I was strongly in the minds of Congressional leaders, and in the minds of the leaders of the other Allied nations, too. Nobody wanted another fiasco in the field of international collaboration for peace but, at the same time, opinion in the United States varied radically from the "One World" thesis to the philosophy of the somewhat shrunken but still smoldering bloc of pure isolationists. Furthermore, as Vandenberg had repeatedly observed, there was the terrible problem of conflicting interests that would arise among the Allied Powers as soon as the shooting ceased. If there was also to be a bitter split or a prolonged home-front battle over the United States position in postwar world affairs the outlook was tragic, indeed.

How strongly Vandenberg was aware of these possibilities, how clearly he saw the circumstances that were slowly forming into an unprecedented opportunity for himself, it is difficult to say. Certainly fragments of the complicated mosaic were constantly in his mind. "We must not fumble the peace . . . as we did after World War No. One," he wrote on February 11, 1943, "[but] there are very definite limits beyond which postwar planning cannot yet go. Ours will not be the only voice at the peace table. Mr. Joseph Stalin will be a very powerful figure. ... Again we do not yet know ... what Mr. Winston Churchill has in mind.... Of course, we shall defend our ideals in peace as well as war; and unquestionably we must prepare ourselves to accept a larger degree of international responsibility. ..."

A month later, he added:

March 26, 1943

I think [the] average American wants to be very sure that American spokesmanship at the peace table is at least as loyal to America's own primary interests as Mr. Stalin is certain to be in respect to Russia and Mr. Churchill ... to the British Empire. This average American is scared by the Vice President's [Henry Wallace's] "international milk route" and by kindred Pollyanna crystal gazing. ... He is neither an isolationist nor an internationalist. He is a middle-of-the-roader who wants to win this war as swiftly and as cheaply as possible; who then wants a realistic peace which puts an end to military aggression; who wants justice rather than force to rule the postwar world; who is willing to take his full share of responsibility in all of these directions; but who is perfectly sure that no one is going to look out for us ... unless we look out for ourselves and who wants "enlightened selfishness" mixed with "generous idealism" when our course is chartered.

This viewpoint — considerably removed from the Vandenberg opinions before Pearl Harbor — had evolved slowly in the Senator's thinking over a long period, but by the spring of 1943 it was well established and, in a way, it was to guide him through the era in which he reached full political maturity and became an almost unique figure in the history of the development of American foreign policy. It is doubtful that ever before a member of a minority party faced the opportunity to mold national policy in the way that was now opening, slowly but surely, for the Senator from Michigan.

The opening wasn't sudden. It was unlikely that it could

even be recognized as an opening for a long time. But it arose out of the determination of millions of Americans that this time we would not — as Vandenberg had said — fumble the peace. It was an aspiration as strong in its way as had been the determination to keep out of other people's wars. It, too, was made to order for the Senator.

3

"Hunting for the Middle Ground"

SENATOR Vandenberg above all was a man of action, and in 1943 he had plenty of opportunity to act in connection with America's search for the answer to an all-important question: What kind of world are we fighting for?

The question touched off a long controversy both in Congress and inside the high councils of the Republican party. In both instances the Senator played a significant role in the decisions that were reached. As a leader of the Party, he was instrumental in shaping what became known as the Mackinac Charter declaration on foreign policy, a declaration that for the first time united the Republicans in favor of responsible participation in a postwar international co-operative organization, and which became the basis of the 1944 party platform's plank on foreign policy.

In Congress he became deeply involved in a long conflict over putting the Senate on record regarding the objectives of the United States in the postwar world. Up until 1943 about the only declaration regarding postwar aims was the Atlantic Charter of 1941, in which President Roosevelt and Prime Minister Churchill opposed territorial or other aggrandizement and pledged recognition of the right of peoples to choose their own governments and to establish a peace that would provide security and freedom from fear and want. But these statements were general in character and early in 1943 there was agitation for an Allied agreement on more definite postwar aims. Vandenberg noted this in a diary from which he later compiled the following "History of the First Attempt To Commit Our Post-war Objectives."

February 4, 1943

Senator Gillette of Iowa introduced [in the Senate] S. Res. 91 which called upon the President to summon an immediate international conference to write a Treaty embodying the principles of the *Atlantic* charter. His primary inspiration was information from the Far East that China et al. feared it was not also a Pacific Charter because of its title. His purpose was to fix world-wide character and officially to commit all United Nations to it. The Resolution was sent to the Foreign Relations Committee and then to a Sub-Committee consisting of Senators George, Gillette and Vandenberg. Nothing was done about it for six weeks.

March 13, 1943

Senators Ball, Burton, Hatch and Hill announced their purpose to introduce a Senate Resolution specifically committing the United States to five peace objectives, and requesting the President to call an immediate international conference for this purpose. This followed a series of speeches by Governor Stassen of Minnesota presuming to outline in much detail the organization of a post-war-league. It also followed much hammering in speeches along this same line by Wendell Willkie and in relentless writings by internationalistic columnists about how the United States must quickly notify the world that all thought of "isolationism" over here is dead. The five proposed commitments were as follows: (1) To assist in coordinating and fully utilizing the military and economic resources of all member nations in the prosecution of the war against the Axis; (2) To establish temporary administrations for Axis-controlled areas of the world as these are occupied by United Nations forces, until such time as permanent governments can be established; (3) To administer relief and assistance in economic rehabilitation in territories of member nations needing such aid and in Axis territory occupied by United Nations forces; (4) To establish procedures and machinery for peaceful settlement of disputes and disagreements between nations; (5) To provide for the assembly and maintenance of a United Nations military force and to suppress by immediate use of such force any future attempt at military aggression by any nation. It further provided that member nations "should commit themselves to seek no territorial aggrandizement." These latter proposals squarely collided with Mr. Stalin's current announcement from Moscow that Russia intends to keep Latvia, Estonia, Lithuania, Eastern Poland, Bessarabia, parts of Finland, etc. They also collided (probably) with what may yet develop as Britain's territorial aspirations in North Africa. This Resolution had been submitted by its authors to Undersecretary of State Welles and apparently had his tacit approval. The announcement regarding it was released the *day before* Secretary of State Hull's return from a Florida recuperation (which may be a significant fact in the light of subsequent events). Welles arranged for the four authors to see the President about it at The White House the following day (Sunday). The latter meeting occurred and the press was given the idea that the President generally approved. (One day later, the President told a press conference he was *not* behind the Resolution; and two days later, the President said his denial was not meant to indicate repudiation of the Resolution).

March 16, 1943

The Resolution was formally introduced in the Senate by Senator Ball who said the four authors had been "delegated" by Senator Truman at a previous luncheon where a number of Senators had discussed the matter. The Resolution was referred to the Foreign Relations Committee. The George Committee promptly asked to be discharged from the Gillette Resolution so that a new and larger Committee could be named to consider *all* of these peace proposals (including one by Senator Thomas of Utah). The new Committee was named consisting of Senators Connally, George, Barkley, Thomas, Gillette, La Follette, Vandenberg and White.

The idea of the Resolution was popular. Sentiment was strongly in favor of some means to prevent future wars, the proposal for a United Nations military force attracted considerable support and the idea of no territorial aggrandizement was one that most Americans liked, especially those who suspected the worst of the British and Russians. But Vandenberg saw other facets of the problem that worried him, especially the fact that the resolution "seeks to particularize prematurely. It could easily re-divide America at home. It could easily divide our Allies abroad. . . . It could jeopardize victory itself. It seems to me . . . that we can successfully generalize to accomplish every good purpose and to avoid the pitfalls."

These confidential comments were unusually revealing not merely in relation to the Resolution but in regard to an approach that Vandenberg was developing toward matters of foreign policy. He had always represented the opposition. Sometimes, perhaps, he had been unnecessarily sharp in his attacks on Administration proposals. But on major issues he had often sought a constructive middle ground from which he could try — sometimes successfully — to force an adjustment of legislative proposals in order to improve them if he could not or did not want to defeat them entirely. Now he was becoming convinced that the adjustment of divergent viewpoints, the development of a conciliatory approach to the postwar issues was essential to the national interest, and he was ready to assist in the conciliating if the opportunity arose — as it did almost immediately.

March 16, 1943 [*continued*]

Two significant things happened. First, British Foreign Secretary Anthony Eden was over here; at a meeting with the Foreign Relations Committee, I asked him this direct question — "Might we not disunite our *war* effort by trying prematurely to unite our peace effort?" He replied in the affirmative and warned against trying prematurely to particularize about peace objectives concerning which there is no specific agreement among the major Allies.

Second: Senators Connally, George, Gillette and I visited the State Department and had a quiet hour with Secretary Hull. The Secretary was greatly disturbed. He frankly said he would have given *anything* to have avoided a precipitation of this issue on the floor of the Senate at the present time. He said the Russian and British situations were delicate; that the war is far from won; that it is impossible as yet to identify specific peace objectives and procedures; that a sharp debate on the subject on the floor of the Senate at the present time might easily divide our own war effort at home and the Allied war effort abroad. He counseled extreme caution in doing *anything*. He said that since the subject had been unfortunately raised in this untimely way, it was probably necessary for the Senate to do *something;* but he hoped it would be confined to a simple statement of general objectives upon which there could be universal agreement. He even made the unique suggestion that the danger of a Senate debate be by-passed by simply having all Senators personally sign a general statement of post-war intentions.

The evolution of the Senator's thinking on the problem of international co-operation apparently speeded up during the postwar objectives negotiations. Under the date of March 24, his "history" of the proceedings expressed opinions on future collaboration that carried him a long step forward and indicated how far he was removing himself — in his private writing — from isolationism.

March 24, 1943

I undertook to see what chance there was to write a general resolution which might meet with general approval and avoid all the yawning pitfalls. *It was my position that the United States obviously must be a far greater international co-operator after this war than ever before;* that we could say so in general terms in keeping with these facts; but that no specific commitments are possible in the absence of *any* commitments by either Churchill or Stalin, and particularly in the presence of statements from Moscow which would make any specific adherence to the Atlantic Charter an act of sheer hypocrisy and sham; that we cannot afford the luxury of quarreling with Russia *now* unless we are prepared even to drive her back into the arms of Hitler and to take on the balance of this war alone; that the *winning of the war* must be our *exclusive* immediate objective. I found it quite possible to get considerable agreement on the following brief Resolution:

"Resolved: that the Senate advises:
"(1) It believes this war must be prosecuted until total victory has been achieved against all the Axis powers by the united efforts of the United Nations;
"(2) It endorses the aspirations of the United Nations to create a world in which military aggression shall be permanently curbed; in which justice rather than force shall prevail; and in which self-governing people shall be free to work out their own destinies in the closest, practical co-operations with each other;
"(3) It is prepared, by due Constitutional process, to consider such co-operations to the full extent of American post-war responsibilities."

I sent this to Hull — telling him frankly that in this immediate emergency I did not propose to do *anything* without his approval. Hull replied most pleasantly and promised a study of the text.

Vandenberg also asked both Senator George and former Senator George Moses, once a power in the Republican party, to write him their opinions of his proposed resolution. To Moses, he added that the Ball resolution was not going to be accepted by the Committee despite a "blitz" that was being conducted in its behalf in which "it seems our friend, Mr. Willkie, is [the] sparkplug." Demands for action had been growing in the Senate and out, and the authors of the Ball resolution indirectly threatened to bring the matter up on the floor if the Committee didn't act.

March 31, 1943

The Sub-Committee held its first meeting. No one favored the Ball Resolution. Each member spoke freely. The consensus was to "go slow." (The external "blitz" in which Willkie announced he would "devote the rest of his life to saving America from the Senate" and in which the four

Resolution authors said they would give us just two weeks to act, had no effect whatever except possibly to slow us down still more; these gentlemen evidently do not know what fire they are playing with in the war situation.) Senator White, probably the most internationally-minded member of the Committee, even suggested that the whole matter might be dismissed with a statement that it is the unanimous judgment of the Committee that the time is not opportune to proceed at all. Senator Gillette withdrew his Resolution. We concluded to wait another week and then see Hull. (One great vice of the situation is that the present precipitation of this issue in the Senate has given the President a perfect alibi for whatever happens hereafter; if we say too much and trouble follows, the *Senate* is to blame; if we say too little and trouble follows, the *Senate* is to blame. *I do not think he has overlooked these possibilities.*)

April 7, 1943

The Sub-Committee met this morning at 9:30 with Secretary of State Hull and we were closeted with him until noon. He continues to be greatly distressed that this subject should have been brought up at all at the present time. He repeatedly warned that we must "go slow" and do nothing which would precipitate an acrimonious debate on the floor of the Senate. Senator La Follette was the most out-spoken in warning him that this is probably impossible. He bluntly said that no matter how wide an advance agreement might be obtained, there was nothing that could stop amendments on the Senate floor regarding such moot points as Russia's territorial aspirations or China's plight or the fate of India or the possible British aspirations in North Africa at the expense of the French.

Hull repeatedly said that anything of this sort could be seriously damaging to our war unity. I frankly stated that if an amendment seeking to guarantee the restoration of the Polish Republic were offered on the floor, I would be forced to support it. Senator Gillette asked just how important it was that the Senate should act at all at the present time. He said all the "cards" should be put on the table — reminding

Hull that Welles had told him "we are sunk unless there is legislative action by June first." Hull asked to be excused from commenting on that but he left no doubts in our minds that he fears a "sinking" of a different sort, and that he and Welles do not see eye-to-eye.

He finally referred to General Pat Hurley's recent escape from a near-air-disaster in the South Atlantic. His plane developed serious trouble and it was a case of deciding whether it was safer to make for Africa or try to get back to Brazil. "You are in the same fix," he said; "you'll have to decide which of your courses offers the lesser danger." He said Europe is beginning to ask whether America will withdraw unto herself again after this war, as she did in 1920, and that they are likely to make their own plans accordingly. He said he would like to prove that we have a "co-operative state of mind" by some sort of Senate pronouncement; but always warning that we *must* avoid "tender" subjects. I finally suggested that we by-pass all Senate discussion by simply reporting that we *and* the State Department find it impossible to write a specific code at the present time; therefore we are recommending a *permanent liaison committee* between the Senate and the State Department to keep intimately in touch with developments pending the time when we can *helpfully* speak. The meeting finally adjourned with quite general agreement that it might be best to try something along this line. Meanwhile, we voted to hear "the four horsemen" themselves next week Thursday.

April 15, 1943

The Sub-Committee held a two-hour conference this morning with Senators Ball, Burton, Hatch and Hill, the authors of the "Ball Resolution" (which one hostile critic cynically described this week as "The Second Battle of Ball's Bluff"). The four Senators asserted they have no pride of opinion in the language of their resolution; that they have never "threatened" independent action if the Committee did not "act within two weeks"; and that they would be very glad to seek agreement with the Committee regarding substitute language if it was not "emasculating." Senator Barkley pointed out that the inter-allied "organization" contemplated by the first three clauses in the Resolution would require that it be formed at once to deal with war problems whereas the other clauses relate to post-war problems which will be handled at the peace table. He questioned the need for the former or the wisdom of confusion in respect to the latter.

When I asked what is meant by proscribing "territorial aggrandizement" — and whether this would mean that Russia is *now* to be notified that Stalin's announced territorial expectations are to be denied — all of the authors of the Resolution were vague and unresponsive. Senator White suggested that any such *present* notification might drive Stalin into Hitler's arms. All four authors insisted that any international agreements made as a result of their Resolution would have to be ratified by the Senate and that they would accept an amendment accordingly. Senator Ball said he thought Secretary Hull is a little *too* cautious in dealing with this matter. He and his associates all argued that our major Allies want to *know* whether America is going to draw back into "isolation," as after World War Number One, when the war is over — and that only the Senate can give appropriate assurances on this score. They admitted that one Congress cannot bind another; but they relied upon a "moral commitment."

Senator Hatch said we must leave "no doubts" about what we intend to do. I replied that I thought the Resolution leaves *nothing but doubts* so long as it skips and dodges all the *real* questions — such as Russia's pre-emption of Poland, Latvia, Lithuania, Estonia, Finland, Bessarabia, etc. — such as China's statement that India must be free — such as Britain's obvious aspirations in North Africa where Senator Gillette said the French are already desperately fearful of permanent British controls.

These things *must* be settled sometime — and I agree the forthright thing would have been to settle them *when this partnership for war was formed*. But now that we are in the war up to our eyes, I think the first job is to *win the war;* and though I concur in the belief that we must have a large measure of post-war co-operation, I am unwilling to do *anything* which might disunite the *war* effort by premature *peace* efforts. That's the nub of this whole controversy. How far is it *safe* to go *now*. I do not want to wind up fighting this war all alone. If we must quarrel with our Allies, I'd rather do it *after victory* — (since the President missed the chance to do it in the first instance, if there was a chance).

April 21, 1943

Only five of the Sub-Committee were able to attend today's session — Connally, George, Gillette, La Follette and myself. As a result we had a very intimate discussion of the whole foreign situation which is involved in *anything* the Senate may do with the Ball Resolution. It was the gloomiest morning I have had since Pearl Harbor. The grape-vine information coming to us is that the war situation has many utterly dangerous phases for America. Senator Gillette reported his information that Germany has made two specific peace proposals to Russia which *might* detach her from the war; that they have been made through Japan; and that evidently there is some sort of a new Jap-Russian accord since Jap divisions are being taken from the Russian sector and diverted to South China.

Senator George said he was almost certain of his information that the relations between Churchill and Stalin are now *worse* than ever. Senator George also said that we are using up our raw materials at such a tremendous rate that we may find ourselves exhausted in another 15 years even as a peace power. Senator La Follette pursued this line to the extent of expressing the fear that we may bleed ourselves so white that we become a second-rate power. The Far Pacific situation was particularly discussed. We were told that the Japs now have a full division at Kiska — although Secretary of the Navy Knox has buoyantly said all along that we can drive the Japs out of Kiska anytime we wish.

As we went over these things — and many more — we became increasingly convinced that the Senate dare not start "resoluting" on any phase of the war (or the subsequent peace) without far more *accurate* information than we now have. There was frank discussion of the almost total lack of *real* information in the Foreign Relations Committee itself. It was stated that one of our general officers has said that when the joint staffs meet, the British and the Russians know *exactly* what their policies and objectives are, but that *our* officers know little or nothing until they are told what to do by the Commander-in-Chief. It was the general opinion that the British have entirely too much to say about *our* strategy.

But the chief thing we informally agreed upon is that the time has come when the Executive must share *real information* with the Congress — at least to the extent that the Committee on Foreign Relations can *know* what it is doing when it starts "passing resolutions." When we adjourned, Chairman Connally was to sound out Admiral Leahy (the President's Chief of Staff) to see if he would be willing to meet with us in confidence. If we are *stopped* in these directions, there *may* be explosive action. . . .

Meanwhile, the recent Associated Press poll was canvassed. This poll asked Senators whether they are ready *now* to commit the country to a post-war international police. Thirty-two said "*No*"; 21 said "yes"; others, non-committal. This would seem to end all Senate chance for the Ball Resolution (including its pledge for an international police) because even its authors agree that it would be fatal to have a sharply divided Senate.

May 1, 1943

The Sub-Committee did not meet this week because only Senators Connally, Gillette and myself were in town. We talked informally. It is obvious that current events are having a definite effect upon our problem.

The summary action of the Russian Government in bitterly breaking off relations with the Polish Government in exile has had a profound effect on the status of the Ball etc. Resolution. The German Government charged that it had unearthed trenches in Poland showing that some 10,000 Polish officers had been murdered in cold blood by the Russian Government in the early occupation. The Polish Government asked the International Red Cross at Geneva to investigate. The Russian Government promptly flew into a rage; charged the whole thing off to German propaganda; and promptly broke relations with the Polish Government in exile. Now Churchill and Roosevelt are feverishly trying to mend the breach.

But the incident poses several questions which are calculated to give our Committee and the Senate further pause in attempting to do anything along the line of the Ball Resolution. Suppose, for example, we were to pass the Resolution — barring all post-war association to nations which indulge in "territorial aggrandizement"; and suppose Mr. Stalin were to ask us if we consider his proposed retention of Latvia, Lithuania, Estonia, East Poland, Bessarabia, etc., to be "territorial aggrandizement." We should have to "fish or cut bait." We should have to say *"Yes"* — which would certainly infuriate Moscow more than this other incident did. If we said *"No"* — we should deny the Atlantic Charter and infuriate tens of thousands of our own people. It's a typical case which shows how we can disunite the war effort by trying prematurely to unite the peace effort. *We must win the war first.* Russia's withdrawal would cost a million needless casualties.

It's a tough thing about which to advocate. But we are caught on the horns of a dilemma. Roosevelt should have been *specific* in the first place when he had a chance to trade our "tools" for the commitments we should have required. To require them *now* is a desperate gamble. The Russian episode has beautifully illustrated what is troubling our Sub-Committee. Russia, on the other hand, took some of the "heat" out of the situation, when Stalin, in his May Day statement sturdily declared against any separate peace. . . .

May 10, 1943

The full Sub-Committee, excepting Senator Barkley who is seriously ill, met this morning with General Marshall. The General gave us a brilliant explanation of the success of the North African campaign and the key part played in it by American troops — with particular emphasis upon the work of Major General Bradley. He said the air attack on Sicily will now be continuous.

Coming to what the Committee wants to know, I asked

him about the Casablanca Conference. He had previously said that at Casablanca the *military* staffs met by themselves and had no part in the *political* (meaning F.D.R. and Churchill) conference. I asked if this meant that the general over-all decisions respecting military strategy were made on the "political" side — and left merely to be implemented by the *military*. He said *No* — without amplifying his answer.

But then he went on to describe what most of us thought was a vitally significant matter. In deciding joint questions with the British, he said we were always handicapped by the fact that when the *British* come to a conference with an idea, it is completely developed to the last degree and has the completely integrated support of the British from Churchill down — including, frequently, a "softening up" of our own American situation through the activity of all the British "Secretaries" here in Washington. He said that this often put us at a disadvantage.

Some of us discussed his testimony later and came to the conclusion that our American spokesmanship is *not* similarly integrated; that our proposals do not always have the joint support of The President, The Staff, etc.; that as a result we frequently get the worst of it; and that the British usually are "on top." He did not say so. Even if this were true, he could not say so.

But while he left us with a new pride in the recent exploits of our troops, he also left us with a new uneasiness about *who* makes our decisions and *how*, and about the British dominion [domination]. I asked him, for example, whether there was any disagreement with the British with the weight to be thrown into the Pacific war. He did not answer directly; but he commented that before Singapore, the British were all for heavy war in the Pacific, whereas they are now "naturally" more interested in the European theater. You can draw your own conclusions.

When Senator Gillette finally sought to find out about our all-out military objectives, the General declined to answer, saying that such things were such complete military secrets that he would not tell them to *anybody* outside half a dozen of his staff. It remains to be seen whether one of his general officers (General Wedemeyer), who heretofore has sought a chance to testify, will still come and still say that our *military* leaders totally disagreed with the commitments made by F.D.R. to Churchill at Casablanca, and that they have little or nothing to say about general strategy — their function being solely to work out the achievement of the military plans upon which F.D.R. and Churchill agree. . . .

May 19, 1943

Winston Churchill addressed a joint session of Congress today — and he made another magnificent speech. His peroration was a plea that we avoid any needless arguments between any of us until we have the victory in hand. He later met with the entire Senate Foreign Relations Committee and submitted himself to questions. He frankly answered one and all.

I asked him, as I had asked Eden, whether we might not disunite the inter-Allied war effort by trying prematurely to settle peace objectives. He replied emphatically *"Yes."* I asked him whether he needed any Senate Resolutions to reassure him or his country that America would cooperate not only in the war but also in the peace. With tears in his eyes and with great eloquence he answered in the negative. I asked him directly whether a Senate discussion now and perhaps a Senate decision now — regarding the meaning of "territorial aggrandizement" and its application to Russia's intentions in Latvia, Estonia, Lithuania, Poland, Bessarabia, etc., might not be a serious hazard to our war-partnership with Russia. He said *"Yes."*

Indeed, his whole attitude left all of us feeling that he was wholly recommending *against any* such action as is contemplated by the Ball etc. Resolution. In the same vein was one of his final sentences in his speech today at the Joint Session: "We must beware of every topic, however attractive, and every tendency, however natural, which divert our minds or energies from the supreme objective of the general victory of the United Nations."

May 22, 1943

Lord Halifax entertained some 15 Senators and 15 Representatives at a "conference" at the British Embassy today.

When we arrived Churchill took me by the arm and walked me off down the lawn by ourselves. He evidently had been under some pressure as a result of the implications of what he had said on Wednesday. He said he hadn't understood the full import of my questions; that, of course, he has no objection to any "general resolutions" in the Senate, etc. But when I pointed out to him that any *"general resolution"* would be subject to any sort of an inflammatory amendment which any member of the Senate might offer on the floor, he went back to his original position and cautioned against "opening Pandora's box."

June 16, 1943

The Sub-Committee talked for an hour this morning with Dr. T. V. Soong, China's Foreign Minister. It had no direct bearing on our own particular task; but it was tremendously informative. Dr. Soong denied that China's resistance was "on the verge of collapse" — although he said that inflation (prices have risen about *60 times* normal) was making his people restless, that the Jap propaganda about "Asia for the Asiatics" was having some effect on the masses. He said the latter, however, would be promptly off-set by the opening of the Burma Road and the evidence that Japan cannot win the war.

The Committee agreed that a prompt repeal of the Chinese Exclusion Act would be the best counter-propaganda. Dr. Soong seemed to have no great faith that the British are very greatly concerned whether China stays in the war, or that General Wavell, in command of British troops in India, is the right man to open the Burma Road. He said America is the only country which *really* understands China — and the Chinese uniformly feel this. He was asked about China's post-war aims and said she, of course, wants all of her original territory back. He seemed to think this might well include Hong Kong. As for China's demand that India must be free, he said they would probably be willing to go along with whatever recommendation America might make upon this score.

He is quiet, keen, able, soft-spoken and amiable — but he certainly gave no ground when Senator Thomas (of Utah) pressed him as to whether his government would consent to some possible "territorial re-arrangements" if found necessary in the ultimate peace. . . .

July 1, 1943

William Phillips, one of our greatest career diplomats and the President's recent personal Ambassador to India, talked freely — and courageously — with us today about the Indian situation. It was one of the most fascinating and illuminating hours I have ever spent.

Phillips minced no words. India's demands for independence are a major factor in the post-war picture, and Churchill's incorrigible refusal to surrender British dominion, now or later, creates one of the greatest dangers to the Allied cause. Further, India has swung over from an opinion that America was her friend to the view that we are supporting British domination and will continue to do so. Most dangerous of all, it is creating a "color consciousness" in India which plays gravely into Jap hands. Of course the native schism between Hindus and Moslems (and lesser sects) makes a "home rule" agreement in India among these native elements difficult. But Phillips said a middle ground can be found for a "limited, representative coalition" if Britain really wishes it.

He traveled the length and breadth of India talking freely to *all* leaders of *all* sects — *except* that he was *not* permitted to interview Gandhi (the greatest of all native leaders) who (with others of his Party leaders) is held incommunicado as a prisoner of State. Phillips was not permitted to see Gandhi (or any of his associated leaders) although Churchill had promised him in London, on the eve of his departure, that he could see everybody and that all doors would be opened to him. The result of all this is a general lack of interest in the Allied cause.

Phillips said that Lord Linlithgow, Governor General, is being replaced by General Wavell (who, he said, will be no improvement upon the absolute autocracy with which the Governor General rules) — although he expressed some hope that General Auchinleck (who succeeds Wavell as Indian Commander-in-Chief) will be helpful. But everything is run from London. He said it often takes four months to get an official reply from these Indian over-lords to the simplest question. He said the Indian army of 2,000,000 is only 30 percent effective; and that the British will expect the Americans and the Chinese to open up the Burma Road.

Senator La Follette bluntly said to Phillips that the fate of India is no longer Britain's own exclusive business, since our American boys are supposed to die there for Allied victory, and that F.D.R. should tell Churchill that he either yields to a reasonable settlement of the Indian independence question (bringing the Indians themselves into this war) or that American troops will be withdrawn from that sector. Phillips substantially agreed and, to our amazement, said he had told F.D.R. that precise thing. All of which moved Senator Connally to say that he himself had told the President that he ought to "turn the heat" on Churchill; that he has too much of a "Churchill complex"; that we ought to be "giving instead of taking" orders. It was clear from Phillips' testimony that India is "dynamite" — and that its destiny will be a bitter bone of contention at the peace table.

As a result of such Foreign Relations Committee sessions the Senator's knowledge of international developments was being widened, but very little progress had been made toward solution of the deadlock over a resolution on postwar objectives. Vandenberg had not given up the idea of drafting a substitute for the Ball Resolution along the lines of the draft he had earlier submitted to Hull, George, and Moses. At that time (March 27) he had written to George, asking for comment on his draft and tentatively suggesting that they might collaborate on it. "I am convinced that an alternative to the Ball Resolution should be introduced in order to let the public see specifically what the precise issue is. . . . If it [Vandenberg's draft] is to be introduced in the Senate, it certainly should appear under bipartisan auspices. . . . I should greatly welcome associating myself with *you* in this connection if you think the step is advisable."

Nothing came of this suggestion for bipartisan collaboration and in late June Vandenberg adopted another approach, joining with Senator Wallace White, Republican of Maine, to draft an alternative to the Ball Resolution. This collaboration was of considerable significance. It was the first all-Republican effort along this line, and Vandenberg apparently had in mind that it would be used as a model for future Republican party policy. As it turned out, the Vandenberg-White effort not only laid the basis for a later Republican declaration on foreign policy but it heavily influenced the final compromise resolution which the Senate eventually adopted.

July 2, 1943

Collaborating with Senator Wallace White of Maine, I introduced today the first all-Republican "foreign policy" Resolution. . . . It will join the others under consideration by our sub-committee. It differs from all others in the following significant particulars: (1) it speaks *only* for "*this*" Congress, thus frankly admitting that one Congress cannot bind another; (2) it pledges post-war co-operation between "*sovereign nations*," thus barring all "World Staters" and assuring the continuance of the American Flag over the Capitol; (3) it limits the *present* exploration of peace aims to such acts as will *not disrupt* the united military war effort, thus frankly recognizing the strategy problem with which our sub-committee is wrestling; (4) it pledges, first of all, the "prosecution of the war to conclusive victory," thus putting first things first, and, by implication, ruling out all meddlers who might threaten victory by premature efforts to consolidate our war aims; (5) it demands that all American peace action shall be "by due Constitutional process," thus eliminating the Roosevelt habit and desire to by-pass Congress in these respects; (6) last, but far from least, it pledges "faithful recognition of *American interests*" (just as Churchill always makes it plain that he is for "Britain first" and just as Stalin always makes it plain that he is for "Russia first"). The Resolution immediately made a profound impression. Writing in The Washington Star, Gould Lincoln said it might well be the pattern for ultimate Congressional action, but also for the next Republican national platform.

July 3, 1943

Senators Ball, Burton and Hill all made speeches in the Senate today, virtually threatening our Committee that we *must* act on *their* Resolution not later than October. But we do not "threaten" easily. Further, these gentlemen will find that *their* Resolution is *not* "the only pebble on the beach." . . .

Meanwhile, Vandenberg had been busy on another and extremely important front. The Republican party, with Harrison E. Spangler as national Chairman, arranged a top-echelon conference at Mackinac Island in September — while Congress was in a brief recess — to draw up over-all plans for postwar policy. The Conference, known as the Republican Advisory Council, was appointed by Spangler as an advisory body to pave the way for the platform makers at the 1944 Republican National Convention. It included all of the Republican governors then in office, representing about half of the States and two-thirds of the population; fifteen members of the House and Senate appointed by the minority leaders in Congress; and ten members of the Republican National Committee.

Vandenberg was one of the members appointed from the Senate and he was primarily concerned with drawing up a statement on postwar objectives. Regarding these he wrote to Thomas W. Lamont:

August 4, 1943

I am hunting for the middle ground between those extremists at one end of the line who would cheerfully give America away and those extremists at the other end of the line who would attempt a total isolation which has come to be an impossibility. I am sure we can frankly assert our purpose to participate in post-war cooperation to prevent by any necessary means the recurrence of military aggression and to establish permanent peace with justice in a free world so far as this is humanly obtainable. But I am equally sure that this has to be paralleled by equally forthright reassurance to our own American people that we intend to be . . . vigilant in the preservation of our legitimate American interests. . . . I do not believe that these two objectives are incompatible in any sense so long as a "rule of reason" is applied to each. . . . I think we must also emphasize the fact that we intend to maintain our own sovereignty in the final analysis. This does not mean that we would decline to restrict ourselves in mutual cooperations which are practical and useful. . . .

Certainly I agree with you that a "super-state will never work." I also agree that we must find "some not too formal method" for helping preserve the peace of the world. . . . Our Republican problem from a political point of view is — as you rightly indicate — complicated by the everlasting recurrence of the "isolationist" theme. . . . Speaking generally, it would be my observation that it is not the so-called isolationists who keep the issue alive, but it is the anti-isolationists who sometimes act as though they were afraid that they might lose their shibboleth.

Vandenberg drew up in advance a resolution to present to the Mackinac Conference and submitted it to Governor Dewey, among others. It was very much like the Vandenberg-White Resolution then before the Senate. The Governor made suggestions for changes in the wording but seemed in substantial agreement. Just before going to Mackinac, the Senator wrote:

August 24, 1943

It seems perfectly fantastic to me that we should attempt to pre-commit America in respect to a peace which as yet is totally in the dark. Furthermore, it grows darker hourly as a result of the Russian attitude. I have no sympathy whatever with our Republican Pollyannas who want to compete with Henry Wallace. . . . On the other hand, I think it is entirely possible for Republicans at Mackinac to avoid all of these nightmares and still declare a forthright purpose to join in the termination (so far as possible) of international piracy — and thus end the miserable notion (so effectively used against us in many quarters) that the Republican Party will retire to its foxhole when the last shot in this war has been fired and will blindly let the world rot in its own anarchy. [These were strong words for the one-time leader of the isolationist bloc, but the next paragraph suggested some of the reasons for Vandenberg's sharp attitude.]

Furthermore, it is my belief (and hope) that we can use the occasion to differentiate between Republican and New Deal foreign policy by asserting also in this connection (1) that we shall remain a totally sovereign country . . . (2) that we shall make all of our own decisions for ourselves by constitutional process; and (3) that we intend to be faithful to American interests. . . . We *must* beat the 4th Term. It is the "last roundup" for the American way of life. I do not believe we can beat it if we split the Party (and its Jeffersonian Democratic Allies) by going either to an isolationist extreme or to an internationalist extreme. . . . I am not talking about a straddle. That would be fatal. I am talking about a rule of common sense. That is my aspiration at Mackinac. I shall probably get kicked all over the lot before and after. But I have at least convinced myself regarding my duty.

Although the Senator went to Mackinac, a beautiful and historic island lying north of the Southern Peninsula in Michigan, ready to wage a determined fight, his anticipation that he would be kicked all over the lot was not realized. He was beginning to hit his stride as a negotiator. He was patient. He was a good listener when that did not defeat his over-all objective. He could keep his eye on the main goal and he was willing to give some ground. As the leadership of the Party gathered at the Grand Hotel, a huge, rambling structure with the "longest porch in the world," Vandenberg found that there was more agreement than disagreement with his idea that the foreign policy declaration should call for a strong, free America to take a full part in the co-operative building of postwar peace and justice. The so-called Willkie bloc, which favored a stronger internationalistic declaration, was not present at Mackinac but virtually all other factions of the party were represented at the sessions. Among those attending were Governors Dewey of New York, Baldwin of Connecticut, Martin of Pennsylvania, Green of Illinois, Bacon of Delaware, Sewall of Maine, Donnell of Missouri, Kelly of Michigan, Warren of

California, Langlie of Washington, in addition to such Congressional leaders as Senator Taft and Senator Austin.

There were advance predictions that, with so many divergent viewpoints represented, it would be difficult if not impossible to secure a meeting of minds on a foreign policy declaration that frankly favored United States participation in a postwar organization of sovereign nations. But Vandenberg was able to reconcile the differences that arose. He managed to accommodate both those who wanted a specific commitment for international collaboration and those who insisted that there should be no infringement on American freedom of action in the postwar world. He ended up with an historic resolution that followed the theme of the Vandenberg-White resolution, putting the party on record as favoring "responsible participation by the United States in postwar cooperative organization among sovereign nations to prevent military aggression and to attain permanent peace with organized justice in a free world." And, of equal importance, he avoided a knockdown battle that might have split the party. Most political observers put emphasis on the importance of Vandenberg's work in bringing about this policy in a spirit of harmony and the Senator himself felt that the conference had been of "profound" significance.

Vandenberg said later in a Senate speech:

> When such a thoroughly representative group — representative not only of our national geography but equally representative of widely differing foreign points of view — when such a group can unanimously recommend a general foreign policy, I submit it is a profoundly significant and prophetic phenomenon in the life of the Republic, and deserves the open-minded consideration of all Americans.
>
> The Mackinac Charter vigorously covers many domestic issues as well. It is by no means confined to foreign issues. But I discuss only the latter tonight because it is the point at which we so sadly need enlightened American unity; and because I happen to have served as chairman of the Foreign Policy Committee, along with Senator Austin of Vermont, Governor Martin of Pennsylvania, Governor Green of Illinois, Congresswoman Bolton of Ohio, and Congressman

Eaton of New Jersey. The well-known pre-Pearl Harbor divergence of views among the group is the conclusive answer to any petty, cheap, and groundless snarl, by an occasional external critic, that the committee was "stacked." It was the exact opposite of "stacked." Yet if it had been "stacked" it could not have finally been more enthusiastically unanimous nor more spiritually unified. That its report should have similarly won the practically unanimous approval of the Nation's editorial opinion is the final, spectacular endorsement of its creed.

It is my view — and you will understand that these are personal reactions not binding upon my colleagues — that the Mackinac Charter has done one basic, superlatively important thing — which is sadly needed if we are to have any sort of common national vision in foreign policy. For the first time, it has plainly been put down in black and white the indispensable doctrine that Americans can be faithful to the primary institutions and interests of our own United States and still be equally loyal to the essential post-war international cooperations which are required to end military aggression for keeps and to create a post-war world in which organized justice shall protect freemen. By the same token, it has put down in black and white the basic truth that Americans can constructively contemplate their world duties without sacrificing their American allegiance. Indeed, their appropriate world duties can become part of their American allegiance when the result is a body of international law and practice which bless us fully as much as they bless others.

In my view, this is what the average American has been waiting to hear. . . .

"Certainly you are entitled to warm personal congratulations on a great job of conciliating the divergent views not only of your committee but of the whole Council," Dewey later wrote to the Senator. "The Party should be grateful to you indeed for a major contribution to its welfare as well as that of the country." In high spirits and beginning to grasp the full possibilities of his role, Vandenberg himself wrote in regard to his hopes for a unified American foreign policy that "I . . . believe when I succeeded in putting forty-nine [different viewpoints] together at Mackinac I discovered the necessary formula. Furthermore, I think it is an utterly sound formula." The Willkie bloc grumbled for a while that the resolution had not gone far enough and that it was time to get down to cases and define methods, but in general the Mackinac formula was accepted by the party. To those isolationists who objected to the implication that the United States would surrender some of her sovereignty, Vandenberg said:

September 17, 1943

We yield some element of total sovereignty (in a literal sense) every time we make any cooperative treaty with other nations. It has been done countless times and it has never occurred to anybody that we were violating a constitutional principle (and, of course, we weren't). It was only this practical fact which I have sought to emphasize by my insistence of the literal word "sovereignty" in the Mackinac Charter.... I thought I was doing a good constitutional job when I succeeded.

The sled-length "interventionists" say to us: "You cannot promise any sort of international cooperation without impairing some small portion of your total sovereignty — therefore when you insist upon sovereignty you prove that you never intend to cooperate at all." The answer to this challenge — in my humble opinion — is the one which I have given. It is a perfectly obvious answer. It was given publicly and was not even remotely challenged by any of our most extreme "non-interventionists." It seems to me that it is simply the recognition of a fact.... Perhaps it is unfortunate that there is no sharp clear line of limitation. But I think that the *total* text of the Mackinac Charter — with its further clear and insistent emphasis upon the Declaration of Independence, the Constitution and the Bill of Rights as our primary and paramount concern — makes the limitation entirely clear.

The importance with which Vandenberg and other Republican leaders viewed the Mackinac foreign policy declaration was emphasized later when Frank Walker, Democratic National Chairman, said in January of 1944 that the country ought to "adopt an international policy that is worthwhile and plan for the peace." Walker was talking in political terms, inviting the voters to support the Democrats and the Roosevelt Administration in the 1944 presidential campaign. But Vandenberg promptly challenged him to accept the invitation of the Mackinac Declaration to eliminate the foreign policy issue from the presidential campaign.

"It would be very interesting if Mr. Walker would implement his wishful thinking by indicating where, when and how the Democratic party either has spoken as definitely on foreign policy as the Republicans did at Mackinac or whether he or it has [moved] or will move to accept the invitation extended to him there last September," Vandenberg said. He pointed out that the resolution concluded with an invitation to "all Americans to adhere to the principles here set forth to the end that our part in helping to bring about international peace and justice shall not be the subject of domestic partisan controversy and political bitterness." What, he asked, had the Democrats done or said that was comparable to that invitation to a bipartisan foreign policy?

Following the Mackinac Conference and the reconvening of the Senate — which had been in brief recess — pressure mounted for the Foreign Relations Committee to make up its mind about the Ball and other postwar resolutions. Representative J. William Fulbright of Arkansas had steered through the House a one-sentence resolution expressing the sentiment of Congress in favor of general postwar co-operative intent and the Administration favored similar Senate action. "The general agitation for some sort of Senate action has reached a point," the Senator wrote in his diary under the date of September 30, "where it may be even worse to longer keep the subject bottled up." Connally suggested on October 6 a compromise resolution along general lines previously discussed but including the two "important factors emphasized by the Republican Conference at Mackinac — sovereignty and constitutional process," Vandenberg recorded, pointing out that the Fulbright Resolution had ignored the sovereignty angle.

These two angles were retained in the final version of the Connally resolution — very similar to the Vandenberg-White resolution — which the subcommittee and the full committee accepted and reported to the Senate.

October 13, 1943

The Sub-Committee completed its labors this morning and all members present voted for the [compromise] resolution. . . .

Those voting for the Resolution were Senators Connally, George, Thomas (Utah), Gillette, Barkley, Vandenberg and White. . . .

It is impossible for us longer to hold the Resolution in Sub-Committee and take full responsibility for non-action in the light of the approaching (British-American-Russian conference at Moscow) — when we are virtually told that the question of Russia making a separate peace with Germany may hang on Stalin's belief that this non-action in the Senate means there will be no form of postwar "collective security" and that he must "look out for himself." We have concluded, for this and other reasons, at least to share our responsibility with the full Foreign Relations Committee.

The Resolutions bow to our Republican "Mackinac" statement in their direct pledge to the use of "Constitutional process" and to the maintenance of "American sovereignty." I believe it is the best thing that could be done under the circumstances. It is personally interesting to me that the Committee Resolution is more like the "Vandenberg-White" Resolution than any of the other proposals that have been before the Committee.

Final: The Sub-Committee's report was adopted by the full Committee by a vote of 20 to 2, after amendments offered by Senator Pepper (acting for the Ball-Burton-Etc. group) had been rejected.

When the Resolution reached the Senate floor it was immediately attacked by the Pepper-Ball-Burton-Hatch-Hill group who successfully prevented that which would have been the most eloquent action of all — namely, *prompt* action without substantial division. This group, abandoning its own original Resolution, sought a specific amendment (which finally was withdrawn). . . .

[While the debate was in progress the Foreign Ministers of the United States, Britain, and Russia had been meeting in Moscow and discussing postwar problems, including the disposition of war criminals, economic and territorial problems, and the question of a United Nations organization among sovereign, peace-loving states to maintain future peace. Their agreement was issued as the Moscow Declaration. Vandenberg incidentally was struck by the reference to "peace-loving states" and later, with his customary phrase-making knack, when the term appeared in the UN Charter he tried to emphasize that it really meant "peace-living states"; that is, states that instead of merely giving lip-service to peace while stirring up trouble abroad actually *lived* peacefully. He never really succeeded in this endeavor, because the newspaper copy editors who handled his statements always assumed that "peace-living" was a typographical error and promptly changed it to "peace-loving," much to the chagrin of the Senator.]

In the midst of the second week of debate, the "Moscow Declaration" was announced. It fell full within the circumference of the Committee Resolution. But, responding to urgent desires that the "Moscow Declaration" should be specifically recognized, the Sub-Committee reassembled for its last meeting; took one paragraph from "Moscow" (making it the fourth paragraph of the Committee Resolution); and added a final paragraph (for which Senator Willis of Indiana was the original author) reasserting the Constitutional authority of the Senate over Treaties and Peace Settlements. I was perfectly willing to accept them because the first of these added paragraphs further under-lined "sovereignty" and the second further emphasized "Constitutionalism."

The Senate debate developed all the dangers we had foreseen and which had caused our Sub-Committee reluctance to turn the subject loose on the Senate floor. Indeed, the confusion and the hazard became so great at one time that there was a wide-spread disposition to recommit the Resolution to the Committee. But the amended report of the Committee finally closed the gaps; and the Resolution went through without change by a Senate vote of 85 to 5. Here is the final Resolution:

RESOLVED, That the war against all our enemies be waged until complete victory is achieved.

That the United States cooperate with its comrades-in-arms in securing a just and honorable peace.

That the United States, acting through its constitutional processes, join with free and sovereign nations in the establishment and maintenance of international authority with power to prevent aggression and to preserve the peace of the world.

That the Senate recognizes the necessity of there being established at the earliest practicable date a general international organization, based on the principle of the sovereign equality of all peace-loving states, and open to membership by all such states, large and small, for the maintenance of international peace and security.

That, pursuant to the Constitution of the United States, any treaty made to effect the purposes of this resolution, on behalf of the Government of the United States with any other nation or any association of nations, shall be made only by and with the advice and consent of the Senate of the United States, provided two-thirds of the Senators present concur.

Nobody could claim full credit for the Resolution as it was finally adopted, but it was unlikely that Vandenberg was as much interested in the question of authorship as he was in the success of a formula for collaboration and conciliation. In the months of labor over the resolution, as well as in the work of the Mackinac Conference, Vandenberg himself had finally emerged as a conciliator who was rapidly learning how to bring together divergent viewpoints and — still more important — how to weight the final result with his own opinions and persuade potential opponents that they liked it that way. It was a talent that he had been slow to discover but he liked it more every day.

Connally, in a kind of backhanded way, summed it up on floor of the Senate when he said: "I wish to thank the distinguished Senator from Michigan ... for the very valuable contribution he made. Being of the minority party, it was probably more difficult for him than for some of the rest of us to go along with the main purpose we had in view, but at all times he manifested a very earnest desire to cooperate, and he gave to the committee wholeheartedly of his talents and leadership in achieving agreement and unity on the resolution. He deserves high credit for his services."

The Senator from Texas was far from the mark in trying to describe Vandenberg's attitude as a minority-party representative. It hadn't been hard for Vandenberg to go along. The Mackinac Conference declaration — in which the Senator took great pride — was strongly reflected in the Senate resolution even though Mackinac was a minority-party declaration and had been engineered by a minority member of the Foreign Relations Committee. Vandenberg may have begun to feel, in truth, that as a minority member he was in a position to do a great deal more than if he had been a member of the majority.

4

Skirmish with the State Department

"I HAVE often recalled to Senator Vandenberg and to others," Vice-President Alben Barkley said at solemn session of the United States Senate after the Senator's death, "how at first he cautiously felt his way, planting one foot ahead of the other, feeling out the ground to determine and test its firmness. When he finally determined the firmness of the ground on which he stood, he planted both feet squarely upon that foundation and became one of the most effective and eloquent advocates of this new effort in human affairs to create an international organization for peace."

The process of planting one foot ahead of the other and feeling out the ground had begun for Vandenberg during the search for a sound resolution on postwar objectives, but it was to take him months to find the place where he could firmly stand. One of the cautious steps that pointed the direction in which he was going was taken in connection with controversy over the United Nations Relief and Rehabilitation Administration. In the early summer of 1943 the darkest days of the war were past, the European struggle was slowly beginning to swing our way with preparations for invasion of Sicily, and even in the Pacific the Allies were starting to strike back effectively at the Japanese. In Washington, there was increasing concern about preparations to relieve the war-devastated areas coming under Allied control, and early in June the draft of an agreement to establish UNRRA was circulated among the Allied governments.

SKIRMISH WITH THE STATE DEPARTMENT

Vandenberg noticed on June 11 that the State Department had published the draft of the UNRRA text. He took it home and read it carefully. Then he wrote a letter to Secretary of State Hull inquiring whether it was intended that the agreement would be submitted to Congress for approval. Hull replied on June 22 that "It has been decided, after consultation with the majority and minority leaders of both houses of Congress, that the United States' participation in the establishment of this United Nations' administration should be through an executive agreement." In other words, the Administration intended to make an executive agreement requiring no formal Congressional approval instead of a treaty, which would be subject to Senate approval by a two-thirds majority.

At this time, Vandenberg was very much absorbed in the Foreign Relations Committee work on postwar objectives and also in preparations for the Mackinac conference but he promptly introduced a resolution in the Senate to have the Committee investigate the draft agreement and to report whether it "partakes of the nature of a treaty and should be submitted to the Senate for ratification." He made no comment on the resolution at the time. But he did write to Senator Charles L. McNary and Representative Joseph Martin, the Congressional minority leaders, asking them if they had approved the agreement as an executive action. To McNary, who was then in Oregon, he wrote:

July 7, 1943

It seems to me that this draft agreement involves the broadest possible commitments for the future . . . and leaves us (as usual) to pay the bills without any adequate control over what the bills ought to be. I think this is clearly a preview of the method by which the President and the State Department intend to by-pass Congress in general, and the Senate in particular, in settling every possible international war and postwar issue by the use of mere "executive agreements." Since introducing the Resolution, I am confronted with a letter from Secretary of State Hull in which he says that the President called in "the minority leaders of the House and Senate several weeks ago and explained this whole thing to them and submitted his preliminary draft agreement and got their approval for the procedure." I should like to know exactly how far the minority House and Senate leaders went in giving their approval (if they did) to this proposition. . . . I think it is significant that the President did not call any members of the Senate or House Foreign Relations Committees into the conference.

Vandenberg later received a telegram from McNary — and a similar one from Martin — saying that they had not agreed that the Congress should be by-passed. "Things have been happening with a vengeance since I introduced my Senate Resolution," Vandenberg wrote to McNary on July 15, after a subcommittee headed by Senator Connally had been named to study the draft agreement. "When the Foreign Relations Committee saw the contents of this draft agreement it unanimously decided upon immediate action (and Connally was even more vehement about it than I was)."

The capital's political reporters also had belatedly discovered that the draft agreement contained the seeds of bitter controversy. Jay G. Hayden, correspondent of the Detroit *News* and a close friend of Vandenberg, wrote that the agreement seemed destined to bring "a first showdown as to where President Roosevelt's treaty-making power leaves off and that of the Senate begins." He quoted Vandenberg as saying that "no one will dispute the worthiness of the purpose [of UNRRA] . . . but it is also true that the pattern contained in the draft proposal . . . could be extended to embrace every other sort of international activity. . . . I do not believe that the Constitution intended to authorize the President to act independently [of Congress] in . . . such matters."

Secretary Hull, accompanied by Assistant Secretary Dean Acheson, appeared before the subcommittee in a tense and controversial session. Hull seemed to give some Senators the impression that he had not been in favor of trying to by-pass the Senate, but tempers were short on all sides and the meeting broke up with a distinct lack of harmony between the Committee and the State Department. This was grist for the mills of the anti-Roosevelt newspapers and especially for the isolationist press. Meanwhile, some of Vandenberg's isolationist-era friends and supporters had been looking unhappily on the Senator's actions and statements in recent months. Isolationist newspapers, which had been strong supporters, began to ask suspiciously what was happening to the Michigan senator. Correspondents were asking, too. "I had wondered for several months," one citizen of Grand Rapids wrote, "just what side of the fence you were on, the internationalist side . . . or the American side. . . . I must be very frank about it, Arthur, you and I have come to a parting of the ways."

On July 8, Vandenberg replied to this letter, saying: "I do not know the basis of your comments. If I have become an 'internationalist' then black is white. It is perfectly clear — it seems to me — that when this war is over we cannot escape certain inevitable international cooperations. . . . The question will be how far we should go and in what fashion. . . . [This viewpoint] is at total odds with Mr. Willkie's 'One World.' It recognizes our new and unavoidable obligations (whether we like them or not). But it speaks up for America first."

In these circumstances, the UNRRA draft agreement provided a kind of rallying point for the anti-Roosevelt isolationist newspapers and they quickly picked up the lead Vandenberg had given them. "The Foreign Relations Committee is being geared for a full-scale investigation of world planning, world WPAing, and world spending of U.S.A. money," remarked the Washington *Times-Herald*. "It is a staggering consideration, isn't it? Especially for us." These comments sometimes ignored Vandenberg's point that he was taking issue only with the "method" of by-passing Congress, but it was obvious that the Senator was now in a position to win his way back into the graces of the isolationists — if he wished to return to his sledgehammer attacks on the President and the internationalists.

But Vandenberg wasn't looking for such an opportunity. Despite his flat statement that he was no internationalist, a process of change had begun during his labors on the postwar objectives resolution and his work in preparation for the Mackinac conference. He had no intention of reversing that process and he made it clear in a statement on the floor of the Senate. It was a significant statement for more reasons than one, because it indicated another and an important facet in Vandenberg's newly developed technique. He was beginning to think ahead, to recognize the first signs of disagreement, to pick out the area where viewpoints would have to be reconciled and — most important of all — to do something about solving disagreements before they had a chance to harden into all-out battles that could end only with the abject defeat of one party or the other. Like everything else, this ability to look ahead was emerging slowly. The Senator, in the summer of 1943, was not in a position to influence the Administration's thinking by persuasion. He had not sufficiently developed his technique. But he did have a pretty good idea of what he was driving toward.

"I have made this statement [attacking the method of executive agreements] not in a spirit of controversy," he told the Senate, "but in a spirit of hope that this very frank disclosure, this very frank discussion of what I believe is a substantial error in the attitude of the State Department and the President in this initial venture, may lead to those contacts between us which may find a better and a happier way in which to solve the remaining problems which will pile in upon us as we liquidate the war and justify our conclusive victory."

His efforts bore fruit and he wrote:

July 15, 1943

Yesterday we had another long conference with Acheson [Dean Acheson, Assistant Secretary of State] which indicated a rather earnest desire on the part of the State Department not only to rewrite the draft agreement in some particulars, but also to concede the necessity for some sort of Congressional approval. It remains to be seen whether this actually develops or whether they are just temporarily being "good boys" under the pressure of almost universal criticism which attaches to any plan to by-pass Congress in an obligation of this magnitude.

As a matter of fact, as it was originally drawn, this draft agreement pledged our total resources to whatever illimitable scheme for relief and rehabilitation all around the world our New Deal crystal gazers might desire to pursue. Of course,

they had to concede in the text of the draft agreement that
their appropriations would *finally* have to come from Congress.
But ... the draft ... clearly intended that there should
be no interference with this world-wide prospectus as it
might be conceived by Roosevelt, Lehman, Hopkins and
Co., until that long last moment when Congress would be
confronted with a "fait accompli." At that late hour it would
be next to impossible for Congress to do anything except
acquiesce.

The State Department, meanwhile, was demonstrating that
it was serious in its offer to give ground. Hull and Connally
had exchanged some harsh words, but, according to the newspapers,
both Vandenberg and Acheson acted as peacemakers,
and after a few days reports circulated that a compromise was
in prospect. It provided for the Department to abandon its
idea of an executive agreement and submit the UNRRA plan to
Congress for approval by a majority of both houses. Vandenberg
agreed to this, giving up his original demand that the agreement
be approved by a two-thirds majority of the Senate, as is
required to put a treaty into effect. Such newspapers as the
Washington *Times-Herald*, owned by Mrs. Eleanor Patterson,
and the Hearst press had been building up Vandenberg's position,
but they quickly switched as soon as word of the compromise
got around. "This so-called compromise, this by-passing
of the Senate, this flouting of the Constitution and surrender
to the Administration at a most critical juncture, is full of peril
to the Republican party," one correspondent of the Hearst
newspapers wrote. "There is justification for the feeling ...
that the 'compromise' has been reached with a view to its inclusion
in the foreign policy resolutions to be adopted at Mackinac
Island. ... The Republican party would be running into
trouble if it should adopt any such proposition. ... Senator
Vandenberg and his associates cannot commit the entire Foreign
Relations Committee to this 'compromise' and the Committee
... will not agree to any such outrageous surrender of the
constitutional rights of the Senate. ... The scheme obviously is
full of peril to the American people."

Vandenberg didn't pay much attention to these open attacks

by the newspapers that had once strongly backed his isolationist viewpoint, although he did try to answer the charges privately. He wrote to one well-known newsman in reply to a letter of complaint against the compromise:

August 24, 1943

If I can force a highly reluctant Administration to submit the UNRRA agreement to Congress for the approval of an enabling Act — as I have already forced it to substantially rewrite the text — I shall consider it a major one-man victory against the precise Executive Dictatorship to which you seem to feel it would be the final symbol of surrender.

You will find the text of the new agreement drastically changed. It ceases to be a general policy commitment as it was when published last June. . . . It is now practically nothing but an authorization for appropriations — with specific statement in the text . . . that we are bound to nothing unless and until Congress makes the subsequent specific appropriations. . . . Thus, in my opinion, it has ceased to be a treaty in any ordinary acceptance of that word. It has become an appropriation authorization which logically and naturally and constitutionally should require the majority approval of both houses and should originate in the House. . . .

I do not consider this to be the "surrender" — I consider it to be the "triumph" of constitutional procedure. It is the first direct and specific defeat of the President's original announced purpose to do the whole job by executive order. I have no assurance that it will succeed — although we are making hopeful progress with the State Department. I have been told that the President is likely to kick it over at the last minute as being an insufferable invasion of his executive prerogatives. If he does, then we can join issue with him on impregnable ground because he will have been the one who spurns an honest effort to thus at least partially simplify the procession of liquidating some of these war problems. I expect his opposition. . . . I have no idea what will happen. I am unable to believe really that the President will sanction what I consider to be the State Department's wholesale surrender in this whole episode.

Later, to another correspondent, he added: "I am personally of the opinion that this procedure — if successful — will clearly simplify the incidental and interim decisions which must be made in connection with the liquidation of the war. It involves a new and direct system of consultation between the State Department and the Senate Foreign Relations Committee which should be able to avoid many of the stalemates of which we are historically aware."

This last sentence summed up the importance, in Vandenberg's mind, of what he was about to achieve. He was looking not merely at the immediate issue of UNRRA but at the long-run problem of postwar settlements and he was obviously hopeful, if not yet convinced, of the State Department's willingness to collaborate with Congress on these problems. Just as obviously, he felt Mr. Roosevelt would avoid such collaboration if possible, but already he had demonstrated that it wasn't going to be possible if Congress remained alert. The negotiations dragged on for weeks before a solution was worked out, but when the Administration finally completed a new draft of the UNRRA agreement the draft met virtually all of the Senator's objections, and it was eventually accepted by the Senate. And, as he noted, it implemented in an almost unprecedented fashion the word "advice" in that section of the Constitution which gives the President "power, by and with the advice and consent of the Senate, to make treaties."

While the UNRRA agreement was not, strictly speaking, a treaty in the Constitutional sense of the word, the advice as well as the consent of a subcommittee of the Senate Foreign Relations Committee had been available to the Administration and it had, furthermore, been acted upon. Not only had Hull shown great willingness to listen to the senatorial advice, but at one point he had offered to send an important Departmental official to the home states of two subcommittee members — Vandenberg was one of them — to consult on a minor point in the revised draft of the agreement during a brief Congressional recess.

The effect of all this on Vandenberg was of high significance. He had at last emerged from the period of frustration, of chafing over inaction, of being on the outside trying to look in at the men who were conducting the war. He had achieved his main purpose in defeating the Executive agreement method, and if his claim of a complete victory was an overstatement — the Administration did avoid the necessity of a two-thirds majority in the Senate — he was at least correct in saying that he had kept the last word on postwar settlements in Congressional hands. But, most important of all, he had won a skirmish in the struggle for collaboration between the Congress and the State Department on foreign affairs.

In the autumn of 1943, Vandenberg was thus getting into stride. The Mackinac Conference, the postwar objectives resolution, and the UNRRA compromise had been of great psychological importance to him at this turning point in his career, and the coming months, in which Hull expanded the idea of collaboration, were to confirm his views. "It is," Vandenberg remarked in a radio speech delivered on September 22, "the wise voice of American intelligence and enlightened American self-interest which [says] that a bad world for others cannot be a good world for us, and which reliably intends to do its full cooperative share in helping to sustain peace and progress in a happier world. So long as both of those objectives remain inseverably linked we can *unite* America on foreign policy. When they are divorced we inevitably fall apart. . . . A rational, tolerant meeting of patriotic minds upon wholly compatible philosophies of action which complement each other . . . spells dependable *unity*. It is the only source of *unity*."

That was an idea which had become firmly fixed in Vandenberg's mind by the winter of 1943–44, and he was going to stick with it for the rest of his career.

5

"The MacArthur Adventure"

VANDENBERG'S satisfaction with the first steps toward collaboration between Congress and the State Department on postwar problems did nothing to change his basic mistrust of President Roosevelt. He had no evidence that the President himself was in sympathy with or believed in the effectiveness of advance foreign policy consultation with Congressional leaders. Mr. Roosevelt had remained silent in regard to Secretary Hull's conversations with Senate leaders on the postwar objectives resolutions and the UNRRA controversy. And Vandenberg was highly suspicious of the Chief Executive's secret diplomatic dealings with Prime Minister Churchill and Generalissimo Stalin.

All of this added up to one thing: the Senator believed that perhaps the most important step that could be taken to assure a satisfactory peace settlement after the war was to defeat Mr. Roosevelt in the 1944 election. Primarily to achieve that goal, he came out for General Douglas MacArthur for the Republican presidential nomination.

It will not be easy for future historians to explain what Vandenberg himself later called the MacArthur "adventure"; but, in appraising the Senator's action, it will be necessary to take into consideration attitudes and events that developed *after* the 1944 campaign, and which disclosed striking differences in his methods and those of the General. It must be remembered that, in 1943, MacArthur had been far removed from the American political scene for seven years; he was generally uninvolved in party affairs and he was a military figure with tremendous appeal to the public in a bitterly fought Pacific War. It is noteworthy that as early as February of 1942, when MacArthur was on Corregidor, the Senator thought of him as a future possibility for the presidency. On that occasion he spoke of the General in a very personal letter to a member of his family — a letter that reflected some of the bitterness and frustration that he felt at the time but which he would never have let creep into his public statements or even into ordinary private letters. In other words, Vandenberg was "blowing off steam" in the letter because he knew that it would be seen only by his immediate family. He was particularly upset by the nation's unpreparedness in the first phase of the war. He wrote:

February, 1942

I certainly envy the guy in uniform who can *see action*. Tydings made a grand speech in the Senate today — giving everybody *hell*. It's too early for us to break loose on our side of the aisle [the Republican side]. But it won't be long now. Come what may, I'm going to "speak my piece" one of these days. Roosevelt . . . hasn't demobilized a single one of his old "social revolution" units. . . . The country is getting ugly — and I don't blame 'em — *so am I*. Even we in the Senate can't find out what is going on. This is Roosevelt's private war! He sends out troops where he pleases — all over the map — and meanwhile MacArthur fights alone! *Ugh!* If he gets out alive, I think he will be my candidate for President in 1944.

Although this letter was emphatically and deliberately an intemperate private outburst to relieve his own very private feelings at a time when he was disturbed and frustrated, it illustrated the peculiar circumstances in which Vandenberg found himself two years later regarding the 1944 election. In the first place, he had definitely decided to deal himself out of the competition for the Republican nomination, and early in 1943 he began searching for a candidate he could support. He was opposed to Willkie. He had developed considerable admiration for Dewey's growth in stature but he lacked confidence that the New York governor could defeat President Roosevelt. He was eager to repudiate any suspicion that he had developed a "me too" attitude. That could best be done by throwing himself wholeheartedly into a campaign for a man who could defeat the President's bid for a fourth term.

In the spring of 1943, the Senator had been invited by Representative Clare Luce to meet two members of MacArthur's staff, Major General Richard Sutherland and Major General George Kenney, who were on a trip to Washington. They talked at length about MacArthur. About this time, too, Vandenberg took public issue with the War Department over an order that no member of the armed forces on active duty could become a candidate for or seek or accept election to any public office not held by him when he entered upon active duty. The Senator regarded this as an attempt to keep the General out of the 1944 campaign and promptly raised the issue publicly. Secretary Stimson then made it clear that the order could not affect MacArthur.

Vandenberg did not, however, communicate directly with MacArthur at this time or later, and he received from the General only one communication — a message written out in the form of a cable on April 13 but delivered by hand. Addressed to Vandenberg (personal and confidential) it said: "I am most grateful to you for your complete attitude of friendship. I only hope that I can some day reciprocate. There is much that I would like to say to you which circumstances prevent. In the meanwhile I want you to know the absolute confidence I would feel in your experienced and wise mentorship. MacArthur."

This communication seemed to take Vandenberg by surprise and it may well have crystallized his attention on the General as a candidate. He pasted the message from MacArthur in his diary and wrote his reactions on the same page.

April 19, 1943

The following message *might* be supremely historic. It was brought to me by hand this morning by Colonel McArdle, who has just flown in from Australia. I have *never* communicated with General MacArthur about the Presidency or anything else. I assume he is commenting on the vigorous statement I made to his Chief of Staff (General Sutherland) and his Air Chief (General Kenney) when they were here a few weeks ago and I met them in Congressman Clare Luce's apartment. Perhaps he also has in mind my prompt repudiation of the recent War Department order which, in my opinion, was aimed at keeping MacArthur out of the next Presidential campaign. At any rate, "Mac" certainly is not "running away" from *anything*. It is typical of his forthright courage.

Not long afterward, in the early summer of 1943, another of MacArthur's staff officers, Brigadier General C. A. Willoughby, was in Washington on a brief visit and had a long talk with the Senator and with other prominent Republicans. One who was most interested was General Robert E. Wood of Chicago. The conversation and subsequent correspondence with Willoughby after his return to the Southwest Pacific confirmed Vandenberg's opinions regarding MacArthur and prompted him to start a quiet boom for the General. There seemed, subsequently, to be one outstanding reason for the Senator's action: he came to the conclusion that MacArthur could defeat Roosevelt and that he was probably the only man who could do it. He obviously admired and respected the General and felt that he was qualified to be President, but throughout the MacArthur "adventure" his emphasis was almost entirely on the idea that he could *win*. In fact, a determined effort was made to keep political issues out of the discussion of MacArthur's candidacy.

"I . . . feel emphatically," Vandenberg wrote, "that our primary obligation to the General is to protect him against any untoward political activities which would in any way embarrass his present status. [MacArthur at that time was Allied Commander of the Southwest Pacific Theater.] I believe that his nomination must essentially be a spontaneous draft — certainly without the appearance of any connivance on his part (of which he would never allow himself to be consciously guilty)."

Even before Willoughby had returned to MacArthur's headquarters in Australia and reported back to Vandenberg by mail, a number of politically minded persons had started booming the General in the midwest. The Senator was fearful that such activities might be premature and might react adversely. He wrote to Joseph P. Savage, president of an Illinois MacArthur-for-President club:

July 2, 1943

I have no right — directly or indirectly — to speak for [MacArthur]. I certainly have no right to assume to direct any national movement in his behalf. It just happens by fortuitous circumstances that the MacArthur movement seems to find me as its focal point because I am the only Senate Republican who has spoken out unequivocally in his behalf. . . . It seems to me that General MacArthur is incomparably our most available nominee and incomparably the best qualified man to lead America in the next administration.

[But he expressed concern about premature political activities and about proposals to enter MacArthur in the Wisconsin, Illinois, and other presidential primaries. Without any strong political organization, the General might be swamped in such primary tests and thus lose all hope of being nominated.]

In my opinion if he is ultimately nominated, it cannot be as a result of the ordinary, normal and traditional political preconvention methods. It will be because of a general rank and file conviction among Republicans of the country that his credentials are paramount. . . . It would be obviously impossible for the General to recognize [the] movement in his behalf, in any way, unless and until he is actually drafted by the next National Convention. The only possible attitude for him to take — and I am sure it is the only one he would ever take — is (and as he himself has already said): "Let's get on with the war."

Early in August Frank Gannett, publisher of a group of newspapers and high in Republican councils, was in Washington, talked with Vandenberg about MacArthur, and thereafter became closely associated with the Senator and Wood in the backstage management of the MacArthur draft movement. About this time Vandenberg heard from Willoughby and later wrote in reply:

August 17, 1943

Thanks for your fine letter of August 3rd. It is more than satisfactory in all of its aspects.

During the last two weeks I have been to Chicago to discuss our matter with General Wood and we are in full agreement. General Wood has offered to underwrite any necessary expense. I have also gone to New York and spent an evening with Governor Dewey. [At this time Dewey had indicated he would not be a candidate for the nomination in 1944.] I doubt if I should quote him other than to say that he is totally sympathetic with the idea of keeping "our candidate" thoroughly available when the time comes (which of course is my own total idea of the essential strategy). He emphasizes the importance of doing absolutely nothing of a promotional nature which would involve "our campaign" in any ordinary political atmosphere or involve us in any of the usual preconvention methods. . . . I have also been to Rochester to see Mr. Frank Gannett. . . . He is for "our man" with an intense enthusiasm. . . .

Jay Hayden is carrying a story . . . today which again puts this whole movement in its proper perspective. . . . I am consulting "our cabinet" regarding the permanent employment of one appropriate man to take over the details of this entire undercover movement. . . . The whole thing, of course, continues to be entirely a gigantic speculation in public opinion and in the evolution of events. Of course, the chances are all against us. I am sure this is fully understood out where you are. It is simply a matter of developing a situation which, in the first instance, produces a national convention in which a majority of the delegates are "uninstructed" so that they are free to make the proper decision when the time comes; then to develop through general consciousness that "our man" is the best answer under all the circumstances. . . .

Tell my friend to just "get on with the war" and to forget this whole political business back here in the States. None of us wants him to do anything else.

In a letter to Wood in September Vandenberg said:

September 15, 1943

I have heard from General Willoughby that the "situation is satisfactory" (which is all I care to put on paper) and that the guidance of friends like you and Edgar Queeny and Frank Gannett and Roy Howard and myself will be satisfactory. Roy Howard seems to be in doubt about the whole matter (although not through any lack of total loyalty to the General). . . .

I am hoping that you will be coming to Washington in the near future. The particular thing . . . that I want to talk to you about is our feeling (when last we talked) that we ought to find some thoroughly capable, competent, experienced and wholly reliable person to take over the responsibility for the general supervision of this entire movement so that it is not left entirely to chance. . . . I am told that we might interest Mr. John Hamilton [former Chairman of the Republican National Committee] to take on this job. In my opinion he has everything which the job requires. He certainly did a beautiful piece of work in producing the Landon nomination in 1936.

Wood and Gannett apparently agreed, because on December 16 Vandenberg wrote Wood that he had "spent last evening with John. His report was encouraging. He agrees that a few of us should get together to make some basic decisions in the near future. . . . It has been suggested that we meet at John's farm at Paoli, Pennsylvania (a Philadelphia suburb), on Saturday, January 15th . . . Mr. Kyle Palmer of the Los Angeles Times will be available for this conference — and he is our key man on the Pacific Coast. It is hoped that you and Gannett and Queeny and Pew [Joseph N. Pew, Jr., a prominent Republican leader in Pennsylvania] and Palmer (and probably Townsend of Arkansas) will be present. . . . By meeting at John's farm, it is felt that we can reasonably hope to keep the entire matter as confidential as it should be."

The Senator did not record which MacArthur supporters finally attended the Paoli conference, but it turned into a weekend affair that included Mrs. Vandenberg and other wives after a rather involved exchange of letters and telegrams. Just what political decisions were made remained unclear in the subsequent correspondence but it was obvious then and later that the group was torn between the fear that they would not do enough to create a MacArthur organization and the fear that they would get the General involved in a premature political battle that might knock him out before the fighting really started. As early as the end of September Vandenberg had written:

September 30, 1943

I think it is desperately important that there should be no signs whatever of any centrally organized activity. It seems to me that the American people are rapidly coming to understand what the General is up against in the Far East [a reference to the Roosevelt-Churchill decision to fight the war in Europe first and the subsequent shortage of men and materials in the Southwest Pacific]. These people can easily *martyrize* him into a completely irresistible figure. So it seems to me more important than ever that we should give our own "commander-in-chief" no possible excuse upon which to hang his own political reprisals. It is obvious on every hand that the movement [for MacArthur] is making solid headway in all directions. ... I cling to the basic thought that if MacArthur can be nominated it will be as the result of a ground swell and not as the result of any ordinary pre-convention political activities. Nevertheless, I am not so naive as to forget that "heaven helps those who help themselves."

The group continued to expand its activities, hired a friend of Gannett's to set up a small central organization, consulted with political sources in California and through the midwestern and various southern states — and worried about reports from the Southwest Pacific. "I am disturbed about one thing which to me is quite inexplicable," Vandenberg wrote to Wood on November 5. "I am constantly hearing reports that veterans returning from the South Pacific are not enthusiastic about our friend. One skeptical correspondent has gone so far as to suggest that there is some sort of diabolical arrangement to see to it that only anti-MacArthur veterans are furloughed home. That of course would be fantastic. I had a V-mail note yesterday from a very intelligent Grand Rapids boy in the South Pacific to whom I had written for a frank canvass of the men out there. He reports growing unpopularity for our friend. What does this mean?" Wood replied, pointing out that MacArthur ran the Southwest Pacific command and the Navy ran the South Pacific command, but he did not offer any further explanation.

Meanwhile, a slate of delegates pledged to Dewey was entered in the Wisconsin primary, and, although some of them later withdrew at Dewey's request, sixteen remained in the race. Vandenberg was hard pressed by various enthusiastic MacArthur supporters to agree to entering the General in this and other primaries, but he insisted it would be a political mistake. An unruly MacArthur fan insisted on running as a MacArthur delegate in the New Hampshire primary and came out last on the list. In Wisconsin, the MacArthur-for-President movement got out of hand and the General's name was entered in the primary against Dewey and Willkie, who made a vigorous campaign in that state. "I have simply had to wash my hands of the Wisconsin situation," Vandenberg wrote on March 18 of 1944. "It is entirely too complex to be handled intelligently at arm's length. But I still hope that we shall be spared a catastrophe at that point. . . . Speaking generally, I should say that . . . the trends have more definitely turned in Governor Dewey's direction. . . . It seems to me that we shall all know the indisputable truth about this situation by the first of June. If it is then clear that Dewey is unquestionably 'in' I think we should all join in giving him the strongest possible send-off."

Dewey won the Wisconsin primary and knocked Willkie out of the presidential race. He also seemed to have ended any chance of a deadlock that would offer an opportunity to bring MacArthur forward as a dark horse at the convention, but "our cabinet" decided to try to keep the General's position firm until the last possible moment. "If people [in Wisconsin] were flocking to Dewey on Dewey's own account then it is all over but the shouting," Vandenberg wrote on April 10. "But if they were flocking to Dewey because he looked like their best chance to 'stop Willkie' then there may be a complete reassessment of values during the next sixty days. . . . I think we should wait until at least the first of May before we take any active step toward joining the Dewey parade. . . . I have written Australia and frankly presented this picture."

They didn't have to wait until May 1, however, to have the question settled. In April Representative A. L. Miller, a Republican of Nebraska, disclosed that he had written to MacArthur about the presidential race and had received a reply. He published the correspondence. Miller's letter attacking the New Deal was so exaggerated, intemperate, and unrealistic that it represented a liability as a political pronouncement. But MacArthur's answer, praising Miller for sagacity and statesmanship, was a devastating, final blow to his own cause, as Vandenberg noted in his diary.

April 30, 1944

The MacArthur Boom Bursts. General Douglas MacArthur announced last night from his headquarters in New Guinea: "I do not covet" the Republican presidential nomination; "nor would I accept it." He gave as his reason for this belated statement the "widespread public opinion that it is detrimental to our war effort to have an officer in high position on active service at the front considered for President." That is not the *real* reason. If it were, he would have said it long ago. The *real* reason is (1) that the tragic mistake made by Congressman A. L. Miller (Nebraska Republican) in publishing his private and confidential correspondence with MacArthur made the latter's position untenable; (2) that the Dewey movement has such momentum that it is remotely likely that any other candidate can overtake him and the General wishes to retire from the scene with dignity and honor. I agree to the statement on both counts. (On the latter count, I have advised it through our mutual friend, Brigadier General C. A. Willoughby, who is G-2 at MacArthur's headquarters.)

Throughout the past twelve months, when I have been the

unofficial head of the "MacArthur movement," I have constantly cautioned all concerned that MacArthur could *only* be nominated as the result of a "pure draft"; that his friends must scrupulously protect his military status; that no ordinary pre-convention methods could be followed; and that any mis-step over here might precipitate an immediate and unequivocal renunciation of the whole movement by the General himself. There is no question that, under such circumstances, the General would have been willing to serve; and I make this statement advisedly. We came dangerously near the necessity for the "unequivocal renunciation" when MacArthur was entered in the Illinois and Wisconsin primaries (both of which events I earnestly counseled against). But the *event* exploded in our faces when Congressman Miller inexplicably made public his *private* correspondence urging the General to run and bitterly assailing the New Deal, and MacArthur's answers in which he (equally inexplicably) praised Miller's statements as the sum total of wisdom. He later said that he merely intended his brief letters to be "amiable acknowledgments" of the letters from the Congressman (whom he scarcely knew) and that they were *intended* to be purely personal. But the publication *hurt* — and threatened even to hurt the General's military status. Miller, in one inane moment, crucified the whole MacArthur movement (and MacArthur with it).

Meanwhile, the Dewey movement some weeks ago had gained such power that his nomination seemed inevitable. I said *then* that the moment this should become indisputable we should *all* get behind him (so as to give him the best possible send-off), and that MacArthur should be formally withdrawn so that he would not be humiliated. I made this recommendation to our "mutual friend" — (I have been scrupulously careful not to exchange so much as *one* letter with the General since the "movement" started). After making his first raw mistake (and getting himself limelighted on all the first pages of the country) Miller proceeded to continue his *public* bombardment of MacArthur (*after* the whole thing was practically all over). I can fully understand why MacArthur found it necessary to act summarily and (deeply as I regret that he cannot be nominated) I applaud his statement (although I have made no *public* statement on this or any other phase of the MacArthur movement from the hour when Miller pulled his magnificent "boner").

I do not believe MacArthur could have been nominated anyway as things now trend. But it is a magnificent tribute to him and his place in American public opinion that, despite the lack of *any* organized campaign in his behalf, he should be "second choice" to Dewey in every part of the country. *Today's* "Gallup Poll" is the final proof. He would have been incomparably the greatest "Commander-in-Chief" we could have had in this war; he would have been our most eligible President, especially in his spokesmanship for America at the peace table. It was impossible, because of his position, to put up a campaign for him. We did the best we could under the circumstances. My chief "allies" were General Robert Wood of Chicago and Frank Gannett (and his man, Raymond Richmond) of Rochester. The most important "free lancers" were Joseph P. Savage of Chicago (who nationalized the "MacArthur Clubs"), General Leach of Minneapolis and Lansing Hoyt of Milwaukee. In a way it is a relief that it is all over. I have paid a "price" for my loyalty (it undoubtedly cost me the Temporary Chairmanship of the Republican National Convention): but I am proud of *everything* I have done in this connection. If MacArthur could have been "drafted" — as we tried to plan it — he would have accepted. The Gentleman from Nebraska finished off that possibility.

Later, he elaborated on the MacArthur letters: "I shall never understand why they were written in the first place." And still later he added: "I was shocked that he should have ever written the letters which Miller made public. If he hadn't written them, Miller couldn't have used them."

The Republican convention at Chicago during the last week of June was almost anticlimactic for Vandenberg, who had long since climbed on the Dewey bandwagon. His chief interest at Chicago was in getting the Mackinac Declaration on foreign policy incorporated in the Republican platform. That was done under the leadership of Senator Warren Austin, chairman of the subcommittee on foreign affairs of the Resolutions Committee. Wendell Willkie raised almost the only serious objections to the foreign policy declaration, asserting that it was ambiguous and indicating belief that it contained "phony phrases." Both Vandenberg and Austin struck back with a defense of the Mackinac formula as a definite commitment and they easily carried the day. The situation was illustrated by the Washington *Star's* famous cartoonist, Berryman, who pictured a smiling Vandenberg leading a slightly worried G.O.P. elephant along a "Mackinac" plank toward the party platform, and saying: "Come on, old girl. If it can hold me, it can hold you." The same idea was expressed in the Senator's diary.

June 26-29, 1944

Chicago National Convention. My job in this connection was much simpler than in the two previous conventions — and yet it involved a desperately serious responsibility. The "foreign policy" problem is still dynamite. But, once more, we got unanimity by sticking to the "Mackinac Idea." As Chairman of the Mackinac Foreign Policy Committee I worked all spring to get my own Committee unanimous (with the splendid aid of Senator Austin). We always felt that if *we* (who had been so far apart in pre-Pearl Harbor days) could agree, it ought to be possible for others to do so too. And that's the way it worked. In addition I consulted Governor Dewey who sent John Foster Dulles to me in Washington. After one very congenial evening, in which I was greatly impressed by Dulles, we found ourselves in complete harmony. I also consulted Senator Taft (speaking for Governor Bricker). So the job was just about done before we ever got to Chicago — and thereafter, it was fairly plain sailing.

Vandenberg's role in the framing of the foreign policy plank was later noted by John Foster Dulles when he wrote the Senator on June 20, 1944: "I want to say how much I feel the Party is indebted to you for the fine preliminary work you did as Chairman of the Mackinac Committee in getting up a foreign affairs plank upon which the Resolutions Committee and the delegates as a whole could substantially unite. Without that assiduous and painstaking advance work by you, which found common ground, there might have been serious disruption." At the bottom of this letter, Vandenberg noted: "Dulles speaks for Dewey in respect to foreign relations — and will probably be his Secretary of State."

The Chicago convention went off smoothly for the most part, with Dewey in command of the situation most of the time, but there was one incident that proved that the ghost of the MacArthur "adventure" was hard to lay. It was the only record of the convention that Vandenberg entered in his diary except for his reference to the foreign affairs plank.

June 26–29, 1944 [continued]

Chicago National Convention. My most interesting experience was when the roll was called for presidential nomination speeches. Bricker and Stassen and Dirksen were withdrawing to make the Dewey nomination unanimous. While this was going on, Senator Townsend rushed over to me to tell me that one of the MacArthur delegates from Wisconsin was about to ruin everything (including MacArthur) by making a 30-minute nominating speech for him. I did not know the delegate; but I pushed my way over to the Wisconsin delegation (after warning Chairman Joe Martin what was coming, and getting him to agree to rush the program into the quickest possible roll call if the unwelcome orator could not be stopped). I felt it would be an insufferable humiliation for General MacArthur to have such a speech made (in view of his total withdrawal many weeks ago) and then to wind up with only one or two votes. I was also afraid the convention would yell down the Wisconsin delegate (which might be a further reflection on MacArthur).

When I got to the Wisconsin delegation and asked for the "orator" they said — "There he goes; he's on his way to the platform." I jammed my way through the crowd and caught him. I said: "I greatly admire your loyalty; but General MacArthur has asked that his name should not be brought up here at all; and I make that request of you in his name."

He belligerently declined to yield. He had his speech in his hand. He said: "I've been instructed by my people to vote for MacArthur and I intend to keep faith." I said: "O.K.; go ahead and vote for him; but your people didn't instruct you to make a 30-minute nominating speech — and humiliate the General." But I could see that the only hope was to hold him in conversation until Chairman Martin could start the roll call. And that's what happened. Before he could get to the platform, "Alabama" had been called and had voted. But it was a narrow escape. . . . The delegate who was going to make the speech was Dr. Koehler of Milwaukee. He did not even vote for MacArthur on the final show-down. Ritter was to make a seconding speech. Of course he never got to *that*; but he *did stick* on the roll call and cast the one vote for MacArthur which kept the ballot from being unanimous.

6

Committee of Eight

THROUGHOUT the abortive campaign to groom MacArthur as a dark horse for the 1944 presidential campaign, Vandenberg had not wavered from his search for a unified approach to questions of foreign policy. The UNRRA agreement discussion lasted for months, and in February the Senator took a leading part in the debate that resulted in approval, by a 47 to 14 vote, of the authorization for an appropriation of $1,350,000,000 for the United Nations Relief and Rehabilitation Administration. Senator McNary, the minority leader of the Senate, died late in February, and Vandenberg was mentioned as a possible successor. But the Republicans, with Vandenberg concurring, selected Senator Wallace H. White of Maine, the acting floor leader, and continued Vandenberg in his post as acting chairman of the Republican Conference. Taft was named chairman of a newly created Steering Committee. Vandenberg was busy during the winter of 1943–44 with various domestic legislative problems, but his chief interest was centered on foreign affairs.

He was disturbed about a number of questions in regard to the organization of the postwar world, some of them questions that were politically important to him in Michigan because of the large Eastern European population there. Furthermore, the closer liaison that had been established with the State Department had not progressed much further than the area covered by the UNRRA agreement. In a letter he wrote:

March 11, 1944

I must confess that I am dubious about the American development of concrete ideas regarding the ultimate European (postwar) reorganization. I am dubious on the one hand because it looks as though our major allies have no intention of surrendering their own primary interests and controls in this connection. I am dubious on the other hand because I seem to detect a resurgence of critical suspicion on the part of our own people in respect to our external postwar obligations. I shall not be surprised [to] find this evidenced in the Congressional reaction to the President's latest request for legislation extending the "good neighbor" policy to the whole world (UNRRA). The trouble is that many of our recent international activities have been so miserably mismanaged — and there has often been such total disregard of economic common sense in the external distribution of our resources — that large sectors of our people are beginning to fear the extension of these trends. In my opinion, the American people can still be counted on to do their full part . . . in connection with the peace; but this will require a corresponding degree of nation-wide reassurance that the legitimate and essential rights and resources of our own United States are vigilantly preserved. . . .

I am frank to say that I have always thought the "unconditional surrender" doctrine — unless it sharply distinguished between "governments" and "peoples" — is dangerous, costly and totally unwise. We must have the equivalent of unconditional surrender so far as Axis authority is concerned. . . . But it seems to me that we can achieve all of these things to a completely adequate extent without robbing the Axis peoples of any and all incentive to stop this war themselves. [And in regard to postwar dealing with Germany, he added:] Our ideas ought to be definitely crystallizing in this connection. But I am pessimistic . . . because of the total lack of Congressional information in respect to the commitments which are being made on our account in all of these various international conferences [the Atlantic Conference, the Casablanca Conference, the Moscow Conference, and the top-level three-power conference: Britain, Russia, and the

United States at Teheran] where the President always acts exclusively upon his own initiative and then maintains totally effective silence upon his return. . . . If there is any Washington planning of a comprehensive nature . . . it seems to me that it must be preceded by a new candor between the White House and the Capitol.

The Senator elaborated on this theme when he wrote:

March 18, 1944

I am totally unwilling to trust these [postwar] negotiations . . . to President Roosevelt's highly internationalistic point of view. I want America to play her full postwar part . . . but I . . . do not believe that Mr. Roosevelt's idea of "protecting American interests" would square with mine for an instant. . . . None of us knows what President Roosevelt's commitments on our behalf have been at Quebec and Moscow and Teheran. We can guess. . . . My guess is that they lean toward Stalin in a degree I would never approve. But in any event I do not see how we could endorse President Roosevelt's undisclosed international purposes. . . . The so-called Atlantic Charter has already been torn to shreds — so far as its promises to little countries are concerned. I deeply fear that there are many sad and tragic disillusionments ahead.

This return to the theme of complaint against the lack of liaison with the Executive branch was not, however, to last long. Secretary Hull was acutely conscious of the necessity for avoiding a Senate fight such as destroyed Woodrow Wilson's League of Nations and he inaugurated at this time a new phase in what he liked to call a nonpartisan approach to foreign affairs. Hull had, in fact, established as early as 1942 an Advisory Committee on Postwar Foreign Policy made up of men and women prominent in public affairs as well as State Department experts, and in May of 1942 the membership was greatly increased to include members of the Senate and House of Representatives. Among the senators were two Republicans — White and Austin — who were definitely internationalists and who could hardly be said to represent the majority views of the Party at that time.

While the Committee provided some guidance for the postwar planning work of the departmental experts, it did not fill the need for an effective liaison with Congress. In the spring of 1944, however, the planning for organization of peace, the Roosevelt-Churchill-Stalin discussions, and the progress of the war against the Axis had reached a point that made imperative some concrete action toward setting up a postwar organization. Both Churchill and Roosevelt, according to Hull's memoirs, originally favored some kind of regional security organizations but gradually they swung around to a world organization along the lines of the United Nations, which Hull had always favored. The Secretary's problem then became that of finding a basis on which the United States could agree on the home front so that a united front could be presented to the other Allied Powers.

In March Hull appeared before the Senate Foreign Relations Committee and went into considerable detail in regard to our foreign relations. He explained that the State Department's postwar planning was at a stage where he wanted to confer with the Committee members on an international organization to maintain peace, and suggested that a committee of members from both parties be appointed to meet secretly and informally with him.

Because of the presidential campaign in the offing, the Republican leaders such as Vandenberg paused to think before accepting the invitation. The Senator explained the situation to Taft and asked his advice. His relations with Taft, incidentally, were unique. They often disagreed publicly; their attitudes and ideas were frequently not in harmony. But Vandenberg entertained a deep respect for the Ohioan and his usefulness in the Republican party and the country. Though not intimate personal friends in the sense that Vandenberg and Senator Millikin were, for instance, Vandenberg always guarded a cordial Taft relationship with the greatest care, and scrupulously refrained from invading what he regarded as Taft's area of major responsibility for domestic problems. Taft put his ideas on the Hull invitation into a letter on March 29, suggesting that if the co-operation was merely to write a blueprint for a League of Nations the question was not important. But he added that, if the proposed committee was expected to confer on all matters of foreign policy, Vandenberg should express willingness to co-operate under certain conditions. These conditions were that the invitation should come from the President — who has primary responsibility for conduct of foreign policy — and should cover every phase of current and postwar activities. He said that in such event the Republicans should be fully informed and given a chance to advise before decisions were made. He also suggested the Republicans reserve the right to consult other minority members of the Senate and that, if the minority advice was consistently ignored, they reserve the right to resign rather than continue a fruitless co-operation. He warned Vandenberg that the newspapers might play up the proposed committee in a way to try to make the Republicans responsible for everything the Administration did and said that steps should be taken to guard against that contingency, because, he felt, the President was not really likely to co-operate.

Vandenberg took Taft's advice, almost literally. In a letter to Connally he spoke for a number of members of the minority when he said:

April 4, 1944
None of us would decline for an instant any effective co-operation. . . . We believe there is serious need for greater liaison . . . in respect to foreign policy. . . . But . . . the creation of this special committee should be accompanied by a clear and explicit definition of its function and jurisdiction. . . . If it is to deal specifically with the application of [the committee's] studies to our actual peace settlements — and no less an effort would seem to be of much practical advantage — I respectfully suggest that we should have the understanding that we shall be fully informed at all times regarding all the facts on which foreign policy depends . . . and that the request for this cooperation . . . should appropriately come from the President himself.

It would, of course, be understood that we would not attempt or presume to speak for or to bind our minority colleagues to any course of subsequent action. . . . If clear and irreconcilable differences of opinion should develop . . . we would reserve the right to resign.

In a final word, we are ready and prepared to do everything within our power to help create an effective "foreign policy" liaison in developing a unified approach to these terrific problems that lie ahead; but the very nature of the talk requires explicit clarification of the obligation which we thus assume.

The President didn't issue an invitation for formation of the Committee but a general agreement was reached, and at the first session in Hull's office on April 25 the Secretary made it clear that the conference would be informal and that no one would be required to assume any obligations. He gave the senators in strict confidence a copy of the United States draft for a United Nations organization, a draft that he hoped to present to the British and the Russians if the senators approved. The senators in the group, which became known as the Committee of Eight, were Connally, Barkley, George, Gillette (Democrats), La Follette (Progressive), and Vandenberg, White, and Austin (Republicans).

May 11, 1944

Our special Senate Committee on Post-War Plans . . . has had three meetings with Secretary of State Hull. The Committee was originally supposed to be six. But when I insisted that La Follette should be on, Connally enlarged it to eight and added Austin on the Republican side on his own initiative (obviously because Austin is so internationally-minded).

At our first meeting, Hull presented the Department's tentative outline for a World Security Organization. The striking thing about it is that it is so *conservative* from a nationalist standpoint. It is based virtually on a four-power alliance. While there is an Assembly in which all nations will be represented with one vote each, the real authority is in a Council of eight upon which America, England, Russia and China shall *always* be represented; and no action looking toward the use of force can be taken if any one of the Big Four dissents. Hull's whole theory is that there must be continued agreement between the Big Four or the post-war world will smash anyway. Also, to his credit, he recognizes that the

United States will never permit itself to be ordered into war against its own consent. He has even gone so far as to suggest that we require this consent to be given by an Act of Congress. This is anything but a wild-eyed internationalist dream of a world State. On the contrary, it is a frame-work (without passing upon details) to which I can and do heartily subscribe. Hull's thought is that, if he can get our tentative congressional consent to the general idea, he will sound out the others of the Big Four — and then come back to us with the results.

The chief difference of opinion, up to date, if any, rotates round the *timing*. I have taken the position that, no matter how acceptable this program for a new League might be, everything depends upon the kind of peace — whether it is a *just* peace — which this new international organization will implement. We are all disturbed by Russia's unilateral announcements from time to time as to what she intends to do, for example, with Poland and the other Baltic States; and by Churchill's constant reiteration of restoring the British Empire intact. The *peace* will create a new status quo in the world. The new "League" will defend this new status quo. It is my position that the United States cannot subscribe to this defense, no matter how hedged about, unless and until we know more about what the new status quo will be. It is my argument that we should go ahead and perfect a plan for collective security; but that we should make it wholly contingent upon a *just* peace (thus strengthening the hands of those who will be seeking a *just* peace). Therefore, in my view, the new "league" must be *contingent* upon the *character* of the *peace*. This is definitely La Follette's view. It is substantially George's view. In varying degrees it has support through the balance of the Congressional committee. I cannot assert it as a fact, but I believe Hull wishes to go ahead and complete the "League" first. If so, it will fail. The point is so fundamental and so important that I have put myself on paper to the Secretary.

This point aside, I repeat that I am deeply impressed (and surprised) to find Hull so carefully guarding our American veto in his scheme of things.

Vandenberg was more or less correct in his interpretation of Hull's desires. The Secretary took up at his second meeting with the Committee, on May 2, the point that Vandenberg raised in relation to committing himself before he knew whether there would be a "good or bad" peace; that is, whether Britain and especially Russia were going to agree to "just" territorial settlements after the war. Hull pointed out that the Senate would have opportunity to pass on the various peace treaties and would, therefore, have a hand in the final settlements. But, he asked, what would the United States do in event these final settlements did not conform exactly to our own ideas? Would Vandenberg want to abandon the whole idea of an international security organization or would he feel that the United States should go ahead with such an organization in the hope that a better peace could be worked out in the future?

The next day, Vandenberg wrote to Hull:

May 3, 1944

I want to leave no doubt in your mind regarding the suggestion which I made. . . . I believe we should earnestly proceed, under your able leadership, with our effort to outline, unofficially, the world organization which we are prepared to support in quest of permanent peace with ordered justice in a free world. . . . But it is my view that it is impossible to disassociate this ultimate formula from the actual physical and specific terms of the peace itself. . . . Otherwise we would be signing the most colossal "blank check" in history.

You have the right to respond, as you did . . . with the question what we would do if the peace terms were unsatisfactory to us and if we therefore should withhold our membership in the international organization. I am frank to say that I do not know the answer. . . . But I consider that situation less hazardous than our advance commitment to help sustain an unjust peace in which we do not believe and which violates our national sense of justice. . . . Therefore, with the greatest respect, I assert the view that our advance action . . . should be contingent upon whether the ultimate peace merits our support. It seems to me that such an attitude immeasurably strengthens the hands of our own Government in urging others . . . to a peace-with-justice.

But, except on this point, Vandenberg's comment in his diary showed enthusiasm for Hull's proposals.

May 11, 1944 [*continued*]

There is nothing remotely approaching a "world state" or a standing "international police force" in his prospectus. He is also manifestly eager to avoid Wilson's mistake of attempting commitments destined for ultimate congressional rejection. All in all, and again reserving details, I think his preliminary scheme is excellent.

At today's meeting I found it necessary to clearly define the limitations under which it must be understood that I proceed as a *Republican* in these conferences; that I am not assuming to bind anyone but myself. I pointed out that there *may* be a new Republican President when the peace arrives and that he will be entitled to *his own* policy. I reminded the Secretary that when President Hoover invited President-elect Roosevelt's co-operation in the dark and desperate days between November, 1932, and March, 1933, the latter flatly *declined* to co-operate, saying that he could not take "responsibility" without commensurate "authority." He was right — in a way. But if we Republicans took his view there could be no present post-war planning at all. I pointed out that we intend to continue to co-operate; but that it must always be remembered that we act under obvious limitations. As a matter of fact, we act with considerable political embarrassment to ourselves because we are largely silenced in our public criticisms. But it is our view that the *country* comes first.

Hanging like a cloud over all of these negotiations is the fact that *none* of us knows what personal commitments may have been made by Roosevelt to Stalin and Churchill — as currently personified by the fact that Churchill, driven into a corner, has just assured the British Parliament that he had a *private* agreement with Roosevelt that the Atlantic Charter does *not* involve "Imperial Preferences" within the British Empire.

The differences between Hull and Vandenberg exploded later in the month when it became obvious that a full agreement could not be reached.

May 19, 1944

We came to our first impasse with Secretary of State Hull today in connection with post-war peace planning. He wants to take his "plan" for an international organization to Churchill and Stalin immediately, and he wants a statement from our Senate Committee virtually *endorsing* the plan. It is a good plan, tentatively speaking; in fact it so surprisingly protects the independent authority of the United States that I am surprised and delighted. But it is impossible for me to *endorse* the plan by specific reference: (1) because it has not been adequately studied; (2) because I have no intention of being drawn into the equivocal position where I would pretend, even by indirection, to commit the next Republican President if there should be one; and (3) it is impossible, from my view-point, to separate the nature of the new "League" from the character of the "peace" which it will assume to sustain.

Being anxious, however, to assist Secretary Hull as much as possible in his contemplated negotiations, the Committee unanimous[ly] agreed to a letter to Hull stating that the Committee "approves your purpose to enter into preliminary conversations with Great Britain, Russia, China and other United Nations to explore a general plan for an international organization as the ultimate means to implement a just and satisfactory peace." We added: "The Committee realizes that there can be no commitments in advance of specific proposals developed in the light of general peace considerations." Also: "The subcommittee reserves its final judgment upon the conversations and any plan which may be adopted until it may be put in final form and terms of peace are known." We further said: "We desire to express our commendation of your efforts to enter into tentative conversations with our comrades-in-arms with respect to this great objective and we give you renewed assurances of our desire to continue to co-operate in the pursuit of these parliamentary studies."

When Chairman Connally advised Secretary Hull of the nature of this intended communication he was both disappointed and angry. He insisted that he must have much more of a commitment from the Committee. For the first time he really disclosed his hand. He asked for a letter specifically referring to his "League" plan and saying that "the members of the subcommittee are inclined to the opinion that the document should be acceptable to the American people and considers that the proposal embodied in it is, in its present status, sufficient to justify your purpose to enter into preliminary conversations etc." The only saving grace was a ponderous sentence which said that "so far as future developments which may affect the present proposal, we will take notice and exercise our judgments in each phase of these developments when they occur and will continue the mutual policy of conference in the light of such developments." Then he wanted to change the final sentence in *our* suggestion so that instead of promising "continued co-operation in the pursuit of these preliminary studies," it would promise "to co-operate further in the development of *this proposal.*"

Practically the entire subcommittee balked at the idea of pretending to commit "the American people." Senator La Follette and I further balked at any reference to any "specific plan" and to the complete omission of any direct reference to the fact that our American responsibility to a new "League" (which would guarantee the post-war status quo) would have to be contingent upon the nature and justice of the peace.

It seemed to be impossible to get an agreement. It was suggested that Hull might better go ahead on his own responsibility with his negotiations — still consulting us for our opinions from time to time for whatever it might be worth. La Follette and I made it plain that we would *not* sign a "blank check." There was much assurance that the Administration intends to take no *political* advantage of our signature; but the protestations merely served to arouse the suspicions. Hull was pressing for action because he wants to get his "plan" out ahead of Churchill's and Stalin's. It was finally agreed to leave the matter open until Monday when the subcommittee will make another effort to agree upon language. The basic trouble with the whole situation is that we do not know what Roosevelt has promised at Moscow and Teheran nor what his private understandings with Churchill and Stalin may be. Constantine Brown flatly charges in The Washington Star that the new map of Europe is *already* agreed upon. I do not intend to be driven into a blind alley.

For the next few days the subcommittee debated various proposals for a letter to Hull, Austin proposing that an international organization should be set up at once without regard to the eventual peace terms. Vandenberg and La Follette opposed this idea. Gillette didn't like the preliminary Hull plan. Vandenberg finally suggested the draft of a letter to the Secretary approving "your purpose to enter into discussions" for an international organization but pointing out that "there can be no commitments on our part in advance." Connally, George, and Austin opposed the letter for various reasons. Barkley wasn't present at that meeting, which Vandenberg described in his diary, and added:

May 23, 1944
It finally became evident that we must do one of two things — either send a split report to Hull or abandon any letter at all. Since none of us wanted to discourage Hull from proceeding at once with his explorations (as a split report might do), it was finally agreed that Chairman Connally should simply make an oral statement to the Secretary that our subcommittee favors his entering upon immediate negotiations with the other United Nations, and stop there. When the meeting finally broke up this afternoon, this was the intended course.

Over all these negotiations — (and there certainly was an earnest effort to find common ground) — hung the shadow of a doubt as to whether we (or even Hull himself) was in possession of *full* information as to what peace terms may have *already* been agreed upon between Roosevelt, Stalin and Churchill. I think it is significant that our subcommittee (although of the highest legislative dignity) has not seen the Chief of State himself in respect to these matters concerning which he is supreme. We have not been told that *he* approves the Hull document — and the newspapers are full of speculations that he harbors quite *different* intentions. We all believe in Hull. But none of us is *sure* that Hull *knows* the whole story. I can simply state for myself that I do not feel I have sufficient authentic information to back *any* specific "League" plan yet (although I heartily favor the principle and the idea); that the Hull proposal is too controversial to deserve even a tentative Congressional o.k. on our part; and that this country will never be willing to join a "League" and accept obligations to implement a peace ahead of any authentic information as to what that peace will be.

At the next meeting of the Committee with Hull there was a renewal of discussion of what Mr. Roosevelt had promised at Teheran, and Vandenberg's fears that the Soviet Union intended to keep control over the Baltic States and Poland after the war were sharply intensified as a result of articles that had appeared in the *Saturday Evening Post*.

May 26, 1944

Although the problem was presumably settled at our last meeting — namely, that Chairman Connally should *orally* tell Hull that we commended his purpose to go ahead with his international conversations — the Chairman called us back together again this afternoon. He had spent two hours with Hull, and he was back *again* asking for a letter. Connally had written *another* letter which was more prolix than the former but which still fought shy of any *real* reservations on our part. It was the same old story over again, and the same old argument. Among the Republicans, Austin was ready to go even farther than Hull asked . . .

I maintained my original position and was backed up by La Follette. This time I went farther with my argument. I pointed out that Forrest Davis has written two articles in the Saturday Evening Post (which Taft subsequently told me had been approved and initialed by the President) followed by another Post article by Demaree Bess in which the *truth* has presumably been disclosed about what happened at Teheran. I said there is no escaping the import of these articles; namely, that Russia and Britain virtually agreed upon what they are to get out of the post-war world and that Roosevelt, by his silence, acquiesced. In other words, the post-war pattern is *already* in sight (the new status quo which the new League will be presumed to guarantee) but that not one word of it has been officially communicated to the American people or to our Committee. I argued that our committee, despite its dignity, is at too low a level of information to justify us in signing *anything* unless we are willing to be stupid. . . . The Post articles to which I refer describe what is to be virtually a three-power alliance (with China added as a pleasant gesture) to run the world; and that is *exactly* what the Hull prospectus envisions. I am unable to underwrite any such plan on the basis of the purely superficial information we have received. Furthermore, I confess that I cannot escape the feeling that the *persistence* with which we are being pursued to sign what could virtually be a blank check has its definite *political* implications in connection with the approaching campaign (although I hasten to absolve Hull of *any* ulterior motives). Perhaps the Hull plan is the *only* workable plan — in view of the tremendous power which Russia (with our aid) has accumulated. But this is no time for Senators (particularly Republican Senators) to "sign up" *in the dark.*

The meeting wound up as did all the others. There was no agreement. Chairman Connally then decided that we should all see Hull next Monday morning. So that is the *next* scene in the drama. Suffice it to say, at this point, that if the Post articles are right, and if Hull's plan is fitted into this pattern, all the ideology of the "Atlantic Charter" is *already* "out the window." Russia and Britain are to *get theirs* — and *we* are to help police the bargain.

Up to this point the secret meetings of the Committee of Eight with Hull had failed to achieve any definite agreement on the nature of the future world organization, but the discussions were an important milestone along the road to United States participation in maintenance of international peace and security. Probably never before had there been comparable advance discussion between the State Department and Congressional leaders in regard to a major international agreement; and probably never had so many viewpoints been canvassed in advance as a safeguard against a later Senate refusal to implement a major step in United States foreign policy. As Vandenberg was to point out at the final meeting, everybody was agreed that Hull should go ahead with negotiations at once and see what he could achieve with the other Allied Powers. The final meeting was interesting, too, because it brought to a head the question of whether the President had made secret commitments at Teheran. In his memoirs, Hull wrote that when he was asked whether any secret agreements existed and whether reports were true that regional European federations had been agreed to by the President, Churchill, and Stalin, he replied that he knew of no such agreements. Vandenberg recorded the same meeting in his diary in greater detail.

May 29, 1944

We wound up our negotiations this morning with Secretary Hull over what he calls "the first phase" of our new international adventure. All the Committee were present except Senator Barkley (who has taken his desperately ailing wife home to Kentucky). Hull had the Post article by Bess on his desk when we entered. Evidently he knew what was coming. Hull immediately addressed his initial questions to me, and I frankly stated that I thought the Post series (all of which post-dated my original letter to Hull) put added emphasis upon the point that the "kind of a peace" (evidently pre-committed by the President at a higher level than *our* conversations occupied) can *not* be disassociated from the "kind of international obligations" we are to assume in underwriting the peace. Hull immediately launched into a long discussion of the Bess comments and a long dissertation on the proposition that we cannot stop in the midst of war to quarrel with Russia regarding peace terms, and, most certainly, that we cannot serve any ultimatums on Russia which would drive her into Hitler's arms. I interrupted him to say that he seemed to misunderstand my view-point; that I was quarreling with *nothing* that had been done (so far as my *knowledge* goes); that I agreed we must not disunite the war effort by premature efforts to unite the peace effort; and that I was simply asserting that this discussion in The Post of what really happened at Teheran (concerning which we have *no official information*) simply emphasizes, as a matter of candor and honesty, that the members of our Committee can make no commitments on his *League* plans until we *know* what has happened — and what is to happen — at higher levels regarding the *Peace* plans (which the League must ultimately underwrite). Hull said: "If we postpone planning our League until after we get a Peace, everything will blow up." I said "You totally misunderstand me, Mr. Secretary: *I want you to go ahead with your League conversations at once and see what you can do;* but, with great respect, I do not think you have any right to expect this Senate Committee either to endorse your plans in advance or to agree that your League shall bind us regardless of whether the Peace satisfies the American conscience or not."

La Follette then made his similar position clear, saying that it would be a misfortune to the post-war planning if we now signed a *general* letter which *could* be construed as carrying our endorsement of his scheme and his evident purpose to complete his League and establish it *ahead* of any definitive peace. Hull kept reiterating that of course, the final peace would have to be satisfactory. But he continued to resist any present statement on the subject.

White finally made a definite statement that he thought it was too much to expect a Senate letter from this group; that the Secretary might better rely upon the Senate's vote of 85 to 5 for the Connally Resolution which, he said, was infinitely stronger than any letter thus far proposed.

Austin had made this latter observation at our last meeting. He now proposed a "compromise"; namely, that the new League should be set up and ratified at once, contingent upon re-ratification after the peace.

George said he thought the most we could do would be to express our agreement that the Secretary should "go ahead" with his foreign contacts.

Then Gillette (who particularly dislikes the four-power-alliance contained in Hull's plan for a League and also, to all intents and purposes, sketched as the presidential purpose in the Post articles) took over. Based on the Post articles, he bluntly asked this question: "Did we make any political commitments at Teheran beyond those of which we have been told?" The Secretary made a long reply, circumscribed at half a dozen points by the limitation "so far as I know," and responded in the negative.

As the time approached for us to leave (to get to the Senate session at noon) Hull finally said that it was clear we would have to give up the idea of a letter, and as we were leaving, he read us a brief press release which *he* would make on his own responsibility. It was *probably* all right. But if improperly interpreted, some of us said we would have to reserve the right to issue statements of our own.

And thus "the first phase" as Hull puts it, came to an end. Connally turned to La Follette and me and said — "Well, the tail wags the dog." I want to make this clear on the record. We have *not* opposed post-war collaboration; we have earnestly approved it. We have *not* sought to postpone the Administration's desire to explore the subject with our Allies at once; we have urged it. But we *have* insisted that we cannot go farther at the moment, that there can be no Senate commitments until the full plan is perfected; and that there can be no final obligation on the part of the United States until we know whether we are to get a peace which *justifies* our obligation to sustain it.

We have all succeeded in keeping these discussions out of

the press. In *secrecy*, at least, the conferences have been a great success. No one would ever know — from Hull's general statement — what has gone on behind the scenes. Hull issued his statement at 8 o'clock tonight. It was printed largely as routine by most of the press (although given prominent attention). . . . But there is *plenty* of discussion coming before this thing is finished.

7

"At the Water's Edge"

THE MEETINGS of the Committee of Eight with Secretary Hull had been conducted so secretly that virtually no reference to them appeared in the newspapers. Even when it was announced that the discussions had been in progress they were given only passing attention in the headlines because so many important news stories were breaking at the time on both the war front and the home front. Political and military affairs were boiling briskly early in the summer of 1944. General Eisenhower was preparing to launch the Allied invasion of France. General MacArthur was maneuvering into position for a return to the Philippine Islands. And preparations were almost complete for the meeting — with considerable fanfare — of the important United Nations Monetary Conference at Bretton Woods, New Hampshire.

The Bretton Woods Conference, incidentally, was a pioneer United Nations session that Vandenberg might have attended, but didn't. Attended by delegates representing forty-four nations, it established the International Monetary Fund, set up the International Bank for Reconstruction and Development (the World Bank), and created other means to foster international financial co-operation on the premise that international trade and development are essential to the economic welfare of the world. The Senator had an opportunity to take part in his first international conference at this time, but he had his eye on the main show — the world security organization — and Senator

Charles W. Tobey eventually represented the Senate Republicans at Bretton Woods.

June 9, 1944

The Administration (speaking through Senator Barkley, majority Senate floor leader) invited me today to become a member of the American delegation at the International Monetary Conference soon to meet in Bretton Woods, New Hampshire. I was forced to decline for the following reasons:

(1). The Conference is to deal with the proposed Post-War International Stabilization Fund (and perhaps with the proposed International Bank). These are subjects within the jurisdiction of the Senate Committee on Banking and Currency — (the same in the House). This is recognized by the President in taking three of his four Congressional delegates from these Committees — Wagner, Democrat, Chairman of the Senate Banking and Currency Committee; Spence [Democrat], Chairman of the same House Committee; Wolcott, Republican, ranking minority member on the same House Committee. Therefore the logical Republican choice from the Senate was Senator Charles W. Tobey of New Hampshire. But the Administration does not want Tobey (for obvious reasons). They tried to get our second ranking Republican from the Committee (Senator John Danaher of Connecticut) but he declined. Then they switched entirely from the Banking and Currency Committee and offered me the place — saying they wanted to broaden the character of the delegation and that *I* could represent the Foreign Relations Committee, the Finance Committee, and the Post-War Economic Planning Committee (all three of which are deeply concerned with the Conference subjects). It was a clear and manifest slap at Tobey (particularly since the Conference is to assemble in his home State). As Chairman of the Republican Conference I could not lend myself to this affront.

(2). While the "American Plan" (to be presented at this Conference) has been twice sketched to some of us in Congress in general terms, none of us have any final information as to what the "American Plan" will be. We have had no part in framing it. There has been no attempt to get a meeting of minds in respect to it. Obviously, the American delegation will have no chance to deal, de novo, with the plan. It will be expected to support the plan at Bretton Woods, and to promote it among the other United Nations. I cannot possibly put myself in a position where my advance assent is thus presumed; nor can I conscientiously accept an assignment which might subsequently embarrass the Administration if I found it impossible subsequently to "go along."

(3). These post-war international fiscal relationships are a matter of great internal controversy in America. There is sharp disagreement, particularly among Republicans, over the so-called "White Plan" which Morgenthau will present. Many feel that it puts entirely too great a burden upon the U.S. Since I would be presumed to speak for my Republican colleagues in such an assignment, I would be in an utterly equivocal position.

(4). I presented all of these considerations to the Senate Republican Steering Committee this morning. The Committee completely agreed. It also agreed that if any Senate Republican was to "go along" it would have to be Tobey....

As a result of Bretton Woods and other developments that crowded the headlines at this time the work of the Committee of Eight attracted attention chiefly on the editorial pages and in the articles of special correspondents and columnists on the Washington scene. Charles G. Ross, veteran St. Louis *Post-Dispatch* correspondent who later served as President Truman's press secretary, looked into the Committee's work in considerable detail, and reported at length on "an extraordinary series of conferences" which, he felt, had upset a hundred and fifty years of American tradition dating from the Presidency of George Washington.

"More than anything else that has occurred in our diplomatic history," Ross wrote, "the recent conferences . . . approximate what Washington originally had in mind. Individual Senators, it is true, have been consulted on treaty negotiations, but there has been nothing comparable to this effort of Secretary Hull's to reach an understanding with a selected group of key men in the Senate on a peace settlement yet to be submitted and, through this understanding, to keep partisanship out of the debates on the settlement and avert such a tragic defeat as Wilson suffered. . . . There are various opinions among the eight as to how far Hull succeeded in his purpose, but apparently all are agreed that at last, in the cautious words of one of them, the Senate and the Administration are much further advanced toward an agreement than they would have been without the conference."

In retrospect, Ross's opinion that an agreement was advanced by the conference seems an understatement. Reporters at the time had only a vague knowledge of the points of conflict, but if the opposing views of Hull and Vandenberg had been brought out in debate on the Senate floor — instead of at conferences so secret that virtually no outsider was aware of them — it is not unlikely that public positions would have been so firmly established that no future compromise would have been possible.

As a result of the measure of agreement that had been reached, however, Hull was able with the advice of his Senate conferees to go ahead with negotiations for an international security organization, starting on August 1 at Dumbarton Oaks. This was basically a job for State Department experts and there was no Congressional representation on the American delegation; but Hull remarked in his memoirs that he had arranged to keep Congressional leaders advised of important developments. He also urged to the Congressional leaders that foreign policy arguments be kept out of the 1944 campaign. One threat of a partisan explosion arose when Governor Dewey issued a statement on August 16 attacking the possibility that the big nations would set up an organization that permanently established their coercive power over the small nations of the world. This concept was denied by Hull, who said he would welcome the cooperation of a representative of Dewey to keep politics out of peace during the campaign. Dewey accepted and sent John Foster Dulles, as his representative, to confer with Hull, starting August 23. The conferences served to clear up various misunderstandings. Later in an interview with the editor of this book, Dewey said he considered that only one major issue in foreign policy was involved — the use of armed force by the proposed security organization. Neither party had taken a position on this question; it could not be decided until the Charter conference was held and therefore Hull and Dulles agreed that the issue would not be debated in the campaign. An official statement on August 25 said that Hull and Dulles had agreed that the subject of future peace should be kept out of politics, but Dulles emphasized that such agreement did not "preclude full public nonpartisan discussion of the means of attaining a lasting peace."

This meeting of minds was an important signpost in the development of unity that begins, as Vandenberg liked to say, "at the water's edge." A responsible group of Republicans, as members of the opposition party, already had joined in creating a situation in Congress that made possible a nonpartisan approach to foreign policy. Then Dewey, as the Republican presidential nominee, was faced with the decision whether to follow this nonpartisan approach toward the problems involved in the establishment of world peace and to abandon whatever political advantage might accrue from traditional campaign attacks on the Administration's activities in that sphere. Dewey clearly recognized the tremendous implications of the problem in relation to the future welfare of the United States and the peace of the world. He chose to keep the issue of world peace out of politics and thereby gave the breath of life to the nascent formula of a nonpartisan foreign policy in the U.S. Vandenberg later was inclined to accept this point as a landmark in bipartisan foreign policy, although he felt that the idea had predated the Hull-Dulles talks. "The origin of 'bipartisan foreign policy' is undoubtedly debatable because it has so many different facets," he wrote subsequently. "In practical operation the Dewey-Dulles-Hull arrangement in the campaign of 1944 was undoubtedly the first formal and formidable exercise of this policy. But of course it was preceded . . . by many expressions of purpose on my own part."

Dewey pointed out later in a statement to the editor of this book that the President violated the Hull-Dulles agreement by making a campaign speech in New York on October 22, in which he declared himself in favor of establishing world security machinery and of having the Congress authorize the United States participation in application of force against an aggressor without specific approval in each case. "The Council of the United Nations must have the power to act quickly . . . to keep the peace by force if necessary," Mr. Roosevelt said. "It is clear that if the world organization is to have any reality at all our representative must be endowed in advance by the people themselves, by constitutional means through their representatives in Congress, with authority to act." Then, referring to statements by the Republican leadership that foreign policy was not an issue in the campaign, the President said that "the question of the men who will formulate and carry out the foreign policy of this country is an issue in this election — very much an issue. It is an issue not in terms of partisan application but in terms of sober facts, the facts that are on the record."

There was, incidentally, a rather stubborn dispute over whether the statement on the Hull-Dulles conferences should use the word "nonpartisan" or "bipartisan." Dulles, according to Hull's memoirs, had wanted to use "bipartisan," which would recognize that the two parties were collaborating. Hull argued that the responsibility for foreign policy could not be shared by both parties, or avoided by the party in power; that the opposition party was merely agreeing not to base its opposition on partisan grounds in this instance. Dulles finally accepted "nonpartisan," a word that Vandenberg, incidentally, preferred in this respect, although in later years he often used the term "unpartisan." His viewpoint, as he sometimes remarked, was that we had bipartisan collaboration in order to achieve a nonpartisan approach to foreign policy.

The Dumbarton Oaks conference, in which the British, Russians, and Americans carved out the foundation for the United Nations, lasted until September 28. After that the British and Americans conferred with the Chinese representatives whom the Russians — still at peace with Japan — were unwilling to admit to the first phase of discussion. There was a large measure of agreement on the world organization, but several deadlocks arose, the chief one concerning the method of voting in the Security Council of the United Nations. The British and Americans argued that in general the vote of a member of the Council involved in a dispute should not be counted. The Russians insisted that it should be counted. (This did not affect an agreement that the vote of the permanent members of the Council should be unanimous on questions involving enforcement action — the veto arrangement which was generally regarded as essential to secure Congressional approval of the security organization.)

On August 22, while the Dumbarton Oaks conference was laboring over this and other issues, Vandenberg laid down in a spur-of-the-moment Senate speech "three or four fundamental points which will be my own continuous impulse in my continuing effort in connection with this great and vital adventure." He expressed the "obvious" conviction that there had to be a sound international organization to create "the mechanisms which shall exhaust the rules of reason before there shall be appeals to might; and ultimately, if all these fail, to mobilize the military cooperation which shall defend the conscience of the world." He called for permanent demilitarization of the Axis powers. But in respect to an international military force he said "there can be deeply conscientious differences of honest opinion" and added that "I am one of those who do not believe that our greatest hope for peace lies in trying to put peace in a steel strait-jacket." The greatest hope, he went on, lay in adequate mechanisms to develop reason and justice. "I doubt whether any hard and fast international contracts looking toward the automatic use of cooperative force in unforeseeable emergencies ahead will be worth any more, when the time comes, than the national consciences of the contracting parties when the hour of acid test arrives." Thus, he felt, the real problem was a just peace that the free nations would be ready and willing to defend in the future.

"I think that in the last year or two our chief difficulty," he added, "has been a lack of adequate public information about some phases of the problem . . . a lack of information particularly regarding postwar understandings at Casablanca, Quebec, Cairo and Teheran."

Three days later, the Senate Committee of Eight met again at Hull's request so that the Secretary could give them news of the Dumbarton Oaks conference. Vandenberg wrote in his diary:

August 25, 1944

Secretary of State Hull called the "Senate Committee of Eight" to the State Department this morning to tell us of what goes on at the Dumbarton Oaks Conference. He renewed his plea that we may continue to deal with this peace problem on a strictly unpartisan basis. The chief question discussed was when and how the use of co-operative force is to be authorized on behalf of the new "League." It appears that the Conference will probably recommend an immediate agreement between the four major powers as to precisely what military force each shall contribute for use when the "League" Council decides to use force. I said that I had no objections to joint staff studies of this sort so that all plans should be ready at all times for an emergency; but that I could not consent that this preparation should raise any presumption that the U.S. will not be entirely free to use its veto in the Council against the use of this joint military force (as clearly contemplated in the draft previously submitted to us by Mr. Hull). I reminded Mr. Hull that he himself had suggested at one of our earliest meetings that he would have no objections if we required our American delegate on the Council to get the consent of Congress (since, under the Constitution, only Congress can declare war) before he voted to thus put us once more into joint war. Hull said that was entirely up to us. Senator George said that he thought America would be morally bound to join in the use of force if we signed up on any present "quota basis." Senator La Follette joined me in insisting that our position must be made absolutely plain at the outset lest we later be accused of bad faith — and that this particularly applies to the Senators on this special Committee. Senator La Follette also requested the Secretary to make it plain to the public that our Committee has been given information *only* respecting the new "League" mechanism; that we have had no information regarding the nature of the peace; that he felt (as I do) that we cannot decide what "League" obligations we are willing to accept until we know the general nature of the peace (which the new "League" must enforce). He said he was afraid the public thinks the State Department is telling us *everything*. Hull agreed that the distinction should be made clear. Then, getting back to the question of the use of force, Hull said there ought to be arrangements by which the "League" would have military force available to it for immediate use in minor disturbances. I agreed that this phase of the matter deserves study; and I suggested that the State Department make a study of the Constitutional question where the power of the Commander-in-Chief to use our military force without consulting Congress ends (as in the sending of Marines to Haiti, Nicaragua, etc.) and where the exclusive power of Congress to declare war begins. I said that it might be possible to deal with these lesser crises on a regional basis; that I would have no objection, for example, to letting the President use our military forces (without coming to Congress) in the Western Hemisphere (under the implications of the "Monroe Doctrine"). But I said that I wanted to make it emphatically plain — so that I would not subsequently be accused of bad faith or of an attempt to "wreck the League" — that I would never consent that our delegate on the new "League" Council should have the power to vote us into a *major* military operation (tantamount to declaring war) without a vote of Congress as required by the Constitution. Secretary Hull said that he expects this present Conference to come to an early agreement; and that he hopes the results of its work may be submitted to a formal, "full dress" Conference of all the United Nations this fall. As I was leaving, he complimented me upon my speech in the Senate earlier in the week."

Later in the same day the Senator further recorded in his diary a reference to talks with Sir Alexander Cadogan and with Dulles.

August 25, 1944 (continued)
Last Tuesday evening I went to a small dinner (six of us) on the terrace of the British Embassy where Ambassador Halifax asked me to be as frank as I could in telling Sir Alexander Cadogan (head of the British Mission to Dumbarton Oaks) what the Republican foreign policy would be in the

event of a Republican victory next November. I stuck close to the "Mackinac Charter" in my reply.

I saw Dulles (representing Dewey) on Wednesday and we fully canvassed his meetings with Hull. We agreed that the great advantage (to us) of these conferences is that they may rob the Administration of its campaign argument that it would "break the continuity" of the peace negotiations if Roosevelt is defeated; also that the great danger is that Dewey may be handicapped in his campaign discussions of foreign policy if he becomes the recipient of too much "confidential information." I am very conscious of this handicap myself as a result of the meetings of our special Senate Committee at the State Department (although we are really told nothing of vital importance in respect to the President's peace plans and his peace commitments).

Four days later Vandenberg put his views on the use of international military forces into a formal letter to Hull, generally repeating what he had told the Secretary at the last conference.

August 29, 1944

It is my view that when our Delegate casts his affirmative vote . . . [for invoking military sanctions], it is a clear commitment on the part of the United States to promptly engage in the joint military action. Therefore it is tantamount to a Declaration of War. I believe our Constitution clearly lodges the exclusive power to declare war in the Congress. Frankly, I do not believe the American people will ever agree to lodge this power anywhere else. . . .

It may be said that it is not for the Dumbarton Oaks Conference, or its successor, to deal with our purely domestic problem as to how our Delegate shall be governed and controlled in the exercise of his "veto" upon the use of military force. That is true. But if we accept and ratify anything like the pending American proposal — and especially if we subsequently accept and ratify the contemplated supplementary agreement defining our share of a joint, international force: if we accept and ratify these Treaties without concurrent notice of our purpose to insist that only Congress can declare war, we may subsequently be accused of bad faith. . . .

There is, of course, a point short of war where our long-time practice recognizes the right of our Commander-in-Chief to use our armed forces without a Congressional Declaration of War. I do not know whether this distinction can be definitely described. I should like to see the effort made. It occurs to me, as I stated Friday, that the discrimination might possibly be made on a regional basis. In other words, we might accept North and South America (under the Monroe Doctrine) as our primary responsibility in respect to the use of military force (just as we have always done); and allow the President and his Delegate to act for us, without Congressional reference, in this primary field. But if the dispute discloses an aggressor who cannot be curbed on a regional basis — if it takes another world-wide war to deal with him I do not see how we can escape the necessity for Congressional consent. (Such a plan would involve similar regional responsibilities for other powers in other areas in the first instance.) My expectation would be, however, that if all our other contemplated "peace forces" become effective and generally accepted by world opinion, any ultimate aggressor would be so clearly criminal and so clearly outlawed that our Congress would not for an instant hesitate to join in his military subjugation. . . . I respectfully express the wish that the opinions of other Senators might be rather freely canvassed on this subject now (before it is too late) to determine what is wisest to propose in respect to this particular point.

A less restrained version of his thoughts on this subject was contained in a letter to Walter Lippmann, who had expressed a similar viewpoint in his newspaper column:

September 14, 1944

Thanks for the "piece." I hope it has *some* effect on the powers that be. I have argued this precise point at the State Department time and time again. Why jeopardize 99 percent of this great adventure in organized security by stubbornly and blindly insisting upon asking for the final one percent of totalitarian power which you do not need and which you would not dare to use in any major crisis if you had it? Why hand the President a blank check which in turn invites the American opponents of all international collaboration to prejudice this total adventure by shouting on the Middle Western hustings — "Are you willing to let the President take you into World War No. Three without regard to the Constitution and without any consultation of your Congress?" It should not require very much imagination to realize what can be done with that sort of an appeal. . . .

I am one of those who deeply believe that we can set up effective peace mechanisms which will reduce the probability of a future aggression to a minimum. . . . I further believe that no President would dare ultimately to take us into one of these subsequent major wars (if one should occur) without the clear and obvious support of the American people. Under such circumstances — as you say — it is not only "unnecessary" but it is the "height of folly" for the architects of this great peace plan to deliberately collide with these realities and thus to hazard the whole magnificent enterprise.

On September 30, after the first phase of the Dumbarton Oaks conference had been completed with several important questions still undecided, Vandenberg wrote a letter to a Michigan constituent summing up his views of the results. To say that he wrote "a letter" sadly misrepresents the Senator's industry in regard to his voluminous correspondence. Throughout his career he answered countless letters from many thousands of persons in Michigan and probably every other state in the union. Sometimes he snapped back at an intemperate critic; more often he tried to explain his own position calmly and clearly. Time after time, he punched out on his portable typewriter a long letter to some man or woman whom he had never seen and would never hear of again. They were not the ordinary politician's letters in most instances. He spent hours every week writing or dictating letters that were really little essays on subjects of national and international importance. Probably they helped clarify his own thinking on important issues, because many times the phrases that he later used in important speeches first appeared in a letter to some obscure student or some inquisitive or cantankerous critic in a distant city or town. His letter of September 30 was merely typical of his vast efforts to keep the people informed, but in this instance it brought into sharp focus his current attitude toward the projected international security organization.

September 30, 1944

The Dumbarton Oaks Conference has had to adjourn, at its present level, with only a 90 percent agreement — and that last ten percent (still in dispute) involves the dreadfully significant question whether we are building a new Peace League in which the four major powers shall be totally immune to discipline. [This was a reference to Russia's demand that any one of the Big Four powers should have the right to veto a charge of aggression against itself.] I am opposed to any such immunity. In my view it would represent a new imperialism. America and Britain are opposed. Apparently Russia favors it. We do not yet have all the official facts disclosed. I comment on the basis of what seem to be authentic news reports. . . .

I can be very definite in respect to many aspects of the [peace] problem. In the light of the horrible progress which science is making in the business of mass-murder, it is clear that another world war would wipe out civilization. I favor every possible human endeavor to prevent it so far as possible by international cooperation and through international organization. . . . It requires the creation of a World Court to which we shall agree to submit all justiciable questions. I heartily favor it. . . . It requires the creation of a new body of international law. . . . It requires, above all else, world education. . . . because our peace engagements, in the final analysis, will be no stronger than the consciences of the peoples of the earth. . . .

I am opposed to what is generally understood by the term "international police force." So I believe, are the President, Secretary Hull and most realistic students of this problem. To be adequate, an international police force would have to be larger than the regular army and navy of any other power on earth. I think it is fantastic to believe that the people would long consent to the maintenance of any such enormous concentration of power in the postwar peace; and I also think that the temptation to reach for its ultimate control could become the greatest possible threat to peace in years to come.

It is obvious that since the major responsibility of the new organization must be carried by the major powers that we must also have a major voice in the decisions that shall be made. But it would be a travesty upon a "new world order" if the smaller states were not given every possible consideration. Under the pending plan seven of them will be admitted to the new League Council. And at least two of them would always have to vote with the four major powers to make a majority. This would seem to be as equitable an arrangement as is possible.

The Senator's concern over a "just peace" was considerably relieved in November when he recorded in his diary a meeting of the Committee of Eight at the State Department, where Undersecretary Edward Stettinius presided because of Hull's illness. The Secretary was soon to resign because of illness and Stettinius was to succeed him.

November 24, 1944
> ... The Oaks agreement was explained in detail. There was nothing new in the presentation. The key question . . . remains unanswered. Can one of the major powers . . . holding permanent seats on the new League Council where a unanimous vote of these permanent members is to be the requirement; can one of these powers vote on (and thus veto) a charge of aggression against it? All but Russia say *"No."* Russia says *"Yes."* Evidently the State Department is hunting for a compromise which, I judge, will seek to get Russia to yield in respect to preliminary stages in the consideration of charges against one of the major powers, but will surrender to Russia's veto when it comes to the use of force. I made my own view very plain. I think any such surrender would be unconscionable. It would immunize all of the

major powers against military discipline. Yet the major powers are the only ones who, as aggressors, can threaten the peace of the world for many years to come. . . . This question evidently is to be settled by Roosevelt, Stalin and Churchill.

I was greatly pleased, however, by another and different development. My chief complaint . . . has been that we . . . through the League guarantee the ultimate status quo in the postwar world even though the status quo shall prove to be wholly unjust (as seems clearly threatened by a new dismemberment of Poland). I have been constantly told by students of the Agreement that these peaceable decisions would not be within the jurisdiction of the new League. I put the question squarely to Stettinius and Pasvolsky [Stettinius' aide] today. After much discussion, they finally answered (to my amazement) that if any State is aggrieved as a result of the peace decisions, and it causes friction and unrest which might lead to trouble, the new League *can* take jurisdiction.

I then made my inquiry more specific: "Suppose Poland is cut back to the Curzon Line by the ultimate peace and theoretically compensated by a slice of Prussia; and suppose this is so repugnant to Poland that serious friction and unrest and potential trouble result; can Poland take this case to the League for redress?" The answer was *"Yes."* (Of course, if this *is* so, it makes a great difference in my attitude; and under such circumstances I would welcome the earliest possible organization of the League.)

Stettinius promised to give me a written memorandum on the subject, and said he thought the State Department had been derelict in not making the point publicly plain. We will wait and see just what the written memorandum says. I am afraid there is a "catch" in it — and I could not imagine that Stalin (who seems to hold the whip hand) would agree to any such interpretation for an instant. But if this *is* true, it offers some hope to the small countries (with Poland particularly in mind) which at this writing seem destined to be the victims rather than the beneficiaries of the much bruised Atlantic Charter. (I wonder if we ever *really speak up* to

Stalin, as is our great right and our equally great responsibility?)

Prior to this conference, the 1944 presidential campaign had drawn to a close without involving the Dumbarton Oaks issues in political wrangling on the home front. But the Senator had been more than a little irritated in the final days of campaigning by the manner in which some candidates pictured the administration as the champion of a battle to keep America from returning to unequivocal isolationism. Of a speech by Helen Gahagan Douglas, he wrote that he had

> thought it was very effective so long as the public does not know the real facts. Of course, the truth of the matter is that all this talk about the "isolationists" is sheer bunk. Every measure for our own national defense for the last twelve years has passed by the practically unanimous vote of Congress — and Arthur Krock recently proved in the New York Times that Congress actually appropriated many millions more for this purpose than Roosevelt ever asked.
>
> His other proposals to "keep us out of war" were opposed by many Republicans (and Democrats) because we were perfectly sure they could not and would not "keep us out of war" — and they didn't. Therefore, he totally failed in the stated objectives of his statesmanship. This failure is now paraded as the consummate proof of his wisdom and vision! I always said during all of these debates that if our purpose was to "keep out of war" we should not do the things which would inevitably take us into war. I always said that *if* this was *our* war we ought to go in through the front door and not through the back door — and we ought to go in as swiftly and conclusively as possible. But that would not have suited Mr. Roosevelt's purposes. He had to re-elect himself in 1940 and in order to do so he *had* to say in Boston on the eve of the 1940 election, "I have said this before, but I shall say it again and again and again: your boys are not going to be sent into any foreign wars." . . .
>
> This story ought to be made plain to the American people. But the whole strategy of the Dewey campaign has been to

soft pedal questions of foreign policy so as not to renew the old cleavage between Western "isolationists" and Eastern "interventionists." I think we stand a fifty-fifty chance of winning. Thus, the fate of America for the next ten generations hangs by a slender thread.

After the re-election of Mr. Roosevelt, Vandenberg expressed in a letter to Dulles the belief that "Governor Dewey made a gallant fight of it. The war was too much for him. That's the whole story as I see it. But there is another day coming." He felt that he had gained something, too — the friendship of John Foster Dulles.

November 11, 1944
One of the most important [compensations] — from my point of view — has been the privilege of coming to know you. I feel that we are already "old friends." I looked forward to working intimately with you in the great "peace adventure." Indeed, I confess to a feeling of "loneliness" as I look ahead to the responsibilities which I still confront. I beg of you always to feel free to send me your advice and suggestions. . . . I suspect you will find me knocking at your door more than once. I really think it is little short of amazing that our views on foreign policy should have proved to be so emphatically harmonious. One of the most interesting and significant things thus demonstrated is the fact that so-called "isolationists" and so-called "internationalists" are not *necessarily* very far apart and *really* may be "brothers under the skin."

Looking back over the record and especially at the Senator's private letters and diary it is remarkable that he was still — late in 1944 — able thus to refer to himself as an isolationist or even as a "so-called 'isolationist.'" His letter to Dulles was written more or less tongue-in-cheek in this respect, but it reflected a viewpoint that was still widely held in regard to Vandenberg and one that he still entertained in a limited fashion in order to separate himself from the "One World" advocates and from the Rooseveltian approach. Actually, the Senator had moved a long way from his "insulationist" attitude of 1941; he had fully accepted in his own mind the extensive future role of the United States in international affairs and he had repeatedly said as much. Yet, because he never forgot that he spoke for American interests first and because he was a persistent and vigorous defender of Constitutional procedure, there was a definite tendency on the part of political reporters and the public generally to continue regarding him as an isolationist at heart; as a man who had merely been forced into acceptance of certain realities regarding foreign policy; as a man who really didn't like the role or believe in it. The Senator's activities as an oppositionist may have contributed something to that feeling; he may have sometimes encouraged it himself because he was not yet fully convinced that there would be a just and acceptable peace, and because he wanted an avenue for political retreat in event the President had secretly given too much ground to Stalin and Churchill.

But everything that he wrote or said in this period showed that he had long since made up his mind without any reservations about one thing: real international co-operation was the only alternative to future wars too horrible to imagine and international co-operation could succeed only if Americans stood firmly united in the world's councils. This was a conviction that Vandenberg was soon going to make unmistakably clear in a fashion so dramatic that even he was to be more than a little surprised.

8

A Speech Heard Round the World

THE BEGINNING of 1945 was a significant time for stocktaking, for washing clean the political slate and for soul-searching decisions as to the future. The Roosevelt Administration was back in power for another four years. The war was almost rushing toward a victorious conclusion for the United Nations. Secretary Hull had stepped out of office after serving longer than any other American in that high position, and Stettinius had been named to succeed him. There had been, late in December, a not-very-happy meeting of the Republican party leaders in New York.

December 21, 1944

This was our first general conference of Party leaders since the November elections. It occurred in Governor Dewey's apartment in the Roosevelt Hotel in New York City. Nothing of any great moment happened — except we agreed that we must have a far more aggressive Party organization than ever before, including a full-time Chairman of the Republican National Committee.

In the course of this discussion, the question arose whether Chairman Herbert Brownell, Jr., would be handicapped by being thought of as "Dewey's man" in connection with a come-back in 1948. Brownell said that if he took the job again it would *not* be as "Dewey's man"; that this was understood by the Governor; that it would be made entirely plain to the country. This caused Governor Dewey to make the most significant statement of the day. I do not presume to quote him literally, but this is approximately what he said.

"I have no illusions about 1948. Intervening time and events will dictate the next Republican Presidential nomination. I have my hands more than full as Governor of New York. . . . I intend to concentrate on this home job. I *honestly* did not want the nomination in 1944, and I *honestly* did everything within my power to avoid it. When it came, I did the best job I knew how. Now I am the titular leader of the Party. I want to do whatever is required of me in *that* assignment. But I intend to leave New York as seldom as possible, and to make as few national speeches as possible. I will co-operate in any way the leaders of the Party wish. But I want solely to do a *Party* job and *not* a *personal* job. As long ago as Philadelphia, in 1940, I deliberately decided that I was *not* going to be one of those unhappy men who yearned for the Presidency and whose failure to get it scarred their lives. Two such men died in New York within the past month — Al Smith and Wendell Willkie. Not for me!

"I can be totally content as a private citizen when I am through with the Governorship of New York. You need not have the slightest worry that if Brownell remains as National Chairman, as I think he should to avoid a bitter Party row over the succession, he will be engaged, directly or indirectly in promoting me for 1948. That would violate not only my orders but also my wishes."

Vandenberg, as well as Dewey, was doing some soul-searching and deciding as the old year faded out. He was making the biggest decision of his life, although at the time he wasn't entirely aware of it and he wasn't completely convinced that he was following the wisest course of action. Basically, he wanted to see an effective international security organization, but he could not escape a deep, haunting fear that the principles that the Big Three had endorsed in general terms might be sacrificed at the altar of postwar aggrandizement. He feared, too, that President Roosevelt by his silence might not prevent such sacrifices. Now at the beginning of 1945, there was soon to be another meeting of the Big Three government heads, this time at Yalta, and preparations were already under way for an Allied conference, later held at San Francisco, to organize the United Nations. What was most strongly in Vandenberg's mind was that decisions soon to be made might result in what he regarded as an unjust peace and in a demand for the United States to underwrite such a peace through the United Nations. The Senator felt not only that it was vitally important to warn the Big Three against such action, which he believed would be repudiated by America, but to force a showdown on the sincerity of London and Moscow toward the principles of justice that they had avowed in general terms in international relationships.

It seemed unlikely to him that Mr. Roosevelt was going to force such a showdown. The President's recent attitude had not been encouraging. There had been a long period of administration silence on postwar problems. Now Vandenberg felt the necessity for what "really amounted to a challenge to the . . . President on the eve of his departure for Yalta." This description of his intent was given by the Senator in 1946 in material he prepared for his campaign in Michigan; but although written for publicity purposes, it seems a reasonable statement of his aims.

There were probably other purposes in his mind as well. Considering the fact that he was an opposition senator, Vandenberg had taken a prominent part during 1944 in helping to shape American policy toward formation of an international security organization. Yet, actually, he had been only chipping at the edges of the problem. The primary responsibility, of course, rested with the President and there was still suspicion between Mr. Roosevelt and the Senator from Michigan. In addition, the Republican party, particularly in the Senate, was widely split on details of foreign policy despite the unanimous agreement that had been reached in framing the broad principles behind the Mackinac Charter.

The Republican leadership in the Senate "is virtually powerless on postwar foreign policy," the *United States News* pointed out as the year 1945 began. "Individual Republican views are too varied and too deeply held. These views range from the unchangeable isolationism of Senator Hiram Johnson of California, to the fervent Internationalism of Senator Joseph H.

Ball of Minnesota. Among the leaders, Senator Vandenberg, a prewar isolationist, now urges extensive collaboration among the nations. Senator Taft is believed heading in the same direction but he stops short of the Vandenberg position at present."

In addition, two new Republicans on the Foreign Relations Committee were Alexander Wiley of Wisconsin, "whose isolationism has been little moderated," and Styles Bridges of New Hampshire, "who places several conditions upon his internationalism." The article concluded that the Republican leadership would have "little effect in the foreign field." This article represented the generally held viewpoint of political reporters at the time and was, naturally, of no comfort to Vandenberg, who definitely desired to have an effect in the field that he believed would decide the destiny of America for years to come. The Senator's reaction to this situation was rather typical; he pulled out his portable typewriter and began writing a speech to be delivered in the Senate. It is interesting but disappointing that he made no comment at all on the preparation of this speech in either his letters or his diary at the time. The only significant letter that he wrote during the preparatory period concerned political affairs in the United States and it reflected his thinking on the subject of the speech only in references to communism at home.

January 2, 1945

I agree that the country desperately needs a major political party which stands at the "right" (instead of the "left" of center). I agree that this is the only hope for the Republican party and — what is infinitely more important — the only hope for the country. On the other hand, I think we have got to be far more realistic about the "social revolution" which has swept the entire world (and to which we cannot expect to be immune) than we were when last we were in power. In my opinion, the postwar world all around the globe is going to trend irresistibly toward social liberalism (if it does not go much farther and actually swing to a Communistic base).

Certainly I do not propose to surrender to any such trends in the United States (although we shall be under greater pressures in this direction than ever before). But I am very certain that the capitalistic system will *not* survive (nor will the Republican Party) unless we meet "social liberalism" with forward-looking "capitalistic liberalism."

Although he wrote nothing at the time bearing directly on the subject, there was no question in the minds of those close to the Senator and especially of members of his family that he was working on an important speech. He worried about it. He rewrote sections of it many times. He expressed concern as to whether he was saying exactly the right thing, whether he was following a wise course, whether he was acting at the proper time. There was no cockiness or overconfidence in him as he bent over his typewriter and puffed on his long cigar until late at night; there was only soul-searching and a touch of uncertainty — and a conviction that there were great dangers ahead for America and the still unborn United Nations. He had once said that he did not want any responsibility for America's entry into World War II, but now he was determined to do everything within his power toward a just peace and an effective international security organization. He wrote long afterward:

July 8, 1948
My advance feelings [were] that the speech *had* to be made in order to clarify and strongly assert the position of America from the standpoint of those of us who had been so-called "isolationists" prior to Pearl Harbor. I further had the deep conviction that it was time to anticipate what ultimately became the "Moscow menace" and to lay down a formula which would make postwar Soviet expansionism as illogical as it would be unnecessary (except for ulterior purposes).

It seemed to me that it had to be a Republican voice from the then minority benches which had to undertake this assignment. This, in turn, narrowed the responsibility to a point where I felt it was a personal challenge to me. Therefore, I proceeded to the event as best I could. . . . I wrote the speech on my own typewriter — as is the case with all of my major efforts (I suppose this is a "throwback" to my old editorial days), I should think I rewrote it at least a dozen times from start to finish before I was satisfied with its final form. In the course of these redrafts I consulted two or three of my intimate newspaper friends, among the Washington correspondents who had particularly intimate experience with foreign affairs. This was chiefly for the purpose of checking facts rather than objectives. In other words, I was anxious to be on firm ground for my "take off" into uncharted territory.

The last sentence of the above letter was probably more hindsight than foresight. When the Senator arose in the Senate on January 10, 1945, he fully realized that he was going to make an important proposal, but he had little idea, as he admitted later, that he was "taking off" into a new era, or perhaps more correctly that this speech would be regarded as the point at which he definitely abandoned forever the last vestige of the isolationism with which the public still associated him.

The January 10th speech was the most memorable in Vandenberg's career, partly because it was generally (although mistakenly) regarded as a great turning point in the Senator's attitude and partly because it was dramatic in content and delivered in a dramatic way at a dramatic time in the nation's history. It demonstrated the remarkable Vandenberg sense of timing. It illustrated his skill as a phrase maker and was freer of clichés and purple passages than many of his earlier efforts. It was the product of intensive labor, as were almost all of his speeches. As a speech maker, Vandenberg was often compared to Henry Clay or Daniel Webster, although as a matter of fact his actual delivery lacked the finesse and the subtle variations of a great orator. He was inclined to pour on the facts, to pound hard at a logical argument and, occasionally, to lean heavily on a strong voice for emphasis. But as a speech writer, he had few rivals in the history of the Senate. He enjoyed the writing, the marshaling of statistics, the coining of catchwords and the careful building of an argument to its logical climax. In speech-writing periods he gave his little typewriter a terrific beating for hours on end. One speech that he prepared — but never delivered — against the Roosevelt Supreme Court packing plan ran to 80,000 words. No speech in his career, however, was prepared with greater care than this one:

January 10, 1945

Mr. President, there are critical moments in the life of every nation which call for the straightest, the plainest and the most courageous thinking of which we are capable. We confront such a moment now. It is not only desperately important to America, it is important to the world. It is important not only to this generation which lives in blood. It is important to future generations if they shall live in peace.

No man in his right sense will be dogmatic in his viewpoint at such an hour. A global conflict which uproots the earth is not calculated to submit itself to the dominion of any finite mind. . . . Each of us can only speak according to his little lights — and pray for a composite wisdom that shall lead us to high, safe ground. It is only in this spirit that I speak today. . . .

The United Nations, in even greater unity of military action than heretofore, must never, for any cause, permit this military unity to fall apart. . . . We not only have two wars to win, we also have yet to achieve such a peace as will justify this appalling cost. Here again an even more difficult unity is indispensable. Otherwise, we shall look back upon a futile, sanguinary shambles and — God save the mark — we shall be able to look forward only to the curse of World War III. . . .

[The Senator then referred, in sympathetic fashion, to the annual message which President Roosevelt had sent to Congress and which spoke of the danger of "differences among the victors" and warned that no nation can assume "it has a monopoly of wisdom or virtue." But trends toward disunity, Vandenberg said, cannot be reversed by "our silence upon the issues that are clearly involved." He went on:]

I hesitate, even now, to say these things, Mr. President, because a great American illusion seems to have been built up — wittingly or otherwise — that we in the United States dare not publicly discuss these subjects lest we contribute to international dissension. . . . But I frankly confess that I do not know why we must be the only silent partner in this grand alliance. There seems to be no fear of disunity, no hesitation in Moscow, when Moscow wants to assert unilateral war and peace aims which collide with ours.

There seems to be no fear of disunity, no hesitation in London, when Mr. Churchill proceeds upon his unilateral way to make decisions often repugnant to our ideas and our ideals. Perhaps our allies will plead that their actions are not unilateral; that our President, as Bevin said, has initialed this or that at one of the famous Big Three conferences; that our President, as Churchill said, has been kept constantly "aware of everything that has happened"; in other words, that by our silence we have acquiesced. But that hypothesis would only make a bad matter worse. It would be the final indictment of our silence — the final obituary for open covenants. We, of course, accept no conception that our contribution to unity must be silence, while others say and do what they please, and that our only role in this global tragedy is to fight and die and pay, and that unity for us shall only be the unity which Jonah enjoyed when he was swallowed by the whale.

I hasten to say that any such intolerable conception would be angrily repudiated by every American — from the President down to the last citizen among us. It has not been and is not true. Yet it cannot be denied that our Government has not spoken out — to our own people or to our allies — in any such specific fashion as have the others. It cannot be denied, as a result, that too often a grave melancholy settles upon some sectors of our people. It cannot be denied that citizens, in increasing numbers, are crying: "What are we fighting for?" It cannot be denied that our silence — at least our public and official silence — has multiplied confusion at home and abroad. It cannot be denied that this confusion threatens our unity — yes, Mr. President, and already hangs like a cloud over Dumbarton Oaks. So I venture to repeat, with all the earnestness at my command, that a new rule of honest candor in Washington, as a substitute for mystifying silence or for classical generalities — honest candor on the high plane of great ideals — is the greatest contribution we can make to the realities of unity at this moment when enlightened civilization is our common stake. . . .

Vandenberg's long-standing concern lest the postwar territorial settlements would violate the rights of small nations, such as Poland, or fail to recognize the urge of such nations as India toward self-government was reflected in his comment on a remark made earlier by Mr. Roosevelt at a press conference, which left the impression that the President was prepared to dismiss "the Atlantic Charter as a mere collection of fragmentary notes." Later, Mr. Roosevelt changed this impression by "correctly and bravely" saying in his message to Congress that the United States would not hesitate "to use our influence — and use it now — to secure so far as is humanly possible the fulfillment of these principles."

"That is the indispensable point," Vandenberg continued. "These basic pledges cannot now be dismissed as a mere nautical nimbus. They march with our armies. They sail with our fleets. They fly with our eagles. They sleep with our martyred dead. The first requisite of honest candor, Mr. President, I respectfully suggest, is to re-light this torch."

Then he said that the United States must appeal to its allies to choose between the alternatives of living in the postwar world on the basis of exclusive individual action in which each tries to look out for himself or on the basis of joint action in which "we undertake to look out for each other. . . . The first way is the old way which has twice taken us to Europe's interminable battlefields within a quarter of a century. The second way is the new way in which we must make our choice. I think we must make it wholly plain to our major allies that they, too, must make their choice."

The Senator then came to what was later called his "confession," although it is unlikely that he thought of it as a "confession" at the time. It was a statement of his personal viewpoint that had developed slowly but positively since Pearl Harbor and had frequently been reflected in his public and private declarations. It was, too, a summary, a kind of definitive explanation of his transition and, as such, it caught in a few paragraphs the whole story of what had happened to America in her relationship with the rest of the world. The Senator was simply adding up the sum of changing circumstances in a changing world. It was not a task that he approached happily, any more than the people of America welcomed the responsibilities of world leadership that were being thrust upon them. But once he had set himself to the task he did it with characteristic vigor. His timing was exactly right to catch the mood of the people.

His words coalesced the doubts and uncertainties and perplexities of America and put into sharply dramatic phrases the answer toward which the people had been fumbling fearfully — but hopefully, too. Everywhere, there was an urgent if almost unrecognized desire to believe, to be reassured that the future was not necessarily a hopelessly sinister mirage of political and military machinations or, alternatively, a hazardous experiment in starry-eyed idealism. With his penchant for practical action to meet an immediate problem, Vandenberg added up the problems and got an answer.

> I hasten to make my own personal viewpoint clear. I have always been frankly one of those who has believed in our own self-reliance. I still believe that we can never again — regardless of collaborations — allow our national defense to deteriorate to anything like a point of impotence. But I do not believe that any nation hereafter can immunize itself by its own exclusive action. Since Pearl Harbor, World War II has put the gory science of mass murder into new and sinister perspective. Our oceans have ceased to be moats which automatically protect our ramparts. Flesh and blood now compete unequally with winged steel. War has become an all-consuming juggernaut. If World War III ever unhappily arrives, it will open new laboratories of death too horrible to contemplate. I propose to do everything within my power to keep those laboratories closed for keeps.
>
> I want maximum American cooperation, consistent with legitimate American self-interest, with constitutional process and with collateral events which warrant it, to make the basic idea of Dumbarton Oaks succeed. I want a new dignity and a new authority for international law.
>
> I think American self-interest requires it. But, Mr. President, this also requires whole-hearted reciprocity. In honest candor, I think we should tell other nations that this glorious thing we contemplate is not and cannot be one-sided. I think we must say again that unshared idealism is a menace which we could not undertake to underwrite in the post-war world.

What was really in Vandenberg's mind was the future position of Russia. Was Stalin in earnest about setting up a workable international security organization with justice for all, or was he out to grab whatever he could for Russia and try to use the security organization to protect the spoils? The attitude of Moscow toward the small states of Eastern Europe had raised grave concern about the peace settlement and the basic importance of Vandenberg's speech was directed toward a showdown on this issue; an attempt to establish whether the United Nations were acting in good faith. His idea of how to get at the truth was, as usual, to propose *action*.

> The real question always becomes just this: Where does real self-interest lie? Here, Mr. President, we reach the core of the immediate problem. Without remotely wanting to be invidious, I use one of many available examples. I would not presume, even under these circumstances, to use it except that it ultimately involves us. Russia's unilateral plan appears to contemplate the engulfment, directly or indirectly, of a surrounding circle of buffer states, contrary to our conception of what we thought we were fighting for in respect to the rights of small nations and a just peace. Russia's announced reason is her insistent purpose never again to be at the mercy of another German tyranny. That is a perfectly understandable reason. The alternative is collective security. . . . Which is better in the long view, from a purely selfish Russian standpoint: To forcefully surround herself with a cordon of unwillingly controlled or partitioned states, thus affronting the opinions of mankind . . . or to win the priceless asset of world confidence in her by embracing the alternative, namely, full and whole-hearted cooperation with and reliance on a vital international organization. . . . Well — at that point, Russia, or others like her, in equally honest candor has a perfect right to reply, "Where is there any such alternative reliance until we know what the United States will do?" . . .
>
> I propose that we meet this problem conclusively and at once. There is no reason to wait. America has this same self-interest in permanently, conclusively and effectively disarming Germany and Japan. . . . It should be handled as this

present war is handled. There should be no more need to refer any such action [use of force to keep the Axis disarmed] back to Congress than that Congress should expect to pass upon battle plans today. The Commander-in-Chief should have instant power to act and he should act. I know of no reason why a hard-and-fast treaty between the major allies should not be signed today to achieve this dependable end. We need not await the determination of our other postwar relationships. This problem — this menace — stands apart by itself . . . I respectfully urge that we meet this problem now.

From it stem many of today's confusions, doubts and frustrations. I think we should immediately put it behind us by conclusive action. Having done so . . . we shall be able, at least, to judge accurately whether we have found and cured the real hazard to our relationships. We shall have closed ranks. We shall have returned infinitely closer to basic unity.

Then, in honest candor, Mr. President, I think we have the duty and the right to demand that whatever immediate unilateral decisions have to be made in consequence of military need . . . shall all be temporary and subject to final revision in the objective light of the postwar world and the postwar peace league as they shall ultimately develop. . . . Indeed, I . . . would write it in the bond. If Dumbarton Oaks should specifically authorize the ultimate international organization to review protested injustices in the peace itself, it would at least partially nullify the argument that we are to be asked to put a blank-check warrant behind a future status quo which is unknown to us and which we might be unwilling to defend.

We are standing by our guns with epic heroism. I know of no reason why we should not stand by our ideals. If they vanish under ultimate pressures, we shall at least have kept the record straight; we shall have kept faith with our soldier sons; and we then shall clearly be free agents, unhampered by tragic misunderstandings, in determining our own course when Berlin and Tokyo are in Allied hands.

Let me put it this way for myself: I am prepared, by effective international cooperation, to do our full part in charting happier and safer tomorrows. But I am not prepared to guarantee permanently the spoils of an unjust peace. It will not work. . . .

Mr. President, I conclude as I began. We must win these wars with maximum speed and minimum loss. Therefore we must have maximum Allied cooperation and minimum Allied frictions. We have fabulously earned the right to be heard in respect to the basis of this unity. We need the earliest possible clarification of our relations with our brave allies. We need this clarification not only for the sake of total Allied cooperation in the winning of the war but also in behalf of a truly compensatory peace. We cannot drift to victory. We must have maximum united effort on all fronts. We must have maximum united effort in our councils. And we must deserve the continued united effort of our own people.

I realize, Mr. President, in such momentous problems how much easier it is to be critical than to be correct. I do not wish to meddle. I want only to help. I want to do my duty. It is in this spirit that I ask for honest candor in respect to our ideals, our dedications, and our commitments, as the greatest contribution which government can now make to the only kind of realistic unity which will most swiftly bring our victorious sons back home, and which will best validate our aspirations, our sacrifices, and our dreams.

The speech was an immediate sensation. The Vandenberg proposal for an Allied treaty guaranteeing future disarmament of the Axis Powers — a proposal that was made to Russia by the State Department, after President Roosevelt's death, and rejected — attracted the first newspaper headlines, but it was the over-all impact of the Senator's declaration that made the speech a turning point, that brought him a sudden and tremendous surge of popular support and led to the emergence of a new and unique figure in the history of American foreign policy. "The important thing about that speech . . . was not that Vandenberg made it but that the American people responded to it with such enthusiasm," James B. Reston of the *New York Times* wrote later in the May 24, 1948, issue of *Life* magazine. "He did not change the American people. He made a tentative public confession in the speech of January 10, 1945, and the American people, by their response to his speech, changed him.

What he did was merely to express and symbolize their change and then stick single-mindedly to the *action* necessary to implement their will. Since then, however, his record is unprecedented."

The idea that Vandenberg was changed by the response to his speech may be questioned on the grounds that the Senator had repeatedly expressed in private correspondence and, to a certain extent, in public statements during 1944 the same basic ideas. "The whole world changed — the factors of time and space changed — with World War II, and I changed with them," he wrote later. But it is a commentary on the public attitude toward him — up until January 10, 1945 — that an able and experienced correspondent who was well acquainted with Vandenberg should regard the speech as a more or less tentative about-face.

Yet Reston's comment could not be questioned as far as the historical consequences of the speech were concerned. The Senator *had* kept open an avenue of political retreat in event of an "unjust" peace and, certainly, it was the unexpected public enthusiasm for his speech that irrevocably confirmed his new course. Still more important, it was this public support that in one great surge gave him the political stature and the strength necessary to carry on his unique role in the following critical years when he not only had to keep in line the obstructionists and die-hard isolationists in his own party but to command the attention of the Administration in framing American foreign policy.

"I confess that I was completely surprised by the nation-wide attention which the speech precipitated," the Senator wrote three years later on July 8, 1948. There was some reason to believe that President Roosevelt was surprised, too. The White House's first reaction was a polite "welcome" to the speech on the following day, but the President was silent on the treaty proposal and, *after* seeing Mr. Roosevelt, Senator Connally expressed the hope that the Senate would not get into any general discussions that would disturb the delicate international situation on the eve of the Yalta conference. This remark prompted the Washington *Post* to comment, while highly praising the address, that the Administration seemed to be "frightened rather than encouraged" by Vandenberg's speech, but if that was true the public approval quickly changed Mr. Roosevelt's mind and in his July 8, 1948, letter Vandenberg was able to add: "President Roosevelt left for his ill-starred conference at Yalta a few days [after the speech]. On the morning of his take-off, he hastily sent to my office for fifty reprints of the speech. I must say this encouraged me to believe that I had struck a helpful note."

The fact that Vandenberg was a leading member of the former non-interventionist bloc in Congress — a bloc that would probably hold the balance of power in any question of ratification of postwar settlements — was emphasized by most newspaper comment. The *New York Times* said: "Whatever reservations or limitations are stated or implied in this proposal, the plan must be described as a real effort to cut through generalities and go to the heart of present problems. . . . Mr. Vandenberg has made an important contribution to the discussion that began at Dumbarton Oaks and now waits upon a further meeting of the heads of government of the chief Allied Powers."

"He was," said the Washington *Star*, "in the role of spokesman for those millions of Americans who want to cooperate fully with our Allies, both in winning the war and writing the peace, but whose minds are beginning to be assailed by doubts and apprehensions. . . . This proposal from Senator Vandenberg, who undoubtedly reflects the views of many of his Republican colleagues, should strengthen the President's hand in the forthcoming meeting with Prime Minister Churchill and Marshal Stalin."

A telegram from Roy W. Howard, head of the Scripps-Howard newspapers, on January 11, said: "In my opinion your speech and your program presented yesterday not only marked a new high in your already admirable career but it was the finest piece of constructive statesmanship offered this country in recent years. We will do our best to back up your program. My admiration and affection are yours."

The New York *Herald Tribune* probably hit most accurately on Vandenberg's basic thinking when it described the speech as "an indication that honest minds, to whatever party they may belong and from however widely separated positions they may begin, can, if they are willing to face the facts, come together upon a firm and common ground. . . . It might be argued that a main reason why the President has confined himself to vague and generalized utterances has been the fear of just that isolationist sentiment to which the Senator has formerly lent aid and comfort; if so, that is water over the dam. . . . The Senator has not found all the answers or achieved a final formula any more than anyone else. That is immaterial. He has made a great contribution toward the forging of a common and non-partisan policy in foreign affairs. He has perceived some, at least, of the fundamental verities and spoken for them powerfully. With this speech, we are, in fact, beginning to 'get somewhere.' "

Political columnist David Lawrence believed that the Senator had "swept away completely any idea that the Republican party in the United States Senate is to obstruct in any way the movement for the establishment of an international organization to assure world peace." He recalled that both Woodrow Wilson and Georges Clemenceau after the first World War proposed a three-power treaty to prevent rebirth of German militarism and concluded that if they had "lived to read the great speech of Senator Vandenberg, nearly 26 years after their historic discussion in Paris, they would have considered themselves vindicated."

"It cannot be said of many speakers that they affect the course of events," observed Walter Lippmann. "But this may well be said of Senator Vandenberg's speech if the President and his lieutenants will recognize promptly and firmly its importance. For this speech can, if it is understood and appreciated, break the vicious circle in which American foreign policy has been revolving so ineffectually. This is high praise but not in the least, I venture to think, an exaggeration. . . . The immense importance of Senator Vandenberg's proposal is that it would end the policy of postponement and thus restore American influence in the settlement of Europe. He has seen what so many of our anguished idealists have not seen, that what our allies are seeking is first of all security against the revival of German militarism. . . . We may hope that Senator Connally will recognize it, and that the State Department will now do what it has thus far hesitated to do — that it will affirm positively its belief that in order to make Dumbarton Oaks work, the arrangements for policing Germany and Japan which are contemplated in Chapter XII of this plan, must be firmly executed."

Columnist Thomas L. Stokes commented that "the strong backing [Vandenberg] has given the President in the major objectives of foreign policy . . . can hardly be exaggerated," and the Detroit *Free Press* remarked that "he has shown America and the world that we cannot dally along the path of destiny. And it can strengthen mightily the President . . . if he, too, can rise above partisan politics." The Nashville *Tennessean* said, "Vandenberg deserves unreserved commendation." The Kalamazoo (Michigan) *Gazette* believed that the speech revealed "qualities of statesmanship, powers of convincing expression and a breadth of understanding which can be of tremendous help in solving the many complex problems confronting America and the world." The Cleveland *Plain Dealer* described it as "a shot heard around the world" and the Providence (Rhode Island) *Journal* said it brought Vandenberg "closer to a niche in history than he has ever been before." The Boston *Herald* said the speech probably was "the most important to come from the Senate Chamber in the last 80 years," and added that it was "sheer nonsense" for the White House to try — as reports hinted — to give the proposals "a brush-off."

The Omaha *World-Herald* felt that "no recent utterance by any public man . . . has been nearly so helpful or been received with such glad and hopeful acclaim by tortured peoples defending themselves against the scourge of brutalitarian aggressive war."

It was not true, of course, that sentiment was unanimous behind Vandenberg's proposals. "There will," said the Chicago *Tribune*, "be general agreement with some of the things Senator Vandenberg said, particularly his denunciation of those who assert that any American who criticizes the power politics of our allies is impairing allied unity. . . . But in his three point plan for unity, Senator Vandenberg must be regarded as speaking for himself, not for his party. He is abandoning the principles of Americanism for which the party must stand if it hopes to regain the confidence of the voters. . . . [He] is apparently willing to make immediate concessions to Britain and Russia, pledging us to maintain a well-nigh permanent police force in Germany, in exchange for vague concessions. . . . We still would undertake the obligations and the Poles, Greeks and other European people would reap the benefits. That is not a program likely to appeal to American parents, nor to their sons fighting now in Europe, and it will be folly for the Republican party, or Republicans in Congress, to embrace it. If the experience of the last 12 years has taught the Republicans anything, which at times seems doubtful, it should have taught the party's leaders that they can't get anywhere by aping Mr. Roosevelt and seconding his policies. . . .

"The Republican party can have but one foreign policy so long as Mr. Roosevelt remains in office. That is that since he has demonstrated that he cannot be trusted to protect American interests Congress dare not give him advance grants of power that he is sure to misuse. It looks more and more like the party is breaking up over failure to recognize this simple fact. Unless its leaders see their error and correct it, the party will cease to perform any useful function and will die of lack of support. America will then have to look to a third party, as yet unorganized, but toward which there are stirrings throughout the nation."

The New York *Daily News* and the Washington *Times-Herald* — closely associated with the Chicago *Tribune* — echoed the third-party idea. In an editorial entitled "Third Party Coming Up," the *Times-Herald* argued along lines similar to the *Tribune* viewpoint but with greater emphasis on the need for a third party. "We think Vandenberg's speech foreshadows the breakup of the Republican party, and the coming of a new party. Why have two major political parties professing the same foreign policy? What we need are the internationalist Democratic party that we already have and a nationalist party which will stand for American interests. . . . For our part, the boys [American soldiers] can't come home and form a nationalist party too soon. We hope that after the war they will speedily get themselves organized, and will take over political control of this country . . . because the present generation of Democratic and Republican leaders have made an ungodly mess both of our foreign policy (if any) and of most of our home economy."

At the other extreme, the Communist *Daily Worker* in New York attacked the speech as showing that "Vandenberg is afraid . . . that the rising new forces of democracy are beyond the control of American reactionaries. . . . Vandenberg has been forced to shift the ground of his attack . . . and it is his deception which has taken in many administration supporters. . . . As Earl Browder pointed out at Madison Square Garden Monday night, Senator Vandenberg has refurbished the old idea of 'carrot and club diplomacy' toward the Soviet Union. He offers the carrot of a military alliance; behind his back is the club of wholesale revision of all European settlements after the war is over."

Later (on March 8) the Moscow journal, *War and Working Class*, said that Vandenberg's "schemes cannot be regarded as expressions of the present foreign policy of the U.S.A., for if American policy were forged along the lines he advocates it could not have found a common language with the other United Nations." The editorial referred not only to the January 10th speech but to other remarks Vandenberg had made in Detroit where he was naturally keenly aware of the Polish problem. "Vandenberg's philosophy is the philosophy of sincere imperialists. . . . [He] already seems to see the whole world on its knees before the entrance to the temple of the almighty dollar. This isolationist of yesterday cannot understand clearly the complexity of international problems, but farsighted people realize that the uncontestable economic might of the U.S.A. cannot be the sole guarantee of peace and security."

Vandenberg himself did not record much about the January 10th speech at the time, except to express his surprise at the reaction to it. "I still don't understand what clicked so terrifically," he wrote his wife late in January. And a few days later he mentioned in another letter to her that the mail he was receiving was "cruel in size." He added, "I wish somebody would psychoanalyze that speech. I can't understand why it has been such an appalling sensation."

Later, when he was at the Paris Council of Foreign Ministers in 1948, he prepared some material for use in his *in absentia* campaign for re-election in Michigan, writing in the third person about himself, probably with political considerations uppermost in his mind. At one point he commented on the January 10th speech:

> Far from resenting the [January 10th] speech, President Roosevelt welcomed it . . . but the Administration evidently

never pressed the program until one year later (after Mr. Roosevelt's death) when Secretary Byrnes (unsuccessfully) made it the central theme of his program. Commenting upon this latter event, former Under-secretary of State Sumner Welles wrote, "At long last — 12 months after it was first proposed by Senator Vandenberg — this plan now gets belated consideration; had it been brought forward at Potsdam [the conference between Truman, Stalin, and Attlee] the recent course of events in Europe might well have been prevented."

The electric effect of the speech was instantaneous. It was printed in full by all the metropolitan press. The Office of War Information promptly beamed it by radio to all our fighting forces. . . . The Gallup Poll reported American public sentiment to be overwhelmingly in line with the Michigan Senator's ideas. . . . It is interesting to note . . . that the Communists immediately took alarm when they saw the nation rising almost as one man behind Senator Vandenberg's leadership. . . . The United Press interpreted this [the Communist] assault as arising from the belief that "it is his [Vandenberg's] purpose to prevent the Communization of Europe."

In all fairness, it should be remembered that in the above comments the Senator was writing a suggestion for the friends and associates who were conducting an election campaign during his absence from Michigan on business of vital interest to all of the country, and that he would not have used even these comparatively immodest phrases if he had been writing in the first person.

One other comment was contained in a letter written that year:

July 8, 1948

I have no evidence whatever that there was any serious followup at Yalta in respect to my basic theme that a four-power military pact (in which we would join) should protect our European allies against any need to fear a postwar resurgence of Axis aggression. I shall always believe that if this program had been aggressively pursued at the time, it would have greatly altered postwar history, and would have deprived the Soviet Union of the major reasons (or excuse or pretense) for the so-called "protective expansionism" which has since become the curse of the world.

9

Yalta: "This Will Raise Hell"

SENATOR Vandenberg's speech on January 10, 1945, was, in later years, regarded not only as a turning point in American foreign policy but as a clear indication that the Senator himself had reached full political stature. After a long search, after a tedious period of testing the firmness of the ground, he had at the beginning of 1945 found a solid footing on which he could and would stand. He was an advocate of a nonpartisan foreign policy and, on February 15, he was able to write President Roosevelt that "you know of my profound conviction that we *must* organize the postwar world on the basis of effective, collective security."

But the mere fact that the Senator from Michigan was ready to collaborate with the Administration on organization of the peace did not solve the problem. It takes two to make a bargain and in this case the other party had to be President Roosevelt. On the basis of the first White House reaction, Mr. Roosevelt seemed to be uncertain of the Senator's intentions in making the January 10th speech. Nor did subsequent events suggest that the extravagant public reaction to the speech pleased the President. Yet Mr. Roosevelt was by no means blinded to the possibilities opened up by the Senator. After what may have been momentary hesitation, he grasped the opportunity offered by Vandenberg's speech to secure greater unity in the vital impending negotiations and, on February 13, the State Department announced that the Senator had been named as a delegate to the United Nations Conference on International Organization at San Francisco, starting April 25.

Vandenberg did not immediately accept. President Roosevelt was at Yalta at the time and the first statement regarding the Big Three Conference there had just been made public. This statement, however, told only part of the story — and some of the vital agreements at Yalta were not revealed until later in piecemeal fashion. Among the points covered, however, in the first statements and press dispatches was an agreement to establish a "general international organization to maintain peace and security" on the foundations laid at Dumbarton Oaks.

The three Allied leaders reaffirmed their faith in the principles of the Atlantic Charter and agreed on reorganization of the provisional (Lublin) government which the Russians had set up in liberated Poland in opposition to the Polish government-in-exile at London. The government was to be broadened to include democratic leaders of Poles abroad (such as the exiled leaders in London) in order to form a new National Unity government, which would be pledged to hold free elections as soon as possible. But the first Yalta statement also pointed out that "boundaries of the new Poland were discussed and it was agreed that the eastern frontier should follow the Curzon Line except for certain specified digressions. It was agreed that Poland was to receive substantial accessions of territory in the north and west." This seemed to make it clear that the Soviet Union would retain control of Polish territory east of the Curzon Line — the approximate line to which Russian forces had occupied Poland early in the war when Germany first invaded that country. "It was announced that President Roosevelt had agreed at the Yalta conference . . . to do the exact opposite regarding Poland of that which the Michigan Senator had urged . . ." David Lawrence noted. "Now to cap the climax President Roosevelt has asked Senator Vandenberg to serve as a member of the delegation to the coming conference of the United Nations where a peace organization is to be set up, presumably to underwrite the very kind of thing against which Mr. Vandenberg inveighed in his speech. . . . Where does this leave the Michigan Senator? Must he turn a somersault?"

That was a question that the Senator was debating, too, and at great length. On the same date that he was announced as a delegate to San Francisco, Vandenberg wrote:

February 13, 1945

We have the report from the "Big Three." I have made a general but brief statement about it in which I welcomed the fact that the ideals of the Atlantic Charter have been restored to good standing (on paper) and that the American people are being told — at long last — what is happening. But I have of course reserved specific comment until *all* the facts are available. I have also reserved all comment on the Polish question. [The large number of Michigan residents of Polish descent gave Vandenberg a special interest in Poland at all times.] On this latter question it looks as though my prophecy . . . has substantially come true. I . . . believe that the "Curzon Line" is indefensible even though it be wangled a bit in some such undisclosed fashion as the preliminary report prophesies. I suppose it is too much to hope that it will be "wangled" to include Lvov and Vilna (which would be something of a consolation). I . . . feel that the recognition of the Lublin government in net effect is unjustified. I am very skeptical about the kind of a plebiscite which will result from the proposed arrangements. In a word, the decision is totally unsatisfactory.

The desperately important question now is "what can we do about it?" Manifestly America will not go to war with Russia to settle such an issue — particularly when the President of the United States has endorsed the settlement. In the final analysis, we could not afford to upset our postwar peace plans on account of this issue. Yet I do not want to surrender to this decision insofar as we have any practical means at our disposal to continue to fight it. It seems to me that the best *practical* hope remaining to us is in my proposal that the new Peace League shall have a right to review all these interim decisions. I note that the statement of the "Big Three" says that "the final delimitation of the western frontier of Poland should await the conference." I still know of no reason why this rule should not apply to *all* "frontiers." The President may tell us, however, when he returns, that he has

already agreed that some of these settlements are *final*. . . .
I am greatly perplexed by the whole prospectus.

A couple of days later Vandenberg wrote to Mr. Roosevelt, who was still away on his Yalta trip:

February 15, 1945
. . . my deepest gratitude for your generous consideration. I think you know of my profound conviction that we *must* organize the post-war world on the basis of effective, collective security and that I generally approve of "Dumbarton Oaks" as a basis for this development. As a member of the American Delegation I should wish to co-operate sympathetically and helpfully. At the same time, I know you will readily realize that, as a representative of the Senate minority, I shall occupy a particularly difficult role if I am to be of *subsequent* utility to this great adventure. [This was a reference to the role that Vandenberg might play in getting Senate approval of the new postwar international organization.] Therefore, for *both* our sakes, I take the liberty of inquiring what specific commitments, if any, would be implicit in my acceptance of this designation; and whether I might feel that it will not violate your commission or your expectations if I freely present my own points of view to our Delegation and if I reserve the right of final judgment upon the ultimate results of the Conference. I add that my prayer will be that the San Francisco Conference may successfully initiate organized peace *and* orderly justice for a free world of free men.

With sentiments of great respect, and with renewed expression of my great appreciation for the honor you have done me in considering my eligibility for this great responsibility. . . .

The contents of this letter were presumably wirelessed to Mr. Roosevelt's party, and the next day Vandenberg received a reply from Joseph C. Grew, Undersecretary of State, who was acting for Secretary Stettinius in Washington. It was a rather strange reply to the Senator's specific questions as to whether he would be a free agent at San Francisco. "I have just received word from Secretary Stettinius asking me to pass on to you the following message: 'Your constructive and helpful comments in regard to our recent efforts are deeply appreciated.'"

If Vandenberg thought this was an evasion or a brush-off, he made no comment on it, but he did sit down and write Grew a long letter outlining his previously expressed attitude toward the Yalta conference and adding:

February 19, 1945

But I want to frankly state my deep disappointment in respect to the Polish settlement (symbolic of the general treatment to be accorded the smaller liberated nations). I am referring not only to the inherent injustice . . . but to the psychological danger which — as a result — may threaten the ultimate attitude of the American people toward their acceptance of the Dumbarton Oaks obligations.

If these Polish decisions are clearly understood to be temporary and subject to subsequent review . . . I think this *purpose* should be made clearly plain to the American people as promptly as possible. There can be persuasive justification for temporary decisions . . . but in my humble opinion "justice" must be the ultimate criterion if there is any hope for permanent peace. . . .

But please let me make the exhibit even more challenging. It is asserted (and I shall be glad to have you affirm or deny this fact) that the Yalta decisions make General Anders and most of his men [Polish soldiers who had escaped early in the war via the Middle East] who bore the brunt of the ghastly Cassino battles virtually homeless and "men without a country" despite the fact that they are our comrades-in-arms upon the battle fronts of Italy today. It is similarly asserted that General Bor and most of his brave and sacrificial "underground" [the elements that rebelled against the Germans in Warsaw] find themselves in a similar status. It is asserted that . . . the Lublin government has outlawed both of these intrepid groups as "traitors" subject to a traitor's penalty. If this is true in any degree it seems to me that it makes it simply unconscionably immoral for us to recognize the Lublin government.

[The Senator also questioned the Yalta arrangement for a three-power committee — Vyacheslav Molotov of Russia, Averell Harriman of the United States, and Sir Archibald Clark Kerr of Britain — to assist in the reorganization of the Lublin government into a Polish Provisional Government of National Unity. The Vandenberg letter continued:]

If it be said that the Yalta Declaration does not recognize the Lublin government, but sets up an entirely new government . . . then I respectfully suggest that the acid test of our present good faith will be tested by the actions of our representative [Harriman] on this present committee. One test will be whether General Anders and General Bor are still "traitors" under it. But in a larger sense, I respectfully submit that these questions dealing with the ultimate independence of Poland are not entitled to be permanently settled by any triumvirate whether at Yalta or in this new Committee.

[In concluding his letter to Grew, Vandenberg said:] I shall greatly appreciate it if you will make these comments available to Secretary Stettinius. I am proceeding on the theory that I can be most helpful to the ultimate peace adventure in which we are all so deeply and desperately concerned by thus frankly asserting my point of view. As an evidence of my good faith I remind you that I am not publicly discussing this matter at the present time. My whole aim and purpose is to seek through intimate cooperation to work out this problem with you and the President and the Secretary of State. I do not want to seem to be dogmatic. I can always endorse reasonable compromises. . . . But it seems to me that we must do more to assure the American people that we are committed to justice as a basis of peace.

While this exchange of letters was still in progress the Senator wrote in less formal terms to John Foster Dulles:

February 17, 1945

I cannot go to this conference as a stooge. If my instructions would bind me to Dumbarton Oaks "as is" I certainly could not go at all. I should have preferred not to have been named. At best, it represents an equivocal role. On the other hand,

I do not think the Republican Party can make a graver blunder than to decline Senatorial cooperation (under appropriate circumstances) when it is tendered by the President in a critical case of this nature and at such a critical moment. I am frank to say . . . I do not believe that this League can produce anything like permanent peace unless it can take ultimate jurisdiction over all the interim decisions that have been made in the course of this war. . . . I might add in passing that I do not know why plebiscites should be denied East of the Curzon Line [the area taken over by Russia] when they are recognized as valid West of the Curzon line.

If I am assured untrammelled freedom to present this point of view (and to render my own independent judgment upon the final results at San Francisco) I think I am called upon to put my head in this noose and take my chances.

Again, in a letter to another person, he wrote:

February 20, 1945

I expect [the President] to say that I am a free agent [at San Francisco]. In that event I shall accept. Otherwise, it would be impossible. I happen to have seen the "instructions" which were given by him to his Bretton Woods delegates. They were bound hand and foot to the Treasury program. . . . I cannot sign any such blank check. It would stultify me and it would sell the Republican Party down the river. That is all there is to it. The speculation in the [newspapers] about the relationship between my decision and the Polish question was without foundation. There are no political considerations (except freedom of action) involved in my attitude. Frankly, I should very much prefer to wind up my public career in a successful contribution to world peace than to suffer six more years in the Senate — if there has to be a choice. If the Polish question is involved in this matter, it is not a question of "popular votes" for me; it is a question whether the American people will ever sanction a Peace League which permanently stratifies the palpably unjust decisions made at Yalta. . . . I agree . . . that the Republican Party will be misunderstood — and so will I — if this invitation is not accepted. My expectation is that it will be accepted. If it isn't I shall have "to tell the world."

Except for an acknowledgment from Grew, there was no further word from the White House until the Senator received a letter, dated February 28, formally extending the invitation to become a delegate. It was signed by the President. In the next day or so, however, there came another note from the President, written February 26, addressed to "Dear Arthur" and signed "F.D.R." At this stage of the game, it was almost as puzzling as the earlier message from Stettinius. It said: "Thanks for yours of February 15th which reached me in mid-ocean. I was, of course, very happy to learn that you are to be a member of the American Delegation at San Francisco. Thank heavens that this whole business is getting to be on a really non-partisan basis. I hope to see you soon after I get back. Always sincerely . . ."

If Mr. Roosevelt believed that the Senator would be so easily satisfied he was overlooking the Dutch in Vandenberg. The Senator wrote again:

March 1, 1945

Please forgive me for pressing the question which I submitted in that letter [of February 15]. I am sure you are totally convinced of my deep anxiety to be of maximum service in the development of the Dumbarton Oaks program for permanent peace through collective security. But for *both* our sakes — and for the sake of my *future* utility in completing this great adventure — I want to be sure we understand each other before accepting your formal invitation. . . . May I understand that it will not violate your commission (as I feel sure is the case) if I feel free to present my own views to my American colleagues . . . and if I reserve my final right of judgment upon the ultimate results?

Mr. Roosevelt replied on March 3: "Dear Arthur: Of course, I expect you freely to present your views to your American colleagues in respect to all problems at San Francisco. We shall need such free expression in the delegation, and in America before and after the conference. I am counting, indeed, on the wisdom I know you can add to our entire effort to secure a program for permanent peace. Always sincerely, Franklin D. Roosevelt."

Vandenberg issued a statement to the press on March 5, saying: "Following an exchange of cordial and satisfactory personal letters with the President, clarifying my right of free action, I am glad to say that I have accepted this invitation. . . . An excellent start has been made [on a security organization]. I am frank to say that my chief anxiety about the tentative Dumbarton Oaks formula is that, except in its brief World Court chapter, it does not once mention 'justice' as a guiding objective or a rule of conduct. . . . I shall have concrete proposals to submit to my colleagues along these lines."

This was almost but not quite the end of the relationship between the President and the Senator from Michigan. There was a later conference at the White House in preparation for San Francisco, and there was a personal talk of which Vandenberg told his family in detail, probably about the middle of March. The Senator had read to the Senate a dispatch quoting remarks by British Foreign Secretary Anthony Eden in the House of Commons on March 7, when Eden warned the Lublin régime against persecution of Poles who were loyal to the rival exile government in London. "The Government of the United States should be equally frank about this situation," Vandenberg told the Senate. "There is no escaping the fact that the treatment accorded Poland . . . will have a large effect upon the success of our ultimate plans for collective security and organized peace." He then repeated some of the views which he had outlined earlier in his letter to Grew in regard to Poland. As a result of this and other speeches the Communist press and radio in New York and Moscow bitterly and repeatedly attacked Vandenberg as an imperialistic obstructionist to the work of forming the United Nations.

After reading these attacks, the Senator called at the White House and discussed them with Mr. Roosevelt. He said that he apparently was going to be a future target for the Russian propagandists and that he could understand why Mr. Roosevelt might wish to accept his resignation as a delegate to the San Francisco conference in order to avoid embarrassment to the

American delegations. "We will have to deal with the Russians and I don't want to make it difficult," the Senator said. "I can conveniently arrange to break a leg — if you wish." Mr. Roosevelt didn't hesitate. "Just between us, Arthur," he answered, "I am coming to know the Russians better, and if I could name only one delegate to the San Francisco conference, you would be that delegate."

This was doubtless the most pleasant phase in the Roosevelt-Vandenberg relations. They seemed to be on a plane of partial agreement for one of the few times in their political careers. It didn't last long. But it may have later served to soften somewhat the Senator's attitude toward the man who had for so long been the object of not only his personal and private fulminations but of his sharpest political attacks.

Meantime, the Senator had been busy preparing for the San Francisco conference, attempting to clarify his own thinking in regard to the Polish question and learning more about the decisions made at Yalta. His thinking on the Polish problem and the broader issue that it symbolized was probably best summed up in a letter to his old friend Frank Januszewski, owner of the *Polish Daily News* in Detroit, with whom Vandenberg often communicated on subjects of special interest to Poles.

March 7, 1945

> I have not altered my view respecting Poland — both for her own precious sake and as a "symbol." I could get no greater personal satisfaction out of anything more than from joining — aye, in leading — a public denunciation of Yalta and all its works as respects Poland. But we *must* ask ourselves whether this is the best service I can render in recapturing some elements of justice for Poland — not merely for Poland's sake but also and particularly for a permanent World Peace which can never survive injustice.
>
> Whether we like it or not (and we don't) we confront a condition and not a theory. We must deal with the realities. . . . The Yalta decisions enjoy . . . President Roosevelt's stamp of approval. . . . Also [they] bear Churchill's stamp of approval. . . . I am forced by the circumstances to believe that

we cannot get results by trying to totally combat decisions which are supported by our own American Administration and by the British Parliament. . . . We must find some other way. . . . What are some of these other ways? One . . . is to hold our own American administration to strict accountability for the kind of a Provisional Polish Government which we shall be parties to imposing on Poland. . . . I agree that it is immoral . . . for us to participate in imposing any government. . . . But . . . which is the better course: to fight the whole idea (with no remote possibility of success) or to accept this much of the inevitable and demand that it function on a just basis?

Then we shall soon confront the San Francisco Conference. It would be a relatively simple matter to dynamite the new Peace League. . . . Then there would be no League. What would *that* do for Poland? It would simply leave Russia in complete possession of everything she wants. . . . There would be no hope left for justice except through World War Number Three immediately. Would it not be better to go along with the New League and make every effort at San Francisco to write the objectives of the Atlantic Charter into its dedications and seek to give it specific authority to examine at any time whatever injustice may have been inherited from the war era and to recommend correction? . . . My own personal role . . . is a troublesome one. I could have refused to sit as a delegate. . . . When I accept the designation, I must primarily work . . . through the Frisco Conference and not in a public campaign of denunciation. . . . I may accomplish nothing. But I shall relentlessly try.

On March 13 the Senator began keeping a more detailed diary of matters concerning the San Francisco conference.

March 13, 1945

First meeting of delegates. All present. Met with Secretary Stettinius and discussed protocol questions at some length. Many pictures and newsreels. Were received briefly at White House by President. He said he was besieged by countless requests from various groups to increase delegation or to name alternates, but that he would "stand pat" on the eight.

It was agreed that widest possible news contacts should be provided press at Frisco — meaning open meetings down to the level of sub-committees.

Each delegate was granted a staff of two. I privately told Stettinius I want to take John Foster Dulles as my lawyer. He said he had great respect for Dulles but that President greatly dislikes "Tom" (Dewey) and Dulles and that it might be obnoxious. On the other hand, he said he had been toying with idea of taking Dulles (in his capacity as head of the Church Group) as an advisor to the whole delegation. He said to "let it ride" for awhile.

I presented my proposed amendments to Dumbarton Oaks — in behalf of "justice." They were referred to Dr. Pasvolsky for study and subsequent conference with me prior to submission to delegation.

Stettinius made a public statement that "each delegate would be free to pursue his own personal views and convictions."

Later in the afternoon I sat with Stassen for an hour and went over my amendments. He agreed to support all of them.

About this time, Walter Lippmann raised a question whether Vandenberg was confusing the "peace keeping" organization to be set up at San Francisco with the "peace making" that would follow the conclusion of the war. San Francisco, he pointed out, was not supposed to be making the peace terms. Vandenberg wrote to him:

March 15, 1945

Your own misunderstanding of my viewpoint proves [the need for clarification]. . . . It is desperately important that the country should not mistake the San Francisco limitations. They have nothing to do with specific peace settlements. They deal solely with mechanisms to maintain the results of the peace settlements and subsequent crises. . . . But I strive for the principle that permanent peace can succeed only on the basis of justice and that any injustice — past, present or future — should therefore be within the jurisdiction of the Peace League's review and recommendation. I strive against the proposition that this jurisdiction starts with the new status quo. That is the crux of the matter. . . .

You say: this wider jurisdiction is already recognized. . . . Unfortunately that proposition is widely challenged. . . . I seek only to make immutably certain that your own interpretation is correct; that we are not intending to make the colossal blunder of putting peace in a strait-jacket and of offering no means of correcting injustice, if there be such, in the present peace settlements (or in any other situation) except by the very process (war) which we presume to discourage.

A week later, the Senator discussed his proposed amendments at his own office with Pasvolsky, and recorded the interview in his diary.

March 20, 1945

Dr. Pasvolsky came to my office and we discussed my proposed amendments in detail. He was very agreeable to all of them and agreed to join in trying to work them in. Very pleasant and instructive two hours. The Doctor (Russian-born) has been the State Department's "expert" on this subject for a long time. He has a face as round as a moon but a head "as long as necessary." When I suggested that the recent Soviet attack on me (last week's 15 minute broadcast from Moscow) might mean that I would be "persona non grata" with the Russians, he said — "Not at all — they respect a fighter — they like to 'be told.'" He said I would be our key man at Frisco for at least one inevitable reason. "The big question mark in every foreign delegate's mind," said he, "will still be the same one that has plagued them in past experience, namely, What will the Senate do? Well — when we are pressing for something we don't seem able to get, we'll send you in to tell 'em that it has to be done if they expect to get their Treaty past the Senate."

I am receiving thousands of letters from service-men who seem to be both amazed and grateful that I should have said I would give their "advice" "top priority."

John Foster Dulles phoned from New York today to say he thought he had better make a public statement asserting his preference to go to Frisco in his private capacity (lest F.D.R. should otherwise embarrass him by declining to appoint him). He sent the letter to me. I gave it out.

Friday, March 23, 1945

We began to get some of the inside "bad news" from Yalta today. It is typical of the baffling secrecy which leaves one eternally uncertain of what "deals" have been made. The Delegates saw the President this morning at 11:30. (He was one hour late.) He told us that at Yalta Stalin demanded six votes in the new League Assembly (to match the "six" of the totalled British Commonwealths, etc.). The President said he talked him out of three of them and got him to agree on "three" in return for which the U.S. shall have "three." He said the Delegates were free to do as they please about it; that he did not "commit" the U.S. but told . . . [Stalin] that if he (F.D.R.) were a Delegate he would vote for it. In response to a question, he said Churchill also agreed.

This will *raise hell*. In the first place, why is this news being held back, when presumably the country was told all about the "Yalta Compromise" on voting (but not a word about this)? In the second place, it will focus attention and put distorted emphasis on the fact that Britain has six Assembly votes while we have only three. This question has heretofore caused no trouble because the Assembly has no powers of action. But if it is important enough to cause Stalin to demand three votes, we will be asked by the country why we are stopped at "three" instead of "six" to match the British. In the third place, this puts all the lesser nations at a further disadvantage. And how about China and France? This is going to be a "tough nut." It looks like bad business to me. The Delegates were rather stunned. . . .

Tuesday, March 27, 1945

The more I have thought about the President's amazing tentative deal with Stalin to get extra votes in the Assembly, the more deadly it has become (1) to American public opinion and (2) to any further pretense of "sovereign equality" among the lesser nations of the earth. I tried to get hold of Stettinius to unburden myself. He is resting in Florida. I tried Grew. He is home sick. I finally spent an hour with Assistant Secretary of State Jimmy Dunn late in the day. We went over the matter. Dunn agrees as to the jeopardy. But what to do? I suggested that the matter ought to be laid before Cordell Hull at once to see if he could not impress the President with the importance of urging Stalin to drop the whole thing (since it *can't* be approved). Or, failing that, that Stalin be left to present his demand de novo — without any reference to any tentative agreement with F.D.R. or Churchill, and certainly without any reference to the fact that F.D.R. wants to "horn in" on the scheme in behalf of the U.S. I do not know what Dunn will do. He made many notes. I think he will try.

The *only* outsider whom I have told about this shocking presidential revelation is John Foster Dulles who is totally trust-worthy. He agrees with me that this effort to "stack" the Assembly could easily dynamite San Francisco — or subsequent Senate approval of the entire Treaty.

Even if Vandenberg and Dulles kept the situation secret, somebody let it leak out in the next twenty-four hours.

Thursday, March 29, 1945

The storm over "extra votes" in the Assembly broke today when the N.Y. Herald Tribune printed a rumor story about it, this morning. The White House was forced to make a confirmatory statement. It was an unfair statement because it did not indicate that F.D.R. had told our Delegates that they were free to do as they please about it. I made the following statement:

I would deeply disagree with any voting proposal, if made, which would destroy the promised "sovereign equality of nations" in the Peace League's Assembly as previously proposed at Dumbarton Oaks. This applies just as much to extra votes for us as for any other nation. This Assembly must continue to be tomorrow's free and untrammeled "town meeting of the world."

"THIS WILL RAISE HELL" 161

The voice of the Great Powers will be amply protected in the Council.

Monday, April 2, 1945

Following the press conference last week in which Stettinius was forced to decline to answer 40 questions put to him about this Yalta mess, the State Department tried over the week end to work up a responsive statement which Stettinius can put out this week. This morning I was called to Connally's office to go over the statement with Stettinius, Acheson and Dunn. It was reasonably satisfactory. But it *committed* our Government (and therefore our Frisco delegation) to "three votes for Russia," leaving us free *only* respecting "three votes for U.S." I immediately objected that this was contrary to the President's statement to the delegation, that we were "free agents" on *both* propositions. The State Department agreed to check again with F.D.R., who has gone to Warm Springs. (Vice President Truman called me in today to tell me that F.D.R. told *him* that our delegates were to be free agents on this question; and he was completely flabbergasted when I told him the other story.)

It also was discussed this morning whether our delegation should not *immediately* announce that we will *not* ask for our "three votes" even if Russia does — so as to establish our *moral* position on this subject even tho F.D.R. may have committed us to support the Russian demand. Connally favors this course. I favor it — if the statement is so drawn as to entirely avoid the "six votes for Britain" issue. It was decided to ask F.D.R. whether he would object to such a statement by our delegation — since it would manifestly weaken the Russian claim. We will get the answers tomorrow. There is a general disposition to *stop this Stalin appeasement*. It *has* to stop *sometime*. Every new surrender makes it more difficult.

Tuesday, April 3, 1945

The Delegation went to the mat this morning over the Yalta episode. Stettinius presented his proposed press release stating that the U.S. Delegation is bound to support the Russian demand for 3 votes but also stating that we would *not* ask 3 compensatory votes for the U.S. Of course this puts Stalin out on the end of a limb. It virtually says to the Frisco Conference — "The U.S.A. is stuck with a bad bargain of which we want no part." I bluntly stated that the idea of binding us to vote for Russia's end of the "bad bargain" was at complete variance with F.D.R.'s statement to the Delegation and that it puts us in a ridiculously equivocal spot. My recollection of F.D.R.'s contrary statement to the Delegation was categorically confirmed by Dean Gildersleeve and Cong. Eaton. The State Dept. obviously sided completely with my point of view but was powerless to escape the presidential commitment. I made it plain that there must be no more of these faux pas. I am grateful, however, that he had the guts to spurn his own deal so far as we are concerned. Otherwise, of course, any further talk of the "sovereign equality of (little) nations" would be a travesty. I feel we have accomplished *something*.

We were introduced to all of our official "advisers." Dulles was not among them. But I talked with him again before he left town and I am sure he will accept in a few days.

We were "documented" today with enough reading matter to keep me up all night for a week.

We got the first pre-view of the assignment of U.S. Delegates to the four main Committees at Frisco. I head one (dealing with the Assembly) and am [on one of those] dealing with the Council. I guess they plan to give me enough work to keep me out of mischief. . . .

At this time, possibly as a result of his exchange of letters with Lippmann, the Senator made public the text of his memorandum proposing eight amendments to the Dumbarton Oaks proposals, intended to assure that the World Security Council should not attempt "to freeze the status quo" but must recommend appropriate measures of adjustment whenever it found any unjust situation threatening the peace. His basic purpose was that the United Nations have the power, not to impose its idea of what was "just," but to recommend changes whenever the organization found any situation in which injustice was a peril.

This was explicit in his proposal to add a paragraph to Chapter Eight, Section A, of the Dumbarton proposals as follows: "If the Security Council finds that any situation which it shall investigate involves injustice to peoples concerned it shall recommend appropriate measures of adjustment which may include revision of treaties and of prior international decisions." Five of the eight amendments were designed to write this principle of "justice" into the Chapter.

Vandenberg wrote to Stettinius:

April 5, 1945

> As I anticipated, the Yalta episode has stirred up the old (and heretofore) latent bugaboo about "six votes for Britain." It is made to order for the purposes of building dangerous prejudice. It is a perfect soap box theme. There is ample evidence that our critics are already going to work on it with a vengeance. I think it is very important that we should promptly begin to mobilize (for use at appropriate times) essential ammunition to the contrary. It will not be enough merely to argue abstractly that the British Dominions are separate entities with independent voices. What we need is tangible proof of this fact. The best proof will be instances where the Dominions have actually differed with the United Kingdom . . . and have actually followed divergent courses. . . . I think this is one of the major hazards which our new enterprise confronts. It is the major tragedy of Yalta (with the exception of Poland).

At the next meeting of the Delegation, Vandenberg began to make some progress with his proposed amendments to Dumbarton Oaks.

Wednesday, April 11, 1945

> Yesterday's Delegation meeting was routine. Today was important. The State Dept. itself recommended the acceptance of my proposed language (Chap. V, Par. 6) to give the Assembly jurisdiction over "measures to establish justice; foster the observance of human rights and fundamental freedoms; encourage the development of rules of international law; and recommend measures for the peaceful adjustment of situa-

tions likely to violate the principles of the United Nations as declared by them on January 1, 1942." The Delegation agreed. Thus the Atlantic Charter is rescued from oblivion; and thus we would *end* the war on the *same* note with which we began it. (It remains to be seen what Russia says to this.)

Charles Taft (Adviser) made his first appearance recommending a change in the language setting up the Social and Economic Council. He wanted to spell out a do-gooder program for the whole world. . . . I suggested that if we did any such thing, we would have to hold last November's election all over again. Even Stettinius jumped the thing. . . . The Delegation unanimously threw out the new proposals and reverted to the simple and general language in Dumbarton Oaks. We are *not* going to try to make over the whole world in one document and at one sitting. In this field, I am quite willing to *plant the seed;* but only time can make it grow.

Thursday, April 12, 1945

Sec. Stettinius *again* brought up the Yalta "votes for Russia." Obviously he and all his Department continue to be both embarrassed and anxious about it. Clearly the President made a commitment which has to be validated. Since the question is likely to arise in connection with the Assembly Chapter of the Charter, and since I am to head this American subcommittee, I demanded *specific* instructions. Are we committed *only* to "vote" for the Russian proposal if offered? Are we committed to "support" it — which is to say, to *argue* for it etc.? It was definitely agreed that we are committed *only* to *vote* for it. The question may rise in different form — namely, whether the Ukraine and White Russia shall be admitted as *members* of the Peace League.

The question of the jurisdiction of the new World Court also came up — and was left open. I reminded them that any form of *compulsory* jurisdiction might endanger American ratification (as it did 10 years ago). It was agreed that we should strive for as much "compulsion" as is calculated to pass the Senate — but no more.

We are getting along famously. The only cloud on the

horizon is Russia (and Yalta). Russia continues to be irksome. She has demanded that there be *four* rotating Chairmen of the Conference (representing the inviting powers). It had been already agreed that Stettinius (representing the host country) should be the *one* Chairman. There *must* be *one* responsible head of the enterprise. We unanimously agreed to support the President in refusing the Russian demand. The revolt against any further Soviet appeasement is growing.

On the same day Vandenberg made a later entry in his diary:

President Roosevelt died today. Thus a truly great and gallant spirit, despite all his flaws, was gathered to his fathers. I shall always feel that Admiral Ross McIntyre, his physician, carries a great responsibility for ever having allowed him to run a fourth time. . . . The gravest question-mark in every American heart is about Truman. Can he swing the job? Despite his limited capacities, I believe he can.

Vandenberg's reference to the death of President Roosevelt poorly expressed his attitude toward the man who, for so many years, was his chief political foe. Actually, the Senator's papers generally present a rather distorted version of his over-all attitude toward Mr. Roosevelt because they were mainly concerned with political affairs. Vandenberg many times fumed at activities in the White House but he had a deep respect for Mr. Roosevelt as a man and for a number of his acts as a statesman. This attitude probably was best expressed at a dinner of the Gridiron Club, a group of Washington political correspondents, in April of 1940, when Mr. Roosevelt, for the majority party, and the Senator, for the minority, were the speakers. At that time the President was generally expected to seek a third term in the White House. Vandenberg was a possible Republican choice to oppose him in the presidential campaign. The Senator also was up for re-election to the Senate that year in Michigan.

The Gridiron speakers were expected to go in for good-humored banter at the expense of the opposition party and Vandenberg that night stuck a number of needles in the New Deal, but he also paused for a serious tribute to Mr. Roosevelt. He said:

First of all . . . I want to present my *personal* — as distinguished from my *political* — compliments to the departing President of the United States. However much we may quarrel over policy, there is *one* point at which I can join his loudest psalm-singers. Speaking of the *man* himself, I do not hesitate to say that I never knew a more gallant soul who has laughed triumphantly at the handicaps of life and given his country a superb example of *personal* courage and a *personal* challenge to "carry on" to victory, no matter what the burden, no matter what the odds. His example to us in this regard has never been equaled and it will never be excelled.

I want to add another touch of the accolade. You see I am in a mellow mood tonight, since this may be *my* last official appearance as well as *his*. Without exploring too closely into dubious details, I do not hesitate to assert that history will accord him credit for making America *social-minded*. Of course, history will have some *other* things to say which I charitably pass in the spirit of the moment. But I think it will say he made us *social-minded*. And it was high-time this phenomenon should come to pass because our best defense of democracy — in a sodden, saddened world of dictators — is to make democracy consciously and intimately advantageous to our whole people.

These are adequate achievements for any man.

Because the Senator's papers do not seem accurately to reflect his mature attitude toward Mr. Roosevelt, it might also be noted here that later in a letter to Mrs. Roosevelt, he paid his respects to the late President's support of a bipartisan foreign policy. "I cordially and emphatically agree with you that [U.S. representation on the UN delegation] should be 'bipartisan.' I think this theory has paid infinite dividends in the last two years [1945–46]. I think it is one of the major reasons why your distinguished husband succeeded in his peace prospectus where the late President Wilson failed."

Continuing his pre-San Francisco diary, Vandenberg commented on Mr. Truman's efforts to establish a cordial relationship between the White House and Congress:

April 13, 1945

Riding to work this morning I got to wondering whether the country wasn't just as anxious and perplexed about the future as I was — and what I could do to sound a note of stabilizing reassurance (because nothing matters at this moment but "our country"). I decided it would help if I called together the Republican Senate Conference and sent Truman a message of trust and faith. This was hastily done. . . . It seemed to make a profound impression.

Truman came back to the Senate this noon for lunch with a few of us. It shattered all tradition. But it was both wise and smart. It means that the days of executive contempt for Congress are ended; that we are returning to a government in which Congress will take its rightful place. There were three Republicans in the small luncheon group besides myself — Martin (House Leader), White and Austin. Indicative of my close relations with Truman, his military Aide (Colonel Harry H. Vaughan) sent me today the last box of cigars they had in the old Vice-Presidential office, with [his] card. [On the card Vaughan had written: "Our swan song."]

. . . No one can fore-tell what the effect [of the President's death] will be on the [San Francisco] Peace Conference. One thing it does is to wash the slate clean of whatever undisclosed commitments F.D.R. has made to Stalin or Churchill. This is all to the good. The "Big 3" no longer exists as a monopoly in respect to world destiny. But it remains to be seen whether, by the same token, we have not lost the strongest voice through which we could hope to argue Russia out of some of the mistakes which it seems determined to make.

With 15 others, I had lunch with Truman this noon. He told me he is *not* going to Frisco personally (as F.D.R. had intended to do) and that he expects to "leave Frisco to our Delegation." Unquestionably we will have greater freedom — but also greater responsibility.

I am puzzled. Stettinius is now Secretary of State in *fact*. Up to now he has been only the presidential messenger. He does *not* have the background and experience for such a job at such a critical time — altho he is a *grand person* with every good intention and high honesty of purpose. *Now* we have *both* an inexperienced President *and* an inexperienced Secretary (in re foreign affairs.) So far as the Peace League is concerned, it means that Dr. Leo Pasvolsky (chief State Dept. adviser on Peace plans) will come close to being the *real* power. He is very able but scarcely representative of American public opinion.

But I liked the *first* decision Truman made — namely, that Frisco should *go on*. Senator Connally immediately prophesied, after F.D.R. died, that Frisco would be postponed. . . . Truman promptly stopped *that* mistake (which would have confessed to the world that there *is an* "indispensable man" who was bigger than America). No more meetings until Monday.

Saturday, April 14, 1945

I attended the White House funeral this afternoon — a simple, deeply impressive service. I sat directly behind Henry Wallace, who missed the Presidency by just three months. I wonder what was going through his head!

Monday, April 16, 1945

The Delegation resumed work today. It accepted my final amendment — intended to avoid freezing the status quo and permitting the new League to look backward as well as forward when correcting injustice and festering frictions. The new language goes into Chap. 5 B6 defining the scope of the Assembly's power of investigation — "including situations arising out of any treaties or international engagements." The Delegation has been unanimous in all these decisions. I am well satisfied.

Commander Stassen joined us today for the first time since we went definitely to work. He came to my office late in the afternoon to say that he had been reading the record and congratulated me on the degree of success I have had.

The formal Frisco assignments were approved today. I head the American Section dealing with the Assembly (along with Bloom and Gildersleeve). I am also on the American Section dealing with the Security Council (along with Hull, Connally and Stassen).

Lord Halifax (British Ambassador) phoned to ask me to drop in at the Embassy tomorrow at six to chat with Anthony Eden (British Foreign Minister). Stettinius urged me to go and to speak to Eden with entire candor.

Tuesday, April 17, 1945
President Truman received the Delegation at The White House this morning. He was modest, unassuming and cordial — as usual. He told us there would be *no changes in the Delegation* — to set at rest reports that Stettinius would be replaced with Jimmy Byrnes and that Eleanor Roosevelt might want to go along. Many pictures were taken.

Our meeting this morning dealt chiefly with Trusteeships (the new device which is to succeed the old mandates). Our government has itself been sharply divided on the subject. The Army and Navy are insistent that we must *keep* full control of most of the Pacific bases taken from the Japs. The State Dept. is afraid this will set a bad example to the other great powers. Secretary of War Stimson made a particularly moving speech — told of the mistake we made after the last war in letting Japan get these mandated islands (which they promptly proceeded to fortify in violation of their trust) — told of his experience as Governor of the Philippines when every "insider" knew that we could *not* hold the Islands against major attack. He spoke of the irony that he should have become Secretary of War at a time when this came true; and vividly urged that this must never happen again. (We all agree with him.) He said he didn't care so much about the "title" to these Islands *if* we have *absolute,* undisputed control over our base needs. Navy Secretary Forrestal backed him up 100%. But the State Dept. is right in insisting that this must be accomplished without setting a precedent for all the other Big Powers to take what they claim they need for their defense (precisely as Russia is already doing). Stassen and Dr. Bowman ("advisor") insisted that, while we *must* follow War and Navy advice, we must also make it plain that we seek no right of social or economic exploitation in respect to any of these peoples. The whole matter was held in abeyance until tomorrow.

Tuesday, April 17, 1945 (evening)

I called at the British Embassy pursuant to the Ambassador's request. Halifax took me to his upstairs study. Anthony Eden came in very soon. We talked for an hour. Eden is somewhat small physically, but handsome and affable and very brilliant. (He said he had just been talking with "Winnie" — Churchill — by trans-Atlantic phone.)

I told him my story: that if I am going to be held responsible for Republican votes in the Senate for the new League Treaty, I must (as Churchill once put it) "be given the tools." I read him my Amendments as approved by our Delegation; and told him I would have to insist upon three "musts." (1) The distinct and specific inclusion of *justice* as an objective; (2) the identification of the pledges in the Atlantic Charter among our purposes; (3) enough "elastic" so the League can look *back* as well as *forward* in correcting injustice and curing potential war festers. (On the latter point, Halifax immediately said — "I suppose you have Poland in mind" — and I said "Yes.") Eden said, on the latter point, he thought it was already implicit in the Dumbarton Oaks Charter. I said, then, there ought to be no trouble in spelling it out. Speaking generally Eden and Halifax agreed with my requests, but reserved the right to study them. They both said there will be no serious trouble about them except with Russia — and that everything will depend on whether Stalin *really* wants this League to succeed. Eden quite frankly said that the League is *not* being organized along the lines he would prefer; but that it is all worth while in order to see if we *can* live with Russia in the post-war world. I think we shall work very well together at Frisco.

Friday, April 20, 1945

Dr. H. V. Evatt, M.P., Minister of External Affairs for Australia, called on me this morning to say that the Australian demands at Frisco are substantially in line with the amendments I have offered and that I can expect Australian cooperation from start to finish. We spoke frankly about Russia. Dr. Evatt expressed the belief that Russia will not wish to see the Conference fail. But he said we might better not have any Peace League at all than to surrender to all of the Russian demands or to permit Russia to veto all of the improvements which he believes with me to be indispensable. Dr. Evatt is frank and vigorous. I was interested in his estimate of Eden and Stettinius. He does not think that either one of them adequately *understands* the problem. He referred to his visit of two years ago when he was here to say that while his country accepted the "Beat Hitler First" formula, it insisted that this must not mean a lack of adequate military strength in the Far Pacific to "hold Japan"; and he thanked me for my part in helping him at that time. I think he is going to be a tower of strength at Frisco.

On that same day, Connally and Vandenberg made their last pre-conference appearance on the floor of the Senate. Connally spoke briefly, warning that the Delegation could not be expected to "bring back perfection" but promising that the Americans would work on a nonpartisan basis and that Dumbarton Oaks would be liberalized. There was a solemn, attentive hush in the crowded chamber and there were tears in the Texan's eyes as he sat down. Vandenberg arose to compliment Connally on his statement and to add: "I have no illusions that the . . . conference can chart the millennium. Please do not expect it of us. . . . But I have faith that we may perfect this charter of peace and justice so that reasonable men of good will shall find in it so much good . . . that all lesser doubts and disagreements may be resolved in its favor. . . . Once more I am asking that your prayers for this great enterprise shall fail neither it nor us. . . ."

As the Senator ended his remarks there was sudden stirring of emotions such as the staid old Chamber had seldom witnessed. On both sides of the aisle men were getting to their feet, clapping their hands in violation of the Senate rules, and, after a moment, surging across the Chamber to shake hands, to put their arms around the shoulders of the two delegates and wish them well. America was going to San Francisco — to the second great international effort to establish lasting peace in the world — in a manner far removed from the lonely pilgrimage of Woodrow Wilson to Paris hardly a generation before.

10

San Francisco Conference: "Town Meeting of the World"

VANDENBERG left Washington on the weekend of April 21 for San Francisco and the "great adventure." None of the historic implications of the impending conference or of his own role escaped him as he set out to write his own "concept of justice" into the preliminary charter that had been drawn up at Dumbarton Oaks. He knew he would represent a viewpoint that "Russia will buck from Hell to Breakfast" but he was going to see it through. "My effort, in an allegorical word, is to give this new International Organization a 'soul,'" he wrote to a close political and newspaper associate. "This holds ultimate hope for the little countries — and it is the only hope I see for them."

To give the organization a "soul" he was determined to emphasize in the Charter the idea of world justice; of an organization that was flexible and changing and would be able to correct injustices that might arise as a result of the peace settlements or of future international agreements.

This approach was to involve Vandenberg in a number of dramatic battles, especially in opposition to the Soviet Union delegation, but it was also to become a dominant factor in his activities in later years; years in which he strove to strengthen the United Nations and to make it a bulwark of a peaceful and orderly world. There was no period in his career that the Senator regarded as more important to the future not only of the United States but of all nations as the two months spent at San Francisco.

He was by no means satisfied with the draft proposals which had been drawn up at Dumbarton Oaks. In the first place, he felt that it was important to get the word "justice" written into the Charter to symbolize the fundamental idea that the new organization would be the basis for world peace with justice. The Dumbarton Oaks proposals, in describing the purposes and principles of the organization, did not include the word "justice." Vandenberg, however, helped to get it into the preamble and Chapter One (Purposes and Principles) of the United Nations Charter. Actually, the word finally appeared three times: first, in relation to the establishment of "conditions under which justice and respect" for international obligations would be maintained; second, in reference to maintaining peace and security in conformity with the "principles of justice and international law"; and, finally, in reference to settlement of disputes "in such a manner that international peace and security, and justice, are not endangered." The insertion of the word "justice" proved comparatively easy but then there arose the question of whether the United Nations Charter would provide not merely the pious words but the working machinery to correct injustices.

One way that such a goal might be achieved was to make the General Assembly — in Vandenberg's words — "tomorrow's Town Meeting of the World" and in that endeavor he ran head on into the Russians. The Soviet delegation wanted to limit the right of the Assembly to discuss matters in the sphere of international relations, a limitation which the Senator and the other American delegates believed would be an infringement on freedom of speech and would cause "tremendous discontent" among the small powers. He waged a long but successful fight to prevent such restrictions.

Vandenberg also wanted to permit the Assembly to consider and make recommendations for solution of any international situation that might be regarded as a threat to peace. In other words, if the Assembly felt that any international agreement or treaty was unjust and thus might lead to war it would have the power to recommend corrective steps — including the review of treaties. Such an arrangement, he felt, was the only hope for the future of such countries as Poland, but it also would make the new organization flexible and adaptable to changing circumstances. Again, he encountered serious opposition, but it was basically a controversy over legalistic terms (the use of the word "treaties") and in the end he achieved his goal.

One of the most significant contributions of the Senator to the San Francisco Conference may have been his work in helping to perfect the formula for regional agreements within the framework of the United Nations by validating the concept of collective self-defense on a regional basis. This not only preserved the effectiveness of the Monroe Doctrine within the framework of the United Nations, but it resulted in Article 51 of the Charter, which was to become the basis for the Western Hemisphere defense treaty and, most significantly, for the North Atlantic Treaty under which the Western World later was organized to oppose the expansion of communism.

In addition, Vandenberg took an interest in liberalization of the veto power that was conferred on the Big Five members of the Security Council as a result of the Yalta agreements. The Russians wanted the right to veto even a discussion of international disputes. In other words, if one of the Big Five desired, it could prevent the United Nations from even talking about a situation that might be a threat to world peace. Vandenberg believed this was a ridiculous infringement on freedom of speech and, in a battle that almost broke up the conference, he played an important part in defeating the Russian proposal.

These were the main interests and contributions of the Senator at San Francisco, but there was another broader development in which he played a leading role — the ending of what he regarded as "appeasement" of Stalin. He went to the Conference convinced that the time had come to put the cards on the table and especially to test whether the Soviet Union wanted to establish machinery for justice in world affairs or whether Stalin merely wanted to use the new organization to foster and protect Communist expansion. Time and again, at critical points, he bolstered and stiffened Secretary Stettinius to stand firm on the Western concept of justice, convinced that the Russians would yield rather than — as some delegates feared — break up the conference. Then and later, it was obvious that Vandenberg believed that the idealist dream of a United Nations was practicable only if America faced the facts of international life and dealt with the Russians on a sternly realistic basis.

Imbued with this idea, he went to work at San Francisco with a kind of spiritual enthusiasm: a stern conviction that the Conference might determine the fate of the world for years to come. And in that spirit — rising above political considerations and personal consequences — he dedicated his heart and mind henceforth, almost to the exclusion of all else, to the concept of permanent peace with justice in a free world of free men.

The plenary sessions of the Conference met in the Opera House but many of the most important meetings among the delegates were in Stettinius' luxurious penthouse atop the Fairmont Hotel, high up on one of the city's steepest hills. The hotel was headquarters for the Americans, and Vandenberg had an office and a suite on the fourth floor. The American delegation met almost every day on the fifth floor and there were sessions, particularly of the Big Five, in the penthouse at all hours. The Fairmont was about ten minutes by automobile from the Opera House, and Vandenberg frequently found himself shuttling back and forth half a dozen times a day to keep up with meetings of his committees and with the penthouse sessions.

There was a great deal of enthusiasm and excitement among the delegates as they gathered at San Francisco. On April 24 the Senator began keeping a detailed diary of the negotiations, writing in it almost every day with the industry of a reporter who had a front row seat at one of history's major dramas. As one might expect, his diary entries deal mainly with those problems which he was given responsibility for handling at the Conference on behalf of the American delegation. They do not therefore tell the full story of what happened at San Francisco.

Tuesday, April 24, 1945 (San Francisco)

Stettinius reached here from Washington this morning (after his Washington week-end with Molotov and Eden). He immediately met our delegation and gave us a *thrilling* message. The new President [Truman] has declined to even wink at a surrender to Stalin on his demand for representation here for the Lublin Poles. He has just sent a blunt message to Stalin including a general demand for Frisco cooperation. Stettinius said Eden could scarcely believe his eyes when he saw a copy — and cheered loudly. Stettinius added that he explained to Molotov that future Russian aid from America depends entirely upon the temper and the mood and the conscience of the American people — and that Frisco is his last chance to *prove* that he deserves this aid. This is the best news in months. F.D.R.'s appeasement of Russia is over. We will "play-ball" gladly with the Russians and "give and take" because we must have unity for the sake of peace *but* it is no longer going to be all "give" and no "take" so far as we are concerned. Stettinius turned to me . . . and said — "*If you* had been talking about Poland to Molotov not even *you* could have made a stronger statement than Truman did." Stettinius does not know what the result will be. Molotov had to report to Stalin and so, pending a reply, they all moved out to join us here. He said that subsequent meetings with Eden, Molotov and Soong were very cordial and that the Russians seemed to be more cooperative. But the crisis will come when Stalin's answer arrives. Russia may withdraw. If it does, the conference *will proceed without Russia.* Now we are getting somewhere! In the absence of Stettinius and Connally, I have been presiding over the Delegation since we reached Frisco. We are continuing to have infinite "press trouble" because of the congenital State Department fear of newsmen. We are *trying* to get things changed.

Wednesday, April 25, 1945

The Conference opens today — with Russian clouds in every sky. I don't know whether this is Frisco or Munich. The Delegation met for three hours this morning. Stettinius opened up the "three votes" issue. It immediately became apparent that Stalin is going to demand *not only* membership in the ultimate Peace League for White Russia and the Ukraine but *also* seats for them *in this conference.* A letter was read from Truman *ordering* the delegation to vote for the former pursuant to F.D.R.'s pledge. He said nothing about the latter. Molotov insists that the former question must be settled tomorrow. (Obviously he will immediately follow with the other demand.) I argued to the finish that *we* have a right to decide for ourselves *when* we shall "keep our promise" on the first proposition; that the American people will swallow this F.D.R. pledge (reluctantly) if it is evident that Russia is willing to "play ball" on other things; that we should demand that the issue be not precipitated until the *whole* pattern (including a settlement of the Polish problem) is in hand; otherwise, we shall be allowing Stalin to pick us off piece-meal (just as Hitler used to do). Ambassador Harriman argued that we must keep the promise made by F.D.R. and *not* permit Russia to break up the Conference on *this* point; but he said he would join me sled-length in declining to yield to Russia on subsequent matters of League policy, even though Russia walked out. . . .

The decision is one of judgment — *At what point is it wisest to stop appeasing Stalin?* Otherwise a new "Munich" will be followed by comparable tragedies.

Vandenberg's pre-conference insistence that he should be a "free agent" at San Francisco, not bound by any Administration decisions, assumed new importance on April 25 when he was a lone dissenter against the admission of White Russia and the Ukraine to the sessions of the Conference.

Wednesday evening, April 25, 1945

The plot thickened tonight — and the American Delegation began to waver. It developed that Molotov is making an issue even of who shall be President of the Conference — altho all other powers agreed that Stettinius (representing the host government) should be President, as is the invariable practice. Molotov wants 4 Presidents rotating. Dulles said this would be an insult to the United States. Various schemes were proposed to compromise the issue. But at least upon *this* point the Delegation voted to "stand pat" and take a chance on voting Russia down tomorrow.

But on White Russia and the Ukraine, the situation shifted. . . . Nelson Rockefeller said that the South Americans will insist upon tieing the admission of the Argentine into any such deal. Truman was reported opposed to admitting the Argentine, and his latest letter of explicit instructions regarding Russia applies *only* to ultimate membership in the League. My position is that none but the United Nations can be admitted to the Conference because otherwise we will throw open the whole question why Italy and Rumania, etc. (to say nothing of all the neutrals) should not be admitted besides, I do *not* believe it is sound policy to surrender to Russia on these unsound propositions. After all, we must answer to the *American people* and to the Senate — as well as to Stalin. We might just as well find out *now* whether Russia intends to work in decent cooperation with this Peace League or whether we are simply launching a perpetual row. Stettinius finally asked for a vote on whether he should tell Truman that the Delegation recommends that we vote to seat White Russia and the Ukraine not only in the ultimate League but also in the Conference (two or three weeks hence) along with the Argentine. For the first time, the Delegation split. I voted *no*. The rest voted *yes*.

On April 26, one of the dramatic sessions of the conference occurred when the Steering Committee took up the chairmanship problem.

Thursday, April 26, 1945

Stettinius, Harriman and Dunn reported to the Delegation tonight on what happened in the Steering Committee of the Conference this morning. It involved the Russian row over the Chairmanship. Molotov moved for four Chairmen (sort of a "Soviet" of Chairmen). Eden was *supposed* to move *one* Chairman and nominate Stettinius. Instead, without any notice to our people, Eden moved for four Chairmen with Stettinius to be the presiding Chairman (a sort of compromise with the Russian view). Padilla (Mexico) then proposed *one* Chairman (Stettinius) and three Vice-Chairmen. Molotov said he wouldn't take a Vice-Chairmanship. Padilla said it was a time-honored custom that the host Government should have the Chairmanship. Smuts of South Africa and Fraser of

New Zealand supported the Eden compromise — to the shocked amazement of our people. In the resultant melee, an adjournment was taken until tomorrow with the subject still open.

Vandenberg's reference to the "resultant melee" told only part of the story. Others who were present at the Steering Committee meeting reported that Ezequiel Padilla had made a gracious speech in support of Stettinius and that Molotov had shocked the meeting by a biting attack on the Mexican Foreign Minister, ridiculing him and denouncing him as a puppet of the United States. The result apparently was not what Molotov expected. The Latin Americans regarded the attack as an insult to all of them and as an expression of contempt for their belief in the dignity and independence of the smaller nations. Padilla was a popular figure among them and Molotov probably could not have done anything that would have more effectively united the Latin Americans against the Russian position.

April 26, 1945 [continued]

Stettinius told us tonight he had talked with Truman and had been told to stand pat (on the chairmanship). The difficulty is that this is more than a row over the Conference Chairmanship. It clearly indicates a Russian purpose to carry this same Sovietizing idea into the ultimate organization of the Peace League itself. Furthermore, the Russian insistence upon the point (a relatively minor one) indicates what trouble we are going to have with Moscow on *every* point — a sort of "rule or ruin" attitude. Connally and I were particularly insistent upon finding out whether Eden and the British had double-crossed us. If we can't count on *them* we'd better find it out. Harriman was particularly insistent in the view that Eden acted in good faith and that it was all the result of a misunderstanding.

It was the consensus of Delegation opinion that we must "stand by our guns" at whatever point we are *sure* of votes enough to win. Preferably, our original position. Otherwise, the Eden compromise. I continue to believe that *this* is the point at which to line up our votes (with a last chance for the

180   THE PRIVATE PAPERS OF SENATOR VANDENBERG

British to prove good faith) and *win* and *end this appeasement of the Reds now before it is too late.*

The matter will be settled in the Steering Committee tomorrow morning. Stettinus has asked Connally and me to accompany him. *Next!*

The "next" test came quickly. On the following day Vandenberg took advantage of an opportunity to stiffen Stettinius' stand against the Soviet bloc and engineered a rebuff of attempts to seat representatives of the Polish Lublin government at the conference.

Friday, April 27, 1945

At 9 this morning we organized in the million dollar penthouse atop the Fairmont (where Stettinius is staying) for the day's battle. Connally and I joined the Secretary for the Steering Committee (consisting of the heads of all Delegations). First we went with him to a private conference with Eden and Molotov. It was my first meeting with Molotov. He is a powerful fellow though not large — greeted me with a very genial smile and said he "knew all about me." The question was whether he would agree to Eden's compromise regarding the 4 Chairmen. He would advance a little and then draw back. Agreement was impossible. It is evident that these Russians have an obsession about the necessity of preserving every semblance of their "equality" with every other nation even in parliamentary forms. Eden and Stettinius stood pat. So the battle was transferred to the full Steering Committee. Everybody except Molotov was agreeable to Eden's compromise of yesterday. Molotov insisted. Eden again stood up. At the last moment when Molotov saw he was clearly in for a beating, he withdrew his latest demands and acquiesced. This means 4 rotating Chairmen (with Stettinius as Chairman of the Chairmen and of the Steering Committee and the Executive Committee and specifically clothed with authority to "run the conference"). It is really a victory for Molotov — even tho he muffed his final objective.

Molotov then immediately brought up the admission of

"TOWN MEETING OF THE WORLD"   181

White Russia and the Ukraine to membership in the ultimate Peace League. Stettinius read Truman's letter agreeing to carry out F.D.R.'s tragically unfortunate pledge at Yalta. Eden and Soong supported. It was voted. (A picture of Anglo-Saxon nations *keeping* faith — altho we *all hated* what we had to do.)

Then we had another example of the typical Russian technique — always crowding for more. Molotov asked that White Russia and the Ukraine be admitted immediately to this Conference. After some maneuvering, this was side-tracked by reference to a Committee.

But then came the worst of all. Masaryk (Czech) read a statement that his Government wanted the Polish Lublin Government admitted to the Conference. He was promptly supported by Molotov. All of which, of course, was in direct *violation* of Yalta. This was *serious*. If any such action had been taken it would have wrecked *any* chance of American approval of the work of the Conference. Someone suggested that this, too, be side-tracked to a Committee (which would have been almost as bad). I was sitting directly behind Stettinius. I told him *this* move *must* be *killed* at once and in the open. I sketched out a quick, brief statement and handed it to Stettinius reading as follows: "I remind the Conference that we have just honored our Yalta engagements in behalf of Russia. I also remind the Conference that there are other Yalta obligations which equally require allegiance. One of them calls for a new and representative Polish Provisional Government. Until this happens, this Conference cannot, in good conscience, recognize the Lublin Government. It would be a sordid exhibition of bad faith." To Stettinius' credit, *he never hesitated an instant*. He took the floor and read exactly what I had written — and with great emphasis. Molotov showed surprise. Eden promptly seconded Stettinius' statement — expressing his amazement, in addition, that Russia should presume to ask for a decision here ahead of an agreement between Britain, America and Russia as pledged at Yalta (which Russia is preventing because it wants a puppet government in Poland).

I forgive Eden for what happened yesterday. He backed

us up today magnificently. Again seeing himself in danger of a beating, Molotov acquiesced in a motion offered by Foreign Minister Spaak of Belgium expressing the hope that this new Polish Government may be organized in time to be represented here before we adjourn.

I am more convinced than ever that we should stand our ground against these Russian demands and *quit appeasing Stalin and Molotov*. Otherwise, this Peace League itself will be nothing but a shambles — with the Soviets bullying it upon every occasion and preventing all constructive work.

Monday, April 30, 1945

The Russian row was pretty well washed up today. I went again with Stettinius to the Steering Committee. Earlier this morning, the Executive Committee had voted Molotov down, 9 to 3, on seating the Argentine. He fought it again in the Steering Committee and was downed 29 to 5 on a motion to "defer it for a few days." Then he took it to the full plenary session and lost 32 to 4. Meanwhile, he got White Russia and the Ukraine seated unanimously. . . . At the same time Molotov took another beating on his effort to have the Conference give special recognition to Sidney Hillman's new World Labor Congress [World Federation of Trade Unions] which was bitterly fought by the A.F. of L. In prospect of sure defeat, he withdrew his motion. The *net* of all this battle is that Molotov won only at those points where he had a commitment from the dead hands of F.D.R. Otherwise, he would have won *nothing*. He lost every other battle. He has done more in four days to solidify Pan America against Russia than anything that ever happened. . . . (The Conference Bulletin embarrassed me tonight by printing a quote from the Washington Times-Herald — "Molotov and Vandenberg are dominating figures of Conference — It looks as if entire history of Conference may revolve around a battle of wits between these two men — it is the hand of Vandenberg that is generally discerned in U.S. moves on Conference chess board.") This isn't true. But I *have* had my part in it — and I am very grateful for the prompt and whole-hearted consideration which Stettinius gives me upon all occasions. . . .

In this period the Big Four powers (Britain, the United States, Russia, and China) arranged to meet and agree privately on as many as possible of the proposed amendments to the proposals drawn up at Dumbarton Oaks. The idea was that a considerable number of them would be acceptable to all four powers and that the four powers would then stand united at the conference behind the amendments they all accepted. At the same time, the consultations would show the points on which the four powers disagreed. One of the latter points that was of vital interest to Vandenberg concerned the right of the General Assembly to examine any situation that might be a threat to peace, including situations arising out of treaties or international engagements. Vandenberg was determined that the United Nations should not become an instrument through which the big powers would merely maintain the postwar status quo, as in Poland, and thus seek to perpetuate whatever injustices might be in the peace settlements. He was convinced that the new world organization must be flexible and able to bring about peaceful changes in the status quo if it was to endure as a guardian of world peace. Discussion of this point brought out considerable opposition to including a provision in the Charter that the Assembly could consider revision of "treaties."

Wednesday, May 2, 1945

The four sponsoring powers met tonight in Sec. Stettinius' Pent-house to compare proposed amendments. Molotov was in great good humor. He has learned the American phrase "O.K." and he used it with obvious amusement whenever he agreed to a proposal — and he agreed quite generally until we hit my key amendment to Chapter V B6 — which revives the pledges of the Atlantic Charter and permits the assembly to explore "situations arising out of any treaties or international engagements." He himself proposed even *better* language for my first sentence — even broader than I had written it — ... But he flatly refused to yield to my second sentence regarding the Atlantic Charter and treaty revision. Eden, for the British, submitted a substitute for this second sentence — "Subject to the provisions of Paragraph IA, the General Assembly should recommend measures for the peaceful adjustment of situations likely to impair the general welfare or to produce results inconsistent with the principles laid down in Chapter II, including situations arising out of any treaties or international engagements." He also agreed to list the Atlantic Charter among the "principles laid down in Chapter II." This was entirely agreeable. Soong agreed for China. I told Molotov that I needed this explicit language (which everyone agrees to be implicit in Dumbarton Oaks) in order to win adequate Senate support. He insisted, however, that this would weaken all treaty obligations. I insisted that it is the only way to escape freezing a status quo and denying any escape from errors made in decisions during the war and at the peace table — denying any escape except by the very armed revolt which we are sworn to resist. Molotov simply kept on repeating "No O.K." The subject was finally passed over for the time being. I later had a long talk with Molotov. He is an earnest, able man for whom I have come to have a profound respect — despite our disagreements.

The dispute over the word "treaties" was settled by an agreement that the Assembly could consider situations "regardless of origin" — a phrase that was put forth by the American delegation and was completely satisfactory to Vandenberg. He also was pleased by a general willingness to accept his proposals to insert the word "justice" into the Charter at various points, although after reading a statement by Stettinius dealing with these amendments but not mentioning the word "justice," he growled to another delegate: "Is the State Department eternally allergic to the word 'justice'?" The May 4th entry in his diary reflected considerable optimism as a result of two days of work which represented, he felt, "an amazing achievement." But there were many big obstacles still ahead.

Friday, May 4, 1945
At the end of two terrific days of constant consultation among the Big Four over Amendments, we finally quit at midnight (the deadline for filing with the Secretariat). We have been in practically continuous session in the "Penthouse" for 48 hours. We (all 4 Great Powers) have agreed

upon 27 amendments. It is an amazing achievement and ought to substantially shorten the work of the Conference. The biggest hurdles are behind us. But we reached the deadline without complete agreement on "regional arrangements" or "treaty revision." Britain, China and the U.S., however, have finally agreed upon the second sentence in a substitute for Chap. V-B-6. This is it:

"Subject to the provisions of paragraph I of this section, The General Assembly should be empowered to recommend measures for the peaceful adjustment of any situations, regardless of origin, which it deems likely to impair the general welfare or friendly relations among nations, including situations resulting from a violation of the Purposes and Principles set forth in this Charter." We have dropped the specific word "treaties" but, to my entire satisfaction, we have broadened the authority to include any situations "regardless of origin." We have also dropped specific reference to the "Atlantic Charter"; but we have covered most of its essential pledges, including "self-determination" by reference to "Purposes and Principles." Meanwhile, of course, everything I want in respect to "justice" and "Human rights" and "fundamental freedoms" is in.

Molotov said tonight at the finish that he was in substantial agreement with the new text but that he wanted 24 hours to think it over. Therefore, the three other powers presented the substitute text on their individual responsibility. (Molotov phoned Stettinius at 9 o'clock Saturday evening that he would accept the substitute.)

A serious shadow fell across the meeting in the pent-house about five o'clock this afternoon when Eden was called to the phone and notified that Russia has now publicly admitted that the 16 Poles (from the Polish underground) invited to Moscow to discuss a broadening of the Polish Provisional Government pursuant to the Yalta agreement have been arrested by the Soviets and flung into jail for "diversive activities." We do not know who the 16 are — except that it is generally understood they include the Poles whom Britain and America have been urging as part of the new Provisional Government. This is bad business. We immediately recessed to permit a consultation between Eden, Stettinius and Molotov. The two former subsequently issued statements peremptorily demanding complete information and calling off all further negotiations under the Yalta Agreement until adequate information is forthcoming. It is said that Molotov was unusually "uneasy" when faced with these facts by the other Foreign Ministers. If it should develop that the 16 are dead — ? ? ? ? ? [Later press accounts indicated that most of the sixteen were sentenced to jail but several apparently were acquitted.]

In the next few days Vandenberg was plunged into his biggest task of the Conference in connection with the provisions relating to regional agreements operating within the framework of the United Nations. It was generally agreed that any nation or nations would, after the war, have complete freedom to take action to prevent any resurgence of aggression by the Axis states. But where did that leave the Monroe Doctrine and the Western Hemisphere? Suppose a European power should endanger the peace of South America. Would the Western Hemisphere states have to act defensively through the United Nations, where effective action might be blocked by the veto? This opened up a whole new field of supposition, and Vandenberg was to spend many difficult days in search of the solution which was of fundamental importance not only to the United States but to all of the small nations of the world.

In the end, a new article (Article 51) was inserted in the Charter in order to make perfectly clear that members of the United Nations always preserved the right to take action either individually or collectively to defend themselves against attack. This reassured the Latin American countries and made agreement possible on the regional provisions of the Charter. Article 51, toward which Vandenberg made an important contribution, was to become a keystone in the later efforts of the Western Powers against the world-wide expansion of communism.

Saturday, May 5, 1945

The pressures of the past week (the hardest working week of my life) relaxed somewhat today since the deadline for amendments passed last night. But it didn't take long for a new crisis to arise. This time it involves "regional arrangements." The Amendment adopted last night included language which permits enforcement action (without reference to the Security Council) under measures (like Russian bilateral defense Treaties with France, Britain, etc.) "against enemy States" or "in regional arrangements directed against renewal of aggressive policy on the part of such States." I could not object to this because it is in line with my January 10th speech demanding a permanent military alliance, outside the Peace League, to keep the Axis disarmed. But, as seems to be inevitable in all these matters, this Amendment opened up serious collateral considerations as we thought it over today. Europe would have freedom of action for her defensive regional arrangements (pending the time when the Peace League shall prove its dependability as a substitute policeman) but the Western Hemisphere would *not* have similar freedom of action under its Pan-American agreements which have a background of a century behind them and which were specifically implemented again by our 21 Republics a few weeks ago at Chapultepec. Therefore, in the event of trouble in the Americas, we could not act ourselves; we would have to depend exclusively on the Security Council; and any one permanent member of the Council could veto the latter action (putting us at the mercy of Britain, Russia or China). Thus little is left of the Monroe Doctrine. Since I am the American member of the Conference Committee dealing with "regional arrangements" I feel a particular responsibility in this matter. It bothered me all day. By a significant coincidence, Nelson Rockefeller (Assistant Secretary of State in charge of Pan-American relations) asked me to join him at dinner where he disclosed these same fears and said the South American Republics are up in arms. . . . The grave problem is to find a formula which will reasonably protect legitimate regional arrangements without destroying the over-all responsibility of united action through the Peace League and without inviting the formation of a lot of dangerous new "regional spheres of influence" etc. In the course of the evening I was able to make a suggestion which seems to answer our needs without exposing the League to these other hazards. It involves a limited extension of the European exemption to the Western Hemisphere. At the end of the latter language it proposes to add: "and with the exception of measures which may be taken under . . . the Act of Chapultepec of the Inter-American Conference on Problems of Peace and War, signed at Mexico City on March 8, 1945, until such time as the Organization may, by consent of the Governing Board of the Pan American Union, be charged with this function." Rockefeller was enthusiastic about this formula. He called in the Cuban Ambassador and the Colombian Foreign Minister to get their reaction. They, too, were enthusiastic. I put the proposal with a supporting argument, into an immediate letter to Secretary Stettinius. It was now midnight. I delivered the letter to Stettinius Sunday morning at 9:30.

Vandenberg's regional proposal encountered opposition not only from other big powers but within the United States delegation as well. An important faction in the State Department and in the delegation was fearful that the United Nations itself would be fatally weakened if various regional groups were empowered to act without going through the Security Council.

Vandenberg recognized this danger by remarking that "the Monroe Doctrine is protected only if we kick the daylights out of the world organization," but he was convinced that this danger could be overcome or at least mitigated. He was supported by Dulles and Representatives Bloom and Eaton and by Nelson Rockefeller. It is interesting to note that, although the war in Europe ended on May 7, Vandenberg's diary entries were so occupied with the Charter Conference that he did not even comment on the German surrender and the end of the long European phase of the struggle.

Monday, May 7, 1945

After Stettinius circulated my letter, "Hell" broke loose. We had a long meeting of the Delegation. Bloom and Eaton agreed with me. But Stassen felt my proposal would gut the international power by emphasizing regional authority. This view was generally held by State Department, particularly by Pasvolsky who was bitter about it. Meanwhile, Rockefeller evidently had taken a trimming at the hands of his Boss for his part in the controversy. The Army and the Navy obviously *wanted* to agree [with Vandenberg] but were "under wraps." Assistant Secretary of War McCloy, speaking for these Services, suggested that the point be met in a separate protocol to be signed by the other four Great Powers (permanent members of the Security Council) that they would *not* vote to veto regional action by Pan-America. Some astonishing statements were made in the debate. Pasvolsky said that if there was a Pan-Am dispute requiring the use of force and any permanent member of the Council votes against it (and thus vetoed it) we would go ahead and use force to suit ourselves (and the Peace League would be all through). I argued that any such latitude as this, reserved to each State, would be a far greater threat to the League than would a frank exemption of Pan-America (under Chapultepec) to use regional force itself in the first instance. Dulles argued that there is nothing in Dumbarton Oaks which prohibits "self-defense" and that under the Chapultepec agreement "self-defense" in the Western Hemisphere is a partnership affair and that the Monroe Doctrine is still part of it. I served notice on the Delegation, as a matter of good faith, that if this question is not specifically cleared up in the Charter, I shall expect to see a Reservation on the subject in the Senate and that I shall support it. I do not see how we could tolerate a possible situation in which (under the Charter) we could not deal with a bad Pan-Am situation at all because (1) we are not permitted to act under Chapultepec and (2) the Security Council is stopped by a Russian or a British or a Chinese or a French veto. Neither do I see how we can desert the demands of our united Pan-Am neighbors in this matter.

At the end of an acrimonious session tonight, the subject was temporarily referred to a special Committee of technicians.

Wednesday, May 9, 1945

The regional row is still unsettled — and grows in magnitude. We had the first meeting of the Regional Committee (of which I am the American member) today. It speedily developed that not only are the South Americans hot about protecting Chapultepec but the Australians are equally anxious not to be left unprotected in their far corner of the earth. They want liberty of regional action if some one of the Big Powers vetoes Organization action on the Council. Other potential regional groups are forming and they could be highly dangerous — particularly the Arabian bloc in its impact on Palestine. Our great problem is to find a rule which protects legitimate existing regional groups (like Pan-Am) without opening up the opportunity for regional balance-of-power groups. Nothing was done at the Conference meeting except to appoint a sub-committee of twelve powers (upon which I represent America).

Our own Delegation is no nearer a settlement. Since it involves basic national policy, the whole thing will have to be put up to the President. . . .

On that same day, Vandenberg won another round in his fight to enable the Assembly to examine any problem relating to maintenance of international peace and security.

Wednesday, May 9, 1945 [*continued*]

Meanwhile the Conference Committee (of which I am also a member) dealing with the Assembly met this afternoon, and the first major action of the Conference was Committee approval of my Amendment to keep the Assembly wide-open for the exploration of any subject "regardless of origin" — thus to make it truly the town meeting of tomorrow's world, and to prevent this Organization becoming an instrument to freeze the status quo in a static world. Thus *justice* gets a forum and *injustice* loses its grip. We had quite a fight. I was ably supported by Mr. Dingle Foot, the United Kingdom delegate. The final vote was 23 to 3 with 2 not voting. The argument chiefly revolved around the clause prohibiting the Assembly from acting if and while the Council might be dealing with the same subject. My amendment included this prohibition. Many wanted to wipe it out. But it stands.

Sunday, May 13, 1945

The great problem this last week-end has been to find an answer to the regional problem. It is now the crux of the Conference. If it is answered to the satisfaction of the South Americans, they will go along with us to clean up all the other problems. If not, we are surrounded by trouble. The question squarely arose in our Regional Committee. The Colombian Foreign Minister made an able presentation of the Pan-American viewpoint, insisting that the Act of Chapultepec must be recognized and that this Western Hemisphere must not be left at the mercy of a default in the Security Council thanks to some alien veto. I followed with an exposition of what I believe to be the American view — namely, that we do not propose to desert the 100-year old Monroe Doctrine, the 50-year old Pan American Union, and the recent Act of Chapultepec, but that we do not propose to give regional arrangements any such supremacy as will destroy the unity of the world organization, and invite a general break-up of the world into regional groups. My statement apparently caught the fancy of the South Americans. Rockefeller reported they were ready for any action within the boundaries of my speech.

Eden goes home tomorrow morning. He is a "great guy." I have come to have a deep affection and a profound respect for him. We have become great friends.

There is much underground chatter about Stettinius. Unfortunately he pretty generally has the press against him. There is increasing gossip about a successor, when this Conference is ended. I agree that there is no longer any strong hand on our foreign policy rudder — neither Truman nor Stettinius nor Grew. I agree that it is a tragic situation in these difficult times. Stettinius does *not* have a seasoned grasp of foreign affairs. He rarely contributes to our policy decisions. We improvise as we go along. Stettinius is not *really* Secretary of State. He is *really* "General Manager" of the State Department (which is a totally different thing). Incidentally, he is the *best* "General Manager" I ever saw. He *gets things done*. But I am afraid that is his chief idea — just to "get things done." He does *not* take the same firm stand in respect to *policy* that he does in "getting things done." President Truman sadly needs a real Secretary of State in the realm of *policy*. But until someone shows me someone whom the President would appoint who is a real improvement in this direction, I am opposed to changing Stettinius.

Actually, Mr. Truman had already decided to replace Stettinius and had told James F. Byrnes early in April that he would be offered the job. Byrnes agreed but they decided not to make the change until after the San Francisco Conference. This decision was unknown to the delegates at the Conference in mid-May when the rumors about Stettinius were circulated and Vandenberg apparently gave them only passing attention.

In the next day or two the American delegation worked over various formulas for a regional solution that would identify the Act of Chapultepec, but the Russians were uncertain and the British refused to accept on the grounds that it invited "group domination." A compromise was then worked out with the British omitting any direct reference to Chapultepec. Vandenberg had "about come to the conclusion that this is the best course — to use general language in the Charter . . . [and] then pass a Delegation Resolution notifying the Senate of our interpretation." This solution, he hoped, would relieve the worries of the small nations, particularly in Latin America. He was keenly aware of the danger that the small nations would feel they were being left out in the cold while the Big Five decided their fate at sessions in the penthouse; he remarked at one point that it was about time to "get them out of the doghouse and into the penthouse" so they would be a vital part of the proceedings.

Tuesday, May 15, 1945

After two more days of wrangling and re-writing, we *finished* the troublesome Regional problem, so far as we are concerned, today. . . . I had a private chat with Stettinius (I called it "fatherly") in which I urged him to take hold of this problem with a firm hand and *to be the Secretary of State* in fact as well as name. I told him this Regional problem involves a decision as to what the *Administration's foreign policy* is in respect to Inter-American relations; that this can't be settled by us Republicans at Frisco; that the *Administration* has got to say what it intends to do to justify the work of the Mexico City Conference (Chapultepec) which *it* sponsored only two months ago. I told him that if he settled *this*, we would have little further trouble with our Latin friends.

Stettinius forthwith took over. Three hours later, we had a meeting with the Latins in the Pent-House and Stettinius *told them* what we would do: (1) propose an Amendment reserving the right of self-defense *including* regional self-defense if and when the Security Council fails to act; (2) propose an amendment including resort to *regional* facilities among the peaceful mechanisms to be embraced; (3) agree to call a new Pan-American Conference (after the Frisco Conference) to implement the Act of Chapultepec (as required by that Act) within the frame-work of the Peace League. The Latins took it. The President gave Stettinius his O.K. over the phone. The Delegation gave its O.K. at 6 o'clock. I announced it to the Regional Committee of the Conference at a meeting this evening. A special meeting of the Sub-Committee has been called for tomorrow to take it up. Meanwhile, we are endeavoring to get the 4 Powers behind it. This has been a great piece of work. It ought to remove the biggest barrier to Conference success. Stettinius is entitled to immense credit for having made a job of it and for having driven it through. It shows what he can do. I hope he continues to *be* Secretary of State.

At this time an old problem was revived in the negotiations. It concerned proposals to write into the Charter a clause that would, under certain circumstances, permit a nation to withdraw from the United Nations. There was in mid-May and later considerable argument over whether a withdrawal clause was necessary, but in the end none was inserted. Vandenberg argued that it was a mistake to omit such a provision from the Charter.

Wednesday, May 16, 1945

For the second time in all of our long Delegation deliberations, I voted a lonesome "*No*" today. It was on the question whether the Charter shall have a withdrawal clause. (There is none in Dumbarton Oaks.) The Delegation voted that there shall be none. It is my position that if any Power (particularly a Big Power) *wants* to get out, it is better out than in because its subsequent reluctance and recalcitrancy is likely to be a liability anyway. I also know that this is calculated to be a tough target of attack in the Senate. I feel that the League should not confess its fears (through withholding a withdrawal clause) that it cannot hold its Members on a voluntary basis. In the long run, if it cannot hold them on a voluntary basis, it cannot hold them at all. Certainly it cannot hold *us*. The counter argument is that we should not make withdrawal too easy; and that if the Charter is silent on the subject, it means that the Council and the Assembly can decide for itself about withdrawals if, as and when the issue arises. But such being the real case, I do not feel that we should take on this added Senate jeopardy by failing candidly to meet the issue *now*. But it's not worth a row.

Saturday, May 19, 1945

Four of us had the most earnestly serious chat since I came to Frisco. The others were John Foster Dulles, Dr. Isaiah Bowman (President of Johns Hopkins), and Hamilton Fish Armstrong (Editor of "Foreign Affairs"). They are our top official "advisors" in all Conference matters. Dulles has come to the conclusion that we *must* have a withdrawal clause. At present there is none. On the other hand, a Uruguayan proposal to *prohibit* a withdrawal clause has been rejected. In Dulles' opinion this means that there *can* be ultimate withdrawal but it will have to occur under arrangements approved by the Security Council. But he has now come to the conclusion that it must be made specific. We dealt in blunt, plain realism. Since coming to Frisco, our relations with Russia have worsened all over the world (as well as here). Russian pledges at Yalta are being everywhere defied.

Yet we are proposing to enter a Peace Partnership with her based upon mutual faith — and she is getting a "veto" (thanks to our fidelity to Roosevelt at Yalta) upon our freedom of action all round the globe to a substantial degree. Dulles said he has been reluctantly driven to the conclusion that America cannot enter such an arrangement without a definite right of withdrawal because we cannot foresee the future. (This has been my view all along — plus the fact that a World Organization *without* a right of withdrawal is too much like a Super-State paraphrasing our own "indestructible Union.")

. . . Dulles will probably circulate a memorandum on the subject to the American Delegates. It is late to raise the issue again — but better late than never. The Delegation has already voted 6 to 1 *against* a withdrawal clause; but I am certain that Senator Connally does not like it any better than I do, and there probably are others. We shall see what we shall see.

The controversy over a withdrawal clause continued but it was finally decided that it would not be possible to get acceptance of the proposal. In the end the Conference approved a declaration of interpretation making clear that members could exercise the right of withdrawal in certain circumstances. The declaration stipulated that "the faculty of withdrawal of the members should neither be provided for nor regulated. . . . It is obvious, however, that withdrawals or some other forms of dissolution . . . would become inevitable if . . . the Organization was revealed to be unable to maintain peace or could do so only at the expense of law and justice."

Meantime, another major issue had arisen parallel with the regional problem. This concerned the veto powers of the Big Five permanent members of the Security Council. The question was divided into three phases. First, there was general agreement that the veto could be exercised to halt any proposal for enforcement action against an aggressor state. This was necessary to assure the big powers a right of decision with respect to use of their armed forces or application of other sanctions which might lead to war. Second, it had been agreed at Yalta

196   THE PRIVATE PAPERS OF SENATOR VANDENBERG

and written into the Charter that the veto could be exercised to prevent the Security Council from acting to bring about a peaceful settlement of a dispute, except that a party to the dispute was not permitted to vote in such instances. The United States delegation now reluctantly accepted this prior agreement, but Vandenberg thought it was "absurd," and merely acquiesced. Third, the main controversy was over a Russian proposal that the veto could be used to prevent even a discussion of a dispute between two states. The United States and other delegations refused to accept this curb on freedom of speech and it resulted in a bitter deadlock.

Sunday, May 20, 1945

Another serious problem arose today. Rockefeller raised it with Dulles who asked that Stassen and I sit in. The Yalta "veto" as *now* interpreted includes a "veto" for the Big Five even on preliminary discussion and investigation of disputes by the Security Council. It does *not* apply, at this point, if one of the Big Powers is a defendant. But that makes it all the more anomalous and fantastic that it should apply to the disputes of others. The "veto" is bad enough under *any* circumstances. But when it can stop the whole process of peaceful inquiry, it becomes at this point, utterly indefensible. The British, through Sir Alexander Cadogan, said yesterday that they do not construe Yalta as requiring a "veto" at this point — (altho their Delegation later rather took this back). Australia, Canada and New Zealand are leading a bitter fight to change the "veto" in this *one* particular. Most of the South American countries threaten to bolt unless it is changed. *We* are in the unfortunate position of being bound by our own State Department interpretation that Yalta includes this *total* "veto" (which, of course, is the Russian position). It means, in plain language that the Russians can raise Hell all over the world, through satellites and fifth columns, and stop the new League from even inquiring into it. It is the *worst* of our legacies from Roosevelt. What a tragedy that F.D.R. could not have lived through this Conference: under the circumstances as they have developed (particularly with Russia violating *her* Yalta pledges all over the world), I do not doubt for an instant that he would force a show-down with Stalin not only on these pledges but also on this critical problem at Frisco. I have recommended that Stettinius put the matter up to Truman, suggesting that *he* ask Stalin to agree to this very modest change in the "veto" lest our stubborn adherence to this repugnant thing may either wreck the Conference or ultimately shock the moral conscience of the country and the world.

Meantime, the regional controversy had been moving toward a solution. On May 18 Vandenberg noted that Stettinius had tried to get the Big Four to agree to presentation of the compromise on regional powers to the Conference Committee, but Gromyko declined for Russia until he had received instructions from Moscow. He even declined to agree that the compromise could be presented merely as an American plan. Vandenberg, who had been forced to put off the presentation until the Committee was becoming impatient, was disgusted because "once more" he had to go down and apologize to his Committee "for another delay." The same thing happened again the next day. Gromyko still had no instructions, and Vandenberg confessed that "by this time I was hopping mad and I am afraid I made a pretty bitter speech to the American delegation. . . . It is insufferable. . . . I bluntly announced that I would not again 'humiliate either my country or myself' by reporting another delay." Gromyko finally got his instructions on May 18 and he merely wanted to make a few changes which Vandenberg felt strengthened the proposed formula. The Big Four and the Latin Americans agreed, and on May 23 Vandenberg was able to proceed.

Wednesday, May 23, 1945

Yesterday our Sub-committee unanimously o.k'ed the final Regional draft. This afternoon, the full Committee did the same. There followed about 20 speeches lauding the results and very generously applauding my part in them. I made a brief acknowledgment at the end.

I am deeply impressed by what has happened. . . . At the outset many of the Nations were far, very far, apart. Our own Delegation was not wholly united. The subject itself was difficult — how to *save* legitimate regionalism (like Pan-Am) and yet not destroy the essential over-all authority of the International Organization. By hammering it out vis-à-vis, we have found an answer which satisfies practically everybody. In my view, that is the great hope for the new League itself. If we do nothing more than create a constant forum where nations must *face* each other and *debate* their differences and strive for common ground, we shall have done infinitely much.

Vandenberg's conviction that the great hope of the United Nations was the creation of a forum for debate on issues that might lead to war was to be severely tested later in bitter disputes with the Soviet Union, but he never wavered in that belief. Even in the midst of Senate controversy over the North Atlantic Treaty four years later, when he charged that the free world had been placed in jeopardy by "embattled, greedy communism," he added that the Charter had "done provably much for peace. I hesitate to think where the world would be today if its [the United Nations'] council table had not been available to talk things out, no matter how inconclusively, rather than to shoot them out."

II

San Francisco Conference: Showdown with Russia

ONCE THE regional problem had been solved in broad outline — further details had to be ironed out later — attention of the Conference centered on a new series of crises in which the veto controversy came closest to causing a breakup. Vandenberg believed that fundamental principles were directly involved in the dispute and he labored to prevent any weakening of opposition to the Russian demands for a veto power so broad that it would have prevented even freedom of speech in the Security Council.

Saturday, May 26, 1945

Every week-end has its crisis. This week it is the revolt of the lesser Powers against an extreme interpretation of the Yalta "veto" which would permit any of the Big 5 to "veto" even a preliminary discussion of a problem in the Council. Led by Dr. Evatt of Australia, the lesser Powers are promising a real rebellion on this point. The trouble, as usual, rotates round the Soviets. Once more our own American problem is to keep faith with F.D.R.'s promises at Yalta. This time the problem is more perplexing than usual because the Big 5 is in disagreement itself over this particular interpretation. Speaking for Britain, Sir Alexander Cadogan says the Yalta "veto" does *not* permit one of the Big 5 to "veto" a discussion of *any* [that is, every] question brought to the Council. That, too, is our American position. China would accept this version. Once more the whole thing hangs on

Gromyko who is "awaiting instruction" from Moscow. He says he is "inclined to go along" — but has to hear from home. It *might* be argued that when all the rest of us agree on an interpretation of Yalta, *our* view ought to govern rather than Russia's. That is *my* position. On the other hand there is much to be said for *not* giving the Russians *any* excuse for running out on Yalta itself. (Of course [Russia] *has* run out; but the rest of us are demanding that it make good — and so we go to painful extremes to "make good" ourselves.) At any rate the answer is up to Moscow — and we are supposed to get the *answer* in the Pent-House tomorrow night. This "veto" bizness is making it very difficult to maintain any semblance of the fiction of "sovereign equality" among the nations here at Frisco and hereafter in the new Peace League. It is fully justified in respect to the use of force because the Powers with the "veto" will be the Powers which must largely furnish the force. But it is immoral and indefensible (except as a legacy from F.D.R. which we are honor-bound to respect) in any other application. But the irony of the situation is that the greater the extent of the "veto," the more impossible it becomes for the new League to involve America in *anything* against our own will. Therefore, the greater the "veto" the easier it becomes to fight off our critics in Congress, in the country and in the press when the new Treaty faces its ratification battle. (Every cloud has a silver lining.)

Wednesday, May 30, 1945
We are still waiting for Gromyko to tell us what Moscow thinks about the "veto." It is desperately irritating to have to wait (and mark time) day after day with everybody else in agreement.

When Gromyko finally got his instructions from Moscow they were of a nature that threatened a breakup of the Conference. In this crisis, Vandenberg's determination not to give ground to the Russians grew stronger despite increasingly serious pressure for some kind of concession on the part of the American delegation. It was a major deadlock of the Conference.

Saturday, June 2, 1945

The *big* crisis broke last night. Gromyko was ready with his answer from Moscow to the main question bedeviling the Conference — namely, shall the Big 5 be able to "veto" even a *discussion* or *consideration* of a question brought to the Security Council? We have been waiting ten days for this. The answer — Russia demands her "veto" even on *free speech* in the Council. This collides with the grim conviction of almost every other Power at Frisco. It is "Yalta" carried to the final, absurd extreme. When Gromyko made his report to us in the Pent-House, we all knew that we had reached the "zero hour" of this great adventure. With what seemed to be finality, the Soviets said they could not accept our proposal for "free discussion." We all knew that none of the rest of us can accept the Soviet view. Did it mean the immediate break-up of the Conference? Did it mean going on to a Charter without Russia? Instead of precipitating a show-down, Secretary Stettinius adjourned the meeting until this morning. Meanwhile he phoned Truman and Hull both of whom said we must irrevocably reject the Soviet position.

In the next few days, the Conference was given a graphic demonstration of the Russian obstructionist tactics, and the Senator put it down with the skill of a reporter on a big story.

Sunday, June 3, 1945

Another futile afternoon in the Pent-House. Any "conference" in the true sense of the word is impossible when the Russian Delegates dare not come to *any* agreement, however trivial, without referring the matter to Moscow. We had eight items on our agenda today (besides the "veto" crisis). We had (1) the French Amendment to the Regional Chapter which all of us (except Russia) including France have approved. [See diary entry of June 8, 1945.] Nothing doing; Gromyko had no "instructions." We had (2) the problem of a fixed meeting of the new League at some future date to rewrite the Charter. Nothing doing; Gromyko had no "instructions." We had (3) the problem of choosing Deputy Secretaries General. Nothing doing;

Gromyko needed "more time to study." We had (4) the Australian effort to "pledge" individual nations to carry out the fantastic objectives which are being written into the Social and Economic Council. Nothing doing; Gromyko "not ready." We had four other relatively minor matters which were settled Gromyko's way by side-tracking them into the Executive Committee. Then came the "pay off." Stettinius said we face an exceedingly difficult situation with the press inasmuch as no official information is being given out regarding the "veto" impasse; that this is resulting in dangerous speculations; that it is periling the morale of the Conference etc. Everybody, except Gromyko, pretty much agreed that Stettinius ought to make an official statement. Gromyko said he would be glad to submit to his government "for instructions" any proposed press statement! And it takes him at least a week to get *any* answer from Moscow! And so—o—o—— we again adjourn while the Soviets push us around.

I proposed that the American Delegation *at least* should make it officially plain to the Conference and the Country that *we* will *not agree* to the Russian "veto" proposal. Gromyko thought that would be "very bad while we are still negotiating." Nothing doing. (Dr. Bowman later told me we should suffer in silence for 48 hours more so as not to give the Russians any shadow of an excuse for complaint if we ultimately break with them on this proposition.) I then made a special plea for settlement of the French Amendment not later than tomorrow because the Plenipotentiaries of 45 other nations at Frisco (having been adjourned for eleven days waiting for the Big 5 to agree) will not much longer be content to twiddle their thumbs while the Big Five impotently palaver in a Pent-House. Gromyko grunted. My view is that we *must* get a Charter whether Russia likes it or signs it or not. It is desperately important that she should sign. But it is no less important that *we* should not stultify our souls.

One of the few times that any domestic political considerations entered into the San Francisco discussions was on June

4 while a solution of the deadlock was still being sought. By this time, President Truman had instructed Harry Hopkins to join Ambassador Harriman in Moscow in an effort to work out with Stalin a solution of the deadlock. Vandenberg, Dulles, and Stassen discussed the probable political effects of the dispute.

Monday, June 4, 1945
Still more of the same. Again the Pent-House. . . . Stassen, Dulles and I had a conference regarding the necessity for making plain our American position on the "veto" matter. We all agreed that we could not possibly sanction any surrender to Russia on this matter because the whole question of American prestige, not only at Frisco but throughout the world, is now at stake. We agreed that this involves a fundamental issue in the Administration's foreign policy; that we Republicans have no right to dictate any such foreign policy for Truman; that the whole thing ought to be put up to him for decision; and that we would reserve our right to speak for ourselves if the policy proved unsatisfactory. Stassen and I agreed that we could no longer go along if there is any surrender to the Soviets upon this score.

Tuesday, June 5, 1945
Still waiting. No news from Moscow. At 3 o'clock this afternoon, Stettinius sent for me. I met with him and Connally and Dunn in the Pent-House. He had an inquiry from the State Dept. asking whether he would agree to a message to Harriman and Hopkins (in Moscow) suggesting that Stalin be told that *if* he could *not* back down on his "veto" stand, would he be satisfied if the Conference went ahead and simply entered on its records the *different* interpretations which we put on the Yalta "veto" formula. The inquiry apparently came via The White House. Stettinius asked Connally and me what we thought of sending such a message. I instantly replied that it was impossible; that it would not only leave the vital Charter question in doubt but also actually would give Stalin the very "veto" for which he is contending; and that it would be a "climax in humiliation" for the United

States. Connally (less vigorously) agreed. Thereupon Stettinius said that was the precise decision which he and his Department had reached. Thereupon he read to us the original message he sent to Moscow three nights ago outlining the American position. I was amazed. It was *magnificent* in its unqualified assertion of our position. It would not have been stronger if I had written it myself. It bluntly denied any justification for the Moscow interpretation of any Yalta agreement against "discussion" in the Security Council, and pointed out that Stettinius so stated in Mexico City four months ago and that Under Secretary Grew so stated in Washington more recently (and without any contradiction from anybody). Furthermore, Sir Alex Cadogan (British) produced the Yalta minutes to show that Stettinius himself made this same statement at the final plenary session in Yalta. I was *proud of my country* when I heard the Stettinius message. It is in the best American tradition. It left no room for doubt that the United States cannot join an International Organization in which the doors are shut upon free speech and free discussion. After *that* message, it would be *impossible* for us to yield, or even compromise, if we *ever* expect Stalin to *ever* have the slightest respect for our American word again. The upshot of the meeting was that, instead of the suggested telegram proposing a weasel-worded compromise, another message was sent to Harriman and Hopkins that we have nothing to add to Stettinius' original telegram. Paul Boncour (former French Premier) made the public statement tonight that if the Moscow "veto" demand is ever put to a vote in the Conference it will be defeated 45 to 5 with only Russia, White Russia, Ukraine, Czecho-Slovakia and Jugo-Slavia supporting it. I think he is right.

The Top Secret message to which the Senator referred in the paragraph above was sent by Acting Secretary Grew to Ambassador Harriman in Moscow on June 2, 1945. In view of the historic importance of the document it has been declassified by the State Department for use in this book and is now made public for the first time. The full text follows:

"The Secretary has asked that the following most important

and urgent message (Topsecret for the Ambassador and Hopkins) be sent you for immediate action.

" 'We have reached a very serious crisis in the Conference in San Francisco. Gromyko told the meeting of Heads of five principal delegations last night that the Soviet Government would not agree to permit even "consideration and discussion in the UN" of any dispute or threatening situation brought before the proposed security council unless formal decision by seven members of the council including the unanimous vote of the five permanent members was taken. We and the other three Governments have taken the position that veto power should apply the moment the council begins to take action even if the first step in the action is a decision to investigate or to make a recommendation. We have maintained however that up to the point of such action no individual member of the council should be in a position to stop the consideration and discussion of a dispute brought before the council. The Soviet proposal carries the principle of the veto against any action not only through the section providing for enforcement action and recommendations as to peaceful means of settlement of disputes but even to the right of a single nation to prevent any consideration and discussion of a dispute. We feel that this would make a farce of the whole proposed world organization.

" 'I have reported this development to the President and he confirms my own feeling as well as that of the U.S. Delegation that the United States could not possibly accept an organization subject to such a restricted procedure which would be entirely contrary to the spirit of the security organization we have had in mind and have been presenting to the American people. The heads of the three other delegations of the five powers have at a meeting this morning stated their position as exactly similar to ours. Neither is it likely that any other of the nations would accept such an organization, and of course we ourselves could not possibly put them or ourselves in the position of even asking the members of the Conference to join an organization subject to such tight and futile restrictions. I stated our position on freedom of consideration and discussion by the security council in a public statement in Mexico City at the close of that Conference early in March and the Acting Secretary in a public statement on March 24 was also explicit in this regard. There has never been any reaction from the Soviet Government which indicated that they had a contrary view until Gromyko's statement of last night.

" 'With the President's approval I am bringing this matter to your attention urgently. I know that in the past Marshal Stalin did not know himself of some of the decisions that were being taken and communicated to us. I feel therefore that it would be most helpful if you and Harry could meet with Marshal Stalin as soon as possible and ask him whether he realizes fully what the instructions sent to Gromyko mean and what effect the Soviet proposal would have upon the character of the world organization we are all trying to work out. Please tell him in no uncertain words that this country could not possibly join an organization based on so unreasonable an interpretation of the provision of the great powers in the Security Council. Please tell him that we are just as anxious as he is to build the organization on the foundation of complete unity but it must be unity of action in the light of a maximum of free discussion. At no stage in our discussions relative to the creation of the world organization at Dumbarton Oaks or at Yalta or at any other time was a provision ever contemplated which would make impossible freedom of discussion in the council or the assembly. This is a wholly new and impossible interpretation.

" 'Please let me know when you think you can put this up to Stalin and when you can give me some word as to his reaction since we will have to take the necessary steps to wind up the conference here if we have nothing favorable from you in this regard.' "

Thursday, June 7, 1945

... The "veto" thing is now being handled by Harriman and Hopkins at Moscow direct. Stettinius whispered to me at a dinner last night that he had a late flash from the State Department that the thing looks encouraging. We shall see.

Meanwhile ... Stassen circulated a memo today in which he said the "veto" crisis is not a *paramount* thing (quite different from Stassen's attitude 2 days ago). He said we might go ahead; leave the "veto" interpretation open; and simply put the rival American and Russian versions on the record. That would be almost exactly what was proposed in Tuesday's State Dept. wire which we all rejected. Dulles and I countered with a memo underscoring the desperate importance of not backing down from our position and pointing out that the "veto issue" is now symbolic of an infinitely larger problem involving American international prestige. To yield, we said, "might make it extremely difficult for the United States again to prevail in any international negotiations with the U.S.S.R. and it would tempt the U.S.S.R. to keep on crowding the United States until dangerous friction developed." We also said: "Many if not most of the nations of the world are under strong pressure by the U.S.S.R. both directly and through internal penetration. They are wondering whether or not there is any nation which feels strong enough to stand up for what it believes as against the U.S.S.R. If the United States — the greatest and most powerful nation of the world — is not willing on this issue and at this juncture and with all of the support that is available, to stand firm, then these other nations will themselves in other matters readily fall in with U.S.S.R. policies. The result will be to leave the United States in a position of greatly increased and dangerous isolation."

The French attack on Syria and Lebanon is being used as a vivid argument against this proposed Charter. It is said that the general "veto" would prevent the new League from taking protective action. That *could* be true because France could "veto" the ultimate use of force against herself. But she could *not* "veto" a preliminary discussion and inquiry by the Security Council and this might well produce conclusive results. Indeed, it probably would. But, beyond that, I would argue that the Levantine crisis would never have arisen in the *first* place if League contacts and consultations regarding *any* and *all* threats to peace and security were in force. I think it stands to reason that France herself would have preferred voluntarily to bring any such problem to her Security Council colleagues for advice and recommendation if the League machinery were available for this purpose.

Later that night, the Senator jubilantly sat down again to write in his diary. The big break had come.

June 7, 1945 (continued)

America Wins! The "Veto" crisis broke today — and it broke *our* way. Gromyko asked Stettinius for a 3 o'clock meeting of the Big 5, at the same time advising him of the Moscow decision. The Secretary immediately sent for Connally and me and told us the news. It is a complete and total surrender. No attempt at any weasel-worded compromise. Just a straight-out acceptance of unhindered hearing and discussion regarding any dispute brought before the Security Council. This *ought* to clear the track for a quick and successful conclusion of the Conference.

I think everyone is convinced that the blunt, unconditional message which Stettinius sent to Moscow turned the trick. I *hope* some of our people have learned a lesson. Many of them were beginning to weaken under the "war of nerves." If Stalin had held out, I am afraid we would have been under heavy pressure from some of our own people to yield. I am equally sure that Stettinius would not have yielded short of instructions from the President. At any rate, we have discovered (I hope) that we can get along with Russia *if and when* we can convince Russia that *we mean what we say*. In my opinion, this victory this afternoon far transcends the limited sphere of the actual decision itself. I think it restores a sinking American prestige at home and abroad; that it gives the new Peace League a chance; and that it recommends an American Foreign Policy which *stands up* for our viewpoints, our ideals, and our purposes. I think it also shows just how we *can* get along with Russia.

Friday, June 8, 1945

Now that the "big battle" is over, I find myself recalling what Marshal Foch said — "He wins battles who holds out the last 15 minutes." That is true with these diplomatic "wars of nerves." On this basis, if Stalin had waited 24 more hours he would have had no difficulty in plowing us under because most of our radio and news commentators and many key newspapers were beginning to say — "This is just a little thing; it's only a matter of procedure; we shouldn't allow it to interfere with the success of the Conference; we might better let Stalin have his way." We had an indication from Washington (previously noted) that the "appeasement" spirit was similarly seeping even into the White House. Of course no one would have admitted that it was "appeasement"; they would have contended that "the end justifies the means" (as at Munich). We had an indication that our own delegation was commencing to crumble (previously noted). (Stassen's memo said — "This need not and must not prevent the completion of the Charter.") Meanwhile Bert Andrews wrote in the New York Herald Tribune that "observers who have watched the Conference were aware that the two men who have most consistently fought against any weakening of the American position are Senator Vandenberg and John Foster Dulles." I believe that's right — adding Stettinius himself and Assistant Secretary Jimmy Dunn. I continue to believe that all the critics who tried to minimize the importance of the issue (in order to justify our surrender) were wrong. I continue to believe that American prestige and a decent Peace League were at stake.

We did not *gloat* over a victory. We made it easy for the Soviets because we hope this means that we can work together hereafter. The Soviets adroitly capitalized their capitulation. "There never has been any desire on our part to handicap this Conference," they said. "Once more we prove our sincerity by showing our good will. You have convinced us and we agree. It is time the world realizes that the Soviet Union wishes this Conference to be a success."

Let's take that at face value — meanwhile continuing to watch our step. I repeat that I am prepared to deal with Russia on a friendly basis. I think it is essential to this great peace adventure. I think our two antipathetical systems *can* dwell in the world together — but *only* on a basis which establishes the fact that *we mean what we say when we say it.*

Meanwhile, there had been unexpected trouble regarding the formula for solution of the regional problem. It had been agreed originally that any necessary action to prevent future Axis aggression could automatically be taken by any state without reference to the Security Council until such time as the various nations "consent" to another arrangement. France on May 30 asked that the language be changed to substitute the word "request" for the word "consent." Everybody agreed except Stassen, who "insists that the new language makes some sort of a fatal surrender to European regionalism — when everybody else completely disagrees with him." Thus when the matter came up the United States delegation was unable to agree with the other Big Five powers on the French proposal. Finally, a compromise was found by Dulles to meet Stassen's position, but then the Russians refused to agree. Action again was postponed until June 9.

Saturday, June 9, 1945

We wound up the "Regional Committee" today. I presented the French Amendment on behalf of the Big Powers at both the sub-committee and the full Committee and got a unanimous vote in both places. It was not without a final flurry when the Soviet Delegate made a deprecatory speech objecting that the remarks of Chairman Camargo (Colombian Foreign Minister) should not be taken as an official interpretation that the Act of Chapultepec qualifies as an eligible Regional Arrangement under the Charter. He said it was only a personal unilateral statement. Literally he was correct. But I immediately followed him and said that his statement was equally personal and unilateral; and that I wanted to make still another for myself — namely that the Pan American Union has been the finest flower of pacific relations for 50 years and that the Act of Chapultepec will become a great cornerstone in the new Organization and will continue to bless the hearts and hopes of men. Whereupon the Latin cheers took the roof off.

Monday, June 11, 1945

We wound up the work of the "Regional Committee" today and quit (thank God!). At the finish this afternoon, Dr. Wellington Koo (China), Chairman Camargo (Colombia), and the Czecho-Slovak Delegate were good enough to praise my contribution to the work of the Committee and I got a vote of thanks. Responding, I said something like this:

"Three weeks ago this Conference was supposed to break on the rocks of these Regional Agreements; it was supposed to be an imponderable mess which could never be resolved; instead, we have a unanimous report this afternoon; this shows what men of good-will can do when they put their hearts and hands to a task; I hope it may be an omen for the future, and that the United Nations may similarly learn to find common ground for the sake of peace and security in the world; in such a pattern this International Organization will become a benediction upon civilization." There was a hearty cheer.

... I understand that Truman will be here next Tuesday and Wednesday and that we *finish then!! Please!!!!*

Thursday, June 14, 1945

The last few days have been largely routine with all attention concentrated on the effort to catch up the tag ends of the Charter, settle the few remaining major problems, and "get out of the trenches" by next week-end when the President is due.

The "veto" formula was finally approved yesterday — at the end of a long battle in which Senator Connally has very ably and patiently pulled the laboring oar. It is perfectly evident that most of the Nations do not like any part of this "veto" business. Led by Dr. Evatt of Australia, they have put up a bitter fight. But it also has been evident from the first that this kind of a League (dependent primarily upon the Big 5 for its real authority) must have the Big 5 veto in all matters involving force. Yesterday the other nations simply surrendered to the inevitable. I agree that there must be this veto on the use of force; but I do *not* agree that it should apply up to and including the point where an aggressor is identified.

Vandenberg's attitude as expressed above was important because later he was to take the lead in putting the United States Senate on record in this connection in the Vandenberg Resolution, which became an important milestone in America's postwar diplomacy. Meantime, the Senator was busy fighting off a new Russian attack on the powers of the General Assembly, which he was determined to preserve as "tomorrow's Town Meeting of the World."

June 14, 1945 [continued]

In the Pent-House yesterday Gromyko renewed his effort to strip the Assembly of its right to "discuss any matter in the sphere of international relations." I fought him vigorously and finally went so far as to say that if the Big 5 were to order this subject reopened in my Committee, it would have to name some one besides me to do it because I would not stultify myself by any such attack on free speech. Stettinius was equally vigorous in defending our position. Britain, France and China joined in. Gromyko was once more left by himself. He said he would take it up with the Steering Committee (but I doubt if he does).

Sunday, June 17, 1945

The last three days has developed the latest and perhaps the worst of the Conference "crises." It has revolved around the Soviet demand to circumscribe the Assembly's power of discussion and recommendation. I was wrong when I prophesied that he [Gromyko] would *not* go all the way through. He now even threatens the Charter itself — having phoned Stettinius late last night that his "instructions" from his government are that they will not sign unless the language is changed to suit his demands. Stettinius phoned me at midnight about it.

This specifically is what it is all about. Committee II–2 wrote the following language into the Charter: "The General Assembly shall have the right to discuss any matter within the sphere of International relations; and to make recommendations — on such matters." When the Committee first acted in May, Russia tried to make it read — "The General Assembly shall have the right to discuss any matter within the sphere of international relations *which affects the maintenance of international peace and security;* etc." The whole amazing row is over these few limiting words. The Committee voted down the limiting words by a vote of 29 to

11. It subsequently adopted the unlimited text by a vote of 42 to 0 (Russia abstaining). The ridiculous part of the whole thing is, from my view, that Chap. V, Sec. B, Par. 6 gives the Assembly the power to discuss and recommend regarding "the peaceful adjustment of *any* situations, *regardless of origin*, which it deems likely to impair the general welfare etc." This is my paragraph — and the basis of my claim that we are proposing to make the Assembly "tomorrow's town meeting of the world" (a phrase which is constantly being quoted and which seems destined to *live*). It is so broad that Gromyko's bitter objection, acting on Moscow's orders, to the other language is wholly inscrutable.

On Friday, Gromyko demanded a meeting of both the Executive and the Steering Committees to hear his protest and they were called for today. Meanwhile on yesterday afternoon Committee II–2 met and Rohstan (Soviet Delegate) moved to amend the text by putting Gromyko's limiting words in a place where they would apply *only* to "recommendations" and not to "discussion."

I reluctantly supported this as a compromise, lest this whole question shall bog down the Conference and postpone the finish next Saturday. But the Committee adjourned without action.

This morning the Executive Committee met. Gromyko and Evatt made opposing statements. At my suggestion, a sub-committee consisting of Stettinius, Evatt and Gromyko was named to seek a composition. Gromyko and Evatt later repeated their arguments before the Steering Committee. As a result the wonder grows as to what Russia is aiming at.

Wednesday, June 20, 1945

After three hectic days, another crisis dies this noon. Once more I find that Foch was right. Whoever holds out for the *last* 15 minutes wins the battle.

On Monday, Gromyko got a text (on the Assembly discussion matter) from Molotov. It proposed to confine discussion to the matters covered in *one* section of the Charter and to matters relating to the "powers and functions of any organs provided in the Charter."

While it might have *technically* met our requirements, its general atmosphere was wholly unacceptable. I insisted that *all* Sections of the Charter, instead of only *one*, should be open to Assembly debate. Gromyko was obdurate. With the constant and invaluable backing of Dulles I refused to yield, insisting that this is the basic question of *free speech*. Stassen again recommended that we accept the Soviet text. We sent for Dr. Evatt, speaking for the smaller powers, and he refused the Molotov "compromise." Then Stettinius sent another of his messages to Moscow. It was "straight between the eyes." He stood up like a concrete column. It is this sort of thing that so endears him to me. He gave Moscow until this noon to accept any one of three alternative texts and told [the Russians] we otherwise would move *alone* this afternoon. We all had a nervous night. There was a chance that the Soviets would kick everything over at the last minute. My personal feeling was two-fold; first, that we dare not abandon "free speech"; second, that, for the sake of future relations with Russia, we *must* make them understand that the United States *means what it says* and that we cannot forever be bluffed down.

At noon today, Gromyko — all smiles and sweetness — met the Big 5 in the Pent House and advised us that he had "instructions" from his government to *accept* one of *our* three texts. I shall always feel that there is a tremendous lesson in this. The Conference track is now clear. The last policy-obstacle has been removed.

Saturday, June 23, 1945

It has been fairly plain sailing since Wednesday. Following the Pent-House agreement, Committee II–2 unanimously adopted the language agreed upon in respect to the powers of the General Assembly, amid many laudatory speeches for Evatt and me. The Commission subsequently adopted it unanimously too.

. . . The plan to sign the Charter today had to be abandoned because Gromyko's "instructions" demanded that Moscow shall have three full days to survey the *completed* text. Therefore, President Truman will hang around three extra days (with Gov. Wallgren up in Olympia) and come down next week. The curtain will fall next Tuesday afternoon.

We had our final meeting of the American Delegation this morning. . . .

Now that we are at the end of our labors and our tensions are relaxed, I look back upon what I believe to be a remarkable performance not only by our Delegation but by the Conference as a whole. To have obtained virtual unanimity under such complex circumstances is a little short of a miracle.

I think Stettinius has done a magnificent job. Without his "drive" we should have been here for two more months.

I think the most valuable man in our entire American set-up has been John Foster Dulles. Nominally just an "advisor," he has been at the core of every crisis. His advice and his labors have been indispensable. I do not know what we should have done without him. He is not only an acute lawyer but he also has a great facility for dealing with diplomatic matters of this nature. He knows more of the foreigners here personally than any other American. Incidentally, he has perfect poise and patience and good nature. He would make a very great Secretary of State.

I want to add a word about the work of Assistant Secretary Nelson Rockefeller. He has been responsible for our Pan-American contacts. I never realized before how important the work of his department is in keeping our "good neighbors" united with us. . . . I do not see how anyone could be more efficient. But it is invidious to try to call this roll. We really have had remarkable team ball. The whole Secretariat has done a stupendous mechanical task with superlative efficiency. If we have sometimes been irritated with Dr. Pasvolsky, let it be recorded that we would have been quite lost without his encyclopedic knowledge of this subject and his indefatigable labors.

I have made some critical observations about Stassen. . . . But, in retrospect, I want to put him down as one of the ablest young men I have ever known; with not only a tremendous capacity for hard work but also with an equal facility for going to the heart of difficult and complex problems; with a fine personality and a superb earnestness in pursuing the highly important assignments which he has carried here; and with the greatest tenacity in his fidelity to his ideals.

We have finished our job. I am proud of it. It has been the crowning privilege of my life to have been an author of the San Francisco Charter. It has an excellent chance to save the peace of the world *if* America and Russia can learn to live together and *if* Russia learns to keep her word.

Vandenberg returned from San Francisco to Washington the last week in June, traveling on an airplane that carried other delegates and dignitaries including Lord Halifax. The British Ambassador and the Senator had become good friends and now called each other by their nicknames. This had led to a familiar joke in the Vandenberg family. When Halifax first suggested that they dispense with formality the Senator agreed that it was a good idea but he neglected to mention it to Mrs. Vandenberg. A day or so later she called the Senator to the telephone to talk to His Excellency and then stopped in horrified silence as she heard her husband say: "Hi, Ed!" She had difficulty even later in getting accustomed to the idea of Vandenberg addressing the tall, austere Britisher as anything but Lord Halifax, and the Senator often chided her about it.

When he arrived in Washington his wife was in Michigan and he wrote her about the delegation's reception.

[*Undated*]

The flight back from Frisco was o.k. We had a very distinguished "load" aboard — including Stettinius, Halifax (Ed!), Velosso, Padilla, etc. . . . We were met at the airport by the Foreign Relations Committee and a band. From that hour to this there has been terrific momentum behind the Frisco Charter. I begin to believe that we did a real job. Later that afternoon Connally and I arranged to appear in the Senate at the same time. There was an immediate "explosion." They took a 15-minute recess while we had a "reception." [Press dispatches described the reception as enthusiastic. Senators crowded around Connally and Vandenberg, slapped them on the back, shook their hands and generally created enough confusion to break up the Chamber's business for fifteen minutes.] Connally spoke the next day and was noisily received. I spoke the following day. . . . The galleries were packed and there were 78 Senators in their seats. You could have heard a pin drop all the way through my speech; and at the finish the whole place broke out in a roar.

Vandenberg's speech was a preliminary report on the Charter conference, which he described as notable not only because it put him in touch with "earnest peace-seeking pilgrims from every corner of the globe but also in its promise of a better world." He praised Connally's role and added:

Without the faintest hint of partisanship at any time, he made it constantly possible for each of us, representing the minority, to play our full role in the deliberations. . . . He was a tower of strength. . . .
I shall support the ratification of this charter with all the resources at my command. I shall do this in the deep conviction that the alternative is physical and moral chaos in many weary places of the earth. . . . I shall do it because this plan, regardless of infirmities, holds great promise that the United Nations may collaborate for peace as effectively as they have made common cause for war. I shall do it because peace must not be cheated of its only collective chance. . . . We must have collective security to stop the next war, if possible, before it starts; and we must have collective action to crush it swiftly if it starts in spite of our organized precautions. . . . The Charter . . . seeks above all else to cure the underlying causes of wars; to correct the frictions which lead to wars; to resolve disputes by peaceful means before they take on the suicidal magnitudes of war; in a familiar metaphor, to "lock the barn before the horse is stolen." . . .
This can be a new emancipation proclamation for the world. . . . I am definitely not saying, Mr. President, that a good league can compensate for a bad peace. . . . But I am saying that . . . the protections for human rights and funda-

mental freedoms inherent in the San Francisco Charter will inevitably make a better, a wiser and a safer job of it in its ultimate impacts upon humankind.

The Senator wrote his wife after this speech that "it is really an amazing situation. Practically all opposition has disappeared. Even La Follette and Wheeler expect to vote 'aye.' Under such circumstances there has been just one thing to do and that is to drive ahead to ratification with the least possible delay."

There was no doubt about the acceptance of the Charter, and the hearings and debate served only to clear up a few questions for members of the Senate. Vandenberg enjoyed newspaper cartoons — a large number of originals were framed on the walls of his study — and he pasted one in his scrapbook at this time. It was a drawing by Clifford K. Berryman from the Washington *Star*, showing a bewhiskered Congress sitting in a rocking chair and happily singing a lullaby to a baby labeled "San Francisco Charter." Vandenberg and Connally were shown in the background and the Texan was saying: "Since we've scheduled the debate I guess we'll have to hold it, but he's practically adopted the baby already."

The end of the story was told in another Vandenberg letter to his wife:

[*Undated*]

Well — the battle is over. . . . 89 to 2! Only Shipstead and Langer in opposition! Hi Johnson couldn't vote because he is in the Naval Hospital again. . . . It really was an amazing outcome. . . . Everybody now seems to agree that I could have beaten the Charter if I had taken the opposition tack. I must confess, now that it's all over, that I am very proud to have been at least one of its fathers. It has stood up amazingly under every possible scrutiny. The things we did at Frisco to remove potential Senate opposition have paid rich dividends.

Heaven only knows whether the Charter will "work." I *think* it will. If not, *nothing* would. Everything, in the final analysis, depends on Russia (and whether we have *guts* enough to make her behave). At any rate, I have "done my bit" for the peace of the world — and I guess that justifies my senatorial existence. Of course, I have no illusions. Today's acclaim can easily be tomorrow's brickbats. But let 'em come! . . . Connally said tonight, very confidentially, that Truman is going to ask the two of us to go along with him when the final peace treaty is written. That's one job I don't want! . . . But I don't suppose any man is entitled to decline such a request from the President if it comes. . . . Weren't you *stunned* by Churchill's defeat? [The Conservative Party had been defeated in a general election in Britain and Clement R. Attlee had succeeded Churchill as Prime Minister.] What a tragic demonstration of "the ingratitude of the electorate"! Here is one of the few men in 2,000 years of history upon whom you could put your finger and say — "*He* saved a nation!" And then the nation slits his throat! Nothing has done more to make me *seriously* consider getting out of this miserable business in 1946. I guess the whole world is on the leftward march. I want no part of it. Yet *Americans* can't surrender. So what? *Ugh!*

12

Atomic Bomb: "Is the Wit of Man Competent?"

THROUGHOUT the Senate debate on the United Nations Charter, Senator Vandenberg repeatedly emphasized that the world must avoid a third great conflict because new weapons of war would virtually desolate the earth. Then, as the Allied drive against Japan reached its climax, his words were underlined with fire by the explosion of the first atomic bomb over Hiroshima on August 6, 1945.

The arrival of the Atomic Age was by no means a complete surprise to the Senator. During the previous March he had been given an oblique glimpse of what was coming when he visited President Roosevelt at the White House prior to the San Francisco Conference. The President was drawn and exhausted following the Yalta Conference and was preparing to go to Warm Springs for a rest at the "Little White House." When Vandenberg sat down beside the Chief Executive's desk, cluttered with gadgets and a disorderly array of souvenirs and gifts, he spotted a copy of the speech he had made in the Senate on January 10, with a heavy line drawn under the words: "If World War III unhappily arrives, it will open new laboratories of death too horrible to contemplate. . . ."

Mr. Roosevelt looked at the Senator gravely, gestured toward the speech, and remarked, "Senator, you have no idea how right you are, but I think you'll discover before the year is over." The discovery didn't come until after the birth of the United Nations, but the fate of Hiroshima gave impetus to the Senator's determination to do everything within his power to make the new international security machinery work effectively as an instrument for world peace.

The effect of the Hiroshima and Nagasaki bombings was immediate. The Japanese — who had previously been trying to feel out a basis for peace — surrendered unconditionally on August 14. With the end of the war top-secret information about development of the atomic bomb was generally made available to the newspapers, which previously had never mentioned the vast project on which America's greatest scientists had been engaged high in the New Mexican mountains at Los Alamos and elsewhere. The project had been under Army control, with Lieutenant General Leslie R. Groves as commanding officer of the "Manhattan Engineering District," which was the code name for the enterprise. Tight security regulations had been set up; scientific workers had been "compartmentalized" or confined to specific phases of the work and only a few men had knowledge of the over-all picture. But, with the war ended, there was a movement for quick return to peacetime procedure. Some scientists wanted to exchange atomic information with colleagues all over the world. Some military men wanted to keep the whole program under close Army control. Half a dozen bills were introduced in Congress aimed at such varied objectives as outright military control of atomic energy and complete abandonment of nuclear fission for military purposes.

Vandenberg's first reaction to the atomic problem was against any hasty move to share the secrets with the world. In a press statement on August 25, he said that such action could not be taken until there is an "absolute free and untrammeled right of intimate inspection all around this globe. That is a freedom which does not yet, unfortunately, adequately exist." In the next few weeks a real Congressional snarl threatened on the subject because various committees were claiming jurisdiction over atomic legislation. The mix-up became so serious that Senator Theodore Bilbo of Mississippi facetiously suggested that the Senate Committee on the District of Columbia be put in charge because it was in the District that "most of our explosions occur." In an effort to resolve this situation, Vandenberg introduced a Concurrent Resolution in mid-September to create a Joint Congressional Committee of six Senators and six Representatives to handle atomic problems. A week later Mr. Truman invited him, with Connally and Senator Scott Lucas of Illinois, to the White House to discuss the legislative problem. Following this conference he wrote to Representative Joe Martin, Jr., the House minority leader:

September 20, 1945

> I have just come from the White House. I want to report the results to you confidentially. The President has promised to speak to his own [Democratic] House leadership along the same line. . . .
> A lot of bills of one kind or another have been introduced. . . . They have gone to various Committees. No one Committee could possibly have clear jurisdiction over a question of such all-embracing import. Soon we shall have rivalry between these Committees and a rush to get somebody's pet Bill reported. This is very dangerous business. To meet this situation I introduced a Concurrent Resolution last week to provide a Joint Congressional Committee . . . to take jurisdiction over the entire question of the development, control and use of atomic energy. My obvious purpose is to concentrate this terrific responsibility in one place where it can be handled in effective cooperation with the President. The only opposition I met in the Senate seemed to me to stem from the fact that this is a Republican Resolution. But the President told our special committee this morning that he thinks my Resolution presents the right way to handle the legislative end of this desperately important matter. I agreed to promptly speak to you about it. . . . I hope you will agree with what we are doing.

Despite the President's attitude, the Congress had a difficult time agreeing on procedure, and it was only after a prolonged Senate debate that a special Senate Committee on Atomic Energy as formed with eleven members, headed by Senator Brien McMahon of Connecticut, whose Resolution for such action was finally accepted. Vandenberg and other high-ranking members of Committees dealing with military, foreign relations and related matters were appointed to the Committee. These senators went back to school for a while to learn the rudiments of atomic science from General Groves, Dr. Edward U. Condon of the Bureau of Standards, and other scientists. They also visited atomic energy projects, before they settled down to try to map out a national legislative policy on the subject.

The Committee was treading unmapped territory. There was an obvious need for action as rapidly as possible, but it was to be a long, hard road before agreement could be reached on an atomic control bill providing for strict government monopoly over fissionable materials and every phase of atomic weapons development. The Senator wrote to the Reverend Edward A. Thompson, his family pastor:

October 26, 1945

I am frank to say that I do not yet know what the answer is to the awful problem which we have brought upon ourselves. It seems perfectly clear that we could not hope to monopolize this secret very long. It also seems clear that atomic energy will have to be put under ultimate international control. This would obviously require a complete and absolute right of worldwide inspection and information. It would be unthinkable, for example, for us to voluntarily permit Russia to take the secret of atomic energy behind its blackout curtain to do with it whatever Moscow pleases. On the other hand, even if we can get a complete and adequate international inspection, we shall still be at the mercy of any brutal aggressor who may suddenly decide to use the atomic bomb against us. So the prospectus is appalling under *any* circumstances and under *any* controls which we might conjecture. I sometimes wonder whether the wit of man is competent to deal with this murderous discovery.

And, on October 29, he wrote to Professor Robert C. Angell of the University of Michigan that "for the time being I can only say for myself that I think the atomic bomb has made the United Nations Organization more essential to the hopes of humankind than ever before. In whatever degree it may have complicated and darkened the international horizon, by the same token it increasingly becomes an ever sterner necessity if the world is to escape a final cataclysm. So far as the atomic bomb itself is concerned, I am sure of just one thing — namely, that the blackout curtain of secrecy must be lifted from every quarter of the globe before *anything* can be done in respect to a constructive program."

He elaborated on this later in another letter:

November 13, 1945

If it were possible to keep this secret in our own possession indefinitely, this would be my first and emphatic choice because we know that America will not use this devastating weapon for aggressive purposes. There are other nations unfortunately which do not deserve this trust. But there is no use in fooling ourselves nor in running away from the facts. . . . Britain and Canada have been our atomic partners and are in possession of [atomic] information. . . . All of our scientists, without exception, testify that any other nation can successfully pursue this scientific secret in the course of the next few years and produce atomic bombs of their own whether we like it or not. Therefore, we confront a condition and not a theory. . . . Our proper course is clear. It is our task to develop through the United Nations Organization a system of complete worldwide inspection which shall guarantee to civilization that no nation (including ourselves) shall use atomic energy for the construction of weapons of war. I know of no other *logical* answer. . . . All that you say about the "iron curtain" in Russia has my complete approval. I am expecting to make a speech on this subject in the Senate within the next few days.

Vandenberg did speak in the Senate two days later, on November 15, which turned out to be a very busy day for him and an important date in the history of development of our atomic energy policy. Stettinius had long since been relieved as Secretary of State — becoming U.S. representative on the Security Council — and Byrnes had succeeded him. "I was shocked," Vandenberg wrote, "by the sudden Presidential decapitation of Stettinius. I think it was grossly unfair. It must have startled the foreign ministers of the other forty-nine nations who saw Stettinius make a spectacular success of his job at San Francisco only to be 'shot at sunrise' as his reward. Incidentally, I think it must have pleased Moscow." The Senator feared that removal of Stettinius had broken up an effective working arrangement between the State Department and Congress. In a letter to his wife he expressed himself more forcefully on the subject.

[*Undated*]

> Of course, you read about Stettinius' resignation. I am entirely disgusted with this act of Truman's. The "new job" assigned to him [Stettinius] is really no job at all — it won't even come into being for many months until after the new international organization is actually under way. He deserved better treatment after his rare performance at Frisco. It just shows how cruel and ruthless "politics" can be. Jimmy Byrnes is a grand guy (for any *other* job down here). But his whole life has been a career of compromise. . . . Just as we have, at long last, got Russia to understand (through Stettinius) that we occasionally mean what we say, Stettinius gets the axe and Jimmy (who helped surrender at Yalta) comes back in! . . . The peace of the world *really* depends on whether Russia and America can live together in this new world. I believe we can if Russia is made to understand that we can't be pushed around. That was our greatest victory at Frisco. Stettinius was its symbol. Now we lose him — and get back Byrnes and Yalta! Oh, well —

Shortly afterward, Vandenberg's fears about Byrnes were given impetus by a conversation on which he remarked in another letter to his wife. He wrote that a former government official had told him that "our new Jimmy is not going to be so strong for 'bi-partisan co-operation.' . . . He says I must also expect a change in the State Department's attitude toward me because Hannegan [Robert Hannegan, Democratic National Chairman] and his crowd have been bitterly complaining that the Administration should have permitted me to get quite so far out in front on foreign policy."

Still another factor entered into the Senator's concern over whether adequate liaison with the State Department would be continued under Byrnes. The new Secretary, a veteran politician under the Roosevelt Administration, had taken over at an extremely busy period that gave him little opportunity to consult with Congress. He left for the Potsdam Conference with President Truman three days after he assumed office; the Senator remained behind. When Byrnes returned there was a tremendous crush of work and he also had to start preparing at once for the coming conference of Foreign Ministers in London and Moscow. All of these developments worried Vandenberg.

His uneasiness with respect to this problem was intensified when the Executive Branch failed to consult with the Senators in connection with the visit to Washington of Prime Minister Attlee of Britain, and Prime Minister MacKenzie King of Canada, to talk over atomic energy problems. It was not until the talks had ended that Connally and Vandenberg were summoned to the White House to be present when the three heads of government announced the results of their discussions to the press. According to Jay G. Hayden, writing in the Detroit *News*, the Senators went to the White House apparently in an unhappy mood. Before entering the President's office they talked briefly with Byrnes. Connally, in blunt Texas fashion, told the Secretary that he and the President were treating atomic energy as if it were their private possession and that they had no authority to propose sharing atomic energy information with other nations or to plan its future control without Congressional consent. Vandenberg, too, made it clear that he was unhappy about the situation and irritated by the fact that they had been rather peremptorily summoned to hear an announcement of which they had no advance knowledge — a procedure of which he complained on many other occasions.

The two Senators and Byrnes were stony-faced as they went into the Presidential office and stood by as Mr. Truman, flanked by his distinguished guests, announced to the press a joint program to seek outlawry of the atomic bomb through the United Nations, international control of the new force for peaceful purposes, and an effective method of safeguards against atomic war through an adequate inspection system. When the press conference ended the Senators departed rather abruptly, not waiting to pose for photographs with the government heads.

"Relations between President Truman and the Senate as respects handling of foreign affairs are in a state of strain which, within the next week, may produce either another try at . . . bipartisan cooperation or a wide-open brawl," Hayden wrote. ". . . Senators Connally and Vandenberg conspicuously absented themselves from a group picture of officials, gathered around President Truman and Prime Ministers Attlee of Britain and King of Canada, after the atomic bomb pact was announced. Vandenberg attributed his departure before the picture was taken to the fact that he was scheduled to speak in the Senate but Connally, supposedly the Administration's chief Senate spokesman as to foreign affairs, offered no explanation and there is no doubt that he walked out in a dudgeon."

Vandenberg probably felt the same way, but it was also true that he had a speech on his mind. He made it that afternoon in the Senate and its theme was the need for a "tonic of universal truths" — an appeal to the Russian bloc of nations to lift the veil of censorship in order to foster international understanding and the progress of international collaboration. "The mutual disclosure of free information and the liberty of a world-wide free press are becoming increasingly indispensable . . ." he said. "This is no longer just an altruistic theory. It has come to be a matter of grim reality. 'Black-outs' make international confidence impossible. When the iron curtain of secrecy falls around an area suspicion is unavoidable, restless conjecture substitutes for knowledge and dependable trust is out of the question."

Vandenberg was more than a little worried at this time that the State Department was erecting an iron curtain of its own as far as the Senate was concerned. This feeling was partly confirmed when Secretary Byrnes invited a group of senators to his office on December 10 and disclosed — only after he had packed his bags and was ready to leave — what plans had been made for the meeting of the Big Three Foreign Ministers in Moscow.

December 10, 1945

Secretary of State Byrnes this afternoon called in the special Committee of Foreign Relations — also three members of the Atom Bomb Committee — and talked with us about his Moscow trip. He said he proposed to suggest an exchange of atom scientists and scientific information with Russia as his first step; then that Russia join us in setting up an Atomic Commission under the United Nations Organization to carry on. His plan was a great shock to the entire Committee. Everyone spoke earnestly.

We agree that Russia can work out this atom science in perhaps two years; but we are unanimously opposed to hastening the day unless and until there is absolute and effective agreement for world-wide inspection and control. This is the crux. We want to banish atom bombs from the earth. But it is impossible unless Russia agrees to a total exchange of information, instead of hermetically sealing herself behind "iron curtains."

We are opposed to giving any of the atomic secrets away unless and until the Soviets are prepared to be "policed" by UNO in respect to this prohibition. We consider an "exchange" of scientists and scientific information as sheer appeasement because Russia has nothing to "exchange." It was our general opinion that we made little impression on the Secretary.

As a result the special Senate Atomic Bomb Committee met immediately and unanimously voted to ask an immediate audience with the President.

The meeting was arranged for the next morning. At 11.45 the senators trooped into the White House — Vandenberg; Connally; Brien McMahon, who though a new senator was Atomic Committee Chairman; Thomas C. Hart of Connecticut, former Admiral in command of the Asiatic Fleet; Edwin C. Johnson of Colorado, an exponent of military control for the new power; Bourke B. Hickenlooper, then a new senator from Iowa; Eugene D. Millikin of Colorado; Millard E. Tydings of Maryland; Richard Russell of Georgia; and Warren Austin of Vermont, who only a little later was to become the nation's top spokesman at the United Nations.

Mr. Truman stood behind his desk, which was long since denuded of the Rooseveltian bric-a-brac, to greet the senators. It was anything but a happy meeting, as Vandenberg wrote in a diary entry.

December 11, 1945

The President received our full Committee this morning. We stated our case and disclosed our fears. The President said he agreed with us, but that he was sure we had misunderstood the Secretary. I asked him if it would be proper for us to see the "directive" he had given Secretary Byrnes for his Moscow errand. He readily produced it and read it to us.

To our amazement we found that the "directive" would fully justify the precise sort of plan which Byrnes told us he intends to pursue. It listed four consecutive steps (with "inspection" and "control" last); and it then specifically asserted that our government considers it quite proper to proceed "a step at a time." We pointed this out to the President — and showed him that, under the "directive," it would be possible for the Secretary to prematurely give away, while in Moscow, at least half of all our "trading stock" when we seek essential controls. It was respectfully suggested that the "directive" be immediately changed by radio (Byrnes already was en route). We do not know whether this was done or not because, for some inscrutable reason, the President seemed to fail to grasp our point in respect to the "directive."

In any event we have made the record — and we shall hold the Executive Department responsible. It is our unanimous opinion that the Byrnes formula must be *stopped*.

The meetings with Byrnes and the President left Vandenberg, and at least a majority of his colleagues, very uneasy. While Byrnes apparently had by no means rejected the theory of proper safeguards through international inspection and control, Vandenberg thought his plans embraced a far too liberal policy on information — sharing in advance of such safeguards. What both the President and his Secretary of State apparently had in mind was an ultimate effort to convince the Soviets of American good faith and a complete lack on our part of any intention of playing "atom diplomacy." Vandenberg, Hickenlooper, and others were less sanguine regarding Soviet intentions. They demanded that the United States assume nothing in this respect prior to ironclad agreement on inspection; and insisted that a stop order be made on atomic energy disclosures until (1) a rigid international control policy had been worked out, and (2) such a policy had been formally approved by Congress.

Once again, as at the time of the Three-Power atomic announcement, Vandenberg was deeply disturbed by the Administration's concept of bipartisanship — a concept that intermittently was to plague him until his illness enforced retirement from Senate affairs years later. Once again, it was the procedure of a hurried call to senators and a last-minute meeting to "inform" them of an impending development or of the execution of a policy, and not to "consult" on the formation of policy. Vandenberg then and thereafter insisted that real bipartisanship meant consultation in advance and not a perfunctory reading to legislators of an impending press announcement or policy statement. He often quoted Harold E. Stassen's observation about the bipartisan approach in roughly these words: "I don't care to be involved in the crash-landing unless I can be in on the take-off." Stassen's comment, the Senator used to say, was such a good statement of the Republican case that he wished it were his.

"It now apparently seems probable that the President will invite me to go to London next month," the Senator wrote to Dulles on December 19, 1945, in reference to the impending first session of the United Nations General Assembly. "He hasn't done it yet. I hope he doesn't. Under all the existing circumstances I do not wish to go. Among other things, I am not at all clear that I could work with Secretary Byrnes. But it may be my duty to go along. I shall feel quite differently about the matter if I find *your* name on the final list."

The "existing circumstances" involved more than merely the atomic legislation tangle. The Senator was forced to look forward to running for re-election in Michigan in 1946 and he was also gravely concerned over the Senate debate on a proposed loan of $3,750,000,000 to Great Britain. He wrote to Dulles:

December 19, 1945

The British loan is a tough conundrum for me and for my Republican colleagues. Of course, I . . . agree that we must face the over-all program and know precisely what we are going to do with other "customers." . . . That tremendously disturbs me. I very much doubt whether a majority of this Congress would vote a postwar loan to Russia — at least not until the "iron curtain" reels up for keeps. Yet it seems that if we grant a loan to England and then deny one to Russia (if she asks for it as she undoubtedly will) we have thereby made further cooperation among the Big Three practically impossible (which, incidentally, would be the end of UNO). In other words, if we are going to ultimately deny a Russian loan, perhaps it would be better not to open up . . . at all.

But there are some other phases of this loan which are pretty bad. . . . Our prospective debtors are already beginning to "shylock" us even before the papers are signed. We are notified in advance that we are to get no good will out of this largesse. If we are not going to get good will what are we going to get?

Senator Brooks of Illinois sounded off with the first anti-loan speech . . . and I must say that it was a *damn good speech*. Somebody will have to sit up nights to answer him — and I have no present inclination to volunteer for any such night work. . . . I have a feeling that we ought to "go along" with this loan for the sake of some nebulous affinity which the English speaking world must maintain in mutual self-defense. But I also confess my feeling that about 90 percent of my constituency will be unimpressed by this ideology . . . and will soon become very vocal against this whole postwar fiscal prospectus. I freely confess my own perplexity. . . . The whole thing has been badly handled. It can easily become a major tragedy.

It was not until much later that Vandenberg finally made up his mind and spoke in favor of the loan to Britain, pleading that it was a matter of "intelligent American self-interest" and that we must accept "the economic as well as the moral leadership in a wandering world which must be stabilized just as necessarily for us as for others." The loan was approved by a narrow margin, but with Vandenberg's constituents the speech was one of the most unpopular he ever made in the field of foreign affairs. He received a flood of letters from Michigan protesting his position.

Meantime, on December 21, 1945, Mr. Truman had advised

the Senator of his appointment as a United States delegate to the General Assembly meeting in London on January 10. The President's letter said that the delegation would be guided by the recommendations of the Preparatory Commission for the meeting, save when "special instructions" were sent by himself. No sooner had the green White House stationery reached his desk than Vandenberg replied, expressing his gratitude but once again bringing up the atomic energy issue.

"You will readily understand that these tight limitations (regarding the delegation's discretionary powers) might commit me to obligations which I would be unwilling to assume, as, for instance, in the control of atomic energy," he wrote. "I anticipate no such crisis. But in any such unexpected event, you have my assurance that your instructions to me as a delegate will continue paramount, and I shall resign rather than run counter to these instructions."

This, too, set a pattern for the future. Vandenberg always regarded as an ace up his sleeve his position as a "minority party" senator, which at all times left the door open to "take a walk" in event of an ultimate showdown. Vandenberg on no occasion resorted to this ultimate weapon, but it was at his side and he knew it.

A week later, on December 27, the atomic problem flared up again. Byrnes, Bevin, and Molotov completed their labors at Moscow and issued a communiqué that outlined a four-point term of reference on atomic energy for the proposed UN atomic control commission. It ordered the commission to formulate the following proposals: (1) for exchanging basic atomic energy information for peaceful purposes to all nations; (2) for control of atomic energy to the extent necessary to assure its use for peaceful purposes alone; (3) for the elimination from national armaments of atomic weapons and all other weapons adaptable to mass destruction; (4) for effective safeguards by inspection and other means to protect complying states against the hazards of violations and evasions.

"I very nearly resigned [from the London delegation] . . . when the Moscow Communique came out because I could not possibly subscribe to what it said about the atom bomb," the

Robinson Studio

1940 — "The leading isolationist choice for the Republican presidential nomination."

Acme Photo

1940 — "The Willkie blitzkrieg hit me just as it hit everybody else." Senator Taft, Wendell Willkie, Senator Vandenberg.

Robinson Studio

"Few recreations save reading." Senator Vandenberg reads the news in his favorite chair at his home in Grand Rapids.

Goodwill Station

1943 — "Beginning to grasp the full possibilities of his role." Senator Vandenberg at the Mackinac Conference.

International News Photo

1944 — "If it is . . . clear that Dewey is unquestionably 'in,' I think we should all join in giving him the strongest possible send-off."

"We have finished our job. I am proud of it." Signing the United Nations Charter, San Francisco, June 26, 1945.

"There was no doubt about the acceptance of the Charter."
C. K. Berryman's cartoon in the Washington *Evening Star*.

Press Association, Inc.

1946 — "Late in April he was to accompany Secretary Byrnes to the meeting of the Big Four Foreign Ministers in Paris." Senator Vandenberg, Senator Connally, and Secretary Byrnes beside the "Sacred Cow," President Truman's plane, just before taking off for Paris.

Senator wrote. "I am unwilling to endorse any atomic disclosures to Russia unless and until we have adequate and dependable methods of international inspection and control which will guarantee the world that atomic weapons are never made again anywhere. The Moscow Communique sounds like one more typical American 'give away' on this subject."

Vandenberg didn't resign. On the contrary, he began scurrying around the capital, to the White House and to the State Department, in order to find out what was going on. Later he pulled out his portable typewriter and made a record of his activities for the benefit of the Special Senate Committee on Atomic Energy. He wrote to Senator McMahon, in reference to the absence of the Committee from Washington at the time:

January 2, 1946

Being unable to get in touch with . . . members of the Committee before leaving, I wish to leave this record with you. . . . I know of the desperately deep interest which you all have in the international phase of atomic controls. . . . When we called upon the President recently I believe we made it clear that we believe this problem must be handled as a whole. . . . Our basic demand throughout was for adequate international inspection and control as the indispensable first step at all times. . . . The President agreed . . . except that he thought we misconstrued his directive [to Byrnes].

Last Wednesday the first news of the Moscow Communique came through. It listed four stages for the work of the UNO Commission — "disclosure" *first* and total "security" *last*. Then it said that "the work of the Commission should proceed by separate stages" and that each "stage" should be completed before the next is undertaken. It seemed to me that this could be read in no other way than that the precise thing is to happen [to] which both our Committee and the Foreign Relations Committee are so earnestly opposed. I felt that I had no right to go to London, as a Senate spokesman, under any such instructions to promote any such objectives.

I immediately presented the matter to Acting Secretary

Acheson who, in turn, 'phoned the President in Missouri. It was arranged that we should meet immediately upon the President's return. We did meet on Thursday. Meanwhile, they had communicated with the Secretary en route home. As a result, I was advised that the Communique should not be read as seemed unavoidable upon its face; that it does not intend to take the "stages" in the order recited in the Communique; that the whole is to be read together; and that complete and adequate "security" must be part of each "stage" of disclosure. This latter is the key. *Each stage of disclosure must be accompanied by adequate arrangements for security.* The President authorized the statement along this line which I issued from the White House *after* it had been approved by Acting Secretary Acheson and prepared in his office.

Under the circumstances, I feel that I can now proceed to London without impairing my obligation to my Senate colleagues. Indeed, the circumstances *now* probably *demand* that I go. . . .

The statement which Vandenberg had issued after his talks with Mr. Truman and Acheson said:

I heartily endorse the immediate creation of a United Nations commission to explore all phases of the problem of atomic energy. The problem is inevitably international in scope. Under recent legislation the American member of the commission will be confirmed by the Senate.

I would not be able to agree that the problem can be handled by separate and unrelated stages. I particularly share what I believe to be the general Congressional opinion that any disclosures regarding the atomic bomb should be part of a complete plan for adequate world-wide inspection and control. For these reasons I have sought additional official information today regarding the program announced in the Moscow Communique.

I am advised by the State Department that while the Communique listed four separate objectives, with inspection and control listed last, it is not intended that these objectives should be taken in the order indicated but that it is intended that the four shall be read together and that each shall be accompanied by full security requirements — all being finally subject to Congressional approval.

This helpfully clarifies the situation. I shall present my own views to the American Delegation in London.

Later, after a conference with Vandenberg, Byrnes announced that Britain, the Soviets, and the United States had agreed that security regulations were to govern all stages of the atomic commission's activities and that the end product would be referred to the American Congress for approval.

In this manner Vandenberg tied down the philosophy that was to dominate the American proposal for atomic energy control later to be advanced at the United Nations but vainly because of Russian opposition. Still, from that day forward he remained vigilantly on guard against any back-slipping and he even emphasized this position by a public exchange of telegrams later with Bernard M. Baruch before Baruch was confirmed by the Senate as United States representative on the UN Atomic Commission.

Meanwhile, the stage was set for Vandenberg to join Byrnes, Stettinius, Mrs. Roosevelt, Connally, and the other delegates in London. Before leaving, he wrote that the "new interpretation" of atomic procedure required his presence in London, rather than his resignation from the Delegation.

December 29, 1945

The fact remains that I am reluctant to leave at this particularly difficult moment. I would not think of it if I did not have the deep conviction that — regardless of all our domestic troubles — nothing is remotely comparable to the importance of stopping World War Three before it starts if this is humanly possible.

I have no illusions about the United Nations organization — and I have been very frank with the American people on this subject. But neither have I any illusions about the fact that the United Nations organization is our only hope as a

basis for developing international peace, security and justice.
I have convinced myself that it is my first duty to see this through.

With this thought in mind the Senator, with Mrs. Vandenberg, stepped aboard the Cunard White Star liner, *Queen Elizabeth*. The ground rules for the United Nations had been drawn at San Francisco; the battle to add substance to the Charter and to make the infant organization work was about to begin.

13

London: "What Is Russia Up To Now?"

VANDENBERG, on the way to London for the first session of the United Nations General Assembly, was beginning a journey into international diplomacy which for two hundred and thirteen days of 1946 was to keep him at conference tables far removed from his Senate desk. London, Paris thrice, and then New York at the year's close brought the Michigan Senator into his closest touch with day-to-day diplomatic negotiations where a single bobble could be fatal not only to his own position, but to that of his nation's foreign policy as well.

It was a year of credits and debits, as Vandenberg himself often put it. It was a year of constantly increasing tension with the Soviet Union in relation to Poland, Greece, Turkey, Iran, Germany, and Central Europe. It was a year in which Vandenberg regarded as his own prime contribution a strengthening and clarification of American foreign policy, particularly with respect to our relations with the Soviet Union. The year began with deep reservations on his part regarding the consistency and clear-sighted self interest of our policy as practiced by Byrnes. It ended with important steps toward a Vandenberg–Byrnes alliance and the development of a more vigorous foreign policy.

Vandenberg — with Stettinius, Connally, Mrs. Roosevelt, and the rest of the party — stepped off the *Queen Elizabeth* in early January to the welcome of the mayor of Southampton, who was attired in the traditional official garb of fore-and-aft hat and fur trimmed coat. London was warmly curious —

particularly about Mrs. Roosevelt and the cigar-smoking senators; it was a field day for the British cartoonists, as well as for some of their more barbed and unfriendly colleagues at home who pictured Vandenberg as a country bumpkin stepping into the British lion's den, wallet stuffed with American dollars, but with precious little else to offer in a game of old world politics.

Vandenberg's first brush with British newsmen was a happy one — he even lauded London's winter weather. He also had a more serious message: "I really had no right to come here for the Assembly, but having helped at the birth of the United Nations in 'Frisco, I wanted to be in on the christening. And I have a desperate feeling that this is the only thing left to save the world." Mrs. Vandenberg, too, had a word: "I'm here simply as a wife; I want to look after my husband." She frequently described her role as that of "a valet and a buffer" for the Senator at such conferences. This was the theme from which she never strayed, despite the blandishments of newspaper women who often sought to edge her into more substantive fields of diplomatic comment.

The Senator's official assignment was to the Assembly's Administrative and Budgetary Committee. It was the housekeeping committee that had to supply the UN with a bank account, to make provisions for its staff, and, infinitely more important, to see that the growing organization lived within its budget. A capital fund for UN's operation of $25,000,000 was set up and a provisional budget for 1946 was set at $21,000,000. The United States' share was set provisionally for the first year at twenty-five per cent until a satisfactory contribution scale could be devised. Even though our contribution was later fixed at about forty per cent of the UN budget, Vandenberg loved to point out that was less spent for peace by his country per year than it had spent per hour for war. Vandenberg stoutly resisted Russian claims that since America's per capita wealth was higher it should pay fifty per cent of UN's cost.

From the start at London, Vandenberg showed a deep distaste for the "fancy" plans of some of his colleagues. Warning against mistaking "pomp for power," he ridiculed suggestions that forty-five square acres of high-priced American real estate be set aside for the organization's permanent headquarters, suggesting instead that the facilities of a moderately affluent college campus would suffice.

"I should consider it fatal to our aspirations," he told his UN Committee, "if the United Nations should permit its aspirations to so far outrun its resources that any peace-loving nation would ever find it financially impossible to maintain its membership and its allegiance or that it should ever lose its vote because of unavoidable arrears. This must never become a so-called 'rich man's club,' it must always remain the 'town meeting of the world.' . . . Let us build carefully and prudently and let us live within our common means for the sake of solvency in connection with this great enterprise to which our efforts are dedicated."

Vandenberg lost a fight against a blanket tax exemption for the salary to be paid the UN's secretary-general; he thought that individual countries and not the UN should determine if the stipends paid UN employees should be taxed. Comparatively, it was a minor point, but minor or major, Vandenberg always hated to lose a fight, and fumed to his colleagues: "They've voted me down nine times today but they can't vote me down in the United States Senate. If the Chief Justice of the United States must pay taxes so must the UN secretary-general."

So important did Vandenberg regard this initial housekeeping job that he urged deferring substantive issues, whenever possible, to later General Assembly sessions. It found the old newspaperman arguing against a subject dear to his heart — Assembly consideration of a Philippine resolution to convene an immediate international conference on freedom of the press to combat rolling down of the iron curtain in much of Central and Eastern Europe.

Though in complete sympathy with the end sought by the Philippine delegation, Vandenberg told the Assembly that its "imperative task" at the first session should be "closely confined to the business of setting up our machinery, putting it in gear, and giving it a chance to get in running order before we attempt its substantive use."

But the Assembly did act on some substantive issues. The resolution authorizing establishment of a UN Commission on Atomic Energy was approved without dissent, a committee was established to facilitate carrying out of a continuing UN Relief and Rehabilitation Administration program to alleviate suffering in war-devastated areas; individual member states were urged to increase food production; the nations voted down a move to sanction involuntary repatriation of war refugees; the Assembly took a stand precluding Spain's membership in the organization. And the Assembly referred to the Security Council two major international political issues — presence of Russian troops in the Azerbaijan, the northern province of Iran; and presence of French and British troops in Syria and Lebanon.

It was also a time of learning for Vandenberg, because he was perfecting the technique which was to make him a successful negotiator at the conference table. It was not without some pain, however. A delegation adviser recalled later that on one occasion Vandenberg spent hours polishing a speech designed to convince some fifty other unwilling delegates that the United States, in normal times, should not contribute more than one third of the UN's budget. He delivered it with his usual vigor and he was somewhat surprised when it was received with polite but stony silence. On leaving the meeting room, he met Connally, who asked how the speech went.

"Well, Tom, I never saw anything like it," Vandenberg replied. "I got all ready for an enjoyable swim. I put on my swimming trunks; I walked out to the end of the diving board; I took a deep breath; I held my nose and jumped. And I'll be dog-goned if the pool wasn't empty!"

The Assembly meeting also marked for Vandenberg the beginning of a friendly association with Mrs. Roosevelt. After seeing her in action the Senator soon acquired a feeling of admiration and respect for her ability. One morning the President's widow was a few minutes late to a delegation meeting. While awaiting her arrival, Vandenberg remarked to a group of his colleagues that "Mrs. Roosevelt is doing a splendid job. She has made a fine impression on all the other delegations. I want to say that I take back everything I ever said about her, and believe me it's been plenty."

Of all his impressions at the first world's "Town Meeting," a night of Security Council debate on the Syria-Lebanon question was the high-water mark of the conference for Vandenberg. It also etched, permanently and deeply, Russia's "new look" of intransigence and truculence. The dispute, Vandenberg told the Senate on February 27, encompassed

> all of our hopes and fears — all of the credits and liabilities — all of the encouragements and warnings of the future. . . .

Two of the newest and smallest and humblest of governments in the world were complaining against two of the five great powers — against two of the permanent members of the Security Council. The difference in relative power and authority could scarcely approach greater extremes. Yet little Lebanon and little Syria were invited to temporary seats at the Council table, pursuant to the mandate of the Charter. There they sat, with the mightiest of earth, to have their untrammeled day in this court of world opinion. It was indeed the triumph of an ideal.

Lebanon and Syria testified that the need for these foreign troops was gone, but that negotiations for their withdrawal had been unsuccessful. Frankly, without rancor, they laid their facts upon the table and petitioned for relief. At long last here, indeed, was at least an approach to the parliament of man. Another large entry on the credit ledger.

When Lebanon and Syria finished, sturdy Ernest Bevin, Foreign Minister of the United Kingdom, promptly announced that he would be willing and glad to withdraw the British troops at once. Monsieur Bidault, the able Foreign Minister of France, immediately followed with a statement in kind . . . the controversy gave promise of amicable composition at one sitting of the Council.

[Then, Vandenberg noted, Stettinius for the United States proposed a resolution asserting the Council's belief that there should be no unwanted troops on foreign soil in peace time and remanding the case to the parties directly concerned for direct negotiation and settlement.]

It appeared to be a prompt and happy and effective composition of the incident. The dove of peace flew in the window. But unfortunately, quickly it flew out again.

At this point the brilliant Soviet Commissar Vishinsky

intervened. He wanted no such easy peace. He was not satisfied, he said, thus to let the matter rest. Long and bitterly he indicted the action particularly of France in Lebanon and Syria. Instead of being closed, the incident then blazed into two more days of intense and futile debate. He offered amendments to the American resolution which both France and Britain — and most of the Council — interpreted as stinging and unwarranted rebukes. This was not oil on troubled waters. It was salt in reopened wounds.

When the President of the Council called for a vote, Vishinsky — the Moscow purge trial prosecutor who was to become such a thorn in the side of American negotiators — insisted that the ballot on the Stettinius resolution and Soviet amendments be taken under Charter provisions prohibiting participation of Council members who themselves were parties to a dispute threatening international peace and security. Bevin and Bidault hotly protested that a "dispute threatening international peace and security" was not involved; they rejected Vishinsky's implication and insisted that they were entitled to vote. But they followed it up by another conciliatory gesture, they would voluntarily refrain from voting.

Vishinsky's amendment was rejected with only the Russians supporting it and the American resolution then was given the seven affirmative votes required by the Charter; but Vishinsky's negative vote vetoed the proposal and it was lost.

"That left little Lebanon and little Syria just where they started," Vandenberg observed. "But then came the thrilling climax. Bevin, for Britain, and Bidault, for France, magnificently asserted that they would voluntarily accept the terms of the resolution and abide by its terms precisely as though it were the law of the Council."

Vandenberg was "proud of western democracy that night. And the life of the United Nations took on new assurance and new expectancy, in the pattern of their attitudes." But for Vandenberg it likewise spelled the keynote to all the trouble ahead: the Soviets' stubborn refusal to act, as well as talk, peace. It was a stern warning of the days to come — days when Vishinsky and Molotov were to argue endlessly about the details and major points of almost every joint endeavor; the stalemated days and months at a dozen conference tables; the hardening Russian attitude toward a settlement with the West.

Vishinsky, Vandenberg said, "seemed less interested in peace at this point than he was in friction. It raised the supreme question of 'What is Russia up to now?' "

It also raised for Vandenberg new doubts about Byrnes. It was an unhappy period. On Byrnes's side there was an unprecedented rush of conference table problems which kept him figuratively and literally in mid-air. Byrnes was harassed by his multiple chores; though he was a governmental jack-of-all-trades, the field of international diplomacy was new to him. Above all — the very quality for which Byrnes had been best known in the Senate was the one that Vandenberg feared might be Byrnes's undoing in the international political field. It had been Byrnes's particular forte in the Senate to be a compromiser, always the leader who could round up a few much-needed votes for President Roosevelt on almost any bill. It was the cloakroom sessions on Capitol Hill where promises were made and compromises worked out at which Byrnes excelled.

Vandenberg confided that it was precisely this characteristic of Byrnes's which he feared might get the Secretary of State into trouble, particularly if he sought compromises and bargains with the hardfisted Molotov-Vishinsky team. Would he "face up" to the Russians; would he insist upon American principles; would he be patient where details were concerned but immovable when a principle was at stake?

The Michigan Senator got off to a bad start with Byrnes on the atomic energy problem, and at London the Polish question brought a new strain on their relationship. By the time of the London conference the new Poland was virtually a Soviet satellite with the postwar election that had been agreed on at Potsdam turned into a one party–one ballot affair to guarantee perpetuation of the Communist régime. New reprisals were taken by the Polish régime against the remnants of the Polish military legions exiled in Italy and Britain, and against the leaders of the non-Communist provisional "government" established in London during the war.

Bevin, whom Vandenberg at the time regarded as one of the strongest of the Western statesmen, was questioned in Commons about repeated murders of opposition party leaders in Poland. His reply to the parliamentary interrogation was described by Vandenberg as keyed to "the blunt candor so typical" of the man, and it warmed the Senator's heart. Bevin said: "I am seriously concerned at the number of political murders that have been committed in various parts of Poland in recent weeks, in circumstances that in many cases appear to point to the complicity of the Polish security police. I regard it as imperative that the Polish government should put an immediate stop to these crimes in order that free and unfettered elections may be held as soon as possible in accordance with the Crimea decisions."

That was blunt language which Vandenberg could understand and approve. The night on which Bevin spoke in Commons the American delegation in London sent an urgent plea to Byrnes, who had returned to Washington, to pursue the Bevin theme on the United States' account. The following day the American Secretary acted by instructing the Embassy at Warsaw: ". . . inform the Polish government that we are relying on that government to take the necessary steps to assure the freedom and security which are essential to the successful holding of free elections."

Vandenberg was greatly dissatisfied. He felt that Byrnes had issued mere *pro forma* instructions in compliance with the UN delegation's request. The Senator, in reviewing the incident later, insisted that it was not enough to "rely" on any other government

> to vindicate the honor and the pledge of the United States of America. We must "rely" on our own initiative. We must "rely" on our own moral authority in a world which, in my opinion, craves our moral leadership. . . .
>
> It does not mean war. . . . It means, first, that we must insistently demand prompt and dependable assurances that the Yalta and Potsdam pledges in behalf of free elections will be effectively fulfilled. It means, in other words, that we shall lift the powerful voice of America in behalf of the inviolable

sanctity of international agreements to which we are a party. If this does not suffice, it means, then, that we shall scrupulously collect our facts; draw our relentless indictment if the facts so justify; and present it in the forum of the United Nations and demand judgment from the organized conscience of the world.

The whole problem of Soviet-American relations with respect to success or failure of the United Nations was coming to a boil in Vandenberg's mind during the London conference. He wrote later:

April 2, 1946

It is obvious that UNO (in its present form) depends upon the temperature of Soviet-American relationships. I do not despair of these relationships if we say what we mean and mean what we say. I think we wrote the proper pattern for these relationships at San Francisco. I would sum it up in two words — "friendly firmness." We cannot blame Moscow for thinking that it can "push us around" because that is precisely what happened during the war in all the Stalin-Roosevelt contacts. In saying this I do not mean to speak critically of our late President. As he himself told me in the last interview I had with him before he died, he was under the awful pressure of a fear that Russia would withdraw from the war and make a separate peace.

The fact remains that we then taught the Russians to believe that "appeasement" was a cardinal factor in our attitudes toward the Kremlin. I feel quite sure that when Russia learns that the "appeasement days" are over — that we intend to stand firmly for peace with justice . . . that we intend to be equally just to Russia herself whenever "justice" is on her side — she will realize that it is not impossible for us to learn to live together in reasonable amity despite the inevitable rivalry between our ideologies. Perhaps I am too optimistic. I hope not. Perhaps my judgment is warped by my ever increasing belief that collective security is the only hope of the world. . . .

Vandenberg was careful to avoid any direct criticism of Byrnes during the London sessions but, as he later remarked in a letter, he felt the Secretary was "loitering around Munich" in this period. Vandenberg "does not consider that the UN is working now in a satisfactory way," the political columnists Joseph and Stewart Alsop wrote. "He fears that it cannot work, so long as it is merely the public forum for debates so bitter as those between Bevin and Vishinsky, and the stage for maneuvers of *Realpolitik* so open as those of the Soviet Union. . . . His remedy will be a much firmer American policy toward Russia. . . . In London, Vandenberg would have preferred much stronger and more open expression of American opposition to the Soviet claims, not in the sense of supporting British interests. . . . Secretary Byrnes and the other makers of American policy have not yet taken a firm line with the Soviet Union because they still hope for local, negotiated settlements of outstanding issues. Therefore, they desire to avoid friction. . . . But domestic political considerations, and especially the fear that a firm policy will not receive public support, now bulk much more largely in the State Department's decisions than the admittedly waning hope that the Russians may be persuaded that they do not want what they say they want."

The results of the London conference were negligible from the standpoint of the United States, and most American newspaper comment reflected a low point in the prestige of Secretary Byrnes. In February Vandenberg came home to speak his mind. Irritable and preoccupied, he closeted himself with his typewriter. As always, it was a battle with the battered little machine. He tried out portions of a speech on a few newspaper friends. The rewriting went on for days. The speech came hard, as it always did. He read it aloud to Mrs. Vandenberg; he read it aloud to himself; the cigar smoke thickened and hung heavily over his broad shoulders as he bent over the typewriter.

On February 27 he called for the speaker's lectern in the Senate, and to packed galleries and an attentive membership he spoke his mind. When he was finished his colleagues rose to their feet in an ovation; as on an occasion a year previously he had touched the electric issue that was worrying the Senate and the nation. There was in his speech criticism, though indirect and by inference, for Byrnes's stewardship to date. But there was a great deal more in his call for a new American policy; a challenge to turn to advantage the progress made in establishing the UN at London — "in 37 days the United Nations turned a blueprint into a going concern. It turned an ideal into a reality." And above all the speech was a call for a new, firm philosophy in meeting the Russian postwar challenge. A forerunner of what some observers — but not Vandenberg — called the "get-tough-with-Russia" policy.

"What is Russia up to now?" was the rhetorical question Vandenberg posed:

We ask it in Manchuria. We ask it in Eastern Europe and the Dardanelles. We ask it in Italy where Russia, speaking for Yugoslavia, has already initiated attention to the Polish Legions. We ask it in Iran. We ask it in Tripolitania. We ask it in the Baltic and the Balkans. We ask it in Poland. We ask it in the capital of Canada. We ask it in Japan. We ask it sometimes even in connection with events in our own United States. "What is Russia up to now?" It is little wonder that we asked it at London. It is less wonder that the answer — at London and everywhere else — has a vital bearing on the destiny of the United Nations. And, Mr. President, it is a question which must be met and answered before it is too late.

[Vandenberg asked his question with heavy shoulders hunched over the lectern, which he grasped with both hands as though to crush it. His only gestures were an occasional deep shake of the head, a hand up, then down, then back to the lectern. His voice, though never harsh, boomed through the Chamber. There were no gratuitous gestures, no toying with glasses, no pushing back the gray-black swatch of hair, hopefully combed to camouflage the bald spot. The Senate had the question; now Vandenberg sought to give the American policy he thought would help find an answer.]

It would be entirely futile to blink the fact that two great rival ideologies — democracy in the west and communism in the east — here find themselves face to face with the desperate need for mutual understanding in finding common ground upon which to strive for peace for both. In the final analysis this means that the two greatest spokesmen for these rival ideologies — Soviet Russia and the United States — find themselves face to face with this same need for mutual understanding, both in and out of the United Nations. Indeed, if this does not oversimplify the problem, it might even be said that the future of the United Nations itself is wrapped up in this question.

If this is so, Mr. President, I assert my own belief that we can live together in reasonable harmony if the United States speaks as plainly upon all occasions as Russia does; if the United States just as vigorously sustains its own purposes and its ideals upon all occasions as Russia does; if we abandon the miserable fiction, often encouraged by our own fellow travelers, that we somehow jeopardize the peace if our candor is as firm as Russia's always is; and if we assume a moral leadership which we have too frequently allowed to lapse. The situation calls for patience and good will; it does not call for vacillation.

Let me make it wholly clear that I do not complain because Russia speaks — indeed, Mr. Vishinsky probably spoke in this Security Council more than the spokesmen of all the other powers combined. I am glad she speaks. She ought to speak. That is what this forum is for. But it is for others, too, Mr. President — just as Mr. Bevin used it upon more than one eloquent and courageous occasion. It is, I repeat, for others, too. . . . It would be impossible to over-emphasize the importance of our own role and our own performance in such epochal events, and the need for positive foreign policies as our consistent guide therein.

[Vandenberg lauded an earlier speech by Lieutenant General Walter Bedell Smith, Ambassador-designate to Moscow, in which Smith stated that while the United States was willing to go far in meeting its international associates, it must be watchful to hold to the line beyond which compromise cannot go. With this, Vandenberg heartily concurred. Then in studied terms, he laid down his own philosophy.]

There is a line beyond which compromise cannot go; even if we have previously crossed that line under the pressures of the exigencies of war, we cannot cross it again. But how can we expect our alien friends to know where that line is unless we re-establish the habit of saying only what we mean and meaning every word we say? I have the deep conviction that this way is the dependable way to permanent peace and concord between us, with its inevitable effect upon the United Nations. Indeed, I have the feeling it is the only way. I have the feeling it is the best way to win Soviet respect and Soviet trust. Respect must precede trust; and both are indispensable to peace.

[In conclusion, Vandenberg called upon the nation to resist a drift in the United Nations toward power politics and to use of the tribunal for self-serving purposes.]

It will require constant, consistent, courageous guidance to keep the United Nations within the main channel of its obligations — and here again is a clear call to America always to act in its traditional character for liberty and justice, and not to lapse, as I fear we may have done on some occasions.

Mr. President, I have endeavored faithfully to report both the credits and the debits on the United Nations' ledgers as a result of the first meeting of the General Assembly. I fear it has been illy and inadequately done. But I want to leave the positive and emphatic conclusion that the credits utterly preponderate with a heavy, a significant, a wholesome and an encouraging balance.

Those, sir, were 37 vital days in London. They are freighted with hope — solidly justified hope — in respect to collective security in this atomic age. In such an age there can be no security which is not collective. With unwavering fidelity we must carry on the great adventure. If there be any failure, let not the blood be upon our hands nor the tragedy upon our souls.

The United States has no ulterior designs against any of its neighbors anywhere on earth. We can speak with the extraordinary power inherent in this unselfishness. We need but one rule. What is right? Where is justice? There let America take her stand.

Once again the press rallied to Vandenberg's support. James M. Haswell of the Detroit *Free Press* wrote from the Senate gallery that "it left you with a sense of history going on right here now." James A. Wechsler, writing for the now defunct New York newspaper *PM*, which had often criticized Vandenberg, said: "There have been few occasions on which a single Senator has so dramatically and so decisively dominated Senate opinion on world-wide issues." The Houston *Post* said it was "the most important speech since the declaration of war"; and the Omaha *World-Herald* said: "This is the voice of responsibility, the voice of statesmanship, the voice that America has been longing to hear."

Others saw it as a direct challenge to the Byrnes approach. Vandenberg himself had informed the Senate that he was speaking earlier than he had expected, but that "events seem to recommend these observations now." He was not unmindful that the Secretary was to speak the following night. Byrnes had reason to be resentful, as he probably was because the Senator's "gun-jumping" violated diplomatic protocol. Some noted that while Vandenberg lauded Connally for "wisdom, vigor, tenacity and success," and Bevin was described as "sturdy," Bidault as "able," even Vishinsky as "brilliant," Byrnes went unmentioned.

Arthur Krock, in the *New York Times*, saw the address as a rebuff to both Mr. Truman and Byrnes for lack of a positive foreign policy. He wrote that the call for a "positive" foreign policy was an implicit though hidden warning that Vandenberg and Dulles were unable to tolerate day-by-day policy improvisations. The text, Krock observed, was "much milder than its implications," perhaps through necessity dictated by Vandenberg's membership on the UN delegation.

The Philadelphia *Inquirer* went even stronger editorially on this theme. It found that Vandenberg, by implication, was charging Byrnes with "lack of a vigorous policy and for not speaking as plainly on world issues as does Moscow." *Time* saw the speech as "a clear challenge to Secretary of State Byrnes."

The next night Byrnes spoke for himself. It was a strong speech; it advocated a firm stand. "If we are to be a great power we must act as a great power." Speaking for the benefit of

Russia, the Secretary denounced aggression "accomplished by coercion or pressure." He castigated maneuvering for "further and undisclosed penetrations of power," and the imposition of troops "upon small and impoverished states."

Byrnes's speech marked a turning point in American policy toward Russia and in the Secretary's relations with Vandenberg. Indeed, the Senator praised the Secretary's remarks as "his . . . evangelical speech. . . . I was . . . happy to find him 'on the march' . . ." *Time* held that Vandenberg had given Byrnes a "firm shove" by his "challenge" and Arthur Krock wrote in the *New York Times* that many passages in Byrnes's speech could have been composed with an eye on what Vandenberg had said twenty-four hours earlier. Krock added that if this were so the Secretary certainly had enunciated a policy that wiped out Vandenberg's points of criticism. The Senator agreed. He told his fellow townsmen at Grand Rapids on March 23 that he endorsed the "new American approach which was voiced in the recent courageous candor of our own Secretary of State Byrnes. I hope it is not too late. I applaud and sustain him in this new vigor."

The estrangement between the two men was ended. The new team was in harness and the nation was to have a firmer approach to the vast problems involved in our relations with the Soviet Union. Never again was there a serious strain on the Vandenberg-Byrnes alliance. Until the Secretary retired from office, the two men stood shoulder-to-shoulder and the idea of nonpartisan co-operation in foreign affairs received new vitality.

14

Atomic Control: Military vs. Civilian

VANDENBERG'S return to his Senate duties was temporary because late in April he was to accompany Secretary Byrnes to the meeting of the Big Four Foreign Ministers in Paris. Nevertheless, he found plenty of action in Washington during March and early April of 1946. The struggle to develop an atomic control bill — later to be known as the McMahon Bill — was nearing an end. The legislation provided for a strict government monopoly over fissionable materials, with licensing arrangements to encourage participation of private concerns in peacetime application of the new force. For senators geared to the principle of private enterprise and opposed to government monopoly it was a new departure but, as Vandenberg pointed out, so was atomic energy. He wrote to a constituent:

April 18, 1946

I agree that it [the McMahon Bill] involves a degree of centralized governmental control which is out of step with all of our essential principles in respect to free enterprise. But I am frank to say that I can see no other answer for the time being which will protect the national security. The use of atomic energy for destructive purposes is the greatest hazard that ever threatened civilization in general and the American way of life in particular. Until we can develop adequate and dependable safeguards against this *destructive* use of atomic energy, I can see no possible justification for *any* latitudes in the control of fissionable material. This inevitably means government monoply at the source of fissionable material. Our "secret" in respect to atomic bombs probably will not be a "secret" for more than five years; but it seems to me that during these five years we must keep it to ourselves through every possible precaution so that we can exercise maximum international pressure for effective and dependable international control. Again this seems unavoidable to require a government monopoly in respect to the sources and production of fissionable material. . . .

Your final paragraph suggests that this problem is so serious that no "precipitate" action should be taken in connection with it. I am sure there is nothing "precipitate" about [the bill]. It comes from a special select Senate Committee which has been constantly at work night and day for five months upon every phase and impact of the problem. Those of us who wrote the bill are jealous advocates of free enterprise. We would not have put atomic energy in a strait jacket (so far as basic material is concerned) if there were *any* alternative. But I am sure you will agree that considerations of national security *must* come first when we are dealing with this life-and-death problem.

Later, commenting on the same problem, he wrote:

July 20, 1946
It is entirely true that the Bill puts all phases of atomic control (including industrial development) in a straitjacket for the time being. It can be called "socialistic." It can even be called "totalitarian." But whatever it is called I hope that it accomplishes a *totalitarian* control of atomic energy for the time being. From my point of view, the most important single need confronting us at the moment is to completely protect the secret of atomic energy until such time as we can get a dependable international agreement to prevent its use for destructive purposes. I am frank to say that I would not care to live in a world in which Russia has atomic bombs. As you know the United Nations Organization is now at work upon this problem of international control to outlaw the destructive use of atomic energy under regulations and disciplines which will be so tight that they will defy bad

faith. You probably have also read from time to time about the arrest of "spies" who are suspected of seeking to steal this secret from us. The net result of this whole situation — so far as I am concerned — is that there can be no latitude whatever in the use and development of atomic energy in our own United States unless and until these international protections are completely and dependably produced.

The Senator's intense interest in protecting the secrets of atomic energy as the big club in the American defense closet until adequate safeguards against misuse were assured led him into a new controversy that had nation-wide repercussions. It began when he suggested an amendment to the bill aimed at assuring the military a full voice in the American atomic energy development program. Accepted on March 12 by the Committee, with only Senator McMahon voting against it, the amendment read:

"There shall be a military liaison board appointed by the President composed of representatives of the Departments of War and Navy, in such number as the President may determine. The commission shall advise and consult with the board on all atomic-energy matters which the board deems to relate to the common defense and security. The board shall have full opportunity to acquaint itself with all matters before the commission. The board shall have authority to make written recommendations to the commission from time to time as it may deem appropriate. If the board at any time concludes that any action or proposed action of the commission, or failure to act by the commission, is inimical to the common defense and security the board may appeal such actions or proposed actions of the commission to the President, whose decision shall be final."

McMahon's opposition was based on belief that the amendment undermined the principle of civilian control, although at one time he had supported placing both the Secretaries of Army and Navy on the over-all control commission. Many American scientists, still raw-nerved from their experiences with General Groves's wartime program, arose in loud protest. The bitterest critic of all, and certainly the unfairest from Vandenberg's viewpoint, was Henry A. Wallace, then Secretary of Commerce.

The Vandenberg-Wallace relations had been personally friendly while Wallace was Vice-President. He had approved of Vandenberg's January, 1945, foreign policy speech. The two men had apartments at the Wardman Park Hotel, and Vandenberg vividly recalled an early morning trip with Wallace to a point of land jutting out into the Potomac River. Here the Vice-President, attired in a sweat shirt, exhibited his prowess with the boomerang. Vandenberg related often how Wallace with deft left-handed tosses sailed the bush weapon far out over the river, the boomerang disappearing into the morning mist, only to return in its circular course a moment later. "Henry was some thrower," Vandenberg said later, "except that on one toss he scared the daylights out of me; the damned thing came back and nearly took my head off. I decided I'd had enough and never went back for more."

No sooner had the Vandenberg amendment been passed than Wallace sought to take Vandenberg's head off again. Opening a Commerce Department atomic energy exhibit, Wallace angrily declared that the Vandenberg provision carried the possibility of delivering the nation into the hands of "military fascism." "I hope that, when the American people realize its significance, they will rise up in their wrath and let the Senate know what that action means," he declared.

Vandenberg was stung by what he told reporters was ill-informed and ill-tempered Wallace criticism. He pointed out that Secretary of War Robert P. Patterson, General of the Army Dwight D. Eisenhower, Army Chief of Staff, and Fleet Admiral Chester Nimitz, Chief of Naval Operations, all had approved his proposal. He said the proposed Military Liaison Committee would have no affirmative powers and that civilians would retain total and final authority over all phases of atomic energy. He argued that Wallace thus was tagging such leaders as Patterson, Eisenhower, and Nimitz with the "potentiality" of fascism. Vandenberg demanded a special meeting of the Committee and a new vote with previously absent senators present. This time the vote was 10 to 1 for Vandenberg, again with only McMahon dissenting.

But far from quieting the storm, it added new logs to the blaze. McMahon, in tones more reasonable than Wallace's, took his case to the public. He claimed the Vandenberg amendment would enable the military to "look into every single telephone call, every single file, every single action" the commission would take. It might be civilian control, the Connecticut senator argued, but it would be such control only with the military looking over the civilians' shoulders and ever able to take over. It meant, for the first time in peacetime history, that the military would have "censorship" powers over civilians, "a right of suspension of action, a right of review. . . . I say that the creation of such a board would destroy the basic concepts on which our government was founded . . . it would be the adoption of a very dangerous policy," he told the Senate.

The scientists in newly formed organizations descended on Washington; a large portion of the press, usually in Vandenberg's corner, came out swinging; and an alarming crosscut of the public joined in the growing opposition. Vandenberg wrote:

March 14, 1946
> [A] little tempest in a teapot . . . has blown up during the last forty-eight hours regarding atomic energy. There is a perfectly legitimate demand in the country (especially among scientists and educators) that final peacetime control of atomic energy should rest in civilian hands. In other words, the peacetime emphasis in respect to atomic energy should be transferred from military uses to civilian uses. I totally agree. But! I do not agree that in the present state of world affairs the Army and the Navy should be totally excluded from consultation when they deem the national security to be involved. It is a parallel conception to say that I want atomic bombs outlawed everywhere and forever and I shall make every maximum effort to this end through UNO. But until we get adequate international arrangements for dependable inspection and control, I do not want to internationalize *our* atomic bombs.

The trouble with those who have been most violently urging civilian control is that they all but ignore the national security factor. Of course, they are supported in this viewpoint by every Communist and every fellow traveller and every parlor pink in the country, because these latter groups would like to make our national security as insecure as possible. I offered a proposal in our . . . Committee to compose these two differing views on a rational and practical basis. I have proposed that our basic Atomic Energy Commission shall be composed exclusively of civilians. Then I have proposed the creation of a Military Liaison Committee . . . which shall have the right to know what is going on in the Civilian Commission and the right to call the attention of the President to any contemplated action . . . which the Army and Navy think might be dangerous to national security. In such an event, the President (himself a civilian) immediately makes the final decision. . . . The only power given to the Army and Navy is to say "stop, look and listen." . . . I cannot imagine how even the most elementary consideration of national security could be protected more modestly and more moderately.

Yet Henry Wallace immediately led the howls of anger. . . . I never heard more fantastic nonsense! . . . A tremendous propaganda machine has already moved into action to condemn my proposal. . . .

Later, on the same day, the Senator wrote that

as the author of the Vandenberg Amendment I can testify that I was under "no pressure from the Military." I never consulted the Military. They never consulted me. All that I know about the "attitude of the Military" in this connection is that I listened to General Eisenhower and Admiral Nimitz discuss national security and atomic energy with amazing restraint on their part in respect to military control and with emphasis upon their desire to establish civilian control to the last possible degree of national safety. . . . Under the Vandenberg Amendment this Military Committee will have no powers at all, in the sense of exercising affirmative authority.

... The proposed Military Liaison Committee ... cannot challenge civilian control. ...

For a week or more, Vandenberg had his hands full answering protests from individuals and organizations and writing to newspapers in rebuttal of arguments against his amendment, despite the fact that he had presented his views on the function of the Military Liaison Committee in a speech March 13 on the Senate floor. In that speech the Senator sought for the first and last time to shed the "Vandenberg label" from a legislative proposal. He explained that the amendment more properly was the work of the ten senators who supported it in committee.

In the second place, as a result of this amendment it is going to be possible to have a completely civilian atomic energy commission in the national management of this new implement. It has resulted in the elimination even of the Secretary of War and the Secretary of the Navy from the Atomic Energy Commission ... under our proposal the civilians have the last word in everything. They even control the amount of fissionable material the Army may have for experimental purposes. They control all the rules and regulations. They control the dissemination of information. In a word, they run the show. I am speaking of a totally civilian commission.

Mr. President, the Military Liaison Board, around which all this controversy roars, has but one function. It makes recommendations to the civilian commission when it believes the national security is involved in the development and control of atomic energy. It has solely the power of recommendation when the national security is involved. If it believes that the civilian commission contemplates some action inimical to national security, it reports that fact to the President. The President, a civilian, has the sole power of decision, and his decision is final. The Liaison Committee has no vote, it has no veto, it has no affirmative power whatever. Its sole function is to require a second look by the President, if it thinks the civilian commission contemplates any error in respect to national security. That is the sum total of the story.

But Vandenberg could convince neither the scientists, the press, nor McMahon. The highly vocal opposition continued; women's clubs, citizens' groups, and others fell into step. The result, Vandenberg wrote, was "the grossest misrepresentation through sudden persistent and hysterical propaganda that I have ever seen in my entire Senatorial career." Something had to be done and Vandenberg did it. He called on Dr. Thorfin R. Hogness, a University of Chicago chemist who had been intimately a part of the atomic project and in whom he had confidence. He told Hogness that he was willing that the scientists "write [their] own ticket" as long as it fell foursquare within the purpose of assuring proper liaison between the military and the ultimate civilian authority, and that the military phases of atomic energy were not to be neglected in an aura of wishful thinking about a brave, new postwar world. Hogness worked as middleman between Eisenhower for the military, the scientists, and Vandenberg. The distilled result was this new version of the now famous military clause:

"There shall be a Military Liaison Committee consisting of representatives of the departments of War and Navy, detailed or assigned thereto, without additional compensation, by the Secretaries of War and Navy in such number as they may determine.

"The Committee shall advise and consult with the Commission on all atomic energy matters which the Committee deems to relate to military applications, including the development, manufacture, use and storage of bombs, the allocation of fissionable materials for military research, and the control of information relating to the manufacture or utilization of atomic weapons.

"The Commission shall keep the Committee fully informed of all such matters before it and the Committee shall keep the Commission fully informed of all atomic activities of the War and Navy departments. The Committee shall have authority to make recommendations to the Commission on matters relating to military applications from time to time as it may deem appropriate.

"If the Committee at any time concludes that any action, proposed action, or failure to act of the Commission on such matters is adverse to the responsibilities of the departments of

War or Navy, derived from the constitution, laws and treaties, the Committee may refer such action, proposed action, or failure to act to the Secretaries of War and Navy. If either Secretary concurs, he may refer the matter to the President, whose decision shall be final."

The new language meant that the Military Committee's authority was narrowed down to "military applications" of atomic energy alone, not to the far broader field of "common defense and security." The military group, also, was placed directly under the control of the War and Navy Secretaries, reporting only through them and with their concurrence to the President.

Vandenberg happily announced that the new version met the "common objective" of all concerned. The Senate Committee unanimously approved the redraft; the military and the scientists were well pleased, and the fight was over. The compromise created a system that on repeated occasions in testimony before Congress has enabled both the military and the civilian commissioners to give assurances that smooth co-operation and mutual understanding had been achieved.

Vandenberg's role in the fight over the Military Liaison Committee had been an interesting and, in some ways, an instructive one. In the beginning he had in mind what seemed to him to be a completely reasonable and necessary objective. The fact that the Committee supported him by votes of six to one and ten to one confirmed his belief that what he was proposing was moderate and constructive. When Wallace promptly struck at his amendment, using extravagant language, Vandenberg was irritated more than concerned and was inclined to believe that he was merely getting the expected left-wing reaction. But as the protest swelled he became angered and stubborn, wrote letters at a furious pace, laid down the law on the Senate floor and argued furiously with the editors of influential newspapers which were generally friendly toward him. He seemed to feel that everybody was wrong but Vandenberg and for a day or two he almost reverted to his old lone-wolf character, striking out on all sides.

This phase, however, didn't last long. Far more tolerant than in 1939, the Senator quickly took a second look at the problem and decided that there must be some reason for the furore, that perhaps the basic trouble was a matter of detail rather than a matter of principle. He had previously discovered and made good use of the idea that compromise on details — if there is a mutual agreement on principle — always can be achieved more easily before the firing starts than after a public battle has been fought. In this case, there was still time to stop the firing, and Vandenberg did just that. It was an important decision because it put him back on the track; it confirmed an attitude that was to be of great significance in the future. Time after time in the difficult foreign policy negotiations still to come Vandenberg spotted controversies in advance and almost invariably he was able to negotiate compromises on details that enabled him to overcome obstacles to the long-range objectives.

It meant that Vandenberg had to move cautiously and in advance of current events; that he had to maneuver in such a way as to maintain control of votes in the Senate; that he had to demonstrate a steadfastness of purpose where basic principles were involved. But it was a quality that eased the path of important legislation by side-stepping the obstacles instead of crashing into them, and it was to become a trade-mark of Vandenberg as a legislative leader. It was a quality, perhaps more than any other, which in the opinion of Francis O. Wilcox, Chief of Staff of the Senate Foreign Relations Committee, stamped him as one of the great "legislative engineers" in the history of the Senate.

15

Paris: "Firmness and Patience" with Russia

THE WATCHWORDS "firmness and patience" toward the Soviet Union were the key to the attitude of the United States delegation which Secretary Byrnes led into the Council of Foreign Ministers, opening at 5:00 P.M. on April 25, 1946, in the lovely Luxembourg Palace. Vandenberg and Connally, as advisers to the Secretary, were becoming old hands at international conferences, but the Paris meetings were to be a trying ordeal for all the participants.

The issue was a peace treaty with Italy and, to lesser degree, treaties with Hungary, Rumania, Bulgaria, and Finland, although in the case of Finland the United States was not directly a party as it had never been at war with the Finns. The preliminary work had begun at the Council of Foreign Ministers' first session at London in September of 1945, a conference that Vandenberg did not attend. But it was at Paris that the basic differences among the Big Four — America, Britain, Russia, and France — were attacked, and Vandenberg recorded the sessions faithfully in his diary. Writing at night in his hotel room, he often turned out from five hundred to one thousand words a day on his portable typewriter or in his tiny, highly legible script. It all started, the first entry showed, peacefully enough.

April 25, 1946

Council of Foreign Ministers organized for Conference today. It met from 5:00 to 8:00 P.M. with Bidault (French) presiding. Meetings are in Luxembourg Palace which Henry IV built for his consort some 250 years ago. The French are making a super-spectacle of it. Police line the street for a block approaching the Palace. Members of the historic Republican Guard [Garde Républicaine] — shoulder to shoulder — line the stairs and corridors, saluting each delegate with drawn sabers. Twenty men sit at the council table (five for each power). The French are headed by Foreign Minister Bidault (who led the French "underground" during the war). The British are led by Foreign Minister Bevin. The U.S. Delegation is Secretary of State Byrnes, Assistant Secretary Dunn, Senators Connally and Vandenberg and "Chip" [Charles E.] Bohlen (interpreter). The Russians are led by Foreign Commissar Molotov and Assistant Commissar Vishinsky. It is the *first* conference which both have attended (which gives the Conference an importance yet to be disclosed).

All was reasonably quiet today — except that disagreement immediately appeared over fixing the agenda. Everybody agreed to *start* tomorrow with the Italian Treaty (which is the hardest nut to crack and which will *really* "tell the story"). But Bidault wanted to add Germany at the foot of the agenda. . . . Bevin objected, saying that *all* powers which fought Germany are entitled to a primary consultation on a German Treaty, and that *all* German questions and *not* just the French anxieties should be considered *together*. Byrnes wanted to add Austria also at the foot of the agenda, seeking primarily to hasten the departure from Austria of all foreign troops including our own. Russia objected — saying Moscow has not yet studied the Austrian settlement. After an hour's wrangle, both of these disputes go over until tomorrow. But it was agreed that we shall start with Italy.

At a private conference with Byrnes this morning, he disclosed to me what I think is an excellent basis for cleaning up Germany. Instead of leaving Allied troops of the four Powers in Germany indefinitely, he proposes a Four-Power Treaty under which Germany shall be permanently disarmed and a system of "inspection" established to assure permanent protection. This goes back to the basis of my proposal in my speech of January 10, 1945, which thus may *yet* be vindicated.

Bidault invited all of us into an adjoining room for champagne and sweets after adjournment. Everybody came except the Russkies. No sign of them!

April 26, 1946

After agreeing today on the preamble to the Italian Treaty, we reached the first hard nut to crack — and stayed with it from 4:30 to 7:30. Molotov presented the Russian demand for $300,000,000 of reparations from Italy, basing his claim entirely on what Italian troops had done in Russia while on the Axis side. Byrnes stated the American position that reparations should be based solely on capacity to pay without outside assistance; the same rule applied to Germany at Potsdam. He pointed out that we have poured half a billion dollars into Italy's post-war rejuvenation; and that to collect reparations from Italy, therefore, would be the equivalent actually of collecting them from us. Bidault agreed for France — adding that if *any* reparations were collected from Italy, France would demand her share. Russia was asking $100,000,000 out of a total of $300,000,000 — most of the balance going to her satellites. Bevin took the same position — no fixed sum of reparations, but if *any* are collected, Britain will expect her dividend. Molotov insisted. Byrnes added that the U.S. has a Big Bill against Italy also; and that although we want no reparations, we shall ask for our share if Russia insists upon reparations. In the face of a deadlock, Byrnes proposed that Italy's "capacity to pay" be immediately examined by experts from the four major powers. To everyone's surprise, Molotov agreed, which is the first suggestion that perhaps the Soviets are prepared to "give ground" in her treaty demands, at long last.

Molotov made a sanctimonious speech about *not* wanting to hurt Italy's economic recovery (but still he wanted his $100,000,000). I told Byrnes tonight that the next time Molotov makes that crack, he should be reminded that it was in Italy where Shylock demanded his "pound of flesh"

— and was then confounded when he was required to take it without drawing a drop of blood.

We and the British and the French will probably laugh the Soviet claim out of the Conference by presenting our *enormous* demands for *our* share *if* there are to be any reparations at all. Making some progress.

Had lunch with the President of France.

April 27, 1946

We decided today upon the Italian fleet which is to be left to Italy — of course a mere skeleton. There was no great controversy. The U.S. proposed that *all* submarines should be sunk. This was agreed — unless a few be retained for "experimental purposes." The *big* question was what to do with the balance of the Italian fleet. Russia wanted one-third of it. Byrnes adroitly maneuvered Molotov into a position where he had to admit that this was not "reparations" but "war booty," which *really* left its disposition in the hands of Britain and America, since we were the ones who captured it. The Russians evidently expected not only to get one-third for themselves, but also a large slice of the balance for Yugoslavia. It was finally settled, without too much difficulty, by referring the disposition to a committee of naval experts with the understanding that the *restitution* claims of Greece and Yugoslavia, when proved, should come first; then the subs should be destroyed, except those saved for experimental purposes; then the balance should be equitably divided *four* ways between Britain, France, U.S.S.R., and U.S. The original Russian proposal had not counted France in. Anyway, this was progress.

Then we took up the new Franco-Italian boundary. With amazing self-restraint, France asked only for four changes in the boundary involving only 750 kilometers of land and 5,000 population. I repeat that the French claim was utterly modest. Bidault asserted that France does not want to invade any area where the inhabitants object. The Soviets again were very acquiescent. They have no interests involved. . . .

The amazing thing about this phase of the business is the

way in which the Western democracies look out for a "square deal" for defeated Italy, which, of course, is not represented in these proceedings, even though she did ultimately switch to the Allied side. It is all so *different* from the Soviet attitude wherever they see something they want.

All in all, I should say it was a very good day — although we *still* have to meet the *real* Italian issues.

April 28, 1946

The Council did not meet today. . . . I went to the races at Longchamps with Byrnes. He told me of some of his difficulties with Secretary Wallace and Senator Pepper — both of whom are more or less constantly in his way. He told me of his current difficulties in respect to an air base in Iceland — the most strategic base on the North Atlantic from either a military or trade view-point. We built a great American base there during the war. Byrnes recently was negotiating with the Iceland officials for a long-term, American operational contract which would fully protect our interests. The Iceland officials suggested that the matter be put off . . . so that it might avoid being dragged into local politics. Everything was quite agreeable — when suddenly Secretary Wallace made a speech in the U.S. in which he said that a base in Iceland could only be intended as a military thrust toward Russia. Pepper also made one of his pro-Russkie speeches, condemning his own Administration's foreign policy as being much too severe with the Soviets. Hell immediately broke loose in Iceland where there is a substantial Communist Party. Pepper's speech was circulated all over Iceland. The matter of an American base immediately became a hot issue in the political campaign. All local parties were forced to declare against any such arrangement — and the whole highly important business is now up in the air. Byrnes considered it so important that he took it up at the next Cabinet meeting — Wallace, unfortunately, was not present — and asserted that he must *not* thus be "shot in the back" by his own colleagues.

Pepper accused me, in this week's *Look* of heading up an "imperialistic, anti-Red Bloc" in the Senate. This is typical . . . smear technique. . . . Byrnes gives every evidence of *"no more appeasement"* in his attitudes, however; and I am *certain* this is the way, if there *is* one to reach common ground with the Soviets. I want to be scrupulously fair and reasonable with them: but I want to be relentlessly firm in our insistence upon these American positions. No more Munichs! If it is impossible for us to get along with the Soviets on such a basis, the quicker we find it out the better. America must behave like the *Number One World Power* which she is. Ours must be the world's moral leadership — or the world won't have any.

April 29, 1946

Bad day! The Russkies were themselves again! All spirits are low tonight.

First came the quarrel over Italian Colonies. The British, in present occupation of these areas proposed: (1) immediate independence for Tripolitania and Cyrenaica (Libya); (2) merger of Italian and British Somaliland, with a study for the future; (3) consultation [with] Ethiopia regarding Eritrea. Bevin pointedly emphasized that this area was largely freed by British, South African, Australian, Indian and native troops; and that the people were solemnly promised independence (in Libya) and that Britain must keep her word. The French proposed trusteeship, under UNO, managed by Italy. The U.S. proposed a general trusteeship under UNO, with a pledge of independence in Libya not later than ten years hence. The Soviets proposed dual trusteeship — a major power in primary control, with Italy as deputy in each instance. Thus Russia would get Tripolitania and either Britain or the U.S. would get Cyrenaica. Tripolitania would get independence in ten years. These trustees would theoretically be answerable to the Trusteeship Council (UNO). The Russian proposition was a slight regression from its previous all-out demand for Tripolitania. But the net result would be quite the same. There were no signs of any compromise in any direction. So we went to the next item on the agenda. . . .

France asked that the internal German situation be put on the agenda. Britain and the U.S. acquiesced provided Austria also were added. Russia wasn't ready to talk about Austria and "stood pat." So we let it go, for the moment, with Germany added to the agenda. By this time Byrnes was *mad*. He made a strong statement about our failure to reach any critical agreements in four sessions and said it showed an ominous lack of mutual trust. He said that Molotov (and the French and British upon some occasions) always argued that Germany has *twice* ravaged his country and that *this* time things must be fixed so it will not occur again. Byrnes pointed out that every Russian move is always explained away in the name of "security." He proposed to deal with this situation with *finality* precisely as I argued more than a year ago in my speech of January 10, 1945. He proposed a treaty between the major powers within the frame-work of the UNO Charter whereby they would mutually guarantee German demilitarization for 25 years, with continuous "inspection" to protect the situation. Bevin and Bidault approved the general idea; but Molotov would have none of it, though Byrnes quoted Stalin as having agreed to the general scheme a year ago. Molotov was maddeningly obdurate, and refused even to understand the proposition. He insisted upon saying that Byrnes wants to talk about "the future" while he wants to talk about "the present." Of course, the Byrnes proposal textually and literally takes care of *both* "present" and "future." This treaty would be the fundamental answer to *all* the Russian "security" pleas. It should have been pressed by F.D.R. at Yalta fifteen months ago. It would have robbed the Soviets of every excuse for seeking territorial expansion, and satellites, in the name of "security." It would *today*. If and when Molotov finally refuses this offer, he will confess that he wants *expansion* and not "security." Perhaps that is why he is so bull-headed on the subject. *Also*, perhaps he is afraid of "inspections" as a precedent. (Looking ahead to atomic bomb control.) Anyway — nothing doing tonight.

I am sure we shall *not* yield to Molotov on any of these major issues. If not, I want the *world* to know the whole story. Then moral conscience all round the globe can face and assess the realities — and prepare for the consequences.

April 30, 1946

Quickly told. We spend an entire afternoon throwing commas and colons at each other. The questions at issue

were the Italian-Yugoslav and Italian-Austrian frontiers. . . .
U.S., U.K. and France were in reasonable agreement. But
the Soviets wanted Yugoslavia to have practically all of the
Istrian Peninsula — and they weren't ready to talk about
Austria at all. As a matter of fact, it was clear that they had
no intention of permitting *any* decisions at the moment. *Apparently* they want to keep *everything* liquid pending a
"grand deal" at the finish. . . .

It was a day's total loss. The Russkies were stalling. But *this* time, they will *not* wear us down.

Mike McDermott, the State Department press representative, had a query from New York tonight wanting to know whether the report was true that I *died* today!!! Last week we had to deny a somewhat similar query from New York as to whether Byrnes had a "stroke." What goes on!

May 1, 1946

Moving toward a show-down. The shadow boxing is about over. There is no sense in carrying on this Punch-and-Judy business. It makes no contribution to better international relations, and it is beneath the dignity of the United States to be shoved around like a fourth-rate power by stubborn, contemptuous, irrational dictators from the Kremlin. As I sit in these Council Meetings, I marvel at the ease with which some of our Allies forget that they would *not* even be on earth if it were not for America. Sure: it took *all* of us to win the war. But we were at least "among those present." We asked nothing then. We ask nothing now. We seek only a decent opportunity to *continue to contribute* to the welfare of a decent world. Yet we are blocked at every turn of the road by Communism-on-the-march. If it is humanly possible, through scrupulous fair-play to Russia and by a super-generous attitude toward her legitimate needs, to bind up a working agreement with the Russkies, this *must* be done. But if the only price is our "unconditional surrender," it is best to find it out before it is too late. It is perfectly evident now that the apparent Russian geniality, relatively speaking, in our initial sessions was only a screen.

Byrnes called Connally and me to his room tonight and said the only thing left to try is a small, closed meeting of the

Foreign Ministers themselves — with a demand on Molotov to put his cards on the table. We heartily agreed. I told Byrnes that I did not even want him to take Connally and me into these secret meetings — particularly me — because they look upon me as one of their chief obstacles, and Connally, too, in lesser degree. This will probably be tried tomorrow. If it fails, we shall seek an amended armistice with Italy to give her a chance — and the world also will know that we here offered a treaty of military alliance against a resurgent axis to satisfy every legitimate Russian quest for "security" — and we have offered a plan to internationalize the *industry* of the Ruhr, without separating the Ruhr politically or economically from Germany.

We were to have had *two* meetings today. But the Deputies could not even agree upon an agenda. So we had one short meeting to consider the comparatively simple American proposal to [extend jurisdiction of] an Inter-Allied Control Commission in the Italian Treaty to administer the terms of the Treaty. The Foreign Ministers had already agreed last September on such a Control Commission in respect to the military phases of the Treaty. . . .

Molotov not only flatly declined thus to extend the jurisdiction: he even refused to validate the *military* controls agreed upon last September. In other words, we not only *made no progress* but we actually slipped backwards. Molotov sanctimoniously argued that *any* post-Treaty controls in Italy would be an invasion of Italian sovereignty (which was little short of laughable in view of the Russian satellite system). *Of course* there must be *some* administrative machinery because the Treaty cannot implement itself. At one point in his "argument," Molotov really "led with his chin." He accused us of wanting post-Treaty controls in order to keep our troops in Italy as long as possible! That was grotesque. Byrnes promptly slammed back at him with a challenge to sign up and accept our proposed "military defense" Treaty — and then *all* of us take *all* of our troops out of Europe at once. But it was all to no avail.

The tragedy of it all is that the rest of this sick world could agree on a total post-war program in twenty minutes.

Only Moscow stands in the way — thus exercising the deadliest of all her "vetoes."

Vandenberg thus was learning the hard way that it was far easier to talk of "patience" with Russia in a speech on the Senate floor than to practice it across the council table from Molotov and Vishinsky. But despite discouraging diary entries, the Americans were "patient" and they were "firm."

Meanwhile, the American delegation in general and Vandenberg in particular were the targets for heavy Communist attacks. The Paris Communist newspaper *L'Humanité* wrote that: "It is possible to say that Mr. Vandenberg and the experts of the American delegation are putting forth great efforts to cause trouble for Mr. Byrnes and to bring about a break-down of the Conference. Unfortunately, Byrnes follows them. It is they who have rejected the realistic proposals of Molotov on Trieste, reparations and the Italian colonies."

Vandenberg wrote in his diary of the attack: "This seems to be the perpetual communist line at home and abroad. I can well imagine that if the Conference fails, the American Reds and their fellow travelers will hold me exclusively responsible. Molotov can do no wrong. I can do no right. Alas!"

The smaller group, as Byrnes proposed, did meet several times; the Secretary refused to abide by Vandenberg's request that the Senators be left behind. With Bohlen, a Department Russian expert as well as a skilled interpreter, they accompanied the Secretary to the private meetings lest the new approach be heralded at home as a scheme to sidetrack the Senate's representation.

Vandenberg described the jockeying for position at the small meetings, even before they could take place, and with it a blowup with Molotov.

May 2, 1946

This *big* and significant day started amusingly. The first question before the Council was whether a little desert island with nothing on it but a light-house should go to Yugoslavia or Italy. On this *at least* there could be *agreement!* It went to Yugoslavia. I do not even remember its name. But even

Molotov had to laugh when the decision was approved. . . .

Then — suddenly — the thing happened referred to in my yesterday notes. Byrnes had arranged for Bidault, as the host minister, to spring it:

Bidault: "We have so many points in disagreement that I wonder whether we are using the right methods. After an encouraging start, we find ourselves bogged down. I suggest we try a different plan; that the Chiefs of Delegation meet for informal discussions to see if we cannot find common ground."
Byrnes: ". . . The U.S. Delegation is willing to try out any method which offers any hope. . . . I am willing to try it now."
Molotov: "Remembering our experience, I agree that meetings of this sort might be helpful."
Bevin: "I have no objections. But neither do I have much hope."
Bidault: "Hope is vital. If we have lost it at this table, we may regain it at some other table."

And thus the new experiment was born. It was agreed to try out the plan this afternoon. . . .

The smaller group met at three o'clock, a total of twelve in all. The chief discussion was about reparations — and the same old ground which had been covered in the larger group was covered again. It made me think of that popular song a few years back — "The Music Goes Round and Round and Comes Out Here." It didn't look like a very successful shortcut. . . . Then we suddenly came close to the finale:

Molotov: "We get 100 millions (of 300 millions) in reparations or there will be no [Italian] treaty."
Byrnes: "If those are the alternatives, then there will be no treaty. We might just as well sign up a new Italian armistice tomorrow and go home."

Molotov *immediately* denied that he had said *what he did say*. In other words, when his bluff was called, he instantly backed water. Perhaps some allowance should be made for difficulties in accurate translations: but there can be no question about the form in which the translations were made. Temporarily, there was a calm — but not for long. Bidault had a tentative scheme for *deferred* reparations, conditional on subsequent capacity to pay without external aid. So did the U.S. The U.K. had a plan also. Then —

Molotov: "I suggest that the French, American and Russian plans be referred to a Committee for study."
Bevin: "I greatly appreciate the courtesy with which Mr. Molotov ignores the British plan. I will not sit in a conference where I am told the views of my government are not entitled to consideration."

Molotov hastily backed away from that one, too. But tempers were getting short. The subject was hastily changed to a discussion of Italian Colonies. Bevin again explained the British plan for the Somalilands. Then —

Molotov: "The British plan is too selfish."
Bevin: "That's a fine comment to come from a nation which has grabbed one-sixth of the surface of the earth."

At this point we quit for the day. But meanwhile Byrnes formally presented a draft proposal for amended armistice terms with Italy — which will at least partially help the situation if we cannot agree on a treaty. Certainly the general situation here is no better. Molotov seems determined to bait Bevin. There is no dove in sight tonight.

I should have noted that before Byrnes flung his ultimatum at Molotov he hastily asked Connally and me whether we would back it — and he got a quick "yes" from both of us. This can't go on much longer. I confess that I admire the way Molotov argues tenaciously for his positions. But the trouble is that they have had so much from us so long that they have not yet sensed the fact that our "surrender days" are over.

May 4, 1946

Molotov led off this morning with a formal statement fully supporting Yugoslavia's boundary demands. He argued that Trieste is a military base from which Italy can infiltrate Yugoslavia; that the proposals of U.K., U.S., and France would rob Yugoslavia of her biggest port and her chief opportunity for development. . . . He summed up his position by saying that we must "meet the national claims of Yugoslavia"; that the causes of friction must be "removed" ("liquidated" would be a more accurate word); that other countries like Poland and Czechoslovakia have already asked that Trieste go to [Yugoslavia], thus simply proving that the "satellites" are still under full control. He wound up with a glorification of the resistance movement in Yugoslavia (which was started by Michaelovich whom Yugoslavia now proposes to shoot for treason).

Bidault replied for France. He said the experts had been instructed to establish an ethnic line seeking to put the least number of people under alien rule. . . . He said the proposed French line came the closest to resolving all the rival claims.

Byrnes opened by challenging Molotov's aspersions on our *motives*. . . . "Any charge," he said, "that we seek to punish Yugoslavia is untrue; we do not question the motives of others, and we do not expect them to question ours." He said that, instead of "tearing anything away" from Yugoslavia (as Molotov had charged), the American proposal would give her the port of Fiume and 1,890 square miles of territory and 375,000 new population. He said we must remember we are hunting for the best ethnic line, and that we are pledged to the principle of "self-determination" for all peoples. . . . He dismissed all the talk of future Italian aggression as based upon the presumption that the United Nations will fail — which he declined to concede. . . .

Bevin followed. He, too, challenged Molotov's reflections upon the "motives" of his colleagues; and generally agreed with what Bidault and Byrnes had said. He was prepared to study any one of the lines proposed by U.K., U.S. or France, but considered the Russian line impossible. . . .

Molotov returned to the attack, saying we could not take the views of the experts (and sought to prove his case with one exhibit from an official Italian map — which Byrnes promptly explained away). This caused "Chip" Bohlen (our long-time interpreter) to whisper to me: "This is a perfect example of the Soviet mind: if facts bother you, just ignore the facts. . . ."

At this point the Council recessed until this afternoon. . . .

"FIRMNESS AND PATIENCE" WITH RUSSIA

May 4, 1946 (afternoon session)
Byrnes opened this afternoon by saying we could agree to let the experts consolidate the British and French lines. . . . He [Molotov] was willing to give this matter further study: but insisted upon immediate answer to the "decisive question." What happens to Trieste? It *must* go to Yugoslavia. . . . Molotov and Byrnes then tangled in an amusing historical debate. Byrnes said Trieste got her first charter in 1472 from the Italians, and has been Italian ever since. Molotov said there was no "Italy" until the 18th century; that Byrnes must be thinking of the Venetian Republic; that even Napoleon (who, he said, was no Yugoslav) put Trieste and Gorizia in a Slovene group as recently as 1810. Of course, the Venetian Republic was Italian — which shows once more how comfortably the Soviets fit their facts to their purposes.) Then Molotov made his *first break*. He suggested a "trading bee" and said that if he got Trieste, *it might make a difference in his attitude toward reparations and colonies*. Then Byrnes . . . proposed a plebiscite between the Russian and the American lines to let the people decide their own destiny, with all Yugoslav and Italian troops withdrawn. He proposed that the plebiscite be conducted by the Council. "Let the people decide."

It was a bomb-shell. Molotov finally countered by saying that a plebiscite should encompass the *whole* area, beyond the Russian and American lines, lest the result be a "chess board." . . . Byrnes concluded the afternoon's argument by saying that after the last war we transferred a peninsula, as a result of which there was great dissatisfaction among minorities. We do not want to repeat this error — so the London meeting determined to recognize an *ethnic* line. If we were to take the plebiscite in the *whole* area, it would simply reproduce dissatisfied minorities, and repeat the troubles of yesterday. Let the people in the *disputed* area express their views. And then we adjourned until tomorrow afternoon.

It is perfectly obvious that old-fashioned "power politics" is at work here. It is equally obvious that much of this show is shadow boxing because, of course, Yugoslavia is a mere puppet of Moscow. It is also obvious that everybody shies away from *realities* because if a plebiscite is dangerous, an *imposed* boundary would be even more dangerous.

I conclude for tonight with this personal observation. Molotov has one of the finest heads I have ever seen on a human being. It is large and magnificently proportioned. It is interesting to note that he has some difficulty even in speaking Russian — because "Chip" Bohlen tells me he stutters.

I don't think we are any farther ahead tonight: but at least we have struck a belated blow for the fundamentals for which our boys *thought* they were fighting.

May 6, 1946

Before we went to a meeting of the smaller group this morning, I was asked by Connally, at Byrnes' request, whether I was prepared to consider trading off Trieste. I said *"No."*

The meeting of Ministers started in dispirited fashion. Byrnes went all over the Italian boundary question again — obviously a futility. Bidault briefly reviewed the French position. . . .

Then Bevin suddenly put all his cards on the table. He called the roll on the issues. He would have to say "No" to the surrender of Trieste because it would violate the London ethnic agreement. On Somaliland, he would give Ethiopia a hearing. On Libya, he would give them independence: or at the very least, remembering the British fight in the desert when they fought alone, he would not retreat "one inch" from the American proposal for a UNO trusteeship. . . .

Byrnes then followed with his summary. Reparations are not insoluble. Greece can get not only the Dodecanese but also Italian assets in Greece. Other external Italian assets to an unexpected substantial sum in Rumania and Bulgaria can go to Russia. Italian assets in Albania should suffice. Yugoslavia gets mines, power plants, etc. which are sufficient. Thus, said he, we really confront only two difficulties — Trieste and the Italian colonies. . . . "We all agree," he said, "on some kind of a trusteeship; but we can't agree who should administer it." He proposed for the present that Italy renounce the colonies; that they be held by the four powers for one year; and if we do not then agree, let UNO decide.

But when we get to Trieste, in view of the basic obligation of the Atlantic Charter to protect unwilling people against transfer, we cannot agree to any proposition which violates the London ethnic agreement. . . .

Molotov said he had not proposed a "bargain" but a "compromise." He said the Soviet argument to give Trieste to Yugoslavia is decisive if we are to consider basic aspects. He said Bevin's proposed "independence" for Libya was modeled on the British "independence" for Trans-Jordan. British troops would remain. It would not be "independence." It would be equivalent to a permanent transfer to Britain. The British plan in Somaliland was the same sort of thing — at Ethiopia's expense. He said Byrnes' proposed "provisional settlement" was no settlement at all — that we must make long range decisions now.

Then Bevin touched off the fire-works. I quote him: "I wish Molotov could understand me about Ethiopia which wants Eritrea. I make no claim for Eritrea. I do not press my suggestion in Somaliland unless it can be done in friendly agreement with Abyssinia and for the benefit of the people. I think in this war Great Britain has set an excellent example in not seeking any territory at all. If I can be given credit for an honest motive, for a moment, it will be seen that I am trying to serve the welfare of these native people. . . . Nineteenth century imperialism in England is dead. We are no longer an expansionist country. I am driven to suspicion sometimes that our place has been taken by others. But as a Social Democrat I am not envious."

Bidault (presiding) briefly referred to the French proposal . . . said we might as well quit for the day.

Not so Molotov. I quote him: "*Nineteenth century imperialism may be dead in England, but there are new twentieth century tendencies. When Mr. Churchill calls for a new war and makes militant speeches on two continents, he represents the worst of 20th century imperialism, and he evidently approves Mr. Bevin's foreign policies.* Of course, one is free to try to divert attention from one's self: but it won't succeed because the facts speak stronger than any slander against another government. Britain has troops in Greece,

Palestine, Iraq, Indo-China and elsewhere. Russia has no troops outside of security zones and their lines of communication. This is different. We have troops only where provided by treaties. Thus we are in Poland, for example, as our Allies are in Belgium, France and Holland. I also recall that Egypt is a member of UNO. She demands that British troops be withdrawn. Britain declines. I wonder how long this sort of thing can continue. The Soviet was astonished when Britain asked that India be admitted to UNO. India was admitted. She is an equal partner. But Britain does not give her her rights. What shall we say of UNO when one member imposes its authority upon another? How long can such things go on? I should not have raised these points but for Mr. Bevin's remarks. Let the truth be recorded."

Mr. Bevin's only reply was this — "Now that you have that off your chest, Mr. Molotov, I hope you feel better."

In an utterly tense atmosphere, Byrnes hastily suggested that since no agreement seems possible in regard to Italy, that we adjourn until tomorrow and then make a survey of the Balkan treaties.

May 11, 1946

We began again on reparations — the old story all over again. It is obviously the easiest point at which to make some concession to Molotov, and yet it involves almost insurmountable obstacles as a matter of principle. The U.S. has put 650 millions into Italy to sustain her since her surrender. We have also spent another 330 millions indirectly (UNRRA, etc.). This is a total of 980 millions. . . . It is simply fantastic that one Ally (Russia) should be stubbornly trying to take out 100 millions in reparations when two other Allies (U.S. and U.K.) have put in 1,100 millions, and are still doing it. I decline to try to explain that one to the American people. Nevertheless we are trying to find a formula which will save Molotov's face. . . .

May 11, 1946 (second session)

We came close to a show-down this afternoon. Before we went in, I had to tell Byrnes that I would be unable to stay here beyond next week; that the Senate's current calendar is too desperately important for me to be away any longer on what seems to be a sort of "pole-sitting contest." Byrnes said it was time to bring things to a head — and he certainly "held Molotov's feet to the fire" in an attempt to do so. The session reverted to its standard pattern — a duel between the U.S. and the Soviets. It ran about like this —

Byrnes: "We have now reviewed most of the points in conflict. It has been helpful. We all want to get together. It is evident that many subjects require further exploration by our Deputies and experts. There is solid hope for new progress in that direction. I now say, earnestly, that since we agreed at Moscow on a date for a Peace Conference, and that date failed, it is now our duty to fix a new date, and seek other advance agreements in the interim. We must rely upon mutual good will. I propose, again, that we call the Peace Conference for July 1 or July 15."
Molotov: "We can easily agree upon a date. But a date is useless unless we can foresee success for the Peace Conference. That requires adequate preparation. I do not expect we can agree upon everything in advance. But we should continue our efforts. . . ."
Byrnes: "Well, if we cannot have a Conference until we are all in agreement, it is a doubtful outlook. . . ."
Molotov: "That is worthy of attention. But we came here to make peace. Let us persist in those efforts. . . ."

He then reviewed all five treaties to show that there are not so many points open. According to his summary, it all really comes down to Trieste and Italian reparations. . . .

As today's second session drew to a close, Byrnes made one more try for an immediate amendment of the Italian armistice. But Molotov was obdurate. And so, as dusk fell on the inexpressibly beautiful Luxembourg Palace and Gardens (where we are meeting), Byrnes said — "Can we at least agree upon adjourning until Monday." And this succeeded!

May 13, 1946

On this dark, glum, grim, chilly day we had exactly that kind of a session of the smaller council. I sometimes think I am entirely too *impatient* for this sort of business; I am sure there is nothing to be gained by continuing the present sittings: that the only hope is a recess in which to think things over and let our irreducible position sink in: that there is nothing to be had except needless irritation in the continuation of these meetings in which the same old speeches are made on the same old themes time and time again — quite as if we were inmates of an Old Ladies' Home where there is nothing to do every afternoon except to chat over the tea: I urged Byrnes yesterday to force a show-down. . . . Anyway, Byrnes is phoning Washington tonight to ask for the "Sacred Cow" on Thursday! Glory be!

Before we broke up Byrnes referred to Molotov's insinuations that Germans are not being adequately disarmed in all zones (an obvious slap at Britain). Byrnes said he had phoned General Clay (our man); that Clay said he had heard no such complaint since December. Byrnes ordered him to ask the Allied Control Council to investigate the matter in all zones, at once. At least, Molotov said that was a good idea. It is still cold tonight. So is the Conference.

May 14, 1946

Byrnes showed me this morning the statement which he is prepared to make today recessing the Council. It is almost word-for-word the same as the statement which I wrote out and gave him Sunday. He expects to use it later in the day after a conclusive and final demonstration that we are deadlocked for the time being. . . . Byrnes talked to Truman last night — the "Sacred Cow" is on her way to Paris!!!

May 14, 1946 (second session)

There was a brief perfunctory discussion of the points in controversy (each of which was "referred to the Deputies" for further study). The track was then clear for Byrnes to toss in our Resolution proposing: (1) a recess of this sitting of the Council until June 15th; (2) the calling of a Peace Conference July 1 or July 15, or, if the Soviets continue to object, putting the responsibility for calling the Peace Conference upon the June 15th meeting; (3) instructing the Deputies to draft a treaty with Austria to go on the June 15th agenda; (4) the immediate promulgation of an amended Italian armistice. Molotov briefly reiterated his objections to discussing Austria but did not comment on the main theme. Bevin asked for a brief recess to study Byrnes' statement. . . . After the recess, Bevin approved the proposal. Molotov merely said he did not wish to discuss it until tomorrow. (I suppose he wants to talk to Stalin.) So the decision goes over until tomorrow. . . .

May 15, 1946

At long last, we got around to Germany (the core of the whole European problem) this morning — but that's all — we just "got around." However, let it be said that the Big Powers have at least started on what promises to be a long and complex debate. The meeting today was called primarily at Bidault's request. This was the essence of his statement:

France has been invaded seven times in 150 years by Germany, each worse than its predecessor. Our need for security is the prime preoccupation of the nation. Security involves three things: (1) concrete guarantees; (2) solid friendships; (3) UNO. Economic factors are important, but the political factor is vital. For example, the Austro-Hungarian Empire was the best economic answer on the Danube: but it had to be broken for political reasons. Thus political considerations must come first, although they need not be economically unsound. The German area in which we are interested consists of three parts: (1) Ruhr; (2) Left Bank of the Rhine; (3) Saar. The Ruhr is an immense factory and the first coal basin of Europe. The Rhineland is an agricultural area which has been the usual corridor of German attack. The Saar is more limited; it was taken away from us after the 4th invasion; but France has had it and its coal mines since World War One. The Ruhr is a great European Treasury. We must guarantee that its natural and industrial resources shall never again be used destructively. It must be internationalized both economically and politically. There should be local administration and policing as far as possible. . . . The Rhineland should be under permanent military control, especially where it directly involves the security of France, Belgium, Holland and the U.K. We will agree to any reasonable political regime so long as it does not involve German sovereignty. . . . Its public administration should be detached from the Reich and put under the political and economic control of France. All of these things are vital to France and to the peace of the world.

When Bidault finished, there was a long silence which caused Bevin, presiding, to suggest the analogy of a "Quaker Meeting." This moved Molotov sarcastically to suggest that since the British are the most closely concerned, they would be the best qualified to speak. So Bevin did. He said we must consider the German problem as a whole and not in sectors. He said he rather shared Bidault's ideas about the Ruhr, except politically. He said we can't deal with the Ruhr until we have dealt with the over-all problem. To discuss the former would defeat the latter. He found two rival problems in the Ruhr: how (1) to get security and how (2) to develop maximum production for the sake of Europe without jeopardizing [security?]. He said it is dangerous to peace to leave a mass of people in Central Europe on a sub-standard basis. Therefore we must balance all factors. Other interested countries must be consulted. He was ready to tackle the studies. More silence. Molotov said he wanted to hear from others (meaning, of course, the U.S.A.). So Byrnes unlimbered. He had with him General Clay who commands the U.S. Zone of occupation in Germany. Clay flew in last night.

Byrnes said he agreed with both Bidault and Bevin. We have to settle both the Ruhr and total Germany. Unless we do, next winter we will have chaotic condition in all zones. . . . He bore down on the need for a permanent plan without further delay. He named five questions which must be speedily answered: (1) will the Ruhr and Rhineland be internationalized and will their resources remain as a unit; (2) will the resources left to Germany be available to Germany as a whole for a balanced economy; (3) can we agree upon machinery for Germany's administration as an economic unit within the next 90 days; (4) shall existing zones be maintained as barriers to a reasonably free internal economy; (5) can the Peace Treaties fix the final western boundary of Germany? He said these questions must be answered by this Council. So he urged his proposal for Special Deputies, with a first report June 15th. Bidault said this statement is worthy of study, but couldn't we at least settle the Saar now. Molotov was quite willing to "think it over"; but first he took off after Bevin again. He said the Soviets took the initiative at the Berlin Conference to discuss the Ruhr, but were told they were out of order in the absence of France. Now France is here. But in the meantime events have marched on. "We read in the press and we hear rumors," said he, "about arrangements the British are making to take over Ruhr industry in the British Zone. We have sought direct information but we have received none. Three-fourths of the military potential of Germany is in the Ruhr. The plans being made by the British and by German trusts and cartels have a great bearing on this military potential. It is obvious that we should discuss Germany as a whole. But I shall not conceal the fact that the Soviet wants to know what goes on in the British Zone and thus in the Rhineland."

Bevin stormed back: "You can have all the information you want about our Zone; and meanwhile we should like to find out what goes on in other zones where we can get very little information. I do not propose to have Britain singled out, for propaganda purposes, for attack. I shall insist upon dealing with Germany as a whole." Molotov interrupted: "I do not understand the reference to propaganda." Bevin replied: "You try to make out that Britain does not act honorably; I get so much of it I must protest." Said Molotov: "If we talk about the Ruhr, which is in the British Zone, we must also talk about Britain." And, finally, with considerable more of the same, Bevin withdrew the reference to propaganda. And so to lunch.

May 16, 1946

Curtains! But it took two sessions today to make the disagreement plain and to fix the responsibility. Bidault opened by expressing the hope the Council might at least make a minimum start on the German problem, by establishing the principle of French control of the Saar. There is little opposition to it, in principle, but the U.S. and the U.K. want the basic German problem handled as a whole. Byrnes insisted that the basic question was his proposal for Special Deputies to make interim reports, beginning June 15th, with a final German Peace Conference in November, and terms of reference covering not only the special and immediate questions which he has raised but also the general problem. To make a long and repetitious story short, Molotov had to have "more time for study." Byrnes withdrew his November date for a final report, suggesting that the date subsequently be fixed by the Council. Molotov — not interested. He finally stripped his proposition to its bare bones — "Could we agree on constituting a Commission of Special Deputies, and then fix their terms of reference later?" Bevin — o.k. Bidault — o.k. Molotov — no. In the course of the long rehash of old arguments, things warmed up twice. Once Molotov intimated there was something dubious about the American proposal of a 25-year mutual alliance; and, again, he took his favorite crack at the British and the suggestion that they are behaving surreptitiously in their German Zone. Bevin again slapped him down on the latter score: and on the former Byrnes bluntly notified him that Stalin had personally approved the principle of the American proposal in a personal conversation with him in Moscow last Christmas Eve. But, after having agreed to disagree on doing anything with the German problem at the present time, the sessions wound up on a pleasant, friendly note as everybody joined in thanking France and Bidault for their gracious and generous hospitality. The score for the series is "no runs, no hits, and a lot of errors" (but not by us).

The "Sacred Cow" couldn't be spared, at the last moment, for our return trip. But we sail at eleven tomorrow in a B-54 which has arrived and is waiting. When we land in Washington I shall issue the following brief statement:

The American Delegation at Paris has been a constant unit in its constructive efforts to seek peace based on human rights and fundamental freedoms. No other Peace can reflect the cause for which we fought. It is unfortunate that greater progress cannot be immediately reported. But delay is preferable to error in such vital matters. We must earnestly persist in seeking common Allied action as soon as possible within the framework of principles which promise peace-for-keeps.

After Vandenberg got back to Washington he received from a friend a long memorandum reflecting the viewpoint of a high French official regarding the attitudes of the delegates at the Paris Conference. The French official was not named and the Senator presumably never identified him, but the memorandum and Vandenberg's comment on it are interesting as an illustration of another way of looking at the proceedings. The French official took the position that Byrnes and Bevin went to Paris determined not to make the slightest actual concession. In London, Byrnes had given the Frenchman the impression of sincerity and willingness to negotiate; in Paris he gave the impression of a clever politician determined not to give an inch but anxious to convince the public that he was trying to reach an agreement despite Russian stubbornness. Neither Byrnes nor Bevin tried to find out how far the Russians would go toward compromise but spent their time trying to put the onus for the deadlock on the Russians. Byrnes seemed most interested in convincing the Russians that the sucker season was ended, and that henceforth the Americans would be tough. Bevin went along with the Americans, as he felt that Churchill had been too soft with Stalin. Actually, the only concessions in the Conference were made by Molotov.

Vandenberg's comment on the above anonymous summary was as follows:

May 28, 1946

> It is hard to be *sure* of anything in connection with this desperately important business. Personally, I think we had to do at least one thing at Paris — namely, speaking loosely, to demonstrate that the "appeasement" days are over. Stalin and Molotov had Roosevelt at a perpetual disadvantage in their war conferences because we were afraid the Russians would quit the war and make a separate peace. As a result, I am sure they got the habit (with justification) of believing that they can always "write their own ticket" in these international meetings.
>
> They had a slight but rather successful jolt at San Francisco. They got another at the first meeting of the Council of Foreign Ministers at London. They received considerable self-confidence at the subsequent Council meeting in Mos-

cow where Byrnes gave away more than he should. I think it was absolutely necessary not only to recover lost ground but also to firmly and conclusively establish at the recent Paris meeting a demonstration of a firm but friendly American purpose to stand by its ideals. Appeasement simply feeds the hazard from which it seeks to escape. Paris was Munich in reverse. We now know that Munich was a ghastly mistake. This at least suggests that "Munich in reverse" was wise at Paris.

I may be wrong but I think Byrnes did a magnificently courageous and constructive job. . . . I do not consider that our American position was at all inflexible. . . . We did relentlessly decline to surrender our principles. We can compromise within principles; but we cannot compromise principles themselves.

There is no doubt that Molotov was in a "trading mood." He constantly referred — day after day — to the fact that he had made a "big concession" (namely Tripolitania) and what was he going to get in return. He asked that question a hundred times. We are in a poor position to enter that sort of a bargaining contest because unfortunately America long since has given away everything it has to give away free, gratis, for nothing. Yes; we can still trade away the rights and lives and destinies of many helpless peoples; but in my opinion it would be an ignominious surrender of America's position of moral leadership in the world and it could easily plant the seeds for future wars. Worse; it could encourage the obvious Russian idea that her expansion — in one guise or another — is irresistible. . . .

We shall have to meet events as they develop. I do not believe that Russia wants war — at least not yet. I do not believe that we are in danger of war by reasonably standing our ground with firmness but with patience. If we are in such danger, the continuing appeasement merely postpones and multiplies the hazard. If Russia is bent upon ruthless expansionism then it is only a question of time before we face a showdown in defense of our own democracy.

Vandenberg reported to the Senate in one of his shortest speeches — nine minutes. The Senate calendar was clogged with labor legislation; it was an election year for Vandenberg; the people of Michigan just might be more interested in how their Senator voted on labor bills than on how he talked world politics; and Byrnes already had reported to the people ably and comprehensively. Vandenberg told eighty-two senators and a crowded gallery that the American Delegation at Paris was "a constant unit in thought and action. It had no differences"; Byrnes's leadership was "distinguished . . . able." This was a far cry from Vandenberg's report after the London Conference. He said that while some agreements had been reached, disagreements prevailed on a number of controlling points. "Eastern communism and Western democracy were unable, for the time being, to see eye to eye in most of these considerations. It is unfortunate that greater progress cannot be immediately reported. But delay is preferable to error in such vital matters. We can compromise within the boundaries of a principle. We can no longer compromise principles themselves."

At home the killing tension and frustration of Paris was relieved, albeit temporarily; the theme of patience and determination could be stressed once again. Despite failures at the Luxembourg Palace "the more important news is that the Council was a complete success in developing, at last, and in disclosing, a positive, bipartisan foreign policy for the United States. It is based, at last, upon the moralities of the Atlantic and the San Francisco Charters. Yet it is based equally upon the practical necessities for Europe's rehabilitation," he told the Senate.

On May 21, Vandenberg wrote Byrnes that the "pattern" of the American attitude was now so clearly set that the presence of the senators for a second round of negotiation of the treaties at Paris might be unnecessary. But on the other hand, Vandenberg wrote, if his absence raised "the slightest doubt" regarding his support of Byrnes or if it might be construed by the Russians as a surrender either on his own part or on the part of Byrnes, he was ready to drop everything else and go.

He reminded the Secretary that he "happened to have" a re-election campaign on his hands in Michigan that fall, and with something less than complete sincerity added: "It does not disturb me in the slightest. I can honestly say that (barring what would be a brief shock of injured vanity) I care very little about the outcome." Vandenberg told Byrnes that he intended to allow nothing to interfere "with my duty which I really owe to the cause of peace (which is my total dedication for the balance of my days)."

Byrnes insisted that the Senators again accompany him, and the upshot was that Vandenberg, Mrs. Vandenberg, Connally and Mrs. Connally, the Secretary and Mrs. Byrnes, and State Department counselor Benjamin V. Cohen boarded the "Sacred Cow" once again, and to the good-by waves of President Truman took off for Paris.

Mrs. Vandenberg arrived at the airport to board the plane with a large hatbox. She was chided by newsmen for taking a new hat to Paris, the hub of fashion.

"Oh, no," she replied. "I've got nothing but doughnuts in there which I made at the apartment last night according to a wonderful Michigan recipe. They're for those sweet boys who've been flying us across the ocean all year in the 'Cow.'"

16

Paris: The Ice Begins To Break

IT WAS mid-June but the weather was "atrociously cold" in Paris when the American delegation arrived for the second round of the Peace Treaty negotiations. Senator Vandenberg had nothing but summer clothes in his suitcase and a straw hat on his head — "the only one in Paris." In contrast to the temporary joviality that prevailed at the first half of the Paris Council session, the delegates gathered in Luxembourg Palace in an atmosphere as frigid as the weather.

The Americans decided to seek an early showdown with the Russians and not to give in to any further "delaying actions" which they felt the Soviets were using to capitalize on European chaos. Vandenberg recorded this showdown in his diary.

June 15, 1946

We had a long Delegation Conference this morning. If possible, we shall seek an early show-down. There is no use playing the Russian game of a "delaying action" while they capitalize on prolonged European chaos. The only palatable compromise at Trieste would be a "free city" in a sufficiently large "free state" to make the "freedom" real. I served blunt notice that I would not agree to any more *fake* "freedoms" such as the "free elections" promised in Poland, Bulgaria and Rumania. The only palatable compromise respecting Italian Colonies would be a UNO Trusteeship with ultimate independence, but not specifying "independence in ten years" (objectionable to the French and British). Instead, we would require the independence question to go on the agenda of the Trusteeship Council the tenth year with freedom of decision at that time. I pointed out that this was the formula used at San Francisco in Article 109 to settle a similar 10-year row over Charter revision. The Delegation's general disposition is to stand pat, and throw any moot questions into UNO's General Assembly. Cohen particularly favors this course. I pointed out that certain sentences in the Teheran Declaration can be used to sustain such a course. So does Article 14 [of the UN Charter] which Molotov and I personally negotiated at San Francisco. . . . In my opinion, this is our last chance to make Stalin understand that we "mean business" and that the "appeasement days" are over. It is also my opinion that when Stalin understands these "facts of life," we can get along with him. . . .

The Council opened up again in Luxembourg Palace at four this afternoon. It was a tense atmosphere. . . . Molotov sprang his first "surprise." He referred to the monarchist riots in Italy (following the election which upset the King). He said the Great Powers cannot ignore these evidences of "Fascist resurgence" and asked for reports from Britain and America (the occupying powers). . . . Then Molotov sprang his second surprise. He proposed that we start on the regular agenda by discussing the *economic* problems in Italy first; and that we *immediately invite Italy to be heard on this matter*. Bevin led the resistance to this proposal. He said he knew of no reason to consult a defeated state on such a problem; and he made his most telling point when he said it was strange that Molotov should be now eager to "consult the enemy" while still refusing to consult the 21 Allied victors in a real Peace Conference, as promised by the Moscow Declaration. Byrnes supported this view. The Deputies have been studying these Italian economic problems for the past month. It was finally decided to first let the Deputies report next Monday. When the session adjourned, Assistant Secretary of State Dunn told me he thought this Russian maneuver was a "tip off" as to Moscow attitudes; that it means Molotov will *delay all decisions* as long as possible; and that we are thus in for a "war of nerves." Well — we shall soon see. Is it a "war of nerves" which also sees the Red Army and the Jugo-Slav Army massing toward the Italian Border? It had better be nothing more than that so far as I am concerned. The Communist Daily (L'Humanité) expressed great regret today that I have returned to Paris, because I once said that I would never "go to Munich."

June 19, 1946

The French enjoyed a noisy celebration last night in honor of General de Gaulle's first challenge to his country to fight the German conqueror. It was the sixth anniversary. Many parades! Much music! (I did not hear it mentioned that it *also* was the anniversary of Napoleon's defeat at Waterloo — the French will have to "sort out" their anniversaries some day.) The Council of Foreign Ministers tied themselves in a wrangling knot today over an utterly inconsequential item and got nowhere. I went, instead, to the opening meeting of the new French Constituent Assembly and saw my friend, Georges Bidault, elected Provisional President of France.

Baruch's report to the Atomic Energy Commission (UNO) is far more important to the peace of the world than anything that happens here. It is *the* "show down" with Moscow. Russia's first response (declining to waive her "veto" in respect to enforcement of the outlawry of atomic bombs) presents us with the *reality* (if she persists) that this will be *two* worlds instead of *one*.

June 21, 1946

. . . The corridors of the Meurice (Hotel) are full of plug-uglies tonight — Molotov's ever present bodyguard. Molotov is dining vis-à-vis Byrnes. Byrnes will tell him what we will and what we won't do. It ought to clear the atmosphere and hasten a show-down. What we want is just enough agreement with Molotov to get his consent to a Peace Conference where 21 Allies (instead of four) can have their say on these moot points . . . told Byrnes this morning that there are two basic principles I want to pursue in dealing with Moscow. (1) I want to make it relentlessly plain that the time is gone by when the Soviets can do as they please with the expansionist program under the guise of peace and security. (2) That, within this rule, we shall prove to Russia that we want to be scrupulously fair and just with her.

No agreement came out of the private dinner. But at least Byrnes was pressing for a showdown.

June 22, 1946

[Today's] was a strange session. Frankly, I do not know what to make of it. For the first time, the United States spoke with the finality which becomes its position in the world. It seemed to me that this was what we were saying in effect: "The time for action has come; the world must have peace; if we cannot get it one way, we shall have to try another; we cannot longer tolerate the delays which make for chaos on the part of those who profit from chaos."

It seemed to me that Molotov was rather stunned to find himself at journey's end. . . . I may be all wrong about it, but he seemed like an animal at bay. What does an "animal at bay" do?

But the next day Vandenberg described as

Blue Monday . . . one obvious delaying tactic after another by Molotov. It was the familiar Moscow technique at its transparent worst. . . . He proposed: (1) Yugoslav sovereignty over the Trieste area; (2) a Yugoslav governor; (3) a local legislature . . . (4) an Advisory Council of the Big Four powers with authority to veto the legislature, and, (5) withal, some sort of a trusteeship arrangement with UNO. This would be oleo-de-luxe! He could not possibly be expected to be taken seriously. He must simply have hoped to precipitate another long debate and another long delay. I doubt if he gets either. The cards are dealt. The bets are down. Somebody's hand is about to be "called."

There came more days of wrangling, but then the ice began to crack.

June 27, 1946

This started out to be the most hopeless of all days and wound up the most hopeful. It was like an unexpected shot of sunshine through the clouds. The session started with another long wrangle over free commerce on the Danube. . . . But, passing to some minor items in the Rumanian Treaty, the Ministers suddenly found themselves in a series of unexpected agreements. Soon this part of the agenda was cleared. They turned to a silly little item in the Bulgarian Treaty (the size of the "Bulgarian Navy"!) which the Russians had held up for days, and agreed that the "Bulgarian Navy" shall consist of one ship not to exceed 7,250 tons. But it was another agreement. Molotov then said: "We might as well clean up the Franco-Italian frontier" — upon which France, Britain and America have agreed from the first but which the Soviets had refused to settle. "We accept," said Molotov. This ended the Tenda-Briga dispute and transferred this area from Italy to France, under guarantees that Italy's use of hydroelectric power from this area shall continue. The pace was rather breathless by this time. It began to look as though perhaps the "stalling" was at an end.

More in humor than in earnest, Byrnes said: "While we are in an agreeing mood, why not finish up the Dodecanese?" Then Molotov, who for two weeks has stubbornly refused to allow a formal decision, bowled everybody over by saying: "Very well; we agree that the Islands shall go to Greece." And thus there was more progress in an hour than we have had in all the rest of the time since we started. Everybody is speculating tonight as to what it means. Have we won our point? Has Molotov decided, at long last, that we do mean what we say? Is he now prepared to go along? Or is he building up what he will call Russia's cumulative "surrenders" (on relatively minor issues) in order to make the world think it is our fault if the Council breaks down over final disagreement on the major issues? Whatever it is, only one who has been through this "war of nerves" can understand our feeling of at least *temporary* relief tonight.

July 1, 1946

After the usual waste of time today, talking about what we shall talk about, the agenda was fixed at the end of half an hour. It started with Trieste — and there it ultimately ended because we got no farther. *But* the Trieste situation greatly changed in the course of the session. Molotov started by proposing a new internationalization scheme which, however, was little more than a paraphrase of his former scheme. . . . Then Bidault "shot the works." He offered a new "compromise": (1) all east of the French line to go to Jugoslavia; (2) an internationalized area in Trieste and adjacent territory from Devin to Novigrad. The latter, of course, would be *entirely* at the expense of Italy and would leave her only a petty segment (perhaps 8%) of Venezia Giulia. Molotov registered prompt interest. . . . [He] abruptly abandoned all of his previous positions and said: "Let us accept the latest French proposal without amendment — the governing statute to be modeled along the lines of the Soviet and French suggestions."

He took Byrnes and Bevin by complete surprise. They asked for a 15 minute recess. Thereafter Byrnes asked that the matter go over until tomorrow — and there it stands. There is much discussion whether Bidault cooked up this "compromise" in advance agreement with Molotov (who had a long private conference with him yesterday). Bidault denies collusion. But on the face of things the facts sustain some such suspicion. It makes no difference. The issue must be settled *on its merits*. . . . My own opinion is [that] I do *not* believe that we can hope to permanently keep the peace in this "cock pit of Europe" by any mixed and complicated responsibility for what happens in Trieste. I think we would merely postpone trouble (and not for long). There is only *one* reason why America is here. We are *not* here to merely help carve up Europe. We are *not* here to white-wash cancers. We *are* here to build *permanent peace*. There will be no peace if Trieste becomes "everybody's business" under a scheme which pins final, effective responsibility in no effective and responsible authority. The "compromise" is not fair to Italy. It is an invitation to a permanent Irredentist movement. I have again stated my views to the Secretary. In my opinion, we should welcome the acceptance, at long last, of the French line. Beyond that we should remit either to the Peace Conference or to the General Assembly the question of (1) whether to internationalize, and (2) if so, *how* to internationalize. This is *definitely* a question which threatens "international peace and security." Such a question should *not* be settled by 4 Big Powers (three of whom have a "balance of power" stake in the decision). It should be settled either by the Peace Conference and thus by *all* of the 21 nations which fought the war, or by the General Assembly and thus by *all* of the 51 nations which have mutually agreed that questions affecting international peace and security are their *mutual* concern.

On July 2 came more sudden agreements. The Italo-Yugoslav border was set, and, most important, an agreement was reached in principle on internationalization of Trieste. Vandenberg wrote in his diary that he foresaw "grave difficulties" in an internationalization scheme for Trieste, but that it was "the only way to break this deadlock in the Council and get this problem out of the monopoly of the four Big Powers and into the larger forum of the 21 nations at the Peace Conference and 51 nations at UNO.... At any rate, I want to make any contribution I can to make the new formula as hopeful as possible, whether I agree with it or not."

The following morning after a conference with Byrnes, Vandenberg went to an anteroom and typed out a specific United States proposal to internationalize Trieste under United Nations protection and provide for drafting provisional and permanent governing statutes. Molotov promptly surprised everybody by announcing that he would accept the American draft as a basis for discussion and with changes in a few words, the Vandenberg "Free Territory" draft was approved. (Actual provisions for governing the Free Territory were not completed until the December meeting in New York, and thereafter could not be put into effect because the Big Powers could not agree on a Governor General for Trieste.)

On July 4 Vandenberg wrote in his diary: "We celebrated Independence Day by placing wreaths at the statues of Washington, Rochambeau and the American volunteers in the French Army. Then we celebrated it again by a session of the Foreign Ministers which lasted eight hours, ran into midnight, and removed the final hurdles in the way of a Peace Conference. The track now is definitely clear...."

But for the next few days Molotov raised "one road block

after another" over who would do the "inviting" to the Peace Conference and who would set the rules for conducting it. Byrnes pressed for sending the invitations out immediately; Molotov insisted that the Big Four powers set the procedural rules in advance of the Conference and before invitations were issued. Senator Connally said Molotov's stubbornness reminded him of the old Texas story of the tipsy lawyer who was going home to dinner. "If it isn't ready," said the lawyer, "I'll just raise hell. If it is ready, I won't eat a damn bite."

Vandenberg reported that the Foreign Secretaries met alone twice on one day during this period:

July 8, 1946

Literally, "the fat was in the fire." Bidault asked Byrnes, Bevin and Molotov to come into his private office. They went. And they didn't come out until 8:30. At that time Byrnes came back into the room in the Luxembourg where we were waiting. He shook his head. He said he could see no daylight. It would be possible, all right, to agree upon the details of rules. But it wasn't possible to hurdle Molotov's continuing demands that the invitations should be tied to the rules, and the Big Powers likewise. In other words, the P.C. [Peace Conference] wasn't to be "free" for anybody — and I am sure Byrnes, who was still grimly "holding the line," felt that his Peace Conference was about to disappear in thin smoke up the chimney. We talked it over. At 9 o'clock Byrnes went back to the secret session. About eleven o'clock he returned — all smiles. The miracle had happened — (as it so often does if we just cling long enough to our ideals when dealing with our Soviet friends). No one seemed to be able to explain just what occurred. In fact, there was some difference of opinion between Byrnes and Bohlen (his interpreter) as to just what *had* occurred. . . .

In any event, all the long and bitter arguments since July 4 were over. And here is the result. France will send out the invitations to the Peace Conference tomorrow morning *without* any rules attached. . . . I consider that the American Delegation has achieved the full *"principle"* of a *"free con-*

ference" for which it has been striving. I also consider that Secretary Byrnes has put up a magnificent battle; that he has "followed through" with infinite patience and yet with relentless courage.

"Patient but firm," had paid off at last. Four days later, after bitter preliminary wrangling over a peace treaty with Germany, the Council of Foreign Ministers adjourned.

Vandenberg returned to the Senate, and this time he spoke at length and in detail.

He told the Senate that the five treaties were far from perfect, he had deep reservations on the Trieste arrangement, but "the end product never can be perfection . . . rather the measure of success is the preservation of essential principles in spite of compromise. . . . I believe the American Delegation at Paris did not compromise with principle in the compositions which made possible this continuing march toward peace."

In detail Vandenberg sketched the major arrangements — the Peace Conference, Trieste, the frontiers, reparations, territories, and all the rest. Ruefully he assured his colleagues that the Senate's rule of "unlimited debate" was "quite painless when compared with unlimited debate in three languages in the Council of Foreign Ministers."

Vandenberg reminded his colleagues that the five treaties now approaching reality lay merely on the perimeter; there had been "appalling disagreement" on Germany. There was no prospect of ending the current administration of Germany in "watertight compartments" with East split from West. "Intense suspicions," then as now, prevailed between Russia and the West in Germany; there was no agreement on any phase. Then speaking to Moscow Vandenberg offered the Russians "a few simple truths."

> You should understand with complete conviction that we deeply respect the great Russian people . . . we are just as determined as you are that military aggression — from any source and no matter what its guise — shall never curse the earth again; and we are enlisted in the cause for keeps. . . .

We are prepared for enlightened, progressive cooperation with every land which invites and deserves our mutual good will. . . .

. . . You should also understand with equally complete conviction, that we cannot be driven, coerced, or pressured into positions which we decline voluntarily to assume; and that we will not bargain in human rights and fundamental liberties anywhere on earth.

There was one more trip to be made to Paris before the summer ended, this time in response to Byrnes's "urgent plea" that Vandenberg participate in the twenty-one-nation conference that would formally draw up the peace treaties for Italy, Finland, Bulgaria, Hungary, and Rumania. The Senator once again boarded the "Sacred Cow" and headed across the Atlantic on August 23. Abandoned were all plans for a personal political campaign for re-election in Michigan; it would be conducted in absentia, because even after the conclusion of the Peace Conference Vandenberg would be called upon to attend the once-postponed United Nations General Assembly session in New York. Thus his activities in the international field were to keep him busy until the very eve of election day.

When he reached Paris for the Peace Conference, Vandenberg ceased to keep up the daily entries in his diary. But at the Conference he took active leadership in a fight for freedom of commerce and navigation on the Danube River waterway. He told the Conference that "it is historically clear that Danubian commerce cannot prosper if it is at the mercy of various uncoordinated, restrictive and discriminatory administrations which respond to the local judgments of the eight national jurisdictions through which the Danube flows. Some of the current trouble — some problems on the Danube — are the result of thus dividing the Danube into unrelated water-tight compartments — in contempt of the lessons of history and experience."

While the United States, Vandenberg maintained, had no direct, commercial interest of its own in the Danube, it had heavy, temporary responsibility because as an occupying power it must act as an "economic trustee for parts of Germany and Austria. . . . But the larger problem of the general peace is our greater concern; and we again assert the conviction that this peace, which is the responsibility of every nation, is substantially related to the avoidance of international trade barriers which invite discrimination and dangerous frictions."

Vandenberg successfully waged a fight to affirm the free commerce and navigation principle and a conference to be called to establish an international traffic régime on the river. Though successful at Paris, along with his efforts to incorporate equal trade and business status in the defeated states for all United Nations members, the growing friction with Russia and the satellite status of Bulgaria, Rumania, and Hungary prevented actual fruition of the efforts.

It was during this third trip to Paris that Vandenberg made his only postwar journey to Germany. With Connally, he accompanied Byrnes to Stuttgart, where the Secretary delivered an address designed to counteract Soviet delays on a German peace treaty and misrepresentation of the American position. Byrnes at Stuttgart once more advocated a twenty-five or forty-year American, British, French, Russian treaty to assure enforcement of German disarmament and nonaggression in the future. It was the idea first advanced by Vandenberg in his January 10th speech of the previous year. Byrnes also assured the Germans that the United States sought to give them primary responsibility for running their own affairs, and, though American security forces would be on call in Germany for a long time to come, his country favored no prolonged "alien dictatorship" enforced by huge alien armies.

Vandenberg was deeply moved by Byrnes's speech, and also by the playing of "The Star-Spangled Banner," "which never before gave me such a thrill," as he told the Secretary. And he was astonished by what he saw in Germany. Traveling on what had been Hitler's personal train, the party visited Berlin, Munich, and other devastated German centers. "What the [war] did to Germany is past comprehension," Vandenberg wrote home. "There certainly won't be any 'German menace' again in my life-time."

"The climax of the trip was Berchtesgaden," he wrote, "and an appalling trip up the side of a mountain (the last 1,000 feet in an elevator going up a shaft hewn from solid rock) where

Hitler had his 'eagle's nest'! Jeez! no wonder he went crazy!"

The party returned to Paris early in September, and the next week the Henry Wallace storm broke. Months before at Paris, Vandenberg had received from Byrnes a tip-off on trouble with Wallace.

But the earlier difficulties were a zephyr compared with the storm that rocked the nation on September 12. On that date, Wallace spoke in New York's Madison Square Garden, asserting that current American policy was too harsh toward Russia; that a more conciliatory approach was necessary; and that the British were adopting an imperialistic course. He attacked the Republican Party as well. While admitting that some individual Republicans "may" hold enlightened views, the Commerce Secretary charged that "the Republican Party is the party of economic nationalism and political isolation — and as such is as anachronistic as the dodo and as certain to disappear. The danger is that before it disappears it may enjoy a brief period of power, during which it can do irreparable damage in the United States and to the cause of world peace."

What made the speech sting was that President Truman at a White House news conference held before Wallace spoke told questioning reporters, who had seen advance copies of the Wallace text, that the speech had his approval. Actually, it came out later, Mr. Truman had not read the speech; but Wallace had read him portions of it in a constantly interrupted conversation. The full impact of the speech and Mr. Truman's endorsement of it were not realized until the press association dispatches reporting it came over the tickers accompanied by the President's advance endorsement.

In Paris Byrnes, Vandenberg, and Connally were hunted men. Peace Conference delegates and foreign ministers of many nations wanted to know if American policy had changed; if the Americans in Paris were reflecting the foreign policy of the United States or if Wallace's interpretation was correct.

Vandenberg promptly issued a statement to the press declaring:

> The authority of American foreign policy is dependent upon the degree of American unity behind it. Rightly or wrongly, Paris is doubtful of this unity this morning. Our bipartisan

foreign policy during the last 18 months had overwhelming bipartisan support in behalf of the unselfish aims for which we fought the war. Although differing on some points, most Republicans have been glad to join most Democrats, thus presenting a united American front to the world. This is the only road to organized peace and collective security. Those who leave this road jeopardize the very objective they profess to embrace.

I am sure that most Republicans, despite inevitable differences, favor a bipartisan foreign policy on a sound American basis, which rejects dictatorship by anybody, which is neither hostile nor subservient to any other power on earth and which defends human rights and fundamental freedoms.

But the situation equally requires unity within the Administration itself. We can only cooperate with one Secretary of State at a time.

Connally declared that while American officials were "striving desperately for peace in the world there should be no controversy or bickering or strife at home." Byrnes made no public statement on grounds that the matter called for correction by the President himself.

All that Vandenberg had worked for now threatened to go up in the smoke of Wallace's charges. The bipartisan approach to foreign policy seemed to stagger under the blows of the Secretary of Commerce. How could Vandenberg keep his own party in line if his co-operation with a Democratic Administration was repudiated by an Administration Cabinet officer?

New fuel was added to the blaze by publication of a memorandum Wallace had written the President on July 23 declaring that the effort for bipartisanship had found Democrats giving in "too much to isolationism masquerading as tough realism in international affairs. . . . Unity [at home] on the basis of building up conflict abroad would prove to be not only unsound but disastrous." This was interpreted generally as a slap at Vandenberg, and reports persisted that Wallace had told Democrats they had been "sucked in" on an anti-Russian Republican policy through Vandenberg's influence.

Vandenberg's position at the Peace Conference clearly was

untenable. So was Byrnes's. Something had to give. The Secretary, supported by Vandenberg and Connally, undertook a transatlantic teletype conference with the President after advising Mr. Truman that his resignation should be accepted immediately if Wallace as a Cabinet member could not be kept quiet on foreign policy.

Byrnes in his own book, *Speaking Frankly*, said that Wallace's subsequent promise to keep silent on foreign policy for the duration of the Peace Conference merely was an unsatisfactory "moratorium" on criticism at the Cabinet level which could be resumed when the Conference closed. "The world is today in doubt not only as to American foreign policy, but as to your foreign policy," Byrnes informed the President. If the criticism of a fellow Cabinet officer could not be silenced permanently, Byrnes said, it would be "far better for the Administration to let us come home now. . . . You and I spent 15 months building a bipartisan policy. We did a fine job convincing the world that it was a permanent policy upon which the world could rely. Wallace destroyed that in a day."

That did it. A day later Mr. Truman obtained Wallace's resignation from the Cabinet.

Wallace was free to criticize bipartisan foreign policy as practiced by the President, Byrnes, Connally, Vandenberg, and, later, General George C. Marshall — but from a position outside of the Cabinet. This Wallace did as a private citizen and as the 1948 presidential candidate on the Progressive Party ticket. But the strong stand of Byrnes and the senators at Paris, and the forthright backing given them by President Truman in the showdown saved the day.

The Paris Conference was concluded the next month; it was not, however, until the New York meetings of the Council of Foreign Ministers in November and December, that final agreement was reached on the treaties after additional weeks of difficult negotiations. In fact, it was a suggestion by Secretary Byrnes that the members of the Council admit failure and go home that brought the Soviet Union to terms. Senator Vandenberg did not keep a diary of the New York meetings.

The following June, behind the leadership of Vandenberg and Connally, the Senate confirmed the Italian Treaty by a vote of 79 to 10, and the pacts with Bulgaria, Hungary, and Rumania by voice vote. The treaties were a reality.

The bipartisan foreign policy, which had withstood all the blows that Russian communism could offer, thus rode out a serious challenge on the home front. It had been challenged by Molotov and Vishinsky and had not been found wanting. It had been challenged by Wallace, and it had prevailed.

17

"More Than a Personal Victory".

WHEN VANDENBERG returned from Paris — for the third time that summer — it was mid-October of 1946, and the United Nations General Assembly was about to meet in New York. There was every reason for the Senator to feel that it was important for him to spend some time in Michigan before the November elections, but he didn't. He had long since decided to take his chances on re-election on the basis of his work at the international conference table. "I am not going to get my work for peace bogged down into politics," he had written. "Politics are important; but peace is indispensable." This decision however had not been an easy one.

As early as December of 1945 the Senator had written to John W. Blodgett that he did not doubt his long absences from Michigan since Pearl Harbor would be a "very serious liability" in the 1946 campaign. "There is an entirely new generation of voters in Michigan since I first ran for the Senate. I must be more or less of a legendary character to many of them. Similar circumstances have been fatal to better men than I. It is an excellent reason why I should have sense enough to 'call it a day' and voluntarily retire.

"Just why I am willing even to consider another campaign — knowing what I do about progressive burdens of the job — is more than I can successfully explain to Hazel [Mrs. Vandenberg], who is all for 'cutting the string.' But I suppose that I will be at it again in response to what is probably a very silly notion about my 'duty.'"

Vandenberg had entered the Senate by appointment on March 31, 1928, following the death of Senator Woodbridge N. Ferris. Later that year he won election in his own right with a 601,301 plurality. In 1934, at the high tide of New Deal strength, he squeaked through by 11,000 votes as the only Republican victor in a populous state, but in 1940 his plurality rose again to 113,364.

He had always been a hard campaigner, but this was not to be in 1946. Vandenberg wrote Kim Sigler, the successful Republican candidate for Governor, that "unavoidable obligations" abroad would keep him out of Michigan during the campaign — "an obligation which transcends all politics and has to have complete priority . . . [though] a source of great embarrassment in terms of our 1946 campaign. . . . Therefore, I am afraid I shall be depending upon you in the fall campaign much more than you can lean on me. I can only hope that the type of service I am trying to render will be something of an offset in attracting the good opinions of the people of Michigan."

The big vote-getting potential of the CIO in Michigan was against him. A suggestion by Vandenberg for a national labor-management conference had met with no success — the conference failed — and he believed it was partially because President Truman did not put "sufficient personal drive behind it." Nor was organized labor happy with the Senator's views on anti-strike legislation. Leftist labor elements rallied to Wallace, who lent his efforts to a "Beat Vandenberg" campaign.

Vandenberg's major effort in the Senate in the months before election, apart from his speeches reporting on trips abroad, had been his address for the generally unpopular British loan. Some had counseled that he keep quiet on the $3,750,000,000 loan since he had little enthusiasm for it; but the good overbalanced the evil, in his mind, and he took the Senate floor to support the loan in a speech that was credited by the Administration and the press as an important factor in winning the close fight. That effort was not an asset in the campaign, especially in a territory such as western Michigan where the Chicago *Tribune* enjoyed a large circulation.

The *Tribune*'s bitter campaign against Vandenberg's "internationalism" worried him and his political advisers. Colonel

Robert R. McCormick's newspaper, which in 1940 had lauded Vandenberg as the most useful member of the Senate, had grown steadily more opposed to him since his January 10th speech in 1945, and by the summer of 1946 it was in full cry against almost everything the Senator was doing. "It is really amazing that responsible journalism can go to such extents in a vendetta," he noted later in a memorandum on an exhibit of *Tribune* editorials.

At least once, in July of 1945, the Senator made a conciliatory gesture toward McCormick because he believed that he saw a trace of "good temper" in an editorial entitled "Senator Vandenberg and Mr. Vandenberg." The editorial recalled that in 1926, "Mister" Vandenberg had written a book extolling "nationalism — not internationalism" and it went on to confess "mystification" at the changed position taken in 1945 by "Senator" Vandenberg. After reading this editorial, the Senator sat down and typed a letter to the editor in which he tried in good-humored fashion to clear up the "mystification." He wrote:

July 20, 1945

> I confess that the world looks like a **very** different place to me in 1945 than it did in 1926. I am trying to adjust my own thinking to the world of today. . . . I still think that the primary obligation of Americans is to America. I doubt that "Mr. Vandenberg" . . . would find any inconsistency in today's attitude of "Senator Vandenberg's" willingness to continue to cooperate with the United Nations on a basis which leaves us totally in control of our own contributions, to the end that peace and security shall be preserved. I doubt that "Mr. Vandenberg" would want "Senator Vandenberg" to oppose our only hope of collective security — which means as much to America as to any other land on earth. I think "Mr. Vandenberg" would agree with "Senator Vandenberg" that 1945 with its robots and its rockets is not 1926 in this regard.

If the Senator hoped that the letter would either soften the *Tribune*'s attacks or get a less bitter presentation of his viewpoint in the newspaper he was disappointed. Throughout the campaign and later the *Tribune* contended that Vandenberg's efforts toward a bipartisan foreign policy represented a "partnership in iniquity"; that he had "gone over to the New Deal body and soul"; that he was "abandoning the principles of Americanism." The newspaper's cartoons portrayed Vandenberg in such roles as Benedict Arnold and as a country bumpkin trying to deal with wily European diplomats. The Senator was careful not to try to strike back in kind during the campaign but later, when the *Tribune* continued its attacks, he occasionally made his feelings clear.

December 20, 1946

I am sorry to say (and I say it most reluctantly) that I have found it less irritating not to read the Tribune any more than I have to. I continue to have the greatest respect for the Colonel and his rugged, relentless fidelity to his own viewpoint (no matter how much I disagree with him). My great regret is that he will not similarly recognize my own good faith. As a matter of fact, this situation dramatizes what I believe to be one of the great hazards to American democracy. I do not know why honest men cannot honorably disagree without resort to bitter personalities which generate "heat" instead of "light." I am afraid that one of the things which keeps our better men out of politics and public service is their reluctance to submit themselves to these muddy tortures. We ought to leave these techniques exclusively to the CIO–PAC [CIO Political Action Committee] and to the Commies. . . .

Again he wrote to a correspondent that "it is quite evident that you are a reader of a Chicago newspaper which is specializing in a personal vendetta against me. I think you will find facts regarding my attitude reported quite differently in other newspapers." In another similar letter, Vandenberg said: "I could not blame you if you scratched me off your list if you rely upon information printed in the newspaper to which you refer. I can give you at least one specific instance (in the editorial which you enclose) of such brazen falsehood that I think it approaches malicious libel. The editorial discusses me along with Senators Aiken and Tobey. Then it says: 'They are against any cut in the budget etc.' On the contrary, I voted to 'cut the budget' four and a half billions with a publicly expressed purpose to try for even more if the facts subsequently warrant. . . . There are many other errors in the editorial — and just as bold. . . . " And again he wrote: "I am well aware of the 'Chicago campaign' to which you refer. It is the most totally vicious and deceptive thing I have ever seen in journalism. Nevertheless, I continue to believe in a 'free press.' I can only hope that my Michigan friends read some other newspapers, too. I hope there is some significance in the fact that these Chicago attacks appear nowhere else."

Vandenberg never ceased to resent the *Tribune*'s attacks, and late in his career he wrote to his wife that "The Chicago Colonel broke loose on me on Sunday and how! This time the column-long editorial was headed 'Judas.' I don't know whether that is 'progress' or not — the last time I was 'Benedict Arnold.' . . . " And later in 1949 he told her that "It's sad news that the . . . Colonel has his hands on the [Washington] Times-Herald. That means some nasty shooting. It's not too pleasant to have it in your own backyard. But I should worry. There's nothing I've got that he can take away and there's nothing I want that he can stop. . . . " A final reference a few days later was: "The whole town seems to dread the . . . Colonel's arrival. One important person said today that within one year it will be impossible to get any self-respecting person to take a job in Washington as a result."

On many occasions during his senatorial career Vandenberg felt called upon to write to the editors of various newspapers both large and small, but almost never did he ask for anything except an opportunity to present his own viewpoint or to clarify an editorial attitude which he felt was based on a misunderstanding. It was only the *Tribune* attacks that seemed to rankle, although as it turned out the influence of Colonel McCormick on Michigan voters was practically nil as far as the Senator's election was concerned. The *Tribune* had a large circulation in western Michigan but Vandenberg ran just as strongly in that section of the state in 1946 as he did elsewhere. Generally, the Michigan press strongly supported the Senator throughout most of his career and, in the country as a whole, Vandenberg enjoyed perhaps the best press of any senator of his era.

In 1946 the Senator met with no primary opposition; his party in Michigan stood behind him. In August, between trips abroad, Vandenberg got home for a few days, visited the harness races at the Ionia Free Fair, and made two speeches on foreign policy, one before the State American Legion Convention and another at the University of Michigan. Both were "nonpolitical," and it was too early to do any campaigning. His 1946 Democratic opponent was James H. Lee, a Detroit utility-rate expert, who waged something less than a vigorous anti-Vandenberg campaign and was himself, for a time, kept outside of the state because of hearings before the Federal Power Commission in Washington.

There were a number of items on the credit side of Vandenberg's political ledger as campaign time drew near. *Collier's Weekly* had given him its $10,000 distinguished service award as the Senate's most valuable member (he was similarly honored in 1949). He turned the check over to the American Red Cross, in which organization Mrs. Vandenberg was very active for years and of which she later served as a national director. The attacks on his "patient but firm" approach toward Russia which were launched by Wallace, Pepper, and others backfired and helped more than they hurt. He was constantly in the news from abroad, and many Democratic and independent voters in Michigan rallied to his support on a basis of his co-operation with Democratic Presidents Roosevelt and Truman in foreign policy.

Vandenberg enjoyed and made capital of the "red hot defamatory Campaign" against him from Moscow and the attacks that continued to be "an almost daily feature of the Communist 'Daily Worker' in New York City." He often called attention to these attacks in writing to Michigan voters, reminding them that he had (1) opposed the original recognition of Soviet Russia, and (2) protested when the Russians violated the Soviet-American agreement that they would keep hands off internal American affairs.

"I am flattered to find myself at the top of the Communist 'purge' list all around the world," the Senator wrote in summing up his attitude. "I fully expect they will break loose with plenty of subversive mud in the Michigan campaign before it is over. But if the people understand that they are 'dropping a letter to Stalin in the mailbox' when they drop their votes into the ballot box, I have no doubt of the outcome."

Campaign headquarters for Vandenberg had been opened in June at the Pantlind Hotel in Grand Rapids. In that month the Senator wrote Republican National Committeeman Arthur E. Summerfield that he had "no illusions about the possibilities of serious and even bitter trouble. The Communists have already put me at the top of their purge list (which of course will be an asset rather than a liability). But I have great respect for their ingenuity, their ruthlessness, their irresponsibility and their cash. I shall be very much surprised if the CIO–PAC does not similarly put all their resources against me — and I have great respect for their potentialities. . . . There is no sure thing when public opinion is in such a state of flux and confusion as it is today."

Vandenberg's 1943–45 Senate voting score card on domestic issues as compiled by James M. Haswell of the Detroit *Free Press*, showed him voting with the CIO position twice, against it five times; seven times for the American Farm Bureau and once against. He voted "conservative" fifteen times, and "liberal" four times.

Vandenberg decided that since he could not be in Michigan during the campaign he had better put all his blue chips on *not* being there and key the campaign to his contributions toward peace. He did not forget that Senator Borah in his later years — and other senators, too — had suffered somewhat by being considered as "world statesmen" who were too remote from the home folks. In some instances, serious political troubles had resulted. Vandenberg, however, had no choice in 1946, and he decided that the best thing to do was to make an asset out of his work at the conference tables. He believed that the people of the midwest had changed their attitude toward international affairs and that he should key his campaign to the theme that Michigan was proud of contributing a senator to the world scene, rather than insisting that he serve as senatorial "office boy" to the home folks' bidding in Washington. The billboards that went up throughout the state, for example, displayed the medallion of the *Collier's Weekly* award to Vandenberg and the words: "The world listens to this man from Michigan."

This idea of emphasizing his work for peace was the theme of many letters that he wrote from Paris to his headquarters in Michigan during the campaign, letters in which he tried to lay down the basic line on which he felt the fight should be conducted.

September 21, 1946

I should like to make *one* statewide broadcast at home from Detroit or Grand Rapids. Its nature would depend upon intervening events. If Pepper or Wallace come into Michigan and make a personal attack upon me (which is entirely likely) I would want to make a direct reply, and I should enjoy making it *hot*. Otherwise, I should report on the peace situation generally without reference to politics. I think it would be highly inadvisable for me to make a final political, partisan Republican speech (after keeping away from it all through the campaign) with no possible result, it seems to me, except to jeopardize the Democratic and the independent votes which we expect to get. Necessity has kept me out of the acute, partisan campaign. We have almost completely built our own campaign upon this thesis. I believe we would have everything to lose and nothing to gain by one last-minute speech which stripped our campaign of its absentee, non-partisan character. I may add at this point that, in the excellent situation we occupy, our greatest anxiety is simply not to make any last-minute mistakes. We must beware of some small but fatal fumble (like Rum, Romanism and Rebellion)....

I certainly shall not make a broadcast under the auspices of the Republican National Committee (unless Wallace-Pepper-CIO have succeeded meanwhile in making a partisan, political issue of our foreign policy). I think it would be sheer political suicide on a national scale for the Republicans, after two years' forbearance, to be the ones who should wreck the non-partisan character of our official attitudes toward America's foreign policy. Since your letter was written, the President has forced Wallace's resignation. The President had declared his complete confidence in "the American Delegation." That means he has declared his confidence in me. Therefore, Michigan Democrats have every reason to vote for me. The press has quite clearly indicated in the interim that Vandenberg has a helluva lot to do with this American foreign policy. In other words, it is just as much a Republican policy as a Democratic one. The country surely wants non-partisan continuity in our foreign policy. . . .

Truman (speaking for his party) prostituted foreign policy to 1946 politics (until he "woke up" and reversed himself). Vandenberg (speaking for his party) made one sharp statement refusing to prostitute foreign policy to 1946 politics. Truman's position was insufferable — and the country rebelled. Truman was driven to a complete about-face. Vandenberg finished where he started — namely, on a plane of dignity and firmness and in complete possession of the field. Nobody can argue me into believing that Vandenberg can do his party any good by sacrificing this sound position after its complete vindication and, at the last minute, duplicating Truman's mistake in mixing "peace" with "votes."

I heartily agree that *other* Republican candidates are entitled to talk to their hearts' content about this record — contrasting the attitudes and actions of Truman (Democrat) versus Vandenberg (Republican), thus proving Republicanism's complete dependability and preferable eligibility in handling foreign affairs. But I do not think Vandenberg himself should rob them of their theme by himself talking politics under partisan auspices in respect to foreign policy (unless the Democratic National Committee first makes the colossal blunder of setting up such a pattern — in which event I will be glad to "hit the roof"). Otherwise — no. Let's not throw away our advantage. The people are not dumb. They understand what has happened. Anyway — I'm not going to get my work for peace bogged down into politics. Politics are important; but *peace* is *indispensable*. . . .

. . . Fortunately, there is *nothing I personally want* in 1948. *This is my last run.*

This letter was an unusual document for several reasons. It was typed out by the Senator, with few corrections, while he was very much occupied with final stages of the Peace Treaty Conferences in Paris. At the same time, he was involved in an election campaign of great significance in his own state some four thousand miles away and, as he wrote, his mind was overflowing with political affairs over which his control was limited by his extended absence from the United States. Furthermore, he was writing to a close relative and campaign worker to whom he was trying to point out circumstances that could be used profitably in the election battle. Thus, he sometimes wrote in the third person in order frankly to make the best use of his own highly developed sense of publicity in behalf of his own candidacy. But perhaps most significant in an uninhibited letter of this nature was his emphatic statement that he had no intention of letting his work for peace get bogged down in politics. At such a time and under such circumstances, it carried a ring of sincerity that rose above political considerations and emphasized a quality of the spirit that was becoming more and more evident in Vandenberg's life. His devotion to bipartisanship was a great deal more than political; a great deal more even than politics in behalf of the United States, although he had no question in his mind that it was in the best interests of America. But in refusing to let politics be a guiding factor he achieved a spiritual quality that was to impress more and more of his friends and associates in the next few years and was to give him both the courage and the strength in difficult times to keep the goal of peace with justice foremost in almost everything he did. It was a kind of dedication from which he didn't waver for the rest of his life.

Something of this idea was expressed in a letter by the Senator commenting on the attitude of 350,000 voters of Polish descent who were angry about the postwar fate of Poland. Frank Januszewski, owner of the *Polish Daily News* of Detroit, sent him an article that had been contributed to the newspaper. It bitterly attacked Vandenberg's role in the postwar negotiation regarding Poland, mainly contending that he had failed to oppose the Russians vigorously. Vandenberg replied to Januszewski:

July 27, 1946

I dislike to pursue this discussion, lest it might seem that I am pleading for votes. I do not care to be further misunderstood or misrepresented. The votes are of no personal consequence to me because the outcome of my personal campaign is a matter of substantial indifference to me. But these same "votes" are, in my humble opinion, a matter of very great importance to the true Polish cause because, no matter how little I may deserve the reputation, I believe I am considered Poland's "first friend" in this and every other capital on earth; I . . . believe that my elimination would serve chiefly to confirm the Soviet and Communist claims that my attitudes do not reflect the opinions either of my country or my large Polish constituency. . . . An eloquent and overwhelming rebuff to the Communist pledge to liquidate me next November would be the most powerful message that Polish-Americans could send to Moscow or to Warsaw. . . .

It seems quite futile to go all through the argument presented in your contributed editorial. The gravamen of my offense seems to be that I have not broken up each international conference because of Russia's presence or that I have not advocated immediate war. . . . Yes; I'll admit that I could have split this country wide open by playing politics with our foreign policy. But by splitting our country wide open, I would have crucified the American unity which is indispensable to "stopping Moscow" and I would have invited Stalin to "divide and conquer." I would also have robbed a new, free Poland of any hope. I would have served the Soviets, not the United States and certainly not a new, free Poland. The price of this unity was a complete reversal of the Administration's appeasement and surrender attitudes at Yalta. Someday we shall overtake Yalta itself. *That* is what the Republican contribution . . . has been.

Meanwhile, in Michigan the campaign was carried on with redoubled enthusiasm because of the dependence which the Senator had placed on his loyal supporters. A news flyer reprinting his Senate speeches and including laudatory newspaper comment was circulated throughout the state. In what was then a new departure, George W. Cushing, of Station WJR, who knew the Senator well and had interviewed him a number of times on the air, prepared a recorded radio program dramatizing his career, speeches, and appointments as an American delegate to world conferences, and it was rebroadcast by numerous Michigan radio stations. Even a theme song — "Battle Hymn of the Republic" — was dubbed in. The "Battle Hymn" was chosen because it was impressive, and along with "Onward, Christian Soldiers," and the Yale University "Whiffenpoof Song," a favorite of the Senator.

As election day drew near the Detroit *News* and other newspapers adopted the theme that "the world will watch Vandenberg's vote." They argued that a vote for Vandenberg was a vote for a patient but firm bipartisan foreign policy, and it was an effective argument. It was not possible for the Senator to make even one speech in Michigan. He had strongly opposed further postponement of the United Nations General Assembly meeting in New York and, as a delegate, he felt that he had to remain there following his return from the Paris Conference. He finally stepped off a train in Grand Rapids on the morning of election day — but there was every reason for political optimism, his cigar was tilted at a jaunty angle, a smile creased his round Dutch face and his eyes twinkled from behind his highly polished spectacles.

That night at the Pantlind Hotel there was nothing but victory in the air and, more important, it was victory on Vandenberg's own terms. The first returns, phoned in from the Grand Rapids *Herald*, were favorable and by early evening it was a cinch. A few hours later it was a landslide. They didn't even bother to tally the county-by-county returns on the carefully prepared vote boards. Campaign headquarters turned into a blissful reunion of family and old friends and nobody worried about the votes which were to give the Senator a margin of 567,647 ballots — the second largest majority of his career and one of the largest in the state's electoral history.

As the vote total bulged, not only for the Michigan Republican ticket but for the Party's candidates across the country, the hotel celebration went all out. Waiters wheeled in huge trays of roast turkey and ham. Floral bouquets made it festive. The man around whom it centered was for the first time in months at home — relaxed, elated, completely joyous.

He was surrounded by his daughters, Mrs. Barbara Bailey and Mrs. Elizabeth Pfeiffer, his wife and son and closest friends. The somewhat reserved characteristics of the Vandenberg nature, which usually kept him from intimate "poker crony" relations with Senate colleagues, melted. Somebody tinkled the little piano left over from some one else's party, a few sang "Hail to the Victors Valiant" — the University of Michigan marching song.

Old friends were there, young friends of a later generation dropped in. One who came was John W. Blodgett, long respected in Republican councils. Howard C. Lawrence, for many years an intimate friend and former State Republican Chairman as well as chairman of Vandenberg political campaigns, was present. Arthur E. Summerfield, loyal political associate and Republican National Committeeman, was there. Dr. A. B. Smith, beloved personal physician and friend, was there with Mrs. Smith. Mrs. Dudley Hay, National Committeewoman; Mr. and Mrs. Heber Curtis; Mrs. Leona Diekema; Mr. and Mrs. David W. Kendall of Jackson — all were there. The Senator's younger friends and his son's contemporaries, such as Louis A. Weil, Jr., publisher of the *Herald*, Mr. and Mrs. John Dregge, Mr. and Mrs. Russell Buck, Mr. and Mrs. Edward Frey, and a dozen others helped celebrate.

It was a time for rejoicing. Seldom before or after that night was Vandenberg as completely happy and carefree; all the months of effort at home and abroad had been well rewarded. The Senator stripped off his dark blue suit coat; the United Nations Delegate identification button sparkled from his vest. He scrawled out this victory statement:

> I am deeply grateful to the people of Michigan for this expression of their confidence and trust. At the end of another term I shall have represented Michigan in the United States Senate for a quarter century. This is honor enough for any citizen.
>
> The outcome means much more to me than a personal vic-

tory. That is secondary. It means unmistakable endorsement of the united, bipartisan foreign policy through which we are striving for national security and for world peace with justice on the basis of sound American ideals. I take it the national returns present a similar mandate. They mean that this policy will continue. Those who may have been led to doubt our unity in this regard now have their eloquent answer from the people of the United States. I am sure the results will facilitate an honorable and just peace.

The Republican party confronts a great challenge. [The Republicans won control of Congress in the election.] It faces a responsibility to the common welfare. I have every confidence it will justify its new rendezvous with destiny.

Three days later, before the United Nations at Lake Success, Vandenberg was able to stand and proudly reassure the world by declaring: "I reassert, with whatever authority I possess, that, regardless of what political régime sits in Washington, you can count upon the wholehearted cooperation of the government of the United States in striving, through the United Nations, for a system of mutual defense against aggression and for organized peace with justice in a better, safer world."

18

Wearing Three Hats

THE ELECTIONS of November, 1946, not only sent Senator Vandenberg back to the Senate, but, after more than a decade of Democratic majorities, brought the Republican party into control of both the Senate and House. It posed the always difficult and perhaps uniquely American problem in two-party statecraft — how the government is to function effectively with the executive branch in control of one political party and the legislative branch in the hands of the other.

No longer was Vandenberg the leading policy spokesman for a party that was a minority in Congress. The Republican victory gave him chairmanship of the Senate Foreign Relations Committee and the post of President Pro Tempore.

Vandenberg actually wore three hats. Firstly, as Chairman of the Foreign Relations Committee he primarily was responsible for foreign policy legislation in the Senate. Secondly, through his contributions to foreign policy, he was the recognized Republican party spokesman in Congress on the subject. Thirdly, as Senate President he was in most intimate touch with the Senate's work. His knowledge of the Chamber's parliamentary situation and prevailing moods were to prove valuable in obtaining prompt action on foreign policy. He constantly had his finger on the pulse of the Senate, and this intensified an almost sixth sense of timing by which Vandenberg knew when to keep silent and when to speak out with telling effect.

In the Eightieth Congress a tacit and informal understanding between Vandenberg and Senator Taft developed. Both men conscientiously sought to avoid direct conflict; Vandenberg devoted his energies almost exclusively to foreign policy and Taft's activities at that time lay mainly in the field of domestic legislation. Vandenberg always expressed great confidence in Taft's leadership in this latter field and it was a factor in his freedom to concentrate on foreign affairs. There were differences between the two leaders at this time, such as on the scope of Marshall Plan aid, but both men sought to minimize them and avoid direct conflict.

Vandenberg also was meticulous in respecting Taft's position as policy chairman. Early in 1947 he wrote President Truman to "respectfully suggest" Taft's inclusion in any Congressional delegation invited to the White House to discuss any matter of "fundamental and far reaching importance."

The letter said:

[*February, 1947*]

My dear Mr. President:

If another Congressional conference is held on any matter of *fundamental* and *far-reaching* importance (as yesterday) I respectfully suggest that the representation of the Congressional majority include Senator Taft because of his position as Chairman of the Republican Senate Policy Committee.

With warm personal regards and best wishes.

The President scrawled his reply to "Dear Van" on the same letter and sent it back, saying that he had had no intention of omitting Taft. And Vandenberg was careful to write formally to Taft in advance — though their offices were but two flights of stairs apart — asking Taft's go-ahead as policy chairman on bringing foreign policy measures to the Senate floor for debate.

Vandenberg in his new position now faced direct responsibility for the fate of foreign policy legislation in the Senate. No longer was it purely a question of his counsel, his prodding, and his advice. The work of translating policy into an established program through the legislative machinery rested heavily on his shoulders.

This task was made more difficult by the constant divisive

tactics and the truculent aggressiveness of the Russians in the agonized postwar world and by the Soviets' use of the veto in the United Nations Security Council. American sentiment was that Russia was abusing the veto and disrupting the United Nations. As Vandenberg put it, the Soviet attitude presented the United States with the danger that "this will be two worlds instead of one." American policy now had to be tailored to the threat of a divided world and this task was very much in the Senator's mind. The evolution of his thinking about the United Nations over a period of months was illustrated by letters he wrote to Colonel Alton T. Roberts of Royal Oak, Michigan, in reference to activities of the American Legion, which was debating resolutions calling for limitations on use of the UN veto.

As early as December 20, 1946, Vandenberg wrote Roberts that

> the American Legion now confronts a greater responsibility than ever before in the life of the nation because it can furnish organized stability to a large sector of our public thinking (and unless I am mistaken we are going to sadly need this sort of rational Americanism). . . .
>
> But when you come to the general subject of amending the Charter of the United Nations, I am afraid I cannot go along with the Legion's suggestions, at least for the time being. I fully recognize the need to reconstruct the so-called "veto." But at this point we face a condition and not a theory. I think it is perfectly obvious . . . that it would be quite impossible to get any fundamental Charter changes at the present time. Even our own Government is opposed to it. So am I. It would break the U.N. if undertaken now or in the immediate future. I think it is very clear that we must first develop a better sense of mutual good faith and good will between the major powers which sit upon the Security Council (and particularly the United States and Soviet Russia). I hope we are moving (slowly but surely) in this direction. . . . It is the theory of most of us who organized the United Nations that the effective use of Chapter Six [for

pacific settlement of disputes] will make it highly improbable that it will ever be necessary to resort to sanctions. . . . U.N. is supposed to be a peace-keeping and not a war-making institution. . . . In a word, I simply say that we should exhaust the pregnant possibilities of the existing Charter before we try to write a new one; and that there is no practical hope of writing a new one if we are unable to find a way to fully utilize our existing possibilities.

Then he again wrote to Roberts:

January 23, 1947
Coming back to the question of the total suspension of the veto in the Security Council. . . . There is a point in the United Nations procedure where the veto becomes of highly important and significant value to our own United States. I refer to the point where the Security Council decides to use force under Chapter Seven. . . . The use of force — as contemplated in this Chapter — goes to the extent of the final mobilization of the armed forces of all member nations. This, of course, is tantamount to defensive war itself. I do not object to this power. I think it finally must be available. But I seriously doubt whether the American people will ever be satisfied to let a majority of the Security Council virtually order us into war without our specific consent. . . . This is the prime reason why I think the American Legion should "go slow" in any sled-length demand for a suspension of the veto. It is for this reason that I am concentrating for the time being . . . upon demanding a suspension of the veto *only* in respect to Chapter Six . . . which deals with pacific settlement of disputes. There can be no . . . rational argument against it (except from the Moscow point of view). Yet it would be a tremendous step in advance.

The continued use of the veto by the Russians as an obstructionist weapon led Vandenberg into a new field of speculation on the future of the United Nations — speculation that he was careful not to express in his public statements.

Another letter to Roberts said:

March 15, 1947

There is absolutely no doubt that the Legion is right when it says "the United Nations organization presents our best opportunity to have an effective and permanent peace." I agree that it is equally right when it says: "inherent weaknesses in the Charter as presently in effect may so weaken the operation of the United Nations as to make it ineffective." Our problem, therefore, is to deal effectively with both of these truths. This inevitably becomes a matter of evolution. . . . We must feel our way. . . . There are many different programs being discussed.

I am particularly interested in paragraph five of your proposed pamphlet. This is really the "guts" of the whole business. Your pamphlet proposes to say that the Legion's proposal can be put into effect "even if one major State vetoes it." How? "By the creation of a special international authority without that major State." The truth of the matter is — and I now very definitely am speaking off the record — that this is a highly prophetic declaration. I think it may well become the method by which so-called Western Democracy ultimately confronts Eastern Communism. In other words, it is my expectation that when some paramount issue (let us say like atomic energy) flatly divides the United Nations, it may well happen that those of us who are in agreement in the United Nations separate ourselves from those who are in disagreement. In other words, we may wind up with a "United Nations" without some of the big powers — just as the old League of Nations wound up without Russia. But the point I want to make is that any such procedure as this is not a means of building up the United Nations. It is inevitably a means of dividing the United Nations. . . . There is no way that you can . . . by-pass the veto in the parent organization without substantially destroying the parent organization and substituting the new international authority as its successor. I agree that this may have to happen — (and again I am speaking in great confidence). But if and when it does happen, I want it to be the plain and obvious result of Soviet intransigence. I would not want it to be the result of an American Legion suggestion made for the paradoxical purpose of trying to strengthen the parent organization which it would actually destroy.

And in a final letter the Senator wrote:

August 12, 1947

It is more than ever evident that for some time to come this is going to be "two worlds" instead of "one" — and the reason is obvious. Bluntly, the $64 question thus becomes whether these two worlds can survive without another war, the most horrible war ever contemplated, perhaps the war that ends this civilization. . . . We must continue to exert every reasonable human effort to avert such a war. . . . But we cannot allow these efforts to blind us to the realities; which means that we cannot, meanwhile, surrender to Soviet aggressions or intransigence which, on the one hand, bring war nearer, or on the other hand, weaken our potentialities in case it comes.

But one or two things seem fairly plain. If there are to be "two worlds" instead of one it becomes *more than ever* necessary to keep the forum of the United Nations available where, so far as possible, we can "talk things out" instead of "shooting them out." Even under the worst conditions, there is some utility in this process — as we occasionally find from time to time. I add, parenthetically, that it seems to me to be worse than futile to talk of some sort of new "world government" under such circumstances. These two worlds cannot fuse. But there still can be a role for an umpire. The hope is that they can learn to "live and let live" — and I refuse to abandon this hope. You cannot expect to rewrite the U.N. Charter under such circumstances — the effort would be waste motion. The best you can do is to provide vivid American leadership in the Security Council seeking to voluntarily circumscribe the use of the veto. But even though this cannot be done, there is this final utility in the United

Nations: it provides self-proof of responsibility if we cannot avoid war, and it provides a ready-made coalition (of the rest of us) if war comes.

So the United Nations is more necessary than ever. But here arises the other dilemma to plague us. We cannot afford to permit the Soviet gang to keep like-thinking nations apart any longer in doing the things that the rest of us conceive to be essential to world restabilization and world peace. Time runs against us and delay encourages the chaos and confusion upon which Moscow thrives. Therefore, I should say, that when we are stymied in such efforts *inside* the Security Council and U.N., like-thinking nations must step *outside* the Security Council and U.N. in accomplishing these other purposes — *always leaving the door open and the option to Moscow and her satellites to enter if they please.*

These letters provided a kind of swift background to the major challenge that the country was to confront in the coming months when the Republicans would be in control of Congress. It was a challenge that brought new departures in the nation's foreign affairs and established a zenith in non-partisan co-operation. Perhaps for the first time in its history the United States was to face up to the requirements of moral and physical world leadership on a more or less permanent basis. Unanimity in the Foreign Relations Committee, overwhelming support by the Congress, and popular acceptance in the nation marked the critical, new departures.

Esther Van Wagoner Tufty, a Michigan newspaper woman and a good friend, put Vandenberg's problem trenchantly, though perhaps in overstated form. In a letter to the Senator she congratulated him on the election victory and his past accomplishments, and added: "But will you be as big (I almost said 'great' but you aren't that yet) when you are the top dog? As the voice of the minority you were magnificent. But now the Republicans are in power and that changes everything. Now there will be more Republican voices and the Party must assume the responsibility of leadership in Congress.

"You are essentially an egotist, and I am glad, to a degree, that you are, or you would not have dared to be so outspoken about the things that matter in this post-war world. This is the moment when you might fail. You must not, because it will not only hurt you personally, but the negotiations of the world are so delicate and important to the point of survival that whether you sneeze in the morning can have earth-shaking results."

It was the very qualities that Vandenberg possessed to such a marked degree as a man of action which now were to serve him well.

He was not what one might call a great innovator of policy; at least that was not his forte. Rather it was in the accommodation of policy to political reality that he excelled. It was in translating policy into the reality of law, the ideal into the practical, the essential process of "removing bugs" from the programs that had been blueprinted in offices far from the realities of Congressional votes. It was in sniffing trouble before it broke out, and moving to avoid — or if necessary to throttle — the trouble, all the while preserving intact the basic principles of a program. After all, as Vandenberg wrote, "Congress itself cannot take the lead in foreign relations because that is the President's job not only by Constitutional requirement but also by practical reality." He could suggest, urge, correct, demand. He could revise and he could prevent — but never could he order.

This role was job enough. It required, in fact, an almost complete dedication and fantastically painstaking care. Precisely at 8.30 every morning of the working week, Hubert, the Negro government chauffeur, would glide the Senate President's big, black Cadillac along the curb at the side door of the Senate Office Building.

The morning papers — two New York newspapers and the Washington *Post* — had been devoured over breakfast at the hotel. Vandenberg nodded to the policeman at the door and slipped into his office suite by a rear door, so quietly that the staff never knew he was there until he rang. Essential correspondence was on the desk. Vandenberg answered every letter brought to his eye and it was a job to keep this within manageable proportions. For an hour and a half he would dictate. Under the pressure of new duties he drafted far fewer letters on his own typewriter, although this newspaper city room habit still prevailed for important correspondence. Vandenberg always regarded his voluminous exchange of letters as a satisfactory substitute for seeing in person the hordes of people descending on his office.

At ten o'clock it usually was committee time — ordinarily in those days a meeting of the Foreign Relations Committee. At 11.45, fifteen minutes before the Senate's noon meeting time, Vandenberg would hurry to the historic crystal chandeliered "Vice-President's" office just off the Senate floor. Since there was no vice-president at that time Vandenberg, as Senate President, used the office. Visiting dignitaries — often a foreign official, sometimes an important constituent of a Senate colleague or a state official — would be ushered in by Dick Deem, a young night school student who was working part time for the Senator, or by the ubiquitous "Tommy," the tiny doorman who has served many Senate presidents.

Just before noon the late Reverend Peter Marshall, a youthful Presbyterian minister and Senate Chaplain, dropped by to exchange a few words with Vandenberg. A close relationship developed between the two — Vandenberg was a deeply spiritual man, though in a very personal and silent way. Together they went to the Senate floor at noon, where after Marshall's minute of opening prayer Vandenberg would drop the gavel for order.

After the Chaplain's death the Senator on November 8, 1949, wrote his widow: "I have just read 'The Exile Heart.' It is a very great evangel — and makes Peter live again. When I opened it at random I immediately came upon a tremendous sentence which belongs to the ages — 'We must not call upon God to be on the side of democracy, but rather let us challenge democracy to be on the side of God.' That is a perfect example of the straight-thinking by which Peter simplified the problems of life. I shall always cherish his deathless inspiration."

The job of President Pro Tempore of the Senate ordinarily was a *pro forma* job. But with no Vice-President in office it had a new meaning, and Vandenberg, who loved the tradition and trappings of the Senate, took the job with great seriousness. He carefully clipped for his scrapbook the newspaper pictures of the Vandenbergs attired in formal clothes arriving at the

White House for the President's traditional dinner tendered the Senate President. The society columns dutifully reported that the red-coated Marine Corps band played after dinner and Frederick Jagel, the Metropolitan Opera star, sang. The Vandenbergs, the White House seating chart shows, sat on either side of the President and Mrs. Truman. Masses of pink roses, pink and white snapdragons, and blue iris set off the State Dining Room's handsome china and gleaming crystal.

Occasionally there was an important parliamentary ruling to be made. Vandenberg would spend hours preparing a ruling on grounds that Senate and legislative precedent were of the highest importance. Charles Watkins, veteran Senate Parliamentarian and informal Senate historian, maintained that Vandenberg's devotion to duty as Senate presiding officer topped that of almost all his predecessors.

Vandenberg buttressed the tradition that a Senate President's business is to preside over the Senate. He always was on the rostrum during important debates. Often he was present, too, when unimportant debates dragged on. It was then that he drew fantastic, lacey networks of intricate "doodles," many of them with a patriotic motif. These have become virtually collector's items, and at least one hangs framed in the offices of a senator who picked it up after the "artist" had abandoned it.

The Senator's knowledge of parliamentary procedure, coupled with his long legislative experience, made him particularly effective in steering important legislation through the Senate. In most cases he was able to outpoint his opponents by the sheer weight of his logic, but sometimes he resorted to other tactics. During the Senate debate on an important bill in 1947, for example, Senator Donnell of Missouri was a persistent critic, raising all sorts of difficult questions. As the last day's debate got under way, Vandenberg came back to his Senate seat with a big grin spread all over his face. "If you stay around here long enough," he said to his chief of staff, "you'll find that there are plenty of tricks of the trade in the Senate. I've just put Senator Donnell in the presiding officer's chair. So long as he's presiding over the Senate he can't get in our hair."

The legislative machinery and Senate traditions were a love as well as a responsibility to him. When he was not in the Chair he was close by, and strict orders were in effect to call him in any untoward event. Lunch was brief — often pie and milk despite his consciousness of the "weight problem" — in the senators' private dining room. Then back to the Chamber. In the late afternoon came consultations, often with State Department officers, usually at the Capitol but sometimes at the Department. At six or shortly thereafter, Vandenberg would return to the office where he often dictated briefly to Geraldyne Creagan, his aide for many years and later his confidential secretary.

At seven, again through the rear door, the Senator was off for his Wardman Park Hotel apartment. By this time the demands of Washington's semiofficial social life had become too much. The Vandenbergs participated only when protocol demanded. Aside from these "starched collar" occasions, they went out once weekly — that occasion at the dictum of Mrs. Vandenberg. Ordinarily there was a brief and never interrupted evening session to read the Grand Rapids and Detroit newspapers, and the Washington evening papers.

Vandenberg had few recreations, aside from reading and card playing. Occasionally, he would take a half-hour off from his duties for a swim in the Senate pool, hardly larger than an oversized bathtub. A couple of afternoons each summer he would go to the ball park, and would have gone oftener had he not become discouraged by the Washington club's long nose dives deep into the second division of the American League. He took it almost as a personal affront that the "Senators" could be that bad. Usually once each fall he would "happen" to find himself within striking distance of Ann Arbor on the weekend of an important Michigan football game. His interest in Michigan football had been heightened by his friendship with the late Fielding (Hurry Up) Yost, famous Michigan coach and athletic director.

But for the most part Vandenberg's day was a dedication to the job at hand. It was not only the speeches that required painstaking care. On every bill he took to the floor Vandenberg was subjected to searching examinations — sometimes for hours on end — by his colleagues. His answers to interrogations were vitally important to both public understanding and subsequent interpretation of Congress' intent. His preparation was so meticulous that seldom if ever was he caught unprepared and off guard. He prided himself on complete mastery of the matter at hand.

In his post as Committee Chairman Vandenberg enhanced his reputation as a man of action. He never liked to leave things undone. He always took pride in the fact that he was usually able to get the Committee to dispose of the items on its agenda with dispatch. And while the legislative process is slow at best, Vandenberg knew, as well as any other Senator, how to get speedy action when the situation required. On one occasion, for example, the Committee approved a resolution shortly before it adjourned for the afternoon. Some five minutes later a member of the Senator's staff went to the Senate floor to consult with him about the kind of report that should be prepared to accompany the resolution. "Well," said Vandenberg, obviously pleased with himself, "I don't think we'll need a committee report this time. The Senate has already passed the resolution."

Vandenberg during this period usually was available to the newspapermen he had come to know and trust. A brush with Vandenberg could be an ordeal for anyone but a Press Gallery old-timer. He could be curt, uneasy, and even testy. But with those reporters in whom he had confidence — "no quotes" unless specifically agreed upon — he completely relaxed, was warm and helpful in the extreme. There were few secrets kept from these newsmen, and no violations of confidence; there was a deep warmth and mutual affection. Probably no senator ever had a friendlier press and no senator ever enjoyed the reciprocal relationship more.

On occasions he "rehearsed" a speech to the criticism of James (Scotty) Reston of the *New York Times*, Bert Andrews of the New York *Herald Tribune*, Blair Moody or Jay Hayden of the Detroit *News*, or columnist Marquis Childs. On Saturday, a partial workday, there was invariably a noon seminar — "school's in session," as Vandenberg called it — with such Senate regulars as Jack Bell of the Associated Press, William Theis of International News Service, John L. Steele of the United Press, the Baltimore *Sun*'s William Knighton or Philip Potter, Ferdinand

Kuhn of the Washington *Post*, Jack Steele of the *Herald Tribune*, the *Times*'s William S. White, and a few others. Often Vandenberg learned more from picking the brains of the newsmen than he told them — but there were few questions that went unanswered, despite the fact that many answers could not be published.

Early in the Eightieth Congress, Vandenberg decided that his new responsibilities required that he withdraw from participating in further international conferences or in United Nations work unless his services were deemed essential for specific tasks by the President. "During the last two years I have considered it my paramount duty to devote practically all of my time to the diplomatic front in seeking to put united American post-war foreign policy on firm foundations," he told newsmen. "I believe these foundations are now soundly established. I shall continue to hold myself available for any further personal labor that may be deemed essential by the President or the Secretary of State. But I am sure that I can now count upon returning to my primary Senate labors without further serious interruption. That is my expectation."

To Mrs. Eleanor Roosevelt, who urged continued bipartisan representation at the conference table and who regretted the decision, Vandenberg wrote that he, too, thought bipartisan representation had paid "infinite dividends" in strengthening the united voice of the United States.

January 9, 1947

It is the question of "Congressional" representation which presents the difficulties. I dare to believe that "Congressional" representation in the General Assembly and in the Council of Foreign Ministers has been distinctly useful to the public welfare — as you yourself are good enough to say. I confess that I am very proud of the privilege I have had to participate in these enterprises. I think perhaps it was indispensable in the initial stages of this great adventure. I am not so sure that it is anything like "indispensable" when the new system of international peace and security starts to mature. On the other hand, I am increasingly impressed with the difficulties confronted by "Congressional" representatives because of their dual capacity. Of course it will always be true that a man cannot serve two masters. Yet that is precisely what I undertake to do — for example — when I, as a Senator, sit in the General Assembly as a delegate. I am helping to make decisions for the United Nations which must pass in review before the American Congress. Having participated in the United Nations in helping to make the decisions, I am not a "free agent" when I return to the Senate to function in my "Congressional" capacity. Indeed, it could be a most embarrassing and difficult situation in the event that I did not approve of some decision made by the United Nations. I should dislike to oppose in Congress anything to which I had given my consent (if only by reluctant acquiescence) in the United Nations.

[Vandenberg pointed out to Mrs. Roosevelt that UN delegates were not "free agents," that by the very commissions which they held they rightfully voted as instructed by the President, and with possibly a subsequent moral obligation to defend this position in Congress. The question, Vandenberg surmised, went to the heart of the traditional "checks and balances" American governmental system. At the same time he urged continuity in American representation at the General Assembly. Vandenberg suggested to Mrs. Roosevelt that delegates to the Assembly perhaps should hold full-time, year-around jobs in order that the nation be "adequately prepared" for Assembly work.] I was deeply impressed — particularly at the recent session in New York — with the fact that the United States was not contributing an adequate measure of moral leadership because our program was essentially one of negation (except in one or two important instances with which you were particularly associated).

I suppose my feeling about the matter is accentuated by the fact that I was attempting the impossible at the recent New York meetings. I was trying to sit both in the General Assembly and in the Council of Foreign Ministers and meanwhile I was pursued by my long distance Senatorial responsibilities. Of course that is an accumulation of responsibilities which is more than any man can adequately carry or to which any man would long be physically equal.

Vandenberg in later years always had the pleasantest recollections of his contacts with Mrs. Roosevelt and praised her United Nations work as "constructive and courageous contributions to the public interest."

As the members of the Senate gathered in Washington during the last days of 1946 the Republican majority faced a heavy responsibility in "organizing" the new Congress for the first time in almost two decades. It did not prove an easy task and the end result was an unusual division of powers among several veteran Republican leaders in the Senate, including Vandenberg and Taft. While Vandenberg became both President Pro Tempore of the Senate and Chairman of the Foreign Relations Committee, Taft was named Chairman of the Republican Steering Committee and Chairman of the Senate Labor Committee. Senator Eugene D. Millikin of Colorado became Presiding Officer at the Republican Conference and Chairman of the Finance Committee. Senator White of Maine took over the job of Majority Floor Leader, and Senator Wherry of Nebraska became Party Whip.

This arrangement among the triumphant Republicans called for considerable skill and tact to maintain a smooth-working organization, and resulted in some friendly ribbing in the newspapers. Cartoonist Berryman in the Washington *Star* pictured a meeting of the new leadership at which two Tafts, two Vandenbergs, and two Millikins met at the conference table, with President Pro Tempore Vandenberg deep in discussion with Chairman Vandenberg, Taft talking happily to his own twin, and Millikin the Finance Chairman chatting with Millikin the Presiding Officer of the Conference. In effect, however, the outcome was to put the Senate organization in the hands of Republican veterans.

"The opening of the 80th Congress at noon on January 3," remarked *Life* magazine, " . . . marked [a] significant shift in the government's center of gravity. In recent years Congress had lost much of its traditional power as part of the American system of checks and balances, had become a combination rubber stamp and whipping boy for the White House and had fallen to dangerously low public esteem. Now it began to reassert its strength and enter into the business of government as a full fledged partner. . . . The eyes of the world were now on men like Senator Arthur H. Vandenberg, the G.O.P.'s dean of foreign affairs, and Senator Robert A. Taft, its domestic leader. Indeed there was something symbolic in the sight of them conferring across a conference table with the intimacy of old friends and the wariness of rivals. . . . "

The organization of the new Foreign Relations Committee under the Congressional Reorganization Act of 1946 was of particular concern to Vandenberg. The Republican vacancies on the Committee were filled with senators who were regarded as friendly to his viewpoint — Henry Cabot Lodge, Jr., of Massachusetts, who had returned to the Senate after service in the army, H. Alexander Smith of New Jersey, and Bourke B. Hickenlooper of Iowa, with whom Vandenberg had served on the Atomic Energy Committee. Hold-over members were Arthur Capper of Kansas, who though senior to Vandenberg chose the chairmanship of the Agriculture Committee rather than the Foreign Relations Committee, Senator White, and Alexander Wiley of Wisconsin. In this connection, it was interesting that Senator Wayne Morse of Oregon vainly sought a seat on the Committee on the grounds that the West Coast had no representation. Vandenberg sympathized with him and, in the end, committed himself to Morse for the first vacancy that should occur in the membership. He also felt that the Republican Conference was committed to Morse, but the Oregon senator was later rebuffed by the Party leadership in favor of Senator Tobey of New Hampshire in accordance with the traditional principle of seniority. Still later, when Senator Vandenberg's death in 1951 left another vacancy on the Committee, Senator Owen Brewster of Maine, whose viewpoint was far removed from that of Vandenberg, was appointed to succeed him.

"Republicans can claim that they follow strict seniority in making the choice," the New York *Herald Tribune* commented on Brewster's appointment, "but this does not obscure the essential fact. A figure standing in foreign policy for the opposite of everything for which Senator Vandenberg fought has been named to succeed him. Party leaders have been concerned not with restoring bipartisanship but with assuring an antagonistic clash. . . . One Republican could complain that the last appointment from the party membership, Senator Tobey, was 'as bad as a Democrat,' and this time there was to be no uncertainty. . . . But in the long run the spirit of Senator Vandenberg will have to prevail."

On the Democratic side of the table were Connally, Walter F. George of Georgia, the late Robert F. Wagner of New York, Elbert D. Thomas of Utah, Alben W. Barkley of Kentucky, and Carl A. Hatch of New Mexico. Francis O. Wilcox, formerly head international relations analyst of the Library of Congress' legislative reference service, who had served as an aide to the senators at international conferences, was selected by Vandenberg as chief of a small technical staff. Vandenberg insisted that the choice of all staff members be made on ability alone, and with no regard to political affiliation.

"Go and get the best people you can find to do the job we have to do," he instructed his chief of staff. "I don't even want to interview the candidates. I am interested only in the net results. But don't forget," he said with a twinkle in his eyes, "I'll hold *you* responsible for everything." As a result one of the most efficient, though one of the smallest, committee staffs on Capitol Hill was organized.

Early in 1947 Vandenberg made a significant address before the Cleveland Foreign Affairs Forum in which he sought both to redefine and explain some limits on bipartisanship. It was one of the few times the Senator made an important speech outside of the Senate. He appeared on the same platform with Byrnes, and the address, coming on the threshold of new duties, struck a responsive chord at home and abroad. Asserting that bipartisanship had been established in the United Nations work and in planning European peace, Vandenberg said:

January 11, 1947

It would be more significant to say we have sought a united American foreign policy so that, despite some inevitable dissidence at home, America could enjoy abroad the enhanced authority of a substantially united front. I dare to believe that, despite some distressing domestic interludes, it has borne rich fruits. In any event, partisan politics, for most of us, stopped at the water's edge. I hope they stay stopped — for the sake of America — regardless of what party is in power. This does not mean that we cannot have earnest, honest, even vehement domestic differences of opinion on foreign policy. It is no curb on free opinion or free speech. But it does mean that they should not root themselves in partisanship. We should ever strive to hammer out a permanent American foreign policy, in basic essentials, which serves all America and deserves the approval of all American-minded parties at all times.

At the same time Vandenberg used the occasion to make clear that a "permanent" bipartisan policy covering all the world by no means had been established. He spoke critically of the two years of delay in calling a conference with the twenty Latin American Republics for negotiation of a hemispheric defense treaty under the Act of Chapultepec. The delay stemmed from alleged failure of the Argentine government to purge itself of Nazi influence. The question of purging the "last vestige" of Nazism from the Western Hemisphere, he said, was a multilateral undertaking, not a matter to be "dictated by us alone."

"There is too much evidence that we are drifting apart — and that a Communistic upsurge is moving in. We face no greater need than to restore the warmth of a new world unity which reached an all-time high at San Francisco," he said of Western Hemisphere problems.

It was significant that Vandenberg also urged at Cleveland that the United States "shift its emphasis" from a policy of seeking unity in China between the Communists and non-Communists, to one of affirmatively aiding Generalissimo Chiang Kai-shek in seeking a coalition of all non-Communist parties under the new Constitution in China. He said:

> While still recommending unity, it might well encourage those who have so heroically set their feet upon this road, and discourage those who make the road precarious. . . . There will never be a minute when China's destiny is not of acute concern to the United States and to a healthy world.

[But as to his opinion on the keystone to the arch of future hopes, Vandenberg left no doubt.]

This record cannot be misread at home or abroad. We have

embraced the United Nations as the heart and core of united, unpartisan American policy. We shall be faithful to the letter and the spirit of these obligations. In my view, this will be true no matter what administration sits in Washington, and it will remain true to whatever extent the United Nations themselves are faithful to our common pledge. That, in general, Mr. Chairman, would be my over-all reply to the world.

But I make the reply with no illusions that now all's well. The United Nations is neither an automatic nor a perfect instrument. Like any other human institution, it will make mistakes. It must live and learn. It must grow from strength to strength. It must earn the ever-expanding confidence and fidelity of people everywhere. It must deserve to survive.

The process of growth "from strength to strength," the conception of the UN as a nonstatic organization, as an instrument for multiple and changing peace-keeping purposes was perhaps not then fully visualized even by the speaker himself. But it was a development in which Vandenberg was to play an increasingly important part.

19

"Calculated Risk"

THE REPUBLICAN-controlled Eightieth Congress hardly had organized when Senator Vandenberg was put to a test in his new role as a leader of the majority and Chairman of the Senate Foreign Relations Committee. Up until this period, at the beginning of 1947, American relief efforts abroad had been largely through the United Nations in an effort to alleviate famine and to start rehabilitation of war-devastated regions or, through the British loan, to unlock restrictive trade situations and re-establish conditions that would facilitate postwar international commerce. The test now at hand involved a basic and untried concept of using American dollars and supplies, military advice and arms shipments to block new Communist inroads against an exhausted, turbulent, and threatened Europe.

Furthermore, the Senator's immediate position was somewhat complicated by the fact that Byrnes, acting on his doctor's orders, resigned as Secretary of State early in January in a move that was not revealed in advance to Vandenberg. The Senator's relations with Byrnes had started on a doubting and critical note but had ended in complete mutual confidence and respect. "I shall never forget," Vandenberg wrote Byrnes in 1949, "our long and intimate and always faithful cooperation during times that tried men's souls. You are a 'great guy.'"

In his 1947 remarks to the Senate Vandenberg described Byrnes as a "very great American." He took an indirect dig at the Administration's "sudden and unusual interruption of the State Department's personnel" but he added that a bipartisan policy would be continued with General Marshall, who had been named to succeed Byrnes. "I think it is highly important that the Senate of the United States, continuing to pursue what has been an effective bi-partisan foreign policy, should make it perfectly clear immediately that there is no interruption to this unity by the episode to which I refer." Vandenberg then demonstrated his ability to get quick and decisive action by calling the Foreign Relations Committee to an immediate meeting, securing unanimous approval of Marshall's nomination and then getting Senate approval, again unanimously, on the same day.

On February 27, 1947, Vandenberg and the other Congressional leaders were called to the White House where Mr. Truman and Secretary Marshall laid before them a top-secret picture of impending disaster in Greece and, in only slightly lesser degree, Turkey. General Marshall briefed the legislators from his up-to-the-minute diplomatic reports, Vandenberg's papers show. Britain, in extreme economic distress herself, now was forced to pull out of Greece and end economic and military aid. Greece was threatened by civil war with the Communists who were — prior to Tito's defection — supported from Yugoslavia, Bulgaria, and Albania. Economic collapse was at hand and the Greek army's morale was deeply shaken.

American interests in Greece, Marshall told the legislators, were by no means restricted to humanitarian or friendly impulses. If Greece dissolved into full-scale civil war it was altogether possible that it would fall to Soviet control. Turkey then would be surrounded; Soviet domination might thus extend over the entire Middle East to India; the effect upon Hungary, Austria, Italy, and France could not be overestimated. It was not alarmist for Marshall to warn that the United States was faced with the first crisis of a series which might extend Soviet domination to Europe, the Middle East, and Asia.

In Turkey the situation was only slightly different, Marshall said. By a war of nerves aimed at the Dardanelles, the Soviets had kept the entire Turkish army mobilized and thus stretched Turkey's economy to the snapping point. The American military establishment believed that an independent Turkey was essential to the security of the eastern Mediterranean and the Middle East.

Neither the President nor Marshall could give the legislators assurances that American assistance would save the situation. But they declared that it was plainly evident that it could not be saved without American assistance. "The choice is between acting with energy or losing by default," Marshall said. And on that phrase — act or lose by default — he struck a responsive note with Vandenberg. The Senator had known nothing of the crisis until he was called to the White House.

June 6, 1947

The President called in a bi-partisan Congressional group prior to his message on the Greece-Turkey situation and apprised us of the general situation. We all made general comments but no commitments. This was the extent of the "bi-partisan technique" in this instance. But it must be remembered that the whole thing was precipitated upon our government so suddenly that there really was very little opportunity for preliminary consultations and studies.

There is a great deal of misunderstanding apparently in the country regarding this whole subject of "bi-partisan foreign policy." Many people seem to think that I act as sort of a Co-secretary of State in connection with foreign policy decisions. This of course is totally erroneous. Indeed, it would be a physical impossibility. Our "bi-partisan foreign policy" has been quite definitely confined (1) to the evolution of the United Nations and (2) to the peace treaties in Europe.

This complaint of a lack of public understanding concerning bipartisan foreign policy often was voiced by Vandenberg. One of the difficulties was that bipartisanship in practice was a continually developing and ever changing thing. It is most unlikely that even Vandenberg in 1947 could foresee that only two years later he was to write in his diary about his own role in actually drafting an important American diplomatic note to Russia on the Berlin blockade. Likewise, the geographical areas covered by his conception of bipartisanship changed with changing policies and problems. Latin America, as already noted, was considered outside the scope of bipartisanship during the years when Vandenberg thought the State Department was stalling on calling a promised hemispheric defense conference. But once the conference was called, Vandenberg was to write that Latin American policy was included in the bipartisan folio.

Another objection Vandenberg was to state repeatedly stemmed from his dislike of crisis diplomacy — typified by a summons to the White House, alarming diplomatic reports, and an urgent plea by the President for action. Vandenberg always believed that a continuing policy developed through continuing consultation with the Congress would largely obviate the necessity for what he termed the "crisis method." Regarding the Greece-Turkey session at the White House, Vandenberg told the Senate that "it is unfortunate when such important decisions have to be made on a crisis basis. But we confront a condition and not a theory. . . ."

The Senator was not immediately clear, however, as to what could be done about confronting the Greece-Turkey "condition." He wrote to Representative John B. Bennett:

March 5, 1947

I am entirely frank in saying that I do not know the answer to the latest Greek challenge because I do not know all the facts. I am waiting for all the facts before I say anything. . . . But I sense enough of the facts to realize that the problem in Greece cannot be isolated by itself. On the contrary, it is probably symbolic of the world-wide ideological clash between Eastern Communism and Western Democracy; and it may easily be the thing which requires us to make some very fateful and far-reaching decisions.

You speak of referring the Greek problem to the United Nations. . . . The Greek appeal is primarily for economic aid; and of course the United Nations is not created or equipped to deal in economic aid. . . . Furthermore, the United Nations is not yet equipped with the military reserve contemplated by its Charter because Soviet Russia has stubbornly refused (in U.N. Committee) to sanction the agreements which are to be submitted to the member nations in respect to military reserves. I should be delighted to have U.N. approval of anything that may be done to save Greece (and thus save the entire Middle East from the Soviet orbit); but I am frank to say that I think Greece could collapse fifty times before the U.N. itself could ever hope to handle a situation of this nature. It is not supposed to handle such situations. But if there is any way to tie it in collaterally, I shall be very glad to see this done.

On March 12 Mr. Truman took his case to Congress, laying the Greece-Turkey crisis before a special joint session. He called for American assistance to "support free peoples who are resisting attempted subjugation." And he asked Congress for an initial grant of $400,000,000 in economic and armed aim, the bulk of it for Greece.

The President's program, and his statement of what became known as the "Truman Doctrine," brought a decidedly mixed reaction from Congress and the country. Americans sensed a radical new departure in foreign policy, and one with perhaps untold implications for the future. Some called it the most significant development in American foreign relations since the Monroe Doctrine. Critics on the left declared that the program was imperialist in nature and would find the United States "bailing out" an outdated and unpopular monarchy in Greece. Critics on the right, including some newly-elected Republican senators, held that it meant unlimited expenditures and that the nation was "bailing out" the responsibilities of the British Labor Government. Many Americans were deeply perplexed and sought enlightenment.

One such was R. F. Moffett, the secretary-treasurer of a Flint, Michigan, wholesale grocery firm. To Moffett, as to others, Vandenberg wrote:

May 12, 1947

You ask me whether there is any "precedent" for the action we are taking in Greece and Turkey. Of course, there are many partial precedents in respect to relief for stricken countries and even for "military missions." But I doubt whether there is any over-all "precedent." But I am afraid we cannot rely upon "precedents" in facing the utterly unprecedented condition in the world today.

Certainly there is no "precedent" for today's world-wide

cleavage between democracy and communism. Perhaps, however, there is something of a "parallel" in remembering what occurred prior to a similar cleavage between democracy and naziism when we surely learned that we cannot escape trouble by trying to run away from it and when "appeasement" proved to be a fatal investment. Of course, we shall never know whether history would have been different if we had all stood up to the aggressor at Munich. But at least we know what it cost to "lie down." Perhaps this is a "precedent" . . .

Greece must be helped or Greece sinks permanently into the communist order. Turkey inevitably follows. Then comes the chain reaction which might sweep from the Dardanelles to the China sea. . . . I do not know whether our new American policy can succeed in arresting these subversive trends (which ultimately represent a direct threat to us). I can only say that I think the adventure is worth trying as an alternative to another "Munich" and perhaps to another war (against the occurrence of which every human effort must be made).

But in another letter Vandenberg complained about the way the problem had been raised.

March 24, 1947

The trouble is that these "crises" never reach Congress until they have developed to a point where Congressional discretion is pathetically restricted. When things finally reach a point where a President asks us to "declare war" there usually is nothing left except to "declare war." In the present instance, the overriding fact is that the President has made a long-delayed statement regarding Communism on-the-march which must be supported if there is any hope of ever impressing Moscow with the necessity of paying any sort of peaceful attention to us whatever. If we turned the President down — after his speech to the joint Congressional session — we might as well either resign ourselves to a complete Communist encirclement and infiltration or else get ready for World War No. Three. I am not prepared to accept either one of these alternatives. I still think there is a chance for Moscow and Washington to "live and let live" if we make it immutably plain that we are the lineal descendants of those rugged old pioneers whose flag bore the motto "Don't Tread on Me." But you may be very sure that I share all of your anxieties and that I have no illusions. Our only choice is the lesser of evils.

Vandenberg faced up to the challenge of "acting with energy or losing by default," which had been posed at the White House by Marshall. Speaking to newsmen after Mr. Truman's address, he said:

[*About March 13, 1947*]

The President's message faces facts and so must Congress. The independence of Greece and Turkey must be preserved, not only for their own sakes but also in defense of peace and security for all of us. In such a critical moment the President's hands must be upheld. Any other course would be dangerously misunderstood. But Congress must carefully determine the methods and explore the details in so momentous a departure from our previous policies.

The immediate problem may be treated by itself. But it is vitally important also to frankly weigh it for the future. We are at odds with communism on many fronts. We should evolve a total policy. It must clearly avoid imperialism. It must primarily consult American welfare. It must keep faith with the pledges to the charter of the United Nations which we all have taken.

We should proceed as far as possible within the United Nations. But that is not practical at the immediate moment because United Nations has no relief funds; and it has not yet concluded agreements with member nations for military support. We should immediately insist in the Security Council that these latter plans be consummated. We should also seek an immediate report from the United Nations Commission investigating alleged external invasion of Greek sovereignty.

The plain truth is that Soviet-American relationships are

at the core of this whole problem. Every effort should be made to terminate these controversies. This effort must occur in plain understanding of basic principles which we shall not surrender. I repeat my own belief that it ought to be possible for Moscow and Washington to "live and let live" since neither wants anything like war. Yet we find ourselves in constant disagreement respecting our mutually pledged objectives. There should be frank consultations between us — with all the cards face up on the table — in final search for mutual understanding. Now, if ever, we must say what we mean and mean what we say. Our persistent offer of an anti-Nazi alliance clearly proves our own good faith.

We cannot fail to back up the President at such an hour — even though many critical details remain to be settled in consultation with the Congress. Meanwhile, we must review our own foreign policy in other directions and make it consistently effective. We must proceed with calm but determined patience to deal with practical realities as they unfold. We must either take or surrender leadership.

For Vandenberg this choice was clear. It represented a far cry from his prewar opposition to amending the Neutrality Act and to lend-lease. Moving speedily, he invited all members of the Senate — members and nonmembers of the Foreign Relations Committee alike — to submit their questions on the Greece-Turkey aid program to him in writing for transmission to the State Department. The four hundred questions submitted were consolidated into one hundred and eleven inquiries, and both questions and official answers were published in what was at that time a unique legislative document. It was a precedent for the extensive background information which was later to be made available to Congress during consideration of other foreign policy programs.

Vandenberg saw one major flaw in the program as outlined by the President. The Administration's draft bill made no mention of bringing the program within the United Nations Charter. No advance notification was given UN regarding the new aid plan; it looked as if the United States were ready to proceed unilaterally and outside of the Charter. For the Senator, who regarded the United Nations as "our first reliance and our prime concern" — as he told the Senate on April 8 — this was a defect to be corrected at once. "The Administration made a colossal blunder in ignoring the U.N." Vandenberg wrote in penciled notes which he filed with his private papers.

Two weeks later and after Vandenberg's insistent urging, the United States, through Ambassador Warren R. Austin, gave the UN Security Council its formal notification that: "The program of economic assistance contemplated by the United States is of an emergency and temporary character. The United States believes that the United Nations and its related agencies should assume the principal responsibility, within their capabilities, for the long-range tasks of assistance required for the reconstruction of Greece . . . the United States is giving momentum to the United Nations by its present policy. . . ."

This was not enough for Vandenberg. In conformity with his statement to newsmen that the aid program should be brought "as far as possible within the United Nations," Vandenberg insisted before the Foreign Relations Committee that the program could be brought directly in line with Charter objectives. He proceeded to draft a new preamble for the bill which referred directly to the United Nations. Phrased in the stilted terms of parliamentary language it stated that:

> Whereas the Security Council of the United Nations has recognized the seriousness of the unsettled conditions prevailing on the border between Greece on the one hand and Albania, Bulgaria, and Yugoslavia on the other, and, if the present emergency is not met, may subsequently assume full responsibility for this phase of the problem as a result of the investigation which its commission is currently conducting; and
>
> Whereas the Food and Agriculture Organization mission for Greece recognized the necessity that Greece receive financial and economic assistance and recommended that Greece request such assistance from the appropriate agencies of the United Nations and from the governments of the United States and the United Kingdom; and
>
> Whereas the United Nations is not now in a position to

furnish Greece and Turkey the financial and economic assistance which is immediately required; and

Whereas the furnishing of such assistance to Greece and Turkey by the United States will contribute to the freedom and independence of all members of the United Nations in conformity with the principles and purposes of the Charter: Now, *therefore be it enacted,* etc.

Though written in legislative jargon, the new preamble was easily understood at Lake Success. News dispatches from the United Nations temporary headquarters reported that UN delegates breathed a sigh of relief that the United States was acting within, not forsaking, the Charter.

One more step remained to be taken. In what Vandenberg described to the Senate as "the greatest act of voluntary allegiance" to the United Nations, he succeeded, with Connally's support, in writing into the bill a provision permitting the Security Council or the General Assembly to terminate the American program whenever it found that "action taken or assistance furnished by the United Nations makes the continuance of such assistance unnecessary or undesirable." And in this respect the amended bill provided that the United States would waive in advance its veto power in the Security Council.

The program thus not only was brought within the framework of the Charter, but the UN was given authority to terminate it through action of its own organs.

With the prime defect remedied, Vandenberg was able to take the Senate floor to urge adoption of the program with a unanimous vote of his committee behind him. In his ornate and somewhat grandiloquent but effective phrasing he told the Senate:

April 8, 1947

Mr. President, in response to the urgent recommendations of the President of the United States, the Senate Foreign Relations Committee has unanimously reported the bill entitled "a bill to provide for assistance to Greece and Turkey."

It could be alternatively entitled "a bill to support the purposes of the United Nations to maintain international peace and security," or it could be titled "a bill to serve America's self-interest in the maintenance of independent governments."

The Committee makes this report primarily in response to direct appeals to our government from heroic Greece which, by her sacrificial world war loyalties, has richly earned the right to perpetuate her proud, historic independence. It does so in response to direct appeals from Turkey, which is the only truly independent nation left on the borders of Soviet Russia from the Baltic to the Black Sea. It also does so in the presence of the overriding strategic fact that the fall of Greece, followed by the collapse of Turkey, could precipitate a chain reaction which would threaten peace and security around the globe. It does so in the profound belief that we Americans have an unescapable stake in all human rights and fundamental freedoms; and that they were better saved — for us as well as others — by adequate and timely support than by waiting for cumulative hazard to magnify the risk. It does so not only in the name of the liberties for which the allies said they fought two world wars, but also in the name of the intelligent American self-interest which prefers an ounce of precaution to a pound of cure, and which believes "that a stitch in time saves nine."

[This was the Vandenberg philosophy. It was the theme of American self-interest and positive action-before-disaster which he was to stress time and again in international undertakings. It was the call to America to act in its own interests because those interests were indivisible from those of the rest of the free world. Vandenberg admitted that the program went beyond previous aid bills which aimed to relieve human suffering.]

... Let us be totally plain about it. It is a plan to forestall aggression which, once rolling, could snowball into global danger of vast design. It is a plan for peace. It is a plan to sterilize the seeds of war. We do not escape war by running away from it. No one ran away from war at Munich. We avoid war by facing facts. This plan faces facts.

But of course there are other facts to face. No plan can guarantee peace. The most it can do is to take the better calculated risk. That, I believe is what this plan does. It is a plan, I repeat, for peace. It is a plan to strengthen the United Nations by supporting its objectives in respect to immediate necessities, pending the time when the United Nations can take over.

[Here, as in almost all of his later "action" speeches, he candidly admitted that the prospective program involved a "calculated risk." He never promised the Senate certain success, but he always held out the certainty of failure through inaction.]

... The problem involved in this bill — like the problem involved in every other phase of languishing peace — is the persistent controversy between what we loosely call eastern communism and western democracy. From it inevitably stem persistent difficulties — difficulties between the Soviet Union and its satellites upon the one hand, and the United States and like-minded non-communist states upon the other.... We plot no offense against the Soviet Union. We are not hunting world domination. We are not seeking a dictation anywhere. But what we deny to ourselves as a matter of morality we also must deny to others as a matter of conquest....

[The philosophic note, the tragedy of failure of the war to bring real peace, was there, too. And Vandenberg emphasized the somber note of disagreements with Russia, differences which he believed could be removed only through mutual good faith.]

In a sense we are a tragic generation, despite our blessings and our place in the sun. We have been drawn into two World Wars. We finally won them both, and yet we still confront a restless and precarious peace. Something has been wrong. It is our supreme task to face these present realities, no matter how we hate them, and to mend the broken pattern if such be within human power....

The Greek crisis or the Turkish crisis or any others among potential crises will largely disappear if the mutual will exists between Washington and Moscow. If it cannot exist, even that ominous knowledge is worth having. While we cannot avoid the interminable rivalries of these incompatible ideologies, there ought to be an honorable way to live and let live within the rules of the United Nations. We should mutually strive to search it out on the basis not only of salvaging the ideals of World War I and World War II, but also and particularly on the basis of the self-interest of the two greatest nations on earth — neither one of whom wants any part of another war. But we, for our part, will never find it through equivocation which will be misread as timidity. We shall never find it except as we succeed in convincing Moscow, first, that we have absolutely no ulterior designs; and, second, that we shall not compromise or whittle away the basic human rights and fundamental freedoms which we both have pledged in the most solemn peacetime commitments of which honorable nations are capable.

[Here too was a theme becoming familiar to Americans: the self-interest of both the Kremlin and the United States in world peace; the warning that timidity in Washington would not lead to this goal; and the deeply spiritual plea that never should the nation compromise on basic freedoms and human rights in pursuit of any false trail toward accommodation with Russia.

Vandenberg defended his United Nations amendments. He pointed out that the United Nations Organization] is not and was never intended to be a relief organization. It has no such funds and was never intended to have such funds. . . . It has no sustaining military force because the Soviet representatives thus far have declined to permit these plans to materialize. If it had either the funds or the force, their use would depend upon the Security Council. In the Security Council this use would face a veto. . . . These are the facts. . . . I know of no better way to destroy the United Nations than to give it a specific job which it is neither intended nor prepared to do.

[The results of a Congressional rebuff for the program, Vandenberg concluded] would be the forfeiture of all hope to effectively influence the attitude of other nations in our peaceful pursuit of international righteousness from now on. It would stunt our moral authority and mute our voice. It would encourage dangerous contempts. It would invite provocative misunderstandings of the tenacity with which we are prepared to defend our fundamental ideals. Mr. President, what would you think if you were a citizen of Athens? Where would you be forced to turn in your hopeless extremity? What would you think if you were a citizen of Ankara? What would you think if you were a citizen of any other of the weary, war-worn nations who are wondering this afternoon whether the torch still burns in the upraised hand of liberty; whether it is hopeless to struggle on toward democratic freedom? And what would you think, Mr. President, if you were the Politburo in Moscow's Kremlin?

The Vandenberg amendment giving the UN power to terminate the program under certain circumstances removed considerable opposition on the part of organizations and individuals who sincerely feared any undercutting of the peace organization's stature. As Walter Lippmann wrote, the amendment cured "the most serious defects of the original Truman proposal . . . exactly, completely and handsomely," and would strengthen the United Nations while reducing the risks involved in American intervention.

But all was not clear sailing although eventual passage of the bill was assured. Gael Sullivan, youthfully eager executive director of the Democratic National Committee, publicly called upon Carroll Reece, Republican National Committee Chairman, to join in a party statement endorsing the "Truman policy" in Greece and Turkey. Sullivan repeatedly used Vandenberg's name in his letter to Reece and in a follow-up public statement.

Infuriated, Vandenberg told the Senate that bipartisan foreign policy was gravely endangered when it got into the rival hands of "partisan national committees." He urged Reece not to accept the proposal and "faithfully" to continue to keep the party out of foreign policy politics. He said:

March 18, 1947

Bi-partisan foreign policy is not the result of political coercion but of non-political conviction. I never have even pretended to speak for my party in my foreign policy activities. I have relied upon the validity of my actions to command whatever support they may deserve. I have never made any semblance of a partisan demand for support and I never shall. What I decline to do myself I cannot permit the Executive Director of the Democratic National Committee to attempt in my name.

It also is necessary, now, to get the record straight. This bi-partisan policy has been confined within relatively narrow limits. It has applied to the United Nations. It has applied to the peace treaties in Europe. It has applied to nothing else. I have had nothing to do, for example, with China policies or Pan-American policies except within the United Nations, and at times I have been satisfied with neither. The first I ever heard of the Greco-Turkish policy was when the President disclosed his thoughts . . . at the White House. I do not complain. But I do not propose to be misunderstood. . . . The quicker last night's appeal, no matter how nobly meditated, is forgotten the better it will be for the United States.

The Greece-Turkey debate dragged on through March into April. Critics of the measure demanded facts and more facts. Repeatedly Vandenberg took the Senate floor in defense. Defeat of the bill meant appeasement of Russia, he said, and more trouble for Secretary Marshall at the then current Moscow Foreign Ministers meeting. The attack came mainly from the left-wing Democratic faction and the far right on the Republican side. Senators Pepper of Florida and Glen H. Taylor of Idaho held that American aid should be channeled through the United Nations. Republican Senators Wherry, Brooks, Malone, and others held that the program would lead either to war or ultimate bankruptcy. Henry Wallace toured Europe attacking the program, and Vandenberg described him on the Senate floor as an "itinerant saboteur." But finally what Vandenberg called a "persistent drumfire" ended. The Senate overwhelmingly approved the bill. The House already had done so by a three-to-one majority and shortly thereafter it was signed into law. It was the first big victory in a Republican-controlled Congress for a bipartisan foreign policy.

Dean Acheson, who was retiring as Undersecretary of State, added a personal note to the trials of the time by writing Vandenberg on May 29: "Your note to me about my resignation is another of the long list of kindnesses which you have shown me. These last six and a half years have not been easy ones. But a vast amount of what feeling of accomplishment I can have and of the pleasure of the work has been in my association with you. I think it is in a play called 'Jimmy Valentine' in which a character engaged in not altogether worthwhile efforts made the tips of his fingers sensitive to the workings of a combination lock by filing them until they were raw. One who has been caught as I have been between the executive and legislative branches of the government at times when neither took an altogether sympathetic view of the other, has his sensitivity increased by friction somewhat differently applied.

"Whether it is for this or other reasons, I think I am peculiarly appreciative of the rare qualities which you have brought to your position of leadership. These are not only your ability and amazing effectiveness on the floor, qualities which everyone recognizes, but your outstanding fairness and your warm generosity in meeting someone who tries to take an objective view. There is also your unswerving loyalty to the project once you are convinced it is right and have started upon it. These are the qualities which you have shown to me in such overflowing measure and for which I shall always be deeply grateful."

While the struggle over Greek-Turkish aid was in progress Vandenberg was also involved during the first half of 1947 in many other important problems, including a sharp wrangle over confirmation of David E. Lilienthal as Chairman of the Atomic Energy Commission. But this time — in contrast to his earlier position regarding the handling of the atomic energy problem — the Senator was ranged alongside the scientists. And this time the fight was primarily over a personality, rather than a principle.

Lilienthal, Chairman of the Board of the Tennessee Valley Authority, had been selected early in 1947 by President Truman to take over the chairmanship of the new commission, but as TVA chairman he had incurred the opposition of Senator Kenneth McKellar of Tennessee. For weeks McKellar paraded a string of witnesses who in many cases made irrelevant charges against Lilienthal before Senate members of the Joint Congressional Committee on Atomic Energy. The Tennessee Senator beseiged Lilienthal with questions regarding his loyalty, his ancestry, his administration of TVA, and charges that Communists had infiltrated the organization. There was irrelevant testimony concerning moonlight dances conducted by nudists in the valley area. Lilienthal patiently endured the experience. At one point in the hearing, he delivered a brief pronouncement on Americanism which was to be widely reprinted under the title, *This I Do Believe*.

The atomic committee heard McKellar out, then approved Lilienthal's confirmation, 8 to 1, Senator John W. Bricker of Ohio opposing. The nomination went to the Senate with a strongly favorable recommendation. But in the seven weeks of wrangling with McKellar something had happened. The Republican leadership — except for Vandenberg — lined up against Lilienthal, and Senate confirmation was in grave doubt.

Senator Wallace H. White of Maine, titular Republican leader of the Senate, announced his opposition on grounds that Lilienthal had ruled TVA with a dictatorial hand. Republican Whip Kenneth S. Wherry of Nebraska denounced Lilienthal on a half-dozen charges; Senator Styles Bridges of New Hampshire, then Chairman of the Appropriations Committee, assailed Lilienthal's advocacy of public power. The big charge was fired by Senator Taft of Ohio, who denounced Lilienthal as soft toward Communists, a "softness" that Taft insisted had seeped into a blueprint for international control of atomic energy drawn up by Acheson and Lilienthal. And the nominee also was condemned for his New Deal background; his alleged contemptuous disregard for Congressional checks and his headstrong administration of TVA.

Vandenberg had voted for Lilienthal's confirmation at the Committee stage and now faced the choice of going all out for the nominee or keeping silent and merely casting an affirmative vote. The former course would pit him against the GOP leadership, of which he was a part and whose support he badly needed for foreign policy measures, and against some powerful voices in his home state. The fight shaped up so sharply that senators on both sides of the aisle concluded that Vandenberg's course would decide the issue. Additionally, there were deep overtones of a Vandenberg versus Taft showdown; a situation both men had worked continually and, in the main, successfully to avoid.

Vandenberg wrote an old Michigan friend in one of his "personal and confidential" messages that in his mind the die was cast.

February 17, 1947

I am willing to say to you that the charges of "communism" (or anything like it) against Lilienthal are a fantastic fabrication highly remindful of the "lynch law." This leaves only the general prejudice growing out of his philosophical attachment to the New Deal and his interest in "public ownership," as opposed to "private enterprise."

Until we have completed the peace treaties and until we have negotiated a competent international agreement to outlaw the use of atomic energy for destructive purposes, it is absolutely vital — in my opinion — that "public ownership" and "public control" of atomic energy should be as completely airtight and fool proof as it is possible to make it. Anything less would be a surrender to the greatest hazard of the ages. We cannot hope for these final treaties and for this international agreement short of another couple of years in all probability. During this time I know — and I am very dogmatic about it — that I am best serving my country when I provide the tightest possible "public control" of atomic energy in the United States. For the time being therefore, Mr. Lilienthal's liability becomes a temporary asset. His appointment is equally temporary. It only runs for 18 months. . . . Under all these circumstances, I confess that I cannot share the contagious apprehension which seems to be attaching to the Lilienthal matter among many of my highly cherished friends like you.

On the contrary, I am inclined to think that the rejection of this nomination at the present time would probably result in the wholesale retirement of our scientists from our atomic organization and that we might lose another incalculably precious year in getting on with our incalculably essential task of developing [atomic power] . . . which will still leave us "out in front" despite what happens elsewhere. This is one of those cases where it is entirely impossible to take the public into our complete confidence.

[Vandenberg told his confidant that he had just received a telegram from Gerald L. K. Smith, a strongly nationalistic extremist with headquarters in Michigan, saying that Vandenberg would be "ruined" if he voted for Lilienthal.] I shall very cheerfully accept this penalty if I conclude that my duty lies in this direction.

Shortly thereafter he reached precisely this conclusion and in an address on April 3, delivered to a tense Senate session, Vandenberg spoke his mind. He said that seven weeks of "utterly exhausting" committee hearings had driven away the "adverse prejudice with which I started. I have been driven to the belief that logic, equity, fair play, and a just regard for the public welfare combine to recommend Mr. Lilienthal's confirmation in the light of today's realities." Then one-by-one he dealt directly with the charges leveled at the nominee. Regarding charges that Lilienthal had "either sympathy toward communism or too easy toleration of it," the Senator said:

After weeks of testimony, I find no basis for this charge. I hope my own record plus the fact that I am in the top bracket of all communist blacklists all round the world, demonstrates that I am not calculated to be "soft" on such a subject. But I do not want to emulate the intolerance of communism itself. . . . It is the opinion of our committee that Mr. Lilienthal is no part of a communist by any stretch of the imagination. There were a few youthful intriguers in one minor department of the Tennessee Valley Authority who were juvenile communists.... I do not minimize these things. They put us on notice as to our necessities for eternal vigilance. I can guarantee that the Joint Congressional Atomic Energy Committee will make this matter its special business. But I am unable to find anything in the record in respect to this phase of the case which indicts Mr. Lilienthal.

[Vandenberg opposed further delays in naming a commission, reminding his listeners that leading scientists had warned against keeping the project in the "twilight zone" between military and civilian control. And once again he spoke out strongly for civilian management of the project, declaring that "in peacetime we cannot drive science into its laboratories with bayonets." Then Vandenberg dealt with a "second charge" against Lilienthal, the complaint that he was a devotee of public ownership and hence would endanger free enterprise in the atomic field.]

We, the Congress, have declared by law that the control of atomic energy must be the tightest government monopoly ever set up in the United States — pending the day when the destructive use of atomic energy shall be outlawed for keeps ... we solemnly and unavoidably decreed that government ownership and management, no matter how much we dislike it in other aspects of our national economy and life, is an indispensable public necessity for the sake of national security in respect to the control of atomic energy.... Therefore one of the most available men to run it is the successful manager of the greatest existing comparable example of public ownership and management. Whether we like it or him or TVA, this sequence leads logically to David Lilienthal's door. His liability under other circumstances thus becomes an asset for the time being.

[He dealt with a "third charge," centered on failure in the Acheson-Lilienthal report to provide for abandonment of the UN veto power when it came to enforcing international safeguards for atomic energy. Insistence on veto-less safeguards had been added to the American plan by Bernard Baruch when he became United States spokesman on the United Nations Atomic Energy Commission.]

It seems to me this criticism is irrelevant, incompetent and immaterial. The Acheson-Lilienthal report was offered, according to its own language, merely as a place to begin. Clearly its authors were charged with the exploration of physical mechanisms for atomic control; not with the exploration of political mechanisms which became the subsequent responsibility of the Baruch group. But they made an invaluable and indispensable report without which the Baruch report and the ultimate finished American plan would have been impossible . . . [it] was a vital milestone on the journey to this final goal.

[Vandenberg wound up his thirty-five-minute address by declaring:] I have no quarrel with those who disagree. I know there is a deep-seated prejudice against Mr. Lilienthal in many earnest and sincere minds. I have no quarrel whatever with those feelings. But for myself, in the presence of the evidence, I have no alternative except to say to my colleagues that I have no doubt that in the interest of the national welfare and for the sake of a square deal, Mr. Lilienthal is entitled to be confirmed.

Seventeen Republicans voted with Vandenberg in defeating, 52 to 38, a motion to recommit the nomination to committee — which would have meant its rejection. Lilienthal was confirmed.

Several years later, Vandenberg indicated that he was in disagreement with some of Lilienthal's acts and attitudes during his tenure as Chairman of the Commission. Throughout the debate on confirmation, the Senator had emphasized that the Chairman was being named for only eighteen months. When he came up for reappointment, Vandenberg supported a Republican move to limit his second term to two years.

In 1949 the Atomic Energy Commission was the subject of a Congressional investigation by a joint committee headed by Hickenlooper, who charged Lilienthal with "incredible mismanagement." One of the points of criticism was that government educational grants in the atomic field had been made to students with Communist affiliations.

"You probably have noticed that we are having 'Lilienthal

troubles' again," Vandenberg wrote to his wife on May 24, 1949. "I really feel sorry. . . . No one can make any sort of an argument for educating young Communists at government expense — and least of all in atomic physics. I can't defend him in this instance and I don't intend to try. Indeed, I am inclined to think he has outlived his usefulness. But I don't intend to join the hysteria which would 'boil him in oil.' " A few days later he added:

May 27, 1949
> We had another struggle with the Hickenlooper show all the morning. The stuff got a little "hotter." But Hickenlooper has got to step up the tempo of his disclosures or he is going to "lose his public." . . . Of course, Lilienthal is not guilty of "incredible mismanagement" (at least not from anything I have yet seen or heard). But I increasingly feel that he is much too loose when it comes to national security. It looks to me as though our final problem will be how to spank Lilienthal for bad security without attempting to find him guilty of incredible mismanagement. The truth of the matter is that he [Hickenlooper] has rendered a very real public service by putting on this show — and the Atomic Energy Commission itself has already greatly tightened up its security defenses as a result.

Still later, on January 25, 1950, Vandenberg wrote to Hickenlooper: "My own considered verdict is that the inquiry disclosed many needs for reforms and improvements and more reliable security in our atomic operations; that the Commission itself — and thus the country — immediately profited from these lessons; and that this whole vast atomic enterprise is bound to be safer and sounder as a result of your courageous activities."

Again, in this same period, he was quoted as saying to Martin S. Hayden, in an article appearing in the Detroit *News*: "I wouldn't say I am off him [Lilienthal] yet. But my confidence is considerably shaken." Hayden quoted Vandenberg as being critical of what the Senator called "Lilienthal's seeming refusal to accept the basic direction of Congress as to the degree of security" required in the atomic program, and particularly the Chairman's contention that safeguards against government educational grants to Communists would be federal intrusion in the educational field. Vandenberg also was quoted as saying that the Commission had used secrecy to "hide" its administrative mistakes.

Apparently these differences never reached the stage of personalities, because when Lilienthal stepped out of the Atomic Energy Commission chairmanship on February 15, 1950, he wrote the Senator: "This is my last act at my desk as I leave: to thank you for past kindness and confidence, and to wish you health and happiness."

Vandenberg's intense interest in atomic energy and his position as Chairman of the Foreign Relations Committee brought him into touch with important negotiations in the period of 1947–49 when there was top-level behind-the-scenes controversy over atomic agreements with Great Britain and Canada. The secret wartime atomic arrangements on which President Roosevelt and Prime Minister Churchill had agreed, at Quebec and Hyde Park meetings, were not entirely clear in the official records, and it was not until 1947 that some high officials acquired detailed knowledge of the agreements. It should be pointed out that knowledge of the agreements was not communicated to the Senate by President Roosevelt. The agreements established a Combined Policy Committee, representing the United States, Britain, and Canada, to regulate matters of mutual interest and concern in the highly secret field of atomic energy. The United States had three members on the Committee, Britain had two, and Canada one. Several changes were made in the American membership on the Committee in the years immediately after the war.

Sometime in the late spring or early summer of 1947, however, Vandenberg and Hickenlooper were startled to discover that Mr. Roosevelt had agreed that the United States would not use the atomic bomb against any other country without the consent of the British. The Senators promptly got in touch with President Truman, Secretary of State Marshall, and Defense Secretary James Forrestal to express their surprise and opposition to any such arrangement and to urge the necessity of an immediate rectification of the agreement. The Senators also raised objections to the fact that large amounts of atomic material were being stored in the British Isles, where it might fall into Russian hands in event of an outbreak of war in Europe and at a time when it was required for the U.S. atomic program.

This situation led to a meeting at the Pentagon on November 16, 1947, with the two Senators, Forrestal, and Undersecretary of State Lovett. They discussed the Roosevelt-Churchill agreements as well as later agreements which, according to the Senator's papers, provided, among other things, for: (1) Sharing of information on atomic development between the United States and Britain and co-operation in atomic development. (2) Problems related to the sharing of uranium ore from the Belgian Congo. (3) Agreement of the United States and Britain not to use the atomic bomb against each other; and not to use it against any other country unless both Britain and the United States agreed.

(*The Forrestal Diaries*, page 338, indicate that Forrestal first heard of the Quebec agreement from Hickenlooper, presumably including the arrangement requiring consent of the British before the bomb could be used. From other sources it was known that the data concerning the atomic agreements had been gathered together by the State Department in two or three months prior to the November 16th Pentagon meeting.)

Lovett, the report on the Pentagon meeting discloses, told the Senators and Forrestal that the information exchange with the British was to cover certain scientific fields, in the opinion of State Department experts, but never to serve as authority for giving the British full information on all phases of atomic energy. The British, Lovett was described as saying, were becoming restless at the failure to obtain a complete exchange of information. And Lovett reportedly said that since the end of the shooting war Britain had received a substantial portion of the Congo ores.

Vandenberg told the conferees that he and Hickenlooper had become aware of the prohibition in the late spring or early summer of 1947 and that he (Vandenberg) had discussed it with President Truman, Secretary of State Marshall, and Forrestal. These discussions, Vandenberg said, dealt with both the prohibition on using the bomb and storage of large amounts of unused atomic material in Britain. Hickenlooper, the report of the Pentagon meeting shows, recalled that he had written Marshall earlier expressing the greatest dissatisfaction with the current situation, urging that it be rectified at once, and stating that he would be unable to support American financial aid to Britain unless this was accomplished.

Vandenberg declared that he thought the Hyde Park and Quebec agreements were "astounding" and "unthinkable," and that he felt a tremendous responsibility as Chairman of the Senate Foreign Relations Committee in this regard. He said that failure to revamp the agreements would have a disastrous effect on Congressional consideration of the Marshall Plan, at that time in a formative stage. Both Senators, noting that discussions with the British and Canadians on revising the wartime agreements were to begin shortly, said that a satisfactory conclusion must be reached before final action on the Marshall Plan program.

In January, 1948, agreement was reached with Britain and Canada in Washington to remove the restriction on use of the bomb. As a result, the final decision for use of the bomb was left in the hands of the President, as specified by American control legislation. The Washington meeting also assured the United States of more adequate ore supplies and clarified the general areas of atomic energy information exchange.

The problem of information exchange was revived later in 1948, however, when Vandenberg and Hickenlooper learned from AEC Commissioner Lewis L. Strauss that Dr. Cyril Smith, an Atomic Energy Commission scientist, had gone to Britain with a letter of authority from the AEC to discuss several matters, including the "metallurgy of plutonium" with the British. Both Senators believed that such a discussion went beyond the authority of the Commission and they took up the question on August 12, 1949, with Forrestal, Dr. Vannevar Bush, Chairman of the Joint Research and Development Board, and Donald F.

Carpenter, Chairman of the Military Liaison Committee established in the Atomic Energy Act of 1946. The meeting, in Forrestal's office, produced another surprise for the Senators, who had been led to believe that the British atomic energy activities were concentrated on industrial power rather than weapons.

Vandenberg's papers said that a distinct difference of understanding was expressed as to the aims of the British atomic energy program. Vandenberg and Hickenlooper insisted that it had been their understanding that British efforts were aimed in the direction of use of atomic energy for industrial power and other nonmilitary purposes. Dr. Bush reported that, for a considerable period of time, the British had been emphasizing weapons production.

Hickenlooper told the conferees, according to the report, that he had just been informed that the Atomic Energy Commission had outlined areas of discussions with the British which entailed disclosures of information far in excess of what he and Vandenberg had understood were embraced in the new American-British-Canadian agreement, and that such new discussions would involve exchange of information on "basic metallurgy of Plutonium," which he considered to be solely bomb and atomic weapon material. Such an information exchange, Hickenlooper contended, was beyond the legal authority of the Atomic Energy Commission, beyond any possible interpretation of the tripartite agreement on information exchange, and that it embraced weapons information possessed exclusively by the U.S. at that time. He added that possession of such information by the British could be a major danger to the United States and a "major target" for Russia. Dr. Bush was then quoted as saying that at that time plutonium had to be considered as exclusively weapons material and that information concerning its metallurgy had to be considered as weapons information.

As a result of this discussion, the visit of Dr. Smith to Britain to discuss the metallurgy of plutonium suddenly became a matter of vital importance. (*The Forrestal Diaries*, page 471, state that Forrestal told Sumner T. Pike, Acting Chairman of the Atomic Energy Commission, that the Defense Department "regarded the conveyance of this information as extremely serious and to be halted if humanly possible.") The conferees in Forrestal's office were described by the report as expressing "genuine concern," and AEC Commissioner Strauss, acting through Pike, attempted to reach Smith in London in order to rescind his authority for discussions with the British. The following day, Vandenberg and Hickenlooper were informed that Strauss, whose original concern was now shared by Dr. Bush and Secretary Forrestal, after cables and transatlantic calls from himself and Pike, had been able to reach Smith and cancel his authority to discuss the metallurgy of plutonium.

At still another high-level conference on July 14, 1949, Vandenberg and Hickenlooper went into the broad subject of atomic co-operation with Great Britain at a Blair House meeting over which President Truman presided. Also present were: other Congressional Atomic Energy Committee members, Vice-President Barkley, Secretary of State Acheson, Defense Secretary Louis Johnson, who had succeeded Forrestal, General Dwight D. Eisenhower, temporarily recalled to Washington as head of the Joint Chiefs of Staff, Atomic Commission Chairman Lilienthal, and several others.

According to the record of the conference, Mr. Truman presided and took part in the conversation, but it should be pointed out that generally the spokesmen for the Administration viewpoint in this instance were the current American members of the Combined Policy Committee. They were Acheson, Johnson, and Lilienthal. The President opened up the evening discussion by relating that the current Anglo-American-Canadian allocation agreement would expire in December and that it was essential to continued operation of the United States atomic program that uninterrupted supplies of uranium from the Congo be assured. The Administration viewpoint was that while the British had been original partners in the atomic program, they now were denied access to some information, including all information dealing with atomic weapon making, and that the British were insisting that a complete partnership was required by the world situation. Mr. Truman reportedly told the conferees that he had reached agreement with the

American members of the C.P.C. for an approach to the British which would assure them a full partnership including sharing the "know how" on weapon making. The position of the Administration, the report stated, was that Anglo-American friendship required such action; the British had able scientific personnel and were ahead of the U.S. in some scientific and chemical fields; that it was only a matter of time until the British proceeding independently developed the bomb; and that Britain's close relations with the Belgians gave her an influential voice in distribution of Belgian Congo ores.

For these reasons, it was stated that the Administration proposed: an atomic partnership with Britain and Canada; an agreement for pooling of information; that the U.S. seek agreement with the U.K. to send all but a limited quantity of source materials to the U.S. for processing and storage; that British and Canadian scientists work in the U.S. with their American colleagues; and that an unspecified number of component weapon parts be stored by the U.S. in the British Isles.

Vandenberg, according to the record of the meeting, stated that he was not prepared to agree to any such an undertaking. He stated that the United States during and after the war had repeatedly and continuously extended its aid to Britain, and without any overwhelming degree of co-operation in return. Vandenberg stated he thought that Britain should reciprocate by permitting the United States to assume full responsibility for atomic weapons production and retain its "know how." Furthermore, the Senator pointed out that the concept of Atlantic Pact defense was based upon avoidance of unnecessary duplication of defense functions by the allied nations plus a specialization of endeavors for which the individual member states were particularly equipped. In atomic energy, Vandenberg said, the United States was particularly equipped to carry the prime responsibility. Furthermore, he maintained that the United States was in a position to morally and honorably insist that Britain co-operate in assuring her a proper allocation of the Belgian Congo ores and that Britain should do this without demanding full information disclosures. A discussion also took place regarding the legality of such a full partnership in light of the restrictions placed on administration of the United States atomic program by Congress.

The question of exchanging information with Britain and Canada in various fields of atomic energy, of course, was not settled at the meeting. It remained a subject of discussion between the three participating governments and between the United States executive branch and Congress.

In late summer of 1947 Vandenberg got a welcome relief from his legislative chores. With Connally, he was appointed a delegate to the long-delayed Inter-American Conference for the Maintenance of Continental Peace and Security held at Petropolis, Brazil, just outside of Rio de Janeiro. For Vandenberg it was a labor of love. He had long objected to the delay in calling the Conference, first promised by Secretary Stettinius in 1945. Moreover, major work centered around Article 51 of the UN Charter, which protected effective regional peace-keeping arrangements by assuring the inherent right of individual and collective self-defense. This was the provision on which Vandenberg and Nelson Rockefeller had labored at San Francisco, shoulder to shoulder with the Latin American delegates.

For many years prior to 1947 the twenty-one American republics had co-operated on behalf of peace in the new world. They had created the Pan American Union — the first international organization of a general character — some thirty years before the League of Nations first saw the light of day. This co-operation, during World War II, culminated in a declaration known as the Act of Chapultepec (1945) which provided that an attack by any state against an American state should be considered an act of aggression against the others; and that whenever such acts or threats of aggression occurred, the parties would consult in order to agree upon the measures to be taken, including the possible use of armed force.

The Act of Chapultepec, however, was a temporary, wartime declaration concluded prior to the creation of the United Nations. The main job at the Rio conference was to put the Act of Chapultepec on a permanent treaty basis and then mesh it properly into the new world organization.

Of all the conferences Vandenberg attended, this certainly

was his most enjoyable. The affection of the Latin American countries, gained through his long-standing advocacy of a strong Inter-American system and his labors at San Francisco, was evident throughout. In this connection, the Senator's remarks two years earlier at the UN Conference at San Francisco on June 13, 1945, were of special importance in regard to the work of the Petropolis meeting. At San Francisco he said that in Article 51 of the UN Charter

> we have found a sound, a practical formula for putting regional organizations into effective gear with the global institution. . . . In my view, we have infinitely strengthened the world organization by thus enlisting . . . the dynamic resources of these regional affinities. . . . We weld these regional king-links into the global chain.
>
> One of these king-links is particularly dear to the hearts of twenty-one Republics in this Western Hemisphere. It is a precious inheritance with fifty years of benign history behind it. . . . We in the Americas are deeply proud of it. We in the Americas are profoundly attached to it. . . . We here [in Article 51] recognize the inherent right of self-defense — whether singly or collectively — which permits any sovereign state among us or any qualified regional group of States, to ward off attack pending action by the parent body [the United Nations].

This speech of 1945, in which the Senator described the regional ties of the American republics as vital to the United Nations, highlighted an idea which Vandenberg promoted with great enthusiasm whenever the opportunity presented itself. "We bring you this bulwark of our strength," he said at San Francisco, "and we build it into the foundations of a better world."

At Petropolis this idea reached full fruition in what is familiarly known as the Rio Pact. The Pact, said Vandenberg later in the rather formal language of the report of the Foreign Relations Committee to the Senate, would accomplish the following: "(1) it imposes an obligation on the contracting parties to take positive action to assist in meeting an armed attack against any American state; (2) it provides for consultation and action, not only in the event of armed attacks and other acts of aggression but whenever any other fact or situation might endanger the peace of the Americas; (3) it outlines the machinery and organs of consultation which the American states will utilize in taking collective measures to meet such threats; (4) it defines a special hemispheric security area; (5) it enumerates the political, economic, and military measures which may be taken against an aggressor; and (6) it provides for the effective integration of inter-American peace machinery into the United Nations."

These principles were agreed upon in an atmosphere of cordial co-operation. Vandenberg had one sharp brush with the Argentine delegation's spokesman, who vainly sought to limit the treaty to attacks launched from outside the Western Hemisphere. But even this clash ended in a lavish display of bear hugs and expressions of good will during which, the press reported, the Senator tried out his very limited Spanish vocabulary.

One important new idea that emerged at the conference was the concept of a well-defined geographic zone within which the Treaty would be operative. While this concept was first put forward by the Mexican delegation, it was Vandenberg who took the lead in working out a satisfactory formula for the zone and in gaining approval for it. Opinion was divided at first among the various delegations on the Mexican proposal, with the majority tending to favor it, and it had a mixed reception among the members of the United States delegation. Therefore, the Senator took the initiative with General Marshall in arranging for an emergency meeting of the delegation on a Sunday afternoon to reach a final decision. Marshall presided and, in his customary democratic manner, requested each one present from Senators Connally and Vandenberg down to the youngest technical adviser to express his point of view. Vandenberg made a persuasive plea for acceptance of the principle of the zone. He argued that it would not be just to expect Latin American states automatically to become involved if United States forces should become engaged *anywhere* in the world.

He pointed out, too, that if the automatic operation of the Treaty were limited to a well-defined geographic area, the signatory parties would understand better the extent of their obligations. At the conclusion of the discussion the final decision reflected in large measure the point of view he had put forward. With the aid of General Matthew Ridgway, who served as Military Advisor to the Conference delegation, the Senator assisted in working out acceptable boundaries for the region so as to include all areas within which any attack directed against the Americas would be likely to occur.

Later, in his speech to the Senate, Vandenberg described the new security zone as follows:

December 8, 1947

... The continental region runs from pole to pole. In the first instance, it is a gigantic, irregular ellipse, a great oval, encompassing North, Central, and South America and the surrounding seas and contiguous lands. Some American island territory, like Hawaii, for example, is geographically outside this contiguous continental region as thus mapped; but all American territory, whether physically within the continental ellipse or not, is declared by article III, section III, of the treaty to be inside the area which is to be given special protections. All the territory of any American State, wherever it may be, is in the area of special protections. It is in the security zone. . . .

A second major "new" idea developed at the Conference was a Peruvian proposal that looked to an immediate cease-fire as the first action to be taken in the case of a conflict between two American States. Again it was Vandenberg who carried the ball for the United States delegation on this problem. As originally put forward the proposal might have appeared as a step backward from the basic concept set forth in the Act of Chapultepec that no distinction should be made between an attack by one American state against another and an attack by a non-American state. It was therefore the Senator's task to reconcile this latter principle with the desire of the Peruvians and several other delegations that there be one last effort at peaceful settlement in connection with an intra-American conflict even after hostilities had broken out. The results of the Conference deliberations on this matter are embodied in Article 7 of the Treaty.

At Inter-American conferences interpreting services are normally supplied only to the United States delegation, since Spanish is spoken or understood by all other delegations. Thus it was that during a session of one of the committees of the Conference only Vandenberg and his two advisers were equipped with earphones. With these clamped over the ears the wearer has a natural tendency to shout when he speaks, as he is unable to judge the volume of his own voice. At this meeting the chairman in giving the floor to one delegate and then another, used the normal polite phrase, "El delegado de —— tiene la palabra" (literally, "The delegate from —— has the word" — i.e., has the floor). The debate was long and one delegate after another expressed his views eloquently and the phrase "tiene la palabra" was frequently repeated. Finally, the Senator turned to his advisers and in a voice made stentorian by his inability to gauge its volume, said "Palabra! He's always saying 'palabra' and then someone starts to talk. Now I know where the word 'palaver' comes from." Unaware that his shouts had been heard by everyone in the room, Vandenberg was naturally puzzled when in the complete silence which followed his advisers, with red faces, made no reply to his trenchant comment.

One of the major features of the Rio Treaty is a provision that a two-thirds majority vote in favor of imposing economic sanctions will be binding on all parties to the Treaty. The United States took the initiative in proposing this far-reaching principle, and the decision was reached in Washington before the Conference convened, with the full consultation and approval of Senators Connally and Vandenberg and other congressional leaders. Vandenberg, conscious of the significance of this "abolition of the veto in the Inter-American system" volunteered "to take on" the burden of defending this provision in the Senate in order to obtain ratification of the Treaty.

Later in defending the treaty before the Senate, Vandenberg pointed out that — unlike the situation in the UN Security Council — no single state could block action by its negative vote. "There is no paralyzing veto," he said, "upon any of these peaceful sanctions. One recalcitrant, one non-cooperator, cannot nullify the loyalties of the others. . . . We are building upon mutual trust. This is a true partnership which represents the greatest advance ever made in the business of collective peace."

The problem of possible Canadian adherence to the treaty also preoccupied Vandenberg and he brought the matter up for special discussion in the meetings of the United States delegation. He firmly believed that every effort should be made to bring Canada into full partnership in the Inter-American system. Although Resolution V of the Buenos Aires Conference of 1936 stated that all inter-American treaties and conventions are open to the adherence of non-signatory American states, the Senator suggested that consideration be given to a special provision in the Rio Pact regarding Canada's adherence. He felt that such a provision might offer Canada an opportunity to cease to be "a ward of the inter-American system" and to become more of a partner, although he recognized the delicacy of Canada's position in view of its membership in the British Commonwealth. It was finally decided that a special provision was not necessary. Article 22 permits adherence by "American States"; the protection of the Treaty is extended to "any American State," and it is generally recognized that the phrase "American State" includes Canada.

At the conclusion of the Conference, a resolution was passed expressing appreciation for Vandenberg's efforts: "The Inter-American Conference for Maintenance of Continental Peace and Security recalls with gratitude the services rendered by Senator Arthur Vandenberg in the Committee on Regional Arrangements of the Conference of San Francisco in obtaining approval of the United States proposal, which later became Article 51 of the Charter of the United Nations, by virtue of which it has been possible to conclude the first treaty which develops the principle of collective self-defense, and it applauds the cooperation which in a lofty and comprehensive spirit he has given the discussion of the Inter-American Treaty of Reciprocal Assistance."

Vandenberg regarded the work of the Petropolis Conference as of greatest importance not only in the future of the American Republics but in connection with future international arrangements elsewhere. "We need to sew up this defense pact [by early approval in the Senate] as a further and highly significant and impressive notification to potential Communist aggressors," Vandenberg wrote to Senator Taft on December 2, 1947. "Those who are responsible for our national defense consider the Treaty to be of vital security value." Vandenberg's viewpoint as to the importance of this action was fully justified later when Article 51 and the Rio Treaty served as the stepping stones to a far more comprehensive undertaking — the North Atlantic Treaty.

On his return to Washington Vandenberg moved with almost unprecedented speed to secure ratification of the Rio Pact. On December 4, 1947, he called the Foreign Relations Committee into session to hold hearings on the treaty, and four days later the Senate approved ratification without amendment by an overwhelming 72–1 vote. The Senator summed up the results of the Rio Conference in the following words to the Senate:

> . . . We have reknit the effective solidarity of North, Central, and South America against all aggressors, foreign and domestic. We have sealed a New World pact of peace which possesses teeth. We have translated pan-American solidarity from an ideal into a reality. We have put the great wartime Act of Chapultepec into an even greater peacetime contract which builds new peace defenses for ourselves and for our good neighbors. With scrupulous regard for the United Nations — acting strictly within articles 51, 52, 53, and 54 of the United Nations Charter — we have demonstrated how like-minded, peace-loving members of the United Nations can make so-called regional arrangements which build peace and security for themselves and for the world, regardless of confusion in higher U.N. councils. This is sunlight in a dark world.

The Rio Conference had one other unreported but important aspect for Vandenberg. It brought a new and close working relationship, as well as abiding friendship, with Secretary Marshall. The relationship, based on mutual respect and affection, was to be at least as valuable to bipartisanship in foreign policy as was the working friendship established earlier between Vandenberg and Byrnes.

An important factor in initial development of the relationship appeared to be the friendship of Mrs. Vandenberg and Mrs. Marshall. Both of them had warm, responsive personalities, and Mrs. Vandenberg's own diary catches the flavor of the developing comradeship. She wrote of a visit to the Marshalls': "... Just to illustrate how wonderful they are with each other, I found them playing Chinese checkers on the porch here after having had a ride to an especially beautiful site. They are completely congenial and a simply grand pair. If nothing else comes out of this conference, it has been a rare privilege to know them better, and Dad [Senator Vandenberg] feels the same way. There is nothing stuffy at all about him [Marshall], in fact, he is a lot of fun, and so human."

Mrs. Vandenberg's report boded well for the difficult tasks both men were to face together in the months to come.

20

The Marshall Plan

BY THE EARLY summer of 1947 it seemed obvious that the economic problems left in the wake of the war could not be solved by the kind of emergency relief the United States had been granting up to that point. Many persons, profoundly disturbed by that fact, were beginning to feel that we had gone about as far as we should go with that type of assistance.

American food, fertilizer, and medicines on an emergency basis could not make Western Europe a going concern. It was, as some senators remarked, the process of trying to patch a badly leaking roof instead of putting on a new one. Billions had been channeled into Europe through UNRRA, the British loan, and the Greece-Turkey program. The Senate in May had overwhelmingly approved a $350,000,000 emergency aid program for Austria, Hungary, Poland, Italy, Trieste, China, and Greece. Vandenberg, again with the unanimous backing of the Foreign Relations Committee, told the Senate that without the emergency aid "famine, disease and disaster will stalk a desperate Europe."

So serious was the situation in France, for instance, that the State Department sent John Foster Dulles on a secret mission to Paris that summer to assess the danger of a Communist attempt to seize power or the possibility of an outbreak of civil war between the leftists and the followers of General Charles de Gaulle, who at that time was making a bid for political power. Dulles found the French torn by strikes, sabotage, and threats of extremist action and he felt that prompt economic help — interim aid pending the inauguration of a long-term program of assistance — was essential to reassure the French and perhaps to avert armed violence. He telephoned Vandenberg in Washington and later conferred with General Marshall, who was at a meeting of the Council of Foreign Ministers in London, and Marshall also telephoned the Senator to explain the situation.

Communist pressure in France, as well as in Italy, Czechoslovakia, and Finland, was increasing. Britain's supply of dollars, essential to industrial recovery, was at the vanishing point. Freak weather of alternate drought and storm was paralyzing European agriculture and mining. Hunger, unemployment, economic stagnation, and resultant despair — all the handmaidens of political unrest — haunted Europe. As at almost no other time since the end of hostilities, the fate of the free nations in Europe hung by a precarious thread. Marshall and Dulles made this situation clear to Vandenberg and asked his assistance in planning stopgap aid as quickly as possible.

The Senator promptly agreed, and as a result of his collaboration it was possible for Marshall to give the French cabinet assurances that encouraged it to hold out and to face the rigors of the coming winter. At a special late fall session in 1947, Congress on December 1 approved interim aid of $587,-000,000 for winter relief in Austria, China, France, and Italy after Vandenberg had told the Senate that it was a fight against "winter hunger and winter cold and against the lurking tyranny which feeds upon such disaster." But the Senator knew that such interim relief was no substitute for the economic revival of Europe. On this subject, Vandenberg wrote to Senator Taft: "There is yet another overriding factor which none of us dare overlook. . . . We now apparently confront the Moscow challenge on every front and on every issue. It is a total 'war of nerves,' at least. . . . At long last we have got to have an integrated foreign policy which is just as comprehensive as that of the Soviets. I am sure that Secretary Marshall is fully alive to this fact. . . ."

As a matter of fact, Marshall had opened up the subject of more substantial long-term assistance as early as June 5, 1947, when he delivered the commencement address at Harvard University — an address that Vandenberg described as a "shot heard round the world" just as another shot fired more than a century and a half earlier at near-by Concord had been heard around the world. Marshall said: "It is already evident that before the United States government can proceed much further in its effort to alleviate the situation and help the European world on its way to recovery, there must be some agreement among the countries of Europe as to the requirements of the situation and the part those countries themselves will take in order to give proper effect to whatever action might be undertaken by this government. The initiative, I think, must come from Europe.

"The role of this country should consist of friendly aid in the drafting of a European program and of later support of such a program so far as it may be practical for us to do so. The program should be a joint one, agreed to by a number, if not all, of the European nations."

It was an idea that captured the imagination of free men in this country and abroad; an idea that challenged the Russians. But it was just an idea and it would require a long period of tortuous work to translate into a reality. For Vandenberg, as Republican foreign policy leader and Chairman of the Senate Foreign Relations Committee, that work of translation was a test of patience, judgment, and physical strength. Again it meant turning an idea into a working agreement; it meant spotting the pitfalls, eliminating the weaknesses, anticipating the opposition, and finding a realistic solid ground regardless of political party. Above all it meant doing these things without losing sight of the goal — without allowing compromises to undermine essential elements of the program.

The Marshall idea fell upon a Republican Congress dedicated to reducing taxes and cutting government spending. There was deep concern, not only in Congress but throughout the country, that scarce American goods would be drained off the domestic market for foreign consumption. There was similar concern lest the United States strain its financial and material resources only to "pour its money down a rat hole," and it was asked whether success of the program would serve only to increase competition for American business.

These doubts had to be met, Vandenberg realized, before any

vast new foreign recovery undertaking could be presented with half a chance for success. Two weeks after Marshall spoke at Harvard, Vandenberg acknowledged the problem posed by the Secretary of State, and proposed that before the United States intelligently could seek an answer it had better learn precisely what the needs were and what its own ability was to meet these needs. He proposed that President Truman appoint a bipartisan advisory council composed of "our ablest and most experienced citizenship" to produce the "facts and recommendations and judgments." And he passed the word to the White House that he would not touch the plan until this had been done, further stating:

June 13, 1947

Current discussion, in and out of official life, is directed toward new foreign programs of large-scale post-war American rehabilitation — as distinguished from direct relief — to prevent social and economic collapse in many parts of the world. It is a good thing that these discussions are under way in the open. But they should not be misunderstood at home or abroad. At home, they should not invite anxieties that we shall rush into imprudent and inadequately seasoned plans. Abroad, they should not be taken as evidence that our foreign friends can depend upon us as a substitute for depending on themselves. . . .

I endorse the importance of facing this problem on an over-all basis instead of dealing with anticipated crises, one by one . . . but equally I recognize that intelligent American self-interest immediately requires a sound, over-all inventory of our own resources to determine the latitudes within which we may consider these foreign needs. This comes first because if America ever sags, the world's hopes sag with her.

He set as an essential task the determination of the over-all extent to which America could "safely and wisely" undertake foreign aid operations; the basis upon which such operations should be undertaken including reciprocal benefits this country was to receive; and "a total balance sheet" covering the over-all needs of the recipient nations so far as American aid was concerned. While the fact-gathering facilities of the United Nations and the State Department were essential, Vandenberg said, there was a "fundamental necessity" for marshaling the nation's best brains in industry, labor, manufacturing, agriculture.

The Vandenberg proposal resulted in the most concentrated, yet broad-scaled, stocktaking in the nation's history. Nine days later, on June 22, President Truman announced creation of three committees, including a nonpartisan Advisory Council, to do the job. A nineteen-man committee, carefully balanced between industry, labor, agriculture, and the professions was formed under the chairmanship of W. Averell Harriman, then Secretary of Commerce and the only government member. This was the committee to review the whole problem of foreign aid and to determine "the limits within which the United States may safely and wisely plan," as President Truman put it, using almost precisely Vandenberg's own words. Additionally, Interior Secretary Julius A. Krug headed a group to study the state of the nation's resources and Chairman Edwin G. Nourse, of the President's Council of Economic Advisors, headed a study group on the impact of foreign assistance upon the domestic economy.

This action was paralleled abroad on the part of European countries by organization of the Committee of European Economic Co-operation at the invitation of Bevin and Schuman. At the first meeting of the Committee the Russians posed what Vandenberg termed "impossible" demands for their co-operation. They withdrew from the consultations, taking the satellite states along, and formed instead the Cominform organization dedicated to wrecking the Marshall Plan. The sixteen free nations of Europe met throughout the summer, not to total up a bill for the United States, but to volunteer their own pledges to reach predetermined industrial and agriculture targets, work toward monetary and economic stability, and to co-operate in removing trade barriers. On the basis of such an undertaking, they estimated that in four and a quarter years of self-help and co-operation, and with an over-all total of $29,000,000,000 in American assistance, the goals could be attained. As a result of careful screening, this figure was reduced to $22,400,000,000 and was later cut to $17,000,000,000.

Throughout the summer and fall the American stocktaking persisted. The sights were set. Under the prodding of Vandenberg and other national leaders, a realistic appraisal of what could be done was made and a program took shape. The reports, the studies, and the findings overloaded a five-foot shelf of books.

In this period Vandenberg labored at a terrific pace, and the strain he imposed on himself was reflected in a series of letters he wrote to his wife telling her of his work on the interim aid bill and — at the same time — on the long-range Marshall Plan. As usual, he did not date the letters to Mrs. Vandenberg, but they covered roughly the autumn weeks, ending in November, 1947, when the interim aid bill was being prepared and enacted.

[*Undated*]
> I am home after a hectic day at the White House and the State Department. . . . About 20 of us met in the Cabinet room this morning. The President is trying to discriminate between "stop-gap aid" for France and Italy to keep them afloat until Spring, on the one hand, and a permanent "Marshall Plan," on the other. (It was this differentiation which I impressed upon Marshall last night as essential to any possibility of success.) We had a fairly harmonious time of it — with this discrimination in mind. . . . The confidential reports from Europe are that the Commies are losing ground (even their satellites are restless). . . . This seems to be the time for us "to make hay." But if our friends in Western Europe are allowed to starve and freeze to death this winter, the Commies will be completely back in the saddle. On the other hand, we must keep our own feet on the ground and avoid commitments that would disrupt our own economy. Where to draw the line!

[*About November 13, 1947*]
> We are dealing at the moment only with the short-range stop-gap relief formula. When that is out of the way, we shall have to dig much deeper in connection with the long-range four-year plan. I am reserving some doubts myself regarding some phases of it — but, in the main, I do not see

how we can avoid the necessity of keeping ourselves insulated against world-wide Communism by maintaining these sixteen nations of the Western Union, and helping them to rebuild an anticommunist, self-supporting society. There's no question we would do it if we were at war with Russia. I'd prefer to do five per cent that much to make it plain to Russia that war would be fatal to her. Evidently I am to have some degree of trouble with Bob Taft. So be it! The world is full of tragedy; but there is no tragedy greater than that we have to have a presidential election next year in the U.S.A. That must be what's biting Robert. . . .

A few days later the letters indicated that there were behind-the-scenes differences with Senator Connally, who had been chairman of the Foreign Relations Committee until the Republican election victory put Vandenberg into that position. This lack of harmony, which never became fully known to the public, was to arouse Vandenberg's concern later as to the future of a bipartisan approach to foreign policy problems.

[*November 18, 1947*]

I have just finished a continuous session of the Foreign Relations Committee which sat straight through from ten this morning until 3:15 this afternoon. . . . Guess I must be getting old. . . . I still have some trouble getting up and down but much less than yesterday when it was just about all I could do to gracefully get up and down on the Speaker's dais during the Joint Congressional session when we repeatedly had to rise — then sit — then rise — then sit. No pain at any other time — and certainly nothing to worry about. . . .

[The letter also referred to a clash with] Connally this morning in the Committee meeting each time I proposed an amendment — I almost blew my top. I *did* get to the point where I said, in offering further amendments, that I hoped they might be considered without prejudice to their source. Sooner or later this feud will explode. I shall still try not to be responsible. . . . If the resistance which is showing up to the little short-range European relief bill . . . is any criterion, our friend Marshall is certainly going to have a helluva time down here on the Hill when he gets around to his long-range plan. It is going to be next to impossible to keep any sort of unpartisan climate in respect to anything. Politics is heavy in the air.

The Senator's fears were relieved late in November, however, and in the end the opposition to the interim aid bill melted away and attention was centered mainly on the long-range Marshall Plan. "The preparations that the State Department has made for this next showdown are amazing. I have never seen better work. Indeed, they have simply overwhelmed us with documentation. I got the report today of the Harriman Commission. . . . It is a magnificent piece of work. But it is three inches thick! I brought it home with me tonight. That'll keep me busy over the weekend (although I will divert long enough to tend to the crossword puzzles). Afraid of a glum Saturday tomorrow because there are so many toplevel football games I'm afraid the Michigan-Indiana tiff won't be on any radio station I can reach."

And, near the end of November:

I think we shall finish [interim aid] Monday afternoon; and I shall be greatly surprised if more than a dozen Senators dare vote against the Bill. Even Taft announced in a speech today that he would vote for it. . . . Did you see that Izvestia (Moscow) put me back at the top of the Communist black list yesterday? . . . That's pretty good. . . . We got thru in the Senate this afternoon in time for a "sweat, swim and rub." While I have had some twinges of the old crink, I must say that it has been nothing like the old plague. . . . Well, that brings me up close to six o'clock. So now I'll get you on the telephone — and then have Hubert take me to the Mayflower for my Lobster Newburg — and then back home and so to bed about 8 P.M.

These letters to his wife were a regular part of the Senator's day whenever she was absent. But during this same period of hard work he was carrying on a voluminous correspondence with others in regard to the Marshall Plan.

To Clark M. Eichelberger, Director of the American Association for the United Nations, Inc., Vandenberg sought to explain the relation of the contemplated program to the United Nations.

June 25, 1947

I wanted immediately . . . to identify the United Nations as a part of any plan of this character. But I must say that I am frankly puzzled to know precisely how it can be worked out . . . The evolution of this vague thing which we now conveniently call the "Marshall Plan" inevitably involves much more than "economics" and inevitably requires a basic meeting of minds between the four great powers covering a number of superlatively vital issues. It will be a miracle . . . if these four great powers can get together on this thing at all. [The Russians had not yet finally decided to oppose the project.] Certainly they cannot hope to get together at anything less than the highest level. In other words, the European Commission [of the United Nations] would be all but impotent in dealing with the realities. I do not think it is any reflection on the United Nations to admit that — in the present state of development — there are some basic questions with which it cannot be expected to cope. This may well be one of them. If it is, it would be a disservice to the United Nations to give it a task which it could not fulfill. On the other hand, if anything could strengthen the United Nations it would be success for the so-called Marshall Plan by whatever means required.

I have no illusions about this so-called "Marshall Plan." . . . Furthermore, I certainly do not take it for granted that American public opinion is ready for any such burdens as would be involved unless and until it is far more effectively demonstrated to the American people that this (1) is within the latitudes of their own available resources and (2) serves their own intelligent self-interest.

To a Detroit constituent, he wrote: "I am entirely willing to admit that America herself cannot prosper in a broken world. But it is equally true that if America ever sags, the world's hopes for peace will sag with her. Meanwhile, however, there are some very realistic problems which we must face — including the basic fact that even our friends in Western Europe will soon be totally devoid of dollar exchange and therefore unable to buy commodities from us which are indispensable to their own self-rehabilitation. I must confess that this poses a tough conundrum in international economics entirely aside from considerations of 'charity' or 'communism'."

To Malcolm W. Bingay, Detroit *Free Press* columnist who had suggested that the program posed impossible conundrums, Vandenberg wrote:

December 29, 1947

... anyone who says "I know the right answer" is way off base. We are dealing with a world in unpredictable flux. To make it worse, half the "flux" is behind an iron curtain where neither the Bingays nor Vandenbergs are allowed to speak. So we have no alternative but to do the best we can, in the absence of certified knowledge, and to balance one "calculated risk" against another. . . .

You are entirely right that an "international WPA" can't save Europe from communism or anything else. Is somebody proposing one? I hadn't heard about it. The so-called "Marshall Plan" is the exact opposite, if it runs true to form — and it's our business to see that it does. It is a program geared to self-help. It requires beneficiary countries to proceed specifically to do the things for themselves which will put them on their own feet (and off ours) by 1951 — and our aid is progressively contingent upon concurrent results. ... I respectfully submit that we do "know enough" to know what will happen if it, or something like it, doesn't work. We know that independent governments, whatever their character otherwise, will disappear from Western Europe; that aggressive communism will be spurred throughout the world; and that our concept of free men, free government and a relatively free international economy will come up against accumulated hazards which can put our own, precious "American way of life" in the greatest, kindred hazard since Pearl Harbor. . . . Let's be equally frank in our "calculations" as to what happens if the iron curtain reaches the Atlantic; if peace and justice are at the mercy of expanding, hostile totalitarian aggression; and if the greatest creditor and capitalist nation on earth should find itself substantially isolated in a communist world where the competition would force us into complete regimentation of ourselves beyond anything we have ever experienced.

As he often did, Vandenberg was thinking out loud, wrestling with himself, facing up to the problems he knew anxious people were asking in good faith. There were, too, letters dealing with more practical details. To General Marshall, Vandenberg wrote that he still was insisting on a "total balance sheet" of all contemplated American foreign aid spending — including Asia and South America. To Undersecretary Robert A. Lovett, who became an indispensable partner in this and other undertakings, he suggested as a practical matter the desirability of obtaining "four or five top-level business executives of the country" as "aggressive witnesses" once the Committee hearings started on the Marshall Plan. This was to be essentially a "business" program.

By November Vandenberg's thinking was clarified to the point where he was able to say at the University of Michigan that "if self-help and self-sufficiency can be made to work, this [the Marshall Plan] objective may well be a bargain. We must find reasonable promise of this success because we cannot indefinitely underwrite the world. . . . There is the calculated risk if we proceed. But let's be honest enough with American destiny not to ignore the calculated risk if we do not proceed. Secretary Marshall correctly says it involves 'the danger of the actual disappearance of the characteristics of Western civilization on which our government and our manner of living are based.' "

As 1948 began the reports, the documents, the figures from the Study Committees were in. The program was deemed well within American capabilities and the committees came up with the conclusion that it should be tried. Draft legislation was prepared and submitted to Congress. The job of steering the Marshall Plan through Congress was at hand.

On New Year's Day, 1948, Vandenberg sought to end the growing talk of a "Vandenberg-for-President" move. Writing to Michigan Republican leaders, he urged that his name be neither presented nor supported for the Republican presidential nomination at the Michigan State Convention or the Republican National Convention in Philadelphia. "I am confident that I can best serve my country by completing my present term in the Senate," he wrote. This did not halt those who sought to advance Vandenberg as the party candidate. But the letter did strengthen Vandenberg's position as a bipartisan foreign policy leader because it represented withdrawal from a very partisan fight over the presidency. It was timed perfectly, coming as the Marshall Plan debate began in Congress.

From January 8 to February 5 the Senate Foreign Relations Committee heard more than ninety witnesses and received for the record scores of written statements. It was perhaps the most comprehensive public hearing on a foreign policy question ever undertaken. Cabinet members, ambassadors, and other government officials were heard; so were leaders in industry, agriculture, and labor. College professors, editors, and trade association representatives appeared; so did the women's clubs, church groups, and organizations interested in various means of keeping the peace. Veterans' groups, civic groups, and such leading citizens as Bernard M. Baruch were heard; plain citizens, One-Worlders, isolationists, socialists, and those who, quite frankly, were not certain where they stood took their turn on the witness stand.

Day after day Vandenberg sat in the huge, marble Senate caucus room, sometimes with the full committee listening attentively to witnesses, sometimes courteously receiving testimony alone when other senators had departed. All witnesses who requested a hearing were heard. Finally, at 11.40 A.M. on February 5, the job was done. Americans had spoken their minds, the Committee could retire behind closed doors to hear confidential testimony and to make up its mind. It was said of Vandenberg that "he killed the opposition to the Marshall Plan with kindness."

Meanwhile, there were rumblings of trouble in the Senate. A group of twenty Republican "revisionists" was meeting regularly at a downtown apartment hotel. Some of the group admittedly were out to "gut" the program; others merely sought to "strengthen" it. All had Vandenberg's ear. Some "revisions" he could accept, thus whittling away at the opposition before the bill reached the Senate floor.

The Administration bill carried a request for a staggering $17,000,000,000 authorization — the total funds estimated for the program over its entire four-and-a-quarter-year span. Vandenberg wrote Secretary Marshall that this should be changed to a generalized authorization for appropriations in amounts deemed necessary by the Administration and Congress until June, 1952. A Congressional authorization is simply a statement of Congress' general intent regarding spending. The specific amounts are not finally determined, and the actual money is not provided until later appropriations are approved. Many times the amounts actually appropriated are well below the authorized amounts.

Vandenberg realized that the huge $17,000,000,000 figure if left in the bill certainly would provide a major bone of contention, and an unnecessary one. It would be a point around which opposition could crystallize. He wrote Marshall that a generalized authorization was common practice in Congress for programs extending from one year to the next. And he said that since one Congress could not bind another on spending, it actually was the yearly cash appropriations which would provide the test. A general, continuing authorization would signify Congress' intention to continue the program beyond a year.

". . . But to express this principal in figures, namely $17,000,-000,000, in the legislation itself may invite a specific reliance abroad which is impossible under our constitutional procedure," he added. "Furthermore, it can only be an educated guess of highly doubtful validity when we thus attempt to assess events for the next four years at home or abroad, and when the entire ERP [European Recovery Program] enterprise is at the mercy of good or bad contingencies."

Three days later Undersecretary Lovett wrote Vandenberg that after consultation with the President, the State Department was ready to accept Vandenberg's language. A potential stumbling block of considerable magnitude had been removed. But the principle of continuity and a four-year program was preserved.

Lewis W. Douglas, Ambassador to Britain, took over the difficult job of liaison between the Committee on Capitol Hill and Marshall and Lovett downtown. It was a fortunate choice. Douglas and Vandenberg established the closest of working relations. Douglas' assistance was invaluable. As a former member of Congress and as a man of great government as well as business experience, he commanded confidence and respect. He knew the problems legislators faced, and he was intimately acquainted with every phase of the Administration program.

The Administration requested a spending authorization of $6,800,000,000 for the first fifteen months of operations. Again with his eye on the Congressional demand for economy, Vandenberg suggested that this initial operation be set at twelve months with $5,300,000,000 as the figure. The monthly spending ration would go unchanged, but the new, Eighty-First Congress in 1949 would have an earlier opportunity to assess results and review progress. The State Department agreed, and Vandenberg thus gained a valuable talking point in the Senate.

The importance of this change was illustrated in a letter Vandenberg wrote to a constituent who asked whether the European Recovery Program would greatly increase taxes, as had been suggested by opponents of the measure. The Senator replied:

March 13, 1948

Of course it is not true that the passage of this Bill will result "in additional taxes as soon as it is passed." Of course, any expenditure from the public treasury is an expenditure and comes out of the common treasury which belongs to the whole people of the United States. But taxes are not going to be increased as a result of the passage of the present Bill. On the contrary, within a week after the passage of the European Recovery Bill, the Senate will vote to reduce taxes by more than four billion dollars a year. . . . This question of "what the Bill will cost" is a very interesting one. Unfortunately, the critics of the Bill have nothing to say about what the failure to pass the Bill will cost. You can get some direct and specific idea on this latter point by reading the testimony before our Senate Foreign Relations Committee by Secretary of Defense Forrestal and Secretary of the Army Royall, who both assert that without legislation of this character they would find it necessary immediately to ask for heavily increased appropriations for military defense. Why? Because it is infinitely cheaper to defend ourselves by economic means. In other words, in the final analysis, peace is cheaper than war. War has no bargains. Peace does. There is no guarantee that this European Recovery Plan will "work." But certainly there is an even chance that it can succeed. In my opinion, we cannot afford not to take that chance.

At Vandenberg's request, sections of the bill dealing with Europe's responsibility and self-help obligations were strengthened. "The continuity of assistance provided by the United States should at all times be dependent upon the continuity of cooperation among the countries involved," was written into the bill. And the administrator was ordered to terminate aid if he discovered that a recipient was not adhering to its agreement with the United States or with its partners in Europe or was diverting American aid from purposes set forth in the act.

Vandenberg wrote in answer to a protest that the money was being spent in subservience to the dictates of foreign countries and alien-minded Americans:

April 9, 1948

I couldn't agree with you more that the "first essential qualification is for the law-making body of the United States to lend this money" and, I would add, to write the rules under which the participating nations shall use our money within their borders. Indeed, I have gone much farther even than that in insisting that the Bill must explicitly spell out these facts. I personally wrote into the Act that continuity of aid is wholly contingent upon satisfying us with the continuity of performance under our explicit specifications in these participating countries. I personally wrote into the Act the requirement for a "Congressional Watch-Dog Committee" to keep in constant and vigilant touch with what goes on. I submit that this is the exact opposite of the thesis which your interpretation . . . attributes to me — namely, that "they (these foreign participating countries) are the controlling factor in the whole matter."

One of the knottiest problems of all dealt with administration of the program. The State Department draft provided for an administrator whose every function, especially those involving foreign policy, would be performed "subject to direction and control of the Secretary of State." Vandenberg, though recalling his own words on a previous occasion that the nation can have only one Secretary of State at a time, was dissatisfied, as were many members of Congress. He thought the Administrator would be too circumscribed under State Department control.

The Senator called upon the Brookings Institution, one of the nation's foremost research organizations, to analyze the administrative problem, and the Institution's findings provided the basis for a compromise acceptable to Marshall, the State Department, the Administration — and, more important, acceptable to the Congress. An administrator of Cabinet rank would head an Economic Co-operation Administration, an independent agency under final Presidential control. Borrowing from the Atomic Energy Act's principles, the Secretary of State and ECA Administrator were to keep each other mutually informed. If consultation failed to solve proposed actions which the Secretary deemed inconsistent with United States foreign policy, the dispute would be referred to the President for final settlement. This opened the door to the "business administration" of the vast economic program, upon which Vandenberg insisted.

Western Germany which was regarded as a key to European recovery was tied into the program. There were numerous other "compromises," accommodations, and changes — some large, some small. Many of them the Senator frankly considered as "window dressing" to get support for the program. Vandenberg demonstrated time and time again his unusual ability to influence senators and win votes. At one meeting of the Committee, someone objected that the words in the bill "impact on our domestic economy" were too general and vague and ought to be omitted. "That's perfectly all right," said the Senator. "Just leave those words in. I can tell nineteen different Senators on the floor of the Senate who are worried about something — your problem is taken care of by that clause in the bill."

The Foreign Relations Committee on February 13 voted 13 to 0 its approval of the undertaking. The bill was cleared for prompt floor action with its passage ultimately assured. Secretary Marshall was able to write that the work, now virtually completed, established Vandenberg in the minds of most informed citizens "as a truly great statesman with wisdom and integrity as . . . cardinal virtues."

On March 1 Vandenberg took to the Senate floor the speech on which he had labored many nights in the Vandenberg apartment. He rewrote the speech seven times. The galleries were packed, corridors and stairways were jammed with people seeking entry; almost a full membership of the Senate was present and House members walked across the Capitol to line the walls of the Senate Chamber. Vandenberg spoke for one hour and twenty minutes. The nine-thousand-word address was one of his longest.

March 1, 1948

Mr. President, with the unanimous approval of the Senate Foreign Relations Committee, I report the Economic Cooperation Act of 1948 in its perfected text. In the name of peace, stability, and freedom it deserves prompt passage. In the name of intelligent American self-interest it envisions a mighty undertaking worthy of our faith. It is an economic act — but economics usually control national survivals these days. The act itself asserts that "disruption following in the wake of war is not contained by national frontiers." It asserts that "the existing situation in Europe endangers the establishment of a lasting peace, the general welfare and national interest of the United States, and the attainment of the objectives of the United Nations."

[He recalled that in the days just past — the last semblance of democracy in Czechoslovakia had been "gutted," and] the kindred fate of brave little Finland may be adding to the ominous score this very afternoon while we debate an axiom, namely that aggressive communism threatens all freedom and all security, whether in the old world or in the new, when it puts free peoples anywhere in chains.

[Vandenberg defended the program as sound American doctrine. He said it could become "a welcome beacon in the world's dark night." And he urged prompt passage because] if a beacon is to be lighted at all it had better be lighted before it is too late. I understand and share the anxieties involved. It would be a far happier circumstance if we could close our eyes to reality, comfortably retire within our bastions, and dream of an isolated and prosperous peace. But that which was once our luxury would now become our folly. This is too plain to be persuasively denied in a foreshortened, atomic world. We must take things as they are.

The greatest nation on earth either justifies or surrenders its leadership. We must choose. There are no blueprints to guarantee results. We are entirely surrounded by calculated risks. I profoundly believe that the pending program is the best of these risks. I have no quarrel with those who disagree, because we are dealing with imponderables. But I am bound to say to those who disagree that they have not escaped to safety by rejecting or subverting this plan. They have simply fled to other risks, and I fear far greater ones. For myself, I can only say that I prefer my choice of responsibilities.

This legislation, Mr. President, seeks peace and stability for free men in a free world. It seeks them by economic rather than by military means. It proposes to help our friends to help themselves in the pursuit of sound and successful liberty in the democratic pattern. The quest can mean as much to us as it does to them. It aims to preserve the victory against aggression and dictatorship which we thought we won in World War II. It strives to help stop World War III before it starts. It fights economic chaos which would precipitate far-flung disintegration. It sustains Western civilization. It means to take Western Europe completely off the American dole at the end of the adventure. It recognizes the grim truth

— whether we like it or not — that American self-interest, national economy, and national security are inseparably linked with these objectives. It stops if changed conditions are no longer consistent with the national interest of the United States. It faces the naked facts of life.

Within the purview of this plan are 270,000,000 people of the stock which has largely made America. . . . This vast friendly segment of the earth must not collapse. The iron curtain must not come to the rims of the Atlantic either by aggression or by default.

Vandenberg then sketched the "chain reaction" which led to formulation of the undertaking. He recalled the postwar aid which found America leaping "from one crisis to another. Bill after bill went through Congress for relief, and billion after billion went from us to them." The process could not go on indefinitely, America "could not longer afford to underwrite futility," Europe could wait no longer for "real emancipation." Through Marshall's Harvard speech, the organization in Europe, the surveys of capabilities and resources at home, the initial drafting of the legislation, the bitter Communist reaction, the legislative compromises, he traced the project. The warnings of Defense Secretary James Forrestal that billions more for American defense would be needed if Europe could not be stabilized, and those from the Harriman Committee regarding new limitations on the American way of life, vividly were recalled. "This is more than a problem of mathematics; it is a problem in peace, stability and human freedoms," Vandenberg said. "It may not work. I think it will. But if it fails let the responsibility rest elsewhere."

The Committee has rewritten the bill to consolidate the wisdom shed upon the problem from many sources. It is the final product of eight months of more intensive study by more devoted minds than I have ever known to concentrate upon any one objective in all my 20 years in Congress. It has its foes — some of whom compliment it by their transparent hatreds. But it has its friends — countless, prayerful friends not only at the hearthstones of America, but under many other flags. It is a plan for peace, stability, and freedom. As such, it involves the clear self-interest of the United States. It can be the turning point in history for 100 years to come. If it fails, we have done our final best. If it succeeds, our children and our children's children will call us blessed. May God grant His benediction upon the ultimate event.

As Vandenberg concluded senators and spectators rose to their feet, flouting Senate rules in a burst of applause. Most senators, led by Connally, filed by Vandenberg's desk to shake his hand. Some observers called it "the climactic role" of Vandenberg's career.

The Senate debated the bill for two weeks. There were challenges on details, met in full by Vandenberg, Connally, Lodge, and others. A move to cut $1,300,000,000 off the first-year authorization, offered by Taft, was beaten back 56 to 31. Finally, five minutes past midnight on March 14, 1948, the Senate voted, 69 to 17, its approval of the program. Shortly thereafter the House agreed to major portions of the Senate bill, the minor differences were ironed out in conference, and very soon thereafter the President signed it into law.

From the start, Vandenberg had insisted that "the business side of this essentially business enterprise shall be under the effective control of adequate business brains which shall be specially recruited for the purpose." He had insisted on a "business" audit before the program was considered; he insisted on a "business" administrator.

Vandenberg had written to a friend:

January 2, 1948

The question of finding a satisfactory administrative formula is perhaps the biggest single conundrum which the Senate Foreign Relations Committee confronts. We all pretty well agree as to our general objective — namely, that the *business* side of this essentially *business* enterprise shall be under the effective control of adequate business brains which shall be specially recruited for the purpose. At the same time we all must also agree that ERP virtually becomes the "foreign policy" of the Government in Western Europe for the next four years. Therefore, our "business administration" of ERP has got to be in successful liaison with the Secretary of State and the President wherever foreign policy decisions are involved. We cannot have "two Secretaries of State" (as I once observed upon a previous historic occasion).

Despite his "greatest respect and affection," Vandenberg moved against appointment of William L. Clayton, Undersecretary of State for Economic Affairs, to the post. He wrote Secretary Marshall:

March 24, 1948

I have had very unhappy repercussions today on the Hill from the story this morning on the front page of the Washington Post that Mr. Clayton is slated to head ERP. This is no reflection on Mr. Clayton. It is simply reflection of the overriding Congressional desire that the ERP Administrator shall come from the outside business world with strong industrial credentials and *not* via the State Department. I want to sound this warning for the sake of ERP itself — now and hereafter. I am sure there would be wide-spread acceptance of Mr. Clayton or Mr. Douglas as "Roving Ambassador" under the terms of the new Bill. They are held in great Congressional respect. But this job as ERP Administrator stands out by itself — as demonstrated in all of the Congressional debates — as requiring particularly persuasive economic credentials unrelated to diplomacy. I think it is seriously necessary — for the sake of ERP — to keep this fact in mind. I am sure I do not need to add that my personal attitude toward Mr. Clayton is one of greatest respect and affection.

Marshall reassured Vandenberg that he (Vandenberg) would be consulted when the President "boiled down" the possibilities to two or three individuals. Vandenberg a little later was called to the White House on the matter by President Truman. The Senator related to a close friend that the President opened up by saying: "Van, I've found just the man for the job and he's willing to take it at a great personal sacrifice."

Vandenberg recounted that he replied: "Fine, who is it?"

Truman's response was to name Dean Acheson, who at that time was outside the government and practicing law. Vandenberg's reply was that he had "no doubt but that Acheson had great ability and might do a fine job — but the Senate won't confirm him for the position."

Precisely how and when Vandenberg became convinced that Paul G. Hoffman, President of the Studebaker Corporation and Chairman of the Board of the Committee for Economic Development, was the man for the job is not clear. Vandenberg later wrote a friend that he had canvassed a hundred-odd business authorities and that in at least half the cases, Hoffman led the list of recommendations for the Marshall Plan post, and he repeated this in his Senate speech urging Hoffman's confirmation. The two men had only a passing acquaintance at the time, though Hoffman had testified convincingly for the ERP bill before Vandenberg's committee, and the Senator was impressed.

Vandenberg urged Hoffman's appointment at the White House, and John Steelman, Assistant to the President, telephoned Hoffman, who was on a brief mission for the Army in Hawaii. Hoffman told the editor of this book that he informed Steelman he didn't want the job and couldn't understand why Mr. Truman would pick a man who did not want the position when so many men did. Hoffman declined to give Steelman an off-the-cuff answer, but agreed to discuss the matter with the President the following week in Washington. When he arrived, he telephoned Vandenberg and bluntly was informed by the Senator, "You've got to take it." Hoffman replied, "I've hired thousands of men in my time, but not a single man by saying that 'you have to take it.'" But Vandenberg was so insistent Hoffman later said, "He knocked all my defenses down and by the time I spoke to the President I couldn't say 'no.'"

"I found him [Hoffman] to be the common denominator of the thought of the nation," Vandenberg told the Senate. The nominee was quickly confirmed by the Senate, and immediately threw himself wholeheartedly into the job.

The choice of Hoffman as Administrator always was regarded by Vandenberg as an extremely fortunate one. Hoffman's performance was highly regarded by all factions in Congress, and although some phases of the Marshall Plan were to come under bristling attack the net opinion was that the job was extremely well done. Such criticism as there was never extended to Hoffman personally. To a constituent who charged that the Marshall Plan administration was a "politically dominated set up," Vandenberg wrote: "It is exactly the contrary. Its administrator, Paul Hoffman, has flatly declined to permit anybody from the President down to dictate the choice of any of his associated personnel; and it has been clearly understood that any such attempts will result in his immediate resignation. As a result, he had the best non-political organization which has ever been put together on a government project."

When, more than two years later, Hoffman resigned from the Marshall Plan post, Vandenberg wrote him:

September 29, 1950

I read of your ECA resignation with regret. But I am bound to say that you have performed so magnificently in your difficult assignment — successfully carrying ECA through all of its major crises — you are entitled to consult your own desires and wishes. I simply want to tell you that you have justified every confidence I ever placed in you and that I shall always be exceptionally proud of having had a key part not only in drafting you for this public service but also in loyally upholding your hands. . . .

I am sure your public career is not ended. You have given the American people the kind of service they desire and demand and I am sure you will face other calls to duty to which you will respond with continuing patriotism and success.

Hoffman summed up his own end of the relationship with Vandenberg in dedicating his book, *Peace Can Be Won*, to: "Arthur H. Vandenberg, Senior Senator from Michigan, whose words and works for peace will always be an inspiration to those who love peace."

And Hoffman later described Vandenberg as "the most perfect example of democratic leadership I've ever seen. He insisted upon getting all the facts, and then following the facts. If America would recognize that the kind of leadership he gave the Senate is exactly the kind of leadership we have to give the world we would be much farther down the line in solving world problems than we are today. It was the kind of leadership which equals can give among equals by selflessness. Senator Vandenberg typified the kind of leadership you have to have in the world today in opposition to the authoritarian type."

Meantime, following Congressional approval of ERP, the House suddenly threatened in June of 1948 to sink the Program before it started. Led by the Chairman John Taber, an economy advocate who was supported by other ranking Republicans, the House ordered a $2,160,000,000 cut in the first-year appropriation, amounting to about twenty-six per cent of the spending request.

The axe fell with a suddenness which left Vandenberg "fighting mad." He wrote Dulles: "I do not know how anything could be more shocking or more subversive of every Republican pretense toward international cooperation. Mr. Molotov told Western Europe last summer not to make the mistake of 'trusting' us. Some of our distinguished colleagues seem bent on proving how right he was."

Ambassador Douglas radioed from London that the House action would result in "additional doubts concerning assurances which Western Europe can place on the reliability and consistency of the United States." New "apprehensions" in France were cited. British Foreign Minister Bevin warned that the action would aggravate fears in Western Europe.

Something had to be done. Breaking with tradition, Vandenberg appealed to the Senate Appropriations Committee for an opportunity to appear before it to protest the House action. It was only a few days before the Republican National Convention at Philadelphia. Some thought the fight over the cut might precipitate an all-out isolationist versus internationalist fight at the convention, and thus perhaps drive Vandenberg, no matter how unwillingly, into the race for the nomination.

In a tense session of the Senate Appropriations Committee Vandenberg made a scorching assault on what he termed the "meat-axe approach" of the Taber group. The cut, he testified, "guts the enterprise" and would "veto" the will of Congress. The House action would brand American policies before the world as "capricious, unreliable and impotent."

Breaking with Congressional tradition against criticizing in one Chamber the action of the other, Vandenberg lashed out with all the strength at his command. It was an angry, impassioned appearance, far transcending in drama any debate over the project on the Senate floor. While granting the Congressional power of review over appropriations, Vandenberg held that by indirection the House sought to repeal the "intent and purpose" of the basic legislation, and to "reverse" American foreign policy as established by Congress itself.

June 9, 1948

I do mean to argue that this Congress, as a matter of intelligent self-interest, cannot afford to throw our attitudes into doubt and thus to multiply the terrified confusion of a world in which the forces of aggression and subversion thrive upon confusion. We must not feed the very fires we would put out.

I do mean to argue that any such cynical reversal would be a major policy decision which should not be made through the back door of an appropriation bill. Indeed, it should not be made at all. . . .

I do not believe that America can afford to be unreliable in a world which is groping for confidence and faith as the basis of security and peace. I would be the last to say that the . . . figures are untouchable. But I do quarrel, Mr. Chairman, with any reductions which subvert the principles and purposes of the original Congressional commitment.

I respectfully submit that, for our own sakes, we dare not deal with this vital problem in the life of the world, including us, in any such cavalier fashion. There is too much at stake. I respectfully submit that any such action is calculated to change the character of ECA from "recovery" to "relief" alone — thus plunging us back into the dreary, hopeless, sterile and utterly costly routines which we must escape.

I respectfully submit that any such action reverses the overwhelming intent of Congress registered two short months ago; and nullifies the Senate's own action in refusing, on a roll call vote, to hack off a comparable arbitrary billion from the original authority. . . . Most desperately important of all, Mr. Chairman, it "keeps the word of the promise to the ear but breaks it to the hope." I respectfully submit that it inevitably undermines that confidence and morale abroad upon which recovery, independent freedoms and peace so heavily lean; and that it serves the alien critics who plot to have these peace plans fail.

[He said that future study, once the program got underway, would disclose] how goes this battle for peace and freedom in which we have such a colossal stake. Then we can make an intelligent audit. We can act without irresponsibility.

Until then I beg of you — for the sake of the hopes by which free men live — that you give ECA a fair chance. Its mere creation already has paid heavy dividends. I ask it for what I believe to be the national interest of our own United States.

Vandenberg's deeply emotional appeal moved the Senate to stand behind him. Most of the funds were restored, the program was saved from an abortive death, and free Europe with American aid and real hope for the future could begin the struggle toward economic recovery.

All in all the ECA was an example of bipartisan foreign policy at its best. With a Republican-controlled Congress and the Administration in the hands of the Democrats anything might have happened. Under such circumstances one might have expected the two parties to divide sharply over an issue of this magnitude. But with the existence of the free world at stake, they joined hands in constructing one of the most complex and far-reaching programs ever designed by a government. Nor did this teamwork end with the Eightieth Congress. After he retired as Chairman of the Foreign Relations Committee, Vandenberg continued to fight for the program he had helped build. It was this continuing support which the Senator and other Republicans gave to the ECA — perhaps as much as any other factor — that enabled the agency to make such a successful record of accomplishment.

21

The Vandenberg Resolution:
"Within the Charter But Outside the Veto"

IN APRIL, 1948, even before the Marshall Plan had been enacted into law by Congress, it was clear that political stability and economic recovery in Western Europe required a good deal more than American-dollar aid. The Russians had challenged the Marshall Plan concept by the Cominform's bristling threats and Molotov's angry denunciations. Much more ominous was the action of the Soviets on March 1, when they snapped on a communication, transportation, and trade blockade against Berlin in an effort to sever that city from the West's occupation zones in Germany. The squeeze was on in a supreme effort to push the Western nations out of Berlin, and for the next fifteen months world peace hung in the balance.

Elsewhere, too, the Communist threat was growing. The last vestige of independence had been eradicated in Czechoslovakia, and new Soviet pressure was brought on Finland and less directly on the remainder of the Scandinavian peninsula. Greece, despite American aid, continued under heavy attack by Communists supported across the borders from satellite states, and there were new Communist efforts to seize power in France and Italy.

At the United Nations Russia had cast some twenty-three vetoes, virtually paralyzing the Security Council's work. American concern over this grave situation was reflected in Congress by introduction of a number of resolutions intended to strengthen the United Nations, but some of which in practice might well have torn the organization apart. These included proposals for federalization of Western Europe, world government, a United States of Europe, an international army, elimination of the veto in punishing aggressors, full-scale redrafting of the Charter, and an immediate bid for world disarmament. The lobbying activities of important private organizations had lined up almost half the Senate membership behind one or another of these reform proposals. It all added up to a period of foreboding and confusion regarding the future of the United Nations.

But, of greatest immediate concern as the Communists intensified their operations was a ghastly realization on the part of State and Defense Department officials that Western Europe and, for that matter, the United States were in a position of relative military impotency in the face of Russian arms. The Western occupying powers in Germany individually and collectively lacked the strength even to parry a Russian blow; the Western European nations individually and collectively represented a military vacuum with the American atomic bomb serving as the main deterring factor against possible aggression from the East.

Facing this crisis, Britain, France, Belgium, the Netherlands, and Luxembourg signed a fifty-year Western Union treaty of collective military and economic co-operation at Brussels in March of 1948. On the day the treaty was signed President Truman told Congress, "I am sure that the determination of the free countries of Europe to protect themselves will be matched by an equal determination on our part to help them do so." But this Western Union represented little more than a sketchy hope; the arms with which the Union could confront Russia were pitiable. Some far more drastic action was essential.

Vandenberg saw the basic problem as that of strengthening the United Nations without destroying it. As early as September, 1947, he had written a Michigan friend:

September 19, 1947
I can fully understand the pessimism about the United Nations which has taken possession of many of our people. It would be both silly and dangerous to ignore the worsening relationships between Moscow and Washington. But there is a way to circumvent the deadly "veto" — as we demon-

strated at Rio [the agreement on regional collective self-defense among the American nations]. There are many other ways to keep the United Nations vigorously alive for essential service even under adverse circumstances. If there were no United Nations today there would be no hope today. This is the simplest possible way of saying that the U.N. must be sustained and strengthened.

By the spring of 1948 — with the Marshall Plan being hammered into shape — he wrote in answer to an inquiry as to whether Russian aggression against the United States was to be expected:

April 6, 1948

I do not know how anybody can dependably prophesy what the Moscow Politburo will do in respect to aggression or in respect to actual war. Under such circumstances, I do not see how anyone can dependably prophesy our own American attitude — except to say that honorable peace is our overriding objective if we are permitted to pursue it. . . .

I have no doubt that Soviet Russia would be very glad to scrupulously avoid direct aggression upon the United States if we are content to let her go without challenge in direct aggression upon everybody else. But I am sure you will agree that our own self-interest could not permit us to complacently await our isolation in a Communist world. On the other hand, I would entirely agree that we must proceed with extreme prudence in assessing indirect aggression.

In the same month he wrote to another constituent:

April 14, 1948

I agree with you that the United Nations must be used in every possible way to create collective security through peaceful means. The great fundamental difficulty is that practically all our American efforts in these directions are aggressively opposed by Soviet Russia and her satellites. This is true in the United Nations where we are constantly met by a Russian veto. It is true in connection with our economic recovery programs. In the case of the European program, for example, the Soviet states immediately met together in Yugoslavia and publicly announced their purpose to "wreck" these economic programs. . . . We cannot hope for peace through appeasement of Russia because appeasement merely multiplies the Soviet contempt for our American attitudes. But I continue to believe that there must be a way by which through friendly firmness we can find a way to "live and let live" in honorable peace.

The Senator did not lose his faith, and in reply to a critic of the United Nations he wrote: "I may be wrong. No one can sanely say 'I know the answers' in these fluxing days of global crisis. But . . . despite all its infirmities (chiefly due to the fact that it has been required to 'run' before it had even learned to 'walk') I have the deep conviction that the world would be infinitely worse off if the U.N. had not been functioning during the last two years."

He elaborated this idea in another letter:

April 22, 1948

I continue to believe that the United Nations offers the best nucleus around which to build international peace and security. Its chief trouble up to date has been the fact that it has been called upon to face major emergencies before it has had a chance even to complete its organization and its mechanisms. . . . I do not believe that Americans are ready to give up their sovereignty in respect to decisions which would take us into war. But I am very sure we are prepared to waive any "veto" upon the pacific settlement of international disputes and I shall continue to work to this end. In the light of existing difficulties under the relatively limited objectives of the United Nations, I am unable to believe that it is in any degree feasible to seek unitary *world Government*. Furthermore, I do not believe that the United States can best serve either its own destiny or the cause of world peace by any such surrender of its independent identity or its free leadership for human rights and fundamental freedoms.

In view of his conviction that an answer to the Russian attitude must be found within the United Nations, Vandenberg took another look at Article 51 of the Charter — an article that he had been instrumental in developing at San Francisco in 1945. Article 51 made clear that nothing in the Charter shall impair the "inherent right of individual and collective self defense if an armed attack occurs," and until the Security Council had taken measures to maintain peace. In addition Articles 52, 53, and 54 of the Charter permitted the existence of regional arrangements for dealing with problems of international peace and security, and the Rio de Janeiro Conference of Western Hemisphere nations had drafted a hemispheric defense treaty under these articles. This sequence of events was assuming more importance in Vandenberg's mind as he noted when he wrote to Nelson Rockefeller on April 28, 1949, that Article 51 was becoming

> the key provision so far as effective hope for organized peace is concerned. I would not be surprised to see it ultimately used as the basis for a complete reorganization of the United Nations inside the Charter and outside the veto. The fact of the matter is that Article 51 has assumed such prominence that I have found it advisable to make a very careful study of its genealogy and I intend to make a speech on the subject in the near future. What will particularly interest you is the fact that I shall identify the hour of its birth as being at that famous dinner party in your hotel room in San Francisco where you were the host and I was the only guest; but where — before the evening was done — we called in the Cuban Ambassador [Guillermo Belt] and the Colombian Foreign Minister [Alberto Lleras Camargo] and sent the note to Stettinius which launched Article 51 upon its potent and significant career.

Again he emphasized his dissatisfaction with the veto arrangements that often made the UN impotent when he commented on a Congressional Resolution that proposed to retain the veto so far as Charter provisions dealing with the pacific settlement of disputes were concerned, but which would seek to remove the Security Council veto over the sterner possibilities of sanctions, including the use of force. He wrote:

April 21, 1948

The United Nations veto should be sharply restricted. Our own government is already moving for its elimination in connection with 32 articles of the United Nations Charter . . . [but] I am frank to say that from my point of view this resolution is entirely unsatisfactory. It would retain the veto on all of the Charter provisions for the pacific settlement of international disputes. It would remove the veto only in case of armed aggression when it would allow others to tell us when we must go to war. It would not "push Russia out of the UN." It would push us out of the UN and leave it exclusively to Russia and her satellites. I do not think this is the proper approach.

The process of finding the "proper approach" involved an unusual and happy collaboration between Vandenberg and Robert A. Lovett, then General Marshall's Undersecretary of State. The two men were already good friends, and Lovett not infrequently called at apartment 500 G, the Vandenberg suite at the Wardman Park Hotel, to talk informally about State Department problems. Now, as they set out to draft a resolution that would define the position of the United States in regard to increasing threats to world peace, this informal collaboration was intensified. For three or four weeks Lovett often stopped at apartment 500 G for an hour after leaving the Department of State in early evening. Sometimes on Sundays the meetings were prolonged; sometimes Vandenberg would try out ideas on his portable typewriter. Essentially the drafting work was left to Vandenberg and Lovett, but Marshall was kept in daily touch with what the three men called "the 500 G meetings."

Vandenberg and his younger collaborator had in common a deep sense of realism, as well as purpose. Lovett understood only too well the desperate need for firm American defense support of our jittery allies in Western Europe. Vandenberg was highly aware that the best laid plans could die a-borning as a result of a hasty move and a subsequent rebuff in Congress. Both men shared deeply-ingrained characteristics of loyalty, devotion to principles, and a saving subsurface sense of humor. Lovett, writing to Vandenberg as he left the State Department in January, 1949, said of the relationships: "If a man is very lucky he has an opportunity once in his life to serve a good cause with men of singleness of purpose, integrity and complete understanding, and with friends whom he both admires and loves. I have had that experience with you and the General [Marshall]. . . ."

Vandenberg, for his part, was at the apex of his power. He was the acknowledged Republican foreign policy spokesman in Congress, Chairman of the Senate Foreign Relations Committee, and, as Senate President pro tem, in a strong tactical position with respect to legislative matters.

Lovett has recalled to the editor of this book that the first and perhaps most difficult task was the definition of the problems to be faced, and an estimate of what could be done practically to meet them. The problems soon were reduced primarily to: (1) formal expression by the Senate in favor of removing the United Nations veto from all questions involving the pacific settlement of disputes and the admission of new members to UN; and (2) a mechanism through which the United States could proceed to the support of such regional and collective arrangements as the Western Union Treaty signed at Brussels. Lovett and his staff experts, with co-operation of the staff of the Foreign Relations Committee, went to work on the problem and came up with several draft resolutions, the preferred draft running to three or four pages. Vandenberg and Lovett, however, agreed that it was much too long and should be boiled down to a single page of easily understood objectives. "We can say all we want to say in one page," Vandenberg insisted.

The work was carried forward privately and quietly in the hotel suite, over the telephone and occasionally in Vandenberg's office just off the Senate floor. During the final stages Washington got a few hints of what was impending. Vandenberg told a Michigan Chamber of Commerce group meeting in Washington on April 27 that: "We would strengthen and revitalize the United Nations which is still the world's greatest peace potential despite the terrific strains which have been put upon it before it has even yet been allowed, thanks to Russian intransigence, to perfect its contemplated peace machinery. We have not yet scratched the surface of the possibilities of its regional arrangements, as exemplified in the Rio treaty. There can be vital progress in this procedure — and I venture to predict there will."

About this time, the Senator told his Foreign Relations Committee colleagues of his work on a new resolution and said that he was determined that the various resolutions for reform of the United Nations were not going to be relegated to "a cold storage plant." He expressed belief that neither the Senate nor the country would be satisfied with a do-nothing attitude and said he believed a single, satisfactory resolution could be offered in the Senate.

In late April, Lovett and Vandenberg met with Marshall, Dulles, and other top Congressional leaders and the high military command. To avoid the goldfish-bowl characteristics of a full dress conference at the State Department the meeting was held at Blair House, the official government residence across the street from the White House.

At the Blair House meeting Vandenberg fished inside his coat pocket and pulled out a preliminary draft of the resolution he had worked over for days with Lovett. Dulles, hearing the single-page resolution for the first time and not realizing the hours of labor that had gone into its preparation, was amazed by the simple and effective language in which every word seemed to say something vital. It was a document that Dulles was to compare to the Monroe Doctrine as a landmark in American diplomacy.

On May 11 the final drafting was completed. Lovett later said that the draft largely was in Vandenberg's phraseology and written on his own typewriter. The result was a Senate resolution advising the President to seek security for the free world through United States support of mutual defense arrangements to operate within the UN Charter but outside the Security Council veto. It also advised the President to attempt to strengthen the Charter through curbs on the veto itself and by providing a United Nations police force together with the regulation and reduction of armaments under dependable guaranty against violation. The text, as finally adopted by the Senate, read:

Whereas peace with justice and the defense of human rights and fundamental freedoms require international cooperation through more effective use of the United Nations: therefore be it

Resolved, that the Senate reaffirm the policy of the United States to achieve international peace and security through the United Nations so that armed force shall not be used except in the common interest, and that the President be advised of the sense of the Senate that this government, by constitutional process, should particularly pursue the following objectives within the United Nations Charter:

(1) Voluntary agreement to remove the veto from all questions involving pacific settlements of international disputes and situations, and from the admission of new members.

(2) Progressive development of regional and other collective arrangements for individual and collective self-defense in accordance with the purposes, principles, and provisions of the Charter.

(3) Association of the United States by constitutional process, with such regional and other collective arrangements as are based on continuous and effective self-help and mutual aid, and as affect its national security.

(4) Contributing to the maintenance of peace by making clear its determination to exercise the right of individual or collective self-defense under Article 51 should any armed attack occur affecting its national security.

(5) Maximum efforts to obtain agreements to provide the United Nations with armed forces as provided by the Charter, and to obtain agreement among member nations upon universal regulation and reduction of armaments under adequate and dependable guaranty against violation.

(6) If necessary, after adequate effort toward strengthening the United Nations, review of the Charter at an appropriate time by a General Conference called under Article 109 or by the General Assembly.

Vandenberg told the Foreign Relations Committee that the various other Senate resolutions concerning the United Nations could be dangerous. The mere introduction of one of the proposals had "raised unshirted hell in France," he recalled, because it proposed that France assume a secondary position in establishment of an international army. His new resolution was designed to indicate the best approach to the over-all problem, he said, and to strengthen the world organization while avoiding the extremes of some of the earlier proposals. Of greatest importance, however, was the intent of the resolution to associate the United States with collective-defense arrangements, especially in Western Europe. The Senator emphasized that American support would be governed by American self-interest and based on principles of "continuous and effective self-help" on the part of the other participating nations in much the same pattern as the Marshall Plan had established.

In three long committee sessions the resolution was reviewed word by word. Paragraphs one, two, and three commanded almost exclusive attention and most of the committee discussion — all of it held behind closed doors — dealt with insistence on the part of senators that automatic commitments be avoided and that actual implementation of the advisory resolution be submitted to Congress for a final determination. Vandenberg and Lovett were able to reassure the Committee on this score, and on May 19 the Foreign Relations Committee by another 13 to 0 vote approved the Vandenberg Resolution — Senate Resolution 239 was its official title — and sent it to the Senate floor for consideration.

On June 11 Vandenberg called the resolution up in the Senate. It was during the closing days of a long session; many senators were involved in last minute committee work and the debate was brief and somewhat desultory. Vandenberg made a ten-minute statement describing the resolution, and then submitted to lengthy questioning mostly from Senators Claude Pepper of Florida, Eugene D. Millikin of Colorado, Kenneth S. Wherry of Nebraska, Arthur V. Watkins of Utah, and J. William Fulbright of Arkansas. He told the Senate:

June 11, 1948

This resolution is a sound answer to several critical necessities in respect of foreign policy which America confronts. It is the unanimous answer of the Senate Foreign Relations

Committee. It is an answer which, after many weeks of earnest consultation, has the wholehearted approval of the State Department. It is an answer which offers new hope for security and peace for us and others, through the United Nations.

What are the necessities which this Resolution is undertaking to answer? The first necessity is this: recognizing the indispensability of the United Nations as the key to collective security, many Senators have earnestly joined in numerous Senate Resolutions proposing new United Nations patterns for a surer collective warrant of just and dependable peace.... We believe the pending resolution is today's best answer to this need.

The second necessity which we have confronted in this connection, Mr. President, is this: up and down this peace-living land, which harbors no thought of conquest against any other power on earth, our people have looked with singular anxiety upon the often unhappy vicissitudes of the scarred United Nations, too often stranded on the veto rocks. They have groped for light with a sense of frustration amid a confusion of well meaning advice. It is a tribute to their instincts that the infirmities of the United Nations have served only to intensify their zeal in its behalf. It is a tribute to their wisdom that they sense its fundamental unity as the only base upon which to build the hopes by which we live. They are entitled to the practical encouragement which this resolution provides.

The third necessity, Mr. President, is this: facing the grim reality that peace may fail through the acts of others, Congress is concurrently driven by prudence to rebuild the minimums of national armed defense in the presence of possible aggression which might sneer at any arguments save those of force. At such a moment it is necessary that the same Congress, if faithful to the spirit of America, should simultaneously renew its relentless dedication to collective peace....

It is necessary to make it plain that we are not preoccupied with bombs and bayonets. It is necessary to make it plain to our own people and to the world that we continue to give unequivocal priority to peace cooperations through a peace fraternity that works. Another war will never be our fault.

This resolution, Mr. President, is the sturdy answer to any misunderstandings upon this score.

There is a fourth and final necessity which we have sought to answer through this resolution. We are embarking upon tremendous efforts to help others to help themselves into economic convalescence which follows independent strength and whatever makes for healthy peace for all nations, America included.

Pending this blessed outcome, it is inevitable that related questions of physical security should arise. This results and has resulted in immediate speculation abroad and at home regarding our American role in this collective-security base. The pending Resolution is the responsible answer, so far as Congress can presently foresee. . . .

. . . it is a plan for our practical American cooperation under specified circumstances, within the framework of the United Nations. It is an answer which encourages individual and collective self-defense against armed aggression within the Charter and outside the veto. It asserts our interest in regional arrangements, specifically invited by the Charter, as a means to renew its effectiveness for peace. It declares our willingness to consider by due Constitutional process our own cooperation, in one way or another, with such regional arrangements, if and when we conclude that our own national interests are involved. But it warns that self-help and mutual aid are prerequisites. Our cooperation must be a supplement and not a substitute for the adequate and continuous defensive activities of others. It is a paraphrase of the Rio treaty which the Senate overwhelmingly approved. It is a plan to make the Charter work in behalf of individual and collective self-defense against armed aggression. It is a potential power for peace. It is another forward move in the indispensable pattern of collective security for us and for others. It never steps outside the United Nations Charter. It never steps outside the Constitution of the United States. It never steps outside the final authority of the Congress. But it steps constructively and hopefully toward a better and a safer world. . . .

The Senate rejected, 61 to 6, a Pepper amendment to strike from the resolution all reference to the possibility of American military aid. And, after eight hours of consideration in a single day of debate, the Senate approved the Vandenberg Resolution, 64 to 6. It is probable that never before in a single day of Senate debate was such a history-making policy underwritten in Congress, one which held out to the non-communist world a prospect of military comradeship, formulated in peace and designed to avoid war, but also to meet war if it came. Less than one month later, Lovett sat down at the State Department with the ambassadors of Canada, Britain, France, Belgium, the Netherlands, and the Luxembourg Minister to begin preliminary discussions that led eventually to the North Atlantic Treaty. Rarely in our nation's history has such a small egg hatched so quickly into such a large chicken.

One who reads the *Congressional Record* of June 11, may well wonder whether some members of the Senate were fully aware of the far-reaching action they were taking on that occasion. The language of the Vandenberg resolution was general — perhaps even a bit vague — and it was impossible to know exactly what the framers had in mind. Vandenberg hastened to reassure his colleagues, both in his remarks on the Senate floor, and in the report he submitted on behalf of the Committee, that the commitments involved in the resolution were limited in scope. On this particular point the Committee report stated that: "The resolution has been designed to avoid open-ended or unlimited commitments and to require reciprocity of aid. The committee is convinced that the three limitations specified in paragraph 3 adequately protect the interests of the United States. These are (1) that United States association must be by constitutional process, (2) that it shall be only with arrangements based on continuous and effective self-help and mutual aid, and (3) that the arrangement be one affecting our national security."

The establishment of the Marshall Plan and the approval of

the Vandenberg Resolution meant a long step forward in the Senator's goal of maintaining the United Nations and of bolstering the free nations against Communist expansion. His correspondence in the following months explained these moves to inquiring constituents and took up various aspects of the broad problem of relations with Russia.

September 27, 1948
   I hope it will not be forgotten that ECA started from scratch about July 1st. It has been working about 90 days. . . . The first 90 days of a four year plan can scarcely test its potentialities. . . . There is something else to remember — I respectfully submit. The utility of ECA is not to be measured exclusively in terms of "currencies" or "commodities" or generally by an economic yardstick. The purpose of ECA is always and forever psychological. It is worth all it costs — at the moment — if it helps keep independent Governments in Western Europe alive and moving forward in united opposition to the Soviet menace which is primarily a menace (when all is said and done) against the United States of America. I hesitate to think how much greater this menace to us would be at this moment if it were not for 90 days of ECA. . . . In my view, ECA is worth more than battalions or battleships in this utterly critical hour of "calculated risks."

Three days later he replied to a constituent who had suggested that the Senator's publicly expressed views were against outlawing the Communist party in the United States:

September 30, 1948
   You will recall that I said Communism in America is not a "party" but a "conspiracy against the government." It inevitably follows that the "conspiracy" is far greater than the "party." In other words, I dealt with domestic Communism as a whole and not with the much narrower subject of the Communist Party. . . . The Party, as a participant in our elections, is of no great importance in respect to the results at the polls. The important thing is the day-to-day subversion of our national life by Communist sabotage which

"WITHIN THE CHARTER BUT OUTSIDE THE VETO" 413

enlists far broader support not only from the "Party" but from "fellow travellers" and from a certain type of so-called "Liberalism" which we might charitably say is too fuzzy to appreciate its own tragic blunders. Furthermore it is, of course, an axiom that if we wiped the Communist Party off of every ballot in the land we would not have destroyed communism and its "conspiracy." We probably would have driven it further underground (where it likes to be and where it flourishes).

But, in a sense, you have the right to say that this begs the question. So, let's go a step farther. I recognize the validity of the argument that there is something which seems to be inconsistent in "fighting the Communist conspiracy tooth and nail," on the one hand, and in admitting the Communist Party to our official ballots on the other hand. Frankly, I have heretofore leaned to this view. So I can fully appreciate the spirit in which you have written.

But, I respectfully submit that we must consult realities before we take our final position. . . . In terms of reality I submit that your question becomes this: "Do we strengthen our battle against the conspiracy by outlawing the Party?" Governor Dewey's answer — out of long experience as a law officer — is "No." That does not make him any less a "tooth and nail opponent" of the "conspiracy." My own final answer (which, again frankly, I am not prepared to give until all the facts are officially explored) will be largely influenced by the recommendations of Mr. J. Edgar Hoover and the FBI upon which we must depend for our active defense against the conspiracy. It is my understanding (I may be wrong) that their answer also will be "No." In other words, there may be a better way to accomplish what you and I desire.

There is always a case to be made for "free speech" and "free ballots" whether we like the way in which these liberties are used or not. There is no case to be made in defense of the Communist conspiracy. Nor can the former be pleaded in behalf of the latter. Let's be sure we get the right answers.

One thing more. If and when our Supreme Court finds that the "Party" is committed as a "Party," to the "conspiracy" to over-throw this government by force, there ceases to be any further argument. The Party would thus automatically become an "outlaw." This question has never been conclusively determined. It ought to be. This is the basic simplification that we need.

In a letter to Senator Ralph E. Flanders, Vandenberg commented on a speech by Flanders and said:

December 6, 1948

Certainly I agree that our case against Russia should always be based on her "emergence as a predatory imperialist power" and not on her Communism (except when the latter implements the former). I have always tried to draw that line — always saying that her Communism is her own business (so long as she doesn't insist upon making it ours). I have always said that my aim is a "live and let live" world.

Certainly I agree that we should smack down the Russkies more effectively in our speeches in the UN Council and Assembly. This situation is a definite weakness. Our spokesmen are much too gentlemanly and homiletical. We lack Vishinsky's opposite number. I plunk with you for "curt decisiveness" mixed with "derision." But (after 216 days across from Mr. Molotov in 1946) I fear I lack your confidence that these Reds would be abashed. Nonetheless, we should gain from adequate oral belligerence. But I would keep it oral. And I think perhaps I find greater value than you do in just "keeping the talking going" — because when we are still talking things out we are not shooting them out. . . .

I do not agree that we are "losing the cold war — definitely losing it on the economic front." I think we are winning it. Indeed, it is for this very reason that I can agree most emphatically that it is possible to "shift from the tactics of a besieged army to that of one waging a successful offensive." . . . I add only the admonition that we do not try to go too far too fast in building regional unities within the UN.

Vandenberg summarized his views on collective security and on the Vandenberg Resolution in a lengthy letter to Senator Lodge. Lodge had asked for comment on a statement by a group of distinguished Massachusetts citizens in regard to limited world government, and was answered:

December 11, 1948

I can completely sympathize with the objective viewpoint presented by the statement you submit to me. We are not making headway fast enough toward a world regime of compulsory peace — although we must tune our impatience to the fact that the United Nations thus far has had only three years in which to overtake and subdue world habits that are centuries old. The practical question is — how can we make progress faster and more dependably?

Can it be done by striving toward some degree of "world government" which forbids the powers to engage in wars? Of course there is nothing to be gained by ignoring realities in searching an answer. It seems to me the realities are that if we cannot get Soviet and satellite cooperation in making the far more limited controls of the United Nations work, or until we do, we could not reasonably expect Soviet cooperation in the conclusive controls of "world government." That looks like an axiom. Therefore, the question really boils down to this: are we ready to organize the world without the Russians, which is to say, against one-sixth of the world which is Russian-controlled? This one-sixth may soon become nearer one-fourth if China falls.

As I shall presently indicate, I am ready to face that overall question under appropriate circumstances. But I am not willing to precipitate it. I want to exhaust more feasible alternatives which I shall identify first. Except as a last resort I do not want deliberately and now to make this a two-world earth and perhaps to make inevitable final war between the two. In other words, it seems to me that your friends have over-simplified their problem. They propose limited world government under which "the power to engage in wars shall be rigidly forbidden by a system of world law." But if their "world government" can not be universal, and clearly it can't at present, then their "world government" surely must become a defensive alliance for war if necessary against the recalcitrants. In other words, it is impossible for anybody to accept "rigid forbiddance" of war unless everybody accepts. Of course, it would be impossible even for us to accept without a Constitutional amendment. Furthermore, even if the Russians did accept, what good is their word in the absence of automatic discipline against bad faith? And again — an ordinance against war is wholly inadequate as a defense against aggression because Soviet aggression depends upon many other devices than war. Indeed "war" is the last implement they want to invoke.

The necessary limitations of a letter make it impossible for me adequately to sustain my case against any present attempt at any degree of "world government" — although I should love to live in a world in which the power to engage in aggression, which is vastly more than the power to engage in wars, would be "rigidly forbidden by a system of world law" — to quote the document you have sent to me.

But this does not mean that we are impotent to move in this Christian direction. On the contrary, we are moving toward this objective but by a different and, if I may say so, more practicable route. I take it that your distinguished petitioners recognize the United Nations in this respect because they frankly assert their loyalty to the UN — adding "but we recognize its grave defects, particularly through the big-power veto and lack of effective police force."

Very good. Now we come to grips with realities. Is not the logical thing for friends of the United Nations to do to tackle these "grave defects" and to see whether something cannot be done about them? At least, should we not exhaust these possibilities before we undertake a new international revolution?

I assert that, to all practical intents and purposes, we can escape the dead hand of the veto, always Russian, and the lack of police equipment, prevented by the Russians, and yet, at the same time, we can live strictly within the literal terms of the United Nations Charter. I assert that this is the objective of Senate Resolution 239 — adopted last summer by a vote of 64 to 4 in the Senate. . . . It is now in process of implementation. I respectfully suggest that the immediate objective of your distinguished correspondents should be their unqualified support of this practical and presently available program.

[Vandenberg pointed out to Lodge that the Vandenberg Resolution stayed within the UN Charter by invoking Article 51 and Chapter VIII to organize regional arrangements and that, if a veto interfered with appropriate Security Council action, the nations banded together in a regional arrangement could act in concert to defeat aggression.]

This is what we have done in the Rio pact in respect to our western world. This is what is contemplated by the "North Atlantic Community." There is no limit to the possibilities. If worse comes to worst, we can organize the whole world of peace-loving nations on this basis — always within the Charter, always outside the veto. If the Russkies wish to join — o.k. If not, they have outlawed themselves.

I, too, am guilty of over-simplification in this statement of the case. But the realities are obvious. My plea is that we deal with realities — and not with wishful thinking, no matter how nobly meditated. . . .

I am sure your distinguished friends will receive these observations in the spirit in which they are written. I am not quarreling with their high-minded ideals. On the contrary, I share them. But "ideals" alone are not enough; and I respectfully submit that this is a time for us to be intensely realistic in mobilizing the presently available forces of peace in behalf of free men and free states in a free world.

Although at that time the collective security problems claimed primary attention, the Senator subsequently urged President Truman to emphasize the Resolution's provisions for limitation on use of the veto curbs and for arms reduction. It was Dulles and Secretary of State Dean Acheson who later carried this fight by working for expansion of the General Assembly's authority in order to curb the veto power in connection with admittance of new members and pacific settlement of disputes.

Concurrently with negotiation of the Atlantic Pact, particularly early in 1949 when Norway and Denmark entered the negotiations despite strong Russian pressure, the subject of American arms shipments became of great importance. Vandenberg was informed by an American official in Paris that French officials indicated that the prospect of such shipments played an important role in their attitude toward the Pact. The Senator sought to counteract what he regarded as a dangerous trend toward overemphasis of an arms assistance program at the sacrifice of broader principles embraced in the Vandenberg Resolution.

Commenting to Harry M. Robbins, Secretary of the Detroit Committee on Foreign Relations, regarding a questionnaire on the Vandenberg Resolution that had been circulated to the Committee membership, Vandenberg wrote:

December 9, 1948

I *hope* those who answer will have in mind the *full* significance of that Resolution. I comment on this phase later on. The explanations on the questionnaire largely (and probably with justification) confine themselves to the subject of whether we shall implement foreign *economic* aid with foreign *military* aid. Indeed, these explanations frankly raise the issue whether "the Vandenberg Resolution implies a moral commitment on the part of the United States" in this direction.

In my opinion, there is *no commitment* of any nature in the Resolution because the Resolution repeatedly refers to procedures "by *Constitutional process*" — which means that Congress reserved to itself complete freedom of action in respect to developments; and this freedom was abundantly spelled out in the debates. In other words, while the Resolution clearly intends to point out what it believes to be desirable areas of *exploration* (and to that extent indicates our hospitality toward such efforts), the right of free and independent decision is equally clearly reserved. I hope, therefore, that when your members answer this series of questions, they will do so entirely on the basis of *merit* (or otherwise) and *not* under any *moral* duress which might flow from the presumption of even a tentative obligation.

I *hope* also that those who answer will have in mind the importance of S. Res. 239 — to my mind the *paramount* importance — which is *not* touched in the questionnaire's explanations. This is it. It is a new formula under which the United Nations Charter can be *made to work without* Charter amendments which manifestly are unattainable under existing UN circumstances and membership.

The procedure contemplated by S. Res. 239 is the extended use of "Regional Arrangements" (specifically invited by the Charter) and Article 51 (spelled out in the Charter itself). The "Rio Pact" is a *working model.* It is a formula which faithfully lives *within* the Charter but *outside the veto.* It permits congenial nations with common interests in peace and security to defend *themselves* (as you know) *"until the Security Council has taken the measures necessary to maintain international peace and security."* That single word "until" is the key to everything. "Until" covers the whole time if, as and when the Security Council is deadlocked. *Yet* the Security Council can instantly resume jurisdiction whenever it is prepared to "take the *necessary* measures."

What I am trying to say, for whatever it may be worth to you, is that the thing of top importance in S. Res. 239 is *not* a trend toward "military assistance" (although I would be the last to ignore it) but it is a device to *unlock the United Nations.*

Your 8th, 9th and 10th questions raise issues about the nature, kind and extent of our "military assistance" to Western Europe. I am sure your members will all understand that there is no proposal to put a joint military machine into present physical being, if I understand the matter, except at a *planning and equipment level.* The purpose is to provide *available potentialities* (to which we would undoubtedly be required to make equipment available in a considerable degree). These "potentialities," however, would never be used except under the terms of the Charter and within its jurisdiction. In other words, this is *not* a "military alliance" in the usual connotation of that phrase.

In another letter written at the same time, the Senator added in regard to regional associations: "Here we can move *outside* the veto. We have done so in the 'Rio Pact' which makes North, Central and South America an autonomous security zone (strictly within the invitation and the jurisdiction of the UN Charter). We shall do the same thing if we succeed in perfecting the proposed 'Atlantic Community Regional Arrangement.' This does not 'amend the Charter.' But it can accomplish most of our peace and security objectives *within* the Charter."

22

On Not Running for President

AS THE 1948 national election campaign warmed up, Vandenberg discovered that it was sometimes even more difficult *not* to run for the presidential nomination than it was to run for the job. Almost nobody would believe his repeated declarations that he was not a candidate. "This business of not running for President is a tough one — if you really mean it," he noted in his diary later. "Perhaps it's because even your best friends feel about it as did the little boy when he saw his first giraffe and said — 'There ain't no such animal.'"

The campaign to put Vandenberg in the White House, regardless of his own views, was remarkable if only for the fact that he was the "internationalists'" candidate, whereas only eight years earlier he had been the outstanding "isolationist" candidate. The boom for him began immediately after his overwhelming victory in the 1946 senatorial election race in Michigan. But not with Vandenberg's consent. "As for 1948 — forget it," he wrote to a friend on November 15 immediately after the 1946 election. "My name has been on a ballot for the last time. I am sick and tired of the 'wear and tear' — and particularly of being maligned, although I suppose I have been amazingly lucky in the latter matter. . . ."

He flatly told reporters that he was not a candidate and, early in 1947, in a speech to the Michigan State Republican Convention at Grand Rapids he repeated his renunciation. But he kept on climbing in the newspaper presidential polls. In March he tried a new technique, writing an unsolicited letter to *Life* for publication. In a wryly humorous vein, he wrote:

I think it is harder *not to run for President* than it is *to run!*

I have tried both. Down to date, neither enterprise has been a success. But in comparing the adventure, I rather think the former is more troublesome than the latter.

I was a candidate for the Republican nomination in Philadelphia in 1940. I was honored with a high score of 72 votes on the third ballot. On the eve of the convention I had prophesied that I would be nominated on the sixth ballot. I named the right ballot but the wrong winner. It was Willkie on the sixth. It all passed off quite painlessly. I simply breezed out with Willkie's blitz — and that was that.

Now, here's the difference. I am *not* a candidate for the nomination in 1948. I do *not* expect to be nominated on the sixth or any other ballot. This is not a temporary stall. This is not pre-convention strategy. It is an absolutely honest statement of my feeling and my wish. But what happens?

[Vandenberg wrote humorously in the letter of his troubles in convincing his newspaper friends that he actually meant that he was not running. He admitted that some of his previous statements had been "pretty cryptic." He then wrote:]

Let's see if I can put it in unmistakable language.

I am not a candidate.

I do not expect to be a candidate.

I shall seek no convention delegates nor approve the efforts of others in this behalf.

I think my place of service is in filling out my tenure in the Senate.

Of course, I would yield to a spontaneous draft (if that hypothesis must be included) because I do not believe any citizen has a right to deny service to his country if and when his service is demanded. But another good journalistic friend of mine, Frank Kent, once proved to me that no presidential nominee is ever drafted unless he connives at it.

I shall not connive.

I am sure, however, that this categorical statement will not assuage the difficulties in *not running for President* because if I am at long last believed, some critics will swiftly rise to say: "It's just as well; he couldn't have gotten it anyway."

The humorous approach was to prove no more successful than the more serious public and private statements, but he kept on trying.

Some months later there occurred an incident that illustrated Vandenberg's interest in the political future of General Eisenhower — an interest that was to grow stronger in the next few years. The Senator went to a dinner given in December at the F Street Club in Washington and attended by several prominent Republican party leaders from Pennsylvania, including Senator Edward Martin, the then Governor James H. Duff, Republican National Committeeman G. Mason Owlett, Joseph R. Grundy, and Joseph Newton Pew, Jr. Also present were Senator Taft and General Eisenhower.

Eisenhower was the center of considerable political speculation then in connection with plans for the 1948 presidential election, but he had kept himself as much as possible out of politics. The dinner-table conversation covered a wide variety of subjects and Eisenhower expressed some of his own views confidentially. Following the dinner, however, a distorted report leaked out to three newspaper correspondents concerning what the General was supposed to have said, including a statement that he favored confiscatory taxes on profits under certain circumstances in order to enable the government to meet its mounting obligations.

When this erroneous account of Eisenhower's remarks appeared in the newspapers, Vandenberg was both surprised and angered. He investigated the circumstances through which the account reached the newspapermen. Then he wrote a letter to Eisenhower about the incident. The letter — and whatever copies there may have been — disappeared later or may have been destroyed, and investigation several years later raised some question as to whether it had actually been delivered to the General or communicated to him orally. But several persons closely connected with it agreed that it said approximately the following: "I would advise you, on the basis of many years of experience in politics, to take no notice whatsoever of the incident involving what you are supposed to have said at the 'Pennsylvania Dinner.' Should you, however, decide to take public cognizance of that incident and clear up the matter, I should regard it as a real privilege if you would permit me to make a public statement, detailing not only what you did or did not say, but also who was responsible for the story."

The contents of the letter — if not the letter itself — were transmitted to Eisenhower by a newspaperman who was a friend of both the General and the Senator. Eisenhower expressed his appreciation. Later he talked by telephone with Vandenberg about the affair, saying that he was not concerned and that he did not intend to say anything publicly about the distortion and did not want anyone else to say anything. Vandenberg, who was much more disturbed by the whole incident, reminded Eisenhower that he had a definite opportunity and responsibility to exert leadership in the highest political places and that he should guard against any false impression of his viewpoint gaining credence. This interest in Eisenhower was increased as Vandenberg became more and more positive in his own decision not to seek the presidential nomination.

On New Year's Day, 1948, after a holiday dinner, the Senator slipped loose his belt and wrote a letter to other Michigan Republicans: "On the threshold of this Presidential election year, I wish to make this statement to my Michigan Republican friends who have been good enough to suggest that Michigan might again propose me for the nomination. Without presuming any such event, I urge that my name shall *not* be presented or supported either in the Michigan State Convention or in the National Convention at Philadelphia. I am confident that I can best serve my country by completing my present term in the Senate. This is said with deepest appreciation of the precious loyalties which Michigan Republicanism has given me through twenty years of public service. . . ."

And in a letter to his close friend, B. E. Hutchinson, of Detroit, he discussed his attitude toward politics and peace and progress in reply to a long communication from Hutchinson concerning current problems.

February 13, 1948

Your long letter of February 9th is a superb statement of your great attachment to the fundamentals that have made us what we are in this blessed U.S.A. I think I, too, am a "funda-

"The world will watch Vandenberg's vote." The Senator, with Mrs. Vandenberg and Arthur Vandenberg, Jr., at the polls, November 1946.

Associated Press Photo

January 1948 — "In the 80th Congress a tacit and informal understanding between Vandenberg and Senator Taft developed."

"He drew fantastic, lacy networks." On this and the following pages are four "doodles" made by Senator Vandenberg while presiding over the Senate in the 80th Congress.

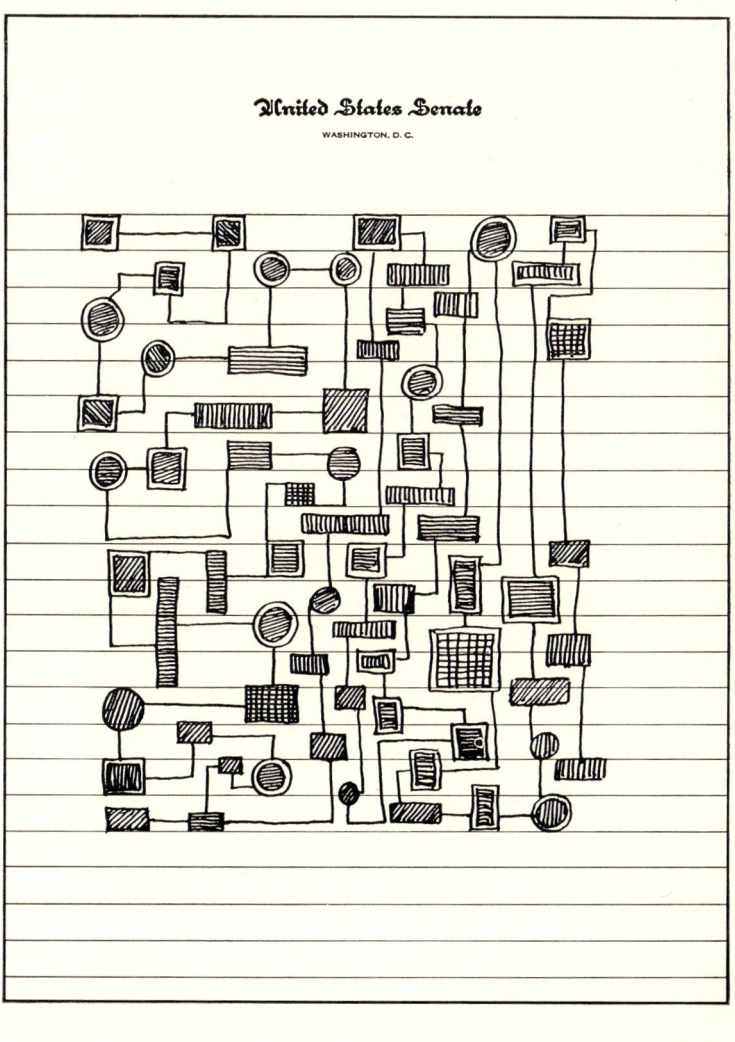

International News Photo

"Such leading citizens as Bernard M. Baruch were heard."
Senators Vandenberg and McMahon with Mr. Baruch.

"Of all the conferences Vandenberg attended, this certainly was the most enjoyable." Off for the Inter-American Conference in Brazil, August 13, 1947.

Kurt Paul Klagsbrunn

"For Vandenberg, it was a labor of love." Senator Vandenberg during the Petropolis Conference, Brazil, 1947.

Pre-Convention Cartoon, 1948, by James T. Berryman in the Washington *Evening Star*

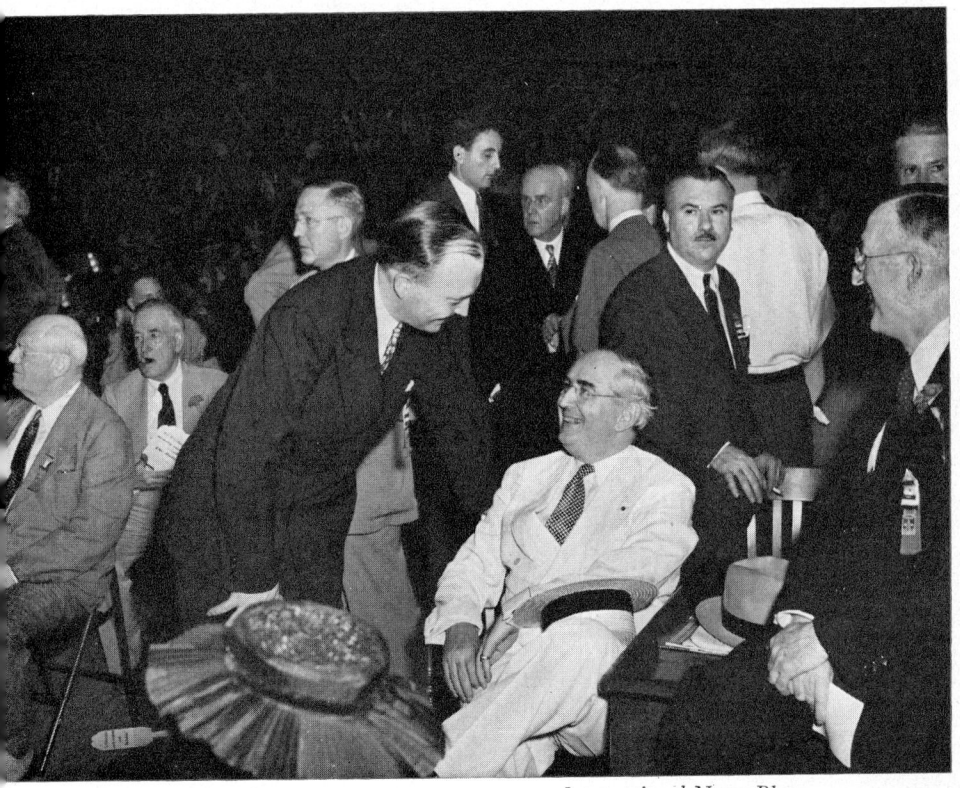

International News Photo

"Harold Stassen came to me . . ." The Republican Convention of 1948.

The Senator and Mrs. Vandenberg boarding a plane for home.

mentalist." My favorite bit of Holy Writ is Isaiah's admonition — "Look ye to the rock whence ye are hewn." Certainly I agree that the disintegration of Constitutional liberty in America would end the hope of the world. I think perhaps you are right that the chief difference between us in these matters may be one of "emphasis," and not one of substance. Perhaps I am not as literal as you are in your "fundamentalism." Yet I am sure you would agree that there is a legitimate and necessary area in which old (and blessed) "fundamentals" must grow in their rational application to a changing world.

For example, I feel deeply that there is a proper degree of "social responsibility" confronting modern government which is the product of changing times. . . . But the mere statement of this fact unavoidably involves the need for greatest prudence and caution lest this evolution shall destroy the "fundamentals" from which I think it logically springs. And at this point our minds completely meet when you say that the present Democratic Party cannot be entrusted with any such responsibilities.

My own preoccupation is *peace*. . . . Another war will come pretty close to being the end of everything. Even the fear of it will intolerably burden our budgets and affect our entire economy. [Vandenberg then commented on the danger that the Administration would exploit the world crisis in order to keep itself in power.] I may be all wrong; but my theory is that I am making it impossible for the Administration to successfully "exploit" any such plea that it alone can be trusted with foreign policy. That is not the reason for my attachment to bipartisan foreign policy — (my reason is that I think it indispensable to our international influence for peace). But, though not the "reason," I believe it is one of the results.

[Then turning to the 1948 presidential race, he added:] . . . your identification of my "mission" [the presidency] fills me with humility and consternation. I *hope* and *pray* you have incorrectly assessed the situation. I am sure you have. I do not believe I could produce the "unity" you crave because I am too bitterly opposed by many important Party elements — and this breach is calculated to widen. I do not believe I possess total qualifications, balancing assets and liabilities, equal to the total, over-all eligibility that can be found elsewhere. I am not at all sure of my qualifications on the basis of sheer physical resistance. Meanwhile, I am sure I am speaking the truth when I say that I can best serve my country by finishing out my term in the Senate. Why? Because a Republican President will be little more than an impotent White House prisoner unless he has effective Congressional leadership, and that's where my vanity comes in. It would be the worst of all tragedies if we won the Presidency and then failed to justify the victory. I know what I can do in the Senate. I've proved it. I do *not* know what I could do in the White House. But I know what a Republican President cannot do if he lacks adequate and effective Senate support.

I think there is probably a good reason why Presidential candidates are so seldom drawn from Congress. My own case is a good example of what I mean. I suppose I have answered ten thousand controversial roll calls in the last twenty years. It would be a miracle if hindsight did not demonstrate that at least twenty percent of them were wrong. This makes "easy picking" for the hostile analyst who "looks at the record" . . .

None of these efforts, however, ended the matter and the Washington *Daily News* summed it up in a headline saying: "Vandenberg Boom Just Won't Bust." Arthur E. Summerfield, national committeeman from Michigan, was hard at work for the Senator. He had made a survey of public opinion throughout the country, beginning in 1946, and was convinced that there was strong popular support for Vandenberg, including the normally Democratic southern states. Regardless of the Senator's personal decision not to be a candidate, Summerfield carefully organized the Republican forces in Michigan to support Vandenberg at the Convention, with the idea of touching off a movement to draft him. At Philadelphia the Michigan delegation was under relentless pressure from other presidential camps, but Summerfield and other delegates remained faithful to Vandenberg until all hope was gone. In later years, one of the Senator's most cherished memories was the loyalty of friends from his home state.

In Congress Senator Henry Cabot Lodge, Jr., of Massachusetts, and others were quietly working for Vandenberg, and there was an effort by sponsors of a "Stop Dewey" movement, spearheaded by Governor James H. Duff of Pennsylvania, to force the Senator to the front as an active candidate. Vandenberg declined to change his position.

In the May edition of *Harper's Magazine,* Richard H. Rovere wrote that Vandenberg was on "the safest and least assailable ground in American politics. Indeed, it is hard to see how a public man could be any better off than he at this moment. His prestige is global. The press of the world, that of Russia excepted, hurries to report everything he says. Here at home he is beyond reproach from his friends and, by the magic of bipartisanship, beyond judgment by his enemies. In fact, he has no enemies; none but the Communists, and they have no friends. . . .

". . . He has said that he does not even want to be President of the United States. . . . Still, Vandenberg has said that he would submit to a draft. One wonders why the Republican leaders don't jump at the chance. Maybe they know what they are doing with all this pulling and hauling over Taft, Dewey, Stassen, MacArthur, Warren, Martin, and the rest, but it certainly puzzles a bystander to see them enduring strife and discord in their search for a good candidate when all they have to do is draft the perfect candidate, Vandenberg, and call it a day."

A *Newsweek* poll of fifty of the nation's leading political writers found Vandenberg predicted as the most likely Republican presidential candidate. The latest Gallup poll prior to Convention time found him among the three top prospects and the predominant choice in event of a deadlocked Convention. He was, as one political writer noted, the candidate favored by the active candidates for the nomination — in event their own hopes died.

The Senator, however, was interested primarily in the foreign policy plank in the Republican platform. "I enclose herewith a first rough draft of a possible platform plank on foreign policy," he wrote Dulles on June 4. "Please give it a quick review — add or subtract — delete or expand. I think it is *very* necessary that we get something down in 'black and white' without too much delay because I think it is quite obvious now that a serious effort will be made in the Resolutions Committee of the Convention to upset any sort of an enlightened foreign policy and return to the 'good old days' when it took two weeks to cross the ocean."

Vandenberg confided to friends that he could be precipitated, however unwillingly, into the Convention race if: (1) it was necessary to block adoption of an isolationist foreign policy plank; or (2) if Governor Green's (Illinois) keynote address to the Convention presaged a knockdown battle between the isolationist wing and those backing the bipartisan foreign policy approach. Those possibilities were averted, however, when the Senator's version of a foreign policy plank was skillfully guided by Lodge through the Resolutions Committee and accepted unanimously by the Convention. Regarding the platform Vandenberg wrote in his diary:

June 20–25, 1948

Philadelphia: My chief interest in this convention at all times was the platform. I was prepared to fight to the finish — on the convention floor if need be — to protect the GOP against a reversion to "isolationism" or against desertion of the peace plans, including "collective security" and the European Recovery Program, which all but went on the rocks when the Republican House leadership (Martin-Taber-Halleck) gutted the ERP appropriation just before Congress adjourned.

It wasn't necessary — thanks to the superb job done by Senator Henry Cabot Lodge, Jr., as Chairman of the Resolutions Committee — thanks also to the fact that it was speedily evident that *nobody* was willing to do serious battle for the antediluvian McCormick, Chicago Tribune, point of view.

Before Lodge (Bless Him!) went to Philadelphia he asked me for a working paper on a foreign policy plank. I gave it to him. He put it all the way through his sub-committee and his full committee and the Convention practically intact. I think it is of historical importance to nail down this fact.

[Vandenberg, in his diary, made a parallel-column computation of the final platform draft and of his own work, and added:]

Thus it will be entirely apparent that the final platform draft on foreign policy is in almost the verbatim pattern of the original working-paper which I gave to Chairman Lodge and also to ex-Governor Brucker of Michigan, who was on the Resolutions Committee.

Before he presented the working paper to his Committee, Senator Lodge, with typical acumen, added four or five more extreme statements (all in harmony with this theme) for the express purpose of giving the little coterie of isolationists on his Committee something to knock out. One was a tacit condemnation of the House Republicans for having voted for European Relief and then against necessary appropriations for it. In due course, the "extras" were knocked down, just as Lodge had planned, and he emerged with what I consider to be a miraculous performance. . . .

Thus *my* platform was adopted by the Convention *unanimously* — which means that the Chicago Colonel and many of my bitter Congressional foes who were Delegates must have voted for it. Life *does* have its amusing consolations. I did not need the nomination in order to be vindicated.

A few examples of the Vandenberg parallel diary compilation on the platform will suffice:

PLATFORM:	MY TEXT:
We dedicate our foreign policy to the preservation of a free America in a free world of free men. With neither malice nor desire for conquest, we shall strive for a just peace with all nations.	We dedicate our foreign policy to the preservation of free America in a free world of free men. With neither malice nor conquest aimed at any other power on earth, we shall strive for an honorable and just peace with all nations. We shall omit no efforts to this end.
We shall erect our foreign policy on the basis of friendly firmness which welcomes cooperation but spurns appeasement. We shall pursue a consistent foreign policy which invites steadiness and reliance and which thus avoids the	We shall erect our foreign policy on the basis of friendly firmness which welcomes cooperation but declines appeasement. We shall pursue a consistent foreign policy which invites reliance and which thus avoids the misunderstand-

misunderstandings from which wars result. We shall protect the future against the errors of the Democratic Administration, which too often has lacked clarity, competence or consistency in our vital international relationships and has too often abandoned justice.	ings from which wars too often flow. Thus we shall protect the future against the errors of the past when the Democratic Administration has too often compromised with our ideals and too often lacked clarity, competence or consistency in our vital international relationships.
We believe in collective security against aggression and in behalf of justice and freedom. We shall support the United Nations as the world's best hope in this direction, striving to strengthen it and promote its effective evolution and use. The United Nations should progressively establish international law, be freed of any veto in the pacific settlement of international disputes, and be provided with the armed forces contemplated by the Charter. We particularly commend the value of regional arrangements as prescribed by the Charter; and we cite the Western Hemispherical Defense Pact as a useful model.	We believe in collective security against aggression and in behalf of justice and freedom. We shall support the United Nations as the world's best hope in this direction. We shall strive to strengthen the United Nations and promote its effective evolution and use. The United Nations should progressively establish international law. It should control atomic energy. It should be freed of any veto in the pacific settlement of international disputes. It should be provided with the armed forces contemplated by the Charter. We particularly commend the utility of regional arrangements as prescribed by the Charter; and we point with pride to the Western Hemispherical Defense Pact as a useful model.
We faithfully dedicate ourselves to peace with justice.	Our faithful dedication is to peace with justice and honor.

On Monday, June 21, at midafternoon and with the Convention already in session, Senator and Mrs. Vandenberg arrived in Philadelphia. While newsmen and photographers waited their arrival for hours in front of the Warwick Hotel where a twelfth-floor suite served as a meeting place for the Senator's friends, the Vandenbergs stopped for a box lunch in a public park, then slipped into a sixteenth-floor apartment on Rittenhouse Square, a few blocks away, which had been offered to them by Mrs. Harrison Caner.

The Senator visited Convention Hall on Monday night, but arranged to go in a side door and take a seat at the rear of the platform in a section reserved for senators. When spotted, he was greeted warmly by the Michigan delegation, was photographed on the platform with Summerfield, Governor Warren of California, and Clare Boothe Luce of Connecticut. He returned to the Hall only after Dewey's nomination and before the balloting for the vice-presidential nomination. He refused appointments with prominent Convention figures; one such balk so angered a state governor that he stomped off announcing he was "off" Vandenberg as a possible nominee. A few old Senate friends were admitted; but they left without any agreement by Vandenberg to lend his support to a draft.

There was, in retrospect, small chance that the "Stop Dewey" movement would succeed or that a deadlock would throw the nomination to Vandenberg. Only quick action at the start of the session could have made that possible — but it was the Dewey forces that acted most quickly and vigorously. They announced that Senator Edward Martin of Pennsylvania would withdraw as a candidate and nominate Dewey — thus splitting the Pennsylvania delegation and starting a swing toward the New Yorker that could not be stopped.

Later, when it was all over, Vandenberg put down his own thoughts about the Convention, writing from notes made in his diary during the sessions.

> Philadelphia — 1948: Many months before the Philadelphia Convention I said I was finding it much more difficult *not* to run than to run for President. This proved increasingly to be the case as the Convention approached. It multiplied during the event. Nor did it adjourn with the Convention. The whole thing still lingers in controversial reminiscence.
>
> I said in March, 1947, that I was not and did not wish or intend to be a candidate for the Republican nomination. I gave my reasons. To me they were conclusive — but, apparently to few others. I said no citizen in my position could decline an honest, spontaneous draft; but that no one was ever drafted without conniving, and that I would not connive. Then on New Year's [1948] I wrote Governor Sigler

... earnestly requesting that Michigan's Convention delegates should "neither present nor support" my name in the national conclave at Philadelphia. It was impossible to speak with a greater finality unless one said, as General Sherman did once upon a time, that he would not run if nominated or serve if elected. Any such statement, in my circumstance, was ruled out as a breach of duty. Furthermore it seemed utterly presumptuous in the light of the improbability of any such event. I further clarified the matter in May after voting in the Senate for the peace-time draft. I said that one who voted to draft others could not decline a draft himself. I shall always believe this put the record straight and clear. But it was not enough. I was relentlessly pursued, down to the final curtain, for something more by (1) those who insisted I owed it to my country to jump all the way in; by (2) those who insisted I must encourage, indeed organize, a draft; and by (3) those who insisted I should take myself all the way out.

There were several different reasons for the alleged "mystery" regarding my attitude. I borrow the word "mystery" from the rash of pre-convention headlines in which my position was the major source of pre-convention speculation.

First, there were those who were unable to believe that any public man could *really* be opposed to his own nomination for President. It happened to be the unequivocal fact so far as I was concerned — for reasons I shall indicate later. I doubt whether my ... son, who was my secretary and closest intimate, believed it until perhaps the final hours of the Convention. Some critics assumed that it was all a matter of "strategy" — which they said was "smart." Some said I was just being "coy." But whenever in the pre-convention days I was waited upon by prospective Delegates in Washington I frankly argued out the case *against* my nomination. I must say it usually failed to produce a convert to my viewpoint. But I think it did gradually establish some degree of integrity for my attitude.

Second, there were those who superficially accepted my attitude but considered it to be temporary and purely expedient. They would say — and this happened countless times — "Well, O.K.; but you've said enough about it; it isn't necessary for you to keep on repeating your disinterest; you should let nature take its course." Then, when I did close up and let nature take its course, these same well-meaning friends, whose precious loyalty I shall never forget, would get the jitters and say that I *must* announce my draft-availability and make it dependably plain because a lot of Delegates still seemed to be in doubt. If I heard it once I heard it one hundred times — "They're afraid they'll get out on the end of a limb and you will saw it off."

Third, there were those who were interested in a deadlock in behalf of their own "dark horses." In the final rounds, there were those who had to "stop Dewey" in order to get a chance for themselves. My intervention was indispensable to any such plans.

Fourth, there was the Michigan Delegation itself, headed by Governor Sigler and Republican National Committeeman Summerfield. It was one of the finest Michigan groups that ever came to a convention. I could never live long enough to re-pay my debt of gratitude for its confidence and loyalty. It was in a tough fix. The Republican State Convention which named it had instructed it to always remember the top-eligibility of the senior Senator from Michigan [Vandenberg]. But the senior Senator from Michigan had asked it not to "present or support" his name. It was the Delegation's own decision to stick to the senior Senator with its highly important 41 votes. It felt that it had just as much of a right to participate in a "draft" as did any other Delegation. It was conscious of the fact that all the pre-convention polls put the senior Senator out in front as the probable nominee. The last of these polls showed 417 out of 815 leading editors in the country prophesied his nomination [United States News]. The Delegation's non-candidate had no headquarters — except a few rooms in the Warwick Hotel. He was refusing to participate in any of the frenzied "conferences" which were constantly going on. I myself saw the Delegation only once when I briefly presented myself Wednesday morning to present my personal compliments. I think they universally agreed with me that morning when I described myself as their "problem child." When Governor Sigler finally decided to put my name in formal nomination, I hastily wrote him a letter begging him not to do so lest it destroy the entire character of my long-sustained position. But, with assurances that he would make my veto abundantly plain, my name went to the [Convention] floor about 3:00 A.M. Thursday morning.

These were the cross currents which bestirred such commotion and controversy and, too often, I regret to say, a great degree of misunderstanding. I was simply standing my ground. I stood my ground to the finish. I would have reluctantly accepted a draft. But there was never a chance for a draft, after Dewey's unexpected show of strength on the first ballot, except as all the other front-runners had been willing to withdraw on the second ballot, and perhaps not even then because Colonel McCormick [Colonel Robert R. McCormick, publisher of the Chicago *Tribune*], hating me a little more than he hated Dewey, would undoubtedly have swung Illinois to Dewey. The other front-runners could not agree on a united program at this point. Later was too late. Governor Stassen, who called on me in my pent-house at 250 18th Street, was, I believe, ready to do so. I think he tried. I also believe there was a last-second effort to draft General Eisenhower — a midnight movement in which Mrs. Ogden Reid of the New York Herald Tribune had something to do. I believe the General would have accepted *if* the track could have been cleared for him. But it could not be cleared for *anybody*.

I had some bitter, scarring experiences during these hectic pressure-hours. One of my dearest friends, from Connecticut, came to me in tears to say that I was "letting my country down" by not jumping in to lead my own battle. There was quite a little of this post-convention comment. In the first place, it would have wiped out the entire integrity of my position for a year. In the second place, in my opinion, it would not have worked. In the third place, it would have been alien to my every instinct and personal conviction in connection with the nomination. So far as I was concerned I was a non-candidate to the end. I considered that a wholly adequate ticket was otherwise available. Such a ticket emerged.

What were my reasons for opposing my own nomination?

First. I had been engaged for three years in fostering bipartisan unity in behalf of collective peace and security for us and the world. I considered it to be the dedication of my life. I thought it to be the greatest cause on earth. I felt it to be never so necessary as in the critical days that lie ahead. I felt that its gravest domestic danger was *not* in the White House but in the Congress. I felt that I should stay on the job where I had demonstrated some degree of competence to serve this cause — perhaps even some degree of *temporary* indispensability. I may have unduly flattered myself. But I said, and deeply meant, that I believed I could best serve my country by finishing out my Senate tour of duty. That was my controlling motive. Indeed, it was more than a motive. It was a passion.

Second. I felt that no man 65 years of age, possessing *any* physical infirmity, should enter upon a White House career — particularly when a total reorganization of the government was on order. If one could know that the worst that could happen to him would be to drop dead — well and good. We have a Constitutional Vice President to meet that crisis. But we have no Constitutional process to cope with permanent incapacity, such as the late President Wilson suffered. [Vandenberg here ignored the Constitutional provision that in case of the President's "inability to discharge the powers and duties" of his office "the same shall devolve on the Vice-President." Presumably he was thinking of the practical difficulties of putting that provision into effect — as in the case of President Wilson.] In the present state of world affairs, the country could not stand that sort of disaster. My personal physician, Dr. A. B. Smith of Grand Rapids, certified that my health was good — despite daily digitalis for an old heart fibrillation, and despite intermittent cervical arthritis which plagued me with persistent headaches. But my own conscience constantly told me that it was an unfair speculation for the country.

Third. Presidential nominees historically rarely come from

Congress — just one in this century. There must be a good reason. I think I personified one of the reasons. In the many legislative battles for the bi-partisan foreign policies for which I have fought, I have unavoidably attracted many bitter enemies both in and out of Congress. . . . Many of my colleagues, sharply differing with my views, are human enough to "remember." I believe we have won our battle against "isolationism." The new Republican platform is clear upon the subject. The new ticket is equally forthright. If this is to be the policy of the next Republican Administration in the White House [Vandenberg had at that time no doubt that his party would win], it is desperately important to make it equally the policy of the Republicans in the next Congress. This new unity is infinitely easier to create and preserve with a *new* White House occupant than it would be if the chief Congressional proponent of these policies were to transfer to the White House. We must think not only of the next *election.* We must think of the next *administration.*

I could add other considerations which weighed upon my mind — the fact that I have had to concentrate so exclusively on foreign policy these last three years that I had some doubts about my own sufficiency in picking up the domestic threads again — the fact that I have had 20 years of continuous Senate service which has separated me from administrative experience — the fact that these 20 years, the last ones superlatively strenuous, have tired me out — the very personal and intimate fact that my good wife, still facing a long recuperation from two major operations, looked with horror upon her own "First Lady" assignment for which ordinarily she would be supremely eligible but from which, under the circumstances and despite her bravery about it, she recoiled.

If I had it to do over again, I think I would irrevocably take myself out of consideration at least six months ahead of the Convention. Perhaps that would exemplify the greater courage — although I felt then and still feel now that I had no right to deny an honest draft. In any event, this business of *not* running for President is a tough one — if you really mean it.

It is perhaps unusual that any national figure of Vandenberg's stature should develop in such logical fashion the reasons why he should *not* be a presidential nominee. These reasons he elaborated upon in conversations with staff members and close friends. Sometimes he joked about it. "When I die," he used to say, "I want the minister to be able to look down on me and say: 'There would have been a great President.'"

In the same vein the Senator recalled the advice which had been given him when, as a young man, he had consulted with his first boss about the desirability of accepting another job that had been offered him. "It is far better to be thought worthy of a job and not take it," the boss told him, "than to take it and be found out."

While at Philadelphia, the Senator also jotted down in his diary some additional Convention notes.

June 20–25, 1948

Philadelphia: . . . I declined to "connive" despite heaviest pressures from many distinguished men and women whose confidence in me I shall never live long enough to justify. I had no part in the "draft" conferences and negotiations which sought to "stop Dewey" — although the Michigan Delegation did so on its own responsibility.

I was not nominated. I got 62 votes on both of two ballots [Michigan's 41, the rest scattered]. I had a big potential following which would have broken to me if there had been a deadlock, which was the only possibility of my nomination which ever existed. But there was no deadlock. Nonetheless I am deeply grateful to my Michigan friends for their loyalty and to many national leaders for their open support. I name a few for the record. Senator Henry Cabot Lodge, Jr., of Massachusetts. Governor [James H.] Duff of Pennsylvania. Senator H. Alexander Smith of New Jersey and Governor Driscoll of New Jersey. Senator Tobey of New Hampshire. Senator Gurney of South Dakota. Senator Young of North Dakota. Senator Morse of Oregon. Senator Cooper of Kentucky. Clare Boothe Luce of Connecticut. Senator Ferguson of Michigan. I should add that Harold Stassen (one of the major candidates) came to me at the last moment and was prepared to give me his full support. Senator Knowland of California also was potentially in my "corner" if the Warren movement dissipated. The only direct word I had from Robert A. Taft was his statement to me, a few days before we came to Philadelphia, that he would wish me to be his Secretary of State.

There seems to be the makings of a perennial argument over the question whether I could have been nominated (1) if I had made a pre-convention campaign, or (2) if I had moved into affirmative action at Philadelphia. The general opinion seems to be that I could. It is argued that my affirmative action would have stiffened up the "favorite son" opposition and created a fighting focus against the frontrunner. I agree that a deadlock for a few ballots would probably have nominated me. But I doubt whether a deadlock was possible.

Governor Dewey was far stronger than anticipated. His "blitz" was a thing of beauty. He crossed the 500 line in two ballots. When the intervening recess failed to produce agreement among others upon one man to face the "blitz" it was all over. But this is the point. If I had been that "one man," Colonel McCormick would have swung his big Illinois Delegation to Dewey, more than enough to nominate Dewey . . . The persistence of his assassination-complex would have been inevitable.

In any event I did *not* "campaign." It would have been impossible if I were to succeed (as I did) in my leadership of bi-partisan foreign policy in the Senate. And I did not "connive" here in Philadelphia. . . .

With a splendid ticket, which believes in what I believe in, and a splendid platform, which says what I believe in, I got *everything* out of Philadelphia that I went there for. . . .

We had no "headquarters" in the usual campaign sense. Arthur, Jr., opened up in the Warwick Hotel as a center for my friends. But I did not go there once until after the nominations. Arthur, Jr., found himself in the middle of the maelstrom which swirled around the speculation as to what I might do. It was a superlatively difficult assignment. He was doing his best to protect the integrity of my position, although I always suspected that he had his own sympathies with those who were trying to get me into action . . . he was ably seconded by a group of loyal "home folks" — Howard Lawrence, Louis Weil, Jr., John Dregge, David Kendall, Robert Wilson and my Secretary, Miss Geraldyne Creagan.

I stayed in a 16th floor apartment on Rittenhouse Square . . . Mrs. V., and my daughters and their husbands were with us. It was a delightful "house party" and a wonderful hideaway. We took most of the Convention by television. . . .

This is certainly the *last* time that I shall figure in the presidential equation. And that suits me! I have four years and six months to go before my Senate term expires. Then — give me a house by the side of the road! Enough is enough! This is specially true when one must suffer the kind of opposition which I have had to suffer for several years — relentless, unscrupulous, bitter. Yet, on balance, I doubt whether any man in public life has enjoyed quite such a friendly press and public as have I.

After Dewey was nominated, Vandenberg for the first time left the Rittenhouse Square hideaway for the Bellevue-Stratford Hotel, heart of Convention activities. He joined a conference of about twenty Republican leaders convened in Dewey's hotel suite, upon Dewey's return from delivering his acceptance speech, to discuss a vice-presidential candidate.

June 20–25, 1948 [continued]
Philadelphia: I was the only one of the erstwhile presidential "candidates" to be invited, until I *insisted* that Taft should be there if I was to stay. He was invited forthwith, but declined — sending word in favor of Bricker for V.P. We were all sworn to absolute secrecy. I shall not break that pledge even for the sake of distant history. But I think I am entitled to record my own part in it. All of the following names were canvassed: Stassen, Warren, Green, Knowland, Bricker, Halleck, Hickenlooper, Ferguson, and two or three easterners who were promptly dismissed for geographical reasons. I was surprised to discover it was generally under-

stood that Stassen and Warren were available despite their previous disavowals. I was entirely frank in urging Dewey *not* to build a *hybrid* ticket — not to choose a V.P. who was not in full harmony with the platform and with his own consistent support of international cooperation. (Wherry's name should have been in that list.) I argued that we could not go to the country with a ticket which did no more than personify the *split* on this issue among Republicans in Congress. I recommended either Stassen or Warren. I wish I were free to record the debate. It was most illuminating and very sharp in spots. I left about 3:00 A.M., before a final decision had been made.

Some years later Dewey himself related, for the purposes of this book, further details of the meeting, saying that he was pleased that the pledge of secrecy had been so well kept by those who attended. He said that the reason for the secrecy pledge was that he wanted all participants to express themselves freely without any fear that what they said would be repeated and thereby cause later political enmities. He added that the meeting included leaders who had been key figures in his preconvention campaign and others except for possible vice-presidential candidates. These included Governors Bradford of Massachusetts, Driscoll of New Jersey, and Langlie of Washington; Senators Saltonstall of Massachusetts and Martin of Pennsylvania; four of Dewey's lieutenants — former New York State Chairman Edwin F. Jaeckel, National Committeeman Russell Sprague, Campaign Manager Herbert Brownell, and John Foster Dulles — and Roy Roberts of the Kansas City *Star*.

The meeting started about 11.00 P.M. and lasted until 4.00 A.M., with a break for coffee and sandwiches at 2.00 A.M. According to Dewey, "We went calmly around the circle and canvassed every possible candidate. We gradually eliminated one after another for one reason or another. I was scrupulous not to express a preference." Dewey said that his part in the meeting was much the same as the role he was accustomed to taking at informal meetings of his chief advisors and party leaders at Albany, where he frequently held Sunday evening sessions to discuss his program and strategy as Governor of New York.

"By process of continuous consultation we arrive at unanimity," he went on. "Pressure is never exerted. Nothing becomes party policy unless it is unanimous. At Philadelphia, Warren was genuinely the unanimous choice of the group. Proponents of other candidates bowed to the arguments of the overwhelming majority." After the decision had been reached, Dewey called Warren on the telephone and the California Governor joined the meeting.

Dewey's memory of the meeting did not agree with Vandenberg's diary comment that he had had to insist on Taft being present; as the Governor recalled it, he had voluntarily invited Taft, but Vandenberg did not know it. A second invitation was issued, however, on Vandenberg's request.

June 20–25, 1948 [continued]

> I went to the Convention Hall the next morning. Governor Sigler told me that Governor Youngdahl of Minnesota had urgently requested him to nominate Stassen from the floor. There was a distinct spirit of rebellion in the air. I think the Convention feared the recommendation of an unacceptable nominee. I advised that no decision regarding a rival nomination should even be discussed until it was known who would be recommended because the Convention could not afford to repudiate its nominee for President twelve hours after naming him unless his V.P. choice was impossible. Then came the Warren news. The rebellion disintegrated. A good job was finished.

Vandenberg recalled a one-hundred-dollar bet with George E. Allen, former administrative assistant to President Truman. Allen had wagered with the Senator that Vandenberg would be the Republican choice long before Convention time. Allen promptly remitted with this note: "After this I am calling off all bets with you. You won't cooperate. Never knew another man who would rather win a hundred dollars than the Presidency of the United States."

There were two noteworthy papers that Vandenberg later

attached to his account of Philadelphia, 1948. Both throw new light on his thinking. One dealt with the remote possibility that, willing or not, he might be drafted as the Party nominee. It was an undelivered speech of acceptance that he had written in advance of the Convention. Such "preparedness" for any eventuality was completely in keeping with the Senator's usual practice. The other was a highly personal memorandum on a post-Convention development in his physical condition.

[*Undated*]

I am preserving the following pages purely as a curiosity. This is the speech I prepared in advance of the Philadelphia Convention — to be available in the totally unexpected event of my nomination. Probably it will be misunderstood as being some sort of proof that I was not sincere, at rock bottom, in my refusal to be a candidate. But that just isn't so. When I went to Philadelphia it was the constant newspaper theme that I stood at least a 50 percent chance of nomination in spite of my flat refusal to be a candidate and my insistent and publicly expressed wish that I should *not* be nominated. I have always believed in "preparedness." I had to be ready for the unexpected and the unsought. I could not trust such an eventuality, however improbable, to the impromptu inspiration of the moment. So I "prepared" — and here it is. Thank Heaven it was and is an *undelivered* speech. It is simply an amusing freak of minor history. Its chief interest to me lies in the rather startling parallel — this speech theme is precisely the one followed, in part, by Governor Dewey in *his* acceptance speech. It may also be interesting to note that I would have wound up with a *one-term* pledge. . . .

The speech that was never delivered began with an acceptance of the "nomination" with the "greatest humility." "I pledge you every devotion of my heart and soul to the best welfare of free America in a free world of free men," Vandenberg would have said.

It embodied a plea for co-operation from all factions in the Party in order to build a "Republican Administration in the best of our traditions which shall serve all our people and save the American way of life." The speech called for a closing of the ranks: "We must seek for our whole people a new era of cooperation and good will." And Vandenberg would have promised to spell out the issues "in unmistakable language" during the course of the campaign.

On the domestic front the written text pledged an administration dedicated to "free enterprise . . . we do not like meddling bureaucrats. We want a minimum of law from Congress. We want a minimum of executive orders from the White House. We want a maximum of freedom." At the same time it pledged prompt action to curb "any monopoly of power which is exercised against the public welfare."

On the international front, the brief "speech" declared: "With neither malice nor conquest aimed at any other power on earth, and with the purpose always to 'live and let live,' we must tirelessly pursue collective security through cooperation and goodwill. We must omit no honorable effort to end this tragic business of war which, in an atomic age, not even the victor can afford to win."

Vandenberg would have called for a "consistent foreign policy — which neither 'zigs' nor 'zags' — so there can be no alien excuse to miscalculate our fixity of purpose. . . . It must always first consult American welfare as its controlling concern. But it must lead courageously and constructively in answer to the prayers that rise from every hearthstone in our land — and I doubt not throughout the world. It must lead for peace."

It encompassed a pledge of fidelity to the United Nations as "the world's best hope. The organized conscience of mankind. . . ." It promised continued American preparedness — "We shall keep our powder dry. . . . We shall be prepared for the consequences of bad faith."

It included a sharp attack on the entrenched Democratic Administration. "After 16 years of New Deal Administration in which an entrenched political dynasty has settled down in the Washington bureaucracy and monopolized the government, it is time for a total audit and a total change. . . ."

And finally, the "speech" that was not to be delivered concluded with the one-term pledge: "I am grateful for your faith. I am conscious of my own limitations. I ask your unremitting aid. I shall ever strive to be the servant of your hopes. I shall pray that we deserve to win. Then, having won as I believe we shall, I want to return to this great Republican convention four years hence and, at the self-chosen end of my public service, hand this commission back to you with a record of accomplishment for the whole American people which will vindicate your judgment here today. God Bless America!"

There was another, and more ominous, diary entry concerning the 1948 Convention.

July 31, 1948

Important: If anything serious should happen to my health in the next few months, I want the following information made public — in fairness to all concerned.

It relates to the fact that I did not positively refuse to allow my name to be considered for the Republican Presidential Nomination at the Philadelphia Republican National Convention although I insisted to the end upon being a non-candidate so far as I was concerned.

My last physical check-up, about eight months prior to the Convention which assembled June 20, 1948, showed a "clean bill of health." Even my so-called "heart condition" (for which I have taken digitalis daily for at least ten years) had stabilized to a point where there was no cause for alarm. It was the professional consensus that there were no physical reasons why I should not be a candidate for President. I re-checked this fact by further inquiries just preceding the Convention.

Following the Convention, I went to Butterworth Hospital in Grand Rapids for my regular routine check-up.

For the first time the X-ray disclosed a tiny spot on one lung. It was so inconspicuous that I was asked to return for another plate. I then left for Washington.

This morning Dr. William A. Morgan (Washington) asked me to stop in at his office. He is an old and cherished friend of mine. He told me that our mutual friend, Dr. A. B. Smith, of Grand Rapids (in whom I have complete and grateful confidence) had sent him these plates; and he told me frankly that they disclosed a lung involvement which might be tuberculosis. He insisted that the matter must be followed up without delay. I agreed to do so just as soon as the Special Session of Congress adjourns.

Events will write their own history in this matter.

The point I want to nail down is that my Doctors never had an inkling of this threat prior to the Convention. I never had the remotest thought of such a thing until this morning, and I do not believe it now.

But it is simply appalling to think of the tragedy of such a thing if I were the Republican nominee for President.

It goes without saying that if I had had any such information, no matter how speculative or inconclusive, I should have gone even farther than I did at Philadelphia in discouraging my candidacy; and I should have taken myself out of *all* consideration with complete finality.

Perhaps I had a sub-conscious warning which moved me to go as far as I did in consistently declining to give any encouragement to the movement in my behalf. Perhaps it similarly inspired my constant comments that *any* man at 64, no matter how well he seemed to be, was inevitably in too hazardous an age-zone to enter upon a White House career.

I write this record because I would not want any citizen to believe I would have gambled with such a chance in *any* degree if I had had the remotest knowledge of this thing which is 100 percent total surprise today. I want it also known that neither my Doctors nor the friends who supported me at Philadelphia could have had any such knowledge. But there's a lesson for the country in this record.

[Then along the left-hand margin of the typed page is found the inked-in notation:]

P.S. Two weeks later a tubercular test proved totally negative.

23

The 1948 Campaign

SENATOR Vandenberg played a relatively minor and behind-the-scenes role in the Dewey-Warren campaign during the fall of 1948.

Before the campaigning began he met with Dewey and Dulles in New York City and issued a statement declaring that America was united against aggressors and determined to protect its "rights everywhere." Despite election-time "internal controversy regarding many phases of foreign policy," Vandenberg said that other nations should be dead certain that there was no controversy over "the basic fact that America is united against aggression and against the loss of freedom." The statement was issued at a time when the Russians were intensifying their blockade of Berlin in an apparent effort to squeeze America, Britain, and France out of the occupied Axis capital.

Vandenberg's relative inactivity in the campaign stemmed from a belief that real campaign slugging, so far as he was concerned, would reduce his effectiveness as a foreign policy leader in Congress, and in the Republican administration that he steadfastly believed would be elected. So sure was Vandenberg of victory that on several occasions during the campaign he wrote Dulles to counsel extreme care against prejudicing the "incoming" Republican administration by campaign foreign policy statements resulting in commitments which would have to be met after election day. Dulles was Dewey's foreign policy adviser and it was assumed he would be Secretary of State in the Republican administration. Vandenberg wrote Dulles:

July 2, 1948

I keenly feel it is very important that "foreign policy" should be handled with highly intelligent skill lest we do more harm than good.

I think you should take over this responsibility or I fear we shall find some of our groups working at cross purposes. I do not mean that you should be too much "out in front." On the contrary, it is to be ever remembered that the next Republican Secretary of State is going to need Democratic votes in the Senate just as badly as the present Administration has needed Republican votes. I have no illusions that the Republican isolationists have surrendered. They will be "back at the old stand" next January.

It is peculiarly our job — yours and mine — to see that bipartisan liaison in the next Congress does not become impossible. Otherwise November will represent a pyrrhic victory. . . .

Vandenberg closely watched the campaign statements dealing with foreign policy emanating from Dewey headquarters. Once he lodged mild objections to a Dewey statement which he thought limited too narrowly the area of bipartisan co-operation. Another time, through Dulles, he took direct though ultra-private issue with a Dewey statement made to Italian-American leaders in which he favored Italian administration of its war-lost colonies through a United Nations trusteeship arrangement. This, Vandenberg wrote Dulles, represented "advance public commitments of the Dewey Administration," without international consultation and perhaps in prejudice of America's future world position at the United Nations.

Dulles, possibly a little concerned by the implied rebuke to Dewey, wrote to Vandenberg that while Dewey and he were sorry that Vandenberg was worried, "he [Dewey] is, of course, competitive by instinct and anyone actually running for office 'presses' a little more, and is somewhat less detached, than one in your position who properly is most concerned with preserving the un-partisan good will needed for future implementation of sound foreign policies. . . . I hope you will be tolerant of the exigencies of the campaign and of political influence from which Mr. Truman does not divorce himself and from which the Governor cannot *wholly* divorce *himself.*"

One campaign development that aroused Vandenberg was President Truman's persistent attack on the Eightieth Congress as "the worst in history." The Senator was particularly incensed because Mr. Truman neglected to draw a line between domestic issues, which might be fair targets for political attack, and the area which he regarded as lying within the bipartisan foreign policy preserve. He wrote to Dulles on August 9, regarding Mr. Truman's attack, that "even his general condemnation is unjustified and untrue on the basis of the record. But his indictment becomes specifically ridiculous in the light of the foreign policy record." After detailing, for Dewey's use, the accomplishments in foreign affairs of the Eightieth Congress, he concluded: "I think it is the most amazing record of constructive cooperation ever written in *any* Congress and I think it is largely responsible for the country's substantial unity in its foreign policy voice, a 'unity' which may well spell the difference between peace and war." And to Herbert Brownell, Jr., Dewey's campaign manager, he wrote on September 22 that he was profoundly shocked by the Truman technique. "Not even Wallace is saying things better calculated to split the country into snarling vendettas at a moment when our destiny cannot afford these soap box luxuries. I think the people will instinctively rally to the Dewey-Warren approach."

In two letters to his wife the Senator remarked again on the Truman technique and the Congressional reaction to it.

July 26, 1948

... Well, we opened up the Joint Session today. It was positively dramatic in its rebuff to Truman. All the Republicans and most of the Southern Dems received him in stony silence. But he really could expect nothing else from the "worst Congress" in history. His message was another hodge-podge. ... Of course nothing much will happen. It just can't. We have been holding almost continuous Republican conferences to decide what we should do. ... A big group wanted to adjourn sine die and go home immediately following his message. But I was one of those who felt the country would expect us to make some sort of a gesture, at least, in the direction of considering his fuzzy recommendations. Dewey strongly felt this same way. . . . Bob Lovett was in for his usual Sunday rendezvous. He said he never knew Marshall to call any but four people by their first names — his wife, his step-daughter, Bob's wife and you. He never calls a man by his first name.

August 9, 1948
. . . I had a long session with Taft this morning about organizing the Republican Senate next January. He hasn't made up his mind whether he wants the leadership. Until he does, there's nothing to be said . . . we have just published a summary of the [Foreign Relations] Committee's labors in the two years of the 80th Congress. It is simply staggering. When I look at it in total I don't see how it could have happened. Yet [Truman] says this is "the worst Congress in history." . . . I had Joe Alsop [the columnist] for another hour . . . he confirmed the report that Dewey said he would first offer the Secretaryship of State to me; then to Dulles if I declined (which I probably would do).

It was mainly to answer the Administration attack that Vandenberg made his one foray during the campaign in a nationwide radio address on October 4. Even the locale of the speech raised some problems so far as bipartisan foreign policy was concerned in Vandenberg's mind. Earlier he wrote Brownell that he saw some dangerous "implications and hazards" in suggestions that the speech be delivered from one of the states in which a hot senatorial contest was taking place.

September 17, 1948
The only "hot" senatorial State where I could be sure that I am not a liability rather than an asset to our senatorial candidate would be Kentucky where I certainly would love to speak up for Cooper. [The reference was to John Sherman Cooper, Republican senator standing for re-election in a usually Democratic State.] He stood by what is now our official Republican foreign policy from start to finish. But! If we choose Kentucky as the locale, let's frankly face the fact

that Barkley was one of the six Democrats on the Foreign Relations Committee who made "bipartisan policy" possible; and what do I say if, in the inevitable press conference, I am asked about Barkley in this connection? . . .

. . . I certainly do not want to *hurt* any of our senatorial nominees. But, again remembering January 20th when you will be asking me to "deliver" in the Senate, and when it can't be done without bipartisan support unfortunately, I submit to your own consideration the argument that this speech should not be localized; that it should either be a studio job or a speech to some national Republican group if that be feasible, preferably the former.

Please acquit me of over-sensitiveness on this subject.

Vandenberg delivered the speech — from a radio broadcasting studio in Washington. In ringing terms he stated the case for Republican responsibility in foreign policy, redefined bipartisan co-operation, and answered President Truman's charges.

Speaking of the four years of efforts to take foreign policy out of partisan politics in the interest of national unity at the water's edge, Vandenberg said:

October 4, 1948

The purpose of this unity is to strengthen American security and sustain American ideals by giving maximum authority to America's voice for peace with justice. In the face of any foreign problem, our unity is as important as our atom bombs. It is particularly important as a discouragement to alien miscalculation which, otherwise, might lead to the mistaken belief that we are vulnerable because of our domestic divisions. It is our best available insurance for peace.

[Referring to the "substantially united American position" on meeting the Russian transportation blockade of Berlin, he said:]

This sort of common action is a vital example of what has come to be known as "bi-partisan foreign policy." It has two vivid advantages at this hour. One: it permits our democracy to speak with a great degree of unity at critical moments when swift decision is vital and when we face totalitarian opponents who can command their own instant unity by police decree. Two: it leaves us free to change our national administration, if such be the peoples' desire and advantages, without affecting the continuity of our foreign policy.

This common action does not mean that we cease to be "Republicans" or "Democrats" at home. It does not mean that we mute our criticisms of mistakes. It does not mean a fake "unity" devoid of popular consent. It means that we strive by consultation to lift foreign policy above partisan issue. It means that we attempt to hammer out the greatest possible measure of agreement so we can speak to the world, not as "Republicans" or "Democrats" but as undivided Americans.

[Vandenberg then related the principles which governed Republican thinking on foreign policy, as embodied in the Party's platform and as practiced during the Republican-controlled Eightieth Congress.] I respectfully suggest that this record makes the 80th Congress, in all that relates to our foreign affairs, not "the second worst in history" as we sometimes hear in general attack, but the best.

[After detailing Republican contributions to the United Nations Charter, the Greek-Turkey assistance program, the Rio Western Hemisphere defense treaty, and the European Recovery Program, he said:]

This, I repeat, is "bi-partisan foreign policy" at its best. It cannot be "bi-partisan" if it is "me too" at either end of Pennsylvania Avenue, or if it is "me too" on either side of the political aisle. It must be what it assumes to be or it will not work. It has "worked" — for a united America — because it wears Republican as well as Democratic trade-marks. These Republican trade-marks are a clue to the kind of action which we shall continue to pursue. . . .

One other thing must be made plain. "Bi-partisan foreign policy" applies only where cooperative consultation and mutual decision exists from start to finish. Historically this has not been the case in China, Palestine or Japan. [Later, in 1951, the Japanese peace treaty was concluded on a bipartisan basis.] Until recently it did not apply in South America. It has nothing to do with military government in Germany —

except that there is closest liaison in respect to the Soviet's vicious challenge to our rights in Berlin and in our Paris answer at the bar of the conscience of the world. Speaking generally, it does apply to most contemporary basic principles with the hearty loyalty of Republicans and Democrats alike, and, I profoundly believe, to the advantage of our own security and welfare.

For Vandenberg, the speech had at least one surprising result. Writing his wife a day or two later, Vandenberg said:

Well — I guess the speech was a success. Dewey called from Albany . . . and was most enthusiastic. Many, many good messages. But here's the confidential "pay-off" of them all. Our Harry phoned from the White House yesterday afternoon and asked would I please slip in the back door at eight last night for a private chat. I did (in the midst of a terrific rain storm). He . . . [said] that he thought it was a "grand speech"; that he deeply appreciated the judicial way in which I had been able to keep my "partisanship" on an unpartisan basis; and that he thought it was more important to retain the "bipartisan foreign policy" than who was elected President. . . . If that isn't a strange reaction to a campaign speech, I never heard one. It almost makes me wonder whether it did the GOP any good.

Throughout the summer months while President Truman and Dewey were trading verbal pot shots across the country, Vandenberg anxiously kept in close touch with the Berlin blockade situation through Undersecretary Lovett. In July the United States dispatched to Russia a note which diplomatic reporters referred to as the stiffest in fifteen years of Soviet-American relations. It demanded that the Soviets lift the transportation blockade; it said the United States was willing to discuss the Berlin situation, but only after the "intolerable" blockade was lifted; and it advised Moscow that the United States would not be forced out of Berlin.

Even as the political campaign raged, the drafting of the note — and in fact the handling of the Berlin crisis on the diplomatic front — proceeded with close bipartisan collaboration. Vandenberg wrote one diary entry concerning the note.

July, 1948

Washington: Undersecretary Lovett came to my apartment five times in connection with this note. He brought me an original and partial draft. After much consideration I drew the final form on my own Corona one midnight. The subsequent changes were very few — although some of it was toned down. However my own language was not belligerent. It explicitly disowned any trends toward war. But it made unmistakably plain that the United States intends to stand upon its rights in Berlin — making it equally plain that, if the siege and blockade first be lifted, we stand eagerly ready to "talk things over." In lieu of agreement between us, the note frankly proposed the "organs of the United Nations" as our recourse, identifying the International Court of Justice for the first time in this connection.

After the Soviet reply was received, Vandenberg wrote Lovett his own further analysis of the crisis situation.

July 19, 1948

The "calculated risk" evidently is becoming more "risky" — and probably deliberately so. I do not see how we can yield our basic position without total sacrifice of every chance we have for peace in Europe, or in the world. But let's always keep in mind that our "basic position" is that we cannot be *forced* out of Berlin by duress. It is *not* that we will not *get* out of Berlin voluntarily under satisfactory circumstances. Our aim, I take it, continues to be the latter.

Unless there are more imminent reasons than I know, I hope we shall not resort to any sort of unilateral force which, in effect, asks for war. If war comes, it must be plain to the world that it is Soviet Russia which has "asked" for it. On the other hand we cannot indulge the luxury of interminable "notes" at a time when the rapidly complicating conditions in the Berlin air can precipitate a miscalculated accident almost any time. . . .

I am simply saying in essence that I would stand fast; but I would *stand fast* for peaceful settlement before ever voluntarily accepting *any* overt responsibility for a needless war.

I hope your Department will keep in touch with Mr.

Dulles on this matter because he, not I, speaks for Governor Dewey. Unity is dreadfully important at home, to whatever extent this asset remain within our reach. . . .

The Berlin blockade crisis, with its inherent threat of war, weighed heavily on Vandenberg's mind in these days as the problem of relations with Russia — perhaps the whole problem of the postwar world — seemed to be moving toward a showdown. After reading an editorial in the Detroit *Free Press*, he sat down and wrote one of his not infrequent letters to the newspapers. But this letter was different because it was intended strictly for the publisher and not for publication. It was addressed to John S. Knight and it was significant for its revelation of the anguished debate which the Senator was carrying on with himself concerning America's approach to vital international problems.

August 17, 1948
My dear Jack,
  This is wholly "between us." I have just read your excellent signed Sunday editorial. With much of it I agree. I certainly was one of those "America Firsters" who wanted to keep out of other peoples' wars — and I went the limit in this direction up to Pearl Harbor. Beyond that, as you indicate, none of us had any option. I shall always wonder whether we might not have stayed out — and forced a peace for others — if we had consciously, deliberately and openly made *peace* the price of our *abstention*.
  But time marches on. We, and the world, are generally speaking in the "fix" which you describe (with reservations at the point where you discuss the so-called "Marshall Plan"). Once more we face the possibility of yet *another* war which, this time, might be the end of everything. Therefore, once more we face ominous decisions as to how we can save a peace worth saving. This brings me to your final paragraph which I shall not soon forget: "Let those who can, find comfort in the knowledge that the blood of our sons is on the heads of the 'statesmen,' present and departed, who inflict these needless and ghastly wars on helpless humans whose souls cry for peace."

I am *not* one of the "statesmen" responsible for the wars of yesterday. But I find myself among the "present" so-called "statesmen" unavoidably responsible for the decisions of today and tomorrow. I can painfully testify that it is a *horrible* responsibility fraught with harrowed days and sleepless nights. It is a *tragic* obligation which sometimes makes life itself all but unbearable. The "blood of our sons" has driven me to subordinate every other objective, in my public service, to the pursuit of honorable peace and to the organization of a global conscience and a global force to stop "the infliction of needless wars on helpless humans whose souls cry for peace." Relatively, nothing else matters.

But how? *How? How?* Everything depends on our poor, fallible human judgments. The next war *should be* "needless" (your word). Worse; it would be the crime of the ages. But, as you yourself have so often said, we do not escape it by running away from it. Appeasement merely precipitates the jeopardy it seeks to avoid. It takes two to keep the peace. We must forever choose between calculated risks. But *how?*

Are our *current* policies wrong? Are they too provocative? Or are they too impotent? What should we do that we are not doing? Or what should we stop doing?

If war comes, I suppose it will be said the "blood" will be on *my* head, in a small way, among others. That simplification of guilt can be no "comfort" to anybody, however, because it does not save the situation. It might even discourage the bold decisions which *could* conceivably save the situation. Be that as it may, I accept my share of responsibility with a sense of grim resolution to do my best, come what may.

But *I want all the help I can get.* I particularly want it from men like you for whose judgment I have the deepest respect and who cannot escape their own share of responsibility for what happens. I earnestly, prayerfully, sincerely ask you to write me in the same confidential spirit in which I am writing you. I want the benefit of your objective view. It will never be repeated or disclosed. It will simply be your comments to an old-time friend who finds himself confronted with many cruel imponderables which affect his nation's destiny. I cannot ask you to share my obligations. I cannot expect you to chart my course for me. I cannot seek more than a *general* indication — friend to friend — man to man — as to what you would advise in pursuit of a foreign policy at the present time which in your opinion would best be likely to encourage the peace we both crave and to prevent the war which your final editorial paragraph infers as "needless" if "statesmen" would adequately perform. God willing — they *must*. But *how?*

I wish I could make you feel that this is written — "Van" to "Jack" — with a deep anxiety for more light in the midst of too much darkness.

In October, 1948, Washington and, indeed, the entire country were startled by Mr. Truman's proposal to send — in the midst of the presidential campaign — Chief Justice Fred M. Vinson to confer with Stalin. Vandenberg wrote an account in his diary.

[*Undated*]

The Famous Truman-Vinson Incident, Etc.: These comments relate to the incident (October, 1948) when President Truman proposed to send Chief Justice Vinson as his personal emissary to Generalissimo Stalin at Moscow to "talk peace" in the midst of the work of the U.N. Security Council while it was considering the American-British-French Resolution condemning the Soviets for their Berlin blockade. Even though the President never went through with it — indeed he dropped it immediately when Secretary of State Marshall objected — the incident did him substantial campaign harm and at least temporarily embarrassed our American Delegation in Paris and our cause before the Security Council: (1) because it looked like under-cutting Marshall, et al., by direct negotiations over their heads; (2) because it would have been unilateral action without consultation of Britain and France who were our partners in the multilateral appeal to U.N. The story got into the newspapers three days after the idea was dead. It leaked through a radio station. Unfortunately when Truman thought of the idea and before he cleared it with Marshall, he evidently told his White

House staff to arrange a nation-wide radio hook-up for later in the week when he would make the dramatic announcement of the Vinson Mission to the country. This would seem to confess a highly political motive in the whole scheme.

The White House staff did contact the radio chains for free time for the subsequent Presidential broadcast. Since it was in the midst of the presidential political campaign, the chains had to know that "free time" was for government business and not for politics (theoretically at least). So at least one of the chains evidently was reassured with confidential news about the Vinson Mission. When the idea died, after its collision with Marshall's unequivocal veto, the request to the chains was withdrawn. But the news belatedly leaked and "the fat was in the fire." Truman did not deny it. But he made additional difficulties for himself by telling several different stories as to what the Vinson Mission was about. First it was just a general appeal to Stalin for pacific cooperation in respect to the Berlin airlift. Truman had in mind Harry Hopkins' somewhat similar mission to Stalin in 1945, when the U.N. Charter was stymied at San Francisco. Finally it was explained as an appeal to Stalin to help us do something about the control of atomic energy. (This was an equally sad excuse because "atomic energy" also was in the Security Council where we and our friends were dealing with it on a multilateral basis.)

Monday, October 4, 1948

I made my nation-wide broadcast presenting the record and the attitude of the Republican Party toward "bipartisan foreign policy."

Tuesday, October 5, 1948

This was the morning when Truman talked to Marshall in Paris and found the Secretary relentlessly opposed to the Vinson Mission because it would break faith with our partners, Britain and France, and subvert the American Delegation in Paris. In the afternoon the White House phoned me and asked me to "slip in" through the East door at 3 o'clock for an off-the-record chat with the President. A few minutes later the White House phoned again and cancelled the date. That evening the President himself personally phoned me at the Wardman Park and asked me if I would run down for a private chat. I went. The only other person present was Senator Connally. We were upstairs in the President's private quarters. He had nothing of any particular importance to say — and I have always wondered whether the meeting was not planned in the first place to break the news to us about the Vinson Mission. But he *never mentioned* the Vinson Mission *at all*. I never heard of it until it broke in the newspapers three days later. After complimenting me on my Monday speech, and saying he wanted to reassure me he was just as much interested in "bipartisan foreign policy" as I was, he said he wanted me to know that he had sent for Secretary Marshall to fly back to Washington the following Saturday for a general survey of Berlin and U.N. and that he hoped I would be available for possible consultations at that time if necessary. Then the President chatted informally about the possibility that he might "call Stalin on the phone" overseas and see what he could do with him. He was *not* announcing his purpose to do so. He was quite casually exploring the idea. I made *no comment* except to say that I thought a bi-lingual phone conversation would be rather difficult. But it was quite evident that the President was earnestly anxious to "do something." Connally and I left at the end of perhaps an hour. The fact that he said *nothing* to us about the Vinson Mission leads me to believe that he had totally dismissed the matter from his mind when he found that Marshall disagreed, and that he had *no intention at any time* of going ahead with the idea except with Marshall's approval. On the other hand, the way in which he was groping for some substitute idea to spectacularly associate himself with the peace crisis abroad left me with the impression that he at least was not "overlooking" the fact that he was coming down the home stretch in a political campaign which sadly needed a "shot in the arm."

Saturday, October 9, 1948

Marshall arrived. He had morning and afternoon conferences at the White House. Marshall, Lovett and I had three hours in between at luncheon in Lovett's secluded Rock Creek Park home. The Vinson Mission was considered by the Secretary as "dead" on the previous Tuesday. No alternative "scheme" was even mentioned. Marshall wanted me to return with him to Paris the next day in anticipation of successful U.N. mediation in the Berlin crisis, and an early meeting of the Council of Foreign Ministers which I had agreed to attend with him. But I felt it would be impolitic for me to suddenly show up in Paris in anticipation of a U.N. decision lest the Russkies should construe it as over-anxiety on our part and thus be encouraged to greater intransigence. The President very kindly phoned late in the day to say that no further White House conference was necessary at the moment.

Friday, October 22, 1948

Jim Reston of the New York Times phoned me (I was in Grand Rapids) from Washington that Arthur Krock (also of the Times) was greatly disturbed because he had heard some sort of rumour that the President was about to try a new version of the Vinson Mission *with my approval*. That certainly "disturbed" me as much as it did Krock. I had no information of any such adventure. The only thing I could conjure in my mind was that two-weeks-old statement about a "phone call to Stalin" and that, because I had not taken it seriously nor offered any argument on the subject, my silence might have been construed as consent. I immediately wired Matt Connolly (the President's Secretary) a message which had to be pretty cryptic; repeated the rumour; expressed my urgent hope that it did *not* involve "the other idea" in my recent "top level conversation" because I thought it, under the circumstances, quite as dangerous as the other.

Saturday, October 23, 1948

The White House phoned me that my wire had been sent forward to the Presidential train upon which Truman had started on another campaign trip. A personal message, direct from the President, was wired back for transmission to me. It said: "Nothing will be done without consultation with you." I thought that was very generous. Nothing further was heard of the Krock rumor.

That is the last pre-election diary entry despite the fact that November 2, election day, was fast approaching. It may be an indication that Vandenberg, like most of Washington officialdom, believed the die was cast; it only remained to tally the votes and count Dewey in. But on November 3, Vandenberg and the nation awoke to find Truman elected in his own right to the presidency. Among the Vandenberg correspondence is found this post-election telegram addressed to the surprise winner:

> I congratulate you upon a victory for which you can take supreme personal credit. I have just issued the following statement: "The people have spoken. The results will be loyally accepted by all Americans. In times like these it is critically necessary that we close ranks behind the nation's chosen leadership. President Truman has won a spectacular victory. Governor Dewey need have no regrets. He made a great campaign which leaves no scars and he received a magnificent vote. While there will still be basic issues upon which there will be honest differences of opinion, we need more than ever the team ball for which Governor Dewey spoke. I am confident President Truman will proceed in this broad spirit."

The next day members of his staff asked the Senator what he thought about the Truman victory. He stopped in the middle of the office, took his cigar out of his mouth and promptly replied in keeping with his general philosophy of giving credit where credit was due. "You've got to give the little man credit," he said. "There he was flat on his back. Everyone had counted him out but he came up fighting and won the battle. He did it all by himself. That's the kind of courage the American people admire."

24

Cracks in Nonpartisan Policy

THE YEAR of 1949 was one of tremendous political change. It was, too, the last year of Senator Vandenberg's active public career. It began for the Republicans, and particularly for the Senator, in an atmosphere of uncertainty because of the stunning election victory of President Truman.

Throughout the Eightieth Congress, Vandenberg had made an impressive record as the key figure in development of a nonpartisan foreign policy. He had convinced the nation that, for him, politics stopped at the water's edge. His prestige had mounted steadily. His position enabled him not only to hold in line the isolationist remnants in his own party but to make it essential for the Administration to seek and respect his collaboration in foreign affairs. To him had come the 1948 Freedom House Award "for service to a free world" and, significantly, his speech on that occasion so reflected nonpartisan thinking that former Democratic Governor Herbert Lehman of New York wrote him to observe that only rarely can one man agree with every part of another man's address, but in this case he [Lehman] could do so without reservation.

But the Truman victory meant change — and uncertainty. The Republicans lost control of the Senate and Vandenberg retired from the chairmanship of the Foreign Relations Committee and the Senate presidency pro tem. General Marshall's health was such that he could no longer continue as Secretary of State, and Lovett planned to retire with his chief. There was discontent within Republican ranks. And there was, in effect, a new President in the White House, because the man who had so humbly and prayerfully succeeded Franklin D. Roosevelt was now Chief Executive in his own right and intended to run his administration with a strong hand. Vandenberg could not escape pondering the future of nonpartisanship in foreign affairs under the changing circumstances.

For one thing, there was the attitude of the President. Immediately after the election Vandenberg had sent him a telegram of congratulations and received in reply a friendly letter praising the Senator's wisdom, courage, and patriotic devotion and stating that the President would continue to rely heavily on his counsel and guidance. But that was all for the time being. Mr. Truman went to Key West to rest, and there was no heart-to-heart talk immediately after the election to assure the future of nonpartisan foreign policy now that the Democrats were back in control of Congress. And it was, of course, inevitable that a period of readjustment in conduct of bipartisanship would follow the election.

Then there was a curious wave of newspaper rumors that Vandenberg might enter Truman's cabinet as Secretary of State — rumors that may have arisen from a recommendation by Marshall or Louis Johnson, who was then close to Truman. The Senator noted them in his diary.

Friday, November 5, 1948

Secretary of State? Today the Detroit Times carried a streamer headline saying that Truman would invite me to head his cabinet as Secretary of State — based, I believe, on pure conjecture. But, reaching Washington, I found the idea seemed to have some reality. A well-known Philadelphia newsman phoned to say that Democratic National Chairman McGrath indicated there yesterday that they would try to get me to take the job. I was also told that Leslie Biffle, Truman's close buddy and the secretary to the Senate Democrats, had said he was recommending it. I felt it was necessary to do something about the matter at once even though I had heard no word and had no reason to believe the President would consider any such idea. But he does so many impetuous things "off the cuff" that I feared he might announce it without talking to me about it.

It would have a tragic effect abroad — and be interpreted as a fatal split in our "bipartisan foreign coalition" — if it were publicly offered and then publicly refused. Without presuming to pass final judgment on an invitation that had not been issued, I felt, nevertheless, that there were powerful reasons why I could not do it; and that these should be known to the President immediately.

Therefore I sent for Biffle, who was about to take off with Truman on his post-election vacation and who has long been one of my own highly cherished and reliable friends. I told Biffle what I had heard. He confirmed the fact that he had recommended it. I pointed out to him — to be relayed to the President — that if my Republican colleagues resented my leaving them, at a moment when they face vital post-election decisions and need every bit of their strength, to head up the Democratic cabinet, it might well be that I would actually lose my best chance to be helpful in supporting "bi-partisan foreign policy." I pointed out that I could not possibly take the place under Truman without substantial freedom of action — and that "freedom of action" for a Secretary of State is really impossible, if not also improper, because the President is constitutionally responsible for the conduct of foreign affairs and the Secretary of State must, in the final analysis, be his servant. I pointed out that the President certainly would want to name his own ambassadors, etc.; and yet I could not operate the Department under personnel chosen for me by someone else. In other words, while the idea had much superficial charm and persuasion, it was not calculated to "work" — particularly remembering the White House habit of going off "half cocked" as in the Wallace and Vinson incidents.

I expressed my profound appreciation of the very high honor contemplated even in the suggestion; and I said I wanted to continue to work in closest possible liaison with Truman in our "team ball" on foreign affairs — but that I seriously doubted whether a scheme of this nature — no matter how nobly meditated by all concerned — could wind up in any other way than in my serving as a "prisoner" in the State Department where I would be just "fronting" for the

Truman administration — with an early resignation the only net result. I told him I was prepared to listen to any arguments to the contrary, if the necessity arose, but that I was simply making sure that no decision or announcement would be made without a full exploration by the President with me. Biffle said he saw my point of view and believed it justified. This is probably the last that will be heard of the matter.

It was, in fact, the last that was heard of the matter. Marshall was to remain in office despite failing health until after the new Congress met in 1949, and meanwhile Vandenberg was very much occupied with a rebellious outbreak within Republican ranks in Congress. The rebellion was directed primarily at Senator Taft, who was on a trip to Europe at the time and whom the rebels sought to oust as Chairman of the Senate Republican Policy Committee. The unrest within the party arose from dissatisfaction of a group of young Republican senators with the leadership of Taft, Senator Kenneth Wherry of Nebraska, and other right-wing senators following the loss of control of Congress. The Senate, for example, lined up with fifty-four Democrats and forty-two Republicans after the 1948 election.

Senator Lodge, one of the rebel leaders, wrote an article for the *Saturday Evening Post* under the title, "What's the Matter with the Republicans?" The article was basically a plea for new and more liberal leadership to rejuvenate the party. Lodge, who was the candidate of the rebels to succeed Taft, sent a copy of the manuscript to Vandenberg, who wrote him that it was "on the beam" but that he wanted to suggest several changes.

November 24, 1948

I miss a basic note of testimony to the inherent power of Republicanism — even in the current debacle. The very question itself seems to imply that we have been all but wiped out — and you do not rebut this implication. It seems to me the *first* thing to be said in response to "What's the Matter" is quite simply that we got 2 million less votes than the other fellow, out of some 50 million votes, in an election which would have gone the other way, presidentially speaking, if only 40,000 votes had been changed in the right places. That's no such debacle as might seem on the surface. That does not call for coroners, even though it does call for soul-searching. We should not *kid ourselves* with any such mathematical solace nor take it as an anaesthetic. But neither should we accept the premise that we have been gutted. On the contrary, if we frankly assess our own shortcomings and if we see to it that we deserve to win, we can do it as soon as 1950 — even on the basis of the 1948 returns. Let's not start the return journey in any sort of a spirit of defeatism.

Vandenberg's position in the Republican internal controversy was a difficult one from the beginning, and he was busy throughout part of November and most of December trying to find an amicable solution. His sympathies were with the young rebels. Lodge was particularly close to him, and the group, including Senator William F. Knowland of California, generally had been the core of Republican enthusiasm for a nonpartisan foreign policy, whereas Taft had more than once opposed Vandenberg on such issues as European recovery funds. Furthermore, Vandenberg recognized the desire of the rebels to shed the "Old Guard" and give the party a "new look" in order to tempt voters away from the Truman Fair Deal band wagon.

But there was much more than that to the problem. Vandenberg had a great respect for Taft's ability in the field of domestic affairs. He also felt confident that Taft could, if he desired, defeat the rebellion, regardless of Vandenberg's position in the fight. Furthermore, his dominating purpose in the coming session of Congress was to maintain a nonpartisan foreign policy and he knew that such a goal would be difficult if not impossible if the Republicans suffered a bitter cleavage among their senior statesmen in the Senate. His hope was that Taft would voluntarily step aside, and, as he recorded in his diary, he worked toward that end.

[*About January 1, 1949*]

The incipient Republican rebellion. I was one of those who thought the Republican organization in the Senate should have at least a partial "new look," and *did* seek to get it by negotiation. I was opposed to an open breach in the Republican Conference which would further decimate our weakened strength at this low moment. But I favored *negotiated* change.

I said to one and all that I would *not* vote against Taft if he chose to seek re-election to his post as Chairman of the Policy Committee, the post of dominant leadership. And I did not. I deeply felt that he has rendered great Republican service; that he has been given a "moss back" reputation which he does not deserve; that we shall need his aggressive wisdom in the 81st Congress; yet that it would be best for the Party, and for him, if he would voluntarily step aside, but not otherwise. . . .

I felt different about Wherry, Floor Leader. While he did a masterful job in the 80th Congress in handling his parliamentary responsibilities on the floor, I never saw the job better done, nevertheless he is widely regarded as one of the last remaining symbols of Republican isolationism — and I felt the Party could not afford to renew any part of this label. (Roscoe Drummond pointed out in the Christian Science Monitor that ten Republican Senators who voted against ECA ran for re-election; that nine were defeated; that only Wherry survived; and that there was little wisdom, to say nothing of political justification, in ignoring what happened to the nine and endorsing the one.) Furthermore, Wherry had been the core and focus of most of the opposition on the Senate floor to the unanimous reports of the Senate Foreign Relations Committee; and while I would ask no Senator to yield up his independence of action to the judgments of others, I think a Senator must be willing at least partially to pay this price if he wants to represent his Party colleagues as a Floor Leader. I said to Wherry and to anyone who inquired that I was opposed to his election as Floor Leader and that I would vote against him — and I did.

But my part in the "revolt" was a rather inactive one. After the [presidential] election Taft went to Europe and did not return until December 15. I counseled many senators, on both sides of the issue, to drop the discussion until Taft's return since his attitude would inevitably be controlling. I thought he might take himself out of the contest if he did not confront a *demand* for his retirement. In these conversations I sounded out the alternatives which would be most generally acceptable. It would have been possible to get practically unanimous agreement on Millikin of Colorado, as either Chairman of the Policy Committee or Floor Leader. I talked with Millikin. He was interested if Taft voluntarily retired — not otherwise. My personal hope was to change the rules to identify the Chairman of the Policy Committee as the Party *leader;* put Millikin here; elect Lodge or Knowland as Floor Leader; and either re-elect Wherry as Whip or make him Chairman of the Caucus (I insisted in spite of my opposition to his Floor Leadership, that he must not be "kicked in the teeth" but that his many good qualities and his Party record should be recognized in some other position).

Taft announced on his return home from Europe that he was a candidate for re-election as Chairman of the Policy Committee. Millikin declined to stand. Lodge ran against Taft. Knowland ran against Wherry. The two latter (Taft and Wherry) won by a vote of 28 to 14. But there will be substantial changes voted into the rules and the "new lookers" will have significant representation on the new Policy Committee. I think probably the "revolt" will prove to have been worth while.

Lodge and Knowland are two *magnificent* young Republican Senators.

I deeply regretted that I could not vote for Lodge in this instance. He is one of my most precious friends. He has been of great assistance to me. He is a superb public servant. I fully expect him to be a Republican President of the United States — and I hope I live long enough to have the chance to help put him in The White House.

The abortive party rebellion ended without having any direct influence on the nonpartisan policy problem that was foremost in Vandenberg's mind but it was promptly followed by Administration activities that boded no good for the future. When the Senator was Chairman of the Foreign Relations Committee he had insisted upon maintaining a ratio of seven Republican to six Democratic members and he had been successful in getting unanimous Committee votes for some forty-eight bills and treaties during the Eightieth Congress. But soon after the Eighty-First Congress met with the Democrats in control they insisted upon claiming eight seats for the majority party and relegating the Republicans to only five Committee posts. Given the number of Republicans in the Senate, this was the smallest minority representation permitted by law, and to Vandenberg it was a serious blow at the nonpartisan approach to foreign affairs. There was no question that the Republicans in the Senate would bitterly resent the action and that Vandenberg's task of keeping them in line behind a nonpartisan foreign policy would be vastly increased as a result.

Shocked and angry, he told the Senate on January 5 that the maneuver was "the first partisan action" in opposition to the spirit of bipartisanship in foreign policy. The new division on the Committee, he insisted, was "implicit with hostility" and carried to the public the implication that the Republican senators were "not quite trustworthy." His protests were in vain. The Democrats refused to budge and some Republican senators who had always been skeptical of nonpartisanship insisted that the Administration had delivered a blow below the belt to their Republican collaborators. Even those who had supported collaboration were upset. Senator Morse of Oregon asserted that "it has been made plain that the Democrats propose to play politics with war and peace."

"Republican Senators see in this 'packing' a very clear indication that they had been taken advantage of in the past and fear that the bipartisan policy will become exclusively a Fair Deal policy," columnist Constantine Brown wrote in the Washington *Star*. And columnist Doris Fleeson described the action as showing that the President "continues to make manifest his determination to exercise strong personal direction of foreign policy.... The Senate group is now constituted in such a way that there can be no interference with Truman foreign policy moves."

"If the bipartisan policy is not breached . . . it will be less because of [the Democrats'] example than because Senator Vandenberg is capable of rising above the affront and carrying on his fight for great principles," observed the New York *Herald Tribune*. And Jay Hayden, writing in the Detroit *News*, reported that "behind this flouting of Vandenberg is very definite resentment of the prominence he has acquired in the public eye. President Truman has winced increasingly because of the popular assumption that someone besides himself was directing American foreign policy, whether this role was attributed to Vandenberg or to his own appointees."

How seriously the Senator took such newspaper comment — Hayden was very close to him — nobody could be sure, but it was certain that he had no intention of abandoning his own convictions as to the necessity of continuing the nonpartisan policy in foreign affairs. He apparently had heard nothing from Mr. Truman in regard to future foreign problems since the election, and with Marshall's retirement, effective January 20, the President did not seek Congressional advice on the appointment of Dean Acheson as his successor. It was not necessary or even customary to do so, but the fact remained that there were important questions of foreign policy — principally the North Atlantic Treaty and the military assistance program — to be decided in the immediate future, and the Administration would need as much friendly Republican collaboration as could be mustered. It was not until an hour or so before Acheson's nomination was announced, however, that the White House informed Congressional leaders of his selection by telephone.

Vandenberg summed up his views regarding the Acheson appointment in a letter to the late Senator Clyde M. Reed of Kansas, promising a thorough review of the appointee's credentials:

January 12, 1949

I am frank to say that Mr. Acheson would *not* have been my choice for Secretary of State. But the President is not choosing an "official family" for me. He is choosing it for himself. I always feel that a President has a wider right of personal choice in naming his Cabinet than in making other appointments. As a general rule, I would let him have his own way in choosing his personal advisers, just as I would insist upon having my own way in choosing my own administrative assistant, and then hold him to strict accountability for the ultimate results. But if there are preponderant considerations to the contrary, the rule should be broken.

Meanwhile — as a matter of elementary fair play — let it be remembered that Mr. Acheson has many affirmative credentials. . . . He has proven himself to be one of the ablest administrators who has served in the State Department. He is one of the few possible Truman appointees who has firsthand knowledge of all the dreadful complexities in our foreign affairs. Incidentally, he has been violently condemned by Moscow for his current points of view.

Meanwhile, certain members of the Senate expressed concern because Acheson had been accused in some quarters of favoring a "soft" policy toward the Soviet Union. In public hearings held on the nomination, Vandenberg tried to set the record straight on that point and later suggested that Acheson issue a statement to the press making clear his attitude toward communism and totalitarianism. On January 14 the Foreign Relations Committee, meeting in executive session, unanimously approved Acheson's appointment. At the same time Chairman Connally released to the press an "excerpt" from Acheson's secret testimony. While it was not announced at the time, Vandenberg revealed to intimates later that he had prepared the statement and it had been agreed to by Acheson. According to the press the excerpt apparently satisfied some senators who might otherwise have opposed the Acheson nomination. The statement read as follows: "It is my view that communism as a doctrine is economically fatal to a free society and to human rights and fundamental freedom. Communism as an aggressive factor in world conquest is fatal to independent governments and to free peoples."

Acheson was the fifth Secretary of State since the idea of nonpartisan foreign policy had been originated five years earlier under Secretary Hull; a series of changes that had always produced a period of uncertainty at the beginning as to whether close liaison could be continued between the legislative branch and the State Department under the new appointee. This time there was the same uncertainty. In contrast to Vandenberg's success in getting Marshall confirmed on the day of his appointment, there was Senate opposition to Acheson and Vandenberg himself supported the new Secretary without any particular show of enthusiasm. He recalled to the Senate that he had opposed Acheson as Administrator of ECA, but he pointed out that his opposition then was based on his determination that the Administrator should have no relation to the State Department and should have been "a proven success in large-scale business management." The Senator's speech reflected his concern that nonpartisanship was in danger of cracking, but he said he had given careful consideration to Acheson's appointment and could find no compelling reasons against it. "We cannot control foreign policy through our action on this or any other nominee," he pointed out. "I want to make that plain. Therefore it should be made wholly obvious that we do not underwrite the results, in terms of foreign policy, which will flow from our confirmation of this or any other nominee."

The Senate confirmed Acheson by a vote of 86 to 6 and the new Secretary later sent Vandenberg a handwritten note thanking him for his support when the going was rough and adding that he would need and ask Vandenberg's advice and help. But the Senator's papers show no immediate follow-up on this letter by Acheson in an effort to assure the continuation of the close, personal collaboration that had existed during the Eightieth Congress.

"Until now," wrote Stewart Alsop, "Truman's role in the making of foreign policy has been with few exceptions confined to an almost automatic approval of what his Secretary of State was doing. This will be so no longer. Truman has no intention of becoming his own Secretary of State. But he does intend that the final authority should be definitely and clearly his. And it was largely for this reason that he appointed . . . a man with whom he was certain that a successful working relationship could be established. . . .

"Yet there is no assurance that the successful relationship

which seems to be in prospect between the State Department and the White House will also evolve between the State Department and the Congress. Two great issues will soon confront the Congress. One is the North Atlantic Pact, designed to form the keystone of American foreign policy. The other is the rearmament of Western Europe, without which the pact will have no meaning.

"Clearly, both measures will require Republican support. Yet the plain fact is that the bipartisan basis of foreign policy has been most gravely weakened. One reason is simply the . . . departure of Marshall and Lovett, with whom the Republican foreign policy leaders and especially Senator Vandenberg have developed an intimate understanding. By contrast, the relationship between Vandenberg and Acheson, who have had serious policy differences in the past, is one of mutual, but distinctly chilly, respect."

In retrospect this estimate appears to be reasonably accurate. Senator H. Alexander Smith of New Jersey, who was a devoted friend and a loyal supporter of Vandenberg's ideas, later told the editors of this book that "I think he [Vandenberg] felt there was a real difference in the attitude of the State Department toward him after Secretary Acheson took over."

But if Vandenberg believed that all of these developments meant a weakening of the nonpartisan effort to which he had long since dedicated himself, he gave no sign of it in public. On the contrary, he was more than ever determined that the damage done to nonpartisanship should be repaired and that the concept of putting peace above politics should be so firmly established that no future Administration or Congress would dare accept any other. He asserted in a Lincoln Day speech at Detroit:

February 10, 1949

Some say . . . the spirit of bipartisan foreign policy is dead. Some say that certain recent unfortunate events — like the Democratic raid on Republican representation on the Senate Foreign Relations Committee — have pronounced its obituary. That is not my view. The form of things, to be sure, has changed, and responsibilities and initiatives have shifted.

But the basic need remains. It will be a sad hour for the Republic if we ever desert the fundamental concept that politics shall stop at the water's edge. It will be a triumphant day for those who would divide and conquer us if we abandon the quest for a united voice when America demands peace with honor in the world. In my view nothing has happened to absolve either Democrats or Republicans from continuing to put their country first. Those who don't will serve neither their country nor their party nor themselves.

A great deal of Dutch stubbornness had gone into the Senator's slow, patient shaping of the policy of nonpartisanship — into what Senator Barkley later described as the cautious process of "planting one foot ahead of the other, feeling out the ground to determine and test its firmness."

On Lincoln's Birthday of 1949, the Senator from Michigan didn't have much time left, but he still had plenty of this stubbornness with which to defend his conviction that a nonpartisan foreign policy was the key not only to America's salvation but to the last, best hope for justice and peace in a jittery world.

25

The North Atlantic Treaty

THE FIRST critical test of nonpartisan collaboration in the Democratic-controlled Eighty-First Congress was on the North Atlantic Treaty, one of the most significant foreign policy decisions in the postwar struggle between the democratic West and the communistic East.

The treaty grew out of the concept of collective self-defense reaffirmed by Article 51 of the United Nations Charter and later reinforced by the Vandenberg Resolution. It was to pave the way for American assistance in the rearmament of Western Europe against the possibility of Soviet aggression and, eventually, for the creation of an international defense force under General of the Army Dwight D. Eisenhower. Thus the ground work in which Senator Vandenberg had had such a prominent part during negotiations on Article 51 at San Francisco provided a foundation four years later for an entirely new departure in American foreign policy, designed to link together this country and the free nations of Europe for mutual self-defense before they were submerged, one by one, by expansion of the Communist bloc.

Throughout 1948 realization had been growing that some drastic action was necessary to unite and strengthen the West. The Vandenberg Resolution was adopted to foster regional and other collective defense arrangements inside the United Nations but outside the veto. Diplomatic discussions were undertaken with the Western European nations. Then, in his inaugural address at the beginning of 1949, President Truman stated that the United States would associate itself by treaty with a "collective defense arrangement" which would include the free nations of the North Atlantic area.

This was a clearing of the ground for the projected North Atlantic Treaty, and Vandenberg's first reaction was cautious. He wrote to a constituent:

January 27, 1949

There is no doubt about the fact that it is a "calculated risk" for us to even partially arm the countries of Western Europe. It is also very much of a "calculated risk" if we do *not*. One risk will have to be weighed against the other. You suggest that it will be a safe thing to do "when the economic stability of these countries shall have improved." The basic question we have to settle is whether "economic stability" can precede the creation of a greater sense of physical security. I am inclined to think that "physical security" is a prerequisite to the kind of long-range economic planning which Western Europe requires. The fact remains that the problem is fraught with many hazardous imponderables. I am withholding my own final judgment until I see the precise terms of the treaty under which this new cooperation will be proposed. I think we ought to have wit enough to write it on a basis which is relatively safe.

The negotiations leading up to conclusion of the North Atlantic Treaty, originally started by Marshall and Lovett, were greeted by Russian charges that the United States and Britain wanted to establish world domination by force. Moscow warned the smaller European nations, particularly Norway, to refuse to co-operate with American "imperialism," but such threats were unsuccessful and plans were well advanced by the time of the President's inaugural address. Acheson, as Marshall's successor, carried the work forward and kept the Senate Foreign Relations Committee supplied with documents detailing the position taken by the United States negotiators. On February 18 and again on March 8, the new Secretary met with the Committee to review in detail the draft language agreed upon by the negotiating parties.

Connally (now Chairman of the Committee) and Vandenberg, who were in fairly close touch with negotiations, believed that there were at least two troublesome points in the draft and they suggested changing them before isolationist senators had an opportunity to use them as rallying points for opposition to the treaty. One was in Article 5, the operating clause, which pledged the signatories to regard an attack against one or more of them in Europe or North America as an attack against all. Each signatory pledged itself to take action, including use of armed force, to restore the security of the North Atlantic area. The Senators insisted upon changing the article to read that each signatory pledged itself to take immediately such action "as it deems necessary, including the use of armed force." This left to the individual signatories complete discretion in determining individual action; each was pledged to act, but the type of action was left to each sovereign nation.

In addition, Vandenberg, Connally, and other Committee members urged that a cover-all provision be added to the treaty providing that the pact would be ratified and its provisions "carried out by the parties in accordance with their respective constitutional processes." With these two changes the Senators believed themselves well prepared to meet any opposition in the Senate. Some senators had expressed concern that the treaty was an automatic commitment by the United States to go to war in case of aggression, and that such a commitment was in violation of the Constitutional provision that Congress alone has the authority to declare war. The cover-all provision made it clear that whatever happened the Constitution would not be by-passed.

Vandenberg's imprint on the treaty also could be found in Article 3, which pledged the parties to develop their individual and collective capacity to resist attack "by means of continuous and effective self-help and mutual aid." This was Vandenberg language that had appeared in the Marshall Plan act and the Vandenberg Resolution. The Senator also considered of special importance his success in relegating reference to the use of force in meeting aggression from a paramount position of emphasis to at least parity with the other methods which might be employed. He feared the treaty might overemphasize the use of force to the detriment of the many other effective steps which could be taken short of this ultimate sanction. On March 18 the final text was made public, and on April 4 it was signed in Washington by the United States, Britain, France, Belgium, the Netherlands, Luxembourg, Portugal, Denmark, Norway, Italy, Iceland, and Canada.

As usual Vandenberg was swamped with letters from those who opposed and those who supported the treaty. And as was his practice he used the correspondence to sharpen his own thinking in behalf of the project and to perfect the arguments he was to make on the Senate floor. To a Michigan correspondent, he wrote:

March 18, 1949

... I am glad to know your preliminary reaction to the North Atlantic pact. I agree with you one thousand percent that "this world cannot stand another war." Every effort of my remaining days will be dedicated to this truth. My greatest fear in this connection is that we will somehow drift into another war. . . . If Soviet Russia does start to march it would seem to be completely inevitable that the United States will be the ultimate target and that we shall inevitably be in that war — Pact or no Pact. So it seems to me that our best insurance is to make our position plain in advance. This includes above all else a clear demonstration that our objectives are totally defensive; that we have no goal except peace with honor and justice in a live-and-let-live world.

If you are right and this proposed North Atlantic Pact is "another provocation to another World War" then the Pact ought to be rejected. If I am right in believing that the Pact is our best protection against another World War then the Pact ought to be ratified. Therefore, our current problem is to fully and publicly explore every phase and every angle of the Pact. You may be very sure that I shall insist upon extensive public hearings which will clarify the issue. I want everything ventilated in this connection so that we may reach the wisest possible decision in a situation where we must take a "calculated risk" whichever way the decision goes.

Vandenberg wrote a South Carolinian who had urged the broadest interpretation of the pact that:

February 22, 1949

I am one of its [the Pact's] authors. I heartily believe in it. I want to give it a maximum chance to help prevent World War Three before it starts. But this requires absolute candor as to what it does and does not promise. I can think of no greater tragedy than to permit our friends in Western Europe to interpret the Pact beyond its actual realities. One reality is that we cannot commit ourselves to automatic war in the future. . . . We are recognizing facts of life as established in the Constitution of the United States. I will go as far as I can within the Constitution. I will not go farther because it would be an imposition upon our own good faith and a false reliance for our friends abroad. I hasten to add that I think we can achieve every essential result for the North Atlantic Pact by staying strictly within the Constitution of the United States and within the Charter of the United Nations.

Other correspondence covered a variety of directly or indirectly related subjects in the following weeks.

April 8, 1949

I emphatically agree with you that the Senate Foreign Relations Committee should hold complete and exhaustive public hearings. . . . On a vital subject of this nature, complete public information is indispensable to "the American way of life." . . . The Pact represents our best "calculated risk" for peace. . . . This is my feeling about the matter. . . . All that the North Atlantic Pact does is to notify Soviet Russia in advance that she cannot start any . . . "armed aggression" with any hope that she can "divide and conquer" western civilization — one country at a time (as both the Kaiser and Hitler undertook to do). . . . But we must make it completely plain that the North Atlantic Pact is solely defensive and that it does not poise any sort of threat — direct or indirect — against the Soviets or anybody else unless they themselves start the armed aggression which is aimed at world conquest for Communism.

April 15, 1949
>I certainly agree . . . [that] the pledges of the Pact must be unmistakable. . . . When it comes to the supplemental arms program (concerning which I really have very little official information up to date), I must confess that I have mixed emotions. Between you and me, I really think I would have preferred to have the Pact stand by itself as an all-out warning sustained by our general pledge but since the State Department has taken this other route (supplementary arms aid) I am not disposed to enter into any *public* argument lest it be misconstrued. On the other hand, I do intend — so far as it lies within my power — to see to it that any such supplementary program is realistic. . . . I think [the answer] lies in making our military aid wholly supplementary to the self-help and mutual aid defense programs of these other countries. In other words, it must be their last reliance rather than their first reliance in their own physical defenses.

In response to a plea from a supporter of the United World Federalists, he wrote:

April 26, 1949
>. . . After long experience at the council table with the representatives of Soviet Russia, I have some very earnest convictions on this general subject. I do not think it is possible to "amend the processes" of the United Nations to transform it into such a World Federal Government. . . . I am perfectly sure in my own mind that a number of other nations would not approve and this emphatically includes the Soviet group. I do not personally believe that there is anything to be gained by pursuing a course which holds no practical hope of accomplishment.

To a Grand Rapids constituent Vandenberg wrote:

February 21, 1949
>. . . in my opinion, when Mr. Hitler was contemplating World War Two, I believe he would have never launched it if he had had any serious reasons to believe that it might bring him into armed collision with the United States. I

think he was sure it would not do so because of our then existing neutrality laws. If an appropriate North Atlantic Pact is written, I think it will exactly reverse this psychology so far as Mr. Stalin is concerned if, as and when he contemplates World War Three. Under such circumstances, I very much doubt whether World War Three happens. . . .

I agree with you that it would be far better to work out all of these things within the general structure of the United Nations and its Security Council. But so long as an arbitrary Soviet veto continues it is impossible to do so. It is equally impossible to remove the veto without Soviet consent unless we scrap the old Charter and write a new one, which perhaps we ought to be considering. The great virtue of Article 51 is that it permits peaceful nations to defend international justice and security scrupulously within the Charter but outside the veto.

The Foreign Relations Committee conducted sixteen days of hearings on the Treaty. The advance consultation with the State Department had removed any possible misunderstandings so far as the Committee was concerned. It voted 13 to 0 to approve the Treaty after hearing ninety-six witnesses in discussion centering primarily on Article 5, and the broad issues of peace, war, and alliances. Two Republican senators who were not members of the Committee and who opposed the Treaty were invited — at their own request — to sit with the Committee and question witnesses. They were Senators Arthur V. Watkins of Utah and Forrest C. Donnell of Missouri. Vandenberg demanded that they be accorded every consideration, and at one time actually considered withdrawing from the hearings when frayed tempers brought some objections by other Committee members to the length of the questioning on the part of the Committee guests.

At the Committee sessions Vandenberg, through his questioning of Secretary Acheson, brought out several important points relating to the interpretation of the Treaty. In the first place, as the following exchange demonstrates, he made clear that the Treaty would operate within well-defined limits. He felt it was necessary to establish this point beyond any shadow of doubt before the Treaty reached the Senate floor.

Senator VANDENBERG. Mr. Secretary, first of all I want to be sure that the record discloses what I conceive to be the very close limitations within which the treaty moves into action. I am not clear about your answer to one question that the chairman asked you. He asked you what happens when an armed aggressor contemplates or undertakes an attack, and I understood you to say that the treaty came into effect under those circumstances. It is not my understanding that it would come into effect on the basis of a contemplation. The armed attack has to occur. Am I wrong on that?

Secretary ACHESON. You are right, Senator. If I gave the other impression, it was inadvertence on my part.

Senator VANDENBERG. And that is not the only limitation. The area of action is completely described within article 51, is it not?

Secretary ACHESON. Yes, sir.

Senator VANDENBERG. And under article 51 even the cooperative effort which is made under the North Atlantic Treaty ceases the first moment that the Security Council has taken the measures necessary to maintain international peace and security, is that not true?

Secretary ACHESON. That is true, both under article 51 and under the express provisions of this treaty.

Senator VANDENBERG. I think it would be well, Mr. Chairman, to print article 51 in the record at this point, because it is the key to the whole situation.

The CHAIRMAN. Without objection, article 51 will be printed in the record at this point.

(Article 51 of the Charter of the United Nations is as follows:)

Nothing in the present charter shall impair the inherent right of individual or collective self-defense if an armed attack occurs against a member of the United Nations, until the Security Council has taken the measures necessary to maintain international peace and security. Measures taken by members in the exercise of this right of self-defense shall be immediately reported to the Security Council and shall not in any way affect the authority and responsibility of the Security Council under the present charter to take it at any time such action as it deems necessary in order to maintain or restore international peace and security.

Senator VANDENBERG. So we confront, then, this series of limitations. In the first place, no nation is the target of this treaty unless it nominates itself as an armed aggressor by its own armed aggression. Is that right?

Secretary ACHESON. Yes, sir; that is correct.

Senator VANDENBERG. Secondly, it is effective only so long as the Security Council fails to take measures necessary to maintain international peace and security.

Secretary ACHESON. That is made repeatedly clear in the treaty itself, Senator.

Senator VANDENBERG. Therefore, if the general membership of the United Nations is faithful to its obligation to the Treaty of the United Nations, this treaty never becomes operative in action at all.

Secretary ACHESON. That is entirely true.

Vandenberg also made clear that if, in the future, any additional countries were admitted to the North Atlantic Pact group, the approval of the Senate would be required as in the ratification of a new treaty. This point assumes interest later in connection with proposals for accession of Greece and Turkey to the Pact.

Senator VANDENBERG. I want to ask specifically about article 10, Mr. Secretary.

The CHAIRMAN. Of the treaty?

Senator VANDENBERG. Of the treaty. This is the article which permits by unanimous agreement other European states in a position to further the principles of this treaty, and contribute to the security of the North Atlantic area, to accede to this treaty. How would the judgment of the United States be expressed upon a question of that character?

Secretary ACHESON. I take it that your question involves the point as to whether this would be done by the Executive alone, or whether there would be the advice and consent of the Senate to it.

Senator VANDENBERG. That is my point.

Secretary ACHESON. Senator, I am authorized by the President of the United States to say that in his judgment the accession of new members to this treaty creates in regard to each new member coming in in effect a new treaty between the United States and that nation, and that therefore the President would consider it necessary to ask for the advice and consent of the Senate before himself agreeing to the admission of a new member.

Senator VANDENBERG. I do not know how you could make a more totally persuasive or righteous answer.

I will pass for the time being.

The CHAIRMAN. I do not want to elaborate on that, but is it not true that with the nations that are now parties to the treaty, any addition of another member would be, in effect, a new treaty?

Secretary ACHESON. That is the President's judgment, sir, which I have just expressed.

The CHAIRMAN. And therefore, being a new treaty, it would have to be ratified by the Senate.

During these hearings Mrs. Vandenberg was ill and was forced to remain in Michigan. The Senator wrote to her regularly, giving her a kind of daily report on his activities. The letters, some of them undated but apparently written in May and June of 1949, concerned public affairs, the Senator's emotional reaction to patriotic band music, his great interest in maintaining good relations with Latin American nations, the state of his health, and his increasingly closer collaboration with John Foster Dulles. Dulles assisted the State Department in connection with a May session of the Big Four Foreign Ministers in Paris and, during this period, was appointed by Governor Dewey of New York to fill a vacancy in the Senate.

[*May 17, 1949*]

General (and Mrs.) Clay flew in today from Germany. He was given the kind of a reception reserved for "heroes" — and he deserved it. At the President's request I joined him at the Airport to welcome Clay. Then to the White House where Harry pinned a Distinguished Service Medal on him. Then to the Capitol where he made separate appearances and speeches before the House and Senate. Then a luncheon for Clay. Clay looks *worn* — but terribly happy to be at "journey's end." . . . He said he never would forget my reaction that day at Stuttgart to the playing of The Star-Spangled Banner by the Army Band.

Tomorrow the Dutra show starts. [President Eurico Gaspar Dutra of Brazil was making an official visit to Washington.] They have put up posters all over the down-town streets — but it's really pretty sad compared with the Rio show for Truman. But they have released all government workers at 3:30 tomorrow afternoon to "see the parade" . . . So there oughta be a good crowd. And I guess all the available Army will be on hand.

[*May 18, 1949*]

I am writing today's "report" *ahead* of the Dutra dinner at the Carlton because I expect I'll be "asleep on my feet" when I get back tonight. Just now I am home from the Airport reception followed by a so-called "parade" through the center of town to the District Building and then to Blair House. (I rode in an open car with Connally and [Secretary of Interior] Cap Krug — hats off — red hot sun — and I am pretty well baked — thank the Lord I wore the midnight-blue fatigue "uniform.") It was really a *pathetic* show (remembering what Rio did for Truman). There were a *few* troops lining the way — standing about 100 yards apart. There were a *few* stragglers on the curb-stones but damn few. There was a smart military show at the Airport (but very limited).

When I got up this morning, cards had already arrived from Fernandez [the Brazilian Foreign Minister] and his wife (who came in ahead of Dutra). That left me in the throes of a dilemma — what to do (in *your* absence)? I thought mebbe I oughta send back *our* cards. But that didn't make too much sense — and besides where are the cards? If you had a phone in your room I would have called you. (These protocol crises are too much for me when I am helplessly all alone.) I finally came to what was probably a unique decision. I went to the office — wrote a hearty personal note to Fernandez — thanked him for his cards — explained that *you* are "out of circulation" or he and his Mme would be hearing from us — expressed the hope that our paths would frequently cross this week — presented my warmest personal compliments — and sent the thing off by hand. When I met the charming, old gentleman at the Airport he seemed quite overcome!

[*May 19, 1949*]

Foster and Janet [Dulles] leave tomorrow afternoon with the Achesons in the new presidential plane for Paris. The last thing this afternoon we had Acheson before the Foreign Relations Committee for an hour outlining the approach which our delegation will take at Paris. I kinda wish I was going along (with you).

One thing is sure — if there ever was any suspicion about his [Acheson's] being pro-Russian it is all different now. As a matter of fact he is so *totally* anti-Soviet and is going to be so *completely* tough that I really doubt whether there is any chance *at all* for a Paris agreement.

[*May 20, 1949*]

I sent you a sweet letter from Dominie Thompson [pastor of the family church in Grand Rapids] regarding the Collier's check. [Vandenberg had received the Collier's award for distinguished Congressional service a second time and the ten-thousand-dollar check was donated to the Park Congregational Church.] It seems to have been quite a sensation. You will, of course, note from the letter that *you* are receiving a large measure of credit for the *idea* — which shows where *you* stand with *your* public. Anyway, the whole thing seems to have been quite a "hit." I notice that the Michigan State Senate passed a Resolution congratulating me on this second Collier's award. There's always something "funny" in connection with such things. I have received something like 100 letters from all over the country — like the one I think

I wrote you about from . . . a Church in Grand Rapids. They all start out with most enthusiastic encomiums about how wonderful it is to have a "great national leader" thus demonstrate his belief in religion and thus to serve the basic "spiritual values" of life, etc., etc. *Then* each correspondent suggests that his or her little church is struggling with some project and wouldn't the great, Christian, senior Senator from Michigan like to pass his benedictions (and his checks) around!

So far as my famous "headaches" are concerned, I can at least report that they are *no worse*. (I haven't had *any* today!) My numb fingers continue numb. (But everybody says — "How well you look!) — and I suspect there's nothing to worry about except the inevitable disintegration of old age.

[*May 25, 1949*]

You will want to see the current "*Look*" for June 7th. They are printing the results of a poll to "Rate Your Senator" as voted by 100 leading correspondents and commentators. Taft is the Senator "who contributes most" and is the "most conscientious" — Pepper the "best orator" — Lodge the "handsomest" — Lucas the "best dressed" — Donnell the "most serious" — Tydings the "most polished" — Millikin the "best sense of humor" and "the noblest dome." It's a good "museum piece" for the scrap book. [Vandenberg did not note that he was "the most statesmanlike" and "the most popular with fellow Senators."]

Well — this was poor, old Jimmy Forrestal's "good-bye" day — and it was one of those things which tore me into emotional bits (as it would have *you*).

It was a beautiful, clear day — but sharp and cold (and I all but froze in the Memorial Amphitheatre at Arlington). I was in a box next to the President. The papers say there were 6,000 present. It was a full, military funeral. Of course Jimmy wasn't very big — but the casket looked *so little!* There were four of the most famous bands in the country. The Marine Band played "Nearer My God to Thee" with infinite pathos. The Navy Band played Handel's "Largo"

— and of course that put me wholly out of commission. The Air Force Band played "Lead Kindly Light" — !!!

And then as they slowly marched from the Amphitheatre to the high hillside where Jimmy finds his peace at last, the big Army Band played "Onward, Christian Soldiers" — and I thought I would expire. There was something about it all which was so intimately tragic and yet so spiritually exalted. I am sure Jimmy did not die in vain. Mrs. F. did not come to the Amphitheatre; but, of course, she was with a rather small group of us at the grave. So be it! And *amen!*

[*June, 1949*]

. . . When Acheson [returning from the Foreign Ministers meeting in Paris] reported to the Foreign Relations Committee yesterday, he paid Foster Dulles very high compliments for his help at Paris. The conferences got nowhere — with the possible exception of an Austrian treaty later in the year — yet it was most significant. It found the Russkies on the defensive for the first time. They evidently know they have lost the cold war in Western Europe and as a result, they are undoubtedly under great pressure from their satellites to get East-West trade going again. It was very obvious that they want to keep the Council of Foreign Ministers meetings going (this was the first in eighteen months) so as not to lose contact. This is the time of all times to keep up our peace momentum in Western Europe and not let down for a single instant — which means ECA, Atlantic Pact and arms implementation. . . .

[*June, 1949*]

. . . Foster [Dulles] brought me down to date re Paris. He says Vishinsky was a different person this time — really a pathetic figure in his obvious lack of liberty to agree even to a comma without phoning Moscow. It was bad enough before, but this was the limit. He is convinced that the Politburo knows that it has lost the cold war in Western Europe; that it's nervous about holding its European satellites; that it's preparing to concentrate largely on Asia; and that its interest in keeping up these four power conferences is largely for face-saving purposes. He thinks that if we can only keep up this peace momentum in Western Europe, the danger of a shooting war is over at least for the time being — well that's my view, too, and I have a hard time tolerating the astigmatism of my colleagues who would subvert our bipartisan foreign policy at this critical period.

[*June, 1949*]

. . . As I told you my trip to Dartmouth was delightful. . . . Geraldyne [confidential secretary] says you know the new 42-year-old prexy — John Dickey. She says he was with the State Department in San Francisco and that he went out on the train with you. He certainly is a grand guy. Our old friend, Prexy Hopkins, was there as my special escort in the graduation parade. I got a laugh from the boys when I told them, in my little speech, that I hoped they would admit me to Fellowship with the Class of 1949 even though I had slipped in the easy way through the back door.

Nothing gave Vandenberg greater satisfaction than invitations to receive honorary degrees. His own education had been interrupted by illness and lack of finances after one year of a combined literary and law course at the University of Michigan. He always regretted that he hadn't earned a degree himself. If circumstances had permitted him to complete his education he undoubtedly would have gone into the legal field. One of the last letters he received just before his death was an invitation to accept an honorary degree from the University of Pennsylvania. Among the degrees he did receive were: 1925, M.A., University of Michigan, Ann Arbor, Michigan; 1926, LL.D., Hope College, Holland, Michigan; 1937, LL.D., Alma College, Alma, Michigan; 1938, D.C.L., Union College, Schenectady, New York; 1939, LL.D., Syracuse University, Syracuse, New York; 1941, D.H.L., Albion College, Albion, Michigan; 1947, LL.D., University of Michigan; 1948, LL.D., Columbia University, New York, New York; 1949, LL.D., Dartmouth College, Hanover, New Hampshire. He also received degrees from American University at Washington, D.C., and from Union College, Schenectady, New York.

[*June, 1949*]

> Here's a cute one on old Tawm [Connally]. You know how he is always trying to talk me out of making Senate speeches. Well — a few days ago he told me he thought it would be smart (when we opened the Pact debate) if neither one of us had much to say until the opposition opens up. He said he thought he'd talk only about ten minutes. "Oh, I can't do that," I said. "This is too important and I personally intend to open up with the speech of my life." That was that. Then one of the Saturday papers had a little piece saying that the Chairman of the Senate Foreign Relations Committee [Connally] was locked up in his office all day, sending out word that he couldn't be disturbed because he was writing "the speech of his life" to open up the Pact debate. I got a great kick out of that.

At this time, while the North Atlantic Treaty was being given its finishing touches prior to debate on the Senate floor, there was also a question of approving appropriations for continuation of ECA. Senator James P. Kem of Missouri introduced an amendment to the appropriation bill so worded that it would automatically withdraw all ECA aid from any country if it (or any subdivision of it) undertook what might be described as government ownership of any basic industry. Vandenberg opposed the amendment — which was later defeated — and wrote several letters to constituents explaining his opposition. He wrote, before the Pact debate had opened in the Senate:

June 27, 1949

> It seems to be the rather general opinion that we are winning this "cold war" through ECA and the North Atlantic Pact. In my opinion, if it were not for these policies, Soviet Communism would today be in substantial control of Europe and this would poise the greatest threat to our own national security in the lifetime of the republic. You evidently disagree both as to the premise and the conclusion. Therefore it is only natural that we should also disagree regarding the so-called Kem Amendment because it would accomplish by

indirection (in my view) the results which I fear would follow the destruction of our Western European program.

Most of the ECA countries in Western Europe have some degree of "socialism" in their governments. Therefore, I suppose it can be said that when we aid their governments we aid "socialism." But in my opinion this is by far the lesser of the alternative evils which we confront as a matter of our own intelligent American self-interest. I believe I am just as much opposed to "socialism" as you are. But there is a vast and ugly gap between Western Europe's kind of "socialism" and Eastern Europe's kind of "Communism." Our Western European allies believe in God and in His free worship. They believe in free and independent governments chosen by free votes. They believe in human rights and fundamental freedoms. They have demonstrated time and again that they believe in peace (American style) and are opposed to armed aggression (Soviet style). The maintenance of their independent self-sufficiency is the greatest practical protection which we in the United States can have.

We are not entitled to dictate to the British what kind of a government they shall freely choose for themselves. (I do not like the Labor Government in many aspects any better than you do.) Our ECA funds are not used for "nationalizing" or "socializing" projects in Britain. They are used for the purpose of stabilizing international dollar accounts which are prerequisite to Britain's economic survival (under any government). I say again that I frankly recognize that this process unquestionably helps whatever British government is in control. But this is incidental to the far more important and overriding concept (in my opinion) of keeping Western Europe independent and free. The Kem Amendment — as I see it . . . would make ECA impossible anywhere else in Western Europe. Since I think that would be a calamity . . . I am opposed . . . although I shall continue urgently to keep ECA out of any of these "socializing" impacts to the last practical degree.

Later, he wrote another letter commenting on the impact of ECA on Europe and on American markets abroad, where some critics feared American goods might be shut out as ECA assisted in the recovery of European industries.

July 16, 1949

> I think there is quite substantial recognition in Washington of the basic economic facts which you present. . . . One finds himself on the "horns of a dilemma" . . . We always seem to be wrestling with some sort of a paradox. On the one hand it is clearly of indispensable interest to the United States to stabilize Western Europe (and particularly Western Germany) as the "holding line" against Soviet aggression (which of course is ultimately aimed at us). On the other hand the effective economic stabilization of Western Europe (and particularly of Western Germany) pours a flood of new competitive commodities into the world's markets and our American producers find themselves menaced in much of our essential export trade. I sometimes wonder whether *this* particular conundrum can ever be resolved except on Hoffman's theory that world peace and stabilization can create new markets for *everybody* by creating higher standards of living at least in the civilized parts of the earth.
>
> I take it, however, that you are thinking more directly about another paradox — namely, that even though Western Europe and Western Germany are *helped* by our existing procedures, they are not *saved;* that on the contrary they are merely invited to temporarily *ignore* their own cancers. I *do* think this is recognized in many places in Washington. The British, for example, have got to produce more for *less* — and then find a market for the "more." (A successful answer of course immediately involves *us* in the *first* paradox to which I have referred.) But how can it be done? My own view is that it is impossible without a successful international stabilization of freely convertible currencies on a basis of true value. But the Lord knows that is easier said than done.
>
> I do not believe that we can *dictate* forms of government to the British or any other *independent* governments with whom we are associated in ECA. Even for *economic* purposes we cannot *impose* political decisions — or these govern-

ments cease to be "independent." Furthermore, any such efforts would probably generate *political* resentments which would drive the people of these countries still farther "left." (This is another paradox.) But certainly we *do* have the right — indeed, it is spelled out in the ECA Act — to require certain net *results* as the price of our continued economic support. It is at *this* point that our best opportunity lies. It is at *this* point that legitimate pressures are possible. But here comes the next paradox. If our friends abroad *refuse* to go along and we withdraw our aid, there will be an early collapse which will be terribly costly to *us* not only in economics but in renewed (and perhaps fatal) encouragement to Communism's cold war.

It seems completely clear that we are *winning* the cold war while we are *losing* the long-range *economic* war. Another paradox! We cannot afford to jeopardize the former trend nor to continue the latter. I sometimes wonder whether the wit of man is equal to the simultaneous solution of both questions.

You have written in *generalities*. I am responding in *generalities*. The question is — what do we do about it? It is so much easier to be critical than to be correct. That is one of the reasons why I regret that I ever left the newspaper business with its glorious freedom to settle things with an editorial.

By the time the North Atlantic Pact was sent to the Senate floor for debate the keystone, Article 5, had been so thoroughly discussed in committee, in advance Senate debate and in the press that there was little more to say about it. Instead the debate swung largely on the impending military assistance program to implement the Treaty and on the question whether Article 3 actually committed the United States to render large-scale arms aid to its Pact allies.

The debate opened on July 5 in the old Senate and Supreme Court chamber, where fittingly enough the Monroe Doctrine was first announced. Repairs to the regular Senate Chamber had forced its abandonment in favor of the old quarters near the center of the Capitol. The room was so small that the public could not be admitted. But the senators worked in an atmosphere of crowded informality with only themselves, a few staff members, and newsmen to hear their words at first hand.

On July 6 Vandenberg spoke for almost two hours on the Pact. It was to be his last full-dress foreign policy speech in the Senate, though he did take the floor later in connection with debate on the Pact and the arms program. Those who heard the speech thought that it was the utter sincerity of Vandenberg's words which drove his message home. The arguments, both pro and con, by that time were old. About all that could be said had been said. But Vandenberg's words were effective because he spoke with the fervor of a man who now saw his work at San Francisco coming to full fruition. He described the Treaty as the

> best available implement to discourage armed aggression and thus to stop another war before it starts. . . .
> My view is that this Treaty is the most sensible, powerful, practicable, and economical step the United States can now take in the realistic interest of its own security; in the effective discouragement of aggressive conquest which would touch off World War Three; in the stabilization of Western Germany; and, as declared by its own preamble, in peacefully safeguarding the freedoms and the civilization founded on the principles of Democracy, individual liberty, and the rule of law. These things, Mr. President, I shall undertake to prove.
> Only those without eyes to see and ears to hear can deny that these precious values — far dearer than life itself — are in jeopardy in today's tortured world. It is the over-riding fact of life. Sooner or later every other problem is over-shadowed by it. It is a condition, not a theory. It must be met as such. That is what this pending treaty undertakes to do.
> This jeopardy does not stem from us. . . . It stems from embattled, greedy communism abroad and at home; from open conspiracies which have frankly sought to wreck the brave self-help and mutual aid which would restore independent peoples to their heritage, with our American cooperation; from kindred saboteurs in the United Nations; from those who have repelled and thwarted our American designs and aspirations for a live-and-let-live world.
> I repeat: the jeopardy does not stem from us. But it

inevitably involves us. Indeed, we are its heart and core. It is aimed ultimately at us. We cannot run away from it. There it is, Pact or no Pact. Every vigilant American knows this is true. We are the final target, though other independent peoples are in nearer jeopardy. We may argue ourselves out of ratifying the Pact. But we cannot thereby argue ourselves out of the jeopardy which the Pact seeks to minimize. . . .

[Vandenberg told his colleagues that the Treaty was not a substitute for the other methods of seeking peace — the United Nations, the Council of Foreign Ministers, and the day-to-day relations carried on with other nations. But he insisted the Pact would strengthen such peace efforts and that it was drafted squarely within the Charter itself. Then, as though referring to his own attitude of other days, he said:]

We might also remember, Mr. President, that times have changed. Once upon a time the oceans were moats around our bastions. Once upon a time it was a miracle to travel round the world in 90 days. Now it is done in as many hours. We might compare old-fashioned muskets with new-fashioned bombs. Once upon a time we were a comfortably isolated land. Now we are unavoidably the leader and the reliance of freemen throughout this free world. We cannot escape from our prestige nor from its hazard.

[Recalling the words of Theodore Roosevelt that the United States had no choice but to play a great part in the world — the choice was whether it was to play it well or ill — Vandenberg said:] I submit to my countrymen that these words were written for the ages. Never did they more accurately define reality, never did they more vividly point the goal than they do this afternoon. Much as we might crave the easier way of lesser responsibility, we are denied this privilege. We cannot turn back the clock. We cannot sail by the old and easier charts. That has been determined for us by the march of events. We have no choice as to whether we shall play a great part in the world. We have to play that part. We have to play it in sheer defense of our own self-interest. All that we can decide is whether we shall play it well or ill.

We played it well in the military climax of World War

I. We played it well in the defeat of our enemies in World War II. We played it ill at Yalta. We played it not so well at Potsdam. We played it ill in China. We played it well at Chapultepec, at San Francisco's Golden Gate, and at Rio. We played it well in Berlin. Our intrepid eagles wrote incalculable American prestige for us across those treacherous skies. We have played it so well in the cooperative rejuvenation of Western Europe that the momentum of confidence and peace is in formidable stride.

This is no time to halt this trend. This is the hour of hours to continue to "play it well." In my deepest conviction that is exactly what the pending North Atlantic Pact will do.

[After describing development of the Treaty the Senator then answered its critics:] There is not one aggressive syllable in the entire contract. There is nothing but peace in its aspirations which give it being and in the self-help and mutual aid which give it life. It is not built to stop a war after it starts — although its potentialities in this regard are infinite. It is built to stop wars before they start. With greatest respect for the counter views of sincere Americans who argue otherwise — but with complete contempt for the hostile, self-serving, self-confessing hysteria against it by communism everywhere — I shall urge the Senate that this is the logical evolution of one of our greatest American idioms, "united we stand, divided we fall."

[Vandenberg referred to the arms aid program and those who emphasized that the Treaty would call for munitions shipments.] I do not agree. Frankly, I should have much less interest in this Treaty if I thought its repressive influence for peace is measured by or dependent on any such implementation. It is not the military forces-in-being which measure the impact of this "knock-out" admonition. In my view its invincible power for peace is the awesome fact that any aggressor upon the North Atlantic Community knows in advance that from the very moment he launches his conquest he will forthwith face whatever cumulative opposition these United Allies in their own wisdom deem necessary to beat him to his knees and to restore peace and security.

It is not the military forces-in-being which measure the

impact of this "knock-out" admonition, important though they are. It is the potential which counts, and any armed aggressor knows that he forthwith faces this potential from the moment he attacks. It is this total concept which, in my view, would give even a reincarnated Hitler pause.

[In precise terms, Vandenberg dealt with the complex and much debated question of the extent of America's commitment under Article 5, the Treaty's one-for-all pledge of mutual assistance in event of attack. It was the heart of the Treaty and the heart of the collective endeavor to maintain peace.]

. . . since this Article says that "an armed attack upon one shall be considered an armed attack upon all," does this automatically commit us to war? It commits us, according to the text to take forthwith, individually and in concert with the other Parties "such action as we deem necessary, including the use of armed force, to restore and maintain the security of the North Atlantic Area." A commitment to take notice and to do something about it is automatic. A commitment to war is not. Indeed, the textual phrase "including the use of armed force" obviously indicates that there are many other alternatives, just as there are in the United Nations Charter.

Everything depends upon the nature of the event. A minor aggression might be stopped by a vigorous warning. An instant appeal to the Security Council of the United Nations might succeed and suffice. If the Security Council defaults, the so-called pacific sanctions described in the Charter might be applied by the partners under the Pact. . . .

But suppose the event is obviously of major and deliberate magnitude and clearly discloses a criminal aggressor deliberately on the march — as Hitler entered Poland or as the Kaiser entered Belgium. Let us say that it is clearly the dread thing which threatens the life and freedom of one of our associated nations, if not ourselves directly. If it is, it threatens the life and freedom of every other associated nation, including our own. If it is, it threatens total war or total surrender, Pact or no Pact. If it is, our commitment is clear as crystal. It is to take whatever action we deem necessary to maintain the security of the North Atlantic Area, which vividly includes the security of the United States. If the only action adequate is war, then it means war. If it does mean war, I venture to assert that, Pact or no Pact, it would mean war for us anyway in this foreshortened world. If it does mean war, I venture to say that we would be infinitely better off for having instant and competent allies. But if it does mean war, only Congress itself, under the specific terms of the Pact, can declare it.

[Vandenberg discussed the century old argument of the extent of a Chief Executive's authority to use military force without a declaration of war by Congress. He defended the Pact as "a supplement to the United Nations Charter, not a substitute. . . ." Then, again returning in conclusion to the major theme of the nature of the Pact, he closed on this note:]

This Pact is a fraternity of peace. It involves us in no obligation not already implicit in our signature to the United Nations Charter. It simply makes the obligation plain and dependable for us and others. It binds potential and indispensable allies to us as well as us to them. It spells it out. This candor can be as powerful as an atomic bomb. This is its terrific authority for peace. It spells out, beyond any shadow of any doubt, the conclusive warning that 300,000,000 people, united in competent self-defense, will never allow an armed aggressor to divide and conquer them pursuant to the pattern of the rapes of yesterday. It spells out the conclusive warning that independent freedom is not an orphan in this Western World, and that no armed aggression will have a chance to win.

Thus we crystallize the most practical deterrent and discouragement to war which the wit of man has yet devised.

We have done our best — for peace. But we recognize our frailty. The wit of man alone is not enough. I quote the final sentence from the findings of the Senate Committee on Foreign Relations: "In tendering this unanimous report on the North Atlantic Treaty, we do so in furtherance of our Nation's most precious heritage — shared in common with the other signatories — continuing faith in our dependence upon Almighty God and His guidance in the affairs of men and nations."

The next morning the Senator found on his desk the following memorandum placed there by his secretary: "Mr. Cordell Hull called to give his warmest congratulations to the Senator on 'one of the greatest speeches ever made.'"

Debate on the treaty lasted twelve days and included an opposition speech by Senator Taft. Vandenberg described the developments to his wife in letters that indicated his satisfaction with the North Atlantic Treaty but suggested that bipartisanship was functioning much less smoothly than in the past.

[*July 11, 1949*]

The Taft speech will lengthen the battle because it lends a certain respectability to the opposition, and some of those who wouldn't have dared stand up on their own will now join the anti parade. But I don't believe it will be serious. . . . I cannot ignore the fact that if Taft thought his negative vote would divide the Party, he would never take that responsibility. . . . I must confess, however, that my friend from Ohio has given me a first class headache tonight. . . .

[*July 20, 1949*]

. . . Senator Graham (of North Carolina), making his maiden speech, gave me a really beautiful compliment and identified the Vandenberg Resolution as the "Magna Carta of new hope for freedom in a Communist-assaulted world." . . . My prophecy is not more than sixteen votes against the Pact. Then comes the still worse battle over implementing it. Here I am in sharp *disagreement* with the President and the State Department. They have gone much too fast too soon. [This was in regard to how much arms should be sent to European nations immediately.] But at least there'll be a breathing spell before this next storm breaks.

[*July, 1949*]

. . . It took us an hour to get a quorum in the Senate and even then we just made it (49). The other half is out of town and of course, all the House is gone. Nice way to run the country! I have never seen such contagious irresponsibility! . . . I sadistically asked Alben [Barkley] today what he thought of all the absenteeism. He allowed it's pretty bad for all except "widowers over seventy."

[*July, 1949*]

I'm sorry you didn't hear the Romberg broadcast last night. . . . I think it was the most thrilling musical program I ever heard. The audience simply went crazy. The announcer said that musical "highbrows" consider Romberg "low-brow" and that "low-brows" consider him "high-brow" and therefore he considers himself "middle-brow." I guess that's about where I land when it comes to music.

Vandenberg played the piano some by ear — in the key of F sharp, which principally involves the black keys. In his early newspaper days he wrote the lyrics to two popular songs that were published. One of them was inspired by a motion picture star — Bebe Daniels — who was a Grand Rapids girl. Its theme was "Bebe, Bebe Be Mine." The signature appearing on the music was a switch of his names — A. V. Hendrick. The music was written by Dr. A. B. Smith, who was Vandenberg's friend and surgeon. One of his daughters, Elizabeth, studied piano seriously, appeared a few times professionally, and at the age of fifteen was piano soloist with the National High School Symphony Orchestra when they performed before President Hoover in Constitution Hall. The Senator's "middle-brow" taste for music included a liking for the "Whiffenpoof Song," particularly the arrangement played by Fred Waring's orchestra. Shortly before Vandenberg's death Waring learned of this and played it for Vandenberg one night on his program, much to the delight of the Senator.

[*July 21, 1949*]

Well — as you know we won the big battle [over the North Atlantic Treaty] today by a vote of 82 to 13 . . . It's a great relief to have the battle over — yet I seem to feel a greater responsibility than ever tonight — how will it all work out? At best, it's a calculated risk. But I have a feeling that this day will go down in history as one of the big dates, and it all stems from the Vandenberg Resolution which you saw a-borning in 500 G [the Vandenberg apartment] with dear old Bob Lovett as the midwife. . . . The Republicans split 32 to 11 my way. But we are going to have a God-awful time with the implementing arms bill a little later.

Vandenberg was always deeply interested in the *size* of the vote by which the Senate approved a foreign policy measure. For important matters like the European Recovery Program and the North Atlantic Treaty a skimpy majority or a bare two-thirds was not enough. He believed it highly desirable — where our national interests are at stake — for the Senate to go on record with overwhelming votes, and he devoted his legislative talents to this end. In this way, he argued, our policy would be firmly established and we would erase any doubt and uncertainty that might exist abroad as to our intentions.

No doubt this was one of the reasons Connally and Vandenberg were anxious, during the negotiations, to clarify the nature of our commitments under Article 5 of the Pact. While the Senators were criticized at the time by some commentators and editorial writers for emasculating the treaty, subsequent events proved the wisdom of their course. The resounding 82–13 vote put the Senate squarely back of the proposition that an attack against one is an attack against all.

[*July, 1949*]

. . . You will be interested in the enclosed note which came by hand this morning from Dean Acheson. But you will be still more interested to know that Dean called up this afternoon and asked if he could drop in at the flat for a drink on his way home — and drop in he did. It was *slightly* reminiscent of the old Lovett days. He came at 5:30 and stayed two hours. . . . He is entirely surrounded with utterly baffling problems. (I wouldn't take his job for a million a week.) Well — he went from one problem to another — China — atom bombs — arms for Western Europe — Korea — Japan — etc., etc. I didn't let him unload them on me in any such fashion as Marshall and Lovett did. But I tried to be both genial and helpful; and when he finally left he expressed deep gratitude and "could he please come again soon." It would be funny if everything were not so desperately serious these days.

We opened up on the ECA appropriations bill in the Senate today — just one more Pandora's box. I think we can save enough of the pieces to keep Hoffman going. But I get so damned sick of that little band of GOP isolationists who are always in the way that I could scream.

Vandenberg was overworked and sick — much sicker than he knew — and as a result, he let his impatience have free hand when he wrote privately to his wife about the "little band of GOP isolationists." He was never impatient with them in public. And it is not likely that he missed the irony of his own position — of how, only a decade before, he had written proudly in his diary of the way "our little band" of arms embargoists fought tooth and nail against President Roosevelt's program for changes in the Neutrality Law that would facilitate aid to Britain.

26

Implementing the Pact

THERE WAS trouble in the air even before the North Atlantic pact was ratified. It blew up around Administration plans to send American arms to the pact nations in Western Europe and it further reflected the deterioration of collaboration under a nonpartisan approach to foreign policy.

Vandenberg, in supporting the North Atlantic Treaty, had specifically reserved judgment on the follow-up arms program. His basic interest in the treaty was that Article 5 provided in advance for co-operative action against aggression, and he regarded this as far more important in the long run than the immediate problem of arms shipments to Europe. Indeed, he feared that too much emphasis on the arms program might turn the mutual defense agreement into an obvious military alliance and touch off a renewed armament race between the East and the West.

This fear was intensified on July 25, 1949, when President Truman sent to Congress a legislative request for a $1,450,000,000 arms program to strengthen not only the signatory nations to the North Atlantic Treaty but certain other nations as well. It was significant that there had been no serious advance bipartisan consultation concerning this program. Congressional leaders had been occupied with the Treaty debate and preferred not to have the controversial arms issue injected into the situation until after the treaty was approved. Furthermore, the State Department was in a hurry because it hoped for action on the arms program before the approaching adjournment of

Congress. Some legislators had been informed by the Department that military assistance would be necessary, with or without the Treaty, and that plans for such assistance were being drafted independently. But it was clear that the problem of military assistance had been discussed with prospective signatories of the Treaty and, for some European nations, the assurance of American arms shipments was a major consideration in their adherence to the pact.

All of these developments disturbed Vandenberg. He seemed to feel that liaison between the State Department and Congress was breaking down and that the legislators were being rushed into important decisions. The North Atlantic Treaty provided for a Council and a Defense Committee to recommend measures — such as arms aid — for implementing the self-help and mutual aid provisions of Article 3. But before the pact mechanism had been set up and before joint defense plans were drafted the Administration was asking approval of arms shipments on a considerable scale. That, he believed, was putting the cart before the horse. Two hours after Mr. Truman's arms program request reached Capitol Hill, the Senator sat down at his typewriter and wrote a statement for the press: "The President's emphasis on collective security is sound. But my first impression is that the program must be rewritten and curtailed to get action at this session. It is too wide in scope and too general in grant of power. It ignores the machinery which the pact provides for its own implementation. Its statement of policy puts too much emphasis upon arms. Since some sort of action is necessary before adjournment, I think study should be given to an interim measure while major plans await reports to the next Congress under Article Nine of the pact."

In a series of letters to his wife at this time Vandenberg stated his viewpoint in plainer words that showed how far nonpartisanship had deteriorated.

[*July 25, 1949*]

. . . The pending arms program is my next big job. I served blunt notice today that I simply would not support the present bill. It's almost unbelievable in its grant of unlimited power to the Chief Executive. It would permit the President to sell, lease or give away anything we've got at any time to any country in any way he wishes. It would virtually make him the number one war lord of the earth. In today's [Foreign Relations] Committee meeting, Walter George, Cabot Lodge, Bill Fulbright and Alex Wiley backed me up one hundred per cent. They have got to write a new bill. The old bipartisan business is certainly "out the window" on this one. Yet I don't want to be shoved over into a position of seeming hostility to the *objective* (in which I deeply believe). So it's a pretty tight "poker game" between Acheson and me.

[*July, 1949*]

... I am not looking forward to next week. It's going to be pretty terrific.... Foster [Dulles] and I must set our pattern for cutting this arms bill down to size. We start Committee hearings Wednesday. It's a tragically serious situation. If this session adjourns with no arms legislation, Western Europe's morale will go into a tailspin. But that is exactly what will happen if the Administration insists upon its present bill.

[*July, 1949*]

I really had a good time at last night's dinner given by the Philippine President. In the first place, I really felt well. In the second place, I landed next to a high officer in the present Manila government and we had a wonderful reminiscence period.... He was a government clerk when we were in Manila and he ran some kind of an errand for you one day. ... He told me a wonderful story.... He was Speaker of the Philippine House when they passed the amended Constitution providing that the President could serve only two four-year terms. It had to have the approval of President Roosevelt. He was deputed to bring it over for FDR's signature. He arrived early in October 1940 when FDR was running for a third term. He reported first to Secretary Ickes who was in charge of our territories. Ickes took one look at the Constitution — saw the two-term requirement and said to the messenger — "Listen Bud, you go up to the Mayflower and get yourself a nice comfortable room and wait until *after* the

November election before you ask FDR to sign anything like that." And that is what he did!

To Hamilton Fish Armstrong, editor of *Foreign Affairs*, he wrote: ". . . I agree emphatically that we must put our joint defenses in potential gear and bring them to a basis of normal sufficiency in our allied countries. On the other hand we must be careful that we do not allow the arms program to overshadow and dominate the non-aggressive character of the pact itself. In other words, we must not let 'the military' now 'move in' and take charge."

The breakdown of nonpartisanship was generally recognized by the press at this time. Some political writers expressed belief that one cause was Senator Connally's antagonism toward Vandenberg, but most observers believed the basic reason was the desire of the White House to run its own foreign policy show. Joseph Alsop, writing in the New York *Herald Tribune*, said that "bipartisanship in American foreign policy, which saved the western world in the postwar years, has been utterly abandoned since the last [1948] election." He pointed out that continuous exchange of information and continuous consultation on policy had made a success of nonpartisanship in the past but that Republicans could not be expected to go along blindly with Administration policies after that system was dropped. "Since his return from Paris," Alsop added, "Secretary of State Dean Acheson had only seen Senator Vandenberg, at least until a few days ago, at two or three purely formal and general conferences. This startling fact is proof that bipartisanship is at an end."

The article went on to say that Connally had "openly resented" Vandenberg's pre-eminence in the past when the Republicans controlled the Senate and that some Administration sources argued that he would "grow very touchy now" if Vandenberg and other Republicans were still consulted. "It is certainly true that Senator Connally's sensitivity constitutes an obstacle to the continuation of bipartisanship. But what is now necessary is not at all the sort of system that prevailed when . . . Under Secretary of State Robert A. Lovett worked for an hour or so with Senator Vandenberg almost every afternoon. . . . The need today . . . is only for a resumption on a reasonable, modified plan, of the normal exchange of information and prior consultation on policy without which any bipartisanship is wholly impossible." Alsop concluded that this was up to the President, and added that "it is certainly not a bad bet that the present situation originated, at least in part, in the White House attitude toward bipartisanship."

Vandenberg pasted the Alsop article in his scrapbook and commented on it in his next letter to his wife.

[*July 31, 1949*]

... I was amused by all the dope stories today to the effect that Acheson is really getting ready to capitulate. They say he is working on an arms compromise. He better had — if he wants any legislation at all this session (and, I repeat, it would be a tragedy to quit with nothing done).

I was also amused at today's Alsop column. This will make old Tawm [Connally] fairly burn in his boots. But I don't object to having it down in record that Lovett and I spent "an hour a day" together during the bipartisan days when we were getting invincible results. I feel rather sorry for Acheson. I think he would like to carry on in the old pattern. But it just isn't possible under the new set-up. Alsop has identified one of the major reasons.

[*August, 1949*]

... I have spent a day in executive sessions of Foreign Relations [Committee] on the arms program for Western Europe. The Administration is doing the best it can to overwhelm me and my insistence on a sharply curtailed program pending the organization of the Atlantic community under the Atlantic Pact.

At this time he wrote in a letter to a constituent:

August 1, 1949

... it would be a supreme tragedy if this session of Congress should adjourn without passing some kind of preliminary "arms bill." Yet that is exactly what is likely to happen unless the Administration sharply changes . . . [the projected bill] because not even the most devoted friends of the pact can swallow the pending arms proposal. If they cannot do so, it becomes a cinch for the "isolationists" to beat the bill.

There are many reasons why the pending bill is impossible. For example, it entirely ignores the fact that the North Atlantic pact, Articles Three and Nine, direct the formation of an "advisory council" and a "defense committee" to develop a plan of "self-help and mutual aid" for implementing the pact. The pending bill totally ignores these treaty articles and proposes to set up the implementation of the pact entirely outside the pact. This is intolerable. The thing we should now do is to provide a very brief interim bill to demonstrate our good faith pending the development of an integrated arms program as directed by the pact itself.

But there is something still more fundamental involved. The President's pending proposal uses the existing situation as an excuse to seek more general peace-time power than was ever concentrated in the White House in the history of the United States. It goes far beyond any necessities created by the pact or by anything else. In Section Three "the President is authorized, upon the request of any nation, to furnish assistance to such nation through grants, or for payment in cash, or through any other means and upon such other terms as he deems appropriate, whenever he deems that the furnishing of such assistance will further the policies and purposes of the Act." In other words, he can sell, loan or give away the entire national defense establishment to anybody at any time and on any terms whenever he thinks it is "important to the national interest in the United States." He would become the top warlord of the earth. Can you imagine that the American people would for an instant surrender any such supreme and exclusive authority to the Chief Executive?

The bill has got to be rewritten if any bill is to pass before this session of Congress adjourns — and I repeat it would be a supreme calamity if Congress adjourns with no bill. This is not merely my own view. It is equally the view of such staunch supporters of collective security as Senator Dulles, New York, Senator Smith of New Jersey, and Senator Lodge of Massachusetts and many others.

Meantime, Vandenberg kept up his pressure for revision of the bill, as he related to Mrs. Vandenberg.

[*August 2, 1949*]

... We had our telltale show-down on the arms program in the joint meeting this morning of the Foreign Relations and the Armed Services committees. I bluntly laid the "facts of life" before Secretary of State Acheson and Secretary of Defense Johnson. I gave 'em an ultimatum — write a new and reasonable bill or you will get no bill and it will be your fault! Both Committees backed me up — and at the end of a rather dramatic session, they went downtown to write a new bill. It was a very tense situation.

[*August 5, 1949*]

... The State Department came up with a new bill today in re arms. They have totally surrendered on eighty per cent of my criticisms. The new bill is really pretty good. But it still has too much money and it does not adequately subordinate itself to the machinery provided in the Atlantic Pact for its own implementation.

The new draft sharply curtailed the President's "blank check" authority to furnish assistance to any nation, or, in fact, to any group within a nation where American security interests were involved. It specified the recipient countries, and it made clear that all aid rendered was to be consistent with the common defense of the North Atlantic area and joint strategic concepts. It also emphasized that the arms aid program was to be consistent with the United Nations Charter. Vandenberg told newsmen that the compromise "substantially narrowed the area of controversy" although some major differences particularly regarding the amount of arms aid, remained to be adjusted. Dulles praised Administration co-operation and said it would contribute to bipartisanship in foreign policy.

Vandenberg wrote Walter Lippmann:

August 9, 1949

... We have killed the "war lord bill" which would have made the President the top military dictator of all time. It did not take the State Department long to surrender after the first meeting of our Joint Committee last week where I think I made the most vigorously candid speech of my life. . . . It would be interesting to know just who wrote the bill. I have been quite amused by the private assurances I have been given by each of the key figures in the transaction that they all were really opposed to the text.

The episode has not been without some collateral advantages — from my point of view. It has publicly demonstrated that the Republican contribution to so-called "bipartisan foreign policy" is not on a "me too" basis. This "me too" charge has been the most successful criticism which the isolationist wing of the Republican Party has been able to throw at me. I have never felt free to answer. Now events have answered for themselves. The truth of the matter, of course, is that the Republican contribution to "bipartisan foreign policy" has always been the exact reverse of "me too." The only difference is that heretofore the "surrenders," if you want to call them that, have occurred in private and in advance.

The new bill is in fairly satisfactory shape — except, from my point of view, the new arms program is being developed on a two-year basis outside and independent of the implementation machinery set up by the North Atlantic pact itself. I do not like this feature. If we believe in "collective security," I think we should embrace it upon every available occasion and avoid unilateral responsibilities. Acheson admitted yesterday in his testimony before the Senate committee in response to my questions the following facts: (1) the North Atlantic pact Council required by Article Nine and its "defense committee" can be set up and can be in operation within 90 days; (2) the pending arms bill runs for two years. It is developed entirely independently of the Council. This does not make sense to me. Furthermore, Acheson admitted that 44 per cent of the proposed expenditures in pact countries will not be made until fiscal 1951. At the very least this means that the budgetary charge against fiscal 1950 can be reduced to $500,000,000 and the balance for fiscal 1951 can be put into "contract authorizations." This would be a big improvement; but still it does not meet my basic point — namely, that this arms program so far as Western Europe is concerned, should be more intimately geared into the machinery of the North Atlantic pact. Arms that are furnished under the pact involve a "self help and mutual aid" obligation which cannot exist in connection with arms that are furnished outside the pact as contemplated by the pending bill.

I do not intend to be dogmatic about this business because it is very important that we get a bill before this session of Congress adjourns. But I continue to believe that the surest way to "get a bill" is to make it as sound as possible.

In another letter he wrote:

August 16, 1949

It is true that I am seeking to sharply restrict the appropriations contemplated for "arms aid" to our friends abroad. On the other hand, I want to be entirely frank in saying that I think *reasonable* cooperation along this line is very essential to our own national security. Of course, there is no doubt about the fact that *we* are the ultimate target of Soviet aggression. Therefore, it seems to me that it is the part of prudence to make sure that we have efficient allies in the event of another war. Indeed, it well may be — and I think it is true — that the best way to stop World War Three before it starts is to make it plain to Soviet aggressors that they cannot win. So far as "economy" is concerned, I know of no better way to "save money" (not to speak of saving lives) than to buy this sort of "peace insurance." . . .

You speak of the money wasted in Greece as compared with the *useful* investment of money in helping Turkey. I emphatically agree with you about Turkey. But Turkey would be lost almost overnight (and with it the Middle East) if the Communists were to control Greece. What we *have* done in Greece during the last two years is to keep her out of the clutches of the Communist guerrillas; and the official reports which we have this week indicate that there is good chance that Greece will be entirely free of this menace within the present year. . . .

You are *completely* right in insisting that we must keep America *solvent* if our peace leadership is to be worth anything to us or to the world. I agree with you that we must be eternally vigilant upon this score. At the same time I respectfully submit that we must take care to avoid "false economy" which undertakes to "save money" *today* at the expense of infinitely greater hazards *tomorrow*.

Again in a letter he emphasized that arms aid was a secondary purpose of the treaty: ". . . I am one of those who wishes to hold this arms implementation to a minimum. I have always felt that the great value of the pact was in its 'potentials' — and that continues to be my view. On the other hand, I think it is very desirable — as one of these potentials — that the existing armed forces-in-being of the North Atlantic countries should be put in gear and brought to maximum efficiency for a minimum force as a nucleus around which effective resistance could be swiftly organized if, as and when the cooperative need might arise. But at the same time and in the same breath I would re-emphasize the fact that this government wishes to lead in universal disarmament under adequate disciplines against bad faith. . . ."

And a letter to James P. Warburg of New York gave Vandenberg's concept of European arms aid at that time:

August 23, 1949
. . . as a matter of logic I think it is perfectly clear that the pending proposals are only an inadequate down-payment on a stupendous future account if the concept and objective are to build sufficient forces-in-being to hold the Russian line. That is not my concept or objective. I think it presents ruinous corollaries both at home and abroad. As you undoubtedly know, I would have infinitely preferred to rely upon the potentials in the North Atlantic Pact as a discouragement to Soviet aggression. My original expectation in connection with Articles Three and Nine was to highlight this potential by putting existing forces-in-being in mutual gear and on a basis of maximum efficiency chiefly for the practical purpose of assuring adequate defense against internal subversion.

Vandenberg, writing Warburg ten months before the outbreak of hostilities in Korea, said he understood Administration plans were calculated to produce a nucleus of nine modernized and effective land divisions in Western Europe, exclusive of American occupation forces. "My concept is the maintenance and integration of this nucleus around which the potentials of tomorrow if necessary can be swiftly organized. Meanwhile, this efficient nucleus will build internal morale and assure control of internal subversion. I do not believe there is any middle ground between this concept which still depends chiefly upon potentials and the complete rearmament which would turn Western Europe and America into an armed camp. . . . It seems to me that we must choose between 'potentials' and 'forces-in-being.' I chose 'potentials.' "

Later the Senator replied to a question from a constituent:

I do *not* think we "are preparing adequately for war" if this question means an adequate defense-in-being against an all-out Russian attack. I do not think it would be *possible* in this sense for us to match the Soviet potentials without turning our country into an armed camp and subordinating our entire national economy to military preparedness on a scale comparable with our efforts in World War Two. But it seems to me that this would be a tragic prospectus which is neither justified nor tolerable.

What we are trying to do is to adequately *prevent* another war before it starts — and it seems to me that this is the supreme challenge of the age. *Certainly* we are making great progress in this direction. There can be no "adequate preparation for war" in this foreshortened world except on a basis of *collective security*. We are vigorously pursuing this latter objective — and with great success. I should say, therefore, that my answer to your question is something of a paradox — namely, that we are "adequately preparing for war" (so far as is humanly possible under modern circumstances) by adequately attempting to stop any new war before it starts.

The correspondence indicated that Vandenberg's objections to the Administration arms proposal included these factors: (1)

it was prepared outside the formula provided by the Atlantic pact; (2) it gave relatively unlimited power to the Chief Executive in determining how much aid should be sent where; (3) the size of the program threatened to engulf and obliterate the concept of self-help and mutual aid embraced in the pact; and (4) it seemed to point toward establishing "forces-in-being" sufficiently powerful to match Russian strength instead of the preparations of "potentials" able to cope with Communist internal subversion and a nucleus for later expansion if necessary. While Vandenberg remained adamant on the first two points, there is later evidence that he sharply altered his position on the fourth point after the Communists showed their readiness to use force to gain their ends in the attack on Korea.

While the senators and the State Department were still wrangling over the final form of the bill, the House voted in mid-August to cut the military assistance funds in half and otherwise showed signs of wrecking the whole program. "The House sure 'put the crimps' into the arms bill!" Vandenberg wrote his wife. "And I don't blame 'em much — the thing has been so miserably handled. Now Acheson and company are yelling to high heaven for help. Foster and I can 'write our own ticket.' But I don't propose to let them belatedly dump their problem in my lap. We'll help 'em trim their bill . . . into possible shape. But it's not going to be *my* bill. At their request, we are meeting . . . on Monday morning at eleven o'clock to survey the salvage job." This development apparently cleared the way not only for revising the bill along the lines proposed by Vandenberg and Dulles, but it appeared to restore at least temporarily a more effective nonpartisan collaboration.

Vandenberg's health was failing at this time, he suffered considerable pain, and his physician wanted him to enter a hospital at Ann Arbor, Michigan, for observation of a lesion in his left lung. The Senator refused to leave Washington during the critical debate over the arms bill, but he promised to enter the hospital as soon as that measure was enacted.

Under such circumstances he worked out with Dulles a series of amendments to the bill, designed to make certain that the arms aid recipients would be obligated to use the aid to promote an integrated defense of the North Atlantic area in accordance with defense plans to be drawn up by the pact's defense committee. Once those plans were agreed upon, no military aid would be given the Pact nations except in conformity with the over-all plans. "This assures that the present program is in fact an interim program to be geared into the North Atlantic treaty procedure just as rapidly as possible," Dulles and Vandenberg said in a joint press statement explaining their amendments. It was proposed that either the President or Congress could cut off arms shipments if, in the light of developments, such shipments would not promote the collective capacity to resist attack and would not fit into the treaty plan for an integrated defense. Congress, by concurrent resolution, as well as the President could terminate aid to any nation for other reasons.

Vandenberg and Dulles proposed that the Administration's request for a $1,160,990,000 spending authorization for the Pact countries be reduced to $1,000,000,000. Of this, $500,000,000 in cash would be immediately available and $500,000,000 could be used to contract for goods to be delivered and paid for the following year. "The net effect of the major amendments to be proposed is to make clear the supremacy of the North Atlantic Treaty. Its procedures for collective area defense must prevail as against any bi-lateral or national system to be inaugurated now. Our proposed amendments will not delay by a day, or substantially reduce in scope, the present program. They do assure that the present program will in reality be only an interim program, to be geared into the integrating processes of the North Atlantic Treaty at the earliest practical date. The amended bill would keep full faith with our partners of the North Atlantic community, assuring them on the one hand a prompt beginning of substantial military assistance, and on the other hand, the transformation of such assistance from national auspices to the collective integrating auspices of the Treaty as soon as this is possible."

The amendments were accepted by the Committee, with an additional proviso that no more than $100,000,000 could be spent before the President certified that the United States had agreed to preliminary defense plans prepared by the pact authority. The Joint Foreign Relations and Armed Services Committees approved the revised draft of the arms legislation 20 to 3, and on September 20 Vandenberg made his last "full dress" Senate speech.

In urging the bill's passage he told the Senate: ". . . the fact that far flung changes have been made in the bill, upon initiatives provided from both sides of the aisle, is the finest possible example of constructive responsibility in collaboration with a responsive State Department. A widely divided Joint Committee sought and found substantial common ground. . . . I think the bill is in honorable keeping with our Treaty obligation. I think it is definitely and specifically in the interests of our own national defense. I think it is recommended by our own intelligent self-interest. I think it is discouragement to war. I think it is prime and vital peace insurance for us and for the free world."

Letters to his wife tell the rest of the story.

[*September 20, 1949*]

This has been a tough day for the "old man." I made a speech this afternoon on the arms bill. It was not one of my painfully prepared "orations." I had no manuscript. I proposed to "take it easy" and just chat for not more than forty-five minutes at the outside. But the usual happened. Questions (mostly from Wherry and Donnell) kept me on my feet for two and a half hours. When it was over I went straight to my hideout and lay down for two hours. This is the last of my really big efforts. I shall be "sliding down hill" from now on until I leave. I think the arms bill will pass this weekend — perhaps by Thursday night. Then I want to wait for the House-Senate conference. The two bills are miles apart. It will take a load of "compromising." . . . But once that is out of the way — I hope not later than the middle of next week — I shall be ready to take off for Ann Arbor and I *mean* that I shall be ready.

[*September, 1949*]

. . . How I wish I could resign this devastating job right now! The whole country is in a state of nerves. Everybody is under tension. Nothing is right. The whole tenor of Senatorial correspondence has changed. Everybody is mad about *something* — and they seem to love to "take it out" on their members of Congress. . . . Oh well — we survived the Civil War and I guess we can survive this. *This too shall pass.*

The words "this too shall pass" were familiar ones in the Vandenberg family and appeared often in the Senator's letters to his wife. A small plaque that was on Vandenberg's desk at the Grand Rapids *Herald* and was later transferred to his office in the Senate bore the inscription: "And This Too Shall Pass." In moments of triumph throughout his career, at times when his family was enthusiastically proud of his accomplishments he often toned down their celebration by reminding them that "this too shall pass." And many times in hours of discouragement he used the motto to point out that tomorrow would be another day. He didn't know the origin of the quotation and in 1947 he asked the Library of Congress to check it. In reply, he received copies of correspondence that had been published in the *New York Times Book Review* in 1935, stating that the phrase "This also passes" came from an Oriental proverb. Akbar, Emperor of Hindustan, asked the Hindu poet, the Rajah Birbal, for a talisman against all sorrow. The Rajah gave him a ring on which was engraved in Persian the word "Mezugrad," meaning "passing away." Arthur Guiterman wrote that "the phrase is proverbial in Hindustan" and that he had used it in a story "Akbar and Birbal," published in the *St. Nicholas* magazine. A poem by Theodore Tilton, entitled "Even This Shall Pass Away," used the same theme. Later, Professor Feliz Howland of Habibia College, at Kabul, Afghanistan, wrote that the expression "this also passes" was of proverbial circulation in Hindustan, Afghanistan, and Persia "where it is commonly employed and where we would be inclined to say 'Wotta life!' The expression itself is more complete and correctly given, 'Een neez meeguzarad' or 'This also passes.'"

[*September 22, 1949*]

. . . The arms bill battle is over (for the time being) and we have won. [The vote was 55 to 24.] It was tough going. But as you have read in the papers, we held the line on all fronts. I made a final twenty minute speech this afternoon — about as hot as they make 'em and I enjoyed it. . . . The Republicans ran out on me right and left — only nine of 'em standing by to help beat the chief amendment with which we had to contend. But eighteen of them came back to support us on final passage. The old dependables were Dulles and Ives, Morse (who came down on a stretcher to vote), Thye (who never left me), Margaret Smith and Wiley. . . . A number of the old standbys are . . . in foreign lands like Alex Smith, Lodge, Baldwin, etc. . . . I have decided that enough is enough. . . . I am going to let 'em "worry along" the House-Senate conference (on the bill) without me. This means — and you may tell our doctor — that I am ready to report at Ann Arbor next Tuesday or Wednesday to suit his convenience.

For some time Vandenberg had been in almost constant pain. He also was deeply worried by the worsening condition of Mrs. Vandenberg who had not recuperated from a series of operations. The Senator suffered from severe headaches which recurred with increasing frequency, and a limp now marked his walk. Friends noted with concern that in order to look over his shoulder he had to turn his body. In this period, too, he seemed reluctant to leave the surroundings of the Senate even when his presence on the floor was not required. Many an evening in the hot Washington summer and fall of 1949 he spent in one of the black leather chairs of the temporary press gallery located in a corridor just off the old Supreme Court chamber. He passed the time reminiscing with newsmen. He seemed almost to be inhaling the atmosphere of the place, determined to savor every remaining minute. Often, despite his pain, he seemed almost to glow with good humor and an inner warmth that was felt by those with whom he talked. But the time had come when he could no longer refuse to obey his doctor's orders. Shortly after the arms bill was passed he slipped out of the Capitol, and he was not to return save for a few brief visits.

Two more letters to his wife completed the account of his last days in Washington, on a somber note. It had just been announced that an atomic explosion had occurred in Russia.

[*September 23, 1949*]

... We had a meeting of the Atomic Energy Committee in secret this morning (and a very solemn one) regarding the Russian development — it's far from certain precisely what the Russians have other than the man-made means of exploding nuclear fission with vast resultant radio reaction. It was [a fairly short time], in our own case, after our original experimental explosion before we tried any actual bomb. Then it's many months before there can be real bomb production in minimum quantities. But the Russians have had [many thousands of] men at work on the job and the benefit of many top notch German scientists whom they virtually kidnapped. In any event, this is now a different world. The new problems are appalling. Where do we go from here and what do we do about it?

The first result, in my personal life, is several insistent official demands that I do not leave Washington during the next few weeks. That was my own immediate reaction. On the other hand, it might be better to get at the job (whatever it is), get it behind me, and be ready for future developments. I have no illusions that I am indispensable but you might read this to the good doctor and get his reaction. If he thinks it's a cold hard fact of life that I have no further option, then let's go ahead as planned and as soon as possible.

[*September 24, 1949*]

[After receiving word from his doctor that the operation was essential] . . . [I have] moved take off day up to Monday. Whatever it is, let's have it over with. . . . Some of the boys who voted to gut the arms program are pretty sick of what they did in the light of the atomic developments twenty-four hours later. But they'll just "play politics" and blame Truman for not telling us sooner although if he had, they would just as readily accuse him of trying to influence the arms vote with a scare. On many counts I don't like him any better than they do. But he is the *only* President and the *only* Commander-in-Chief we have got or are going to have for three more critical years. I want to help lick him when the time comes — but not at the expense of the national security, meanwhile.

27

China: "The Conundrum of the Ages"

SENATOR Vandenberg was fully aware of the gravity of the China Problem and of the serious implications raised by the spread of Communist influence in Asia, particularly after 1946. He gradually came to believe that the Administration had sold Generalissimo Chiang Kai-shek's Nationalist government "down the river" and — although he acknowledged the war pressures under which President Roosevelt labored in his conferences with Stalin — he believed that the China debacle was due in part at least to the Big Three agreement at Yalta.

By the time Vandenberg became Chairman of the Senate Foreign Relations Committee in 1947 the China situation was deteriorating so rapidly that it appears unlikely he ever formed, even in his own mind, a positive program for United States policy in the Far East except to oppose Communism. It is not, of course, the responsibility of Congress to initiate foreign policy and, in addition, Vandenberg never regarded China as coming within the sphere of bipartisan collaboration because of a lack of adequate advance consultation at the time when basic China policy decisions had been made.

The Senator later expressed himself on this subject in conversation with Senator H. Alexander Smith of New Jersey. "In 1949," Senator Smith recalled to the editors of this book, "I was very much concerned about the Far Eastern situation and he was also. We felt that our Far Eastern policy was completely futile and yet we were not entirely clear at that time in what direction we should move. [Vandenberg] had the confidence of the State Department on most matters and especially in such important matters as the United Nations Charter and the situation in Europe, but when it came to the Far East, he told me constantly that he was not consulted and that he simply was handed a program of decisions already made to which he was expected to give his official approval."

The problems that confronted the United States after the war in relation to China were some of the most perplexing and controversial in the field of foreign policy. In general, the United States had long been deeply interested in maintaining the integrity and independence of that country, regarding a stable China as essential to peace in the Far East. But hopes that the Chinese Republic would serve as a stabilizing force in the postwar era were shattered by the deadly impact of a long armed struggle and by the attitude of the Soviet Union. Twelve years of fighting and eight years of Japanese occupation had weakened and divided the country. Inflation steadily increased and production was discouragingly low. The Nationalist government failed to hold the confidence of the masses and appeared unable to solve China's many grave problems. In addition, the Soviet Union, which had agreed in 1945 to support the Nationalist government and extend it economic assistance, permitted huge quantities of Japanese war matériel to fall into the hands of Chinese Communists. The Russians also removed some $2,000,000,000 worth of industrial equipment from factories in Manchuria after the Japanese surrender.

The United States, on the other hand, had extended to the Nationalist government of China substantial military and financial assistance. The State Department estimated that this aid amounted to approximately $1,469,400,000 from 1937 to the date of the Japanese surrender in 1945. This assistance was continued after the war in the form of lend-lease, Export-Import Bank credits, and UNRRA funds amounting to an additional $1,436,900,000 by 1948, plus an estimated $181,900,000 (sales price) in surplus property sales.

In the postwar period, however, the Administration decided that, if large-scale aid was to be made effective, some kind of unity had to be achieved in China itself, where the Communists were the principal and most threatening rivals of Chiang Kai-shek's régime. There were various proposals for creating some kind of coalition government, and this objective, in fact, was advocated by the Nationalists at that time. President Truman sent General Marshall to China in 1946 to try to assist the Chinese leaders in forming a coalition — including Communists — that would foster national unity and stability.

The Marshall mission to China eventually became the center of considerable controversy, owing largely to the question of whether an attempt should have been made to bring Communists into the government. The General later explained to the editors of this book that his instructions were merely to assist the Chinese in carrying out their own decision to form a coalition and emphasized that his mission had no responsibility for the decision to negotiate with the Communists. Not only did the Marshall mission fail in respect to its effort to form an effective coalition, but the General was frustrated in his attempts to get American assistance into what he regarded as the proper hands in China. On one occasion, for example, he secured a shipment of U.S. Army winter equipment and clothes which the Nationalist troops desperately needed. But in this case, as in so many others, Marshall's efforts to aid the Nationalists were subverted and the equipment never reached the soldiers of Chiang Kai-shek, but fell into the hands of the Communists instead. On other occasions substantial shipments of ammunition from the United States, intended for the Nationalists, ended up in Communist camps.

After more than a year of futile negotiations, the mission had not achieved its goal and was withdrawn. Following Marshall's return home, the Chinese civil war broke out in earnest.

It was during the course of this experience that Administration leaders apparently became convinced that corruption and inefficiency in the Nationalist government nullified American assistance to Chiang Kai-shek. President Truman then placed an embargo on the shipment of arms to China for a period of about ten months.

Meanwhile, the first major indication in Vandenberg's papers that he was gravely concerned about Chinese developments had come shortly after the Republicans won control of Congress in 1946 and the Senator became chairman of the Foreign

Relations Committee. In a speech at Cleveland he urged the Administration to "shift its emphasis" away from Communist participation in the government.

January 11, 1947

Here lies a vast and friendly republic, rich in wisdom, equally rich in its democratic promises for tomorrow, and historically fixed in the orbit of our good will. Since 1911, when Dr. Sun Yat-sen gave China her new vision, she has been struggling, against bitter odds, toward the light of a new day. While recognizing the Nationalist Government of Chiang Kai-shek, we have — through a year's mission headed by our distinguished General Marshall — been impartially urging that it produce unity with a rival armed party, the Chinese Communists.

Under the determined leadership of Chiang Kai-shek, a National Assembly has just produced a new Constitution and the government has been reorganized with a coalition of non-Communist parties. We can hope that this Nanking charter, with its first, great national election promised before next Christmas, will weld together a strong and competent China. It is my own view that our own Far Eastern policy might well now shift its emphasis. While still recommending unity, it might well encourage those who have so heroically set their feet upon this road, and discourage those who make the road precarious. Our Marines, having finished their task, are coming home. But there will never be a minute when China's destiny is not of acute concern to the United States and to a healthy world.

This pronouncement, though brief, was given significance by the fact that Marshall had just returned from China. Vandenberg's words also were aimed at the theory, sometimes advanced then, that the Chinese communists were really just an agrarian party and not actually Moscow-type Communists. "There can be no doubt whatever," he wrote later, "that our own Government was tragically misled by the propaganda that Chinese Revolutionists were just 'earnest agrarians' and not actual Communists." The Senator had been dealing with the Russians and watching Communist expansionist tactics in Europe, and he was interested in the strongest possible democratic opposition to such expansion everywhere in the world, including China.

"I am sure," he wrote shortly after the Cleveland speech, "the time has come for us to firmly sustain the Chinese nationalist government — even though at the same time we insist that the Chinese nationalist government shall put its own house in better order. It seems to me that we might just as well begin to face the Communist challenge on *every* front." The withdrawal of United States forces from China was not, Vandenberg believed, an abandonment of Chiang Kai-shek. He wrote:

February 10, 1947

Frankly, I do not believe that the withdrawal of our troops from China "abandons the Chinese to the Communists." . . . We have had only a token force in China. . . . This new American policy actually releases the Chinese Nationalist Government to "clean out" the armed Chinese Communists. Heretofore, we have been trying to force Chiang Kai-shek to take these Communists into his coalition Government. Personally I think it is far more hopeful for China that we have abandoned these pressures because I never knew a Communist to enter a coalition government for any other purpose than to destroy it. If we now give the Chinese Nationalist Government (which has written a good constitution and which has coalesced all Chinese Parties except the armed Communists) the moral support it deserves, I would expect China to have a better chance (if any) to stabilize itself. But I have no illusions about China's future under any prospectus. It is the greatest speculation of the ages.

In the next two years Vandenberg was often concerned with problems relating to China. His main conclusion was that the over-all problem was so big and complex that it was close to insoluble so far as the United States was concerned — particularly in the face of a mounting crisis in Europe. But, in spite of the increasingly fluid situation in China, he believed it desirable to continue our program of assistance to Chiang Kai-shek so long as such aid could be used effectively against Communism.

He did not, however, desire to take any action that might involve the United States militarily on the mainland of Asia. He made these two points unmistakably clear on March 29, 1948, when he presented the China Aid Bill to the Senate. Earlier American aid to the Nationalist government had been suspended, and by 1948 many members of Congress had become seriously concerned about the Administration's policy toward China. Vandenberg strongly backed the China Aid Bill, which authorized appropriation of $338,000,000 for economic assistance to the Nationalists, in addition to approximately $100,000,000 that was to be used for military assistance.

In his speech before the Senate he outlined the many difficulties that had beset the Nationalist government, and added:

March 29, 1948

... Mr. President, the wonder is not that all these pyramiding burdens and all these accumulated hazards should have driven hard-pressed China to the brink. The wonder is that prior crises have not been able to break her intrepid spirit to carry on. We would be inexcusably less than frank if we did not admit that, as of the moment, the situation is touch and go. But, in my view, we would be inexcusably less than loyal to our own objectives if, at such a moment, we did not do what lies within our power, taking account of our other responsibilities, to help sustain and to encourage the Chinese Government and the Chinese people to reject aggression and to sustain their independence. ...

[Still later in his speech Vandenberg referred to the military aid recommended for China in the Committee's bill:]

... It proposes to make military supplies available, at China's option. For this or any other purpose, at China's option, a grant of $100,000,000 is included in the bill. This implements a heavy program of transfers of military surplus, at nominal prices, already under way, and to be extended. Your committee believes, as a matter of elementary prudence, that this process must be completely clear of any implication that we are underwriting the military campaign of the Nationalist Government. No matter what our heart's desire might be, any such implication would be impossible over so vast an area. Therefore, for the sake of clarity, we prefer to leave the initiative, in respect to these particular funds, in the hands of the Nationalist Government. The current net result is no less effective. But we also want no mistake about the nature of our obligations. Congress must retain freedom of decision as events may recommend. . . .

The attitude of Vandenberg and the other Committee members was succinctly summarized in the report of the Foreign Relations Committee which the Senator submitted to the Senate. "China is a maze of imponderables," said the report. "It is impossible to know the quantity and type of aid necessary for the restoration of a stable and independent China. The Committee is convinced, however, that the assistance contemplated in this bill should appreciably strengthen the position of the National Government without, at the same time, involving the United States in any additional commitments of a military nature."

Some months later, after receiving through Senator William F. Knowland of California a long and gloomy report from an expert on the Chinese political and financial situation, Vandenberg wrote on October 21, 1948, that it presented

a situation which is well nigh imponderable. Its conclusions seem to be predicated on the fact that China is lost unless "the United States takes on a positive policy of military aid" . . . and that this military aid is forthcoming at once (which is prior to the new year). . . . I should say that it is impossible for us to enter the Chinese equation on any such all-out basis . . . without new Congressional action. If we are to give [such] military aid to China . . . it would involve an enormous obligation. . . . This burden (of unpredictable size) would be superimposed upon what appears to be the unavoidable necessity of military aid to Western Europe. In other words, this raises the fundamental question (of which we are all partially conscious) as to the total drain upon our own resources which we dare contemplate.

It seems to me that this poses a problem of paramount concern to the Dewey Administration which will be the one that must implement any such immediate commitments on the part of the Truman Administration. . . . [This was just before the 1948 election, which Vandenberg, like most other Americans, assumed Dewey would win.] I have no doubt that the general trend in China is . . . going from bad to worse and that perhaps this Communist trend is calculated to continue. . . . The vital importance of saving China cannot be exaggerated. But there are limits to our resources and boundaries to our miracles. . . .

After Mr. Truman had won the election, Vandenberg felt that the China situation was still on the downgrade. "The situation has deteriorated to such a tragic extent that it is exceedingly difficult to know just what we can *effectively* do at this final moment in the crisis," he wrote on November 22. "The mere appropriation of money — without a practical and feasible plan of cooperation — is sheer waste of our own substance. Furthermore, I am forced to say that the Nationalist Government has failed to reform itself in a fashion calculated to deserve continued popular confidence over there or over here. Under the circumstances, it is *not* an easy thing to chart an appropriate course of emergency action."

Early in December of 1948, former Governor Alf Landon of Kansas attacked the Administration for its blunders in China and remarked that as a result of the bipartisan foreign policy the Republicans were being "gulled" and kept from talking in regard to foreign affairs. This remark of Landon's caused Vandenberg to react sharply because he felt that it involved a misunderstanding about bipartisanship. In other words, he did not feel that bipartisan foreign policy was involved in China, because there had not been advance consultation with Republicans in regard to that policy on a scale comparable to the bipartisan consultation on European questions.

The Senator wrote a long and revealing letter to Knowland in which he commented on Landon's statement and set forth his attitude generally toward China, where Chiang Kai-shek's position was steadily growing worse as a result of mounting Communist army attacks. Landon had attacked "the Marshall program" as partly responsible for this debacle because it tried to "force Chiang Kai-shek to take in the Communists," and he criticized the failure of "bipartisan" Republicans to speak out against the Administration's China policy. Attention at the time was also centered on charges that the Administration had suppressed a report on China by General Wedemeyer because it was suspected that the report was contrary to Administration policy. Vandenberg wrote Knowland:

December 11, 1948

Mr. Landon may be of the opinion that we "gulled" Republicans should have yelled our heads off about China and the Generalissimo during the past year or two, but in my opinion it would only have precipitated and underscored a discussion of Chiang's weaknesses and would have nullified any remnant of his prestige. It is easy to sympathize with Chiang — to respect him . . . — as I always have and still do. But it is quite a different thing to plan resultful aid short of armed American intervention with American combat troops (which I have never favored and probably never shall).

I think our China policy was wrong (and always said so) in striving to force a Communist coalition on Chiang. . . . I think we should have taken realistic steps long ago to sustain the Nationalist Government — but certainly it is now evident that this "realism" also involved an indispensable house-cleaning in Chiang's government. I envy Mr. Landon's freedom to criticize what wasn't done and his freedom of responsibility for deciding specifically what should have been done then and what ought to be done now. When practically all of our American-trained and American-equipped Chinese divisions surrender without firing a shot — where do we go from here? I am afraid I totally miss Mr. Landon's point when he volunteers to take Republican responsibility for these Democratic decisions which never were, and are not now, any part of the bipartisan liaison.

You ask me two specific questions. The anwers necessarily are totally confidential to you. (1) I never actually saw the Wedemeyer Report. But I listened to a complete paraphrase of it from General Marshall and I was satisfied that its release would have been a serious blow to Chinese-American relations. It is my opinion that some of his recommendations would have gotten us into serious trouble — even the fact of their proposal. [The Wedemeyer Report was not published in full until 1951.]

(2) Of course I do not know who wrote the Marshall "directive" [the Presidential directive to General Marshall concerning his mission to China and covering his instructions to assist the various parties in their purpose of bringing about a coalition government]. But I have always understood (I have no dependable authority for this statement) that *he wrote it himself.* Personally I do not believe he would have undertaken the mission on any other basis. I can understand your suspicions about some of the men in the lower echelons of the [State] Department at that time in respect to China. I always shared those suspicions and I think I have had some small part in forcing some changes. But it is my opinion that the "directive" was Marshall's *own* — and represented a point of view which was a clear conviction with him and still is. . . .

It should be noted here that Marshall later explained for the purposes of this book that unusual circumstances surrounded the actual writing of the directive. At the time he was preparing to depart for China, it was also necessary for him to spend much time before a Congressional committee investigating the circumstances of the Japanese attack on Pearl Harbor in 1941. As a result, Marshall said, he had no time to participate in the drafting of the directive, but he was represented at the drafting by two Army generals. He added that he did not actually have an opportunity to study the document until he was on an airplane en route to Chungking, although presumably he was already familiar with its contents and with the purpose of his mission.

As the China problem became more acute in 1948, Vandenberg's role as Foreign Relations Committee chairman lent special importance to his attitude toward Far Eastern developments. The Senator believed that the situation was so complex and so muddled that the Truman Administration by this time really had no policy toward China. In a letter he wrote:

December 14, 1948

We must deal with today's conditions in China as they are and we must be realistic about it. Appropriations alone are not enough. They must implement a plan which offers at least some small degree of hope for success. . . . We have poured more than two billion dollars into China in the last few years. But pouring money is not enough — as we have learned to our sorrow. For example, a number of Chinese divisions — fully trained and equipped by America — have surrendered without firing a shot. And all of the American equipment is in the hands of these Chinese Communists. There can be plenty of argument as to why this happened. But the point is that it did happen — and no plan for the future is any good unless it can avoid such happenings again. This is simply one example out of many to demonstrate the extreme difficulty which the most ardent friends of China (among whom I hope I am enrolled) confront in searching an answer to the current crisis.

He wrote a month later:

. . . the situation in China has disintegrated so rapidly that [we] . . . confront the grave question as to how any sort of American aid can be made effective and not be a waste of American resources. . . . It . . . seems to be apparent that this progressive disintegration has cost the National Government the support and sympathy of a large portion of all the Chinese people. Indeed, it is now probable that the Nationalist Government will fall before we could ever sustain it with a new program of aid. . . . If we made ourselves responsible for the Army of the Nationalist Government, we would be in the China war for keeps and the responsibility would be ours instead of hers. I am very sure that this would jeopardize our own national security beyond any possibility of justification. . . .

Vandenberg's basic idea during this period was that China should be kept out of Communist hands. In conversations on the subject, particularly with Dulles, he gave the impression that he had little faith in Chiang Kai-shek's administration but, on the other hand, he felt that Chiang had been loyal to the Allied cause during the war and that the United States was honor bound to meet obligations to his government. He believed, too, that the State Department could have more vigorously carried out these obligations. This impression became stronger as the Chiang régime lost ground rapidly early in 1949. On January 22 the Nationalists surrendered Peiping and turned over American-made war matériel there to the Communists. On February 4 the Senator was invited to an off-the-record conference at the White House on the following day, to be attended — according to the telephoned invitation — by Dean Acheson, Senator Connally, Senator Barkley, Representative Eaton, and Representative Bloom. The next day he recorded the meeting in his diary.

Saturday, February 5, 1949

This meeting proved to be about China where the Nationalist Government (which we support) has all but collapsed and is now trying to negotiate peace terms with the Chinese Communists. Under ECA we granted $125,000,000 of American military aid to Chiang Kai-shek. About half has been delivered this past year. The other half (about 60 millions) is now in process of delivery — some on ships ready to sail.

The President met us in the Cabinet Room. He was very serious. He said that his National Security Council and his military advisors had recommended this week that he suspend all export licenses on all further shipments to the Nationalists because of their imminent collapse and, therefore, that these supplies probably would simply fall into the hands of the Chinese Communists (or, in the event of Chiang's fall, be sold by the Chinese in the black market). He asked our view. Two or three of the gentlemen immediately fell in with the idea of stopping all export licenses forthwith. I kept silent until the President asked for my view. This is substantially what I said.

Chiang and his Nationalist government may well be on their last legs. They probably *will* collapse in the near future. Our shipments to them, therefore, might well fall into the hands of the Northern Chinese Communists (as has been the case with American equipment furnished to eight American-trained Nationalist Divisions which surrendered without firing a shot). But there is something here vastly more important than what happens to $60,000,000 worth of supplies. The American Government already is charged with a large share of responsibility for Chiang's Government's fate because of our previous policies and our failure to give it adequate military supplies. (This charge is only partially justified up-to-date.) But if, at the very moment when Chiang's Nationalists are desperately trying to negotiate some kind of a peace with the Communists, we suspend all military shipments to the Nationalists, we certainly shall make any hope of a negotiated peace impossible. We shall thus virtually notify the Communists that they can consider the war ended and themselves as victors. We virtually withdraw our recognition of the Nationalist Government. We seal China's doom. Regardless of the justification of previous charges that our American policy has been largely responsible for China's fate, if we take *this* step at *this* fatefully inept moment, we shall never be able to shake off the charge that *we* are the ones who gave poor China the final push into disaster. Millions of our own people will be shocked; and we shall seriously lose prestige throughout the world. I decline any part of any such responsibility. I beg of you, at the very least, to postpone any such decision for a few more weeks until the China question is settled *by China* and *in China* and not by the *American government in Washington*. This blood must not be on *our* hands. My point is further emphasized by the fact that the title to almost all of this 60 millions in supplies has already passed to the Nationalist Government which is waiting for these export licenses. Therefore your order will be much more than a withholding of American supplies in American hands. It will be a ban on the Nationalist Government — and that will be "the last straw." I make it plain that I have little or no hope for stopping the immediate Communist conquest. That is beside the point. I decline to be responsible for the *last push* which makes it possible.

After a moment of silence, the President said that, of course, I had posed the real question. Then he asked the Vice President for his view. Barkley said he agreed with me.

That ended the conference. I doubt whether the President will issue any "orders" for a while to come.

As a matter of fact, Vandenberg's papers of later date show that Mr. Truman did gradually cut off aid to the Nationalists after the surrender of Peiping, acting in a manner that was intended to avoid the shock of any sudden cessation of American support of Chiang. And in the next few months the Communist surge in China became an increasingly explosive issue in Washington, with Republicans strongly attacking the Administration for the debacle. Vandenberg tried to keep more or less on the sidelines for a while, but this proved difficult.

In the summer of 1949 circumstances arose that forced him to take an active part in the debate. R. Walton Butterworth, a State Department expert on China, was promoted to be Assistant Secretary of State for Far Eastern Affairs, subject to Senate confirmation. A number of Senate Republicans decided to make an issue of China by what proved to be a vain effort to defeat the Butterworth nomination. Vandenberg, who was opposed to Butterworth only because of his past connection with our China policy, voted "present" in the Foreign Relations Committee when the nomination was considered. Later, on the Senate floor, however, he was asked by Senator Brewster of Maine, why he had taken that position. Vandenberg replied that he thought it was

> a very great mistake . . . not to bring a fresh point of view to the assignment, rather than simply to continue the regime which . . . is inevitably connected with a very tragic failure of our policies in the Far East. . . . It seemed to me it would have been the course of wisdom to cut the string, so to speak, in the continuity of a policy that has failed.
>
> [Pressed by Brewster in the same debate, he added that the bipartisan foreign policy did not apply to China.] On previous occasions I have categorically replied that there was no such liaison in respect to China policy. I wish to reiterate it, because I disassociate myself, as I have publicly done upon previous occasions, from the China policy which we pursued. It is a very easy, simple matter to disassociate one's self from

a policy. It is not quite so easy to assert what an alternative policy might have been. I concede that it is far easier to be critical than to be correct. . . . I am quite willing to testify that I think the President and the State Department would do extremely well to continue the attitudes they have displayed so generously in other directions by making very sure that any evolution of a new policy in the Far East and China comes completely into contact and review, at least with the Senate Foreign Relations Committee, before any commitments are concluded, because in this area we obviously face the conundrum of the ages. . . .

I say quite frankly that I hope . . . there will be no consideration of a recognition of a Communist government in China without complete preliminary contact and exploration.

This speech prompted Vandenberg's close friend, Jay Hayden of the Detroit *News*, to write that the Senator's "present" vote in the Committee had, for the first time in two and a half years, cracked the 13–0 bipartisan solidarity of the Foreign Relations Committee. "And," he added, "it was precipitated by the man who, more than any other, prompted and cherished this solidarity. It tended to confirm reports for some time that Vandenberg . . . is greatly dissatisfied with the way [foreign] issues have been handled in Congress. . . . The real meaning of all this is that the bipartisan relationship as to foreign affairs has undergone a subtle but unmistakable change since Acheson took over as Secretary of State. Senator Vandenberg has been consulted often enough, but always in an atmosphere of restraint and stiff formality — in marked distinction to his easy and friendly contacts with the two previous Secretaries of State, Byrnes and Marshall."

Vandenberg's letters at this time also suggest that he hesitated to be drawn into the China dispute because it would show that he opposed what General Marshall had tried to do on his mission to Chungking. He admired Marshall and valued his personal friendship and he did not want to disturb that relationship. Yet there were indications in the Senator's letters to his wife during the summer of 1949 that he — apparently mistakenly — believed that differences of opinion regarding China may have resulted in a less cordial friendship with Marshall, a change that Vandenberg would have deeply regretted. The letters to Mrs. Vandenberg, as usual, were not dated, but they begin apparently in June of 1949.

[*June, 1949*]

... The New York Sunday [crossword] puzzles challenged me for a couple of hours. But I can't get very far with them today. ... I did the baseball game by radio as usual. ... I presume you have been reading about the flare-up in the Senate over our China policy. I *had* to get into it — couldn't stave it off any longer. But I hate to have any part of it because I dislike to say *anything*, however indirectly, which reflects on anything that George Marshall ever did. ... I think he was somewhat misled by the boys on the Far East desk in the State Department. In any event, our China policy has been a tragic failure and, now that the chips are down, I can't help saying so. Acheson precipitated the issue when he chose this particular moment to promote Walton Butterworth from the China desk to Assistant Secretary of State in Charge of all Far Eastern affairs. If we ever needed a "fresh view" it's in *that* spot. If we ever needed to "cut the string" and take a fresh start, it's here. So I have no alternative but to oppose the Butterworth confirmation, although he is personally a very fine chap. But it's tough going for me because I am so anxious not to reflect on the General.

Soon afterwards the controversy became so widespread that the State Department early in August issued a White Paper reciting (and defending) the history of American diplomatic actions in China. "The unfortunate but inescapable fact," the Department said in pointing out that the heart of China was in Communist hands, "is that the ominous result of the civil war in China was beyond the control of the government of the United States. Nothing that this country did or could have done within the reasonable limits of its capabilities could have changed that result; nothing that was left undone by this country has contributed to it." The White Paper made clear that the Nationalist government could expect no further active support or substantial aid from the United States. It also urged that we should do what we could to encourage those developments in China by which democratic elements there might reassert themselves and throw off the communist rule. The document was criticized by Republicans for failing to tell the whole story, as noted by Vandenberg in another letter to his wife.

[*August 7, 1949*]
 . . . You will find an interesting article about the Marshalls in the New York Times Magazine. I don't know what has happened to us in that direction — unless it be China. Whatever it is I am deeply sorry, and I certainly don't understand because I wouldn't have thought that anything short of a major crisis could have made any difference. I hope we find out some day. . . . Speaking of China, I am . . . [on] the front pages here today with my brief statement on the "White Paper." . . . Nothing that I said about China warranted any such attention. I simply wanted to nail down the fact (among others) that the China "crime" goes back to Teheran and Yalta where F.D.R. sold Chiang Kai-shek down the river in order to get Joe Stalin into the Jap war (just four days before the Japs surrendered). But it's very easy to criticize, looking backward, and I am not disposed to do much of it. . . .

[*August 12, 1949*]
We had a disgraceful meeting of Foreign Relations this afternoon to pass on Bill Knowland's resolution inviting MacArthur to return and testify on the Far Eastern situation. [Connally] was violently opposed to it. It carried by one vote with two Democrats (Russell and Byrd) on our solid Republican side. . . . I have no idea MacArthur will come back. He has said as much already. But we sure are going to find a way to find out what he thinks about China and the Far East enigma.

[*August, 1949*]
 . . . You said you thought the recent silence in the Marshall direction might be the result of my absence at the dinner in his honor. No; I feel pretty sure it's the result of the neces-

sary and unavoidable attack I have had to make on China policy. Too bad — but there was no way to get around it although I never mentioned his name.

[*About August 15, 1949*]

... [Senator] Alex Smith ... has a [strong concern] about doing something for China. ... He doesn't know what — and neither do I, because China aid at the moment is like sticking your finger in the lake and looking for the hole. ...

Although he was perplexed, Vandenberg didn't stop trying to find a solution for the China conundrum. In a letter of August 25, 1949, to a constituent, he wrote that

the White Paper is supposed to be a recital of facts. In addition, however, it "adds up" to a defense of Administration policy in China. I do not agree with this policy. I think we virtually "sold China down the river" at Yalta and Potsdam and in our subsequent official demands for coalition [the Marshall mission] with the armed Chinese Communists. I have always opposed this program. ... I favor an affirmative policy of vigilance and helpfulness in the Far East. I frankly concede the difficulty of determining precisely what this policy ought to be because the China situation itself is in such a constant flux. ... What we need is a "new look" at China which can disclose the realities. We must *not* surrender the Far East to the Soviets.

About two months after the issuance of the White Paper, the Chinese Communists announced establishment of the People's Republic of China and, on December 8, 1949, Chiang Kai-shek moved his Nationalist government to Formosa. This raised still another vital question for the United States: What should our attitude be in event the Communists launched an attack against Formosa, which was an island of considerable strategic importance to defense of the Pacific area? The attitude of the Administration toward this question appeared to be defined on January 5, 1950, when President Truman issued a statement saying in effect that the United States had no intention of establishing bases on Formosa or of interfering in the current situation or of pursuing a course that would lead to involvement in the civil conflict in China. He added that the United States would not provide military aid or advice to the Nationalists on Formosa, but would continue the ECA program of economic assistance to Chiang. Most observers interpreted this statement as removing Formosa from our Pacific defense perimeter — a decision that was widely and rather bitterly debated and which was to be reversed by the outbreak of war in Korea six months later.

Meanwhile, the China problem was complicated further by the fact that some twenty-five nations extended diplomatic recognition to the Communist régime late in 1949 or early in 1950. The United States did not recognize the Communists, however, and took the lead in opposing an effort to unseat the representatives of the Nationalist government in the United Nations. In this connection, the United States government took the position that we would vote against seating the Communists as representatives of China but that we would abide by the will of the majority in event any United Nations organ should vote to seat them.

Vandenberg was both puzzled and worried about these developments in Formosa and the admission of the Communist régime to the United Nations. He frequently telephoned Dulles to consult about the situation which involved President Roosevelt's agreement at Cairo that Formosa (then a Japanese colony) should be restored to the Republic of China. Dulles suggested to the Senator that, at least pending a Japanese Peace Treaty, the United States should continue to assert that Formosa was affected by an international interest and was not purely a China problem because the Cairo Declaration, he argued, was not itself an operating document but merely a statement of future purpose. Since that Declaration was made, the Charter of the United Nations had come into force as a superseding document and under it the welfare of the eight million inhabitants of Formosa had been made a relevant consideration, and this was a problem which might well be brought within the scope of United Nations concern. It might not find that the welfare of the inhabitants would be promoted by subjecting them to Chinese civil war and possible Chinese communist rule. This viewpoint was at the time rejected by the State Department when Dulles proposed it to Secretary Acheson in the latter part of 1949, after discussing it with Vandenberg. Dulles was never clear as to whether Vandenberg fully accepted his idea. "He did not dissent," Dulles said later, "but neither did he publicly or affirmatively push the idea."

"I do not presently favor the recognition of the Communist regime in China," the Senator wrote on January 5, 1950. "I think primary 'recognition' requires proof of competent control of the country and satisfactory evidence of a willingness and purpose to recognize the obligation of international law. I am unable to prophesy when these factors will be present. So long as we continue to recognize the Nationalist Government in China, I favor continued support of this Government in Formosa but not through active American military action which could involve us in war responsibilities." A few days later he wrote:

January 9, 1950

I . . . deeply dislike the present abrupt abandonment of the Nationalist Government (no matter what its weaknesses) without some sort of alternative program in Formosa (where the Formosans ought to have a right to say a little something about their own fate). I am opposed to recognition of the Communist regime in China at this immediate moment — although realities may force an early abandonment of this position. . . . I may be wrong. But I cannot escape the feeling that the "Ward episode" [detention of U.S. Consul Angus Ward by Communists in Manchuria] and many others require some sort of assurances that the Communist Government in China will respect our rights under international law. Perhaps the assurances (even though given) would prove as futile as the promises in the Roosevelt-Litvinov correspondence preceding our recognition of Soviet Russia. But it seems to me that at least as a matter of self-respect we must keep the record clear. This may prove to be impractical. But I want to explore it to a finality.

A week later he added:

"THE CONUNDRUM OF THE AGES" 539

January 17, 1950

We must face things as they are and make the best of it. This inevitably requires us to face the total Far Eastern situation rather than China and Formosa by themselves. This means that our policy must concern itself not only with salvaging what we can in China and Formosa, but also in doing what will best keep another billion of Asiatics out of the Soviet order. I am convinced that we would seriously impair our status among the latter billion if we were to join ourselves in any military action. ... I should ... like to find a way to give the Formosans some degree of self-determination in respect to their own destiny; and I should like to see some means provided through which the United Nations can take collective action. But the whole thing is desperately complicated and we must proceed (at long last) with prudence as well as courage in this critical area.

Dulles' proposal regarding Formosa was obviously still in Vandenberg's mind when he wrote:

January 23, 1950

I am inclined to agree ... that we can sustain a legal claim that Formosa cannot be permanently separated from Japan except by terms of the ultimate Japanese peace treaty. I confess, however, that I was somewhat jolted in this concept when I discovered that this treaty reservation was not a part of the official proceedings at Cairo and Potsdam. The situation is somewhat further complicated by the fact that Japan's formal surrender ... included a cession of Formosa to the Chinese Republic; and that the first of General MacArthur's executive orders after the surrender confirmed this cession. The fact remains that a strong argument can still be made in behalf of [the above] viewpoint (which I have always held myself). ... Thanks to the tragic mistakes which have been made ... the United States is now in a position where it must consider the Communist threat to all of Asia and the Far East as a whole. ... There still remain one billion people in the Far East who are still resisting Communist aggression; and whatever our policy now is to be we must make sure above everything else that it does not alienate this remaining free billion. In my opinion, any militaristic action on our part in respect to Formosa could seriously jeopardize our successful contacts with India and Indonesia and Indo-China, etc. This all adds up to a pretty sad "mess." . . . We must not "bite off more than we can chew." We certainly must not precipitate World War Three. Yet we must do everything within reason to preserve an anti-Communist Formosa. . . .

Just before the start of the Korean war in June of 1950, interest centered on whether the United States, while actively opposing admission of the Communist régime as the representative of China in the UN Security Council, would nevertheless permit the Council to unseat the Nationalists and seat the Communists if the required majority in the Council so voted. Vandenberg wrote to Acheson in this connection:

June 5, 1950

I understand our tentatively announced position to be that we will vote no, but waive our "veto." While this may superficially preserve a consistent American attitude regarding the use of the "veto" on questions of admissibility, it may be also calculated finally to result in actual victory for the Soviet objective. . . . I agree that we should vote no when the role is called. . . . We should keep the public record totally straight and pin subsequent responsibilities where they belong — hoping always for a new era in which international good faith may provide a dependable basis for peace. In the present instance, our affirmative vote in the Security Council would be tantamount to "recognition" of the Communist Chinese Government without even a pretense of commitments on its part to honor the Charter's peace machinery or to observe civilized diplomacy. . . .

Then comes the even more significant question whether we should use our negative vote as a "veto" even though seven affirmative votes be secured for the Chinese Communists. On the general question of admitting new members to the United Nations, the Soviet Union has consistently entrenched its minority position by using its no vote as a "veto." . . . The historical American position is exactly the opposite. . . . I have heard it argued that the United States must waive its "veto" in order to preserve the integrity of its own position as thus stated. Certainly I agree that we must consistently honor our own precedents. But I emphatically call attention to the fact that "our own precedent" requires "voluntary agreements" [to remove the veto from the admission of new members] . . . it requires multilateral action — to create a universal rule to waive the "veto." It seems to me that the precedent, if it applies at all, expressly negatives unilateral action. It could be as dubious for us to abandon our "veto" — all alone and without reciprocity — as it would be for us to seek disarmament by mere unilateral example. That would be unthinkable.

The letter acknowledged that the question in regard to China was "not completely analogous" to the election of a new member of the United Nations, but Vandenberg insisted that "before our position is formalized" the United States should determine whether Russia and other permanent members of the Council were prepared to act on removing the veto from all questions relating to the admission of new members.

Acheson opposed the seating of the Chinese Communists but, in reply to Vandenberg, he said that it was the State Department's view that decisions by the Security Council on the seating of rival claimants seeking to represent an existing member nation were not subject to the veto. That was about the way matters stood in mid-June of 1950, when the Communist régime in North Korea was secretly completing preparations for an outbreak that would upset everybody's calculations in the Far East.

After World War II, the United States had occupied the area of Korea south of the Thirty-Eighth Parallel, with the Russians occupying the area north of that line. Efforts on the part of the United States to eliminate the dividing line and unify Korea were not successful. A United-Nations-sponsored election was then held in the southern zone, the Republic of South Korea was established and, on January 2, 1949, recognized by the United States. American troops were withdrawn in July of 1949. Moscow had previously announced on December 31, 1948, that Russian troops were withdrawn from the northern zone, where a Korean Communist régime had been established.

The United States gave both economic and military assistance to the Koreans. From 1945 to 1949 we spent more than $1,000,000,000 in occupation of and assistance to South Korea. In 1949 Congress approved arms shipments to the South Koreans, and an American military mission was established to advise and assist in defense efforts. The arms shipments were slow in getting under way, however, owing in part at least to higher priorities on military equipment badly needed in other parts of the world. But there was more to the picture than just lack of defense preparations, because the United States took a position vis-à-vis the Soviet Union in Korea that was in contrast with the position we had adopted in Europe.

In Europe, the United States warned potential aggressors that they would be met with armed force. Some Administration leaders warned of the danger of war if aggression occurred in the Far East, too, but there was in regard to Korea a failure to take the same positive stand we had taken with respect to Europe. On the contrary, the over-all impression given by the Administration was generally regarded as a "write-off" of certain areas in the Far East. Certainly the speech given by Secretary Acheson before the National Press Club on January 23, 1950, together with the statements of other Administration leaders, left the impression that we would not defend Korea in event of a Communist attack.

Vandenberg's health was failing in the summer of 1950 when the North Korea Communist armies, well equipped with tanks and heavy artillery, launched a surprise offensive against the lightly-armed South Korean army below the Thirty-Eighth Parallel. But from his sickroom, the Senator closely followed every move in the drama that began so unexpectedly in Korea, in Washington, and at the United Nations. He strongly felt that the Korean war was due to mishandling of the situation by the Administration; that the mishandling was largely a matter of failure to act firmly and wisely in the preceding months. His correspondence in the following weeks particularly emphasized the fact that — in contrast to the policy pursued in Europe — the Administration had permitted a dangerous situation to arise in Korea at a time when strong leadership might have avoided the events that led up to military hostilities. On the other hand, Vandenberg was ready to face the war situation, once it had arisen, and he strongly approved President Truman's decision to reverse his field in the Far East and meet the North Korean aggressors with force.

Shortly before the fighting started, the President had written Vandenberg a friendly note expressing hope for his recovery and saying that he wanted to talk things over when the Senator was able to call on him. Vandenberg replied on July 3, 1950: "I shall look forward to the opportunity to talk with you. . . . I think you have done a courageous and indispensable thing in Korea. As you know, I have heretofore disagreed with our official attitude toward many phases of the Far Eastern situation. I regret that we could not have filed our ultimatum (through the United Nations) sooner. But I think I understand the many complexities which you have confronted in this campaign. In any event, when the time came for you to act in behalf of free men and a free world you did so with a spectacular courage which has revived the relentless purpose of all peaceful nations to deny aggression."

This did not, however, cancel out the Senator's belief that the Korean war might have been avoided. A few weeks later he elaborated this idea in a letter to a constituent.

August 5, 1950

There is no doubt that the "Korean mess" has been "mishandled" from the start. I hope you understand that none of the Administration's Far Eastern policies were ever part of our bipartisan program. Under that program, however, America took positive action against Communist aggression in Western Europe, Greece, and Turkey; and our warning to aggressors has thus far succeeded in peacefully holding them at bay. For some unaccountable reason, we pursued an opposite course in the Far East — and particularly in Korea — where the Administration virtually notified any Communist aggressors that they could have the right of way. As a matter of fact, we never even sent the South Koreans the military supplies which Congress ordered to be made available to them. It is small wonder that Communist aggression came as a result; and still smaller wonder that even we ourselves were unprepared for what happened when the Administration reversed its policy overnight. . . .

God knows this is no time to "play politics" with foreign policy or with national security — and I shall never do so. But I believe it is important to keep the record straight. Certainly, it is vital business of a minority party to hold the majority party to strict accountability lest mistakes shall duplicate themselves.

A subsequent letter said:

October 20, 1950
. . . It would be easy for me to point out that we followed a different policy in Asia than we followed in Western Europe; and — with the benefit of hindsight — I think it may be argued that the Administration's Asiatic policies were at least partially responsible for the crisis which resulted in Korea. . . . But it is only fair to say that the crisis might have developed anyway (if not in Korea then somewhere else). It is only fair to add that our Government did meet the crisis bravely when it arose. Sooner or later some such showdown was inevitable because of the inherent nature of communism. At least it is now totally unmasked and I hope we have learned that we must fight it to the finish — either at home or abroad — for the sake of our own security.

And another letter written a few days later:

October 24, 1950
I hope the Korean situation does not wind up in an anticlimax which finds President Rhee [of South Korea] at any sort of odds with either the United Nations or Washington. I very well remember his call upon me. Certainly he has been a great patriot. Frankly, however, I do not think he should

expect to inherit the civilian control north of the 38th parallel unless a northern referendum establishes this design. It is undoubtedly true that he shares some tentative rights of quest north of the 38th parallel because of the magnificent fighting of the South Koreans . . . but fundamentally the entire Korean liberation is a United Nations enterprise and the conclusion of total Korean independence must set a United Nations pattern. The United Nations and the United States interest in driving the Communists to the Manchurian and Chinese borders obviously involves vastly more than extending the status of the South Korean Republic. It involves the total fate of Asia and must be handled as such. . . .

A November 15th letter said: "I think the Korean War was inevitable (under the circumstances) if the United Nations are to become in any degree effective against communist aggression. Certainly America and the world needs united collective action against communist aggression. Perhaps we could have avoided actual hostilities if we had been firm in notifying the communist aggressors that we would oppose any aggression in Korea as we have made it plain we will do in Western Europe."

A final letter was written when he was ill in Grand Rapids:

January 17, 1951

You probably noticed the statement I issued a few days ago in regard to "unity" as the indispensable bulwark not only of the United Nations but also and particularly of our own national security. I hope the Government of the United States does not directly or indirectly recognize Red China for membership in the United Nations. It is clearly an aggressor in Korea and clearly in conflict with every pledge and aspiration of the United Nations Charter. Time and circumstances may ultimately correct this situation. But the prospect, it seems to me, is not yet in sight and I think it would be a grave blow to the United Nations in American public opinion if this were to happen now. In other words, I am suggesting — in this letter which is purely personal to you — that our support of the United Nations must be coupled with its adequate support of the things for which it and we stand.

28

"And This Too Shall Pass"

SENATOR Vandenberg underwent a serious operation at the University of Michigan Hospital at Ann Arbor on October 3, 1949, for removal of half of his left lung. He was sixty-five years old, and the more than five hours required for the operation were a tremendous drain on his strength. It was described as highly successful and the Senator came through in excellent condition. His physicians ordered him to rest for at least three months — but for Vandenberg that was a difficult if not impossible assignment. There were so many things that he yet had to do.

"Our job," he wrote to Winston Churchill in reply to a telegram of good wishes, "is *not* finished until we have stabilized a *free world* of *free men*."

For one thing, Vandenberg was gravely worried about the future of bipartisanship. It had suffered setbacks during the previous Congress and there were growing threats of resurgent Republican isolationism that promised greater trouble in the future. John Foster Dulles, who had been expected to play a helpful role in developing Republican foreign policy in the Senate, was defeated that fall by Democrat Herbert H. Lehman in a special election to fill the unexpired term of Robert F. Wagner of New York. Senators were beginning to talk about a reduction in arms aid and ECA funds for Europe and a real partisan battle was in the making over the loss of China to the communists, with opinion hardening against recognition of the new régime.

"I hope and expect to be back on the firing line when Congress reassembles in January," he wrote on October 8, 1949. "My 'job' is far from finished — if we are to have a decent peace without World War Three. The G.O.P. shows signs of 'splintering' into various degrees of isolationism which could be ominous for a free America in a free world. I hope to play my full part yet in making collective peace effective. That is what keeps me going. But it will have to be by the end of 1952 because — regardless of what you may read to the contrary — I am retiring when this term ends."

A few days later he received a letter from President Truman, who expressed his pleasure that the Senator had come through the hospital ordeal with "flying colors," and added: "The country needs men like you and I certainly don't want anything to happen to you. Take good care of yourself."

In such circumstances, Vandenberg had difficulty in obeying his doctor's instructions to do nothing. Even when he was able to stop thinking about national affairs his mind was constantly on the book that he had long planned to write — the book for which he had collected voluminous data and written countless diary entries throughout the years in Washington. In his mind, it had become a far more important book than he had anticipated because it would be an attempt to clarify and explain the thing that had become most important to him — bipartisanship in foreign policy.

Bipartisanship — or as Vandenberg preferred to call it "nonpartisanship" — was an ideal which in a limited field was transformed into a reality in the postwar years. But it was often misunderstood and it was always in danger of political attack. The main purpose of the book that the Senator hoped to write was to strengthen nonpartisanship and make clear its vital importance in the future of America — make it so clear that the people would never again tolerate political infringement on this principle to the detriment of the national interest.

As has been mentioned earlier, Vandenberg was always interested in making ideas work — putting them into effect, and he seldom resorted to a purely philosophical approach to problems of government. But in one of the few philosophic letters he ever wrote, he took up the question of bipartisanship with

Robert E. Hannegan, a political realist, and at that time Chairman of the Democratic National Committee. Just before the 1946 election the Senator was representing the United States at the United Nations General Assembly and in the Council of Foreign Ministers in New York. He was also a Republican candidate for re-election from Michigan. This combination of responsibilities caused him to do some serious thinking about nonpartisanship and on October 28 he wrote his thoughts to Hannegan, saying he would be "eternally grateful" if the Democratic chairman answered him *after* the election.

He began by saying that bipartisanship in foreign policy was of indispensable importance, but he asked whether such a thing was

> permanently possible. I want to discuss it seriously after November 5th [election day]. I am trying to figure out whether the equally important and equally indispensable maintenance of a two-party political system does not inevitably collide with the foregoing.
>
> Current events offer the clinical exhibit I want to dissect. During my foreign policy collaboration with President Truman and Secretary Byrnes (Democrats) I have flatly refused to make any speeches on a partisan (Republican) basis because I have considered that this would tend to destroy bipartisan, which is to say, united American foreign policy. I have been severely criticized in some sectors of my own party as a result. It has been argued that this trends toward the "one party system" which would spell the negation of American political liberties, transfer the infirmities of totalitarian elections to the United States and thus defeat for us the achievement of what Secretary Byrnes calls a "peoples' peace." It has been argued that this helps the "ins" to keep the "outs" out. Unquestionably there is a powerful argument to be made along these lines — particularly if and when the majority party takes "foreign policy" into election politics. It is, of course, offset by considerations of national interest which ought to be paramount . . . but again we find ourselves

plagued by the fact that the "national interest" also requires the maintenance of the two-party political system.

This immediately poses an equally embarrassing and perhaps imponderable question for the political majority — the administration in power. Having been the beneficiary of minority cooperation . . . what is its ethical and essential attitude when election time rolls around: Shall it keep "foreign policy" out of its campaign appeal? Shall it forego the partisan capitalization of its leadership in what, for the sake of argument, is a successful "foreign policy" even though this "success" stems from bi-partisan cooperation? . . . Does not that immediately transfer all the political advantage of a bi-partisan "foreign policy" to the minority?

Now, reluctantly, I use myself as a "guinea pig" in this clinic. I write ahead of the November 5th results so that we can keep this discussion at the academic level. For 18 months I have spent most of my time cooperating with two Democratic Presidents and three Democratic Secretaries of State — at their solicitation — in developing a bi-partisan, American foreign policy. All five of them have been kind enough to express their gratitude and appreciation. I am a candidate for re-election on the Republican ticket on November 5th. On the same day that I receive President Truman's commission as an American delegate to the second session of the General Assembly of the United Nations — a commission which says that he "reposes special trust and confidence in my integrity and ability" — his party's national committee. . . . sends two of its most prominent orators (whom I shall not name because this is a purely impersonal inquiry) into Michigan to seek my party's defeat in general and my defeat in particular. Bang! "Foreign policy" is back in politics! Do I still keep still, which I am doing? Or do I shove "foreign policy" still further into politics — and probably for keeps?

To still further complicate the situation, if I am defeated it is the Administration's "foreign policy" which really takes the licking because I am so closely identified with it. Yet, if I win, I may contribute to a major political defeat for the Administration. So the Administration loses in either event.

These were difficult questions that he had posed, but in Vandenberg's mind there was only one answer and he became more firmly convinced of it each year. Some critics suggested that bipartisanship gagged free debate in Congress, but Vandenberg answered: "I do not believe this is the result in actual practice. It may shorten 'free debate' through the effective advance clarification of the issues involved — thus eliminating in some degree some of the controversy which otherwise would require exploration. But I think there is a vast difference between shortening debate and gagging debate." And to the criticism that his efforts to get unanimity in the Foreign Relations Committee might mean unquestioned acceptance of measures on the Senate floor, he replied: "I would not deny the inevitable fact that a unanimous bipartisan Committee report . . . creates an impetus which discourages partisan attack. On the other hand, I think it encourages factual attack if such be warranted through a clarification of the real issues involved."

But above all, Vandenberg vigorously objected to charges that nonpartisanship represented a slavish "me too" parroting of the Administration in foreign policy issues. He often cited the record of accomplishment in Congress that was different from the Administration's original foreign policy proposals and pointed out that the very fabric of many important foreign policy undertakings bore the unmistakable imprint of the Republican party. He said in a Lincoln Day speech at Detroit:

February 14, 1949

During the last two years, when the Presidency and Congress represented different parties, America could only speak with unity, and therefore with power, through some instrument of liaison. So-called bipartisan foreign policy provided the connecting link. It did not apply to everything — for example, not to Palestine or China. But it did apply generally elsewhere. It helped to formulate foreign policy before it ever reached the legislative stage. Otherwise it would not have worked. Let's be clear about that. It was not a carbon-copy process. There are outstanding Republican trade-marks in every act that Congress passed. It was a meeting of minds. Thus we achieved substantial unity. Our

Government did not splinter. It did not default. It was strong in the presence of its adversaries.

Shortly after he had undergone the operation at Ann Arbor, the Senator went home to recuperate. On November 19, he wrote to Dulles that he was "getting sick and tired of the increasingly persistent attempts to support the fiction that bipartisan foreign policy is entirely 'me too' on the part of its Republican participants. There is evidently a rugged fight ahead of our own party to break down the unity which we have created for the voice of America at the water's edge. I do not have the remotest idea of surrendering to any such self-serving isolationism."

The outlook for continuation of nonpartisanship was very much on his mind in the following weeks and he wrote Senator Lodge that he did not like some "current G.O.P. trends . . . utter distortions of facts in respect to the kind of 'bi-partisan' foreign policy you and I have sustained. This could develop into very serious business for the country — and it could needlessly wreck our party's future." By the middle of December, 1949, Congress was preparing to get back to work and the trend against nonpartisanship appeared to be growing rather than diminishing.

"For some time," said the Washington *Star* in an editorial, "there has been a restless stirring in the Republican ranks, a rising revolt against the 'me-tooism' which some hold responsible for the succession of G.O.P. disasters at the polls. And there is more than a suspicion that some influential Republicans have been playing with the idea of carrying this revolt to the extent of junking the bipartisan foreign policy in the hope that some partisan advantage could be salvaged from the resulting discord. Senator Vandenberg has served notice that he will have no part of this. . . . [He] has a gift of setting such matters in their proper perspective in language that everyone can understand."

Abandoning his rest schedule, Vandenberg flew back to Washington on December 20, accompanied by his wife. Neither had by any means recovered from their illnesses. The Senator was in severe pain much of the time. He moved about with considerable difficulty at any time. Many of his friends urged him to go somewhere and recuperate in the sun. But he didn't want to go and his doctors apparently decided that a revival of limited activity in Washington might give him the impetus to regain his strength. It didn't. His first night in Washington was a painful one, and around midnight he called his doctor, asking for a sedative so that he could get some sleep.

"I have a press conference scheduled for tomorrow," he explained, "and I want to be ready for it."

"You're making a mistake," the doctor replied. "You can't hold a press conference or anything else tomorrow."

"Look here, Doc, let's get this straight," Vandenberg said. "I'm paying you to fix me up so I can get there — not to keep me away."

He made the press conference, at which he reaffirmed faith in nonpartisanship and opposed immediate recognition of Spain. But the reporters observed that he was not the old Vandenberg. He had lost weight. It was difficult for him to get in and out of his automobile. He said he would be in the Senate on January 3, but he couldn't make it. He listened to the radio in his hotel apartment when President Truman delivered his State of the Union message to Congress.

The newspapers had editorially welcomed Vandenberg back to the Senate, and a number of Washington political columnists wrote of the role he was expected to play in a revival of bipartisan collaboration on foreign policy, but the days went by and the Senator could not leave his apartment except for sojourns in the Georgetown Hospital. He didn't give up trying to get back into the stream of things, but about all he could do was to write letters. In January he wrote to a constituent what was perhaps the most concise definition he had yet composed of bipartisanship.

January 5, 1950

To me "bipartisan foreign policy" means a mutual effort, under our indispensable two-Party system, to unite our official voice at the water's edge so that America speaks with maximum authority against those who would divide and conquer us and the free world. It does not involve the remotest surrender of free debate in determining our position. On the contrary, frank cooperation and free debate are indispensable to ultimate unity. In a word, it simply seeks national security ahead of partisan advantage. Every foreign policy must be *totally* debated (and I think the record proves it has been) and the "loyal opposition" is under special obligation to see that this occurs.

Late the same month he resigned from the Joint Congressional Atomic Energy Committee because he was unable to take an active part in its work. He was interested at this time in efforts to write a Republican party statement on foreign policy, and he rallied his strength to discuss the proposed statement with members of a drafting committee. He occasionally wrote letters to friends or to Senate colleagues who had asked his views on current legislation. He suggested through the press on February 1 that the President notify the United Nations that we were ready to abandon the new hydrogen superbomb project as soon as Russia permitted effective international control of atomic energy. But, for the most part, Vandenberg made no attempt to "lecture" his Senate colleagues from the sanctuary of a sickbed where he would be more or less immune to counterattack, and he made only one entry in his diary — the last he was to make — during 1950. It bore no date, but apparently was written about the second week in February.

New statement of Republican principles: On February 6, 1950, a Joint Committee representing the Republicans in the House and Senate and on the G.O.P. National Committee agreed upon a new statement of the G.O.P. "Principles." The instigators of this movement were primarily seeking to get away from what they (often erroneously) called a "Me Too" attitude toward Administration policies. Many of them were frankly aiming at so-called "Bi-Partisan Foreign Policy" in general — and, I suspect, at *me* in particular. The ultimate question of chief curiosity was what *I* would do under the circumstances and what the net result would be.

I immediately determined not to accept the urgent invitation of Chairman Millikin of the Republican Senate Conference to serve among the Senate representatives on the Committee. I wanted the Party to speak for itself. I wanted the net result to be free of any attack based on the presumption that I "dominated" it. Therefore I also declined an invitation to submit "written suggestions." (As a matter of fact the state of my health recommended this action anyway.) Of course, at the same time, I offered to "consult" with anybody at *any* time in connection with the Foreign Policy "plank."

The first to come to me was Senator Taft who very generously showed me his brief text and sought my comment. To the surprise, I think of both of us, we quickly came into substantial agreement. He promptly accepted a few additional sentences of mine; and this became the basic "working paper" upon which the balance of the Committee labored in respect to Foreign Policy.

Senator Brewster, who was Chairman of the Senate group, came to me subsequently several times — once accompanied by Congressman Halleck — and very considerately sought my further comment.

The big Committee's final agreement was not, of course, what I would have wished because it had to be the "common denominator" of many rival view-points. But, under such handicap, I considered it to be far better than I had ever thought possible. At least it did not repudiate "bi-partisan co-operation" in Foreign Policy and it *did* recognize and validate some of the *fundamentals* underlying it.

In my opinion, the misguided effort to wreck this "bi-partisan approach" to Foreign Policy was utterly stupid even from the stand-point of practical politics. If it had succeeded, Truman could have gone on the hustings this Fall in the '50 campaign and devastatingly said — "The Republicans ask you to elect a Republican Congress; but if you do, you will still have a Democratic President for two more years; therefore, since they warn you in advance that they will refuse foreign policy co-operation, this means a stalemate; it means you will be voting for *no foreign policy* during the two most critical years in the life of the Republic; you had better not swap horses in the middle of *this* stream."

Bi-partisan co-operation in Foreign Policy (which involves no remote suggestion of withholding vigorous and vigilant criticism when and where deserved) is not only "good patriotism" in my book; it is also the best kind of *Republican politics.*

An interesting exhibit is the following mimeograph issued the night of February 6th. This is the new Foreign Policy "plank." The underscored [italicized] words are mine:

The American people face the hard fact that though they won the war nearly five years ago they have not yet won the peace. We offer them leadership in new efforts to achieve this vital end.

We favor a foreign policy in which all Americans, regardless of party, will join to assure peace with justice in a free world while maintaining the independence and the rights of the American people.

We insist upon restoration of our foreign agreements to their proper place inside the Constitution and we insist that the United States shall not be bound to any course of action unless the spirit and letter of our Constitutional procedure are followed.

We oppose secret commitments, and we denounce the refusal of the Administration to furnish accurate and adequate information to the Congress.

Under our indispensable two-party system, we shall be vigilant in critical exploration of Administration Foreign Policy. We favor consultation between the Executive and Members of both major parties in the Legislative Branch of Government in the initiation and development of a united American Foreign Policy; and we deplore the tragic consequences of the Administration's failure to pursue these objectives in many fields, particularly in the secret agreements of Yalta, subsequently confirmed at Potsdam, which have created new injustices and new dangers throughout the world.

We favor full support of the United Nations and the improvement of its Charter so that it may be an effective international organization of independent states prepared to mobilize public opinion and the armed forces of the world against aggression. We favor full support of the inter-American system as an integral part of the international organization, and of our treaty obligations in the North Atlantic Community.

We advocate a strong policy against the spread of Communism

or Fascism at home and abroad, and we insist that America's efforts toward this end be directed by those who have no sympathy either with Communism or Fascism.

We support aid to those states resisting Communism but such aid should be given only if it is essential to our national security, *if it is within the total limits which the American economy can afford,* if it will be effective, if it is beyond the ability of the aided nation to supply for itself, and if there is a program for progressive reduction.

The Senator's satisfaction that the Republican statement did not repudiate bipartisanship indicated his growing concern over the future of that basic policy. The newspapers at the time reported that Administration leaders were making efforts to revive bipartisanship which, according to the Associated Press, had been "sagging in the continued absence from Congress of Senator Vandenberg." The Washington *Post* added that "it is chiefly Senator Vandenberg that the country must thank for what success has been achieved so far in bipartisanship. Now Vandenberg is ill, and the yawning rift testifies to the loss of his disinterested service." Columnist Doris Fleeson wrote on March 22 that Vandenberg's absence was "remarked on fearfully by supporters of the present foreign policy, especially ECA and the military assistance program. . . . As of now such forebodings are unjustified, according to Republicans in a position to speak with knowledge and authority. It is predicted that the Foreign Relations [Committee] Republicans . . . can be depended on for reasonable support of Administration policy. . . . It is stressed that to date the McCarthy charges [attacks by Senator Joe McCarthy of Wisconsin, on alleged Communist influence in the State Department] and the demands for Secretary of State Acheson's resignation are personal to Senators and neither widespread nor a matter of party policy."

But the *New York Times* said editorially that "even the Democrats miss the clear, authoritative voice [of Vandenberg] that rises above the buzz of party politics to define American policy to the world. For Senator Vandenberg's distinction is that he has given leadership to both parties in the development of foreign policy, and more than any other American has lined up behind it the massive popular support that has been our greatest asset in the post-war years. This leadership is lacking today. . . . We have to go forward . . . and where the vision, experience and good-tempered statesmanship of Senator Vandenberg are needed is in the hard transitions like the present, when new issues arise and policy has to evolve to meet fresh tests and changing conditions. The wish for his speedy recovery is a wish not for him alone but for the country he serves so well."

Only once during the spring of 1950 did Vandenberg make a major effort to influence Congress, and on that occasion he was careful to adopt an indirect method of expressing his views in a letter to ECA Administrator Paul G. Hoffman on the second anniversary of the European Recovery Program. At the time a Republican attack on Secretary Acheson was gaining momentum, and some observers feared that the whole concept of bipartisanship would go down under a partisan search for a 1950 campaign issue. "I have tried to be scrupulously careful not to 'lecture' my colleagues from behind the 'iron curtain' of my stubborn convalescence," Vandenberg wrote to a newspaper friend. "It did seem to me that I could (and should) 'sound off' to Mr. Hoffman on the occasion of the Second Anniversary of ECA and that this could be done without too much friction and yet perhaps with some effectiveness. But I do not feel entitled to go much farther with that sort of thing until I am personally back on the firing line where I can be legitimately challenged and where I can defend my position."

The letter to Hoffman was an appeal to both parties to support ERP and a proposal to create an unpartisan commission that would recommend a long-range U.S. economic and political peace policy. He wrote:

March 24, 1950
> The least I can do is to take advantage of this occasion to say that, in my humble opinion, you and your ECA associates, at home and abroad, have rendered incalculably vital service to our country and its indispensable leadership for liberty. You have paid off in current dividends of freedom. ECA was launched as an unpartisan enterprise — established by a Republican Congress in full and free cooperation with a Demo-

cratic Executive. This working unity typified our finest traditions and our greatest safety in the presence of external hazards to all Americans, regardless of Party. . . . As one citizen to another, I thank you for this service from a grateful heart. United, we stand. Divided, we fall. I want America to *stand*. . . .

In all candor can it be successfully denied that ECA has been substantially responsible for reversing the corroding gloom which threatened Western Civilization two years ago, and which might have brought the "iron curtain" to the very rims of the Atlantic but for this brave adventure? How much is that worth in liberties and lives and dollars to our own United States? Let us not ignore any of the lessons we have learned . . . emphatically including the lesson that free nations must continue as free nations to work together in closest, practical harmony for the effectual defense of their mutual heritage.

A few days after the letter to Hoffman was published, Vandenberg received a long letter from President Truman, expressing his appreciation for the Senator's attitude, discussing various foreign problems, and giving his own version of the origin and development of bipartisan foreign policy. Addressing Vandenberg as "Dear Arthur," the President wrote on March 27: "I appreciated most highly your letter to Mr. Hoffman, supporting continuation of the full appropriation for E.C.A. I have been very much disturbed about the situation as it has been developing in the Congress with regard to the whole bipartisan foreign policy.

"As you know, that bipartisan foreign policy was inaugurated back in the time when Cordell Hull was Secretary of State, and when I was Chairman of the Committee to Investigate the National Defense Program. In fact, I was one of the Senators who worked diligently on the B2H2 resolution. The first great result of our bipartisan policy was the setting up of the United Nations, and all of us are grateful for your own great contributions at that time. As a continuation of that policy, the salvation of Greece and Turkey was first inaugurated at the suggestion of the then Secretary of State, Mr. Byrnes, and General Marshall.

"As you remember, we had a conference on the matter in the White House, at which you were present with several other Senators and Representatives of the Foreign Affairs and Foreign Relations Committees of the Congress. The European Recovery Program was a follow-up of the approach to the salvation of Greece and Turkey.

"You remember, Dean Acheson, then Under Secretary of State, made a speech on the subject at Cleveland, Mississippi, in May 1947, which was followed by General Marshall's commencement address at Harvard University in June 1947. After that, several conferences were held by the President and Members of the Foreign Affairs and Foreign Relations Committees of the House and Senate, and the European Recovery Program was inaugurated.

"There isn't any question in my mind that it has been a very successful Program, and that it must be continued to its logical conclusion. Still later, the North Atlantic Pact and the Military Aid Program were worked out on a bipartisan basis.

"The approach of several Senators to the foreign policy program, in an effort to find an issue for the coming campaign this fall, is unfortunate. I am sorry that they can't find a domestic issue on which to carry on the campaign. It seems to me that that could be done if an intelligent approach were made to the subject.

"I sent a communication to Chairman Kee of the House Committee on Foreign Affairs at about the same time you were writing to Mr. Hoffman. I am glad the letters were publicly distributed at the same time. They should have a very salutary effect in the effort to save the foreign policy. I am enclosing a copy of a letter which I have just sent to Styles Bridges on this same subject. As I said to Senator Bridges, the breakup of the bipartisan foreign policy at this time would mean but one thing — victory for Russia in Europe, and in all probability a definite approach to a shooting war, which none of us wants.

"The unfortunate situation in the Far East, which came about as a result of the corrupt Chinese Nationalist government, has caused us much difficulty, through no fault of ours that I have been able to discover. I believe that the Chinese and Far Eastern situation eventually will be rescued from the totalitarian regime at Moscow. One of the most awful situations, as a result of the overthrow of the Nationalist government, will be the starvation of millions of innocent people in China. I am now endeavoring to find a way to alleviate that condition. The Chinese, as you know, are fundamentally anti-foreign, and we must be exceedingly careful to see that this anti-foreign sentiment is not turned in our direction.

"I am making every effort possible to negotiate a treaty with Japan, which would be very helpful if we could get the cooperation of the Russians. We have never had that cooperation since hostilities ceased, and those of us who are familiar with the movements and the historical procedures following the German surrender know that every agreement made between us and Russia seems to have been made only to be broken at the convenience of the Russian government. You of course know this bit of history as well as I do.

"You will notice in my communication to Senator Bridges that I told him I would be glad to talk with any group at any time on any subject which affected the foreign relations of the United States. Irresponsible attacks on the Secretary of State, I think, are the greatest asset that the Kremlin has in this country.

"I sincerely hope that the Lord will be good to the country and hurry along your physical recovery, so that you can come back and take your proper place as the Minority Leader of the Program."

Vandenberg answered the President's letter and, on March 31, 1950, received still another one from Mr. Truman. "You just don't realize," it said, "what a vacuum there has been in the Senate and in the operation of our foreign policy since you left. That has always been one of the difficulties in the continuation of policy in our Government.

"I am sincerely hoping that you will recover completely and have an opportunity to train some of the young men in the Senate who are anxious to carry on with what you, Cordell Hull and other Secretaries of State visualized with regard to a continuing foreign policy for this great Government of ours.

"I mentioned you yesterday in a press conference as one of those who could appreciate exactly what the country needs in its foreign relations.

"Personally, I am not confining that need to foreign relations alone. It is very seldom that men really become statesmen while they are yet alive, in the minds of the people and their associates. As you well know, I have always held you in that category. Take good care of yourself, and if there is anything I can do to contribute to your welfare and recovery, all you need do is name it."

The President's words were echoed at this time by newspaper comment on Vandenberg's letters to Hoffman. Many editorials emphasized that his absence from Congress was one of the main reasons for the impairment of nonpartisanship. One of his favorite cartoonists, Berryman of the Washington *Star*, illustrated the letter with a picture of Vandenberg in "Our Foreign Policy Shop" — filled with chinaware — trying to bar the door to a rambunctious G.O.P. elephant who seemed intent on breaking all the merchandise. "The Republican opposition in Congress is now in open rebellion against the men who have led the Republican party since Pearl Harbor," wrote Walter Lippmann. "Vandenberg and Stimson represent . . . the bipartisan policy of national unity for war and for peace. . . . The men who have captured the leadership of the Republican party are the old isolationists. . . . In the last analysis, McCarthy and the more important Republicans who are backing him do not believe in a foreign policy in which the United States plays a responsible and cooperative role in the world."

On some occasions, Vandenberg attempted to answer those Senate Republicans who were opposed to or who pondered the effects of bipartisanship. To Senator Homer Ferguson, his Michigan colleague with whom he long had a warm relationship, he wrote:

May 31, 1950

> It seems to me that the fundamental point is that we are discussing an attitude rather than a formula. This "attitude" recognizes that, even under the most favorable circumstances, a democracy like ours is under heavy handicap when imperiled by an autocracy like Russia where decisions require nothing but a narrow Executive mandate. We are seeking

to prevent a shooting war; but the success of the effort is calculated to be in exact ratio to the impressiveness with which our "unity" makes for our own security. Therefore the reciprocal need for "team ball" calls for maximum cooperation at both ends of [Pennsylvania] ... Avenue in searching a final, unified foreign policy. This does not detract one iota from the need for searching legislative scrutiny in the making of these policies. ... It is to be noted that this bipartisan liaison is much simpler (as in the 80th Congress) when each major party controls one end of the executive-legislative process involved in foreign affairs. There has to be cooperation under such circumstances or America would be devoid of any foreign policy at all. We both confront unavoidable and obvious responsibilities in such cases. The situation (and the procedures) are far less clear (though no less imperative) when one party controls both Congress and the White House and has the total primary responsibility for what happens to us abroad.

It is for this reason that I have feared the possible results of any wholesale and total repudiation of the basic bi-partisan (unpartisan is a better word) attitude. We may not successfully ask the American people to elect a Republican Congress in 1950 (under two more years of a Democratic President) if we notify them in advance that there can be no bipartisan foreign policy whatever from such a Republican Congress, which in effect means no foreign policy at all during these two vitally important years when our "cold war" for honorable peace will be won or lost. ... I have no complaint in the world against fair challenge to anything which this Administration does (and there are plenty of grounds). But I do not believe it is good for the country or the party to belligerently forsake the bi-partisan attitude and the unity label.

On April 11 the Senator had to return to Georgetown Hospital in Washington for removal of a tumor near his spine. His condition after the operation was described as good, but his recovery was slow and he was in and out of the hospital for weeks. On May 20 he limped from his apartment to his automobile and was driven to the Senate Chamber, where a fight was in progress to break a filibuster by Southern senators against the bill to set up a Fair Employment Practices Commission. It was an issue on which many senators were more than willing to find some excuse for not casting a public vote, but Vandenberg took the opposite viewpoint and made a great effort in order to be present. A roll call was in progress when he arrived unexpectedly, thin and pale but smiling broadly. A buzz of whispers swept around the Chamber as he entered. Vice-President Barkley, presiding, looked up in surprise and then waved his hand. Senators left their seats to greet Vandenberg. Barkley interrupted the roll call to welcome him back and, as he finished speaking, everybody in the Chamber stood up and applauded.

Vandenberg stayed only a short time, but the visit was a severe drain on his strength. He didn't go again. And on June 10 Mrs. Vandenberg died after a long illness. Her loss was a staggering blow to Vandenberg. She was a warm, devoted woman who for thirty years had been an indispensable "partner" in the Senator's career. For several years before her death she had suffered almost constant pain, and her incredible courage in this period gave her husband the inspiration to carry on after his own health began to fail.

In this period, he received many letters from his friends, and some of the most cherished ones were from General Marshall, who wrote several times in an informal way to express his feeling of friendship and respect. Marshall almost never addressed anyone by his first name, but now he started his letters with "Dear Arthur," and if there had been any cleavage between the Marshalls and the Vandenbergs their friendship was long since restored. On July 10 the Senator wrote Marshall: "I loved your reminiscence — 'It would have been a great relaxer to sit down and have a drink with you and Bob Lovett and decide just how we were going to manage the world and then have done it.' Those were truly 'great days.' My part in them will always be my proudest record. Looking backward, it is really quite amazing how well we and the world got along together."

But the Senator's health was getting no better and by late

September he had been forced to return to Grand Rapids, where he entered Butterworth Hospital for an examination and then went to his home on Morris Avenue for convalescence. The Senate passed a resolution in which the membership expressed its "high esteem" for Vandenberg and his "zeal for the cause of world peace" and its hope for his "speedy and complete recovery."

In October Senator H. Alexander Smith, with whom he had worked closely and in warm harmony, returned from a trip abroad and wrote Vandenberg that he had talked with Winston Churchill, who asked "very especially how you were." Smith added that the British statesman remarked that he had not seen Vandenberg many times but that he nevertheless felt very close to the Michigan Senator because they had a "community of soul" and saw the world in much the same way.

Vandenberg was pleased that fall by the appointment of Senator Lodge to the American delegation to the United Nations and to Committee Five — the so-called "housekeeping" committee — of the General Assembly, where, he pointed out, "you can take over the responsibilities which I had to initiate in the first two General Assemblies." He wrote Lodge on October 4, 1950, to assure him: ". . . if you ever face an 'imponderable' which needs the advice of 'the old man' I shall be delighted to hear from you. . . . The Doctors tell me I am progressing. That may be. It is not surprising if I am a bit more cynical than they are since I am on the receiving end of their advice. But I am hoping — if it is humanly possible — to be back in reasonably complete Senate activity when the next session convenes."

And on the fifth anniversary of the United Nations, he wrote to a newspaper friend, Michael A. Gorman of Flint, Michigan:

October 24, 1950

I feel somewhat like "an ancient mariner" this afternoon as I think back to five years ago today. It seems more like fifty, so much has happened in the interval. The U.N. has hit bottom and survived. I sincerely believe it now stands an excellent chance of justifying the hopes and aspirations with which we wrote and signed the Charter. . . . I am still confined to my home by my stubborn convalescence (which now includes a busted rib!) but if it is humanly possible I intend to resume my Senate responsibilities on the spot. . . .

[Mr. Truman had made a speech that day saying that the United Nations had given grounds for faith in the future and that Korea had proved that the international organization could meet a challenge. Everywhere men were seeking a better life, he said, and the United Nations was helping them toward this objective. And Vandenberg added a P.S. to his letter in which he said:] I thought the President made a great speech this morning. . . . I wish the Administration had made fewer mistakes, particularly in the Far East; but he certainly "delivered the goods" at the finish.

On November 21 he wrote Senator Taft: "Please do not be 'upset' (your word) by anything that appears in the papers involving our relationships. We have lived through several years of press efforts to put us at odds. It has never succeeded and I am sure it never will. We may not always agree on policies. But I dare to believe that we will always agree that we are dependable friends."

Late in November Edward R. Murrow, radio commentator, asked Vandenberg for help in preparing a documentary radio program based on American foreign policy since 1945. Vandenberg replied on November 24 that

my untimely illness has kept me out of the bi-partisan foreign policy debate for more than a year. The opponents have pretty well confused the country on the subject. The President himself has not helped any by his resurrected habit of castigating the "no good 80th Congress" when I was Chairman of the Senate Foreign Relations Committee. He has tried to somewhat discriminate between domestic and foreign policies in this respect; but it has been a feeble discrimination which has left a sadly erroneous impress with the country. Of course, I am prejudiced but I think the 80th Congress made the greatest of all records in projecting a new foreign policy for the United States and a new national unity on foreign policy. . . . In my opinion the great achievement was to create confidence in our foreign policies both at home and abroad. In my opinion there is vital need — greater than ever — to recreate this procedure (expanded to cover all major foreign policy considerations) and this resultant unity. It will be more difficult because our critics have had a lively vocal season. . . . The grave need is to find a "meeting of minds" which will reassure our own country and the world that our democracy can function in times of crisis. The need is to consult national rather than political destiny.

There was in the early months of 1951 only one issue before the Senate that prompted Vandenberg to write extensively to his colleagues. Even then he wrote only in response to their inquiries, because he still felt that it was improper for him to try to exert his influence directly while he was an invalid in Grand Rapids. The issue arose as an aftermath of the European arms aid bill, which had marked the end of Vandenberg's twenty-three years in the Senate, and it involved the sending of additional American infantry divisions into an integrated European army under command of General Eisenhower. President Truman insisted that he had authority under the Constitution to send four additional American divisions abroad to join the two already there in the Eisenhower army. The President said that as Commander-in-Chief he could send the troops without Congressional assent, although he would be happy to consult with legislators on the matter. This led to the "Great Debate" in the Senate early in 1951. Senator Wherry of Nebraska insisted that no troops should be sent until Congress established an over-all policy covering the question and he formulated a Resolution emphasizing the necessity for prior Congressional approval. This raised the old question of whether Congress could or should tie the hands of the President in a way that might handicap him in meeting an emergency.

Vandenberg originally had been opposed to overemphasis on maintenance of "forces-in-being" in Europe because he believed that the great strength of the North Atlantic Community lay in the fact that it represented "potential" military strength that would deter a possible aggressor. He modified that viewpoint, however, in view of such developments as the Korean war, and in the "Great Debate" he felt that the Wherry Resolution might dangerously handicap the Chief Executive.

Vandenberg wrote:

January 23, 1951

I have been watching "the great debate" with interest. I greatly appreciate what Chairman Connally had to say about me. He has a tough job on his hands and I wish I were there to help. Just strictly between us, I think it is very necessary for the Senate to clarify its position regarding the North Atlantic Pact because the present state of controversy invites disunity both at home and abroad. Personally, I feel that the theory of the North Atlantic Pact is our salvation. Our friends in Western Europe must understand that they must do their part. But so must we.

In the same period, Wherry asked Vandenberg by telegram for clarification of various questions concerning the North Atlantic Treaty, and Vandenberg replied:

February 2, 1951

... I deeply respect your views although we disagree regarding the fundamentals of peace for national security. [He added that the proposed Wherry resolution might be interpreted] in some quarters as Congressional approval of the original challenge to the President's general Constitutional power (a challenge which I do not believe can be successfully sustained). Furthermore, I believe it is dangerous and futile to attempt to keep us out of potential war by any one such Presidential limitation. For example, the President is the only officer (military or civil) who can release the atom bomb. This leads immediately to war — and we would undoubtedly need every facility at our command in instant defense of the nation. ... I think it would be preferable for the President and Congress to voluntarily agree by legislation on the general basis of our reciprocal support without reference to the President's Constitutional prerogative (which has been in dispute for 150 years).

I make no proposal. I am not on the ground, to my great regret, because of my stubborn convalescence. I do not know whether this is feasible. It would require complete Presidential cooperation. (He is the only President we shall have and this is the only Congress we shall have during the next critical two years; the quicker we reach a working relationship so that we can have a united policy, the safer our country will be.)

On February 12, 1951, impressed by what he described as "some invincibly great speeches" made by Eisenhower in Washington on the troops issue, Vandenberg wrote W. S. (Doc) Gilmore, publisher of the Detroit *News*, regarding his concern over the turn of events. "Between you and me, I do not like the idea of complete Presidential freedom, without a reference to Congress, to send American troops abroad. But we confront a condition and not a theory. He is Commander-in-Chief. His constitutional function must not be impaired lest it tie our hands behind our backs. Yet when it comes to implementing Article Three of the North Atlantic pact, there ought to be time for him to frankly consult Congress in advance and that is what he should do voluntarily."

And a few days later Vandenberg dictated a long letter to Senator James H. Duff of Pennsylvania, who had proposed a visit on a scheduled Detroit trip. Duff, in writing Vandenberg, had enclosed a statement on the troops issue which stimulated Vandenberg's interest and moved him to set down in detail his current views on relations between the President and Congress, and on the collective defense of the free world. He wrote:

February 17, 1951

My dear Senator Jim:

Thanks for your letter of February 14, and the telephone message from your office which preceded it.

I cannot begin to tell you how sorry I am that I had to tell your office that my weekend is committed to some final consultations regarding my stubborn convalescence and it was simply impossible for me to arrange any sort of conference with you. This is a source of deepest regret to me — not only because I should like nothing better than to discuss the "state of the union" with you but also because I so deeply cherish your generous personal friendship.

The things which you say about me in your letter are much too kind. Nevertheless I like them. They are good for my morale. I only hope that I may at least partially justify your confidence and faith.

I am expecting to get back to Washington this spring, although I cannot tell when. It will not be in time for "the great debate." I have deliberately refrained from making any public statements regarding foreign policy except very generally and briefly — but I hope with sufficient finality to make it clear that I still consider collective security the only possible way that our own United States can contribute to the prevention of the awful course of World War III (which would scar victor and vanquished alike).... I think I have made it quite plain ... that I consider the North Atlantic Pact to be the indispensable key to our own national security as well as to the peace of a free world.

I have been somewhat distressed by some Republican suggestions which trend in the opposite direction. But it seems to me that the situation has been clearing itself by the sheer force of the logic of the condition. Now comes your fine letter to confirm my expectations! I hope you are saying in Detroit exactly what you have said in the advance excerpt which you have sent to me. I think your position and your argument are invincible. I am now surer of my own views because you have reached the same net conclusion to which I should subscribe without reservation. I do not know how any one could state the case better than you have done. Governor Dewey took substantially the same position in his broadcast last Sunday when he drew a nice distinction between the "commitment" of troops and the "deployment" of troops when once committed. The latter (namely, the deployment) is necessarily a prerogative of the Commander-in-Chief.... He must not be robbed of his "deployment" prerogatives or we may find that we have tied our own hands behind our own backs....

I add one other thought. To transfer any portion of this authority to Congress is to subordinate military decision to the political judgments of Congress. We partially tried that system in the Civil War when the Committee on the Conduct of War set a tragic precedent against any such bitter mistake. This leads inevitably to the final question whether this logic does not deny the constitutional authority of Congress "to declare war." This is a fair subject for argument. But we find one constitutional question thus colliding with another, namely, the constitutional prerogative of the President as Commander-in-Chief to defend the United States. It is unfortunate that we find ourselves in this twilight zone which has existed for 150 years and which has never been resolved because the force of current circumstances — which is to say the law of self-preservation — has always resulted in sustaining the President's prerogative. Never did the force of circumstances more definitely recommend this same position than under the circumstances which exist today.

Nevertheless a rule of conduct — as well as a rule of accommodation — requires some sort of unity between the legislative and the executive branches of Government. We found it before. We must find it again. Or we shall have no foreign policy worthy of the name during these next two critical years.

I think you have admirably stated the constitutional case when you say "it is a constitutional duty of the President to consult the Senate with respect to policy for the use of troops unless the situation is so immediately critical that to spend time in consultation and debate might increase the national peril." In other words — as you have said — "when there is time there ought to be consultation."

This particularly applies to Article 3 of the North Atlantic Pact, because, in the course of normal events, there should be and there is "time for consultation" before the event. Yet this might not be true. The Senate's action, therefore, should comprehend all of these contingencies so that under no circumstances shall America be handicapped by itself in defending its own national security.

This leads me to one inevitable conclusion — as it does you. The Senate should recognize (1) our full obligation to the

North Atlantic Pact and (2) it should frankly recognize the President's ultimate prerogative as Commander-in-Chief; but it could well restate the great responsibility of Congress in decisions of this character and it should urge the President to submit recommendations under Article 3 to the Congress *when not incompatible with the public interest.* . . .

I am sure the President will recognize that Congress ultimately has the inevitable power to control appropriations. I would expect this to be vigilantly used. Therefore, we had best know in advance where we are going and what we are going to do when we get there. Furthermore, the President will recognize (as does no one else) the awful responsibility which he assumes if he precipitates combat action without Congressional okay. The Congress itself might well underscore this responsibility by its present action.

I beg your indulgence for this insufferably long letter. But I have wanted you to know my exact state of mind and I hope this letter may substitute for the interview which we have been unable to arrange. I do not care to be quoted on this subject except as I am making my own statement for publication. But if there are any thoughts contained herein which would be of the slightest use to you (in sustaining your own position), you are more than welcome to borrow them without credit.

Thanks again for your great generosity in proposing to come to Grand Rapids. I hope to see you soon in Washington.

The same month he discussed the Wherry Resolution in detail in a letter to Lodge:

February 26, 1951

I have publicly been keeping still about the Wherry Resolution. . . . I have carefully watched all that you have had to say on the subject and — as usual — your concepts have been close to my own. We both believe in our primary responsibility to our own United States; but intelligent self-interest tells us that certain phases of "collective security" are absolutely indispensable to our own "self-interest." . . .

If I could have my way about it, the Senate resolution which evolves from the "great debate" would do the following things:

1 — It would re-examine our fidelity to the North Atlantic Pact so that this may stand as the unequivocal basis of our foreign policy.

2 — It would recognize that we ratified the North Atlantic Pact by an overwhelming vote for a Senate Resolution which required the exercise of due constitutional process in implementing the Treaty.

3 — It would recognize the fact that "due constitutional process" involves 150 years of indecisive debate regarding the power of the President summarily to deploy troops abroad — although throughout these 150 years the President's prerogative has governed our procedures.

4 — The Senate also recognizes and sustains the exclusive Congressional prerogative to "declare war" and the great responsibility which Congress must assume in implementing Presidential action.

5 — Therefore, the Senate resolves (with particular reference to Article Three of the North Atlantic Pact) that we must now accommodate our national policy to these facts and it urges the President:

A — To seek advance Congressional approval for the deployment of American troops abroad whenever long range planning is not incompatible with our public interest for national security; and

B — That the President should immediately notify the Congress whenever an emergency requires the summary use of his personal responsibility.

This is a very rough outline but I am sure you will see what I am trying to get at. I simply want to face facts as they are and honestly assert the truth. . . . The obvious need is for a "modus vivendi" under which we strive for unity. Perhaps there is a better way. I am far from dogmatic on the subject. . . . But in the absence of an acceptable "modus vivendi" we shall have no foreign policy at all for the next two years. . . . The President's great mistake was in not bringing his Korea decision to the immediate attention of Congress (as Wilson did at Vera Cruz). At *that* time, the country and the Congress overwhelmingly agreed with him and would have said so. Much of the intervening controversy would itself have been avoided. Above all things we must not try to substitute political decisions for military decisions in the deployment of troops which is an inevitable and indispensable prerogative of the Commander-in-Chief. Otherwise, we shall trend toward the errors of the Senate "Committee on the Conduct of the War" back in Civil War days. ... Finally, I do not want to turn my back on all of the great military leaders whom we so recently trusted to win World War II for us.

One of the military leaders of World War II was very much in the Senator's mind in this period when he felt that heroic efforts were essential to preserve the national unity that begins at the water's edge. Vandenberg frequently talked about General Eisenhower in conversations with close friends who visited him during his illness. One of these was Louis A. Weil, Jr., the son of one of the Senator's closest newspaper cronies (Louis A. Weil of Port Huron, Michigan) in the old days and now Vandenberg's successor as publisher of the Grand Rapids *Herald*. The Senator always was keenly interested in the ideas and activities of the younger generation and in the weeks when he was confined to his sickroom he often had his secretary ask Weil to drop in and talk over the news developments of the day. "During those days," Weil recalled later, "his conversation centered more and more on the need for restoration of national unity, which he felt had sharply deteriorated. The Senator constantly emphasized the necessity for leadership of the kind that only Eisenhower could provide."

These conversations and the letters that he wrote served to bring into focus Vandenberg's long-standing admiration of Eisenhower and his belief that they had much in common in their viewpoints toward America's world position. He knew, incidentally, that in 1948 the General had expressed himself favorably toward efforts to draft Vandenberg for the Republican presidential nomination.

In the following year, after Eisenhower had made a speech at St. Louis in his capacity as President of Columbia University, the Senator wrote him on September 8, 1949: "Your St. Louis speech was 'swell.' The sane philosophy of the 'middle road' is indispensable to the preservation of our threatened American unity. No one can lead this indispensable 'revival' quite so well as you. This means more than meets the eye. I am one of those who deeply believes in you."

On September 14 the General replied: "Praise from you on the content of a public talk is praise from a master. I am grateful for your thoughtfulness in writing and deeply gratified that your thinking upon the American future roughly parallels my own. We live in serious times, and I assure you that I always look forward to any opportunity, even of the briefest, that allows me to listen to an expression of your beliefs and convictions."

A few months later when a friend expressed to Vandenberg the belief that Eisenhower was the strongest possibility for the 1952 Presidential contest, Vandenberg had replied: "Thanks for your long distance squint at 1952. We *may* find ourselves 'riding the same horse.' I think the specifications call for a personality of great independent magnitude who can give our splintering American people an 'evangel' instead of an ordinary campaign."

And over a year later, on January 15, 1951, he had occasion to remark — without any political implications — on the General's ability. "I feel that General Eisenhower's frank assessment of the first hand information which he is now collecting [in regard to the defense of Western Europe] may well prove to be a decisive factor in our plans and in our public opinion. I wish I could be there when he arrives in Washington but I am afraid this is quite impossible."

When Eisenhower arrived back in the United States following his survey of the North Atlantic Treaty Organization defense problem, he reported to Congress and then, on February 2, 1951, made a radio-television report to the nation. In that speech he re-emphasized his belief that the United States must help Western Europe to rearm. According to press accounts of the speech, the General took issue in this respect with arguments that had been advanced not long before by former President Herbert Hoover and by Senator Taft. Eisenhower said that he believed "preservation of a free America requires our participation in the defense of Western Europe." He added that success in this project "is attainable" and that "while transfer to Europe of American military units is essential, our major and special contribution should be in the field of munitions and equipment."

Vandenberg had a television set in his bedroom at home and he listened enthusiastically to General Eisenhower's address. Later, a newspaper reporter called him from Philadelphia to get his comment on the speech, and the Senator praised it. Then he added: "I feel as though a great load had just been lifted from my back. Things will be all right with Ike at the helm."

"I agree with you that the national attitude toward foreign policy has somewhat changed," he wrote to a constituent on February 13. "But I think that General Eisenhower will help to put us back on the main track of collective security in the Western world. I know of no other way that we can anticipate anything like national security."

Vandenberg made another reference to Eisenhower in his correspondence when on February 10 he began — but never finished — a letter to former Representative Clare Boothe Luce. It was probably the last letter he actually wrote himself instead of dictating. The never-completed letter said:

> First, forgive the pencil and paper. I am sitting up about two hours a day but I have not yet reached the "pen and ink" or the "typewriter" stage of my stubborn recuperation.
>
> Second — forgive me for the intolerable delay in acknowledging your thoughtful holiday greetings.... The fact simply is that I have been having an unusually tough time. My aches and pains (now 16 months of them) have precluded correspondence. But you and Harry have often been on my mind.
>
> Suffice it to say that I still have three nurses "round the clock." I spent January in the hospital again, fighting an immobility which attacked my right leg, and an angry chest which insisted upon reminding me of the Spanish Inquisition.

But things are getting a little better — and I am still aiming at a return to the Wardman Park this Spring *sometime*.

My two daughters are here. Their paternal fidelity is really beautiful. They are a good antidote for the lonesomeness with which I am surrounded. But I still selfishly think that wives should outlive their husbands. I have too much time to "think things over." Yet every cloud has a silver lining — and the spiritual values in life come surging to the fore. They are so much more important than anything else. (I have a little "prayer meeting" all by myself each night.)

I send an occasional suggestion to my more stable Republican colleagues in the Senate. But what a mess our blessed nation is in. (Thank God for Eisenhower!) What the whole free world (including us) needs is more confidence and faith. Why can't they all see that there is no security for us (or for them) except in the security of others! But I seem to sense a returning realization of Republican responsibility — which I hope may continue. We must not let the country down —

The winter of 1951 was an agonizing period for Vandenberg, brightened only by the expressions of friendship and respect which came to him regularly from the men with whom he had worked so desperately to establish his country's position in a world dedicated to justice and peace. Senator Smith flew out to see him. Senator Lodge and other colleagues telephoned or wrote to him repeatedly. General Marshall sent him informal, chatty messages. President Truman dashed off several expressions of friendship and hope for his early return to the Senate. Occasionally, in answering these letters, the Senator would express his viewpoint on current affairs.

To General Marshall he wrote: "I have no illusions — just between you and me — as to what contribution I might make during this desperately critical era. But I should like to try. My 'internment' is a source of constant and keenest regret to me. I want to be on the 'firing line' again. These times call for everything that any of us can do with an eye to the 'next generation' rather than the 'next election.'"

As the Korean situation continued critical, he wrote on January 15 to President Truman that "nothing matters in this crisis except the welfare of our country. It calls for the greatest possible meeting of minds in behalf of invincible unity against an aggression which is clearly aimed at us. I deeply regret . . . my stubborn illness. . . . Your generous personal references are deeply appreciated. . . . You may be sure that you have all my prayers in the midst of the indescribably heavy burdens which you are carrying."

The President on March 6 sent Vandenberg a telegram from Key West, saying: "All of your friends are disturbed by reports that you have not been getting on so well lately. This is just a line to let you know that I am thinking of you and hope you will be back in your old place soon. The country needs you. Best of luck always."

It was typical of the Senator from Michigan that once, late in February, he found the strength to write a longer letter to a Princeton University student — probably the last of those thousands of persons with whom he corresponded but whom he never knew — in answer to questions about foreign policy and his own role in the Senate. With old problems momentarily crowding the bitter problems of 1951 from his mind, he wrote:

February 26, 1951

My attitude toward international affairs in general and toward collective security for our own national defense was sharply altered by World War II. Prior to World War II, the oceans were virtual moats around our continental bastions. All this changed progressively at Pearl Harbor and thereafter. It became very obvious to me that this was a different world in which we had to sustain our own freedoms. The climax in this trend was demonstrated this past week in a continuous Atlantic flight in something like four hours and thirty-seven minutes from England to America. Meanwhile, the atom bomb sharply altered the problem of national defense. These things — and all their related circumstances — rendered obsolete all of our prior thinking regarding our own national security. In other words, I believe I have only been keeping abreast realistically with the progress of our times.

I certainly *was* what might have been called a "nationalist" prior to Pearl Harbor — although even then I supported a certain degree of international cooperation as evidenced by my willingness to join the League of Nations under reservations of Article 10 and my vote to enter the World Court. I suppose I am now called an "internationalist." But I still think that our first American fidelity must be to our own American security. . . . This is only another way of saying that I think the "nationalist" of yesterday still recognizes this axiom when, as a matter of intelligent self-interest, he demands "collective security" as the only means to defend our own American welfare and to pursue our freedoms in a free world.

By this time — it was late February of 1951 — the Senator probably had a pretty good idea that he wasn't ever going back to the Senate floor. He wasn't going to admit it, but his condition was becoming steadily worse and his doctors and family knew that there was no hope for his recovery. There wasn't anything anybody could do.

Early in March the Senate adopted by a rising vote a resolution expressing its respect for Vandenberg and its hope that he would eventually resume his seat. "I do not think things will come out too badly at Washington," the Senator wrote that week to an old newspaper friend, Carl M. Saunders, who got his start under the Senator's tutelage and always called him "boss." "I am in touch with a number of my key colleagues. I could wish for greater unity. But — as you say — it will be better that the G.O.P. should have hammered out its policy on the anvil of debate. I do not think that my seat in the Senate is entirely 'unoccupied.' I was touched — more than I can tell you — by the unanimous resolution adopted Monday in the Senate by a rising vote. It really makes all of my efforts over the years worthwhile."

On the same day, March 7, 1951, he answered a message from the President, and for the first time addressed him informally as "My dear Harry." The letter to Mr. Truman said: "I am deeply touched by your telegram of March 6. I know it is inspired by a long-time personal friendship which you and I enjoy. It moves me to greet you in this personal way. Your message is good for my morale. I hope you enjoy your Key

West outing and that it will reinvigorate you for the heavy burdens which you carry.

"I have abiding faith in the future of our good old U.S.A. . . ."

About nine o'clock on the evening of April 18, 1951, Arthur Hendrick Vandenberg died of cancer at his home on Morris Avenue in Grand Rapids, Michigan.

Notes and Index

Notes

Page

1. "In my own mind. . . ." Letter to Charles M. Rowan, New York, June 24, 1949.
3. Feb. 2, 1940, letter to Albert F. May, Jr., Lansing, Mich.
11. "I fought it. . . ." Letter to Carl M. Saunders, Editor, Jackson (Mich.) *Citizen Patriot*, Mar. 19, 1941.
15. "It is dangerous. . . ." Letter to Irving Glasband, Los Angeles, Nov. 18, 1941.
    "not too tense. . . ." See Robert Sherwood, *Roosevelt and Hopkins*, p. 431 (Harper & Bros., New York, 1948).
26. Jan. 12, 1942, letter to Charles H. McBride, Holland, Mich.
29. Feb. 20, 1942, letter to Henry Hazlitt.
34. Feb. 11, 1943, letter to James Kennedy, East Lansing, Mich.
35. Mar. 26, 1943, letter to Maj. George Fielding Eliot, New York.
40. "seeks to particularize. . . ." Letter to Maj. George Fielding Eliot, Mar. 26, 1943.
56. Aug. 24, 1943, letter to Samuel B. Pettengill, South Bend, Ind.
59. "I . . . believe. . . ." Letter to Henry R. Luce, New York, Sept. 24, 1943.
60. Sept. 17, 1943, letter to Harry A. Jung, Chicago.
69. July 8, 1943, letter to Henry K. DeHaan, Grand Rapids, Mich.
70. July 15, 1943, letter to Sen. Charles McNary, Salem, Ore.
71. "This so-called compromise. . . ." Letter of George Rothwell Brown, Aug. 21, 1943.
72. Aug. 24, 1943, letter to John T. Flynn, New York.
73. "I am personally of the opinion. . . ." Letter to the Editor, Grand Rapids *Herald*, Aug. 25, 1943.
    And, as he noted. . . . Interview with Paul Ward, Baltimore *Sun*, Sept. 24, 1943.

76. Feb., 1942, letter to Mrs. Vandenberg.
78. "I . . . feel emphatically. . . ." Letter to Gen. Robert E. Wood, Chicago, Sept. 15, 1943.
82. Sept. 30, 1943, letter to Frank E. Gannett, Rochester, N. Y.
83. "I have simply had to wash my hands. . . ." Letter to Gen. Robert E. Wood, Mar. 18, 1944.
"If people [in Wisconsin]. . . ." Letter to Gen. R. E. Wood, April 10, 1944.
86. "I shall never understand. . . ." Letter to Gen. R. E. Wood, May 1, 1944.
91. Mar. 11, 1944, letter to Raymond L. Buell, New York.
92. Mar. 18, 1944, letter to Monroe Shakespeare, Kalamazoo, Mich.
112. "The origin of 'bipartisan foreign policy'. . . ." Letter to Charles M. Rowan, New York, June 24, 1949.
120. Sept. 30, 1944, letter to Mrs. John K. Ormond, Birmingham, Mich.
123. "thought it was very effective. . . ." Letter to B. E. Hutchinson, Detroit, Oct. 28, 1944.
129. Jan. 2, 1945, letter to James H. Sheppard, Grand Rapids, Mich.
130. July 8, 1948, letter to Fred S. Robie, Ann Arbor, Mich.
139. "The whole world changed. . . ." Letter to Charles M. Rowan, New York, June 24, 1949.
"I confess that. . . ." Letter of July 8, 1948, to Fred S. Robie, Ann Arbor, Mich.
145. July 8, 1948, letter to Fred S. Robie, Ann Arbor, Mich.
148. Feb. 13, 1945, letter to Frank Januszewski, *Polish Daily News*, Detroit.
152. Feb. 20, 1945, letter to Howard C. Lawrence, Grand Rapids, Mich.
172. "My effort. . . ." Letter to Frank M. Sparks, Grand Rapids *Herald*, Apr. 17, 1945.
192. Actually, Mr. Truman. . . . See James F. Byrnes, *Speaking Frankly*, p. 49 (Harper & Bros., New York, 1947).
198. "embattled, greedy communism. . . ." Senate speech, July 6, 1949.
220. "Senator, you have no idea. . . ." Quoted from Vandenberg in United Press dispatch, Aug. 25, 1945.
224. Nov. 13, 1945, letter to L. F. Beckwith, Lapeer, Mich.

NOTES 585

224. "I was shocked. . . ." Letter to John Foster Dulles, New York, July 3, 1945.
226. Jay G. Hayden in Detroit *News*, Nov. 19, 1945.
232. "I very nearly resigned. . . ." Letter to B. E. Hutchinson, Detroit, Dec. 29, 1945.
235. Dec. 29, 1945, letter to B. E. Hutchinson, Detroit.
238. "I really had no right. . . ." British press dispatch, Jan., 1946.
239. "imperative task. . . ." *New York Times* dispatch by Sydney Gruson, London, Jan. 14, 1946.
241. Feb. 27, 1946, Senate speech.
243. "seemed less interested. . . ." Senate speech, Feb. 27, 1946.
    Vandenberg confided. . . . Letter to Hamilton Fish Armstrong, New York, Apr. 2, 1946.
244. "inform the Polish government. . . ." Vandenberg speech, Grand Rapids, Mich., Mar. 23, 1946.
245. Apr. 2, 1946, letter to H. F. Armstrong, New York.
246. "loitering around Munich. . . ." *Ibid.*
250. "If we are to be a great power. . . ." Speech of James F. Byrnes, New York, Feb. 28, 1946.
251. "his . . . evangelical speech. . . ." Letter to H. F. Armstrong, New York, Apr. 2, 1946.
252. Apr. 18, 1946, letter to L. G. Carmick, Detroit.
253. July 20, 1946, letter to L. T. Girdler, Muskegon, Mich.
256. Mar. 14, 1946, letter to Carl M. Saunders, in the Jackson (Mich.) *Citizen Patriot*.
257. "as the author. . . ." Letter to the Editor, Baltimore *Sun*, Mar. 14, 1946.
259. "the grossest misrepresentation. . . ." Letter to Ulric Bell, New York, Mar. 16, 1946.
285. May 28, 1946, letter to Henry R. Luce, New York.
304. "I am not going. . . ." Letter to Arthur Vandenberg, Jr., Grand Rapids, Mich., Sept. 21, 1946.
    'Just why I am willing. . . ." Letter to John W. Blodgett, Grand Rapids, Mich., Dec. 24, 1945.
305. Letter to Kim Sigler, Lansing, Mich., July 16, 1946.
306. July 20, 1945, letter to the Editor, Chicago *Tribune*.
307. Dec. 20, 1946, letter to Howard Ellis, Chicago.
    "it is quite evident. . . ." Letter to Chester Arnt, Benton Harbor, Mich., Mar. 17, 1947.

307. "I could not blame. . . ." Letter to William C. Michaels, Kansas City, Mo., Mar. 15, 1947.
308. "I am well aware. . . ." Letter to L. E. Osmer, Grand Rapids, Mich., Mar. 18, 1947.
309. He often called attention. . . . Letters to Gordon McDonald, Ann Arbor, Mich, May 23, 1946, and to Allen B. Crow, Detroit, and other constituents, June 4, 1946.
"I am flattered. . . ." Letter to J. W. Blodgett, Grand Rapids, Mich., Aug. 23, 1946.
310. Letter to Arthur E. Summerfield, Flint, Mich., June 4, 1946.
311. Sept. 21, 1946, letter to Arthur Vandenberg, Jr., Grand Rapids, Mich.
317. "I reassert. . . ." Speech before the United Nations General Assembly, New York, Nov. 8, 1946.
324. "But you will be. . . ." Letter of Esther Van Wagoner Tufty, Nov. 7, 1946.
325. "Congress itself cannot take. . ." Letter to C. Reid Webber, Grand Rapids, Mich., Oct. 14, 1947.
330. "During the last two years. . . ." Press conference, *New York Times*, Dec. 18, 1946.
Jan. 9, 1947, letter to Mrs. Franklin D. Roosevelt, New York.
337. "I shall never forget. . . ." Letter to James F. Byrnes, Spartanburg, S.C., Oct. 26, 1949.
339. June 6, 1947, letter to Prof. Kenneth Colegrove, Northwestern University, Evanston, Ill.
340. "it is unfortunate. . . ." Senate speech, Apr. 8, 1947.
342. Mar. 24, 1947, letter to Bruce Barton, Phoenix, Ariz.
343. About Mar. 13, 1947, press statement.
346. "the greatest act. . . ." Letter to R. F. Moffett, Flint, Mich., May 12, 1947.
351. Mar. 18, 1947, Senate speech.
"itinerant saboteur." Debate in Senate, Apr. 16, 1947.
352. "Your note to me. . . ." Letter from Dean Acheson to Vandenberg, May 29, 1947.
354. Feb. 17, 1947, letter to B. E. Hutchinson, Detroit.
373. Dulles found the French. . . . Editors' interview with John Foster Dulles, 1951.
374. "There is yet another. . . ." Letter to Robert A. Taft, Washington, Oct. 8, 1947.

NOTES 587

376. "our ablest and most experienced. . . ." Press statement, June 13, 1947.
June 13, 1947. *Ibid.*
"safely and wisely" . . . Senate speech, May, 1947.
the basis upon which. . . . Senate speech, Nov. 24, 1947.
"a total balance sheet". . . . Letter to Robert A. Taft, Washington, Oct. 8, 1947.
377. "impossible" demands. . . . Senate speech, Mar. 1, 1948.
381. "I am entirely willing. . . ." Letter to R. C. Sackett, Detroit, June 20, 1947.
383. "a total balance sheet". . . . Letter to Gen. George C. Marshall, June 24, 1947.
"four or five top-level business executives. . . ." Letter to Robert A. Lovett, Washington, Dec. 10, 1947.
"if self-help and self-sufficiency. . . ." Speech at the University of Michigan, Ann Arbor, Nov. 3, 1947.
384. "I am confident. . ." Letter to Arthur E. Summerfield, Flint, Mich., and others, Jan. 1, 1948.
385. Vandenberg wrote Secretary Marshall. . . . Letter to Gen. George C. Marshall, Washington, Dec. 31, 1947.
. . . Undersecretary Lovett wrote Vandenberg. . . . Letter of Robert A. Lovett, Jan. 2, 1948.
386. Mar. 13, 1948, letter to Harmon E. Chamberlin, Battle Creek, Mich.
387. Apr. 9, 1948, letter to Merwin K. Hart, New York.
389. "as a truly great statesman. . . ." Letter to Vandenberg from Gen. George C. Marshall, Washington, Feb. 24, 1948.
392. Jan. 2, 1948, letter to Carl M. Saunders, Jackson, Mich.
393. Marshall reassured Vandenberg. . . . Letter of Gen. George C. Marshall, Mar. 25, 1948.
394. "no doubt but that. . . ." Editor's interview with Paul G. Hoffman.
Hoffman recalled later. . . . *Ibid.*
395. "It is exactly the contrary." Letter to Fred G. Stanley, Detroit, Sept. 24, 1949.
Peace Can Be Won by Paul G. Hoffman, Doubleday & Co., Inc., New York, 1951.
"the most perfect example. . . ." Editors' interview with Paul G. Hoffman, Oct. 9, 1951.

NOTES

396. "fighting mad." Associated Press, Washington *Star*, June 5, 1948.

"I do not know. . . ." Letter to John Foster Dulles, New York, June 4, 1948.

"meat-axe approach". . . . Testimony before Senate Appropriations Committee, June 9, 1948.

400. Sept. 19, 1947, letter to Dr. John W. Dunning, Grand Rapids, Mich.

401. Apr. 6, 1948, letter to Prof. John B. Waite, Ann Arbor, Mich.

Apr. 14, 1948, letter to E. H. Sawyer, Homer, Mich.

402. "I may be wrong." Letter to Clarence H. Booth, Detroit, Apr. 16, 1948.

Apr. 22, 1948, letter to Robert L. Warren, Ann Arbor, Mich.

404. Apr. 21, 1948, letter to the Rev. D. D. Brady, Jackson, Mich.

405. "If a man is very lucky. . . ." Letter of Robert A. Lovett, Jan. 7, 1949.

412. Sept. 27, 1948, letter to B. E. Hutchinson, Grosse Pointe, Mich.

Sept. 30, 1948, letter to Charles A. Macauley, Detroit.

424. "On the threshold. . . ." Letter to Sigler, Summerfield, *et al.*, Jan. 1, 1948.

428. Vandenberg confided to friends. . . . Confidential statement to reporters, June, 1948.

441. "After this I am calling off. . . ." Letter of George E. Allen, June 27, 1948.

453. July 19, 1948, letter to Robert A. Lovett, Washington.

475. Jan. 27, 1949, letter to James H. Sheppard, Grand Rapids, Mich.

477. Mar. 18, 1949, letter to W. J. Cooper, Mt. Pleasant, Mich.

478. Feb. 22, 1947, letter to R. B. Wilson, Isle of Palms, S.C.

Apr. 8, 1949, letter to Benjamin G. Pinx, Detroit.

479. Apr. 15, 1949, letter to Henry Hazlitt, New York.

Apr. 26, 1949, letter to Prof. Charles C. Price, Notre Dame, Ind.

Feb. 21, 1949, letter to Glenwood C. Fuller, Grand Rapids, Mich.

489. June 27, 1949, letter to Boyce K. Muir, Grand Rapids, Mich.

491. July 16, 1949, letter to John Francis Neyland, San Francisco.

505. ". . . I agree emphatically. . . ." Letter to Hamilton Fish Armstrong, New York, July 25, 1949.

506. Aug. 1, 1949, letter to Carl W. Saunders, Jackson, Mich.

510. Aug. 16, 1949, letter to the Rev. Ronald A. Brunger, Stephenson, Mich.

511. ". . . I am one of those. . . ." Letter to John Scott Everton, Kalamazoo, Mich., Aug. 25, 1949.
512. I do *not* think we. . . . Letter to Clyde Beck, Detroit, Sept. 14, 1949.
522. "There can be no doubt whatever. . . ." Letter to Mrs. H. M. Harrington, Sault Ste. Marie, Mich., Feb. 5, 1951.
523. "I am sure. . . ." Letter to J. B. Montgomery, Detroit, Jan. 27, 1947.
Feb. 10, 1947, letter to William Loeb, publisher, Manchester *Union-Leader*, Manchester, N.H.
526. "The situation has deteriorated. . . ." Letter to Frederick W. Newton, Saginaw, Mich., Nov. 22, 1948.
529. Dec. 14, 1948, letter to the Rev. Allen J. Lewis, Lake Odessa, Mich.
. . . the situation in China. . . . Letter to Eugene F. Zeimet, Detroit, Jan. 18, 1949.
533. "And . . . it was precipitated. . . ." Jay G. Hayden article in the Detroit *News*, June 27, 1949.
536. Aug. 25, 1949, letter to Donald F. Zorn, North Adams, Mich.
538. "I do not presently favor. . . ." Letter to Donald F. Zorn, North Adams, Mich., Jan. 5, 1950.
Jan. 9, 1950, letter to Roger D. Lapham, San Francisco.
539. Jan. 17, 1950, letter to Bernard C. Yunck, Detroit.
543. Aug. 5, 1950, letter to H. Tom Collord, Detroit.
544. Oct. 20, 1950, letter to Edwin F. Wilsey, Marquette, Mich.
Oct. 24, 1950, letter to George Maines, Flint, Mich.
545. "I think the Korean War. . . ." Letter to Jo Anne Iden, Ceresco, Mich., Nov. 15, 1950.
Jan. 17, 1951, letter to Mrs. Leon DeVel, East Grand Rapids, Mich.
546. "Our job. . . ." Letter to Winston Churchill, London, Oct. 31, 1949.
547. "I hope and expect. . . ." Letter to Albert L. Miller, Battle Creek, Mich., Oct. 28, 1949.
550. "I do not believe. . . ." Letter to David Lawrence, Washington, Nov. 17, 1949.
"I would not deny. . . ." *Ibid.*
552. Jan. 5, 1950, letter to Mark Wells, Detroit.
557. "I have tried to be. . . ." Letter to Jack Bell, Washington, Apr. 5, 1950.

563. "I loved your reminiscence. . . ." Letter to Gen. George C. Marshall, Washington, July 10, 1950.
564. The Senate passed a resolution. . . . Senate Resolution 359, Sept. 23, 1950.
567. Jan. 23, 1951, letter to Francis O. Wilcox, Washington.
574. "Thanks for your. . . ." Letter to Dr. Isaiah Bowman, Baltimore, Dec. 15, 1949.
"I feel that General Eisenhower's. . . ." Letter to Dean Acheson, Washington.
576. "I have no illusions. . . ." Letter to Gen. George C. Marshall, Washington, Jan. 2, 1951.
577. Feb. 26, 1951, letter to John L. Bell, Jr., Princeton, N.J.
578. "I do not think things will come out. . . ." Letter to Carl M. Saunders, Jackson (Mich.) *Citizen Patriot*, Mar. 7, 1951.

Index

Acheson, Dean, 70, 363, 475, 485, 487, 530, 557; letter to Vandenberg, 352; questioned by Vandenberg on limits of North Atlantic Pact, 480–83; informal visit to Vandenberg, 500–501
American Legion, debate in, on use of veto in UN, and Vandenberg's letters concerning, 320–24
Argentine Republic, seating of, at San Francisco, 182
Arms Embargo, battle over, 2–3
Armstrong, Hamilton Fish, 194
Atomic control, question of military vs. civilian, 252–61
Atomic co-operation with Great Britain, 363–65
Atomic Energy Committee, 222–23, 228–29
Auchinleck, General Sir Claude, 52
Austin, Senator Warren, 58, 92, 95, 101, 102, 106, 167, 228

Baldwin, Governor Raymond E., 6, 57
Ball, Senator Joseph H., 38, 39, 44–45, 55, 62, 128–29
Barkley, Senator Alben, 17, 39, 48, 62, 66, 95, 101, 104, 334, 364, 473, 530, 531
Baruch, Bernard M., 235
Beaverbrook, Lord, talks with Vandenberg, 13–15
Beneš, Dr., President of the Czecho-Slovak government-in-exile, views of, on internal situation in Germany, 22–23
Bevin, Rt. Hon. Ernest, British Foreign Secretary, on Poland, 243–44, 263, 272–74, 277–78, 282–85, 294, 296
Bidault, Georges, 262–63, 268, 272, 281–84, 291, 294, 296
Bilbo, Senator Theodore, 221
"Bi-partisan foreign policy," 339–40, 351–52, Vandenberg's review of, in theoretical sense, in letter to Hannegan, 547–51, and further comments and reflections of Vandenberg on, 551–55, 561–62; Republican "plank" on, 555–56
Blodgett, John W., 304, 316
Bloom, Representative Sol, 168, 188, 530
Bohlen, Charles E., 263
Bolton, Frances, Congresswoman, 58
Bone, Senator Homer T., 10
Bowman, Dr. Isaiah, 169, 194, 202
Bradley, Major General Omar, 48
Bretton Woods, International Monetary Conference at, 108–10
Bricker, John, 88
Bridges, Senator Styles, 129, 353, 559
Brooks, Senator Charles W., 231, 351
Brownell, Herbert, Jr., 126
Bulgaria, U.S. declares war on, 31–32
Bulgarian navy, 293
Burton, Senator Harold H., 38, 44, 55, 62
Bush, Dr. Vannevar, 362, 363
Butterworth, R. Walton, 532, 534

Byrd, Senator Harry F., 535
Byrnes, James, Secretary of State, 169, 192, 224–35 *passim*, 334; at the Luxembourg Palace conference, 262–84, 289–97; address at Stuttgart, 299; resignation, 337

Cadogan, Sir Alexander, 116–17
Camargo. *See* Lleras
Capper, Senator Arthur, 333
Carol, ex-King of Rumania, efforts of, to enter United States, 26
Carpenter, Donald F., 361–62
Carr, Governor Ralph, 6
Chapultepec, Act of (1945), 187, 188, 189, 191, 192, 193, 335, 365
Chavez, Senator Denis, 10
Chiang Kai-shek, Generalissimo, 335, 522, 523
Chicago, Republican Convention of 1944 at, 86–89
Chicago *Tribune*, 305–09
China, policy of U.S. toward, in civil war, 519–45; Marshall mission in, 521, 522; State Department White Paper on, 534–35
Chinese Communist régime, question of admission of to UN, 540–41
Churchill, Rt. Hon. Winston Spencer, 27–29, 35, 37, 41, 93, 98, 99, 101, 102, 104, 133; at the Foreign Relations Committee, 50; conversation with Vandenberg at British Embassy, 51; inquiry after, and remarks on, Vandenberg, 564
Clay, General Lucius, 282, 483–84
Cohen, Benjamin V., 288
Collier's Weekly, 310–311; award of, for distinguished Congressional service, given to Vandenberg, 485
Combined Policy Committee, 359, 363
Committee of the Senate, on postwar economic policy and planning, 34; on peace proposals, 39
Condon, Edward U., 223
Connally, Senator Thomas, 25, 32, 39, 40, 46, 47, 61, 62, 64–65, 95, 100, 101, 102, 103, 139, 168, 219, 263, 288, 299, 300, 301, 334, 476, 489, 505, 530, 535

Convention, Republican, of June 1940, some "inside" history concerning, 5–7

Danaher, Senator John, 109
Danube River, navigation on, 298–99
Darlan, Admiral Jean François, 33
Degrees, Honorary, List of, awarded to Vandenberg, 488
Detroit Free Press, analysis of Vandenberg's votes on domestic matters, 310
Dewey, Governor Thomas E., 5, 57, 59, 76, 83, 84, 86, 87–88, 111–13, 117, 124; statement in 1944 on nomination in 1948, 126–27
Dickey, John, 488
Dodecanese, 293
Donnell, Senator Forrest C., 327, 480
Douglas, Lewis W., U.S. Ambassador to Great Britain, 387
Duff, Senator James H., 423 (as Governor); letter of Vandenberg to, on relations of President and Congress and collective defense of free world, 568–71
Dulles, John Foster, 87–88, 111–13, 117, 124, 159, 160, 188, 194, 195, 483, 485, 487–88, 507, 517, 538, 546
Dumbarton Oaks, Conference at, 111–23
Dunn, James, Undersecretary of State, 160, 161, 263
Dutra, Gaspar, President of Brazil, 484

Early, Stephen T., 16
Eaton, Representative Charles A., 59, 162, 188, 530
Eden, Rt. Hon. Anthony, British Foreign Secretary, 40, 50, 168, 169–70, 176, 178–81, 185–86, 191
Eisenhower, General Dwight, 33, 255, 257, 363, 423–24; Vandenberg's views on future possible role of, 573–76
Eliot, Major George Fielding, 33
Evatt, Dr. H. V., M.P., Australian Minister of External Affairs, 170–71, 199, 211, 214

INDEX 593

Ferguson, Senator Homer, letter of Vandenberg to, on bipartisanship, 561–62
Fernandez, Senhor, Brazilian Foreign Minister, 484–85
Flanders, Senator Ralph E., 414
Foot, Dingle, 190
Foreign Ministers, Council of, at the Luxembourg Palace, 262–84; Italian Treaty: reparations, 264–65, 272–73, 278; Italian fleet, 265; Franco-Italian frontier, 266; colonies, 267, 273, 277, 289–90; Italo-Yugoslav and Italo-Austrian frontiers, 268–69, 293, 295; Inter-Allied Control Commission to administer treaty, 270; Trieste, 273–77, 292, 293–95. Smaller informal meetings agreed on, 272. Germany, 281–83; concluding sessions and adjournment, 283–84; second part of Conference (June, 1946), 289–297
Foreign Policy, Republican Resolution on, introduced by Vandenberg, 53–54; compromise resolution amended, accepted and passed by Senate, 62–65; Advisory Committee on Postwar, 92
Formosa, 536–40
Forrestal, James, Secretary of the Navy, 169, 360, 363, 486–87
Fulbright, Senator William, 408; as Representative, 61

Gannett, Frank, 79, 80, 86
George, Senator Walter F., 34, 38, 40, 42, 46, 53, 62, 95, 96, 101, 106, 334
Gildersleeve, Dean Virginia C., 162, 168
Gillette, Senator Guy M., 38, 39, 40, 43, 46, 47, 49, 62, 95, 101, 106
Glass, Senator Carter, 17
Graeco-Turkish situation (1947), 338–52
Graham, Senator, 498
Green, Governor Dwight H., 58
Grew, Joseph C., Undersecretary of State, 149–50, 153; Vandenberg's letter to, on Poland and on Yalta decisions in connection with forthcoming UN Conference at San Francisco, 150–52; message to Harriman on veto power in UN, 204–6
Gromyko, Andrei, at San Francisco, 199–208, 214
Groves, General Leslie R., 221, 223
Grundy, Joseph R., 423

Halifax, Lord, 116, 168, 169–70; conversation with Vandenberg, 21–23; invites certain Senators and Representatives to British Embassy, 50–51
Hannegan, Robert E., letter to, on bipartisanship, from Vandenberg, 547–50
Harriman, Averill, 177; message to, on veto power, from Acting Secretary Grew, 204–6
Hart, Thomas C., 228
Hatch, Senator Carl A., 38, 44–45, 62, 334
Hickenlooper, Senator Bourke B., 228, 333; on questions connected with the atomic bomb, 358–59, 360–65
Hill, Senator, 38, 44, 55
Hiroshima, 220–21
Hoffman, Paul G., 394–95; letter of Vandenberg to, on second anniversary of ECA, 557–58
Hogness, Dr. Thorfin R., 259
Hopkins, E. M., President Emeritus of Dartmouth, 488
Hopkins, Harry, 15–16
Hull, Cordell, Secretary of State, 111, 112, 113, 168; on pending Senate peace resolutions, 40–41; establishes Advisory Committee on Postwar Foreign Policy, 92; appears before Senate Foreign Relations Committee, 93; meetings with "Committee of Eight," 95–107, 115–16
Hungary, U.S. declares war on, 31–32

"Insulation." See Isolation
Isolation, Vandenberg's views on, 1, 3–4; finally abandoned by Vandenberg in speech of Jan. 10, 1945, 130–45

Italian Treaty, 264–77, 289–90, 292–93, 293–95. *See also* Foreign Ministers, Council of
Ives, Senator, 517

Januszewski, Frank, 155, 313
Johnson, Senator Edwin C., 228
Johnson, Senator Hiram, 128
Johnson, Louis, Secretary of Defense, 363

Kee, Representative John, Chairman of House Committee on Foreign Affairs, 559
Kem, Senator James P., 489; amendment (to Appropriation Bill for ECA), 489–90
Kenney, Major General George, 77, 78
Kiska, 46
Knowland, Senator William F., 465, 535
Knox, William F., Secretary of the Navy, 19, 46
Koehler, Dr., 89
Koo, Wellington, 210
Korean War, 541–45
Krock, Arthur, 123, 250

La Follette, Senator Robert M., Jr., 10, 39, 43, 46, 96, 100, 101, 103, 105, 106, 115, 218; on India, 53; appointed to "Committee of Eight," 95
Langer, Senator William, 10
Langlie, Governor Arthur B., 58
Lawrence, Howard C., 4
Lend-Lease Bill, Vandenberg on, 9–12
Lilienthal, David, Chairman of the Atomic Energy Commission, 363; disputes concerning confirmation and work of, 352–59
Linlithgow, Lord, Viceroy of India, 52
Lippmann, Walter, 118, 141
Lleras Camargo, Colombian delegate to San Francisco Conference, 210
Lodge, Senator Henry Cabot, Jr., 333, 427, 428, 507, 517, 576; letter from Vandenberg to, on world government, 414–17, and on Wherry Resolution, 571–73; Vandenberg's comment on article on Republican party by, 464–65
Long, Breckinridge, Assistant Secretary of State, 26
Lovett, Robert A., Undersecretary of State, 360, 361, 505–6; sees Vandenberg on Berlin blockade, 452–54
Lublin, Poles, President Truman's message to Stalin on, 175–76. *See also* Poland
Lucas, Senator Scott, 222
Luce, Representative Clare Boothe, 77, 431

MacArthur, General Douglas, candidacy for President (1944) of, supported by Vandenberg, 75–89
McCloy, John J., Assistant Secretary of War, 189
McCormick, Colonel Robert R., 305–308
McIntyre, Marvin, 16
McKellar, Senator Kenneth, 353
Mackinac, Republican Conference at, 55–62
McMahon, Senator Brien, 222, 228, 254, 256
McNary, Senator Charles, 67, 68, 90
Malone, Senator George W., 351
Marshall, General George, 14, 48, 359, 361, 367, 576; remarks of, to Senate Subcommittee, 48–49; succeeds Byrnes as Secretary of State, 338; speech at Harvard on long-term assistance to Europe, 374–75; on directive for China mission, 528; Vandenberg's attitude toward, in connection with Chinese mission, 533–34, 535–36
Marshall Plan, 373–98
Marshall, Reverend Peter, Chaplain of the Senate, 326
Martin, Representative Joseph, 67, 68, 88, 89, 167; confidential letter of Vandenberg to, on conference at White House about atomic energy legislation, 222
Masaryk, Jan, 181
Military Liaison Committee, 259–61, 362

INDEX

Miller, Representative A. L., 84–86
Millikin, Senator Eugene D., 228, 332, 408, 553
Molotov, Vyacheslav, Russian Foreign Minister, in Washington, 32–33; at San Francisco, 175–98 *passim*; at the Luxembourg Palace conference, 262–84, 290–97
Morse, Senator Wayne, 333, 517
Moses, Senator George H., 42, 53

Nagasaki, 221
Neutrality Law of 1937, 2
Nimitz, Admiral Chester, 255, 257
North Atlantic Treaty, 475–98, 499–500; Vandenberg's speech to Senate in favor of, 493–98; arms program in connection with, 502–18; Vandenberg's answer to Senator Wherry's questions on, 567–68
Nye, Senator Gerald P., 10
Nye Munitions Investigating Committee, 2

Owlett, G. Mason, 423

Padilla, Ezequiel, Mexican Foreign Minister, 178, 179
Pasvolsky, Dr., 158, 168, 188, 189
Patterson, Robert P., Secretary of War, 255
"Peace Through War by Proxy," 8
Peace Treaties (with European Allies of Germany), Conference at Paris, 298–302
Pepper, Senator Claude, 62, 266–67, 311, 351, 408, 411
Petropolis, Inter-American Conference at, 365–72
Pew, Joseph N., Jr., 6, 81, 423
Phillips, William, U.S. Ambassador, on India, 52–53
Pike, Sumner T., 362, 363
Poland, questions in connection with Yalta decisions on, 147–56; Bevin on political murders in, 243–44
Poles, the sixteen "Underground," imprisoned in Russia, 185–86
Polish Daily News of Detroit, letter on Polish question from Vandenberg to Editor, 155–56; Vandenberg's reply to article contributed to, on Polish question, 313–14
Postwar objectives, 34–65; Gillette Resolution, 38–39; Ball Resolution, 38–47
Pryor, Samuel F., Jr., 6

Republican National Committee, resolution of April 21, 1942, 30
Rhee, President (of South Korea), 544
Ridgway, General Matthew, 368
"Rio Pact," 366–72
Robbins, Harry M., 418
Robin Moor, sinking of, 12–13
Rockefeller, Nelson, 177, 187, 188, 215–16
Roosevelt, President Franklin D., 16, 23–25, 37, 39, 73, 75, 92, 93, 98, 99, 101, 102, 123, 128; accused of violating Dewey-Hull-Dulles arrangement, 112–13; reaction to Vandenberg's speech of Jan. 10, 1945, 139, 146–47; exchange of letters with Vandenberg about San Francisco commission, 153–55; death of, 165
Roosevelt, Mrs. Franklin D., 8, 169, 238, 240
Rumania, U.S. declares war on, 31–32
Russell, Senator Richard B., 228, 535

San Francisco, Conference at, 172–98; question of chairmanship, 179–80; of admission of White Russia and the Ukraine, 180–82, and of the Argentine, 182; the regional problem, 186–93, 210–11; the withdrawal clause, 193–95, 197–98; the veto power, 195–97, 199–210, 211; the powers of the Assembly, 212–14; summary of accomplishments, 214–19
Savage, Joseph P., 79
Ships, German and Italian, in American ports, 12
Smith, Dr. Cyril, authority of, to discuss metallurgy of plutonium with the British, 361–63
Smith, Gerald L. K., 355
Smith, Senator H. Alexander, 333, 507, 517, 519–20, 536, 564, 576
Smith, Senator Margaret, 517

596   INDEX

Smith, Walter Bedell, 248
Soong, T. V., Chinese Foreign Minister, 51–52, 176
Spence, Representative Brent, 109
Stalin, Marshal Joseph, 35, 39, 41, 92, 98, 99, 101, 102, 104
Stassen, Commander Harold E., 88, 168, 215–16
Stettinius, Edward, Secretary of State, 121, 126, 156, 157, 161, 164, 167, 169; at San Francisco, 175–98 *passim*; criticism of, 191–92; dismissal of, 224–25
Stimson, Henry, Secretary of War, 169
Strauss, Lewis L., 361, 363
Sutherland, Major General Richard, 77, 78

Taber, Representative John, attempt of, to cut funds for ERP Program, and failure, 397–98
Taft, Charles, 164
Taft, Senator Robert A., 58, 87, 332, 423; the Convention of 1940 and, 5, 6–7; on Hull's proposed bipartisan committee, 93–94; relations with Vandenberg in 80th Congress, 318–19; against confirmation of Lilienthal, 353; opposes North Atlantic Pact, 498; consults Vandenberg on new statement of Republican principles, 553; letter from Vandenberg to, 565
Taylor, Senator Glen H., 351
Thomas, Senator Elbert D., 39, 62, 334
Thye, Senator Edward J., 517
Tobey, Senator Charles W., 109, 334
Truman, President Harry S., 39 (as Senator), 167, 168, 178, 192, 359, 361, 363–64, 393–94, 547, 576; invites Vandenberg and others to White House to discuss atomic energy legislation, 222; and resignation of Wallace, 300–302; letter to Vandenberg on bipartisan foreign policy, 558–61; exchange of letters with Vandenberg during latter's illness, 576–77, 578–79
"Truman Doctrine," 341

Tufty, Esther van Wagoner, letter of, to Vandenberg on his re-election, 324
Tydings, Senator Millard E., 228

Ukraine, seating of, at San Francisco and in UN, 176–78, 180–82
"Unconditional surrender" doctrine, 91
United Nations, formation of. *See* Dumbarton Oaks. *See also* San Francisco Conference
United Nations Assembly, first meeting in London, 238; case of Lebanon and Syria, 240–42; Vandenberg appointed U.S. delegate to (2d session), 549
United Nations Charter. *See* Dumbarton Oaks. *See also* San Francisco
United Nations Relief and Rehabilitation Administration (UNRRA), draft of agreement to establish, published, 66–67; Vandenberg's resolution to investigate draft agreement concerning, 67; Vandenberg's views and actions on method of dealing with draft agreement concerning, 67–74; agreement passed by Senate, 90

Vandenberg, Senator Arthur Hendrick, isolationist views, 1–4; attitude toward nomination for Presidency (1940), 4; presented to King George VI, 5; at the Convention of 1940, 5–8; criticized by Mrs. Roosevelt, 8–9; on lend-lease, 9–12; on the sinking of the *Robin Moor*, 12–13; talks with Beaverbrook, 13–15; views on war with Japan, Germany, and Italy at time of the Declarations, 16–20; conversation with Halifax, 21–23; exchange with President Roosevelt on creation of Joint Congressional Committee on War Cooperation, 23–25; on Churchill's speeches to the Commons, 27–29; on Russia as our Ally, 31–33; appointed to Committee on Post-War Economic Policy and Planning, 34; on postwar objectives and relevant Senate resolutions, 34–52; on William Phillips' report on India, 52–53; seeks alternatives to the Ball Resolution, 53–55; role in the Mackinac foreign policy resolution, 55–62; and in final compromise resolution passed by Senate, 62–65; introduces resolution to investigate UNRRA draft agreement, 67; views and further actions on method of dealing with UNRRA agreement, 67–74; supports MacArthur presidential candidacy (1944), 75–89; doubts about Administration's postwar plans, 90–93; asks Taft's advice on informal bipartisan committee suggested by Hull, 93–94; accepts idea resulting in "Committee of Eight," 94–95; on Hull's plans for World Security Organization, 95–107; declines to attend Bretton Woods Conference, 108–10; on negotiations at Dumbarton Oaks, 111–23; on Roosevelt's proposals to keep out of war, 123–24; feels need for a party "of the right," 129–30; speech of Jan. 10, 1945, and comments of the Press concerning, 130–45; named as delegate to UN Conference at San Francisco, 146–47; and debates acceptance, 147–54; exchange of letters with President Roosevelt on acceptance of San Francisco commission, 153–55; views on the Polish question, 147–56; amendments to Dumbarton Oaks draft, 157–58, 163; on question of "extra votes" in the UN, 159–65; on the death of President Roosevelt, 165; general attitude toward President Roosevelt, 165–66; remarks in Senate on eve of San Francisco meeting, 171; at San Francisco, 172–98, 199–219; attitude toward atomic energy control, 220–36; appointed to Committee on atomic energy, 222–23; on dismissal of Stettinius, 224–25; with atom bomb committee has special audience with the President, 228–29; on loan to Great Britain, 230–32; appointed delegate to General Assembly meeting in London, 232–36; work in London on UN Budgetary Commission, 238–39; change of view on Mrs. Roosevelt, 240; views on the case of Lebanon and Syria, 240–42; relations with Byrnes, 243–51; speech of Feb. 27, 1946, on Russia; U.S. and UN and press comment, 246–51; on the McMahon (atomic control) bill, and amendment thereto, 252–61; role in formation of Military Liaison Committee, 259–61; at the Luxembourg Palace conference, 262–84 and report and comment on, 285–87; at second part of Luxembourg conference, 289–97, and speech to Senate on, 297–98; attends Paris Peace Treaty Conference, 298–302; role in Senate confirmation of treaties with European Allies of Germany, 302–3; campaign of 1946 and re-election, 304–17; position in 80th Congress, 318, 332–34; relations with Taft in new Congress, 318–19; correspondence with Col. Roberts about debate in American Legion on limitations of use of veto in UN, 320–24; on the death of the Rev. Peter Marshall, 326; as President *pro tempore* of the Senate, 326–29; as Committee Chairman, 329; attitude to reporters, 329–30; views on a dual rôle in Congress and the UN, 330–31; address at Cleveland on bipartisanship, on the UN and aid to Chiang, 334–36; letter to Byrnes on his (Byrnes's) resignation, 337; quickly secures Senate approval of Marshall's appointment as Secretary of State, 338; on Graeco-Turkish situation, 339–52; praised by Acheson, 352; supports appointment of Lilienthal to chairmanship of AEC, 352–58; later doubts concerning Lilienthal, 357–59, on the atomic bomb and Great Britain, 359–65; attends Inter-American Conference at Petropolis, 365–72; secures ratification of Rio Pact, 371–72; argues in behalf of Marshall Plan, 373–98; proposes bipartisan advisory committee, 376; at Foreign Relations Committee hearings, 384; suggests changes in language of Administration bill, 385; discusses effect of Marshall Plan on taxes, 386–87; on administration of Marshall Plan, 388; speech in Senate (Mar. 1, 1948) in behalf of ERP bill, 389–92; opposes appointment of Clayton or Acheson to be head of ERP, 393–94, and favors Paul G. Hoffman, 394–95; argues in Senate against House view, 397–98; prepares (with Lovett) a resolution to strengthen the UN "outside the veto," 399–420; speech in Senate on S.R. 239, 408–11; on outlawing the Communist party, 412–14; on possibility of being a candidate for the Presidency, 421–45; statement on Foreign policy given to Lodge paralleled in Republican party platform (1948), 428–30; exchanges with Dulles on foreign policy during 1948 campaign, 446–48; on President Truman's criticism of 80th Congress, 448; speech on bipartisan foreign policy (Oct. '48) 450–52, 457; on Berlin blockade, 452–54; on proposal to send Vinson to Moscow, 456–60 and on an analogous rumored proposal, 459; on the reelection of President Truman, 460; on being suggested for President Truman's Secretary of State, 462–64; on an article by Lodge concerning Republican party, 464–65; position in Republican internal controversy, 466–67; views on Acheson, 469–72; first reactions to proposal for North Atlantic Treaty, 475–80; questions Acheson on limits of North Atlantic Pact, 480–83; comments on visit of President Dutra, 484–85; attends Forrestal's funeral, 486–87; receives Honorary degree at Dartmouth, 488; on giving funds to countries partly socialist, 489–90; on effect of ECA on American markets abroad, 491–92; speech in Senate in favor of North Atlantic Treaty, 493–98; on arms aid to Europe in connection with North Atlantic Treaty, 502–18; failing health, 513, 517; on Russian atomic explosion, 518; on Chinese question, 519–45; presents China Aid bill to Senate, 524–25, comments on London's statement about Administration's blunders in China, 526–27; on Wedemeyer Report and directive to Marshall, 527–28; at White House meeting after fall of Peking, 530–32; against appointment of Butterworth to be Asst. Secretary for Far Eastern Affairs, 532; dissassociates himself from U.S. China policy, 532–33; attitude to Marshall in connection with Chinese mission, 533–34, 535–36; on White Paper on China, 536; on Formosa and recognition of Communist régime in China, 537–41; on Korean War, 542–45; reflections on bipartisan foreign policy in letter to Hannegan, 547–50, and further reflections on, 551–55, 561–62; opposes immediate resumption of full diplomatic relations with Spain, 552; resigns from Joint Congressional AEC, 553; consulted by Taft and also by Brewster on "New Statement of Republican Principles," 553–54; letter to Hoffman in support of ERP, 557–58; exchanges of letters with President Truman on bipartisan policy and Vandenberg's role, 558–61; letter to Senator Ferguson on bipartisanship, 561–62; undergoes operation, 562; last visit to Senate, 562–63; on Senator Lodge's appointment to American Delegation to UN and Committee Five, 564; letter to Taft, 565; on 80th Congress, 565–66; on Senator Wherry's resolution concerning sending troops abroad, 566–67; replies to Wherry's questions on North Atlantic Treaty, 567–68;

INDEX 599

views on relations between President and Congress and collective defense of free world, 568–71; to Lodge on Wherry Resolution, 571–73; views on Gen. Eisenhower and his possible future role, 573–76; Senate resolution expressing respect for and wishes for recovery of, 578; death of, 579
Vandenberg, Mrs. Arthur, 238, 288; on the Marshalls, 373; illness and death of, 563
Vaughan, Colonel Harry H., 167
Vishinsky, Andrei Y., 242–43

Wagner, Senator Robert, 109, 334
Walker, Frank, Democratic National Chairman, 61
Wallace, Henry, 168, 257, 266, 311; relations with Vandenberg, 255–56; speech in New York on foreign policy and resignation from Cabinet, 300–302; tours Europe attacking aid measures to Greece and Turkey, 351
Walsh, Senator David, 10
Ward, Angus, U.S. Consul, 538
Warren, Governor Earl, 57, 431
Watkins, Senator Arthur V., 408, 480

Watkins, Charles, 327
Wavell, General, 82
Welles, Sumner, Undersecretary of State, 39, 44
Wheeler, Senator, 218
Wherry, Senator Kenneth S., 332, 351, 353, 354; resolution on sending troops abroad, 566; Vandenberg's reply to questions of, on North Atlantic Treaty, 567–68; Vandenberg's views on Resolution of, 566–67, 571–73
White, Senator Wallace H., 39, 45, 62, 90, 92, 95, 167, 332, 333
White Russia, seating of, at San Francisco and in UN, 176–78, 180–82
Wilcox, Francis O., 261, 334
Wiley, Senator Alexander, 129, 333, 517
Willis, Senator Raymond E., 63
Willkie, Wendell, 5, 29–30, 60, 76, 83, 84, 87
Willoughby, Brigadier General C. A., 78, 79–81
Wolcott, Representative Jesse P., 109
Wood, General Robert E., 78, 80–81, 86

Yalta, 145, 147–68

/973.917V227P>C1/

Date Due

MAR 1 3 '59			
APR 3 '59			